FUTURE
English for Results

1

TEACHER'S EDITION
AND LESSON PLANNER

Daniel S. Pittaway

Series Consultants

Beatriz B. Díaz

Ronna Magy

Federico Salas-Isnardi

PEARSON
Longman

Future 1
English for Results
Teacher's Edition and Lesson Planner

Pearson Education, 10 Bank Street, White Plains, NY 10606

Staff credits: The people who made up the **Future 1** team, representing editorial,
production, design, and manufacturing, are Rhea Banker, Nancy Blodgett,
Maretta Callahan, Elizabeth Carlson, Aerin Csigay, Dave Dickey, Nancy Flaggman,
Irene Frankel, Mike Kemper, Katie Keyes, Linda Moser, and Liza Pleva.

Cover design: Rhea Banker
Cover photo: Kathy Lamm/Getty Images
Text design: Lisa Delgado
Text composition: ElectraGraphics, Inc.
Text font: Minion Pro

ISBN-13: 978-0-13199145-3
ISBN-10: 0-13-199145-0

Printed in the United States of America

3 4 5 6 7 8 9 10—V009—14 13 12 11

Contents

Lesson Planner

The instructional design of *Future* has been carefully crafted and draws on tried-and-true methods. In *Future*, current research findings are put into practice. Each of the skill sections reflects sound pedagogy and offers a logical progression from unit to unit within a level as well as from one level to the next throughout the series. The instructional design is tailored to meet the interests and needs of students at their language level and at the same time, to fulfill curriculum mandates.

Future has been designed to help students persist in their English studies. The program motivates students to keep coming to class through its situational contexts that reflect students' real lives, its touches of humor, and its community–building group work and team projects. If outside factors cause students to miss classes, the strategies and study skills presented in the Student Book, along with the Practice Plus CD-ROM, help students continue their studies until they are able to return to class.

Future also helps students make a successful transition into academic programs. The levels of *Future* progressively introduce academic skills so that students feel empowered to continue their education. By continuing on into academic programs, students improve their chances of entering the job market with all the skills and tools they need to be successful.

Future is truly an integrated-skills course: listening, speaking, reading, and writing are woven together throughout the lessons, just as they are naturally woven together outside the classroom. For example, students practice their listening skills not just on the Listening page, but also in the Life Skills lesson, and in other lessons throughout the unit.

Following are some of the key pedagogical features of the skill sections of *Future 1*.

Vocabulary

- **Picture-dictionary layout.** Presenting vocabulary through clear, colorful photos and illustrations helps students quickly understand new words and phrases.
- **Elicitation before presentation.** New words are set to the side of the pictures. Teachers elicit what their students know by using the pictures first, and then focusing on text. This helps teachers to engage their students, and it empowers students by letting them say what they already know.
- **Recycling of new words.** After new vocabulary is introduced, it is used again and again throughout the course, giving students the maximum exposure to the new words in a variety of situations. Current research shows that the more encounters learners have with a target word, the more likely they are to retain that word.[1]
- **Strategies for learning outside the classroom.** Learning Strategies in the Vocabulary lessons support persistence by giving students ideas for continued learning outside the classroom. These strategies can be used with any new words students encounter.

Listening

- **Multiple genres.** Throughout *Future*, students are exposed to a variety of listening types such as conversations, interviews, and radio talk shows.
- **Natural language.** Natural discourse is presented so that students hear authentic models. The listening selections model high-frequency words and expressions from the Longman Corpus of Spoken English database.
- **Pre-listening activities.** Before students listen to each selection, they complete pre-listening activities, which pre-teach new vocabulary and help activate students' background knowledge. Students are also asked to make predictions about what they will hear. This helps develop students' critical thinking skills[2] and is an important strategy for successful listening in a second language.[3]
- **True listening practice.** Students listen to the audio without seeing the audio script on the page. This serves two purposes: 1) It ensures that the listening exercise is truly checking students' listening skills, rather than their reading skills; and 2) It helps students prepare for standardized tests in which they are asked to listen to audio selections and answer questions without seeing the script. Students who need extra support can read the audio script printed in the back of the Student Book.
- **Multiple exposures to the same listening selection.** Students listen to selections multiple times. This helps them develop their listening skills and allows them to be successful with the listening task.
- **A variety of listening tasks.** A wide variety of comprehension exercises check students' understanding of both the meaning and the details of the listening selection.

Speaking

- **Careful scaffolding to promote success.** The Listening lesson that precedes the Speaking lesson exposes students to the language they will use in conversation. Students then practice the model conversation through activities that progress from controlled to more open. Speaking lessons culminate in guided role plays, which allow students to have fun expressing themselves in the new language using vocabulary and structures they are familiar with.
- **Negotiation of meaning.** Many of the exercises in each unit require students to work together to negotiate meaning. Giving students the opportunity to interact and negotiate meaning supports development of their language skills.[4]
- **Problem-solving tasks.** In each unit, students have the opportunity to discuss solutions to a particular problem related to the unit theme. These tasks engage students' critical thinking skills and allow them to focus on fluency.

---

[1] Folse, K. (2006). The Effect of Type of Written Exercise on L2 Vocabulary Retention. *TESOL Quarterly*, Vol. 40, No. 2, 273–93.

[2] Bloom, B.S. (1956). *Taxonomy of Educational Objectives, Handbook I: The Cognitive Domain*, New York: David McKay Co Inc.

[3] Rost, M. (2002). *Teaching and Researching Listening*. Harlow, England: Pearson Education.

[4] Mackey, A. (1999). Input, interaction, and second language development: An empirical study of question formation in ESL. *Studies in Second Language Acquisition, 21*, 557–587.

Pronunciation

- **Systematic pronunciation syllabus.** Pronunciation presentations and practice exercises precede many of the speaking lessons. Students practice isolated sentences from the model conversation that follows.
- **Focus on stress and intonation.** While some pronunciation lessons highlight specific sounds like *th*, students focus on the natural stress, intonation, and rhythm of the language.
- **Emphasis on receptive skills.** *Future* encourages students to notice the natural patterns of English to aid their comprehension as well as their production.

Grammar

- **Grammar naturally embedded in the spoken language.** Grammar in *Future* is first presented receptively through the conversation in the Speaking lesson. Then, grammar charts at the beginning of the grammar lesson explicitly show the target structures.
- **Minimal metalanguage.** The charts use little metalanguage in order to ensure that the forms and the meaning of the target structure are clear and comprehensible.
- **Practice with both meaning and form.** Presentations focus on meaning as well as form, a practice that can help learners incorporate more new structures into their language use.[5]
- **Progression from controlled to open practice.** Practice activities progress from very controlled to open, providing ample written and spoken practice in the target structure.
- **Contextualized activities.** Exercises are contextualized, recycling themes and vocabulary from the unit, so that grammar practice is authentic and meaningful.
- **Numerous pair and group activities.** Pair and small group work allows students to work with new language structures in a safe, motivating environment, as well as offering further opportunities for them to negotiate meaning.
- **Opportunities for students to show what they know.** *Show What You Know* activities at the end of every grammar lesson allow students to put together the vocabulary, structures, and competencies they have learned.

Reading

- **High-interest, useful articles.** The reading articles in *Future* present interesting, useful information related to the unit theme. The structures and vocabulary in the texts are controlled so students can be successful readers.
- **Pre-reading activities.** As in the Listening lessons, the Reading lessons have pre-reading activities to help build students' cultural schema, an important factor in successfully completing a reading task.[6] New vocabulary is also pre-taught so that students can focus on improving their reading fluency and skills.

- **Recorded reading selections.** The readings in *Future* are recorded so that students can listen as they read along. Research has shown that listening while reading can have a positive effect on reading fluency.[7]
- **Opportunity to apply the information.** A *Show What You Know* activity at the end of the reading lesson allows students to synthesize and apply the information they have just learned.
- **Building of reading skills.** Comprehension questions check students' ability to find the main idea as well as important details in the text.
- **Inclusion of document and environmental literacy.** In addition to high-interest articles, *Future* gives students practice reading and completing forms and other documents that they are likely to encounter in their everyday lives.

Writing

- **Step-by-step writing syllabus.** Offered in a natural progression, writing tips throughout *Future* introduce students to the mechanics of writing.
- **Personal writing.** Students learn to write sentences and short paragraphs using material they are familiar and comfortable with. Sentence- and short-paragraph-writing is integrated throughout the lessons of *Future*.
- **Modeling of writing tasks.** Models for all writing activities in *Future* allow students to complete each task successfully.
- **Authenticity of purpose.** In addition to the personal writing, students complete several authentic genres such as forms, lists, notes, and letters.

Review and Assessment

- **Checkpoints to track progress.** Every unit begins with a list of competencies to be covered. As students complete each lesson, they check off the goal they have completed. At the end of the unit, students are directed to review the goals list to see their progress. Keeping track of goals completed motivates students and reinforces their sense of success and accomplishment.
- **End-of-unit review.** Every unit in *Future* ends with a review of the language and skills presented in that unit. By re-visiting the vocabulary, structures, and competencies they have learned, students can retain the information more easily and assimilate it into their pre-existing knowledge.
- **Opportunities for ongoing assessment.** The *Show What You Know* activities at the end of most lessons and at the end of every unit can be used by teachers to assess their students' progress in particular language skills and competencies. For teachers who want to do a more formal assessment of what their students have learned, the *Tests and Test Prep Book* provides unit tests as well as a midterm and a final test.

---

[5] Ellis, R., Basturkmen, H., & Loewen, S. (2001). Learner uptake in communicative ESL lessons. *Language Learning, 51,* 281–318.

[6] Burt, M., Peyton, J. K., & Adams, R. (2003). *Reading and adult English language learners: A review of the research.* Washington, DC: Center for Applied Linguistics.

---

[7] Kruidenier, J. (2002). *Research-based principles for adult basic education reading instruction.* Washington, D.C.: National Institute for Literacy, Partnership for Reading.

Each unit begins with a **list of course components** that can be used in class or assigned for homework.

5

Shop, Shop, Shop

Classroom Materials/Extra Practice

CD 2
Tracks 23–42

T
Transparencies 5.1–5.6
Vocabulary Cards Unit 5

MCA
Unit 5

Workbook
Unit 5

Interactive Practice
Unit 5

Unit Overview

Goals
- See the list of goals on the facing page.

Grammar
- Simple present affirmative statements
- Simple present *yes/no* questions and short answers; contractions
- Simple present negative statements; contractions

Pronunciation
- Sentence rhythm: stress on important words

Reading
- Read an article about U.S. dollar coins

Writing
- Write sentences about problems with clothing
- Write sentences about things people need, want, or have

Life Skills Writing
- Write a personal check

Preview
- Set the context of the unit by asking questions about shopping (for example, *Do you like to shop? Where do you shop?*).
- Hold up page 85 or show Transparency 5.1. Read the unit title and ask the class to repeat.
- Explain: *Many people like to shop.* Shop, shop, shop *means that people shop a lot.*
- Say: *Look at the picture.* Ask the Preview question: *What do you see?* If students call out various types of clothing, tell them they will learn more words for clothes in this unit.

Unit Goals
- Point to the Unit Goals. Explain that this list shows what the class will be studying in this unit.
- Tell students to read the goals silently.
- Say each goal and ask the class to repeat. To explain any unfamiliar vocabulary, bring in the following items or show them from the book: receipts (page 93), price tags (page 93), and personal checks (page 257) to illustrate. Explain the following term:

  Return something: *To take something that you do not want back to the store and get your money back*
- Tell students to circle one goal that is very important to them.
- Call on students to say the goal they circled.

T-85   UNIT 5

A comprehensive **list of competencies and skills** provides an overview of the unit.

Teaching ideas for the unit opener picture help teachers establish the context of the unit and get students ready for the unit theme.

Step-by-step teaching notes help teachers give **clear grammar presentations**. Corresponding **transparencies with discovery exercises** can be found in the *Transparency and Reproducible Vocabulary Cards* component.

Teaching notes are organized in a **lesson plan**: Getting Started, Presentation, Controlled Practice, Communicative Practice. **Suggested times** for each part of the lesson plan are based on a 60 minute class. This time may vary depending on class size.

Lesson 3 Talk about things you need, want, or have

Getting Started 5 minutes

- Say: *We're going to study* want, need, *and* have. *In the conversation on page 89, Zofia used this grammar.*
- Play CD 2, Track 27. Students listen. Write *He needs new clothes, but he wants a backpack!* on the board. Underline *He needs* and *he wants.*

Presentation 10 minutes

Simple present affirmative

- Copy the grammar charts onto the board or show the charts on Transparency 5.3 and cover the exercise.
- Read the sentences in the left chart and ask the class to repeat.
- Read the sentences in the right chart and ask the class to repeat.
- Read the first point in the Grammar Watch note. Circle *wants* and *needs* in the chart. Then write: *He wants a new shirt.* Make the -*s* large for emphasis. Read the sentence and ask the class to repeat.
- Read the second point in the Grammar Watch note.
- Ask students to close their books. Remove any visual aids for the chart. On the board, write the following incomplete sentences:

    You _____ new clothes. (want)

    He _____ new clothes. (need)

    We _____ new clothes. (have)

    She _____ new clothes. (have)
- Students call out answers. Write answers on the board.
- If you are using the transparency, do the exercise with the class.

Language Note

Students often do not hear the final -*s* on third-person singular present affirmative verbs. Pronounce it clearly when modeling sentences. Further, provide a variety of examples so that students begin to recognize subjects that fall within the third-person singular category (for example, *The teacher _____ new clothes. Christina _____ new clothes.*).

Controlled Practice 30 minutes

1 PRACTICE

Ⓐ Underline the correct word.

- Read the directions.
- Ask students to look at the picture of Mr. Garcia. Point to the blue shirt he is wearing and say the example item with emphasis on *has.*
- Say: *Look at the subject of the sentence before answering. Also, look at the grammar chart to help you answer.*
- Walk around as needed to help students make connections between the subjects in the exercise items and the subjects in the chart (for example, *Amy and Jeff = They*).
- Students compare answers with a partner.
- Call on students to say answers.

Ⓑ Complete the sentences. Use the verbs in parentheses.

- Read the directions and tell students to look at the picture of the woman. Read the example and ask the class to repeat it. Write it on the board.
- Ask: *Why is the answer* needs *and not* need? (Because *My sister* is the same as *she.*) Point to the example on the board and circle *My sister.* Write *she* under it, saying: *They are the same. Remember—look at the subject of the sentence before answering.*
- Students compare answers with a partner.
- Call on students to write answers on the board.

▬▬ Expansion: Vocabulary and Graphic Organizer Practice for 1B

- To provide extra practice with *need, want,* and *have,* tell students to make three lists with the headings *Need, Want,* and *Have* in their notebooks. Students then write three clothing items they need, three they want, and three they have.
- Students compare lists with a partner by reading the items they listed (for example, *I want new shoes. I need a new jacket.*).
- To practice ordinal numbers, students can also list their items in order of importance (for example, *First, I want new shoes. Second, I want . . .*) and share these with their partner.

UNIT 5 **T-90**

Language Notes offer insightful and helpful information about English. The notes also offer ideas for **Community Building** in the classroom and **Networking** activities to help students get to know their classmates.

Expansions provide more practice with specific skills.

Ideas for multilevel instruction help teachers meet the needs of all learners in a classroom.

Teaching notes for the Life Skills Writing section on pages Txi–Txii help teachers work with students on understanding and completing real-life writing tasks.

Lesson 4 Use U.S. money

3 TALK ABOUT PRICES

Listen. A customer in a clothing store...

- Tell students to look at the pictures. Ask: *What do you see?* (a skirt and a pair of jeans) Say: *Look at the price tags.* Ask: *How much is the skirt?* ($15.99) *How much are the jeans?* ($17.99) *Is the skirt a lot of money? Are the jeans a lot of money?*
- Say: *When you are in a store, you can ask How much . . . ? to learn the price.*
- Read the first line of the directions.
- Play CD 2, Track 31. Students listen and repeat.
- Say: *Remember, say How much is this . . . ? for singular items and How much are these . . . ? for plural items.* Write these two questions as headings on the board. Ask students for clothing items for each one and write them on the board.
- Resume playing Track 31. Students listen and repeat.
- Pair students and tell them to take turns playing the customer and the assistant.
- Call on pairs to perform for the class.

4 PRACTICE

A Listen. Fill in the price tags.

- Read the directions. Write the first answer on the board as an example so students remember to write a dollar sign and a decimal point.
- Play CD 2, Track 32. Students listen and write.
- Call on students to write answers on the board.

Communicative Practice   15 minutes

B PAIRS. Practice the conversation above. Use...

- On the board, rewrite the conversation from Exercise 3 with blanks for the prices and items.
- Read the directions. Play the assistant and practice the conversation with an above-level student.
- Pair students. Say: *Practice the conversation with the clothes and prices from Exercise 4A.*
- Ask: *Which things are singular?* (blouse, watch) *Which things are plural?* (shoes, jeans) Say: *Take turns playing the customer and the assistant.*
- Call on pairs to perform for the class.

T-93   UNIT 5

■■ MULTILEVEL INSTRUCTION for 4B

Cross-ability Tell above-level students to play the customer so they control the flow of the conversation.

C Look at the receipt. Answer the questions.

- Read the directions. Ask the question in item 1. Tell students to point to the date on the receipt. Quickly scan the room and check that students are able to find the date. Say: *Ask the student next to you for help if you can't find it.*
- On the board, write *sales tax.* Say: *In most states in the United States, we pay sales tax on clothes and other things we buy.* Ask: *What is the sales tax here?* Write it on the board.
- Explain: Change *is money you get back when you pay for something. For example, if the total is $18.00 and I pay with a $20 bill, then the change is $2.00.*
- Read the directions.
- Walk around and spot-check students' answers. Students compare answers with a partner.
- Call on students to say answers.

5 LIFE SKILLS WRITING

Turn to page 257 and ask students to complete the personal check. See pages Txi–Txii for general notes about the Life Skills Writing activities.

Progress Check

Can you . . . talk about prices and read price tags and receipts?

Say: *We have practiced talking about prices and reading price tags and receipts. Now, look at the question at the bottom of the page. Can you talk about prices and read price tags and receipts?* Tell students to write a checkmark in the box.

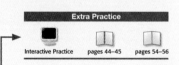

Extra Practice

Interactive Practice   pages 44–45   pages 54–56

Cross-references to relevant pages in course components at the end of each lesson allow the teacher to plan additional in-class or at-home activities.

Progress checks allow students to reflect on their ability to use the competencies presented in the lesson.

Lesson 8 Return something to a store

Getting Started 5 minutes

1 BEFORE YOU LISTEN

CLASS. Read the information. Answer the question.

- Say: *Look at the picture.* Ask: *What is happening?* (The woman is returning clothes.)
- Say: *Remember that* return *means to take something that you do not want back to the store to get your money back.*
- Read the directions and the paragraph. Ask: *Do you ever return clothes?*

 Expansion: Speaking Practice for 1

- If possible, ask students to tell stories about what they returned. Ask: *What did you return? Why?*

Culture Connection

- Say: *In the United States, many stores allow you to make returns.*
- Ask: *What about in your country?*

Presentation 20 minutes

2 LISTEN

A Look at the pictures. Why do people return...

- Read the directions.
- Hold up the book. Point to each picture, and ask about the article of clothing: *What is it? What's the problem?* Students identify the clothing (for example, *pants*) and read the reason (*They don't fit. They're too big.*).
- On the board, write the singular and plural forms of each reason (for example, *It's too big. They're too big.*). Tell students to copy them into their notebooks.

- Finally, hold the book up and point to the circle next to the title of the art, which says *On the air.* Say: On the air *means that a show is on the radio. We will now listen to a radio show.*

B Matt Spencer is interviewing people...

- Read the directions. Point to the picture on page 101 and explain: Customer service employees *are the people in a store who answer your questions and help you when you have a problem.*
- Read the question and the answer choices.
- Play CD 2, Track 39. Students listen.
- Call on the class to say the answer.

Teaching Tip

Optional: If pre-level students need additional support, tell them to read the Audio Script on page 284 as they listen to the conversations.

C Listen again. Number the reasons...

- Read the directions.
- Play CD 2, Track 39. Pause after the first reason (*My husband doesn't like it.*) and ask: *Which reason did you hear?* Students put a *1* in the circle next to *It doesn't look good. I don't like it.*
- Resume playing Track 39. Students number the remaining reasons.
- Students compare answers with a partner, using *first, second, third,* and *fourth.*
- Call on students to read the reasons in order. Ask: *Which one is first/second/third/fourth?*

UNIT 5   **T-100**

EXPAND Show what you know!

3 ACT IT OUT

STEP 1. Listen to the conversation.

- Play CD 2, Track 42. Students listen.
- As needed, play Track 42 again to aid comprehension.

STEP 2. You are in a clothing store. Student A,...

- Read the directions and the guidelines for Students A and B.
- Pair students. Students practice at their desk with their partner.
- Walk around and check that Student A is correctly asking *yes/no* questions in the simple present and that Student B is giving correct short answers.
- Call on pairs to perform for the class. While pairs are performing, use the scoring rubric on page Txiv to evaluate each student's vocabulary, grammar, fluency, and how well they complete the task.
- *Optional:* After each pair finishes, discuss the strengths and weakness of each performance either in front of the class or privately.

STEP 3. Review the conversation...

- Tell students to review the conversation on page 101.
- Play CD 2, Track 40. Students listen.
- As needed, play Track 40 again to aid comprehension.

STEP 4. It's the next day.

- Read the directions and the guidelines for Students A and B.
- Pair students. Students practice at their desk with their partner.
- Walk around and check that Student A is correctly using the negative of *be* and that Student B is asking about the reason for returning the sweater.
- Call on pairs to practice for the class.
- While pairs are performing, use the scoring rubric on page Txiv to evaluate each student's vocabulary, grammar, fluency, and how well they complete the task.
- *Optional:* After each pair finishes, discuss the strengths and weakness of each performance, either in front of the class or privately.

4 READ AND REACT

STEP 1. Read about Luis's problem.

- Say: *We are going to read about a student's problem, and then we need to think about a solution.*
- Read the directions.
- Read the story while students follow along silently. Pause after each sentence to allow time for students to comprehend. Periodically stop and ask simple *Wh-* questions to check comprehension (for example, *When is Luis's birthday? What does Paula give him?*).

STEP 2. PAIRS. Talk about it. What is Luis's...

- Pair students. Read the directions and the question.
- Read the ideas in the list. Give pairs a couple of minutes to discuss possible solutions for Luis.
- Ask: *Which ideas are good?* Call on students to say their opinion about the ideas in the list (for example, S: *I don't think he can keep the tie because he doesn't need it.*).
- Now tell students to think of one new idea not in the box (for example, *He can sell it on the Internet.*).

MULTILEVEL INSTRUCTION for STEP 2

Pre-level For more support, students work in groups of 3.
Above-level Ask pairs to discuss the pros and cons of each idea. Call on pairs to say the pros and cons of each (for example, *He can return the tie and buy a wallet. Pro: This is an easy way to get a wallet. Con: Maybe the wallets at the store are all expensive. He will pay more money for it.*).

5 CONNECT

Turn to page 248 for the Community-building Activity and page 268 for the Team Project. See pages Txi–Txii for general notes about teaching these activities.

Progress Check

Which goals can you check off? Go back to page 85.
Ask students to turn to page 85 and check off any remaining goals they have reached. Call on students to say which goals they will practice outside of class.

UNIT 5   **T-104**

Supporting Persistence in the Classroom

Persistence activities, Life Skills Writing activities, and Team Projects for each unit are in the back of the book. Cross-references within the unit indicate at what point each activity should be completed. Detailed notes for each activity can be found on the *Future* Companion Website at www.longman.com/future. Following are some general notes that apply to all of the activities within each section.

Persistence Activities

The Persistence activities are classroom-tested activities that support students in continuing their studies. Recent research has shown us that students are more likely to persist when they feel they are part of a learning community and when they are able to set educational goals they believe they can achieve. Programs can also support student persistence by showing students how to study efficiently and how to monitor their learning. Each Persistence activity in *Future* fits one of these categories: community building, setting goals, or developing study skills.

Step 1: Introduce the activity
- Say the name of the activity. Then explain the objective of the activity. For example, for Unit 1, say: *We're going to learn each other's names* or, if students have already been introduced to each other, say: *We're going to practice remembering each other's names.* For Unit 2, say: *We're going to talk about our goals for learning English.*
- Put students in groups, if necessary, for the activity.

Step 2: Get ready
- Read the directions for the first part of the activity and make sure students understand what they need to do.
- Review any language students need for the activity. If the activity requires a lot of the unit vocabulary, have students take a few minutes to review the words and phrases in the vocabulary lesson. If students will need to write sentences, write an example sentence on the board.
- Model the activity for students. If the activity has students working in groups of three, call two on- or above-level students to the front of the room. Model the activity with them, taking one part yourself. If the activity requires students to work independently, write the exercise on the board and call on a few students to give sample responses. Write their responses on the board.

Step 3: Start the activity
- Have students start working in groups or independently, as necessary for the activity. Walk around the room while students are working, checking to make sure they are on task and providing help as needed.
- If the activity has a second part, check to make sure all students have had sufficient time to complete the first part before moving on. When students are ready, repeat Steps 2 and 3 for the second part of the activity.

Step 4: Wrap up
- After students have completed all parts of the activity, call on a few students to share their work with the class. If the activity had students working in pairs or groups, call on one or two pairs or groups to perform the activity for the class. If students were working independently, call on a few students to share their responses.

Life Skills Writing

The Life Skills Writing activities consist of completing forms and other documents. Students first look at a model and answer comprehension questions about the model; they then complete the writing task using their own personal information. These activities often appear at the end of the Life Skills Lesson, but may appear at different points in a given unit.

Step 1: Introduce the activity
- Say the name of the activity. Then explain the objective of the activity. For example, for Unit 1, say: *You are going to complete a form with your personal information.* For Unit 4, say: *You are going to complete an emergency contact form.*
- Ask students why they might need this kind of form or other document.

Step 2: Present the model
- Read the directions for Exercise A. Hold up the page or use the transparency for that page. Have students complete the activity as a class.
- Read the directions for the comprehension exercise for the model. Have students complete the task.
- Call on students to provide their responses for the comprehension exercise. Go over any questions that students may have.

Step 3: Complete the writing task
- Read the directions and make sure students understand the task.
- Depending on the level of your class, you may wish to use the transparency to have students complete the task together before having them work independently.
- As students work, walk around the classroom and check for accuracy. Give students help as needed.

Step 4: Check progress
- Say: *Look at the question at the bottom of the page. Can you _____?* For example, for Unit 1, say: *Can you complete a form with your personal information?* For Unit 4, say: *Can you complete an emergency contact form?*
- Tell students to write a checkmark in the box.

Team Projects

The Team Projects give students an opportunity to use the language they have learned throughout the unit to produce a product such as a booklet, poster, or chart. Students work in teams of 3 or 4. Each team member is assigned a specific role: Captain, Co-captain, Assistant, or Spokesperson. The teacher can assign roles that match each student's strength. For example, since the tasks performed by the Co-captain are not language-intensive, the teacher may want to assign this role to a pre-level student.

Step 1: Introduce the objective

- Say the title of the activity. Then explain the objective of the activity. For example, for Unit 1, say: *We're learning our classmates' names and countries.* For Unit 2, say: *We're making a diagram about where people work.*

Step 2: Form teams

- Form groups of 4 students. Ask them to sit with each other.
- Assign students the roles of Captain, Co-captain, Assistant, or Spokesperson. You can also make cards with the titles Captain, Co-captain, Assistant, or Spokesperson and give each team the cards so students can select their own roles.
- If necessary, students can share one role. For example, a pre-level student and an above-level student can perform the role of the Assistant together. Also, one student can have two roles. For example, an above-level student can perform the roles of both the Assistant and the Spokesperson.

Step 3: Get ready

- Gather the materials in the note and have them ready for students to use.
- Read the directions for all team members and the materials note.
- You may want to provide the key question(s) students need to ask during the activity. For example, for Unit 1, say: *What's your name? Where are you from?* For Unit 2, say: *Who works in a _____?*
- Tell the co-captain to watch the classroom clock to track the time and to tell the team when they have one minute left.
- Have students complete the task. Monitor teams to make sure students know their roles.
- Walk around and help as needed.

Step 4: Create

- Have Co-captains retrieve needed materials.
- If the activity includes a chart or graph, hold up the example provided and go over it with the class. Encourage teams to sketch the chart or graph on a piece of notebook paper before creating it on a poster.
- Read the directions for the Co-captains and team. Each team can decide who will do what to create the poster, chart, or booklet.
- Have the Co-captain watch the clock and tell the team when they have one minute left.
- Walk around and check that all students have a role. If it seems that a student is not involved, ask the team, *What is _____ doing?*

Step 5: Report

- Call on each Spokesperson to tell the class about the group's project. The goal of the presentation is to make sure the audience (the other students) understands all the information presented.
- Have the other students in the class write down a question for the team that is presenting. Call on students to ask questions that the spokesperson can answer. For example, for Unit 2, a student may ask, *What jobs are at a construction site?* For Unit 5, a student may ask, *How many people shop on the Internet?*

Speaking Activities

The final page of every unit of *Future* contains an Act It Out activity and a problem-solving activity. These activities offer students an opportunity to practice their spoken fluency and to demonstrate their understanding of the unit vocabulary, grammar, and competencies.

After students have practiced the activity in pairs or small groups, allow some students to perform the activity in front of the whole class. If you wish to use this activity for evaluation purposes, use the Speaking Rubric on page T-xiv to make notes about each student's performance. An example of this rubric is shown below. For each category listed in the rubric (Vocabulary, Grammar, Fluency, and Task Completion), include comments about both *strong points* and *weak points*. You can then use those comments to give each student a rating of 1, 2, or 3 for each category.

The purpose of this kind of evaluation is to give fair and clear feedback to students and to give them specific points to work on so they can improve their fluency. It is important to use language that a student can understand and to give examples of what the student did or didn't say when possible. For example, you might say, *You used a lot of vocabulary from the unit* or *You need to work on forms of be. Review the grammar charts in the unit.* Feedback should be given to students in a timely manner in order to be most effective and helpful.

Vocabulary	Score	Comments
Uses a variety of vocabulary words and expressions from the unit	3	
Uses some vocabulary words and expressions from the unit	2	
Uses few vocabulary words or expressions from the unit	1	
Grammar	**Score**	**Comments**
Uses a variety of grammar points from the unit; uses grammar with control and accuracy	3	
Uses some grammar points from the unit; uses grammar with less control and accuracy	2	
Does not use grammar points from the unit; uses grammar with little control or accuracy	1	
Fluency	**Score**	**Comments**
Speech is authentic and fluent; there is authentic communication with partner	3	
Speech is overly rehearsed at points; not true communication	2	
Speech is not authentic; is not really listening to and communicating with partner	1	
Task completion	**Score**	**Comments**
Student completed the task successfully	3	
Student mostly completed the task; student went off topic at various points	2	
Student was not able to successfully complete the task: see comments	1	

Speaking Rubric

Name: _____

Class: _____ Date: _____

Activity: _____ Unit: _____ Page: _____

Vocabulary	Score	Comments
Uses a variety of vocabulary words and expressions from the unit	3	
Uses some vocabulary words and expressions from the unit	2	
Uses few vocabulary words or expressions from the unit	1	
Grammar	**Score**	**Comments**
Uses a variety of grammar points from the unit; uses grammar with control and accuracy	3	
Uses some grammar points from the unit; uses grammar with less control and accuracy	2	
Does not use grammar points from the unit; uses grammar with little control or accuracy	1	
Fluency	**Score**	**Comments**
Speech is authentic and fluent; there is authentic communication with partner	3	
Speech is overly rehearsed at points; not true communication	2	
Speech is not authentic; is not really listening to and communicating with partner	1	
Task completion	**Score**	**Comments**
Student completed the task successfully	3	
Student mostly completed the task; student went off topic at various points	2	
Student was not able to successfully complete the task: see comments	1	

FUTURE
English for Results

1

TEACHER'S EDITION
AND LESSON PLANNER

Acknowledgments

The authors and publisher would like to extend special thanks to our Series Consultants whose insights, experience, and expertise shaped the course and guided us throughout its development.

Beatriz B. Díaz Miami-Dade County Public Schools, Miami, FL
Ronna Magy Los Angeles Unified School District, Los Angles, CA
Federico Salas-Isnardi Texas A & M University—TCALL, College Station, TX

We would also like to express our gratitude to the following individuals. Their kind assistance was indispensable to the creation of this program.

Consultants

Wendy J. Allison Seminole Community College, Sanford, FL
Claudia Carco Westchester Community College, Valhalla, NY
Maria J. Cesnik Ysleta Community Learning Center, El Paso, TX
Edwidge Crevecoeur-Bryant University of Florida, Gainesville, FL
Ann Marie Holzknecht Damrau San Diego Community College, San Diego, CA
Peggy Datz Berkeley Adult School, Berkeley, CA
MaryAnn Florez D.C. Learns, Washington, D.C.
Portia LaFerla Torrance Adult School, Torrance, CA
Eileen McKee Westchester Community College, Valhalla, NY
Julie Meuret Downey Adult School, Downey, CA
Sue Pace Santa Ana College School of Continuing Education, Santa Ana, CA
Howard Pomann Union County College, Elizabeth, NY
Mary Ray Fairfax County Public Schools, Falls Church, VA
Gema Santos Miami-Dade County Public Schools, Miami, FL
Edith Uber Santa Clara Adult Education, Santa Clara, CA
Theresa Warren East Side Adult Education, San Jose, CA

Piloters

MariCarmen Acosta American High School, Adult ESOL, Hialeah, FL
Resurrección Ángeles Metropolitan Skills Center, Los Angeles, CA
Linda Bolognesi Fairfax County Public Schools, Adult and Community Education, Falls Church, VA
Patricia Boquiren Metropolitan Skills Center, Los Angeles, CA
Paul Buczko Pacoima Skills Center, Pacoima, CA
Matthew Horowitz Metropolitan Skills Center, Los Angeles, CA
Gabriel de la Hoz The English Center, Miami, FL
Cam-Tu Huynh Los Angeles Unified School District, Los Angeles, CA
Jorge Islas Whitewater Unified School District, Adult Education, Whitewater, WI
Lisa Johnson City College of San Francisco, San Francisco, CA
Loreto Kaplan Collier County Public Schools Adult ESOL Program, Naples, FL
Teressa Kitchen Collier County Public Schools Adult ESOL Program, Naples, FL
Anjie Martin Whitewater Unified School District, Adult Education, Whitewater, WI
Elida Matthews College of the Mainland, Texas City, TX
Penny Negron College of the Mainland, Texas City, TX
Manuel Pando Coral Park High School, Miami, FL
Susan Ritter Evans Community Adult School, Los Angeles, CA
Susan Ross Torrance Adult School, Torrance, CA
Beatrice Shields Fairfax County Public Schools, Adult and Community Education, Falls Church, VA
Oscar Solís Coral Park High School, Miami, FL
Wanda W. Weaver Literacy Council of Prince George's County, Hyattsville, MD

Special thanks to Sharon Goldstein for her invaluable contribution to the pronunciation strand.

Reviewers

Lisa Agao Fresno Adult School, Fresno, CA
Carol Antuñano The English Center, Miami, FL
Euphronia Awakuni Evans Community Adult School, Los Angeles, CA
Jack Bailey Santa Barbara Adult Education, Santa Barbara, CA
Robert Breitbard District School Board of Collier County, Naples, FL
Diane Burke Evans Community Adult School, Los Angeles, CA
José A. Carmona Embry-Riddle Aeronautical University, Daytona Beach, FL
Veronique Colas Los Angeles Technology Center, Los Angles, CA
Carolyn Corrie Metropolitan Skills Center, Los Angeles, CA
Marti Estrin Santa Rosa Junior College, Sebastopol, CA
Sheila Friedman Metropolitan Skills Center, Los Angeles, CA
José Gonzalez Spanish Education Development Center, Washington, D.C.
Allene G. Grognet Vice President (Emeritus), Center for Applied Linguistics
J. Quinn Harmon-Kelley Venice Community Adult School, Los Angeles, CA
Edwina Hoffman Miami-Dade County Public Schools, Coral Gables, FL
Eduardo Honold Far West Project GREAT, El Paso, TX
Leigh Jacoby Los Angeles Community Adult School, Los Angeles, CA
Fayne Johnson Broward County Public Schools, Ft. Lauderdale, FL
Loreto Kaplan, Collier County Public Schools Adult ESOL Program, Naples, FL
Synthia LaFontaine Collier County Public Schools, Naples, FL
Gretchen Lammers-Ghereben Martinez Adult Education, Martinez, CA
Susan Lanzano Editorial Consultant, Briarcliff Manor, NY
Karen Mauer ESL Express, Euless, TX
Rita McSorley North East Independent School District, San Antonio, TX
Alice-Ann Menjivar Carlos Rosario International Public Charter School, Washington, D.C.
Sue Pace Santa Ana College School of Continuing Education, Santa Ana, CA
Isabel Perez American High School, Hialeah, FL
Howard Pomann Union County College, Elizabeth, NJ
Lesly Prudent Miami-Dade County Public Schools, Miami, FL
Valentina Purtell North Orange County Community College District, Anaheim, CA
Mary Ray Fairfax County Adult ESOL, Falls Church, VA
Laurie Shapero Miami-Dade Community College, Miami, FL
Felissa Taylor Nause Austin, TX
Meintje Westerbeek Baltimore City Community College, Baltimore, MD

Thanks also to the following teachers, who contributed their ideas for the Persistence Activities:

Dave Coleman Los Angeles Unified School District, Los Angeles, CA
Renee Collins Elk Grove Adult and Community Education, Elk Grove, CA
Elaine Klapman Venice Community Adult School, Venice, CA (retired)
Yvonne Wong Nishio Evans Community Adult School, Los Angeles, CA (retired)
Daniel S. Pittaway North Orange County Community College District, Anaheim, CA
Laurel Pollard Educational Consultant, Tucson, AZ
Eden Quimzon Santiago Canyon College, Division of Continuing Education, Orange, CA

About the Series Consultants and Authors

SERIES CONSULTANTS

Dr. Beatriz B. Díaz has taught ESL for more than three decades in Miami. She has a master's degree in TESOL and a doctorate in education from Nova Southeastern University. She has given trainings and numerous presentations at international, national, state, and local conferences throughout the United States, the Caribbean, and South America. Dr. Díaz is the district supervisor for the Miami-Dade County Public Schools Adult ESOL Program, one of the largest in the United States.

Ronna Magy has worked as an ESL classroom teacher and teacher-trainer for nearly three decades. Most recently, she has worked as the ESL Teacher Adviser in charge of site-based professional development for the Division of Adult and Career Education of the Los Angeles Unified School District. She has trained teachers of adult English language learners in many areas, including lesson planning, learner persistence and goal setting, and cooperative learning. A frequent presenter at local, state and national, and international conferences, Ms. Magy is the author of adult ESL publications on life skills and test preparation, U.S. citizenship, reading and writing, and workplace English. She holds a master's degree in social welfare from the University of California at Berkeley.

Federico Salas-Isnardi has worked for 20 years in the field of adult education as an ESL and GED instructor, professional development specialist, curriculum writer, and program administrator. He has trained teachers of adult English language learners for over 15 years on topics ranging from language acquisition and communicative competence to classroom management and individualized professional development planning. Mr. Salas-Isnardi has been a contributing writer or consultant for a number of ESL publications, and he has co-authored curriculum for site-based workforce ESL and Spanish classes. He holds a master's degree in applied linguistics from the University of Houston and has completed a number of certificates in educational leadership.

AUTHORS

Marjorie Fuchs has taught ESL at New York City Technical College and LaGuardia Community College of the City University of New York and EFL at the Sprach Studio Lingua Nova in Munich, Germany. She has a master's degree in applied English linguistics and a certificate in TESOL from the University of Wisconsin–Madison. She has authored or co-authored many widely used books and multimedia materials, notably *Focus on Grammar: An Integrated Skills Approach* (levels 3 and 4), *Longman English Interactive 3 and 4*, *Grammar Express* (*Basic and Intermediate*), and workbooks to the *Oxford Picture Dictionary*.

Lisa Johnson has taught ESL and EFL for 20 years in the United States, Taiwan, and Russia, and is currently an instructor at City College of San Francisco. Based on her experience teaching VESL courses, she co-authored *Apply Yourself: English for Job Search Success*. She also co-authored or edited the Communication Companions for the *Longman English Interactive* series and contributed to *Talking Business Intermediate: Mastering the Language of Business*. In addition, she co-authored a large-scale curriculum for health care professionals. Ms. Johnson holds a master's degree in TESOL from the University of Northern Iowa.

Sarah Lynn has taught ESL and EFL for 20 years in the United States and abroad, and she currently teaches ESL at the Harvard Bridge to Learning and Literacy Program in Cambridge, Massachusetts. Ms. Lynn holds a master's degree in TESOL from Teachers College, Columbia University. She has trained volunteers and given workshops on the teaching of reading, kinesthetic techniques in the classroom, and cross-cultural communication. She has developed curricula for adult education programs in the areas of reading, life skills, and civics, and she is the co-author of *Business Across Cultures*. She has also contributed to numerous teacher resource materials, including those for *Side by Side*, *Foundations*, and *Word by Word*.

Irene E. Schoenberg has taught ESL for more than two decades at Hunter College's International English Language Institute and at Columbia University's American Language Program. Ms. Schoenberg holds a master's degree in TESOL from Teachers College, Columbia University. She has trained teachers at Hunter College, Columbia University, and the New School University, and she has given workshops and academic presentations at ESL programs and conferences throughout the world. Ms. Schoenberg is the author or co-author of numerous publications, including *True Colors*; *Speaking of Values 1*; *Topics from A to Z*, Books 1 and 2; and *Focus on Grammar: An Integrated Skills Approach* (levels 1 and 2).

Scope and Sequence

UNIT	VOCABULARY	LISTENING	SPEAKING AND PRONUNCIATION	GRAMMAR	
Pre-Unit **Getting Started** *page 2*	Classroom instructions; Asking for help	• Listen to classroom instructions • Listen to ways of asking for help	• Follow classroom instructions • Ask for help	• Introduction to imperatives	
1 **Getting to Know You** *page 5*	Countries	• Listen to an introduction • Listen to a conversation about countries of origin • Listen to a conversation about classes	• Introduce yourself • Shake hands when you meet someone • Greet and say goodbye • Identify people and ask where they are from • Talk about school • Sentence stress • The different sounds in *he's* and *she's*	• Subject pronouns • Simple present of *be*: Affirmative and negative statements • Contractions with *be*	
2 **A Hard Day's Work** *page 25*	Jobs; Workplaces	• Listen to someone introducing two people • Listen to a conversation about jobs • Listen to a conversation about workplaces	• Introduce others • Talk about jobs • Talk about workplaces • Falling intonation in statements and *Wh-* questions • Pronunciation of *-s* and *-es* endings in plural nouns • Rising intonation in *yes/no* questions	• *A/an* • Plural nouns • Simple present of *be*: Yes/no questions and short answers • Simple present of *work* and *live*	
3 **Time for Class** *page 45*	Things in a classroom; People and places at school	• Listen to a teacher giving instructions for a test • Listen to a conversation about things in the classroom • Listen to a conversation about people and places at school	• Give and follow classroom commands • Talk about things in the classroom • Identify people at school • Get someone's attention and ask for information • Voiced *th* sound • Word stress	• Imperatives • *This, that, these, those* • Object pronouns	
4 **Family Ties** *page 65*	Family members; Physical descriptions	• Listen to a conversation about family members • Listen to a conversation about what someone looks like • Listen to a conversation about children's ages and grades in school	• Talk about family members • Describe people • Give age and child's grade in school • Understand the U.S. school system • Understand cultural appropriateness of asking about age • Pronunciation of possessive *'s* • Linking words together: consonant to vowel	• Possessive adjectives and *'s* with names • *Be* and *have* with descriptions • *How old is/are . . . ?*	

LIFE SKILLS	READING	WRITING	NUMERACY	PERSISTENCE
• Learn the letters of the alphabet • Learn numbers	• Locate the U.S. map in your book	• Identify capital and lowercase letters	• Learn numbers	• Learn about your book • Learn about working in pairs and groups
• Give first and last name • Give spellings • Use appropriate titles • Complete a personal information form	• Read a paragraph about class attendance • Read an article about immigrants in the U.S. • Problem-solving: Read a paragraph about class placement	• Write sentences about your name and marital status • Write sentences about yourself, a classmate, or your teacher • Start country names with capital letters • Start people's names with capital letters • Start sentences with capital letters • End sentences with a period	• Interpret a pie chart • Take a class survey	• Talk about attendance • Persistence Activity: Name game • Project: Make a poster about your classmates
• Use cardinal numbers 0–9 • Give phone number and area code • Read a telephone directory • Listen to a message and write a phone number • Complete a form at work • Project: Create a Venn diagram of jobs and workplaces	• Read an introduction of two people • Read an article about talking to a job counselor • Problem-solving: Read a paragraph about work schedules	• Write a sentence about someone's job • Write sentences about your job and workplace • End questions with a question mark	• Learn cardinal numbers 0–9	• Network Activity: Find classmates with the same job as you. • Persistence Activity: Goal setting: Why learn English?
• Use cardinal numbers 10–100 • Give locations of places around school • Complete a school registration form	• Read a paragraph about arriving late to class • Read a letter of advice about good study habits • Problem-solving: Read a paragraph about test-taking	• Write sentences about things in your classroom • Write tips for learning English	• Count classroom items • Learn cardinal numbers 10–100	• Understand classroom rules • Learn good study habits • Set study goals • Network Activity: Find classmates who want to practice the same study skill as you. • Identify learning strategies • Project: Make a booklet about your school • Persistence Activity: School supplies
• Use ordinal numbers 1st–31st • Identify day, date, and month • Read calendars • Write dates in numbers and words • Give date of birth and birthday • Complete an emergency contact form • Project: Make a calendar of holidays	• Read an article about blended families • Read a paragraph about the physical characteristics of family members • Problem-solving: Read a paragraph about personal phone calls at work	• Write sentences about yourself and your family • Start months with capital letters	• Interpret a calendar • Learn ordinal numbers 1st–31st • Count students and categorize by physical description • Interpret a pie chart • Understand percentages • Calculate age based on date of birth	• Network Activity: Find classmates with the same birthday month as you. • Persistence Activity: My friends and family

Text in red = Civics and American culture

UNIT	VOCABULARY	LISTENING	SPEAKING AND PRONUNCIATION	GRAMMAR
5 **Shop, Shop, Shop** *page 85*	Colors and clothes	• Listen to a conversation about shopping for a gift • Listen to a customer asking about sizes and colors • Listen to interviews with people returning clothing to a store	• Talk about needs and wants • Ask about sizes • Read size labels • Talk about likes and dislikes • Return something to a store • Sentence rhythm (weak words)	• Simple present affirmative • Simple present: *Yes/no* questions and short answers • Simple present negative
6 **Home, Sweet Home** *page 105*	Rooms of a house, furniture, and appliances	• Listen to a conversation about a house for rent • Listen to a conversation with a building manager about features of an apartment • Listen to directions on an automated telephone recording	• Describe a house or apartment • Ask about apartment and house rentals • Give directions • Stress in compound nouns	• *There is/There are* • *There is/There are: Yes/no* questions • Prepositions of direction and location
7 **Day After Day** *page 125*	Daily routines and leisure activities; Clock times	• Listen to a conversation about schedules • Listen to a conversation about weekend activities • Listen to a radio show about ways of relaxing	• Talk about daily routines • Ask when something happens • Talk about leisure activities • Talk about frequency of activities • The weak pronunciation of *do you* in questions • Pronunciation of -*s* and -*es* endings in third-person singular present tense verbs	• *Wh-* questions and prepositions of time • Adverbs of frequency • *How often?* and expressions of frequency
8 **From Soup to Nuts** *page 145*	Common foods	• Listen to two friends talking about food they like and dislike • Listen to someone ordering a meal in a restaurant • Listen to a call-in radio show about nutrition	• Talk about likes and dislikes • Read a menu • Order meals in a restaurant • Talk about the nutritional value of common foods • Talk about different ways to prepare food • Pronunciation of *I like* and *I'd like* • Intonation of choice questions with *or*	• Count and non-count nouns • Choice questions with *or* • *How much/How many*

LIFE SKILLS	READING	WRITING	NUMERACY	PERSISTENCE
• Use U.S. money • Talk about prices • Read a receipt • Understand sales tax • Write a personal check • Project: Talk about where classmates shop for clothes	• Read a paragraph about a birthday gift • Read about clothing sizes • Read an article about presidential dollar coins • Identify presidents • Problem-solving: Read a paragraph about returning gifts	• Write sentences about problems with clothing • Write sentences about things people need, want, or have • Use hyphens in amounts on personal checks	• Learn values of U.S. money • Count U.S. money • Understand prices • Understand a shopping receipt • Make a bar graph about where classmates shop	• Network Activity: Find classmates with the same favorite color as you. • Persistence Activity: Class jobs
• Read addresses • Give addresses • Read an Apartment for Rent ad • Understand how to rent an apartment • Address an envelope • Project: Make a floor plan for your dream house	• Read an article about smoke alarms and fire safety at home • Read a paragraph about furnished apartments • Problem-solving: Read a paragraph about rent increases	• Write sentences about houses and things in them • Write directions to a place • Use abbreviations in addresses	• Talk about numbers of rooms in a home • Compare rents of two homes	• Network Activity: Find classmates who live in your neighborhood. • Persistence Activity: My vocabulary learning stategies
• Identify abbreviations for days of the week • Interpret a work schedule • Read and complete a time sheet • Understand Social Security numbers • Write a note to request time off	• Read about weekly schedules • Read an article about how Americans spend their free time • Problem-solving: Read a paragraph about busy schedules	• Write sentences about your schedule and free-time activities • Use capital letters for days of the week • Use abbreviations for days of the week	• Tell time • Count hours worked in a day or week • Interpret bar graphs • Conduct a survey about classmates' free time and make a bar graph • Project: Create a schedule	• Network Activity: Find classmates with the same free-time activity as you. • Persistence Activity: Daily planner
• Read store flyers and compare prices for food • Read food labels • Understand U.S. measurements of weight • Write a note listing things to buy • Project: Create a menu	• Read a paragraph about what someone eats for lunch • Read an article about expiration dates on food • Problem-solving: Read a paragraph about healthy eating habits	• Write a shopping list • Write a sentence about the nutritional value of foods • Write sentences about food your classmates want • Use commas between things in a list	• Learn weights of food • Compare prices • Understand nutritional information on food labels	• Network Activity: Find classmates who shop for food near your home. • Persistence Activity: Getting-to-know-you tea

Text in red = Civics and American culture

UNIT	VOCABULARY	LISTENING	SPEAKING AND PRONUNCIATION	GRAMMAR
9 **Rain or** **Shine** *page 165*	Weather, seasons, and temperature	• Listen to a conversation about weather and current activities • Listen to a conversation about preparing for a storm • Listen to a weather report for different U.S. cities • Understand temperatures in degrees Fahrenheit	• Talk about activities taking place now • Talk about the weather • Pronunciation of *–ing* ending • Project: Give a weather report	• Present continuous: Affirmative and negative statements • Present continuous: *Yes/no* questions and answers • Adverbs of degree: *Really, very, pretty*
10 **Around** **Town** *page 185*	Places in the community	• Listen to a conversation about the location of a place • Listen to someone giving directions by bus • Listen to a radio show about weekend events • Learn how to get information about events in your community	• Ask where places are • Ask about bus routes, schedules, and fares • Talk about activities in the immediate future • Word stress • Sentence stress	• Prepositions of place • Simple present: Questions with *how, how much,* and *where* • Present continuous for the future
11 **Health** **Matters** *page 205*	Parts of the body; Symptoms and illnesses	• Listen to a mother calling school about a sick child • Understand and follow procedures for a child missing school • Listen to a conversation with someone who missed work • Identify appropriate reasons to miss work • Listen to a call-in radio show about remedies for illnesses	• Call to explain absence • Describe symptoms • Call in sick to work • Talk about past activities • Give advice • Pronunciation of *was/were* and *wasn't/weren't*	• Review: Simple present statements and questions • *Be* simple past: Statements • *Should*: Statements
12 **Help** **Wanted** *page 225*	Job duties	• Listen to someone asking about a job and talking about his skills • Listen to a conversation about availability • Listen to an interview with the owners of a new business	• Respond to a Help Wanted sign • Talk about ability and inability • Ask a co-worker to work your shift • Respond to personal information questions in a simple job interview • Ask and answer questions about past experience • Sentence stress: *Can* and *can't* in statements • Sentence stress: *Can* and *can't* in short answers	• *Can* for ability: Affirmative and negative statements • *Can* for ability: Questions and short answers • *Be* simple past: *Yes/no* and *Wh-* questions

LIFE SKILLS	READING	WRITING	NUMERACY	PERSISTENCE
• Talk about weather conditions • Respond to weather emergencies • Create an emergency plan for your family • Write a postcard to a friend	• Read a paragraph about the weather in two cities • Read an article about small talk • Understand how to make small talk • Problem-solving: Read a paragraph about weather emergencies	• Write sentences about activities you or others are doing currently • Write sentences about today's weather • Use the degree mark for temperatures	• Read a thermometer in degrees Fahrenheit	• Network Activity: Find classmates who spend their day off the same way as you. • Persistence Activity: Important dates in school
• Identify forms of transportation • Identify traffic signs • Interpret destination signs on buses • Read bus schedules • Write directions to get to a place	• Read a paragraph about the location of a new supermarket • Read an article about resources available at the public library • Get a library card • Problem-solving: Read a paragraph about items left on a bus	• Write sentences about your weekend plans • Write sentences about your classmates' weekend plans	• Understand a bus schedule	• Network Activity: Find classmates who get to school the same way as you. • Persistence Activity: Things I read in English • Project: Make a booklet about places in your community
• Make a doctor's appointment • Read an appointment card • Follow instructions during a medical exam • Interpret medicine labels • Complete a medical information form • Project: Make a poster about healthy habits	• Read a paragraph about illnesses • Read an article about the health benefits of walking • Problem-solving: Read a paragraph about a sick child	• Write sentences comparing two pictures • Write suggestions for health problems	• Read medicine labels and understand correct dosages	• Talk about attendance • Persistence Activity: Individual barriers, group support
• Read want ads • Identify different ways to find a job • Complete a job application • Project: Make a list of skills needed for your dream job	• Read a paragraph about a busy day at a clothing store • Read an article about appropriate body language for a job interview • Problem-solving: Read a paragraph about recommending someone for a job	• Write a want ad for a job you want • Write sentences about your job experience and skills • Use commas in short answers to *yes/no* questions	• Calculate weekly earnings based on hourly wages	• Network Activity: Find classmates with the same work shift as you. • Persistence Activity: Now I can

Text in red = Civics and American culture

Correlations

UNIT	CASAS Reading Basic Skill Content Standards	CASAS Listening Basic Skill Content Standards	
1	**U1:** R1.2; 1.3; 1.4; 2.2; 2.4; 2.5; 3.1; 3.3; 3.8; 6.1; **L3:** R1.1; 2.6; 2.4; **L4:** 1.4; **L5:** 2.5; **L6:** 3.10; 3.12; **L7:** 3.1; 3.2; **L8:** 3.10; SWYK Review: 3.10	**U1:** L1.1; 1.2; 1.4; 2.1; 3.1; **L1:** L1.2; 2.3; **L3:** 3.4; **L4:** 1.3; **L5:** 3.2; **L6:** 3.3; **L7:** 1.2; 1.4; 3.1; 3.4; 4.2; 4.10; SWYK Expand: L3.3; 3.4; 4.1; L4.2	
2	**U2:** R1.2; 1.3; 1.4; 2.2; 2.4; 2.5; 3.1; 3.3; 3.8; 6.1; **L2:** R3.12; **L3:** 6.1; **L4:** 4.1; **L7:** 3.2; 3.3; SWYK Expand: 3.3; 3.10	**U2:** L1.1; 1.2; 1.4; 2.1; 3.1; **L1:** L1.1; 3.1; 3.4; 4.1; **L2:** 1.2; 1.4; **L3:** 3.1; **L4:** 3.6; **L5:** 3.3	
3	**U3:** R1.2; 1.3; 1.4; 2.2; 2.4; 2.5; 3.1; 3.1; 3.3; 3.8; 6.1; **L1:** R3.12; **L2:** 3.3; 3.6; 3.10; **L3:** 3.6; 3.12; **L4:** 3.3; 3.6; 3.12; 7.1; 7.8; **L6:** 3.10; 3.12; **L7:** 4.1; 4.9; **L9:** 3.10; SWYK Review: 3.10; SWYK Expand: 7.1; 7.8	**U3:** L1.1; 12; 1.4; 2.1; 3.1; **L1:** L1.1; 1.2; **L2:** 2.1; 2.5; 4.1; **L4:** 3.4; **L7:** 1.1; 1.2; 2.3; **L8:** 2.1; 3.3; 3.4; SWYK Expand: 5.2	
4	**U4:** R1.2; 1.3; 1.4; 2.2; 2.4; 2.5; 3.1; 3.1; 3.3; 3.8; 6.1; **L1:** R3.10; **L2:** 3.10; **L3:** 3.10; **L4:** 2.2; 4.9; **L5:** 3.11; **L7:** 4.1; 4.3; **L9:** 3.12; SWYK Review: 3.12; SWYK Expand: 3.11	**U4:** L1.1; 12; 1.4; 2.1; 3.1; **L1:** L3.4; **L2:** 3.4; **L3:** 1.3; **L5:** 3.3; 3.4; **L7:** 3.4; **L8:** 3.4; 4.2; **L9:** 3.4; SWYK Expand: 3.4	
5	**U5:** R1.2; 1.3; 1.4; 2.2; 2.4; 2.5; 2.12; 3.1; 3.1; 3.3; 3.8; 4.1; 4.4; 6.1; **L3:** R6.1; **L4:** 4.6; 5.1; **L5:** 6.1; **L6:** 2.5; 6.1; **L7:** 6.3; SWYK Expand: 3.11; 4.9	**U5:** L1.1; 12; 1.4; 2.1; 3.1; **L1:** L3.4; **L2:** 5.1; **L4:** 3.5; **L5:** 3.3; **L7:** 3.3; 3.11; **L8:** 5.2; 6.1; SWYK Review: 3.4; SWYK Expand: 3.3	
6	**U6:** R1.2; 1.3; 1.4; 2.2; 2.4; 2.5; 3.1; 3.1; 3.3; 3.8; 6.1; **L1:** R3.12; **L2:** 2.7; 3.12; 4.1; 6.2; **L3:** 2.7; 3.12; 6.2; **L4:** 3.3; 3.11; 3.12; 4.1; **L5:** 3.3; 3.12; **L6:** 3.12; **L7:** 2.7; 4.1; 6.2; **L8:** 4.9; **L9:** 3.12; SWYK Review: 3.12; SWYK Expand: 3.3	**U6:** L1.1; 12; 1.4; 2.1; 3.1; **L1:** L3.3; **L2:** 5.1; 5.2; **L3:** 3.4; **L5:** 3.2; 3.3; 3.4; 4.3; 6.5; **L6:** 3.2; 3.3; **L7:** 3.1; 3.4; **L8:** 3.4; 4.3; 5.1; SWYK Review: 3.3; 3.4; SWYK Expand: 3.3; 3.4	
7	**U7:** R1.2; 1.3; 1.4; 2.2; 2.4; 2.5; 3.1; 3.1; 3.3; 3.8; 6.1; **L1:** R2.7; 4.1; **L2:** 4.2; **L3:** 4.2; 4.6; **L4:** 4.2; 4.6; **L5:** 4.6; **L6:** 4.2; 4.6; **L7:** 3.3; 3.11; **L9:** 4.6; SWYK Review: 4.6; SWYK Expand: 3.3; 3.11	**U7:** L1.1; 12; 1.4; 2.1; 3.1; **L1:** L1.1; 3.1; **L2:** 3.3; 3.4; **L3:** 3.4; **L4:** 3.4; **L5:** 3.1; 3.4; 4.1; 4.2; **L7:** 3.1; **L8:** 3.1; 5.1; 5.2; **L9:** 3.4; SWYK Review: 3.43.1; 5.1; 5.23.1; 3.4; 4.1; 4.2	
8	**U8:** R1.2; 1.3; 1.4; 2.2; 2.4; 2.5; 3.1; 3.1; 3.3; 3.8; 6.1; **L1:** R4.1; 4.8; **L2:** 3.3; 4.2; **L3:** 4.1; **L4:** 3.3; 3.11; 4.1; 4.3; 4.9; 6.2; **L5:** 4.1; 4.4; **L7:** 3.11; 4.1; 6.2; 7.8; **L8:** 4.1; 4.8; SWYK Review: 4.1; SWYK Expand: 3.3; 3.11; 4.4	**U8:** L1.1; 12; 1.4; 2.1; 3.1; **L1:** L1.1; 3.1; **L2:** 3.4; **L3:** 1.3; **L5:** 1.3; 3.3; 5.1; **L6:** 3.4; **L8:** 5.1; SWYK Review: 1.3; SWYK Expand: 3.3	
9	**U9:** R1.2; 1.3; 1.4; 2.2; 2.4; 2.5; 3.1; 3.1; 3.3; 3.8; 6.1; **L1:** R4.8; **L2:** 3.12; 4.9; 6.1; **L3:** 7.13; **L4:** 2.12; **L5:** 6.1; **L7:** 6.1; 7.7; 7.8; **L8:** 6.1; SWYK Expand: 7.8	**U9:** L1.1; 12; 1.4; 2.1; 3.1; **L1:** 1.1; 3.4; **L2:** 5.1; **L4:** 1.1; **L5:** 3.1; **L7:** 3.4; **L8:** 1.1; 5.1; SWYK Expand: 5.2	
10	**U10:** R1.2; 1.3; 1.4; 2.2; 2.4; 2.5; 3.1; 3.1; 3.3; 3.8; 6.1; **L1:** R3.13; **L2:** 3.3; 4.9; 6.1; **L3:** 4.9; 6.1; **L4:** 2.1; 4.8; **L5:** 4.8; **L6:** 3.12; **L7:** 3.12; 6.2; SWYK Review: 2.5; 4.6; SWYK Expand: 4.9	**U10:** L1.1; 12; 1.4; 2.1; 3.1; **L1:** L1.1; **L2:** 3.4; 4.1; 5.1; **L4:** 2.4; 3.4; **L5:** 3.4; 3.5; **L6:** 3.4; 3.5; **L8:** 5.1; **L9:** 3.4; SWYK Review: 3.4; SWYK Expand: 3.4	
11	**U11:** R1.2; 1.3; 1.4; 2.2; 2.4; 2.5; 3.1; 3.1; 3.3; 3.8; 6.1; **L1:** R2.12; **L2:** 2.12; **L4:** 3.6; 3.7; 3.11; 4.6; 6.2; **L5:** 3.14; 7.4; **L6:** 7.4; **L7:** 6.1; 6.2; 7.8; **L8:** 6.1; **L9:** 2.1; SWYK Review: 3.14; 7.4; SWYK Expand: 3.14	**U11:** L1.1; 12; 1.4; 2.1; 3.1; **L1:** L1.1; 2.1; **L2:** 5.11; **L4:** 1.3; 3.7; 3.8; 5.1; **L5:** 1.3; 3.7; 3.8; **L7:** 3.3; **L8:** 5.1; **L9:** 2.5; SWYK Expand: 2.5; 3.4	
12	**U12:** R1.2; 1.3; 1.4; 2.2; 2.4; 2.5; 3.1; 3.1; 3.3; 3.8; 6.1; **L1:** R3.2; 3.3; **L2:** 6.1; **L4:** 2.7; 2.12; 4.6; **L5:** 3.12; 3.14; **L6:** 3.14; **L7:** 3.11; 7.1; **L9:** 4.6; SWYK Review: 4.6; SWYK Expand: 4.6	**U12:** L1.1; 12; 1.4; 2.1; 3.1; **L1:** L1.1; 3.4; **L2:** 5.1; **L3:** 3.8; **L5:** 5.1; 7.1; **L6:** 3.4; **L8:** 5.1; **L9:** 3.4; 3.5; SWYK Review: 3.4; 3.5; SWYK Expand: 3.4; 3.5	

CASAS Competencies	LAUSD ESL Beginning Low Competencies	Florida Adult ESOL Course Standards
U1: 0.1.4, 0.1.5; **L1:** 0.1.6, 0.1.7, 0.2.1; **L2:** 0.1.1, 0.1.6, 0.1.7, 0.2.1; **L3:** 0.1.7, 0.2.2, 0.2.3; **L4:** 0.1.2, 0.2.1; **L5:** 0.1.2, 0.2.1; **L6:** 2.7.2, 2.7.3, 6.4.2, 6.7.4; **L7:** 0.1.2, 0.1.7, 0.2.1; **L8:** 0.1.2, 0.1.7, 0.2.3; **SWYK Review:** 0.1.1, 0.1.2, 0.1.7, 0.2.1, 0.2.3, 7.3.1; **SWYK Expand:** 0.1.2, 0.1.7, 0.2.1, 0.2.3, 0.2.4	1; 5; 6; 7; 9a; 9b; 9c; 11a; 11b; 11c; 16; 58a; 58b; 60	2.01.01, 2.01.02, 2.01.03, 2.01.04
U2: 0.1.4, 0.1.5, 0.1.7, 4.1.8; **L1:** 0.2.1, 0.2.4, 7.4.1; **L2:** 0.2.1, 0.2.4; **L3:** 0.2.1, 0.2.4; **L4:** 0.2.2, 2.1.7, 6.0.1, 6.0.2; **L5:** 0.2.1, 0.2.4; **L6:** 0.2.1, 0.2.4; **L7:** 0.2.1, 0.2.4, 4.4.1; **L8:** 0.2.1, 0.2.4, 4.4.1; **L9:** 0.1.2, 0.2.1, 0.2.4, 7.4.3; **SWYK Review:** 0.1.2, 0.2.1, 0.2.3; **SWYK Expand:** 0.1.2, 0.2.1, 0.2.3, 0.2.4, 6.6.5, 7.1.1, 7.3.1, 7.3.2	4; 7; 9a; 9b; 19; 22; 50; 51; 60	2.01.01, 2.01.02, 2.01.07, 2.01.10, 2.03.14, 2.04.01
U3: 0.1.2, 0.1.4, 0.1.5, 0.1.7, 0.2.1, 0.2.4; **L1:** 7.4.1; **L3:** 0.2.3, 2.8.5; **L4:** 0.2.3, 7.1.1, 7.4.1; **L7:** 2.8.3, 6.0.1, 6.0.2; **L8:** 2.8.3; **SWYK Review:** 0.2.3; **SWYK Expand:** 0.2.3, 2.8.2, 2.8.3, 7.1.1, 7.3.1, 7.3.2	5; 7; 9b; 9c; 9d; 10; 12; 15; 16; 17; 18; 23a; 60	2.03.16, 2.04.01
U4: 0.1.2, 0.1.4, 0.1.5, 0.1.7; **L1:** 0.2.1, 0.2.4, 6.7.3, 7.4.1; **L2:** 0.2.1, 0.2.4, 6.7.3; **L3:** 0.2.1, 0.2.4; **L4:** 0.2.1, 0.2.4, 2.7.3, 6.4.2, 6.7.4; **L5:** 0.2.1, 0.2.4; **L6:** 0.2.1, 0.2.4; **L7:** 0.2.1, 0.2.4, 2.3.2, 2.3.4, 6.0.1, 6.0.2; **L8:** 0.2.1, 0.2.4, 2.1.2, 2.5.1, 2.8.1; **SWYK Review:** 0.2.1, 0.2.3, 0.2.4; **SWYK Expand:** 0.2.1, 0.2.3, 0.2.4, 2.3.2, 2.3.4, 2.7.1, 7.1.1, 7.3.1, 7.3.2	3; 4; 6; 7; 26; 40; 60	2.01.02, 2.01.04, 2.01.05, 2.02.07, 2.02.08, 2.04.01
U5: 0.1.2, 0.1.4, 0.1.5, 0.1.7, 0.2.1, 0.2.4; **L1:** 1.2.9, 7.4.1; **L2:** 1.2.9; **L3:** 1.2.9, 7.4.3; **L4:** 1.1.6, 1.2.1, 1.2.4, 1.2.9, 1.6.4, 1.8.1, 5.4.2, 6.1.5; **L5:** 1.2.9; **L6:** 1.2.9; **L7:** 1.1.6, 5.2.1; **L8:** 1.3.3, 1.6.4; **L9:** 0.2.3, 1.2.9; **SWYK Review:** 0.2.3, 1.2.9; **SWYK Expand:** 0.2.3, 1.2.1, 1.2.2, 1.2.5, 1.2.6, 1.2.9, 1.3.1, 1.3.3, 7.3.1, 7.3.2	14a; 30a; 30b; 31; 33; 34; 41; 60	2.01.03, 2.02.02; 2.04.03, 2.04.06, 2.04.07
U6: 0.1.2, 0.1.4, 0.1.5, 0.1.7, 0.2.1, 0.2.4; **L1:** 0.2.3, 1.4.1, 7.4.1; **L2:** 1.4.1, 1.4.2; **L3:** 0.2.3, 1.4.1, 1.4.2; **L4:** 1.4.1, 1.4.8, 6.4.2, 6.7.4; **L5:** 1.4.1; **L6:** 1.4.1, 1.4.8; **L7:** 0.2.3, 1.4.2, 2.4.1; **L8:** 2.1.7, 2.1.8, 2.2.1; **L9:** 2.2.1; **SWYK Review:** 0.2.3, 1.4.1, 1.4.2, 2.2.1, 7.1.1, 7.4.1; **SWYK Expand:** 0.2.3, 7.3.1, 7.3.2	2; 4; 8; 21; 22; 23a; 23b; 38; 39; 60	2.01.02, 2.01.03, 2.01.09, 2.04.04, 2.06.03, 2.07.01
U7: 0.1.2, 0.1.4, 0.1.5, 0.1.7, 0.2.1, 0.2.4; **L1:** 2.3.1, 7.4.1; **L2:** 2.3.1, 2.3.2, 2.6.1; **L3:** 0.2.3, 2.3.1, 2.3.2; **L4:** 0.2.3, 4.2.1, 3.1, 2.3.2, 4.4.3, 4.6.2; **L5:** 2.3.1, 2.6.1; **L6:** 2.3.2; **L7:** 6.7.2; **L8:** 0.1.8, 2.6.1; **SWYK Review:** 0.2.3; **SWYK Expand:** 0.2.3, 2.3.1, 7.1.1, 7.3.1, 7.3.2	4; 12; 13; 25; 26; 55; 60	2.01.02, 2.03.09, 2.03.10
U8: 0.1.2, 0.1.4, 0.1.5, 0.1.7, 0.2.1, 0.2.4; **L1:** 1.2.8, 3.5.1, 3.5.2, 7.4.1; **L2:** 0.1.8, 1.2.8, 2.3.1; **L3:** 0.1.8, 0.2.3, 1.2.8; **L4:** 1.2.8, 1.4.1, 1.6.1; **L5:** 1.2.8, 2.6.4, 3.5.1; **L6:** 1.2.8, 2.6.4; **L7:** 0.2.3, 1.2.2, 1.2.4, 1.6.1, 1.6.5, 3.5.1, 3.5.2; **L8:** 1.2.4, 1.6.1, 3.5.1, 3.5.2; **L9:** 1.2.4; **SWYK Review:** 0.2.3, 1.2.4; **SWYK Expand:** 0.2.3, 2.6.4, 7.3.1, 7.3.2	14a; 31; 35; 36; 37; 38; 60	2.01.02, 2.01.03, 2.04.02, 2.05.06
U9: 0.1.2, 0.1.4, 0.1.5, 0.1.7, 0.2.1, 0.2.4; **L1:** 2.3.3, 7.4.1; **L2:** 0.1.8, 2.1.8, 2.3.3; **L3:** 0.2.3, 7.4.3; **L4:** 0.2.3, 2.1.2, 2.3.3, 2.5.1, 3.4.8; **L5:** 2.3.3, 2.5.1, 3.4.8; **L6:** 1.2.9; **L7:** 0.1.8, 0.2.3, 2.3.3; **L8:** 1.2.9, 2.3.3; **L9:** 0.2.3, 2.3.3; **SWYK Review:** 0.2.3; **SWYK Expand:** 0.2.3, 1.2.8, 2.3.2, 2.3.3, 3.4.8, 7.3.1, 7.3.2	12; 13; 14a; 19; 28; 29; 33; 47; 48; 60	2.01.01, 2.01.02, 2.02.05, 2.02.09
U10: 0.1.2, 0.1.4, 0.1.5, 0.1.7, 0.2.1, 0.2.4; **L1:** 0.1.6, 1.2.6, 1.2.7, 2.2.1, 2.5.1, 7.4.1; **L2:** 1.2.6, 1.2.7, 2.2.1; **L3:** 1.2.6, 1.2.7; **L4:** 1.9.1, 2.2.2, 2.2.3, 2.2.4; **L5:** 1.1.6, 2.2.2, 2.2.3, 2.2.4; **L6:** 1.3.1, 2.2.1; **L7:** 0.2.3, 2.5.6; **L8:** 2.6.1, 2.6.3; **SWYK Review:** 0.2.3, 2.6.3; **SWYK Expand:** 0.2.3, 2.6.3, 7.3.1, 7.3.2, 7.4.1	2; 9d; 11a; 11c; 22; 23b; 24a; 24b; 30a; 42; 60	2.02.01, 2.02.02, 2.06.01, 2.06.02
U11: 0.1.2, 0.1.4, 0.1.5, 0.1.7, 0.1.8, 0.2.1, 0.2.4; **L1:** 3.6.1, 7.4.1; **L2:** 3.6.1, 3.6.3, 3.6.4, 3.6.5; **L3:** 3.1.3, 3.6.3, 3.6.4; **L4:** 0.1.6, 0.2.3, 3.1.2, 3.2.1, 3.3.1, 3.3.2, 3.3.4, 3.6.3, 3.6.4; **L5:** 2.3.2, 3.1.2, 3.6.3, 3.6.4, 3.6.5; **L6:** 3.6.3; **L7:** 3.4.2, 3.5.2, 3.5.9; **L8:** 3.4.2, 3.5.4, 3.5.9, 3.6.3; **L9:** 0.1.3, 3.3.2, 3.4.1; **SWYK Review:** 0.1.3; **SWYK Expand:** 0.1.3, 3.5.2, 3.5.4, 3.5.8, 3.5.9, 7.1.1, 7.3.1, 7.3.2	11b; 18; 19; 26; 27; 43; 44; 45; 46; 48; 57; 58b; 60	2.01.02, 2.01.03, 2.01.05, 2.01.06, 2.03.06, 2.03.09, 2.05.01, 2.05.02, 2.05.03, 2.05.04, 2.05.05, 2.07.03
U12: 0.1.2, 0.1.4, 0.1.5, 0.1.7, 0.2.1, 0.2.4; **L1:** 0.2.3, 4.1.6, 4.1.8, 7.4.3; **L2:** 4.1.2, 4.1.3, 4.1.6, 4.1.8, 4.1.9; **L3:** 4.1.2, 4.1.3, 4.1.6, 4.1.8; **L4:** 0.2.3, 4.1.2, 4.1.3, 4.1.6, 4.1.8; **L5:** 4.1.6, 4.1.8, 4.8.3; **L6:** 0.2.3, 4.1.2, 4.1.3, 4.1.6, 4.1.8, 4.1.9, 4.8.3; **L7:** 0.1.8, 4.1.2, 4.1.5, 4.1.6, 4.4.1; **L8:** 0.1.8; **L9:** 0.1.6, 0.1.8, 4.1.2, 4.1.5, 4.1.6, 4.1.8; **SWYK Review:** 0.1.6, 4.1.2, 4.1.5, 4.1.6, 4.1.7, 4.1.8; **SWYK Expand:** 0.1.6, 4.1.2, 4.1.5, 4.1.6, 4.1.7, 4.1.8, 7.1.1, 7.3.1, 7.3.2	12; 13; 14b; 50; 51; 52; 53; 54; 55; 56b; 60	2.01.01, 2.01.02, 2.01.03, 2.01.04, 2.01.10, 2.01.14, 2.03.01, 2.03.02, 2.03.03, 2.03.04, 2.03.09, 2.03.10

All units of *Future* meet most of the **EFF Content Standards**. For details, as well as for correlations to other state standards, go to www.pearsonlongman.com/future.

To the Teacher

Welcome to *Future*
English for Results

Future is a six-level, four-skills course for adults and young adults correlated to state and national standards. It incorporates research-based teaching strategies, corpus-informed language, and the best of modern technology.

KEY FEATURES

Future provides everything your students need in one integrated program.

In developing the course, we listened to what teachers asked for and we responded, providing six levels, more meaningful content, a thorough treatment of grammar, explicit skills development, abundant practice, multiple options for state-of-the-art assessment, and innovative components.

Future serves students' real-life needs.

We began constructing the instructional syllabus for *Future* by identifying what is most critical to students' success in their personal and family lives, in the workplace, as members of a community, and in their academic pursuits. *Future* provides outstanding coverage of life skills competencies, basing language teaching on actual situations that students are likely to encounter and equipping them with the skills they need to achieve their goals. The grammar and other language elements taught in each lesson grow out of these situations and are thus practiced in realistic contexts, enabling students to use language meaningfully, from the beginning.

Future grows with your students.

Future takes students from absolute beginner level through low-advanced proficiency in English, addressing students' abilities and learning priorities at each level. As the levels progress, the curricular content and unit structure change accordingly, with the upper levels incorporating more academic skills, more advanced content standards, and more content-rich texts.

Level	Description	CASAS Scale Scores
Intro	True Beginning	Below 180
1	Low Beginning	181–190
2	High Beginning	191–200
3	Low Intermediate	201–210
4	High Intermediate	211–220
5	Low Advanced	221–235

Future is fun!

Humor is built into each unit of *Future*. Many of the conversations, and especially the listenings, are designed to have an amusing twist at the end, giving students an extra reason to listen—something to anticipate with pleasure and to then take great satisfaction in once it is understood. In addition, many activities have students interacting in pairs and groups. Not only does this make classroom time more enjoyable, it also creates an atmosphere conducive to learning in which learners are relaxed, highly motivated, and at their most receptive.

Future puts the best of 21st-century technology in the hands of students and teachers.

In addition to its expertly developed print materials and audio components, *Future* goes a step further.

- Every **Student Book comes with a Practice Plus CD-ROM** for use at home, in the lab, or wherever students have access to a computer. The Practice Plus CD-ROM can be used both by students who wish to extend their practice beyond the classroom and by those who need to "make up" what they missed in class. The CD-ROM also includes the entire class audio program as MP3 files so students can get extra listening practice at their convenience.
- The **Workbook with Audio CD** gives students access to more listening practice than ever before possible.
- The **Tests and Test Prep** book comes with the *Future Exam View® Assessment Suite*, enabling teachers to print ready-made tests, customize these tests, or create their own tests for life skills, grammar, vocabulary, listening, and reading for students at three levels—on-level, pre-level, or above-level.
- The **Teacher Training DVD** provides demo lessons of real teachers using *Future* with their classes. Teachers can select from the menu and watch a specific type of lesson, such as a grammar presentation, or a specific type of activity, such as an information gap, at their own convenience.
- The **Companion Website** provides a variety of teaching support, including a pdf of the Teacher's Edition and Lesson Planner notes for each unit in the Student Book.

Future provides all the assessment tools you need.

- The **Placement Test** evaluates students' proficiency in all skill areas, allowing teachers and program administrators to easily assign students to the right classes.
- The **Tests and Test Prep** book for each level provides:
  - **Printed unit tests** with accompanying audio CD. These unit tests use standardized testing formats, giving students practice "bubbling-in" responses as required

for CASAS and other standardized tests. In addition, reproducible test prep worksheets and practice tests provide invaluable help to students unfamiliar with such test formats.

o The *Future* **Exam***View*® *Assessment Suite* is a powerful program that allows teachers to create their own unique tests or to print or customize already prepared tests at three levels; pre-level, on-level, and above-level.

- **Performance-based assessment:** Lessons in the Student Book end with a "practical assessment" activity such as Role Play, Make it Personal, or Show What You Know. Each unit culminates with both a role-play activity and a problem-solving activity, which require students to demonstrate their oral competence in a holistic way. The **Teacher's Edition and Lesson Planner** provides speaking rubrics to make it easy for teachers to evaluate students' oral proficiency.

- **Self-assessment:** For optimal learning to take place, students need to be involved in setting goals and in monitoring their own progress. *Future* has addressed this in numerous ways. In the Student Book, checkboxes at the end of lessons invite students to evaluate their mastery of the material. End-of-unit reviews allow students to see their progress in grammar and writing. And after completing each unit, students go back to the goals for the unit and reflect on their achievement. In addition, the CD-ROM provides students with continuous feedback (and opportunities for self-correction) as they work through each lesson, and the Workbook contains the answer keys, so that students can check their own work outside of class.

Future addresses multilevel classes and diverse learning styles.

Using research-based teaching strategies, *Future* provides teachers with creative solutions for all stages of lesson planning and implementation, allowing them to meet the needs of all their students.

- The **Multilevel Communicative Activities Book** provides an array of reproducible activities and games that engage students through different modalities. Teachers' notes provide multilevel options for pre-level and above-level students, as well as extension activities for additional speaking and writing practice.

- The **Teacher's Edition and Lesson Planner** offers pre-level and above-level variations for every lesson plan as well as numerous optional and extension activities designed to reach students at all levels.

- The **Transparencies and Reproducible Vocabulary Cards** include picture and word cards that will help kinesthetic and visual learners acquire and learn new vocabulary. Teachers' notes include ideas for multilevel classes.

- The **Practice Plus CD-ROM** included with the Student Book is an extraordinary tool for individualizing instruction. It allows students to direct their own learning, working on precisely what they need and practicing what they choose to work on as many times as they like. In addition, the CD-ROM provides all the audio files for the book, enabling students to listen as they wish to any of the material that accompanies the text.

- The **Workbook with Audio CD**, similarly, allows students to devote their time to the lessons and specific skill areas that they need to work on most. In addition, students can replay the audio portions they want to listen to as many times as necessary, choosing to focus on the connections between the written and spoken word, listening for grammar pronunciation, and/or listening for general comprehension.

- The **Tests and Test Prep** book, as noted on page xiv, includes the *Future* **Exam***View*® *Assessment Suite*, which allows teachers to print out prepared tests at three levels (pre-level, on-level, and above-level) and to customize existing tests or create their own tests using the databank.

Future's persistence curriculum motivates students to continue their education.

Recent research about persistence has given us insights into how to keep students coming to class and how to keep them learning when they can't attend. Recognizing that there are many forces operating in students' lives—family, jobs, childcare, health—that may make it difficult for them to come to class, programs need to help students:

- Identify their educational goals
- Believe that they can successfully achieve them
- Develop a commitment to their own education
- Identify forces that can interfere with school attendance
- Develop strategies that will help them try to stay in school in spite of obstacles
- Find ways to continue learning even during "stopping out" periods

Future addresses all of these areas with its persistence curriculum. Activities found throughout the book and specific persistence activities in the back of the book help students build community, set goals, develop better study skills, and feel a sense of achievement. In addition, the Practice Plus CD-ROM is unique in its ability to ensure that even those students unable to attend class are able to make up what they missed and thus persist in their studies.

Future supports busy teachers by providing all the materials teachers need, plus the teacher support.

The **Student Book**, **Workbook with Audio CD**, **Multilevel Communicative Activities Book**, and **Transparencies and Reproducible Vocabulary Cards** were designed to provide teachers with everything they need in the way of ready-to-use classroom materials so they can concentrate on responding to their students' needs. The **Future Teacher Training DVD** gives teachers tips and models for conducting various activity types in their classroom.

Future provides ample practice, with flexible options to best fit the needs of each class.

The Student Book provides 60–100 hours of instruction. It can be supplemented in class by using:
- Teacher's Edition and Lesson Planner expansion ideas
- Transparencies and Reproducible Vocabulary Cards
- Workbook exercises
- Multilevel Communicative Activities
- Tests
- CD-ROM activities
- Activities on the Companion Website (longmanusa.com/Future)

TEACHING MULTILEVEL CLASSES

Teaching tips for pair and group work

Using pair and group work in an ESL classroom has many proven benefits. It creates an atmosphere of liveliness, builds community, and allows students to practice speaking in a low-risk environment. Many of the activities in *Future* are pair and small-group activities. Here are some tips for managing these activities:
- Limit small groups to three or four students per group (unless an activity specifically calls for larger groups). This maximizes student participation.
- Change partners for different activities. This gives students a chance to work with many others in the class and keeps them from feeling "stuck."
- If possible, give students a place to put their coats when they enter the classroom. This allows them to move around freely without worrying about returning to their own seats.

- Move around the classroom as students are working to make sure they are on task and to monitor their work.
- As you walk around, try to remain unobtrusive, so students continue to participate actively, without feeling they are being evaluated.
- Keep track of language points students are having difficulty with. After the activity, teach a mini-lesson to the entire class addressing those issues. This helps students who are having trouble without singling them out.

Pairs and groups in the multilevel classroom

Adult education ESL classrooms are by nature multilevel. This is true even if students have been given a placement test. Many factors—including a student's age, educational background, and literacy level—contribute to his or her ability level. Also, the same student may be on-level in one skill, but pre-level or above-level in another.

When grouping students for a task, keep the following points in mind:
- *Like-ability* groups (in which students have the same ability level) help ensure that all students participate equally, without one student dominating the activity.
- *Cross-ability* groups (in which students have different ability levels) are beneficial to pre-level students who need the support of their on- or above-level classmates. The higher-level students benefit from "teaching" their lower-level classmates.

For example, when students are practicing a straightforward conversation substitution exercise, like-ability pairings are helpful. The activity can be tailored to different ability levels, and both students can participate equally. When students are completing the more complex task of creating their own conversations, cross-ability pairings are helpful. The higher-level student can support and give ideas to the lower-level student.

The *Future* Teacher's Edition and Lesson Planner, the Teacher's Notes in the Multilevel Communicative Activities Book, and the Teacher's Notes in the Transparencies and Reproducible Vocabulary Cards all provide specific suggestions for when to put students in like-ability versus cross-ability groups, and how to tailor activities to different ability levels.

Unit Tour

Unit Opener

Each unit starts with a full-page photo that introduces the themes and vocabulary of the unit.

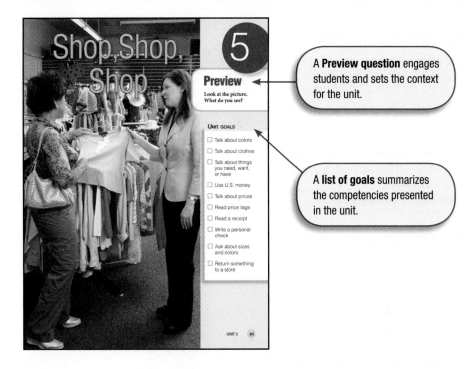

A **Preview question** engages students and sets the context for the unit.

A **list of goals** summarizes the competencies presented in the unit.

Vocabulary

Theme-setting vocabulary is presented in picture dictionary format.

Oral and written activities provide abundant vocabulary practice.

Show what you know activities allow students to use new words in conversation and provide an assessment opportunity for the teacher.

Vocabulary learning strategies give students the tools to continue learning outside of class.

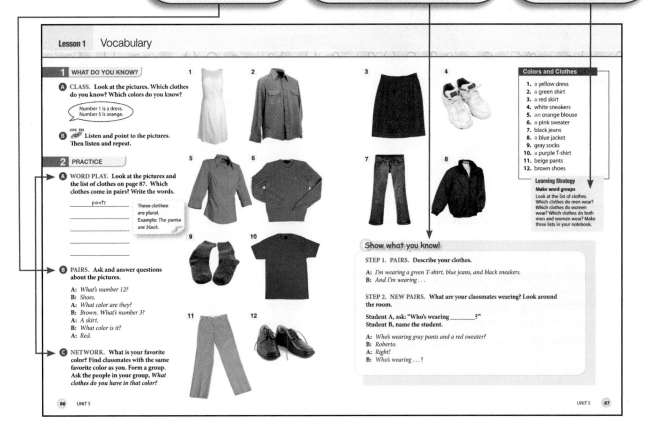

Listening and Speaking

Three listening lessons present the core competencies and language of the unit.

Before You Listen activities introduce new language and cultural concepts.

Prediction questions focus attention on the context-setting photo and encourage critical thinking.

The **Pronunciation Watch** and exercises focus on the sound patterns, stress, and intonation of English.

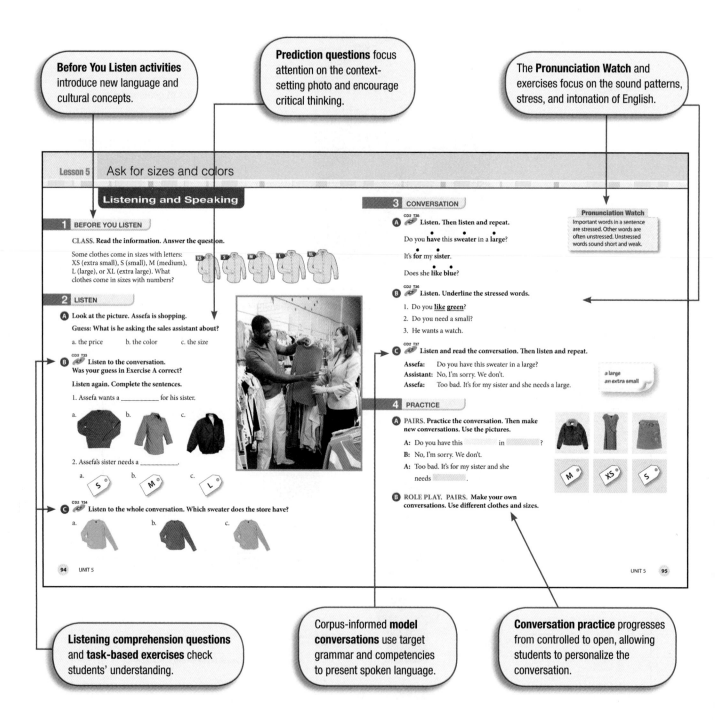

Listening comprehension questions and **task-based exercises** check students' understanding.

Corpus-informed **model conversations** use target grammar and competencies to present spoken language.

Conversation practice progresses from controlled to open, allowing students to personalize the conversation.

Grammar

Each unit presents three grammar points in a logical, systematic grammar syllabus.

Grammar charts present the target grammar point with minimal metalanguage.

Grammar Watch notes call attention to specific aspects of the grammar point.

Lesson 6   Ask about sizes and colors

Grammar

Simple present: Yes/no questions and short answers

Do	I we you they	need new shoes?	Yes,	you we I they	do.	No,	you we I they	don't.
Does	he she			he she	does.		he she	doesn't.

Grammar Watch

Use the base form of the verb in questions with *do* or *does*. In the chart, *need* is in the base form.

Contractions
don't = do not
doesn't = does not

1 PRACTICE

A Match the questions with the short answers.

1. Do you have these shoes in a size 9? __d__   a. Yes, he does.
2. Does your son like his new sneakers? ____   b. No, she doesn't.
3. Does Ms. Cho have a backpack? ____   c. Yes, they do.
4. Do your sisters want new clothes? ____   d. Yes, we do.

B Complete the conversations. Use *do, does, don't,* or *doesn't*. Use capital letters when necessary.

1. A: ___Do___ you have this jacket in black?
   B: Yes, we ___do___. Here you go.
2. A: _____ Cindy want a new watch?
   B: No, she _____. She likes her old watch.
3. A: _____ you need these jeans in a size 14?
   B: No, I _____. I need a size 12.
4. A: _____ you have this shirt in an extra small?
   B: No, we _____. But we have it in a small.
5. A: _____ Mr. Miller like this green sweater?
   B: No, he _____. He likes the blue sweater.

C PAIRS. Practice the conversations in Exercise B.

96   UNIT 5

2 PRACTICE

Complete the questions. Use *do* or *does* and the verbs in parentheses. Use capital letters when necessary. Then look at the pictures. Answer the questions.

1. A: ___Does___ Ben ___have___ an extra-large white T-shirt?
   (have)
   B: _Yes, he does._
2. A: _____ Ben and Tina _____ blue shirts?
   (have)
   B: _____
3. A: _____ Tina _____ a large red jacket?
   (need)
   B: _____
4. A: _____ Ben and Tina _____ red sweaters?
   (need)
   B: _____
5. A: _____ Tina _____ a small green sweater?
   (have)
   B: _____

BEN'S CLOTHES

TINA'S CLOTHES

Show what you know!   Ask about sizes and colors

STEP 1. Write *yes/no* questions. Use *you*.

1. like / red ties   _Do you like red ties?_
2. have / a favorite color   _____
3. need / new clothes   _____
4. want / new jeans   _____

STEP 2. PAIRS. Ask and answer the questions in Step 1.

Paula: *Do you like red ties?*
Ed: *Yes, I do.*

STEP 3. NEW PAIRS. Ask your new partner about his or her old partner.

Dan: *Does Ed like red ties?*
Paula: *Yes, he does.*

Can you...ask about sizes and colors? ☐

UNIT 5   97

Controlled practice leads to lively **pair and group activities**.

Show what you know activities invite students to demonstrate their mastery of the listening, speaking, and grammar skills they have learned.

Checkpoints at the end of the lesson allow students to mark their progress.

Life Skills

The Life Skills lesson in each unit focuses on functional language, practical skills, and authentic printed materials, such as schedules, labels, and signs.

Short conversations model functional language related to the Life Skills topic.

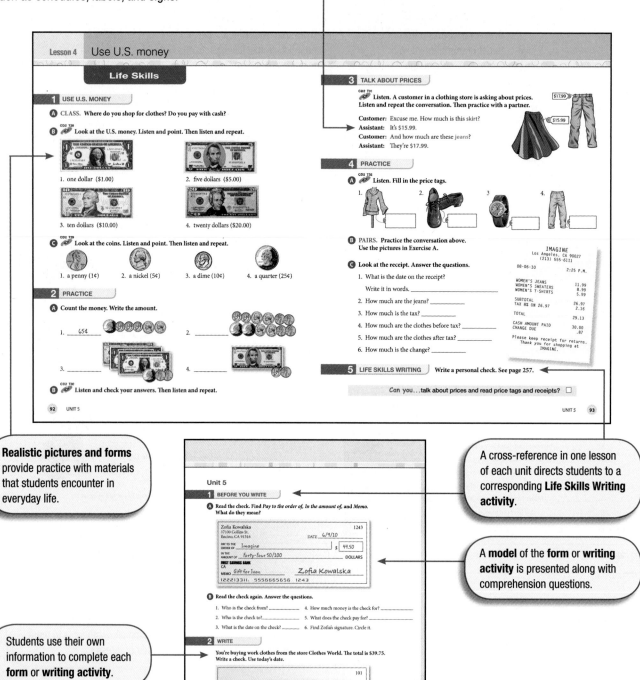

Realistic pictures and forms provide practice with materials that students encounter in everyday life.

A cross-reference in one lesson of each unit directs students to a corresponding **Life Skills Writing** activity.

A **model** of the **form** or **writing activity** is presented along with comprehension questions.

Students use their own information to complete each **form** or **writing activity**.

Reading

High-interest articles introduce students to cultural concepts and useful, topical information. Students read to learn while learning to read in English.

Pre-reading questions accompanied by pictures pre-teach vocabulary and activate students' background knowledge.

The **article** recycles language that students have learned.

Lesson 7 Read about U.S. dollar coins

Reading

1 BEFORE YOU READ

A CLASS. Look at the $5 bill. Who is the man in the picture?

B Look at other bills you have. Who are the people on the bills?

C Look at the U.S. presidents on the coins. Which presidents do you know?

1 2 3 4

D GROUPS OF 3. Look at the coins again. Answer the questions in the chart.

	Which president is on the coin?	When was he president?	Which president was he?
1	George Washington	1789–1797	first
2			
3			
4			

98 UNIT 5

2 READ

CD2 T38
Listen. Read the article.

The New One-Dollar Coin

Many Americans don't know the names of the U.S. presidents. But now people can learn their names. How? With money! The U.S. government is making four new $1 coins every year. Each coin shows a different U.S. president.

The new George Washington $1 coin

The front of each coin has a lot of information about the president. It has the president's picture, his name, the dates he was president, and which president he was. For example, the George Washington coin says that he was the president from 1789 to 1797. It also says he was the first president.

The back of the coin shows the Statue of Liberty. The date of the coin is on the edge.

Some people like the new coins. But other people don't like them. In the past, the U.S. government made other $1 coins. Those coins were not popular. Will the U.S. president $1 coins be popular? We'll have to wait and see.

3 CHECK YOUR UNDERSTANDING

A Read the article again. What is the main idea? Complete the sentence.

The U.S. government is making new _____.

B Read the sentences. Circle *True* or *False*.

1. Most Americans know all the U.S. presidents.	True	(False)
2. The new $1 coins show different U.S. presidents.	True	False
3. On the front of the coin, you see the Statue of Liberty.	True	False
4. The old $1 coins were not popular	True	False

Show what you know!

PAIRS. Talk about it. Do you have any $1 coins? What is on them? Do you use them? Do you like them?

UNIT 5 99

Comprehension questions check understanding of the article and build reading skills.

Show what you know activities allow students to internalize, personalize, and apply the information they have learned.

Review

The Review page synthesizes the unit grammar through contextualized cloze or dictation activities.

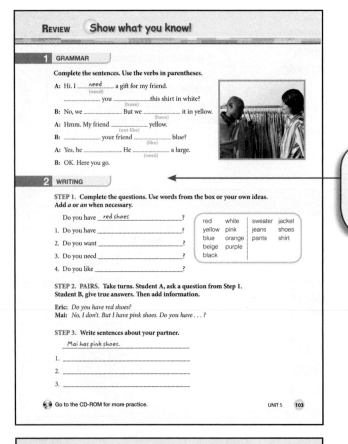

REVIEW **Show what you know!**

1 GRAMMAR

Complete the sentences. Use the verbs in parentheses.

A: Hi. I ___need___ a gift for my friend.
   (need)

   _____ you _____ this shirt in white?
      (have)

B: No, we _____. But we _____ it in yellow.
              (have)

A: Hmm. My friend _____ yellow.
        (not like)

B: _____ your friend _____ blue?
         (like)

A: Yes, he _____. He _____ a large.
            (need)

B: OK. Here you go.

2 WRITING

STEP 1. Complete the questions. Use words from the box or your own ideas. Add *a* or *an* when necessary.

Do you have _red shoes_ ?

1. Do you have _____ ?
2. Do you want _____ ?
3. Do you need _____ ?
4. Do you like _____ ?

red	white	sweater	jacket
yellow	pink	jeans	shoes
blue	orange	pants	shirt
beige	purple		
black			

STEP 2. PAIRS. Take turns. Student A, ask a question from Step 1. Student B, give true answers. Then add information.

Eric: *Do you have red shoes?*
Mai: *No, I don't. But I have pink shoes. Do you have . . . ?*

STEP 3. Write sentences about your partner.

Mai has pink shoes.

1. _____
2. _____
3. _____

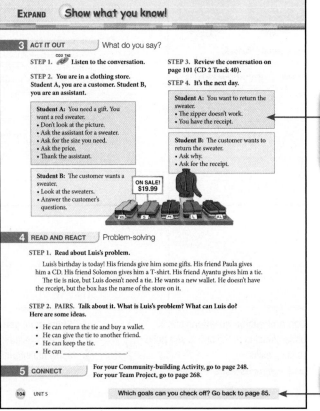

Go to the CD-ROM for more practice.

A **Writing section** helps students build writing skills by using the unit grammar in sentences and short paragraphs.

Expand

The final page of the unit allows students to review and expand on the language, themes, and competencies they have worked with throughout the unit.

EXPAND **Show what you know!**

3 ACT IT OUT What do you say?

STEP 1. Listen to the conversation. [CD2 T42]

STEP 2. You are in a clothing store. Student A, you are a customer. Student B, you are an assistant.

> **Student A:** You need a gift. You want a red sweater.
> • Don't look at the picture.
> • Ask the assistant for a sweater.
> • Ask for the size you need.
> • Ask the price.
> • Thank the assistant.

> **Student B:** The customer wants a sweater.
> • Look at the sweaters.
> • Answer the customer's questions.

ON SALE!
$19.99

STEP 3. Review the conversation on page 101 (CD 2 Track 40).

STEP 4. It's the next day.

> **Student A:** You want to return the sweater.
> • The zipper doesn't work.
> • You have the receipt.

> **Student B:** The customer wants to return the sweater.
> • Ask why.
> • Ask for the receipt.

Lively **role-play activities** motivate students, allowing them to feel successful. Teachers can use these activities to assess students' mastery of the material.

4 READ AND REACT Problem-solving

STEP 1. Read about Luis's problem.

Luis's birthday is today! His friends give him some gifts. His friend Paula gives him a CD. His friend Solomon gives him a T-shirt. His friend Ayantu gives him a tie. The tie is nice, but Luis doesn't need a tie. He wants a new wallet. He doesn't have the receipt, but the box has the name of the store on it.

STEP 2. PAIRS. Talk about it. What is Luis's problem? What can Luis do? Here are some ideas.

• He can return the tie and buy a wallet.
• He can give the tie to another friend.
• He can keep the tie.
• He can _____.

5 CONNECT For your Community-building Activity, go to page 248.
For your Team Project, go to page 268.

Cross-references direct students to the **Persistence Activity** and **Team Project** for that unit.

Which goals can you check off? Go back to page 85.

Checkpoints allow students to see the unit goals they have accomplished.

Persistence Activities

Persistence activities build community in the classroom, help students set personal and language goals, and encourage students to develop good study skills and habits.

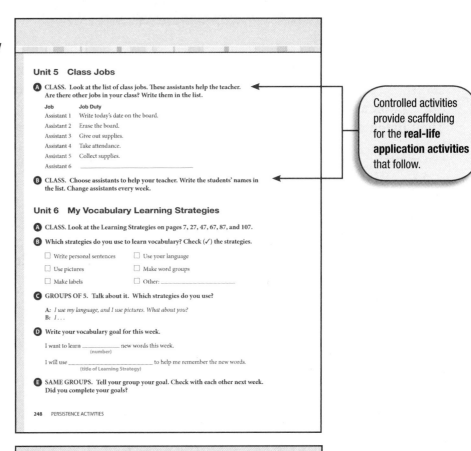

> Controlled activities provide scaffolding for the **real-life application activities** that follow.

Unit 5   Class Jobs

A CLASS. Look at the list of class jobs. These assistants help the teacher. Are there other jobs in your class? Write them in the list.

Job	Job Duty
Assistant 1	Write today's date on the board.
Assistant 2	Erase the board.
Assistant 3	Give out supplies.
Assistant 4	Take attendance.
Assistant 5	Collect supplies.
Assistant 6	_____

B CLASS. Choose assistants to help your teacher. Write the students' names in the list. Change assistants every week.

Unit 6   My Vocabulary Learning Strategies

A CLASS. Look at the Learning Strategies on pages 7, 27, 47, 67, 87, and 107.

B Which strategies do you use to learn vocabulary? Check (✓) the strategies.

☐ Write personal sentences   ☐ Use your language

☐ Use pictures   ☐ Make word groups

☐ Make labels   ☐ Other: _____

C GROUPS OF 5. Talk about it. Which strategies do you use?

A: *I use my language, and I use pictures. What about you?*
B: *I . . .*

D Write your vocabulary goal for this week.

I want to learn _____ new words this week.
       (number)

I will use _____ to help me remember the new words.
    (title of Learning Strategy)

E SAME GROUPS. Tell your group your goal. Check with each other next week. Did you complete your goals?

248   PERSISTENCE ACTIVITIES

Team Projects

Each unit includes a collaborative project that integrates all of the unit themes, language, and competencies in a community-building activity.

> A **graphic organizer** helps students collect the information they need for the task.

> Students work in teams to create a **poster**, **chart**, **graph**, or **booklet** that relates to the unit theme.

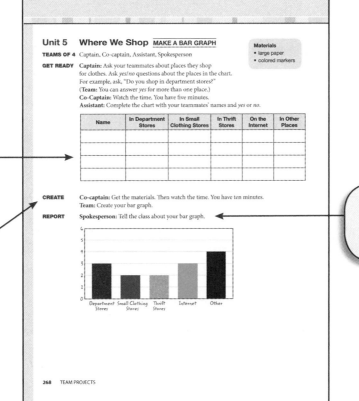

Unit 5   Where We Shop   MAKE A BAR GRAPH

Materials
• large paper
• colored markers

TEAMS OF 4 Captain, Co-captain, Assistant, Spokesperson

GET READY Captain: Ask your teammates about places they shop for clothes. Ask *yes/no* questions about the places in the chart. For example, ask, "Do you shop in department stores?"
(Team: You can answer *yes* for more than one place.)
Co-Captain: Watch the time. You have five minutes.
Assistant: Complete the chart with your teammates' names and *yes* or *no*.

Name	In Department Stores	In Small Clothing Stores	In Thrift Stores	On the Internet	In Other Places

CREATE Co-captain: Get the materials. Then watch the time. You have ten minutes.
Team: Create your bar graph.

REPORT Spokesperson: Tell the class about your bar graph.

> Teams give **oral presentations** to share their project with the class.

268   TEAM PROJECTS

Getting Started

Welcome to Class

1 USE THE ALPHABET

- Letters can be *capital letters.*
  Examples: A, B, C
- Letters can also be *small letters.*
  Examples: a, b, c

CD1 T2

A Look at the letters. Listen and point. Then listen and repeat.

Aa	Bb	Cc	Dd	Ee	Ff	Gg	Hh	Ii	Jj	Kk	Ll	Mm
Nn	Oo	Pp	Qq	Rr	Ss	Tt	Uu	Vv	Ww	Xx	Yy	Zz

B PAIRS. Look at the letters again. Student A, say a letter. Student B, point to the letter.

CD1 T3

C Listen. Circle the letter you hear.

1. (A) E   2. (F) S   3. I (Y)   4. (B) V
5. K (Q)   6. C (Z)   7. (H) A   8. G (J)

CD1 T4

D Listen. Write the letter.

1. __A__   2. __E__   3. __I__   4. __O__   5. __U__

These letters are vowels. Other letters are consonants.

2 USE NUMBERS

CD1 T5

A Look at the numbers. Listen and point. Then listen and repeat.

1	2	3	4	5	6	7	8	9
10	20	30	40	50	60	70	80	90

B PAIRS. Look at the numbers again. Student A, say a number. Student B, point to the number.

CD1 T6

C Listen. Write the number you hear.

1. __5__   2. __70__   3. __9__   4. __50__   5. __2__
6. __8__   7. __10__   8. __90__   9. __40__   10. __6__

Getting Started

Welcome to Class   5 minutes

- Write the alphabet on the board. Use capital letters.
- Point to individual letters and say: *Letter. This is a letter.* Then indicate the whole alphabet.
- Then indicate the whole alphabet and say: *Alphabet. This is the alphabet.*

Presentation   10 minutes

1   USE THE ALPHABET

A **Look at the letters. Listen and point....**

- Read the directions and the note.
- Play CD 1, Track 2. Students listen and point.
- Resume playing Track 2. Students listen and repeat.
- To wrap up, write some letters on the board. Some letters should be capital and others small. Point to a letter and ask the class: *What letter is this?* Then ask: *Capital or small?* Repeat with other letters.

> **Teaching Tip**
> Play the CD as often as necessary for students to complete each exercise.

Controlled Practice   30 minutes

B PAIRS. **Look at the letters again. Student A, say...**

- Read the directions.
- Model the activity. Call on an above-level student to come to the board. Say a letter and ask the student to point to it on the board. Repeat with a couple of other letters. Then switch roles, and ask the student to say a letter while you point to it.
- Pair students. Walk around and check that Student A is not pointing while saying letters.

MULTILEVEL INSTRUCTION for 1B
Cross-ability Form groups of 3. The highest-level student in each group plays Student A first while the other two students take turns as Student B. Then students switch roles.

C **Listen. Circle the letter you hear.**

- Read the directions. Play CD 1, Track 3. Students listen and circle the letters they hear.
- Call on a student to write the answers on the board. To wrap up, say each answer and ask the class to repeat.

D **Listen. Write the letter.**

- Read the directions. Play CD 1, Track 4. Students listen and write the letters they hear.
- Call on a student to write the answers on the board.
- Say each answer and ask the class to repeat. Read the note.
- To wrap up, write several consonants and vowels on the board in random order. Point to each one and ask the class: *Vowel or consonant?*

2   USE NUMBERS

A **Look at the numbers. Listen and point...**

- Read the directions. Play CD 1, Track 5. Students listen and point.
- Resume playing Track 5. Students listen and repeat.
- To wrap up, write some letters and numbers on the board in random order. Point to each one and ask: *Letter or number?*

B PAIRS. **Look at the numbers again. Student A, say...**

- Read the directions. Write the numbers from Exercise 2A on the board. Play A and model the activity with an above-level student. After practicing a few times, switch roles.
- Pair students. Walk around and check that Student A is clearly pronouncing the numbers. Model correct pronunciation as needed.

C **Listen. Write the number you hear.**

- Read the directions. Play CD 1, Track 6. Students listen and write.
- Call on a student to write the answers on the board. Say each answer and ask the class to repeat.

Controlled Practice   15 minutes

3   **FOLLOW INSTRUCTIONS**

Look at the pictures. Listen to your teacher. Repeat...

- Read the directions.
- Say each instruction and ask the class to repeat. To aid comprehension, demonstrate each instruction as you say it (for example, cup your hand behind your ear and tilt your head to signify *Listen to your teacher*).
- To check comprehension, say a few instructions and direct students to perform them.

Expansion: Listening Practice for 3

- Pair students.
- Student A says an instruction and B performs it (for example, A: *Point to the picture.* B: [Points to a picture in the book.]).
- Student A says three instructions before partners switch roles.

4   **ASK FOR HELP**

Read the question. Listen to your teacher and repeat.

- Read the directions.
- Say: *Can you repeat that, please?* Ask the class to repeat.

- Say: *When you don't understand, say,* Can you repeat that, please?
- Demonstrate the usefulness of this question by play-acting with a student. Mumble something and prompt the student to ask you to repeat. Then repeat yourself clearly (for example, T: [Mumble: *Take out your book.*]. S: *Can you repeat that, please?* T: *Take out your book.*).
- Pick up a book or another common classroom object and ask an above-level student what it is called in his or her native language. For example, ask: *How do you say* book *in Spanish?* (libro). Then ask the student, *How do you say* libro *in English?* (book)
- On the board, write: *How do you say* _____ *in English? Ask a volunteer to write a word in his or her native language in the blank.* Then say: *When you don't know how to say a word in English, say,* How do you say [the word] in English? *Ask the class to repeat.*
- To wrap up, repeat both questions a few times and ask the class to repeat.

Community Building

Write the Ask for Help questions on the board for easy reference for students on a daily basis. During class, if students say either question incorrectly, point to the model on the board, say it, and ask the student to repeat.

Look at the pictures. Listen to your teacher. Repeat the sentences.

Take out your book.

Point to the picture.

Read the information.

Put away your book.

Look at the board.

Listen to your teacher.

Open your notebook.

Write sentences.

Use a pencil./Use a pen.

4 ASK FOR HELP

Read the questions. Listen to your teacher and repeat.

Can you repeat that, please?

How do you say _____ in English?

5 WORK WITH YOUR CLASS

Look at the pictures. Listen to your teacher. Repeat the sentences.

Work in pairs.

Work in groups.

Work as a class.

6 LEARN ABOUT YOUR BOOK

A CLASS. **Turn to page iii. Answer the questions.**

1. How many units are in this book?   12

2. Which unit is about families?   Unit 4

3. Which unit is about health?   Unit 11

B CLASS. **Some activities are in the back of the book. Answer the questions.**

1. Look at page 245. Which activities start on that page?   Persistence Activities

2. Look at page 253. Which activities start on that page?   Life Skills Writing

3. Look at page 265. Which activities start on that page?   Team Projects

C PAIRS. **Look in the back of your book. Find each section. Write the page number.**

Map of the World __296__   Postal Abbreviations __295__

Grammar Reference __273__   Word List __275__

Map of the U.S. and Canada __294__   Audio Script __280__

D CLASS. **Where is the Practice Plus CD-ROM?**

Getting Started   3 minutes

- On the board, write the word *pair* and draw two stick figures next to it. Then write the word *group* and draw three stick figures next to it and a plus sign (+). Finally, write the word *class* on the board and draw several stick figures in a cluster next to it.
- Point to each word, say it, and ask the class to repeat.

Presentation   5 minutes

5 **WORK WITH YOUR CLASS**

Look at the pictures. Listen to your teacher. Repeat...

- Read the directions.
- Point to each picture and say each sentence.
- As needed, point to the drawings on the board and explain: Pairs *means two students.* Groups *means three or more students.* A class *means all students.*
- Explain: *It is important to work with other students to practice English.*

Controlled Practice   5 minutes

6 **LEARN ABOUT YOUR BOOK**

Ⓐ CLASS. Turn to page iii. Answer the questions.

- Read the directions.
- Explain: iii *is a Roman numeral. Sometimes books use Roman numerals in the beginning of a book.*
- *Optional:* Write the following conversion list on the board and ask students to copy it into their notebooks:

i	= 1
ii	= 2
iii	= 3
iv	= 4
v	= 5
vi	= 6
vii	= 7
viii	= 8
ix	= 9
x	= 10

- Ask each question and tell the class to call out answers.

Ⓑ CLASS. Some activities are in the back of the book...

- Read the directions.
- Read item 1 and ask the question. Answer: Persistence Activities. Explain: *Persistence activities are things you can do to help you stay in school.*
- Read item 2 and ask the question. Answer: Life Skills Writing. Explain: *Life Skills Writing activities will help you learn how to fill out forms and do other writing that is helpful in your everyday life.*
- Read item 3 and ask the question. Answer: Team Projects. Explain: *Team Projects are a good way to practice English with your classmates and to use what you learn in each unit.*

Communicative Practice   10 minutes

Ⓒ PAIRS. Look in the back of your book. Find each...

- Ask: *Where is the map of the world?* Say: *Find the page where it starts.* If no one can find it, show students where the page is. Make sure that everyone opens to that page. Write it on the board for students to copy.
- Pair students.
- Write the sections on the board. Then call on six students to each write an answer. If there are mistakes, call on the class to say the correct page. When calling out answers, students may say each digit (for example, *2-3-1* for page 231).
- Correct any mistakes on the board as needed.
- *Optional:* Ask: *Where is the Practice Plus CD-ROM?* (At the back of the book) Explain: *The CD-ROM has extra practice for each lesson in your book.*

MULTILEVEL INSTRUCTION for 6C
Pre-level For additional support, students work in groups of 3.
Above-level Ask students to also find the page numbers for Unit 3 and Unit 5.

Ⓓ CLASS. Where is the...

- Have the class find and point to the CD-ROM (in the back of the book).

Getting to Know You

Classroom Materials/Extra Practice

CD 1
Tracks 7–26

T
Transparencies 1.1–1.5
Vocabulary Cards Unit 1

MCA
Unit 1

Workbook
Unit 1

Interactive Practice
Unit 1

Unit Overview

Goals

- See the list of goals on the facing page.

Grammar

- Affirmative of *be* with *I, he,* and *she;* contractions
- Negative of *be* with *I, he,* and *she;* contractions
- Affirmative of *be* with *we, you, they,* and *it;* contractions
- Negative of *be* with *we, you, they,* and *it;* contractions

Pronunciation

- Sentence rhythm: stress on important words
- Consonant sounds: *he's* vs. *she's*

Reading

- Read an article about immigrants in the U.S.

Writing

- Write sentences about your name and marital status
- Write sentences about yourself, a classmate, or your teacher

Life Skills Writing

- Complete a personal information form

Preview

- Set the context of the unit by greeting the class and introducing yourself (for example, *Good morning. My name is . . . It's nice to meet you.*).
- Hold up page 5 or show Transparency 1.1. Read the unit title and ask the class to repeat.
- Explain: Getting to know you *means that we will learn about everyone here.* Write on the board: *get to know a person = learn about a person.*
- Say: *Look at the picture.* Ask the Preview questions: *Where are the people?* (in a classroom) *Who are they?* (adult students and a teacher) Write the correct answers on the board and ask the class to repeat.

Unit Goals

- Point to the Unit Goals. Explain that this list shows what the class will be studying in this unit.
- Tell students to read the goals silently.
- Say each goal and ask the class to repeat. Explain unfamiliar vocabulary as needed:

    Introduce: *When you introduce two people, you tell them their names for the first time. For example:* Ana, this is Ken.

- Tell students to circle one goal that is very important to them. Call on several students to say the goal they circled.
- Write a checkmark (✓) on the board. Say: *We will come back to this page again. You will write a checkmark next to the goals you learned in this unit.*

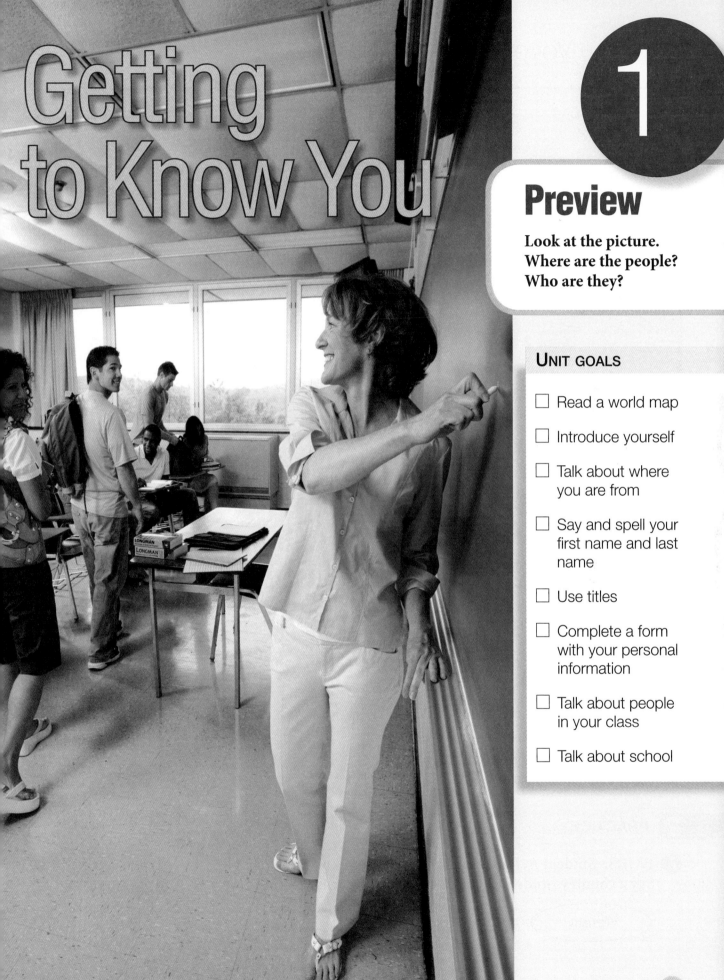

Getting to Know You

Preview

**Look at the picture.
Where are the people?
Who are they?**

UNIT GOALS

- ☐ Read a world map
- ☐ Introduce yourself
- ☐ Talk about where you are from
- ☐ Say and spell your first name and last name
- ☐ Use titles
- ☐ Complete a form with your personal information
- ☐ Talk about people in your class
- ☐ Talk about school

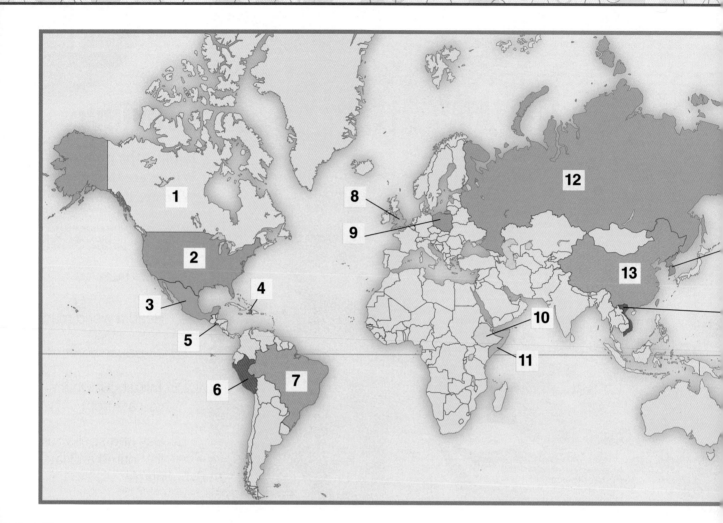

1 WHAT DO YOU KNOW?

A CLASS. Look at the map. Which countries do you know?

> Number 3 is Mexico.

CD1 T7

B 🎧 Listen and point to the countries.
Then listen and repeat.

2 PRACTICE

A PAIRS. Student A, look at the list of countries on page 7.
Say a country. Student B, point to the country on the map.

> Vietnam.

Getting Started   5 minutes

1   WHAT DO YOU KNOW?

Ⓐ CLASS. Look at the map. Which countries...

- Show Transparency 1.2 or hold up the book. Tell students to cover the list of words on page 7.
- Write on the board: *Number _____ is _____.*
- Point to number 3 on the map and ask: *What country is this?* Read the example with the class.
- Say: *Look at the other numbers.* Ask: *Which countries do you know?* Students call out answers as in the example. Point to the board if a student needs help forming the sentence.
- If students call out an incorrect country, change the answer into a question for the class (for example, *Number 8 is Poland?*). If nobody can identify the correct country, tell students they will now listen to a CD and practice the names of the countries.

Presentation   10 minutes

Ⓑ 💿 Listen and point to the countries....

- Read the directions. Play CD 1, Track 7. Students listen and point to the countries. Pause after number 15 (Vietnam).
- Walk around and check that students are pointing to the correct countries.
- To check comprehension, say each country in random order and ask students to point to the appropriate one.
- Resume playing Track 7. Students listen and repeat.

▬ Expansion: Pronunciation Practice for 1B

- Say countries in random order and ask the class to repeat.
- Ask an above-level student to come to the front of the room and lead this activity. Tell the student to say the country again if the class does not repeat it clearly.

▬ Expansion: Writing Practice for 1B

- Tell the class to close their books. Say a country and tell students to write it. Repeat for several countries.
- Students compare answers with a partner.
- Walk around and spot-check students' answers. If many students have difficulty, tell them they will practice spelling later in the unit.

Controlled Practice   10 minutes

2   PRACTICE

Ⓐ PAIRS. Student A, look at the list of countries....

- Read the directions. Tell the class you are A and they are B.
- Say a country and tell the class to point to the correct country on the map. Repeat with one or two additional countries.
- Pair students and tell them to take turns playing A and B.

▬ MULTILEVEL INSTRUCTION for 2A

Pre-level Pair students. Perform the activity with them to make sure they understand what to do.
Above-level Student A says two or three countries in a row, and Student B points to them in succession.

Community Building

Show students how to correct each other's mistakes by modeling the activity again with an above-level student. Ask the student to play A and say a new country. Play B, as follows:
  A: *Mexico.*
  B: (Points to Brazil.)
  A: *No, point to Mexico.*
  B: (Correctly points to number 3.)
  A: *Yes. Good!*

Communicative Practice   30 minutes

B Look at the map. Find your country. Write...

- Write the name of your country on the board (for example, *the United States*). Say it and ask the class to repeat.
- Point to the capital letter(s) in your country and say: *Use a capital letter for countries.*
- Ask: *Where are you from?* If students say a country not listed on page 7, write it on the board.
- Students write their country on the line provided.
- Walk around and help with spelling and capitalization as needed.

C PAIRS. What country are you from? Point...

- Read the directions. Play A and model the example with an above-level student.
- Pair students. Walk around and check that students are pointing and asking/answering correctly.
- Tell students to stand, mingle, and repeat the activity with several partners.
- Ask pairs to perform for the class.

▆▆▆ **MULTILEVEL INSTRUCTION for 2C**

Cross-ability The higher-level partner plays A first, and then students switch roles.

D GROUPS OF 3. Meet your classmates.

- Read the directions and the example. Ask the class to repeat the example.
- Model the activity with two other students (at least one above-level). Use real information.
- Form groups of 3 and walk around the room, joining groups as they practice.

▆▆▆ **Expansion: Vocabulary Practice for 2D**

- Point to the list on page 7 and ask: *Are you from a country on this list? Are you from a different country?* Ask those students from countries not on the list: *What country are you from?*
- Write those countries, and ask the class to copy them into their notebooks.
- Hold up Transparency 1.2 and point out where these countries are. Ask students to help you identify the countries by pointing to them for you.

Learning Strategy: Write personal sentences

- Read the directions.
- On the board, rewrite the example to make it true (for example, *My teacher is from the United States*).
- Tell students to copy the sentence into their notebooks. Say: *You can remember* the United States *because I am from there.*
- Walk around as students write their sentences. If misspellings occur, tell students to check the list on the board or on page 7.
- Call on a few students to read their sentences out loud.
- Say: *You can remember new vocabulary when you write sentences that are important to you.* Remind students to use this strategy to remember other new vocabulary.

Show what you know!

STEP 1. SAME GROUPS. Write the names...

- Read the directions and the example.
- Ask two students where they are from. Write the answers on the board as in the exercise (for example, *Renato is from Brazil. Hong is from China.*).
- Remind students to capitalize names and countries. Tell students to ask, *Can you write it for me, please?* if they are not sure about spelling.
- Walk around and check capitalization.

STEP 2. Tell your class about one classmate...

- Read the directions and the example. Ask the class to repeat the example.
- Call on each student to talk about where one classmate is from (for example, S: *Carlos is from Peru.*).
- Ask for confirmation from the student being talked about (for example, T: *Carlos, are you from Peru?* Carlos: *Yes.*).

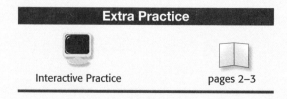

Extra Practice

Interactive Practice   pages 2–3

B Look at the map. Find your country.

Write the name of your country.

_____Answers will vary._____

14

C PAIRS. What country are you from?
Point to the map. Tell your partner.

A: _I'm from Ecuador. What about you?_
B: _I'm from Sudan._

15

D GROUPS OF 3. Meet your classmates.

A: _Hi. I'm Monica Cruz. I'm from Mexico._
B: _Hi. I'm Loc Tran. I'm from Vietnam._
C: _Hi. I'm Joseph Duval. I'm from Haiti._

Countries

1. Canada
2. the United States
3. Mexico
4. Haiti
5. El Salvador
6. Peru
7. Brazil
8. England
9. Poland
10. Ethiopia
11. Somalia
12. Russia
13. China
14. Korea
15. Vietnam

Learning Strategy

Write personal sentences

Write three sentences in your notebook
about people from different countries.

My teacher is from Canada.

Show what you know!

STEP 1. SAME GROUPS. Write the names of
your classmates from Exercise D and their countries.
Answers will vary.

For help, ask:
"Can you write it
for me, please?"

_____Monica_____ is from _____Mexico_____.

1. _____ is from _____.

2. _____ is from _____.

STEP 2. Tell your class about one classmate from your
group in Exercise D.

Monica is from Mexico.

Listening and Speaking

1   BEFORE YOU LISTEN

CLASS.   **Look at the picture. Read the information.**

In the United States and Canada, people shake hands when they meet for the first time. What about in your country?

2   LISTEN

A   **Look at the picture. Luisa and Ilya are new students.**

Guess: What are they saying?

CD1 T8

B   **Listen to the conversation. Was your guess in Exercise A correct?**

Listen again. Choose the correct picture.

a.

b.

CD1 T9

C   **Listen to the whole conversation. Complete the sentences.**

1. Ilya is from __a__ .   (a.) Russia   b. Poland
2. Luisa is from __b__ .   a. Mexico   (b.) Peru

Lesson 2 Introduce yourself

Getting Started   5 minutes

1 BEFORE YOU LISTEN

CLASS. Look at the picture. Read the information.

- Read the directions. Read the passage, while the class reads along silently.

Culture Connection

- Demonstrate shaking hands with a student. Make eye contact and shake firmly. Say to the class: *In the United States, people shake hands when they meet.*
- Ask: *When you meet someone in your country, what do you do? Do you shake hands?*
- If possible, ask students to demonstrate acceptable greeting rituals (for example, bowing) in their countries.

Expansion: Speaking Practice for 1

- Walk around and shake hands with students. Demonstrate a firm handshake and eye contact. Tell students that these are important when shaking hands.
- Ask students to turn to the person next to them and practice shaking hands. Tell them to say *Hello* or *Hi* when they shake hands.

Presentation   25 minutes

2 LISTEN

A Look at the picture.... Guess:...

- Tell students to look at the picture of Luisa and Ilya. Ask: *What is Luisa saying? What is Ilya saying?* (Note: In Exercise B, students will be given the answer.)
- Write the headings *Luisa* and *Ilya* on the board, and under them write students' answers, correcting grammar as you write.
- Read students' answers from the board. Explain unfamiliar vocabulary as needed.

B Listen to the conversation. Was your....

- Read the directions. Play CD 1, Track 8. If anything on the board is similar to the actual conversation, circle it.
- Give students the answer to Exercise A: *Hi, I'm Luisa. Hi, I'm Ilya.*
- Play Track 8 again, as needed for students to hear the answer to Exercise A.

Teaching Tip

Optional: If students need additional support, tell them to read the Audio Script on page 280 as they listen to the conversations.

Listen again. Choose the correct picture.

- Ask students to look at the two pictures. For each picture, ask: *What is happening?* (a. Saying goodbye. b. Saying hello.)
- Read the directions. Play Track 8 again. Students circle the letter of the correct picture.
- Ask the class to call out the correct answer.

C Listen to the whole conversation....

- On the board, write: *Ilya is from _____. Luisa is from _____.*
- Read the directions. Play CD 1, Track 9. Tell students to listen for the countries that Ilya and Luisa are from.
- Call on a student to fill in the blanks on the board.

3 CONVERSATION

A 🔘 Listen and read. Look at the pictures.

- Ask students to look at the cartoon. Ask: *What is he doing?* Tell students they will listen to a student practicing an introduction.
- Read the directions. Play CD 1, Track 10. Students read along silently.
- To check that students understand the humor of the conversation, ask: *Why is Hong surprised?* (Because the mirror talks to him.)

Expansion: Learning Strategy for 3A

- Ask: *Are you like Hong Li? Do you repeat things to practice English?*
- Ask students to share other strategies they use to improve their English (for example, *I talk to my kids. I watch TV.*). Make a list on the board for students to copy into their notebooks.

B 🔘 Listen. Then listen and repeat.

- Read the directions and Pronunciation Watch note.
- Write the sentences and questions on the board.
- Say: *Nice to meet you.* Say *nice* and *meet* slowly and more loudly than the other words. Tell students these words are stressed.
- Ask: *Where are you from?* Say *where* and *from* slowly and loudly. Tell students these words are stressed.
- Play CD 1, Track 11. Students listen.
- Circle the stressed words on the board.
- Resume playing Track 11. Students listen and repeat.

Controlled Practice   5 minutes

4 PRACTICE

A PAIRS. Practice the conversation. Use your own...

- Read the directions.
- Practice the conversation with an above-level student. Use real information. Emphasize the stress patterns practiced in Exercise 3B.
- Pair students. Walk around and check that students are using the correct stress patterns.

MULTILEVEL INSTRUCTION for 4A

Pre-level Ask pairs to write in their information before they practice.

Above-level Tell pairs to practice without looking at the conversation.

Communicative Practice   25 minutes

B MAKE IT PERSONAL. CLASS. Walk around...

- Read the directions.
- Ask students to stand, mingle, and practice the conversation with several partners for five minutes.
- Walk around and participate in the activity. Model clear pronunciation.
- After five minutes, tell students to return to their seats. Call on students to say how many students they met.

Expansion: Speaking Practice for 4B

- Challenge students by asking: *Who remembers where everyone is from?* To refresh students' memories, first have all students take turns saying their names and where they are from.
- Then ask for volunteers to say each student's name and country of origin (for example, S: *Irene is from Mexico. Bao is from Vietnam. . . .*).

Culture Connection

- Say: *Many people in the U.S. come from other countries or from other parts of the U.S. It is common to ask where someone is from when you are getting to know them.*
- Ask: *In your home country, when you meet people, do you ask where they are from?*

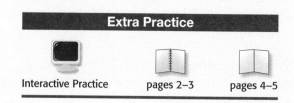

Extra Practice		
Interactive Practice	pages 2–3	pages 4–5

3 CONVERSATION

CD1 T10

A  **Listen and read. Look at the pictures.**

Hi. I'm Hong Li.
Hi. I'm Hong Li.

I'm from China.
I'm from China.

Nice to meet you.
Nice to meet you.

Nice to meet
you, too!

CD1 T11

B **Listen. Then listen and repeat.**

Nice to **meet** you.

Nice to meet **you, too**.

Where are you **from**?

What about **you**?

> **Pronunciation Watch**
>
> In English, important words in a sentence are stressed. Stressed words sound long and strong.

4 PRACTICE

A PAIRS. Practice the conversation. Use your own information.

Answers will vary.

A: Hi. I'm _____.

B: Hi. I'm _____.

A: Nice to meet you.

B: Nice to meet you, too.

A: Where are you from?

B: I'm from _____. What about you?

A: I'm from _____.

B MAKE IT PERSONAL. CLASS. Walk around the room. Meet other classmates.

Say and spell your name

Life Skills

1 SAY AND SPELL YOUR NAME

A Review the alphabet on page 2.

CD1 T12

B 🔘 Listen to two students talking. Read the conversation. Then listen and repeat.

A: What's your first name?

B: My first name is Loc.

A: How do you spell that?

B: L-O-C.

A: L-O-C?

B: Right.

A: And what's your last name?

B: Tran.

A: OK. Thanks.

> *last name = family name*

2 PRACTICE

CLASS. Practice the conversation again. Walk around the room.
Talk to three classmates. Write their names.   Answers will vary.

First Name	Last Name
Loc	Tran

> **Writing Watch**
>
> Start names with capital letters. Example: *Loc*

3 USE TITLES

CD1 T13

🔘 Listen and point to the pictures. Then listen and repeat.

Mr. Johnson

Miss Chan (Ms. Chan)

Mrs. Brown (Ms. Brown)

Can you...say and spell your first name and last name? ☐

Lesson 3 Say and spell your name

Getting Started 5 minutes

Culture Connection

• Write your first name and last name on the board. Point and say: *My first name is _____. My last name is _____.* Ask a few students: *What is your first name? What is your last name?* Write them on the board under the headings *First Name* and *Last Name*.

• Say: *In the U.S., use your first name with friends and family. Use your full name when you fill out forms.* Write some situations on the board, for example: *register for school, fill out a form at the doctor's office, apply for a driver's license.* Say: *When you register for school or apply for anything, use the last name that is on your official identification, for example, residency papers, social security card, or driver's license.*

• Ask: *In your home country, when do you use your first name? Your last name?*

Presentation 10 minutes

1 SAY AND SPELL YOUR NAME

A Review the alphabet on page 2.

• Tell the class to turn to page 2 (Pre-Unit).
• Say: *Look at the alphabet.*
• Say each letter and ask the class to repeat.

Language Note

Identify pairs of letters that students have difficulty distinguishing (for example, *B* and *V* for Spanish speakers). Provide a sustained pronunciation drill for these pairs.

Controlled Practice 10 minutes

B Listen to two students talking. Read...

• To warm up, write your first name and last name on the board and write *first* and *last* above them. Say: *My last name is my family name.* Ask the class to spell your first and last name out loud.
• Read the directions. Play CD 1, Track 12. Students listen and read along silently.
• Resume playing Track 12. Students listen and repeat.

Communicative Practice 10 minutes

2 PRACTICE

CLASS. Practice the conversation again. Walk...

• Using real information, model the conversation from Exercise 1B with an above-level student. On the board, write the student's first and last names after the student spells them for you.
• Read the directions. Say: *After you write, show your partner your book to make sure the names are correct.*
• Read the Writing Watch note: *Start names with capital letters.*
• With their books, students stand, mingle, and talk to three classmates. They write first and last names in the chart.

3 USE TITLES

Listen and point to the pictures. Then listen...

• To warm up, on the board write your last name with an appropriate title (for example, *Mrs. Smith*). Read it and ask the class to repeat. Point to *Mrs.* and say: *This is a title.* Point to your last name and say: *This is my last name, or family name.*
• Explain: *Use a title to be formal.*
• Read the directions. Play CD 1, Track 13.

Expansion: Pronunciation Practice for 3

• On the board, write: *Mr., Mrs., Ms.,* and *Miss.* Pronounce each title and ask the class to repeat.
• Point to each title in random order and ask the class to say it.

Progress Check

Can you . . . say and spell your first name and last name?

Say: *We have practiced saying and spelling first and last names. Now look at the question at the bottom of the page. Can you say and spell your first name and last name?* Tell students to write a checkmark in the box.

Controlled Practice   25 minutes

4 PRACTICE

Ⓐ Look at the pictures. Check (✓) the correct title.

- Read the directions.
- To warm up, ask students who they see in the picture: a man, woman, boy, or girl.
- Read the note about titles to the class. Explain: Ms. *doesn't say if the woman is married or single.*
- To check answers, say both names and ask which one is correct (for example, T: *Mr. Lopez or Mrs. Lopez? Ss: Mr. Lopez. T: Right!*).

> **Culture Connection**
>
> • Say: *In the U.S., many women like to use the title* Ms. Ask: *In your first language, do you have a title like* Ms.*?*
> • Call on students to say titles in their native language. Repeat them and ask the class to repeat.

▮ Expansion: Writing Practice for 4A

- Tell students to think of an appropriate title for themselves and to write that title with their last name in their notebooks.
- Students then show their name and title to a partner and practice pronouncing each other's names and titles.

Ⓑ 💿 Listen. Some students are signing up...

- Ask students to look at the forms. Tell them that each one already has a first or last name.
- Read the directions. Play CD 1, Track 14.
- Play Track 14 again if students have difficulty listening for the important information.
- Students compare answers with a partner.
- Call on a few students to say answers.

▮ Expansion: Listening Practice for 4B

- Dictate titles while students write them in their notebooks (*1. Mr. 2. Miss 3. Ms.*). Repeat each title once.

Ⓒ READ AND WRITE. Read about Elsa Medina....

- Read the directions.
- Read the paragraph about Elsa and ask the class to repeat.
- Read the Writing Watch note about capitalization and punctuation. Write the paragraph on the board without capitals or periods, and with the class correct it.
- As students write, walk around and help with capitalization, spelling, and punctuation.
- Ask for volunteers to read their paragraphs to the class.

5 LIFE SKILLS WRITING

Turn to page 253 and ask students to complete the personal information form. See pages Txi–Txii for general notes about the Life Skills Writing activities.

Progress Check

Can you . . . use titles?

Say: *We have practiced using titles. Now, look at the question at the bottom of the page. Can you use titles?* Tell students to write a checkmark in the box.

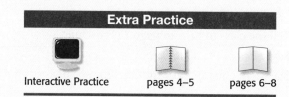

Extra Practice		
Interactive Practice	pages 4–5	pages 6–8

4 PRACTICE

Use titles with last names, not first names.
Example: *John Smith = Mr. Smith, not* Mr. John
• Say Mr. for both married and single men.
• Say Ms. for both married and single women.

A Look at the pictures. Check (✓) the correct title.

1.

2.

3.

1.
- ✓ Mr. Lopez
- ☐ Mrs. Lopez

2.
- ✓ Miss Parker
- ☐ Mrs. Parker

3.
- ✓ Ms. Lee
- ☐ Mr. Lee

CD1 T14

B Listen. Some students are signing up for classes. Write the first or last name. Circle the correct title.

1. (Mr.) Mrs. Ms. Miss
First Name: ___Michael___
Last Name: ___Chen___

2. Mr. Mrs. Ms. (Miss)
First Name: ___Darya___
Last Name: ___Kotova___

3. Mr. Mrs. (Ms.) Miss
First Name: ___Ana___
Last Name: ___Lopez___

C READ AND WRITE. Read about Elsa Medina. Then write about yourself in your notebook.

> My first name is Elsa. My last name is Medina. I'm from Ecuador. I'm married.

Writing Watch

Start sentences with a capital letter. End sentences with a period.

5 LIFE SKILLS WRITING

Complete a personal information form. See page 253.

Can you...use titles? ☐

Listening and Speaking

1 BEFORE YOU LISTEN

A READ. Look at the pictures. Read and answer the questions.

It's time for class. Ana is at her desk. But two students are not there. Jae Yong is absent. Artur is late.

1. Who is absent? _____Jae Yong_____

2. Who is late? _____Artur_____

B CLASS. What about *your* class? Who is absent today?

2 LISTEN

A Look at the picture. Luisa and Sen are classmates.

Guess: What is Luisa's question?

a. What's that?   b. Who's that?

CD1 T15

B   Listen to the conversation. Was your guess in Exercise A correct?

Listen again. Complete the sentences.

1. _____Nikolai_____ is the man in the picture.
   a. Nikolai   b. Ilya

2. Nikolai is from _____Russia_____.
   a. Russia   b. Poland

CD1 T16

C   Listen to the whole conversation. Choose the correct picture of Ilya.

a.

b.

Getting Started   10 minutes

1 BEFORE YOU LISTEN

A READ. Look at the pictures. Read and answer...

- On the board, write *Here, She's absent,* and *He's absent.* As needed, explain that *absent* means *not in class.* Then take attendance in your class. Tell students to say *Here* when you call their name and to say either *He's absent* or *She's absent* for students who are not present.

- Read the comic strip out loud while the class reads along silently. Call on students to say what is happening in each of the three frames of the comic strip. As needed, explain the action by saying: *First, the teacher calls Ana. Ana says, "Here." Then the teacher calls Jae Yong. A student says, "He's absent." The teacher calls Artur, but he is outside. He says, "Oh, no. I'm late."*

- Explain that *Oh, no* is something to say when there is a problem.

- Explain *late* by drawing two clocks, one that says 10:00 and one that says 10:10. Say: *Class starts at 10:00* and point to the first clock. Say: *Artur came to class late* and point to the second clock.

- Read the paragraph while the class reads along silently.

- Ask the two questions and call on students to answer. Tell students to write the answers. Walk around and check that students wrote the correct names. If many students have difficulty, reread the paragraph to them.

B CLASS. What about *your* class? Who is absent...

- On the board, write: _____ *is absent today.*

- Ask: *Who is absent today?* Students call out names. Point to the sentence on the board to help students say their answers in a complete sentence.

Presentation   25 minutes

2 LISTEN

A Look at the picture.... Guess:...

- Ask students who is talking in the picture. (Luisa)
- Read the directions.
- Ask: *What is Luisa's question?* Write the answer choices on the board and read them.
- Poll the class: *Who thinks the answer is* a? *Who thinks it is* b?
- As needed, explain: What *is for things.* Who *is for people.*

B Listen to the conversation. Was your...

- Tell students they will now listen to Luisa and Sen's conversation.
- Read the directions. Play CD 1, Track 15.
- Circle the correct answer on the board. Ask: *Was your guess correct?*

> **Teaching Tip**
>
> *Optional:* If students need additional support, tell them to read the Audio Script on page 280 as they listen to the conversations.

Listen again. Complete the sentences.

- Read the directions. Play Track 15 again.
- Students compare answers with a partner.
- To check answers, call on two students to write the full sentences on the board. Correct as needed.

C Listen to the whole conversation....

- Ask students to look at the two pictures. For each picture, ask: *What is happening? (Possible answers: a. He is sick. He is at home. He is in bed. b. He is at school. He is late.)*
- Read the directions. Play CD 1, Track 16. Students circle the letter of the correct picture.
- Students compare answers with a partner.
- Ask students to raise their hands if they checked *a.* Repeat for *b.*

3 CONVERSATION

A Listen. Notice the different sounds...

- Hold up the book and point to the note at the top right. Elicit from students: He *is for a man*. She *is for a woman*. Write He *is* and She *is* on the board.
- Cross out the *i* in He *is* and in She *is* and replace each with an apostrophe. Pointing to the apostrophes, explain that in a contraction we combine two words into one with an apostrophe. Say: He's *is a contraction of* he is. She's *is a contraction of* she is.
- Say *he's* and *she's* and ask the class to repeat several times. Say: *People use contractions when they speak.*
- Read the example sentences. Strongly contrast *She's* vs. *He's*. Model the formation of the lips and mouth needed to pronounce each contraction.
- Play CD 1, Track 17. Students listen.
- Play Track 17 again. Students listen and repeat. Check that students are saying /z/ at the end of *he's* and *she's* and not mispronouncing it as /s/.

■■■ Expansion: Pronunciation Practice for 3A

- On the board, write sentences similar to the examples. Use several countries to reinforce the Lesson 1 vocabulary (for example, He's *from Brazil.* She's *from Vietnam.*).
- Say each sentence and ask the class to repeat.

B Listen. Which word do you hear?

- Read the directions. Tell students to listen carefully for *he's* or *she's*. Play CD 1, Track 18.
- Call on students to say answers.

C Listen and read the conversation....

- Note: This conversation is the same one students heard in Exercise 2B on page 12.
- Play CD 1, Track 19. Students listen and read along silently.
- To explain the meaning of *not*, practice the following conversation with a student: T: *Are you Ilya?* S: *No.* T: *No, you're* **not** *Ilya. You're _____!*
- Explain: You're right *means* You're correct.
- Play Track 19 again. Students listen and repeat.

Controlled Practice   10 minutes

4 PRACTICE

A PAIRS. Practice the conversation. Then make new....

- Pair students and tell them to practice the conversation in Exercise 3C.
- Then, in Exercise 4A, point to each picture, say the name, the pronoun (*he* or *she*), and the country. Ask the class to repeat.
- Copy the conversation onto the board with blanks, and read it. When you come to a blank, fill it in with information from the first row (*Jin Su, he, Korea*).
- Ask a pair of on-level students to practice the conversation on the board for the class. Erase the words in the blanks and ask two above-level students to make up a new conversation.
- Pair students and tell them to take turns playing A and B and to use the information in the boxes to fill in the blanks.
- Tell students to stand, mingle, and practice the conversation with several new partners.
- Call on pairs to perform for the class.

■■■ MULTILEVEL INSTRUCTION for 4A
Cross-ability Pre-level students should play A until they become more confident with the activity. Then students switch roles.

Communicative Practice   15 minutes

B MAKE IT PERSONAL. PAIRS. Make your own...

- Read the directions. Tell students that for B's last line they need to say their classmate's country. Pair students and tell them to create a table with names and countries using true information they learned about classmates from previous activities.
- Say: *If you don't know where a student is from, say* I don't know.
- To check comprehension, while other pairs continue to practice, sit with students and play A.

Extra Practice

Interactive Practice

3 CONVERSATION

A CD1 T17

Listen. Notice the different sounds in _he's_ and _she's._
Then listen and repeat.

He's from Mexico.   She's absent.

he = 👤   she = 👤

he's = he is   she's = she is

B CD1 T18

Listen. Which word do you hear?

1. a. He's   (b.) She's

2. (a.) He's   b. She's

3. (a.) He's   b. She's

C CD1 T19

Listen and read the conversation. Then listen and repeat.

Luisa: Who's that?

Sen: That's Ilya.

Luisa: No, that's not Ilya.

Sen: Oh, you're right. That's Nikolai.

Luisa: Nikolai? Where's he from?

Sen: He's from Russia.

4 PRACTICE

A PAIRS. Practice the conversation.
Then make new conversations.
Use the information in the boxes.

A: Who's that?

B: That's the teacher.

A: No, that's not the teacher.

B: Oh, you're right. That's _____ .

A: _____ ? Where's _____ from?

B: _____ 's from _____ .

Jin Su	he	Korea
Laura	she	Mexico
Ubah	she	Somalia

B MAKE IT PERSONAL. PAIRS. Make your own
conversations. Use the conversation in Exercise A.
Ask about a classmate.

Talk about people in your class

Grammar

Affirmative of *be* with *I*, *he*, and *she*

I	**am**	from Russia.
He		a student.
She	**is**	in level 1.
Nikolai		

Grammar Watch

We usually use contractions in conversation.

Contractions

I am = **I'm**
he is = **he's**
she is = **she's**

---

1 PRACTICE

A Change the underlined words to contractions.

1. My name is Luisa Flores. ~~I am~~ *I'm* in level 1.
   ~~I am~~ *I'm* from Peru.

2. That's Emilio. ~~He is~~ *He's* in my class.

3. Ms. Reed is the teacher. ~~She is~~ *She's* from Canada.

4. Carlos is a new student. ~~He is~~ *He's* from Mexico.

5. Gabriela is from Mexico, too. ~~She is~~ *She's* in level 3.

CD1 T20

B Listen and check your answers.

C Look at the pictures. Complete the sentences. Use capital letters and contractions.

1. ___*I'm*___ from Mexico.   2. ___*She's*___ from Vietnam.   3. ___He's___ from El Salvador.

4. ___I'm___ from Peru.   5. ___She's___ from Korea.   6. ___He's___ from China.

Getting Started   5 minutes

- Say: *We're going to study the verb* be *with* I, he, *and* she. *In the conversation on page 13, Sen used this grammar.*
- Play CD 1, Track 19. Students listen. Write *He's from Russia* on the board. Underline *He's.*

Presentation   10 minutes

Affirmative of *be* with *I, he,* and *she*

- Copy the grammar chart onto the board or show the chart on Transparency 1.3 and cover the exercise.
- Point to yourself and say *I.* Tell students to point to themselves and repeat *I.* Point to a male student, say *he,* and ask the class to repeat. Point to a female student, say *she,* and ask the class to repeat. Explain: *These words are* pronouns. *Pronouns are words you use when you do not say a person's name.*
- On the board, write several sentences from the chart (for example, *I am from Russia. He is a student. Nikolai is in level 1.*). Read each sentence and ask the class to repeat.
- Ask students which pronoun to use for Nikolai and why. (*He,* because you use *he* when you talk about a man or a boy.)
- Say: *Use* am *with* I. *Use* is *with* he, she, *and the name of one person.*
- Write more sentences but leave out *be* (for example, *Juanita _____ from El Salvador.*). Call on students to fill in the correct form.
- Read the Grammar Watch note while students read along silently. Write *I am* on the board. Cross out the *a* and replace it with an apostrophe. Call on students to come to the board to transform *He is* and *She is* into *He's* and *She's.*
- If you are using the transparency, do the exercise with the class.

Controlled Practice   10 minutes

1 PRACTICE

A **Change the underlined words to contractions.**

- Read the directions. Read the example in item 1.
- Remind students to capitalize the beginning of a sentence. Write a sentence in lowercase (for example, *he is in my class.*). Point to the *h* and ask: *What is the problem?* (We need to change *h* to *H.*) Make the correction on the board. *Optional:* Explain that *I* is always capitalized.
- Write the first item after the example on the board (*I am from Peru.*) and ask the class to repeat. Write *I'm* above the uncontracted *I am,* read the sentence with the contraction, and ask the class to repeat.
- As you walk around helping students, ask individuals why item 3 uses *She.* (The title is *Ms.*) If students don't understand this, review titles.

B **Listen and check your answers.**

- Read the directions. Play CD 1, Track 20.
- Play Track 20 again to aid comprehension.
- Call on students to write the sentences with contractions on the board. Correct as needed.

C **Look at the pictures. Complete the sentences. Use...**

- Ask students to look at the pictures. For pictures 2, 3, 5, and 6, ask: *Do you see a man or a woman?*
- Read the directions. Then read each example and ask the class to repeat.
- Students compare answers with a partner.
- Call on students to say answers.

Expansion: Speaking and Writing Practice for 1C

- Form groups of 3. A asks B and C: *Where are you from?* B and C respond: *I'm from _____.* A writes their response (for example, *Sen is from Vietnam. Manuel is from Mexico.*). Students switch roles and repeat.
- Pre-level students can simply write their partner's name and country.

Presentation   10 minutes

Negative of *be* with *I*, *he*, and *she*

- Copy the grammar chart onto the board or show the chart on Transparency 1.3 and cover the exercise. Say several sentences from the chart (for example, *He is from Mexico. I am not from Mexico.*) and ask the class to repeat.

- Say: Negative *means* no *or* not.

- To demonstrate the difference between affirmative and negative, write on the board and say: *I **am** the teacher.* Ask the class to repeat. Then point to a student and say: *He/She is not the teacher.* Write the sentence on the board and ask the class to repeat.

- Write the headings *Negative* and *Affirmative* on the board. Elicit other examples and write them on the board under the appropriate heading.

- Read the Grammar Watch note. On the board, show how *he is not* and *she is not* can form contractions in two different ways (*he + is + not = he's not* or *he isn't*). Say: *These contractions mean the same thing. You can use* he's not *or* he isn't.

- If you are using the transparency, do the exercise with the class.

Controlled Practice   5 minutes

2 PRACTICE

Ⓐ Look at the identification cards. Underline...

- Read the directions and the example while students read along silently.

- Tell students to check the identification cards before they choose answers.

- Students compare answers with a partner.

- Call on students to say the correct sentences.

Expansion: Writing Practice for 2A

- Using blank index cards, students make identification cards like those in Exercise 2A.

- Form groups of 3 or 4. Students exchange cards and write two sentences as in Exercise 2A (for example, *Juanita is/isn't from Colombia. She is/isn't in Beginning-High ESL.*).

- Students exchange cards again and underline the correct words. Make sure that they do not answer items about themselves. Have one person in each group check answers.

Communicative Practice   20 minutes

Ⓑ PAIRS. Look at the chart. Student A, choose....

- Read the directions. Practice the example with an above-level student.

- Go over the chart with the students by asking questions (for example, *What is Carlos's last name? Who is absent? Who is here? Who is from Korea?*).

- Pair students. Walk around and check that Student A is giving clues correctly.

- Call on students to ask the class questions.

▮▮ MULTILEVEL INSTRUCTION for 2B

Pre-level Sit with pairs and do the activity with them, helping them interpret the chart.

Above-level Pairs add real information for students in the class and continue the game.

Show what you know!

GROUPS OF 3. Student A, say a true or false....

- Read the example conversation with two students.

- Students may need practice making up information. Make a couple of true and a couple of false statements about yourself. Then call on a few students to say a false sentence about themselves.

- Form groups of 3. Tell students to take turns playing A, B, and C after each conversation.

- Walk around and check that students are saying a variety of true/false statements.

Progress Check

Can you . . . talk about people in your class?

Say: *We have practiced talking about people in the class. Now, look at the question at the bottom of the page. Can you talk about people in the class?* Tell students to write a checkmark in the box.

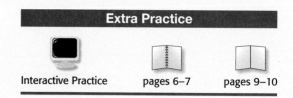

Extra Practice		
Interactive Practice	pages 6–7	pages 9–10

Negative of *be* with *I*, *he*, and *she*

I	am		from Mexico.
He		not	the teacher.
She	is		in level 3.
Luisa			

· · · · · · · ·

Grammar Watch

Contractions
I am not = **I'm not**
he is not = **he's not** OR **he isn't**
she is not = **she's not** OR **she isn't**

2 PRACTICE

A Look at the identification cards. Underline the correct word.

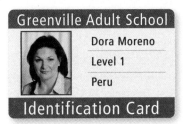

Greenville Adult School
Dora Moreno
Level 1
Peru
Identification Card

Greenville Adult School
Dawit Solomon
Level 1
Ethiopia
Identification Card

1. Dora **is** / **isn't** from Peru.
2. She **is** / <u>**isn't**</u> from Ethiopia.
3. Assefa **is** / <u>**isn't**</u> in Level 3.
4. He <u>**is**</u> / **isn't** in Level 1.

B PAIRS. Look at the chart. Student A, choose a person. Make sentences about the person. Student B, guess the person.

A: *She's from Peru. She's absent.*
B: *Luisa?*
A: *No! Dora.*

Level 1 Attendance				Monday
Name	**Country**	**Here**	**Absent**	**Late**
Mr. Carlos Delgado	Mexico			✓
Ms. Luisa Flores	Peru	✓		
Ms. Hae-Jin Lee	Korea	✓		
Ms. Eun Young Lim	Korea		✓	
Ms. Dora Moreno	Peru		✓	
Mr. Emilio Vargas	Mexico	✓		

Show what you know!   Talk about people in your class

GROUPS OF 3. Student A, say a true or false sentence about yourself. Use *I'm* or *My name is*. Students B and C, guess *True* or *False*.

A: *My last name is Garcia.*
B: *True.*
C: *I think it's false.*
A: *It's true. I'm Carmen Garcia.*

Can you…talk about people in your class? ☐

Reading

1 | **BEFORE YOU READ**

CD1 T21

A 🔘 **Listen and read. Point to the pictures.**

1. Mr. Addis is in the U.S. to be safe.
His country isn't safe.

2. Mrs. Sarit is in the U.S. for work.
Her job here is good.

3. Mrs. Medina is in the U.S. to be with her
family. Her brother and his family are here.

B PAIRS. Talk about it. Why are *you* here?

C CLASS. Some people are happy to be in the U.S. 🙂

Some people are not happy to be in the U.S. 🙁

What are some reasons people are not happy to be in the U.S.?

Getting Started

10 minutes

1 **BEFORE YOU READ**

A **Listen and read. Point to the pictures.**

- Read the directions. Play CD 1, Track 21. Students listen, read along, and point to the pictures.
- Ask: *What does* safe *mean?* (not in danger; not hurt; protected) Write both the question and answer on the board for reinforcement. As needed, explain further: *We are safe in class. We are not in danger.*
- Play Track 21 again to aid comprehension.

> **Teaching Tip**
> Tell pre-level students to use their finger to follow along the text while the CD is playing.

B **PAIRS. Talk about it. Why are *you* here?**

- To warm up, brainstorm reasons why students have come to the U.S. To begin, list the reasons from Exercise 1A (to be safe, for work, to be with family) on the board.
- Call on on-level and above-level students to suggest more reasons (for travel, for freedom) if possible. Allow L1 peers to translate for pre-level students. Write all possible reasons on the board.

- Pair students. Say: *Use the reasons on the board or say other reasons. Student A, ask:* Why are you here? *Student B, say a reason.*
- Walk around and help students interact and indicate a clear reason they are in the U.S.

MULTILEVEL INSTRUCTION for B

Pre-level Point to the three reasons on the board (*to be safe, for work, to be with family*) and ask students to choose one. Listen in on pairs and ensure that they are able to communicate. If not, model how to do the activity with a partner and then continue to observe the pair.

Above-level If applicable, ask pairs to discuss more than one reason why they came to the U.S.

C **CLASS. Some people are happy to be in the...**

- Read the directions. Ask: *What are some reasons people are not happy to be in the U.S.?* As students call out answers, write them on the board. Keep reasons to short phrases or sentences (for example, *Houses are expensive. Too many cars/lots of traffic.*).
- As needed, explain any unfamiliar vocabulary through simple explanations, drawings (for example, a simple house with a dollar sign over it for *Houses are expensive*), or miming (tapping a wristwatch while pretending to be in a car to demonstrate *traffic*).

Lesson 6 Read about immigrants in the U.S.

Presentation 10 minutes

2 READ

 Listen. Read the article.

- Tell students they will read an article. Explain: *An article is a short piece of writing in a magazine.*
- Ask: *What is the title of the article?* Explain that *the title is the name of the article and it usually appears in larger letters than the rest of the article.*
- Ask: *What is an immigrant?* As needed, explain: *An immigrant is a person who came from another country to the United States to live.*
- Read the directions. Play CD 1, Track 22. Students listen and read along silently.
- Say: *When you are reading, pictures help you understand important ideas in the article. Look at the pie chart.* Ask: *Why is it called a pie chart?* (Because it looks like a pie.)
- Copy the pie chart from the article. Say: *Look at the green part of the pie chart.* On the board, write *80%* in the large part of the pie. Write *20%* in the small part. Point to the large piece and say: *Most people, 80%, are happy to be in the U.S.* Point to the small piece and say: *Fewer people, 20%, are not happy to be in the U.S.*
- Explain that the colors next to each line in the box match the colors in the chart. Ask: *Are most immigrants happy to be in the U.S.?* (Yes.)

Controlled Practice 15 minutes

3 CHECK YOUR UNDERSTANDING

Read the article again. Then read the sentences....

- Read the directions. Tell students to circle *Some* in sentence 1, *always* in sentence 2, and *Most* in sentence 3. Tell students that these are the important words in the sentences.
- As needed, explain *some*, *most*, and *always* by drawing a diagram on the board, for example:

```
1___2___3___4___5___6___7___8___9___10
|_____always_____|
|_____most_____|
|__some__|
```

- Say: *Read the article carefully to yourself to see if these sentences are true.*
- Call on a few students to say answers.

Communicative Practice 25 minutes

Show what you know!

CLASS. Take a survey. Ask your classmates...

- Read the directions. Explain: *Your pie chart will have three pieces—yes, no, and sometimes. Write down how many students answer yes, no, and sometimes. Then make a pie chart.*
- On the board, model how to make a pie chart by working with made-up numbers. Show that 10 students = 100%, 6 students = 60%, 3 students = 30%, and 1 student = 10%. Create a proportional pie chart. Label each piece with the number of students and its percentage of the whole (for example, 6 = 60%).
- As needed, simplify the task by telling students to talk to ten classmates.
- Walk around and help students as they survey their classmates. Check that they are writing how many students answer *yes*, *no*, and *sometimes*. Check that their pie chart pieces represent the correct proportions based on the number of students asked.
- To wrap up, ask a few students to show their pie chart to the class.

Expansion: Math and Speaking Practice

- Ask a few students where they are from and make a list on the board (for example, *Mexico: 12, Peru: 3, Korea: 4*).
- Then draw a simple pie chart to represent the number of students from different countries. *Optional:* Write the percentages in each piece.
- Tell students to stand, mingle, and ask at least ten other students *Where are you from?* Students record their answers in their notebook and then create a pie chart like the one on the board.

Extra Practice	
Interactive Practice	page 11

CD1 T22

Listen. Read the article.

Immigrants in the United States

Many immigrants come to the United States. Why?
- Some people come for work. They get jobs here.
- Some people come to be safe. They are not safe in their countries.
- Some people come to be with their family. For example, a man comes first. His wife comes later to be with him.

Are immigrants happy to be in the U.S.? It is difficult to come to a new country. But 80% of immigrants say they are happy to be here.

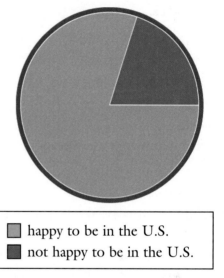

☐ happy to be in the U.S.
■ not happy to be in the U.S.

Source: U.S. Census Bureau

3 **CHECK YOUR UNDERSTANDING**

Read the article again. Then read the sentences. Circle *True* or *False*.

1. Some immigrants come to the U.S. for work. **(True)** False

2. Families always come to the U.S. together. True **(False)**

3. Most immigrants are happy to be in the U.S. **(True)** False

Show what you know!

CLASS. Take a survey. Ask your classmates, "Are you happy to be here?" You can answer *yes, no,* or *sometimes*. Make a pie chart for your class. Use the pie chart in the article as a model.

Listening and Speaking

1 BEFORE YOU LISTEN

A Look at the words in the box.
Then look at the pictures.
Match. Write the words
on the lines.

1. ___good___ 2. ___great___ 3. ___interesting___

boring   easy   ~~good~~
great   hard   interesting

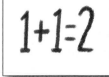 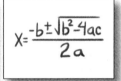 

B PAIRS. Compare answers.

4. ___easy___ 5. ___hard___ 6. ___boring___

2 LISTEN

A Look at the picture. Min Jung is asking
Ilya and Kamaria about their class.

Guess: How is the class?

a. hard   (b.) good

CD1 T23
B Listen to the conversation.
Was your guess in Exercise A correct?

Listen again. Complete the sentences.

1. Ilya and Kamaria are in ___level 1___.
   (a.) level 1   b. level 2

2. The students are ___great___.
   a. good   (b.) great

CD1 T24
C Listen to the whole conversation.
Complete the sentence.

Ilya says: "English is ___hard___."

Lesson 7 Talk about school

Getting Started
5 minutes

1 BEFORE YOU LISTEN

A **Look at the words in the box. Then look...**

- Read the directions. Explain: *Choose the word that matches each picture. For example, the English test says 85%, so number 1 is good. It's not great, but it's good.*
- Ask: *Can you find a test that is great?* (2)

Language Note

As needed, explain the rest of the vocabulary in the box by giving examples the students can relate to. For example, to explain *boring*, mime falling asleep at your desk or acting completely uninterested. Explain *hard* by writing a very difficult math problem on the board ($3x^2 - 6y = 56$), then pointing at it looking confused. Explain *great* by pointing to an example of student work that is flawless. Explain *interesting* by opening a textbook and being attentive and excited.

B **PAIRS. Compare answers.**

- Students compare answers with a partner.
- For each picture, call on students to raise their hands if they chose a certain answer, for example, *Who put* great *for number 2?*

■■ MULTILEVEL INSTRUCTION for 1B

Cross-ability The higher-level partner uses the art to illustrate the meaning of the vocabulary words in the box if the lower-level partner makes mistakes.

■■ Expansion: Vocabulary Practice 1B

- Think about the expressions you use to praise students (for example, *Great job! Wonderful!*). Write these expressions on the board. Say them and ask the class to repeat and to copy them into their notebooks.
- As needed, explain any unfamiliar expressions by illustration (for example, have a student read the directions to an exercise and then praise him or her: *Excellent reading!*).

Presentation
15 minutes

2 LISTEN

A **Look at the picture.... Guess:...**

- Read the directions.
- Tell students to look at the picture. Ask: *Where are the students? What are they doing?*
- Ask: *Do you see Ilya? How is Ilya's class? Guess.* Write the answer choices on the board and read them.

B 💿 **Listen to the conversation. Was...**

- Read the first part of the directions. Play CD 1, Track 23.
- Ask: *Was your guess correct?* Circle the correct answer on the board.

Teaching Tip

Optional: If students need additional support, tell them to read the Audio Script on page 280 as they listen to the conversation.

Listen again. Complete the sentences.

- Play Track 23 again. Students complete the sentences again.
- They compare answers with a partner.
- Call on two students to say answers.

C 💿 **Listen to the whole conversation....**

- Read the directions. Play CD 1, Track 24. Tell students to listen to the new information at the end of the conversation.
- Call on a student to read the answer.
- Ask: *The class is hard, but Ilya is smiling in the photograph. Why?* (He likes the teacher, the class, and the students.)
- Ask: *Is English hard? Why?* Write answers on the board. End the discussion with some words of encouragement for the class, such as fun ways to study English (practicing with a friend or neighbor).

Controlled Practice   25 minutes

3   CONVERSATION

Listen and read the conversation. Then...

- Note: This conversation is the same one students heard in Exercise 2B on page 18.
- Play CD 1, Track 25. Students listen and read along silently.
- Explain unfamiliar expressions as needed:

    How is it? means *What do you think?*

    What about the _____? is a common way to continue a conversation.

- Play Track 25 again. Students listen and repeat.

4   PRACTICE

Ⓐ GROUPS OF 3. Practice the conversation. Then...

- Form groups of 3 and tell students to practice the conversation in Exercise 3.
- Then, in Exercise 4A, point to each picture, read its caption, and ask the class to repeat. Use the drawings to explain *helpful*, *smart*, and *friendly*.
- To check comprehension, ask: *Who is helpful? Who is friendly? Who is smart?* Call on students to answer using real information (for example, *The teacher is helpful.*).
- Read the directions.
- Copy the conversation onto the board with blanks. Read through the conversation. When you come to a blank, fill it in with a word from the first column (*easy* and *helpful*).
- Ask a pair of on-level students to practice the conversation on the board for the class.
- Erase the words in the blanks and ask two above-level students to make up a new conversation in front of the class.

- Pair students and tell them to take turns playing A and B and to use the words in the boxes to fill in the blanks.
- Walk around and check that students are using falling intonation.
- Tell students to stand, mingle, and practice the conversation with several new partners.
- Call on pairs to perform for the class.

■■■ MULTILEVEL INSTRUCTION for 4A

Pre-level Provide extended modeling and repeating practice by saying each line of the conversation and having pairs repeat after you before they take roles and practice together.

Above-level After practicing a few times, students cover the conversation in Exercises 3 and 4A and practice only by looking at the information in the boxes.

Communicative Practice   10 minutes

Ⓑ MAKE IT PERSONAL. GROUPS OF 3. Make...

- On the board, erase *level 1* from the conversation and replace it with the name of your class.
- Ask students to think of additional words to describe the class (for example, *fun*, *nice*). Write them on the board.
- Form groups of 3 and ask them to create original conversations using words on the board.
- To check comprehension, sit with individual groups and encourage students to create original conversations, using a wide range of vocabulary.

Extra Practice

Interactive Practice

3 CONVERSATION

CD1 T25

Listen and read the conversation. Then listen and repeat.

Min Jung: Hi! So, what class are you in?

Ilya: We're in level 1.

Min Jung: Oh. How is it?

Kamaria: It's good. The teacher is great.

Min Jung: What about the students?

Ilya: They're great, too.

4 PRACTICE

A GROUPS OF 3. **Practice the conversation.
Then make new conversations. Use the words in the boxes.**

A: Hi. What class are you in?

B: We're in level 1.

A: Oh. How is it?

C: It's _____. The teacher is _____.

A: What about the students?

B: They're _____, too.

easy	great	interesting

helpful	smart	friendly

B MAKE IT PERSONAL. GROUPS OF 3. **Make your own conversations.
Use the conversation in Exercise A. Talk about your English class.**

Grammar

Affirmative of *be* with *we, you, they,* and *it*

| We
Luisa and I
You
They
Sen and Ilya | **are** | in level 1.
friendly. |

| It
The book | **is** | interesting. |

· · · · · · **Grammar Watch**

Contractions
we are = **we're**
you are = **you're**
they are = **they're**
it is = **it's**

you   you

---

1 PRACTICE

A Look at the pictures of some new students at Greenville Adult School.

Complete the sentences. Use the correct form of *be*.

1. **Mr. Salas:** You _____ *are* _____ in level 1.

   Tai-Ling: Thanks.

2. **Mr. Salas:** Here. You _____ *are* _____ in level 2.

   Paulo: Thank you.

   Ai-Lun: Thanks. Bye.

   Paulo: Goodbye, Mr. Salas.

3. **Paulo:** So, you and Meseret are in level 1.

   Tai-Ling: Yes. We _____ *are* _____ in level 1.

4. **Paulo:** So, how is your class?

   Tai-Ling: It _____ *is* _____ interesting.

   Ai-Lun: And how are the students?

   Meseret: They _____ *are* _____ great.

B ROLE PLAY. GROUPS OF 5. Practice the conversations in Exercise A. Student A, you are Mr. Salas. Students B, C, D, and E, you are the new students. Remember: Use contractions in conversation.

Getting Started   5 minutes

- Say: *We're going to study the verb* be *with* we, you, they, *and* it. *In the conversation on page 19, Ilya and Kamaria used this grammar.*
- Play CD 1, Track 25. Students listen. On the board write: *We're in level 1.* Underline *We're.*

Presentation   10 minutes

Affirmative of *be* with *we, you, they,* and *it*

- Copy the grammar charts onto the board or show the charts on Transparency 1.4 and cover the exercise.
- Demonstrate the meaning of each pronoun by pointing to students (for example, motion with your hands to include yourself and two other students, look to the class and say *We*).
- Read sentences from the left chart and ask the class to repeat.
- Read sentences from the right chart and ask the class to repeat.
- Write a few new sentences on the board to review and contrast when to use *is/are.* Leave the verb space blank and call on students to tell you the correct answer (for example, *He _____ in English 1. Ruben and Osvaldo _____ in English 1.*).
- Read the Grammar Watch note. Ask: *What are the contractions from Lesson 5?* (I'm, he's, she's) Ask: *What are the contractions in this Grammar Watch note?* (we're, you're, they're, it's)
- Ask students to look at the pictures below the note. Say: *You say* you *when you talk to one person or a lot of people.* Point to one student and say *you.* Then point to the whole class and say *you.*
- If you are using the transparency, do the exercise with the class.

Controlled Practice   15 minutes

1 **PRACTICE**

A **Look at the pictures of some new students...**

- Read the directions. Say: *Look at the pictures before you write the answers.*
- Tell the students to look at picture 1. Then read the example with the class.
- Tell students to do item 2. Say: *First, look carefully at picture 2. Who is talking?* (Mr. Salas and two students) *What are they talking about?* (the students' classes) *Next, read the whole conversation and then write in the answer.*
- Students complete items 3 and 4 by themselves and then compare answers with a partner.
- To check answers, call on pairs or groups to perform the completed conversations for the class.

B **ROLE PLAY. GROUPS OF 5. Practice the...**

- Role-play the completed conversation with four students. Play Mr. Salas and assign roles to the four students.
- Form groups of 5. Students choose their own roles and practice.
- Walk around and ask students to switch roles and continue practicing. If students aren't pronouncing their lines clearly, model correct pronunciation and ask them to repeat.

MULTILEVEL INSTRUCTION for 1B
Pre-level Groups say each line together before taking roles.
Above-level Groups practice the conversation by using contractions instead of full forms.

Expansion: Speaking Practice for 1B
- Ask the same groups to create new conversations. Students can recycle expressions from Exercise 1A. Groups can first write out a script that they practice, or they can improvise. Call on each group to perform for the class.

Presentation 10 minutes

Negative of *be* with *we*, *you*, *they*, and *it*

- Copy the grammar charts onto the board or show the charts on Transparency 1.4 and cover the exercise.
- Read the sentences in the left chart and ask the class to repeat.
- Do the same for the right chart.
- Write a few new sentences on the board to help students understand when to use the negative forms of *is/are*. Leave the verb space blank and call on students to tell you the correct answer (for example, *Evelia and I _____ not late. He _____ not in English 1. Ruben and Osvaldo _____ not in English 1.*).
- Read the Grammar Watch note. Remind the class that they already know how to contract *is + not* two different ways and ask for a sample sentence. Write it on the board (for example, *She isn't from Peru. She's not from Peru.*). Tell them we can also contract *are + not* in two ways. Write *we are not* and make the contraction both ways on the board.
- If you are using the transparency, do the exercise with the class.

Controlled Practice 10 minutes

2 PRACTICE

Ⓐ Read the conversations. Underline the correct...

- Read the example in item 1 with the class.
- Say: *Read the conversation before you answer.*
- Students complete items 2–4.

▬▬ **Expansion: Listening Practice for 2A**

- Tell the class to close their books. Dictate some sentences from the conversations while students copy them into their notebooks (for example, *1. We're late.*).
- Students compare answers with a partner. Walk around and check spelling and punctuation. Look for missing periods and apostrophes and point to places that need a period or an apostrophe.
- Say: *Open your books and check your answers. Look at the conversations in Exercise A.*

Ⓑ PAIRS. Practice the conversations.

- Read the directions. Practice the conversation in item 1 with an above-level student.
- Pair students. Tell them to practice each conversation and to switch roles.
- Walk around and, as needed, model pronunciation and ask students to repeat.

Communicative Practice 10 minutes

Show what you know!

PAIRS. Look at the picture of Jin-Hee and Antonio....

- Call on a student to describe the problem in the picture. (Antonio is not happy about his class.)
- Create two headings on the board: *Positive* and *Negative* (or + and –). Call on students to say adjectives from the word box that fit each category (for example, *friendly* goes under *Positive*).
- Pair students and ask them to create a conversation. Model the example and call on students to finish it.
- Walk around and check students' pronunciation. Encourage use of vocabulary by asking students to use specific words in the box.
- Call on pairs to role-play for the class.

▬▬ **MULTILEVEL INSTRUCTION**

Pre-level Form groups of 4 and tell students to prepare B's answer together before they take turns practicing the conversation.

Above-level Ask pairs to practice without a script. Encourage them to use other vocabulary they know to complete B's answer.

Progress Check

Can you . . . talk about school?

Say: *We have practiced talking about school. Now, look at the question at the bottom of the page. Can you talk about school?* Tell students to write a checkmark in the box.

Extra Practice

Interactive Practice   pages 10–11

Negative of *be* with *we, you, they,* and *it*

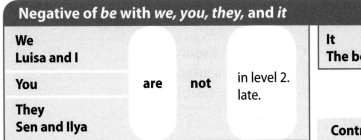

We Luisa and I			
You	are	not	in level 2. late.
They Sen and Ilya			

It The book	is	not	easy.

Grammar Watch

Contractions

we are not = **we're not** OR **we aren't**
you are not = **you're not** OR **you aren't**
they are not = **they're not** OR **they aren't**
it is not = **it's not** OR **it isn't**

2 PRACTICE

A Read the conversations.
Underline the correct words.

1. **André and Li:** Oh no. **We're** / **We're not** late.
   Teacher: It's OK. You're on time. **You're** / <u>**You're not**</u> late.

2. **Teacher:** Where are Maria and Carmen? **They're** / <u>**They're not**</u> here.
   Maria and Carmen: Oh. <u>**We're**</u> / **We're not** here. Sorry we're late.

3. **Solomon:** My class is good. <u>**It's**</u> / **It's not** interesting. How is your class?
   Irina: My class <u>**is**</u> / **is not** interesting, too.

4. **Solomon:** How are the students?
   Irina: They're great. <u>**They're**</u> / **They're not** friendly.

B PAIRS. Practice the conversations.

Show what you know! Talk about school

PAIRS. **Look at the picture of Jin-Hee and Antonio.
Student A, you are Jin-Hee. Student B, you are Antonio.
Talk about school. Use words from the box.**

boring   easy   friendly   good   great   hard   helpful   interesting   smart

A: *How is your class?*
B: *It isn't good . . .*

Can you . . . talk about school? ☐

1 GRAMMAR

A Some students are talking about their classes. Complete the sentences with the correct form of *be*. Use the affirmative in the first sentence and the negative in the next sentence. Use contractions where possible.

1. **Claude:**   I __'m__ in level 2. I __'m not__ in level 1.

2. **Sook:**   The book ___is___ hard. It __'s not / isn't__ easy.

3. **Paula:**   My teacher ___is___ from the U.S. He __'s not / isn't__ from Canada.

4. **Santiago:** Paula and I ___are___ from Mexico. We __'re not / aren't__ from El Salvador.

5. **Lei:**   I __'m__ in level 1. I __'m not__ in level 2.

6. **Tamar:**   My classmates ___are___ helpful. My class ___isn't___ hard.

B PAIRS. Look at the pictures. Complete the conversations. There is more than one correct answer. Remember, start sentences with a capital letter. End sentences with a period. Answers will vary but could include:

1.

Hi. I'm Bill.

Hi. I'm Pia.
Nice to meet you.

2.

Where are you from?

We're from Mexico.

3.

Where's Dawit?

He's absent.

4.

Where are they from?

I think they're from Korea.

C SAME PAIRS. Practice the conversations.

Show what you know!

1 GRAMMAR

A **Some students are talking about their classes....**

- Read the directions and the example.
- Tell students to refer back to the grammar charts on pages 14 (affirmative of *be* with *I*, *he*, and *she*), 15 (negative of *be* with *I*, *he*, and *she*), 20 (affirmative of *be* with *we*, *you*, *they*, and *it*), and 21 (negative of *be* with *we*, *you*, *they*, and *it*) as needed.
- Walk around and check students' word choice and spelling.
- Students compare answers with a partner.
- Call on students to say answers. Correct as needed.

B **PAIRS. Look at the pictures. Complete...**

- Read the directions. Copy the speech bubbles from picture 1 on the board. Read the bubbles and ask the class to call out an answer (it doesn't have to be the same as in the example). Write it in the blank, say it, and ask the class to repeat.
- Pair students and say: *First, practice each conversation. Make up answers. Then write a sentence in each blank.*
- Walk around and check that students are using language learned in the unit or other language appropriate for the cartoons. Also, check that they are using capital letters and periods correctly.

C **SAME PAIRS. Practice the conversations.**

- Pair students and tell them to practice the conversations. Walk around and check pronunciation.
- Encourage students to use a wide range of vocabulary.
- Call on pairs to perform for the class. Write any new and interesting vocabulary you hear on the board for students to copy into their notebooks.

MULTILEVEL INSTRUCTION for 1A

Pre-level Monitor pairs (or assign an above-level student to monitor them) and model the conversations for them so they can repeat before they practice together.

Above-level Tell pairs to continue the conversations so each person has at least three things to say, for example:

A: *Hi. I'm Bill.*
B: *Hi, I'm Pia. Nice to meet you.*
A: *Nice to meet you, too.*
B: *Where are you from?*
A: *I'm from the United States. And you?*
B: *I'm from Brazil.*

Show what you know!

D **DICTATION. Listen. Complete...**

- Tell students they will listen to a conversation twice. The first time they will just listen. The second time they will listen and fill in the blanks.
- Play CD 1, Track 26. Students listen.
- Play Track 26 again. Students listen and fill in the blanks. If students cannot keep up, pause the CD to allow more time.
- Now tell students they will listen to the conversation again and check their answers. Play Track 26 again.

Expansion: Speaking Practice for 1D

- Pair students and ask them to practice the completed conversation.

2 WRITING

STEP 1. Complete the sentences. Choose the correct...

- Read the directions and the example. Call on a student to finish item 1.
- Look at item 2 with the class. Ask why the first answer is *She*. (Because *she* is the pronoun to use when you talk about *Luisa*, who is a woman.) Ask similar questions about the other two answers in item 2.
- Complete the exercise with the students.

STEP 2. Write two or three sentences about yourself,...

- Read the directions. Say: *Remember to capitalize your sentences.* Point to the capital letters at the beginning of the sentences in Step 1.
- Say: *Remember to use a period at the end of your sentence.* Point to several periods in Step 1.
- Walk around and check capitalization and use of periods.
- Call on students to read their sentences to the class.

CD-ROM Practice

Go to the CD-ROM for more practice.

If your students need more practice with the vocabulary, grammar, and competencies in Unit 1, encourage them to review the activities on the CD-ROM. This review can also help students prepare for the final role play on the following Expand page.

Extra Practice

pages 10–11

D 🔊 DICTATION. **Listen. Complete the conversation.**
Use capital letters when necessary.

Luisa: This is Bao and Hanh. ___They're___ from Vietnam.

Ilya: Nice to ___meet___ ___you___. ___I'm___ Ilya Petrov.

Luisa and I are students at the Greenville Adult School.

___We're___ in level 1.

Hanh: Nice to meet you, Ilya. Where ___are___ you ___from___?

Ilya: ___I'm___ ___from___ Russia.

Luisa: Bao and Hanh ___are___ students at Greenville, too.

___He's___ in level 5, and ___she's___ in level 6.

Ilya: Really? That's great.

---

2 WRITING

STEP 1. Complete the sentences. Choose the correct word.

1. My name ___is___ Ilya Petrov. I ___am___ from Russia.
   _(is / are)   _(is / am)

2. Luisa is my classmate. ___She___ ___is___ from Peru. (She's)
   _(They / She)   _(is / are)

   ___We___ are in level 1.
   _(We / She)

3. Ms. Reed ___is___ the teacher. ___She___ ___is not___ (She's not / She isn't)
   _(is / are)   _(He / She)   _(are not / is not)

   from my country. ___She___ ___is___ from Canada. (She's)
   _(He / She)   _(is / are)

STEP 2. Write two or three sentences about yourself, a classmate,
or your teacher. Use the sentences in Step 1 as examples.

Answers will vary.

_____

_____

_____

3 ACT IT OUT What do you say?

STEP 1. Review the Lesson 2 conversation between Luisa and Ilya (CD 1 Track 9).

STEP 2. PAIRS. You are at a party. Say hello and introduce yourselves. Shake hands. Talk about where you are from.

4 READ AND REACT Problem-solving

STEP 1. Read about Roberto's problem.

Roberto Cruz is a new student at the Riverside Adult School. He is in a level 1 class. He thinks the other students in his class are friendly. He thinks the teacher is great. But there's one problem. The class is too easy. He thinks he needs level 2.

STEP 2. PAIRS. Talk about it. What is Roberto's problem? What can Roberto do? Here are some ideas.

- He can talk to the teacher.
- He can go to a different school.
- He can stay in level 1.
- He can _____.

5 CONNECT

For your Community-building Activity, go to page 245.
For your Team Project, go to page 265.

    Which goals can you check off? Go back to page 5.

3 ACT IT OUT

STEP 1. Review the Lesson 2 conversation...

- Play CD 1, Track 9. Students listen.
- As needed, play Track 9 again to aid comprehension.

STEP 2. PAIRS. You are at a party. Say hello and...

- Form like-ability pairs. Say: *Practice introducing yourself as if you are meeting for the first time. When you introduce yourself, look at the eyes of your partner.*
- Walk around and observe students interacting. Check that students are introducing themselves, shaking hands, and stating where they're from.
- Call on pairs to perform for the class. While pairs are performing, use the scoring rubric on page Txiv to evaluate each student's vocabulary, grammar, fluency, and how well they complete the task.
- *Optional:* After each pair finishes, discuss the strengths and weaknesses of each performance either in front of the class or privately.

Teaching Tip

The "Show what you know!" role play allows students to demonstrate what they've learned in the unit. Therefore, when you discuss students' performances with them, it is important to evaluate carefully and provide specific feedback (for example, *I think you need to use more vocabulary words from the unit.*).

4 READ AND REACT

STEP 1. Read about Roberto's problem.

- Say: *We are going to read about a student's problem, and then we need to think about a solution.*
- Read the directions.
- Read the story while students follow along silently. Pause after each sentence to allow time for students to comprehend. Periodically stop and ask simple *Wh-* questions to check comprehension (for example, *Who is the new student? What level is the class?*).

STEP 2. PAIRS. Talk about it. What is Roberto's....

- Read the directions and the question.
- Read the list of ideas. Ask: *Which ideas are good?* Call on students to say their opinion about the ideas in the box (for example, S: *I think Roberto can talk to the teacher.*).
- Pair students. Tell them to think of one new idea not in the box (for example, *He can read the book for level 2.*) and to write it in the blank. Encourage students to think of more than one idea and to write them in their notebooks.
- Call on pairs to say their additional solutions. Write any particularly good ones on the board and ask: *Do you think this is a good idea? Why or why not?*

▮▮ MULTILEVEL INSTRUCTION for STEP 2

Pre-level Students work in groups of 3 to come up with an idea.

Above-level Ask pairs to write at least two new solutions.

5 CONNECT

Turn to page 245 for the Community-building Activity and page 265 for the Team Project. See pages Txi–Txii for general notes about teaching these activities.

Progress Check

Which goals can you check off? Go back to page 5. Ask students to turn to page 5 and check off the goals they have reached. Call on students to say which goals they will practice outside of class.

# A Hard Day's Work

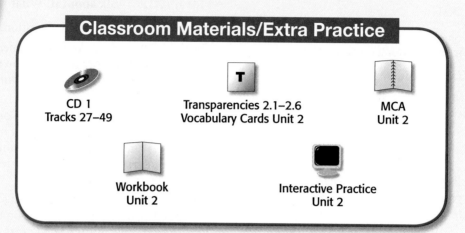

Unit Overview

Goals

- See the list of goals on the facing page.

Grammar

- Indefinite article: *a/an*
- Singular and plural nouns
- *Be: Yes/no* questions and short answers
- Simple present affirmative: *Work* and *live*

Pronunciation

- Falling intonation in *Wh-* questions and statements
- Rising intonation in *yes/no* questions

Reading

- Read an article about job skills

Writing

- Write sentences about what you do, where you work, and where you live

Life Skills Writing

- Complete a work form with your name, title, and phone numbers

Preview

- Set the context of the unit by asking questions about jobs and work (for example, *Do you work? Do you have a job?*). Write the word *work* on the board and check that students understand. Then ask several students: *Do you work?*

- Hold up page 25 or show Transparency 2.1. Read the unit title and ask the class to repeat.

- Explain: A hard day's work *means that you worked hard all day.*

- Say: *Look at the picture.* Ask the Preview question: *Who are the people?* As students call out job titles, write them on the board. If students miss any people, point to each one and ask: *Who is this?* If students cannot identify the job, say the correct response, repeat it, and point to the appropriate picture.

- Tell students these are some of the words that they will study in this unit.

Unit Goals

- Point to the Unit Goals. Explain that this list shows what the class will be studying in this unit.

- Tell students to read the goals silently.

- Say each goal and ask the class to repeat. Explain unfamiliar vocabulary as needed.

- Tell students to circle one goal that is very important to them. Call on several students to say the goal they circled.

- Write a checkmark (✓) on the board. Say: *We will come back to this page again. You will write a checkmark next to the goals you learned in this unit.*

A Hard Day's Work

2

Preview

Look at the picture.
Who are the people?

UNIT GOALS

- ☐ Introduce someone
- ☐ Talk about jobs
- ☐ Use numbers 0–9
- ☐ Give phone numbers
- ☐ Complete a form at work
- ☐ Ask about jobs
- ☐ Talk about where you work

Lesson 1　Vocabulary

1　WHAT DO YOU KNOW?

A CLASS. **Look at the pictures. Which jobs do you know?**

> Number 3 is a doctor.

CD1 T27

B  **Listen and point to the pictures. Then listen and repeat.**

2　PRACTICE

A PAIRS. **Student A, look at the list of jobs on page 27. Name a job. Student B, point to the picture.**

> A cashier.

B WORD PLAY. **GROUPS OF 3. Student A, act out a job. Students B and C, guess the job.**

B: *You're a homemaker.*
A: *No.*
C: *You're a gardener.*
A: *Right!*

C **Write your job. Use true or made-up information.**

Answers will vary.

Lesson 1 Vocabulary

Getting Started   5 minutes

1 WHAT DO YOU KNOW?

Ⓐ CLASS. Look at the pictures. Which jobs...

- Show Transparency 2.2 or hold up the book. Tell students to cover the list of words on page 27.
- Write on the board: *Number _____ is _____.*
- Point to picture 3 and ask: *Who is this?* Read the example with the class.
- Say: *Look at the other pictures.* Ask: *Which jobs do you know?* Students call out answers. Point to the board if a student needs help forming the sentence.
- If students call out an incorrect job, change the answer into a question for the class (for example, *Number 8 is a manager?*). If nobody can identify the correct job, tell students they will now listen to the CD and practice the names of the jobs.

Presentation   10 minutes

Ⓑ 💿 Listen and point to the pictures....

- Read the directions. Play CD 1, Track 27. Pause after number 16 (an electrician).
- To check comprehension, say each job in random order. Students point to the appropriate picture.
- Resume playing Track 27. Students listen and repeat. Explain: A waiter *is a man.* A waitress *is a woman.* A server *can be a man or a woman.*

Teaching Tip

Allow students to use their first language to explain any unfamiliar jobs to one another.

Controlled Practice   15 minutes

2 PRACTICE

Ⓐ PAIRS. Student A, look at the list of jobs...

- Read the directions. Tell the class you are A and they are B.
- Say a job and tell the class to point to the correct picture. Repeat with one or two additional jobs.
- Pair students and tell them to take turns playing A and B.

Community Building

Show students how to correct one another's mistakes clearly and politely (for example, A: *A driver.* B: [Points to the homemaker.] A: *No, please try again.*).

▬ MULTILEVEL INSTRUCTION for 2A

Cross-ability Ask the higher-level partner to play A a few times to check that B understands the vocabulary before they switch roles.

Ⓑ WORD PLAY. GROUPS OF 3. Student A, act...

- Read the directions. Read each line in the example and ask the class to repeat.
- Play A and model the example with two above-level students. Change roles and ask an above-level student to model a new job while you and the other student guess the job.
- Form groups of 3. Tell students to switch roles after they guess A's job.
- Walk around and check that students are using the language in the example (*You're a _____.*).

MULTILEVEL INSTRUCTION for 2B

Pre-level Tell groups to focus first on the jobs on page 26, and then on the jobs on page 27.
Above-level Brainstorm additional jobs with students, for example, *a manager, a receptionist, a construction worker, a nursing assistant, a landscaper, a tax preparer, a tutor, a teacher, a nanny, a hairdresser, a chef.* Ask groups of students to act them out.

Communicative Practice   20 minutes

Ⓒ Write your job. Use true or made-up...

- Write *teacher* on the board. Point to it and say: *This is my job.* Ask the class to repeat.
- Ask: *What is your job?* If students are not working, encourage them to say a job they want. Write students' answers on the board.
- Tell students to write their job on the line provided. Tell them they can make up information (for example, they can write a job they want or plan to have).
- Call on several students to say the job they wrote.

Learning Strategy: Use your language

- Provide each student with four index cards or tell students to cut up notebook paper into four pieces.
- Read the directions. If you have students with low first-language literacy skills, pair them with more capable peers if possible.
- Walk around as students work. If misspellings occur, tell them to check the list on page 27.
- Say: *You can use your language to help you remember new words in English.* Remind students to use this strategy to remember other new vocabulary.

Community Building

As you visit with students, show them you are an active language learner yourself by trying to pronounce job titles in their native languages.

Expansion: Speaking Practice

- Ask several students to present their cards to the class and teach the class to say jobs in their native languages. This is a fun way to build class community and value other students' languages.

Show what you know!

STEP 1. Walk around the room. Ask three...

- Copy the chart onto the board. Tell students that *What do you do?* means *What is your job?* Ask two students: *What do you do?* Write their jobs next to their names.
- Tell them to copy the chart into their notebooks with enough space to write the answers of three other students or more if they wish.
- Tell students to stand, mingle, and ask at least three classmates about their jobs.
- Walk around and check that students are interacting, writing, and capitalizing names.

STEP 2. Introduce one classmate to your class.

- Tell students they will now introduce someone from their chart.
- Using the language in the example, choose a student to play "Antonio," but use the student's real name.
- Write the example on the board, but substitute real information based on the student you introduced. Read the example and ask the class to repeat.
- Check pronunciation: Say *he's* and *she's* and ask students to repeat.
- Call on volunteers to stand and introduce a student from their chart while the class responds: *Nice to meet you, _____.*

Language Note

If you notice that students are omitting the article *a* or *an* when saying a job, do a mini-review by using examples from the chart in Step 1 on the board.

Expansion: Speaking Practice for STEP 2

- Divide the class into two teams and direct them to continue the Exercise 2B word play. To begin, select a student from Team 1 to play A.
- The rest of the team members have 10 seconds to guess the job. If they are successful, they get one point. Then ask Team 2 to perform.
- Continue the game for at least five turns. For each turn, select a new A from the performing team. Compare points and declare the winner.

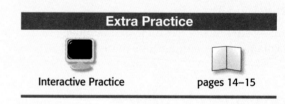

Extra Practice

Interactive Practice   pages 14–15

3

4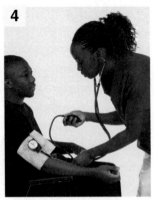

5

6

9

10

Jobs

1. a cook
2. a waiter / a waitress
3. a doctor
4. a nurse
5. a gardener
6. a driver
7. a cashier
8. a sales assistant
9. an accountant
10. an office assistant
11. a homemaker
12. a child-care worker
13. a housekeeper
14. an artist
15. a painter
16. an electrician

Learning Strategy

Use your language

Look at the list of jobs. Make cards for three or four words. On one side, write the word in English. On the other side, write the word in your language.

Show what you know!

STEP 1. Walk around the room. Ask three classmates about their jobs. Complete the chart.

Soo-Jin: *What do you do?*
Antonio: *I'm a cook.*

Name	Job
Antonio	a cook

STEP 2. Introduce one classmate to your class.

Soo-Jin: *This is Antonio. He's a cook.*
Class: *Nice to meet you, Antonio.*

Listening and Speaking

1 BEFORE YOU LISTEN

CD1 T28

A 🔊 **READ.** Look at the picture. Emilio, Gabriela, and Pierre are at a party.

Listen and read the conversation.

B **GROUPS OF 3.** Introduce two classmates.

A: _____, this is _____.
_____, this is _____.
B: Hi, _____. Nice to meet you.
C: Hi, _____. Nice to meet you, too.

Pierre, this is Gabriela. Gabriela, this is Pierre.

Hi, Pierre. Nice to meet you.

Hi, Gabriela. Nice to meet you, too.

2 LISTEN

A Look at the picture again. After the introduction, Gabriela asks Pierre a question.

Guess: What is Gabriela's question?

a. What do you do?   b. How is your class?

CD1 T29

B 🔊 Listen to the conversation. Was your guess in Exercise A correct?

Listen again. Complete the sentences.

1. Pierre is a gardener and _____*a student*_____.
   a. a driver   b. a student

2. Gabriela is a student and _____*an artist*_____.
   a. an artist   b. a nurse

CD1 T30

C 🔊 Listen to the whole conversation. What is Emilio's job?

a.    b.

Introduce someone and talk about your job

Getting Started 10 minutes

1 BEFORE YOU LISTEN

A  READ. **Look at the picture. Emilio,...**

- Tell students to look at the picture and to point at the correct person when you ask: *Who is Emilio? Who is Gabriela? Who is Pierre?*
- Say: *Pierre and Gabriela are meeting for the first time.*
- Ask three above-level students to play the roles of Emilio, Gabriela, and Pierre and perform the conversation for the class.
- To warm up for the listening, tell students to read the conversation in the speech balloons silently, starting with Emilio's lines.

Listen and read the conversation.

- Play CD 1, Track 28. Students listen and read along silently.

B GROUPS OF 3. **Introduce two classmates.**

- Copy the conversation with blanks onto the board. Tell the class you will introduce two students to each other.
- Call on two students to join you at the front of the class. Write their names in the blanks. Play A and practice the conversation with them.
- Form groups of 3. One person in each group plays A.
- Walk around and check that Student A is introducing B and C to each other.
- After each group has successfully performed the introduction, ask them to switch roles and repeat.

MULTILEVEL INSTRUCTION for 1B
Cross-ability. Ask the higher-level student to play A first.

Presentation 20 minutes

2 LISTEN

A **Look at the picture again.... Guess:...**

- Read the directions. Write the answer choices on the board.

- Say: *What do you do?* and ask the class to repeat. Ask: *What does this question mean?* As needed, remind students that it means *What is your job?*
- Say: *How is your class?* and ask the class to repeat. Ask: *What does this question mean?* (Do you like your class?)
- Ask: *What is Gabriela's question?* Tell students to circle the letter of Gabriela's question.

B  **Listen to the conversation. Was your...**

- Read the directions. Play CD 1, Track 29.
- Circle the correct answer on the board. Tell the class to raise their hands if their guess was correct.

Teaching Tip

Optional: If students need additional support, tell them to read the Audio Script on page 280 as they listen to the conversations.

Listen again. Complete the sentences.

- Tell students to read the sentences silently. Tell them to listen for Gabriela's and Pierre's jobs in the conversation.
- Play Track 29 again. Students listen and complete the sentences.
- To check answers, call on two students to write the sentences on the board. Correct as needed. Read them and ask the class to repeat.

Culture Connection

- Ask: *When you meet someone in your home country, do you ask about the person's job?*
- Tell students that in the United States it is normal to talk about jobs after an introduction.

C  **Listen to the whole conversation....**

- Ask students to look at the two pictures. For each picture, ask: *What job is this?* (an artist, a painter)
- Play CD 1, Track 30. Students listen for Emilio's job.
- Play Track 30 again as needed.
- To check the answer, ask: *What is Emilio's job?* (a house painter)

3 CONVERSATION

A 🔘 Listen. Then listen and repeat.

- Write the example sentences on the board. Say them, pointing to the arrows as you say the last word in each one.
- Read the Pronunciation Watch note. As needed, explain that a *Wh-* question begins with *What*, *Where*, *Who*, *When*, *Why*, or *How*. Tell the class they will practice *What* in this unit.
- Play CD 1, Track 31. Students listen for falling intonation.
- Resume playing Track 31. Students listen and repeat.

Controlled Practice   10 minutes

B 🔘 Listen and read the conversation....

- Note: This conversation is the same one students heard in Exercise 2B on page 28.
- Play CD 1, Track 32. Students listen and read along silently. Pause the track. To explain *Really?* practice the following conversation with a student: T: *Are you from Mexico?* S: *Yes.* T: **Really?** *I'm from Mexico, too!* To explain *too*, say information that your students have in common (for example, *Aricelis is a student. Kyung is a student, **too**.*).
- Check comprehension by asking: *What does Pierre do?* (He's a gardener and a student.) *What does Gabriela do?* (She's a student and an artist.)
- Resume playing Track 32. Students listen and repeat.
- Check that students' voices go down when they repeat *Wh-* questions and statements. If not, model correct pronunciation or replay Track 32.
- Ask: *What job do Gabriela **and** Pierre have?* (They're students.)

Communicative Practice   20 minutes

4 PRACTICE

A PAIRS. Practice the conversation. Then make...

- Pair students and tell them to practice the conversation in Exercise 3B.

- Then, in Exercise 4A, point to each picture and ask students what job it is. Tell students to write the name of the job next to each picture. Students can refer to page 27 to check spelling.
- Read the directions.
- Copy the conversation onto the board with blanks. Read through the conversation. When you come to a blank, fill it in with a job from the first pair of photographs (*a homemaker* and *a nurse*). Point out that A and B are both homemakers.
- Ask two on-level students to practice the conversation in front of the class. Tell pairs to take turns playing each role and to use the pictures to fill in the blanks.
- Walk around and check that students are using falling intonation. Tell students to stand, mingle, and practice the conversation with several new partners.

▬ MULTILEVEL INSTRUCTION for 4A

Pre-level Tell students to first fill in the blanks lightly in pencil before practicing. After practicing, students can erase their choices and write new ones.

Above-level Tell students playing A to mix and match jobs from different rows (for example, *a waiter* and *a nurse*).

B MAKE IT PERSONAL. PAIRS. Make your own...

- Read the directions. Tell students to write several jobs to use in the conversation. Students can use jobs on pages 26–27 and any additional jobs they know. Call on students (especially above-level) to say additional jobs they know. Write them on the board and explain any unfamiliar ones.
- Pair students and tell them to practice the conversation. Walk around and check that students are using falling intonation and are correctly identifying one job they both have and one job that is different.
- Call on pairs to perform for the class.

Extra Practice

Interactive Practice

3 CONVERSATION

A CD1 T31

🔘 **Listen. Then listen and repeat.**

A: What do you do?

B: I'm a student.

Pronunciation Watch

In *Wh-* questions and in statements, the voice goes down at the end.

B CD1 T32

🔘 **Listen and read the conversation. Then listen and repeat.**

Gabriela: So, what do you do?

Pierre: I'm a gardener. And I'm a student at Greenville Adult School.

Gabriela: Really? I'm a student there, too. And I'm an artist.

Pierre: Oh, that's interesting.

4 PRACTICE

A PAIRS. **Practice the conversation. Then make new conversations. Use the pictures.**

A: What do you do?

B: I'm   .

A: Really? I'm   , too.

    And I'm   .

B: Oh, that's interesting.

B MAKE IT PERSONAL. PAIRS. **Make your own conversations. Use the conversation in Exercise A. Use true or made-up information.**

Grammar

A/An		
Pierre is Paula is	**a**	gardener. driver.

Gabriela is Tal is	**an**	artist. electrician.

Grammar Watch

- Use **a** before consonant sounds.
- Use **an** before vowel sounds.

1 PRACTICE

A Underline the correct word.

1. **A:** That's Lily. She's **a** / **an** office assistant.

   B: Oh, really? I'm **a** / **an** office assistant, too.

2. **A:** Paul is **a** / **an** teacher, right?

   B: No. He's not **a** / **an** teacher. He's **a** / **an** nurse.

3. **A:** I'm **a** / **an** gardener. What about you?

   B: I'm **a** / **an** electrician.

4. **A:** This is Dr. and Mrs. Silver. He's **a** / **an** doctor

   and she's **a** / **an** accountant.

   B: Nice to meet you. I'm Teresa Castro.

   I'm **a** / **an** child-care worker.

5. **A:** What do you do?

   B: I'm **a** / **an** homemaker. I'm also **a** / **an** artist.

CD1 T33

B 💿 Listen and check your answers.

C PAIRS. Practice the conversations in Exercise A.

D WRITE. Complete the sentences. Use *a* or *an*.
Then write a sentence about someone you know.

1. Bob is ___a___ cashier.

2. Lucia is ___an___ electrician.

3. Kevin is ___a___ driver.

4. John is ___a___ cook.

5. Sarah is ___an___ office assistant.

6. Hai is ___an___ accountant.

7. Genet is ___a___ student.

8. Answers will vary. _____

Getting Started 5 minutes

- Say: *We're going to study a/an. In the conversation on page 29, Pierre and Gabriela used this grammar.*
- Play CD 1, Track 32. Students listen. Write on the board: *I'm a gardener.* Underline *a gardener.*

Presentation 10 minutes

A/An

- Copy the grammar charts onto the board or show the charts on Transparency 2.3 and cover the exercise.
- Read sentences from the charts and ask the class to repeat.
- Read the Grammar Watch note while the class reads along silently. To review consonant and vowel sounds, write some letters in random order (for example, *a, d, e, g, o, p*). Point to each one, and ask students to call out if it is a vowel or consonant.
- If you are using the transparency, do the exercise with the class.

▬ Expansion: Grammar Practice

- Write several jobs from page 27 on the board. Point to each one and ask: A *or* an? Students call out the appropriate article.
- Write and say the correct answers while the class repeats.

Controlled Practice 15 minutes

1 PRACTICE

A **Underline the correct word.**

- Remind students about the information in the Grammar Watch note.
- Read the directions and the example. Call on a student to read B's line, choosing *a* or *an*. Ask: *Why is* an *the answer?* (Because *office* begins with a vowel sound.)
- Students compare answers with a partner.

B 🎧 **Listen and check your answers.**

- Read the directions. Play CD 1, Track 33.
- *Optional:* Play Track 33 again, pausing after each item to allow students to repeat.

C **PAIRS. Practice the conversations in Exercise A.**

- Form cross-ability pairs and tell them to practice the conversations.
- Walk around and check for correct pronunciation of *a/an*.
- Call on pairs to perform for the class.

Language Note

If students aren't clearly pronouncing *a/an*, conduct a mini-review by saying the article with its noun and asking the class to repeat (for example, T: *A child-care worker.* Ss: *A child-care worker.*).

▬ MULTILEVEL INSTRUCTION for 1C

Cross-ability The higher-level partner models pronunciation of each line before the other partner repeats it.

D **WRITE. Complete the sentences. Use *a* or *an*....**

- Read the directions and the example.
- Remind students about the information in the Grammar Watch note.
- Call on students to say answers. Correct as needed.

▬ Expansion: Writing Practice for 1D

- Ask students to write an extra sentence for each item in Exercise D and say what the person is **not** (for example, *1. Bob is a cashier. He's not an office assistant.*).
- Walk around and check that students are using *a/an* correctly.

Lesson 3 Talk about jobs

Presentation

Singular and plural nouns

- Copy the grammar charts onto the board or show the charts on Transparency 2.3 and cover the exercise.
- Point to *cook* and say: Cook *is a noun. A noun is a person, place, thing, or idea.* Give examples by pointing to various objects in the classroom and identify them by name (for example, *chair*).
- On the board, write *singular = 1* and *plural = 2 or more.* Say: *A singular noun is one thing. A plural noun is two or more things.* To illustrate, hold up one pencil and say: *I have a pencil.* Then hold up two pencils and say: *I have pencils.*
- Read the Grammar Watch note. Use more examples of classroom objects to illustrate singular vs. plural. Ask the class to call out how to spell these words and write them on the board.
- If you are using the transparency, do the exercise with the class.

Controlled Practice   10 minutes

2 PRACTICE

A Write the plural form of these words:...

- Read the directions and the example (*nurse → nurses*) and ask the class to repeat.
- Tell students to read the Grammar Watch note before they write.

B Listen and check your answers....

- Play CD 1, Track 34. Students listen and check their answers.
- Resume playing Track 34. Students listen and repeat.
- Call on individual students to pronounce the plural forms. Correct as needed by modeling.

C Look at the pictures. Complete the sentences.

- Read the directions and the example. Ask the class to repeat the example. Remind students to use *a* or *an* if there is one person in the picture and to use plural nouns if there is more than one person.
- Call on students to read their completed sentences.

Communicative Practice   10 minutes

Show what you know!

STEP 1. Look at the jobs. These jobs are the five...

- Explain: *A common job is a job that a lot of people have.* Write the jobs on the board. Say: *Look at the five jobs.* Ask: *Which job is most common?*
- Tell students to put the number 1 next to the most common job, the number 2 next to the next most common job, and so on. Encourage them to guess. They will find out the answers in Step 3.

STEP 2. GROUPS OF 3. Talk about your answers.

- With two students, read the example. A and B say what they think is the most common job. When responding in agreement, students say: *Yes, I think . . .*
- Say: *When you talk about the jobs, use the plural as in the example.*
- Ask two or three more students to say which job they think is number 1.
- Form groups of 3 and tell students to talk about their answers.
- Walk around and check that students are interacting and saying complete sentences.

STEP 3. Listen and check your answers...

- Read the directions. Play CD 1, Track 35.
- Write the answers on the board and read them. Ask: *Were your guesses correct? Are you surprised?*

Progress Check

Can you . . . talk about jobs?

Say: *We have practiced talking about jobs. Now, look at the question at the bottom of the page. Can you talk about jobs?* Tell students to write a checkmark in the box.

Extra Practice		
Interactive Practice	pages 12–13	pages 16–17

Singular and plural nouns

John is	**a cook.**	John and Linda are	**cooks.**
Amy is	**a waitress.**	Amy, Ana, and Luz are	**waitresses.**

Grammar Watch
- Add **-s** to form most plurals.
- Add **-es** to words that end in s, sh, ch, and x.
- For a list of some irregular plural nouns, see page 273.

2 PRACTICE

A Write the plural form of these words: *nurse, gardener, cashier, waitress,* and *driver*.

___nurses___   ___gardeners___   ___cashiers___   ___waitresses___   ___drivers___

CD1 T34

B Listen and check your answers. Notice the pronunciation of the –s and –es endings. Listen again and repeat.

C Look at the pictures. Complete the sentences.

| 1 | 2 | 3 | 4 |

1. They're ___drivers___.
2. Rosa is ___a gardener___.
3. Jill, Mei, and I are ___waitresses___.
4. Bob is ___a nurse___.

Show what you know!   Talk about jobs

STEP 1. Look at the jobs. These jobs are the five most common jobs in the U.S. Guess: Which job is number 1, 2, 3, 4, and 5? Write a number next to each job. (The answers are given in Step 3.)

__3__ driver   __4__ teacher   __5__ cashier   __1__ sales assistant   __2__ office assistant

STEP 2. GROUPS OF 3. Talk about your answers.

A: *I think cashiers are number 1.*
B: *No, I think . . .*

CD1 T35
STEP 3. Listen and check your answers in Step 1.

Can you . . . talk about jobs? ☐

Give phone numbers

Life Skills

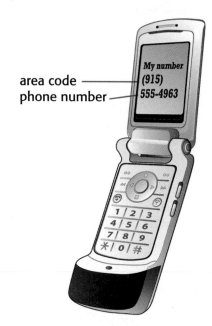

area code
phone number

My number
(915)
555-4963

1 USE NUMBERS 0–9

A **CLASS.** Think about numbers in your life. When do you use numbers? Do you use numbers at work?

CD1 T36

B Look at the numbers. Listen and point. Then listen and repeat.

0 zero	1 one	2 two	3 three	4 four
5 five	6 six	7 seven	8 eight	9 nine

2 PRACTICE

CD1 T37

A Listen. Circle the area code you hear.

1. 212 (512)   3. (305) 315   5. (919) 915
2. 713 (714)   4. 408 (708)   6. (786) 706

*We often say
oh for O.*

B **PAIRS.** Look at the pictures. Which places do you know? Write the words from the box on the lines.

~~a hospital~~   an office   a restaurant   a child-care center

1. ___a hospital___

2. ___a child-care center___

3. ___a restaurant___

4. ___an office___

Lesson 4 Give phone numbers

Getting Started 　　　　10 minutes

1 USE NUMBERS 0–9

A CLASS. Think about numbers in your life....

- Read the questions.
- Encourage students to think about places in their everyday life where they use numbers. If students have difficulty answering, prompt them with the following questions: *Do you have a phone number? Do you have a student ID number? Do you use numbers at work?*
- If students use numbers at work, ask them to explain how. Above-level students may be able to say, for example, *I'm a cashier. I use numbers to count money and make change.*

Presentation 　　　　5 minutes

B **Look at the numbers. Listen and point....**

- Ask students to look at the numbers in the box.
- Play CD 1, Track 36. Students listen and point.
- Resume playing Track 36. Students listen and repeat.

Controlled Practice 　　　　30 minutes

2 PRACTICE

A **Listen. Circle the area code you hear.**

- Ask students to look at the picture of the cell phone. Ask: *What is the area code? What is the phone number?* Tell students to pronounce each digit in an area code (for example, 915 → 9-1-5).
- Explain: *With area codes and phone numbers, you can pronounce 0 in two ways—either* zero *or* oh.
- Ask: *What is the area code here?* Write it on the board. Say it and ask the class to repeat.
- Explain: *When you write a phone number, use parentheses around the area code. Use a dash after the first three digits of the phone number.* Write a complete telephone number on the board.

- Play CD 1, Track 37. Students listen and circle the area code they hear.
- Play Track 37 again if students need to hear it twice before they answer.
- Students compare answers with a partner.
- Call on students to say answers. Correct pronunciation as needed.

Expansion: Writing Practice for 2A

- Pair students. Student A reads one area code from each item in Exercise 1A. Student B writes it in his or her notebook.
- Student B can also practice writing parentheses around each area code.

B PAIRS. Look at the pictures. Which places...

- Read the workplaces in the box and ask the class to repeat (for example, *a hospital . . . an office . . .*).
- Read the directions. Ask: *What is number 1?*
- Pair students and tell them to cross out each item that they use in the box.
- Students work together to match the pictures and the words.
- Call on students to say answers.

MULTILEVEL INSTRUCTION for 2B

Cross-ability The higher-level students point to each picture and ask their partners to identify each place before writing the answers.

Expansion: Vocabulary Practice for 2B

- Ask students who works in each of the places in Exercise B (for example, T: *Who works in a hospital?* Ss: *A nurse. A doctor.*).
- Write answers on the board, but tell students to spell the words before you write them (for example, T: *How do you spell* doctor? Ss: *D-O-C-T-O-R.*).

3 GIVE PHONE NUMBERS

 Listen to the messages on the answering....

- Tell students to look at all four of the messages and read them silently. Explain: *Someone called you about a job. Listen to the messages. Listen for the area code and phone number.*
- Play CD 1, Track 38. Students listen and write.
- Play Track 38 again. Students check their answers.
- Call on students to write answers on the board. Check that students include the parentheses and the dash. Correct as needed.

4 PRACTICE

A **Listen and read the conversation....**

- Play CD 1, Track 39. Students listen and read along silently.
- Resume playing Track 39. Students listen and repeat.
- Explain: *555 is for made-up phone numbers. In textbooks, television, and movies, people use 555.*

Expansion: Listening Practice for 4A

- Dictate several made-up phone numbers with area codes to students. Ask a few students to come to the board to do the exercise while the others remain at their desks.
- Students compare answers with a partner.
- Look at the students' answers on the board. Correct as needed. Check that they have put parentheses around the area code and a dash between the first three and last four digits of the phone number.

Communicative Practice   15 minutes

B **CLASS. Walk around the room. Ask two...**

- Write the headings *Name* and *(Area Code) Phone Number* on the board. Practice the conversation in Exercise 4A with an above-level student. Tell the student that he or she can use real or made-up information. Write it under the appropriate heading on the board.

- Read the directions. Emphasize that students can use made-up information if they want.
- Give the class a strategy for making sure they have the correct numbers: Tell them to repeat phone numbers back to the student to check them. If they miss part of a phone number, tell them to ask, *Excuse me, could you repeat that?*
- Walk around and help students confirm the information they write.
- Call on students to say the phone numbers they wrote.

5 LIFE SKILLS WRITING

Turn to page 254 and ask students to complete the form for work. See pages Txi–Txii for general notes about Life Skills Writing activities.

Progress Check

Can you . . . use numbers 0–9 and give your phone number?

Say: *We have practiced using numbers 0–9 and phone numbers. Now, look at the question at the bottom of the page. Can you use numbers 0–9 and phone numbers?* Tell students to write a checkmark in the box.

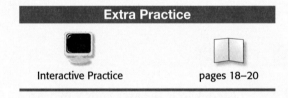

Extra Practice

Interactive Practice   pages 18–20

3 GIVE PHONE NUMBERS

CD1 T38

Listen to the messages on the answering machines.
Write the missing numbers.

1.

Call Mr. Fernandez
at Center Hospital
about the gardener
job.

(562) 555-1 ___349___

2.

Call Grace Simms
at Grace's office
Supplies about the
cashier job.

(_40_ 8) 555-7 _821_

3.

Call Jin Heng Wu at
Riverside Child Care
about the child-care
worker job.

(_773_) 555- _960_ _2_

4.

Call Ms. Rodriguez
at Carla's Restaurant
about the waiter job.

(_339_) 555 - _8851_

4 PRACTICE

CD1 T39

A Listen and read the conversation. Then listen and repeat.

Elena: What's your phone number?

Asad: 555-4963.

Elena: And what's the area code?

Asad: 915.

B CLASS. Walk around the room. Ask two classmates for their phone number and area code. Write the numbers. Use true or made-up information.

	Name	(Area Code) Phone Number
	Asad	(915) 555-4963
1.		
2.		

5 LIFE SKILLS WRITING   Complete a form at work. See page 254.

Can you...use numbers 0–9 and give your phone number?   ☐

Listening and Speaking

1 LISTEN

A Look at the picture. Ilya and Claudia are at a party. They're talking about Sara.

Guess: What does Sara do?

(a.) Sara is a student.

b. Sara is a teacher.

CD1 T40

B Listen to the conversation. Was your guess in Exercise A correct?

Listen again. Complete the sentences.

1. Sara is ___a cashier___.
   (a.)   b.

2. Ilya is ___a cook___.
   a.   (b.)

CD1 T41

C Listen to the whole conversation. Complete the sentences.

1. Claudia says, "I'm _____." (Check (✓) all the correct answers.)

   ☐ an electrician   ☑ a cook   ☑ a waitress

   ☑ a child-care worker   ☐ a cashier   ☑ a doctor

2. Claudia is _____. (Check (✓) one answer.)

   ☑ a homemaker   ☐ a gardener   ☐ a housekeeper

Getting Started   5 minutes

 1   LISTEN

A   Look at the picture.... Guess:...

- Say: *Look at the picture.* Ask: *What do you see?* As needed, prompt students: *How many people do you see? Where are they?*
- Ask students to name each of the three people in the picture. (Ilya, Claudia, and Sara)
- Say: *Guess: What does Sara do?* Write the answer choices on the board and read them. Tell students to guess the correct answer.

■ Expansion: Speaking Practice for 1A

- Ask students why they think Sara is either a student or a teacher. (*Possible answers:* Her bag looks like a teacher's bag. She is dressed like a teacher/a student.)

Presentation   35 minutes

B **Listen to the conversation. Was...**

- Read the directions. Play CD 1, Track 40.
- Circle the correct answer on the board. Ask: *Was your guess correct?*

> **Teaching Tip**
>
> *Optional:* Remember that if students need additional support, tell them to read the Audio Script on page 281 as they listen to the conversations.

Listen again. Complete the sentences.

- Point to each picture and ask: *What is the job?* to check that students understand what each picture shows (1. a. cashier, b. waitress; 2. a. waiter, b. cook).
- Read the directions. Play Track 40 again. Students listen and choose *a* or *b* to complete the sentences.
- Students compare answers with a partner.
- Call on students to say answers.

C 🖊 **Listen to the whole conversation....**

- Ask students to read the sentences and all the answer options.
- Play CD 1, Track 41. Students listen and complete the sentences.
- Play Track 41 again if students have difficulty.
- Students compare answers with a partner.
- Call on students to say answers.

■ Expansion: Writing Practice for 1C

- Ask students to write three sentences about what Claudia is not (for example, *She is not a waitress.*). Students can use the jobs they didn't check to write their sentences.

■ Expansion: Listening and Speaking Practice for 1C

- Pair students and tell them to take turns dictating their sentences from the above writing expansion activity to each other.

Lesson 5 Ask about jobs

2 CONVERSATION

A Listen. Then listen and repeat.

- Read the Pronunciation Watch note. Ask: *What is the answer to a yes/no question?* (Yes or no.)
- Write the example sentences on the board. Say the sentences, pointing to the arrows as you say the last word in each one.
- Play CD 1, Track 42. Students listen.
- Resume playing Track 42. Students listen and repeat.

B Listen to the sentences. Does the voice...

- Review falling intonation by saying a couple of *Wh*- questions (for example, *What time is it?*).
- On the board, draw the checkboxes as shown on the page. Read the directions. Tell students they will check (✓) the box for Up or Down for each sentence they hear.
- Play CD 1, Track 43 and pause after the first item. Check the Up box on the board. Make sure students understand the activity before continuing.
- Call on students to say answers. To wrap up, play Track 43 again and ask students to repeat.

C Listen and read the conversation....

- Note: This conversation is the same one students heard in Exercise 1B on page 34.
- Tell students that the conversation has both *Wh*-questions and *yes/no* questions.
- Play CD 1, Track 44. Students listen and read along silently.
- Resume playing Track 44. Students listen and repeat.
- Model the conversation if students have difficulty.

Controlled Practice   10 minutes

3 PRACTICE

A PAIRS. Practice the conversation. Then make...

- Pair students and tell them to practice the conversation in Exercise 2C.

- Then, in Exercise 3A, point to each word in the boxes, say it, and ask the class to repeat. As needed, tell students to look back at pages 26–27 for pictures of these words.
- Ask a pair of on-level students to practice the conversation in front of the class.
- Tell pairs to take turns playing each role and to use the pictures to fill in the blanks.
- Walk around and check that students are using rising and falling intonation correctly.
- Tell students to stand, mingle, and practice the conversation with several new partners.
- Call on pairs to perform for the class.

MULTILEVEL INSTRUCTION for 3A

Pre-level Tell students to draw an upward arrow above the end of *yes/no* questions and a downward arrow at the end of *Wh*- questions and statements.

Above-level Ask pairs to continue practicing by looking only at the information in the lists.

Communicative Practice   10 minutes

B MAKE IT PERSONAL. PAIRS. Make your own...

- With two above-level students, practice the conversation using true information. Play A while B tells you about the other student.
- If possible, quickly review everyone's job (students can use real or made-up information) by asking each student in the class, *What do you do?*
- Pair students. Say: *Student A, ask about a student who you and Student B can see.*
- Walk around and check that students are using accurate job information.

Expansion: Speaking Practice for 3B

- Pairs continue by asking where their partner is from. For example, A: *So, where are you from?* B: *I'm from Canada.* A: *That's interesting. I'm from Poland.*).

Extra Practice

Interactive Practice

2 CONVERSATION

A 🔘 **Listen. Then listen and repeat.**

Are you a student?   Is he a cook?

B 🔘 **Listen to the sentences. Does the voice go up or down at the end?**

	1.	2.	3.	4.
Up	☑	☐	☐	☑
Down	☐	☑	☑	☐

C 🔘 **Listen and read the conversation. Then listen and repeat.**

Claudia: Who's that? Is she a teacher?

Ilya: No, she's not. She's a student.
And she's a cashier at Al's Restaurant.

Claudia: Oh, that's interesting. And what do you do?

Ilya: I'm a cook.

3 PRACTICE

A PAIRS. **Practice the conversation. Then make new conversations. Use the words in the boxes.**

A: Who's that? Is   a teacher?

B: No,   's not.   's a student.
And   's   .

A: Oh, that's interesting. And what do you do?

B: I'm   .

she	a cashier	a sales assistant
he	an electrician	a painter
she	a nurse	an accountant

B MAKE IT PERSONAL. PAIRS. **Make your own conversations. Use the conversation in Exercise A. Student A, ask about a classmate. Student B, give true answers.**

Grammar

Be: Yes/no questions and short answers

Are	you		a teacher?
Is	he she Sara		
Are	you they		teachers?
Is	your job it		hard?

Yes,	I **am.**
	he **is.**
	she **is.**
	we **are.** they **are.**
	it **is.**

No,	I'**m not**	OR	
	he'**s not**		he **isn't.**
	she'**s not**		she **isn't.**
	we'**re not** they'**re not**		we **aren't.** they **aren't.**
	it'**s not**		it **isn't.**

Writing Watch

End questions with a question mark.

1 PRACTICE

A Write *yes/no* questions about jobs.

1. cook / she / a / Is   Is she a cook?

2. they / Are / sales assistants   Are they sales assistants?

3. a / Are / waitress / you   Are you a waitress?

4. Is / painter / he / a   Is he a painter?

5. John / a / gardener / Is   Is John a gardener?

6. the job / easy / Is   Is the job easy?

Is she a cook?

B Complete the conversations. Use capital letters when necessary.

1. **A:** ___Are___ they waiters?

   B: No, _they're not_. (OR _they aren't_.)

2. **A:** ___Is___ she a cook?

   B: Yes, ___she is___.

3. **A:** ___Are___ Marta and Kim office assistants?

   B: Yes, ___they are___.

4. **A:** ___Are___ you an electrician?

   B: No, ___I'm not___.

5. **A:** ___Is___ he an accountant?

   B: No, ___he's not___.OR he isn't

6. **A:** ___Is___ Mr. Garcia a painter?

   B: Yes, ___he is___.

Getting Started   5 minutes

- Say: *We're going to study yes/no questions and short answers with the verb be. In the conversation on page 35, Claudia used this grammar.*
- Play CD 1, Track 44. Students listen. Write *Is she a teacher?* on the board. Underline *Is she.*

Presentation   10 minutes

Be: Yes/no questions and short answers

- Copy the grammar charts onto the board or show the charts on Transparency 2.4 and cover the exercise. Add the words *student* and *students* and some of your students' names to the left chart.
- Ask questions from the left chart (for example, *Are you a student?*). Model rising intonation and ask the class to repeat. Say: *These are yes/no questions.*
- Read the Writing Watch note and point to the question marks in the chart.
- Form both affirmative and negative answers for each question you asked the class (for example, *Yes, I am. No, I'm not.*). Model falling intonation and ask the class to repeat as they did for the questions. Point to the middle and right charts and say: *These are short answers.*
- Ask students to form and call out questions from the left chart. Remind students that a form of *be—Are* or *Is*—comes first.
- Ask students some *yes/no* questions that they can answer affirmatively (for example, *Are you a student? Are you in class?*). Guide students to form appropriate affirmative short answers (without contractions).
- Then ask students some *yes/no* questions that they can answer negatively (for example, *Are you a teacher? Are you at home?*). When students answer, first write out the uncontracted negative first-person form on the board (*No, I am not.*). Since students learned how contractions are formed in Unit 1, call on a volunteer to rewrite the answer as *No, I'm not.*
- Remind students to use an apostrophe to show that two words are combined.

- Ask third-person questions about your students (for example, *Is Julio a teacher?*). Students should call out an appropriate negative short answer (*No, he's not* or *No, he isn't*). On the board, demonstrate that a contraction can be formed with *he* and *is* (*he's*) or with *is* and *not* (*isn't*). Say: *Both contractions mean the same thing.*
- If you are using the transparency, do the exercise with the class.

Controlled Practice   35 minutes

1 PRACTICE

Ⓐ Write *yes/no* questions about jobs.

- Read the directions and the example. Tell students to look for the capitalized word to begin each question.
- Ask students to look at the grammar chart so they remember how to form *yes/no* questions. Remind them to end questions with a question mark.
- Walk around and check word order, capitalization, and use of question marks.
- Students compare answers with a partner.
- Call on students to say their answers.

Ⓑ Complete the conversations. Use capital letters...

- Read the example and ask the class to repeat.
- Remind students to capitalize the first word of sentences.
- Ask students to look at the pronoun or the names in each question to decide whether to use *are* or *is.*
- Students compare answers with a partner.
- Call on students to write the completed conversations on the board. Correct as needed.
- Call on pairs to perform the conversations.

▬▬ Expansion: Writing and Speaking Practice for 1B

- Tell students to write answers to the questions in Exercise 1A in their notebooks. Students write affirmative short answers to three questions and negative short answers to the other three.
- Then pair students and ask them to practice asking and answering the questions in 1A.

2 PRACTICE

Look at the pictures. Complete the conversations....

- Read the directions and the example.
- Tell students to look carefully at the pictures before they write the answers.
- Remind students to use *he* for a man and *she* for a woman. Also remind students to use *a* or *an* for one person.
- Walk around and check for proper capitalization and use of periods, use of *a/an*, and appropriate short answers.
- *Optional:* Pair students and ask them to practice the completed conversations. Call on pairs to perform the completed conversation for the class.

Expansion: Speaking Practice for 2

- Pair students. If magazines are available, ask students to cut out pictures of people working and have a short conversation based on the ones in the exercise (for example, A: *Is she a doctor?* B: *No, she isn't. She's a nurse.*)

Communicative Practice   10 minutes

Show what you know!

GROUPS OF 3. Student A, think of a famous singer...

- Ask students to identify all three people in the photographs (from left to right: Shakira, Pele, Jackie Chan). Ask students why each person is famous. (Shakira is a singer. Pele was a soccer player. Jackie Chan is an actor.)
- As needed, explain unfamiliar vocabulary by giving examples that your students can relate to (for example, singers: *Gwen Stefani, Beyoncé, Bono*; athletes: *Venus Wiliams, Derek Jeter, Kobe Bryant*; actors: *Christian Bale, Angelina Jolie, George Clooney*).

- Read the directions and the example conversation and ask the class to repeat the conversation.
- Play A and ask two above-level students to perform the activity with you for the class. To make it easier to guess, write three names on the board and tell the two students you are thinking of one of them (for example, *Christian Bale, Beyoncé,* and *Derek Jeter*).

MULTILEVEL INSTRUCTION
Cross-ability The higher-level student asks questions first to provide a model for his or her partner.

Expansion: Writing and Speaking Practice

- Ask students to gather information about three classmates. Students need to write their classmates' jobs, where they are from, and if they are men or women.
- Pair students. Student A thinks of one of the students. Student B begins asking *yes/no* questions to identify who it is.

Progress Check

Can you . . . ask about jobs?
Say: *We have practiced asking about jobs. Now, look at the question at the bottom of the page. Can you ask about jobs?* Tell students to write a checkmark in the box.

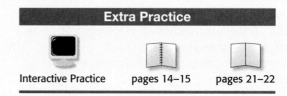

Extra Practice		
Interactive Practice	pages 14–15	pages 21–22

Look at the pictures. Complete the conversations. Add *a* or *an* when necessary.
Use capital letters and periods when necessary.

1. **A:** <u>Is she an</u> accountant?

   B: <u>Yes, she is.</u>

2. **A:** <u>Are they</u> artists?

   B: <u>No, they aren't.</u>

3. **A:** <u>Is she an</u> electrician?

   B: <u>Yes, she is.</u>

4. **A:** <u>Is he a</u> nurse?

   B: <u>No, he isn't.</u>

5. **A:** <u>Are they</u> gardeners?

   B: <u>Yes, they are.</u>

6. **A:** <u>Is she a</u> waitress?

   B: <u>No, she isn't.</u>

Show what you know! Ask about jobs

**GROUPS OF 3. Student A, think of a famous singer, athlete, or actor.
Students B and C, ask *yes/no* questions and guess the famous person.**

B: *Is it a woman?*
A: *No, it isn't.*
C: *Is the man an athlete?*
A: *Yes, he is.*
B: *Is he from Brazil?*
A: *Yes, he is.*
C: *Pele?*
A: *Yes!*

Can you...ask about jobs? ☐

Reading

1 BEFORE YOU READ

A Look at the pictures. Read the sentences about job skills. Check (✓) the sentences that are true for you.

Answers will vary.

☐ I use a computer.

☐ I take care of children.

☐ I cook.

☐ I clean.

☐ I pay the bills.

☐ I'm organized.

B GROUPS OF 4. Talk about your answers. Who has the same job skills?

A: *I cook and clean, and I'm organized. What about you, Ken?*
B: *I'm organized, too. And I . . .*

Lesson 7 Read about job skills

Getting Started   20 minutes

1 BEFORE YOU READ

Ⓐ Look at the pictures. Read the sentences about...

- Read the directions.
- Explain: *To do a job, you need skills. A skill is a special ability, something you do well.*
- Point to each picture and call on individual students to read the skill statements (for example, *I use a computer.*). Explain any unfamiliar vocabulary (for example, Organized *means that you keep everything in order.*).
- For each picture, ask students to call out jobs that match each skill (for example, T: *What jobs use a computer?* Ss: *An accountant. An office assistant.*).
- Say: *Check the skills that are true for you.*

> **Expansion: Vocabulary and Speaking Practice for 1A**

- Call on students to say their real-life jobs (or jobs they want in the future). Write skills needed for those jobs on the board (for example, *restaurant busperson: I clean tables. I organize dishes and plates. I work well with other people. I help the server.*).
- Individual students copy the skills needed for their job and repeat them.

Ⓑ GROUPS OF 4. Talk about your answers. Who...

- Read the example.
- Call on a few above-level students to say their skills. After the first student answers, prompt additional students with *What about you, _____?* as in the example.
- Form groups of 4. Students take turns stating their skills (A: *I use a computer.* B: *I use a computer, too.*).
- Walk around and check that students are taking turns.

> **MULTILEVEL INSTRUCTION for 1B**

Pre-level To encourage conversation, first point to the pictures and ask students which skills are true for them. (*Do you use a computer? Do you take care of children?*)

Above-level Ask students to identify additional skills not on the page (for example, *I drive a truck. I solder. I pack boxes. I help customers.*). Call on students to share these skills with the class. Write them on the board. To explain unfamiliar vocabulary, give simple definitions, draw stick figures, or mime behavior.

Culture Connection

- Say: *Job skills are very important in the United States. The more skills you have, the more opportunities you have.*
- Ask: *What job skills are important in the United States? Are the same job skills important in your home country? Do you have skills that you learned in your home country that you use here in the United States? What are they?*
- Ask: *What skills can you learn here at school?*
- Write students' suggestions on the board. As needed, suggest the following: *organization, teamwork, speaking and writing in English, special language training* (if your school offers vocational ESL courses), and *problem-solving skills.*

Presentation 15 minutes

2 READ

 Listen. Read the article.

- Ask: *What is the title of the article?* As needed, hold up the book, point to the title, and say *title*. Write on the board: *title = Homemaker Finds a Job.*
- Tell students to look at the picture. Read the caption. Ask: *What is a job counselor's job?* (He/She helps people find a job.)
- Play CD 1, Track 45. Students listen and read silently. Explain: Online *means* on the Internet.
- *Optional:* Play Track 45 again. Pause the CD after each of the following paragraphs and ask:

    First paragraph: *What does Li Chen do?* (She's a homemaker.) *Does she want a new job?* (Yes.)

    Third paragraph: *What can Li Chen do?* (Take care of children, cook, clean, pay bills online)

    Fourth paragraph: *What are Li Chen's skills?* (She's good with children and numbers. She's organized, and she uses a computer.)

Community Building

If there are job counselors at your school, ask for handouts, pamphlets, and other level-appropriate materials to share with your students. Discuss with students the importance of studying English to reach their job goals.

Controlled Practice 15 minutes

3 CHECK YOUR UNDERSTANDING

A Read the article again. Answer the questions.

- Read the directions. For item 1, underline the first activity (*I take care of the children.*) for the class.
- Call on students to say answers.

Expansion: Speaking Practice for 3A

- Ask students to explain their answer to question 2 (for example, S: *Li can do many things because she has many skills.*).

B What is the main idea of the article? Complete...

- Read the note about the main idea.
- Students complete the sentence. Call on a student to write the completed sentence on the board.

C PAIRS. What do you think? What is Li's new job?

- Pair students. Tell students they should guess. Tell them to think about Li's skills and to look at the jobs on pages 26–27.
- Call on pairs to say their answers.

MULTILEVEL INSTRUCTION for 3C

Cross-ability The higher-level student asks the question first to make sure that the lower-level partner can answer. The higher-level student can suggest a job (*Is Li an office assistant? Why?*).

Communicative Practice 10 minutes

Show what you know!

PAIRS. Talk about it. What are your job skills?...

- Pair students. Ask: *What are your job skills?* Write their answers on the board (*I can . . .*).
- Ask: *What jobs can you do now?* Write their answers on the board (*I can be a . . .*).
- Ask: *What job do you want in five years?* Write their answers on the board (*I want to be a . . .*).
- Walk around and sit with pairs. Check that students are taking turns asking and answering.

MULTILEVEL INSTRUCTION

Pre-level Tell students to refer back to previous lessons in this unit if they need help identifying jobs they can do now or want in the future.

Above-level Ask pairs to discuss at least three job skills they have now and three jobs they can do now, and to explain why they want a particular job in five years.

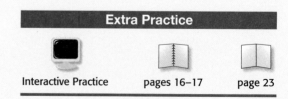

Extra Practice

Interactive Practice   pages 16–17   page 23

CD1 T45

💿 **Listen. Read the article.**

Homemaker Finds a Job

Li Chen looks at job information in a job counselor's office.

Li Chen is a homemaker. Now her children are in school. She wants a job. But she's a homemaker. What kind of job can she do? She talks to a job counselor.

The job counselor asks Li, "What do you do at home every day?"

"Well," Li says, "<u>I take care of the children</u>. <u>I cook</u>. <u>I clean</u>. <u>I pay the bills online</u>."

The counselor says, "You can do a lot of things! You're good with children. You're organized. You're good with numbers. You use a computer!" She helps Li find a job.

3 **CHECK YOUR UNDERSTANDING**

Ⓐ **Read the article again. Answer the questions.**

1. What does Li do at home every day? Underline four activities in the article.

2. What does the counselor think?

    (a.) Li can do many things.   b. Li can be a cook.   c. Li can't get a job.

3. What are Li's job skills?

    She is __good with children__, __good with numbers__, and __organized__.

    She can use __a computer__.

Ⓑ **What is the main idea of the article? Complete the sentence.**

Your skills at home are also good ___job___ skills.

> The *main idea* is the most important idea in an article.

Ⓒ **PAIRS. What do you think? What is Li's new job?**

Show what you know!

PAIRS. Talk about it. What are your job skills? What jobs can you do now? What job do you want in five years?

Talk about where you work

Listening and Speaking

1 BEFORE YOU LISTEN

CLASS. Look at the picture. For some jobs, like security guards, people need uniforms. What other jobs need uniforms?

2 LISTEN

A Look at Miriam's uniform. What is her job?

_____nurse_____

CD1 T46

B 🖸 Look at the picture. Dora is at a party. She is talking to Miriam and Pierre.

Listen to the conversation. Was your answer in Exercise A correct?

CD1 T46

C 🖸 Listen again. Where does Miriam work?

a.

b.

CD1 T47

D 🖸 Listen to the whole conversation. Complete the sentences.

1. Pierre is a _____student_____.
   a. nurse   b. teacher   (c.) student

2. Pierre says, "It's _____a hard job_____."
   a. an interesting job   (b.) a hard job   c. a great job

E **CLASS.** Read and discuss.

Miriam says, "That's not a job." Pierre says, "Yes, it is."
Who is right, Miriam or Pierre?

Getting Started   10 minutes

1 BEFORE YOU LISTEN

CLASS. Look at the picture. For some jobs,...

- Explain: *A* uniform *is special clothing that you must wear to do a job.* Hold up the book and point to the security guard's uniform.
- Read the directions. If students have difficulty coming up with jobs, tell the class to turn back to pages 26–27. For each job picture, ask: *Does this job have a uniform?*

■ **Expansion: Speaking and Vocabulary Practice for 1**

- Ask students if they wear a uniform for a job they have now or have had in the past.
- If possible, ask students to sketch a picture of their uniform in their notebooks and write the job below it. Students who have never held such a job can make one up, draw its uniform, and label it.
- Students compare drawings with a partner and state the job (for example, A: *I'm a cook.* B: *That's interesting. I'm a sales assistant.*).
- Walk around and look at students' drawings. If possible, display the drawings.

Presentation   15 minutes

2 LISTEN

Ⓐ **Look at Miriam's uniform. What is her job?**

- Ask students to look at the uniform and guess Miriam's job (*a nurse*).
- Call on a few students to say their guesses. Write them on the board.

Ⓑ 💿 **Look at the picture. Dora is at a party....**

- Read the directions.
- Ask: *Who is Miriam?* Point to Miriam (the woman in orange). Say: *What is Miriam talking about?* (her job)

Listen to the conversation. Was your answer...

- Play CD 1, Track 46. Students listen.
- Circle the correct answer on the board. Ask: *Was your guess correct?*

> **Teaching Tip**
>
> *Optional:* Remember that if students need additional support, tell them to read the Audio Script on page 281 as they listen to the conversations.

Ⓒ 💿 **Listen again. Where does Miriam work?**

- Ask students to look at the pictures. For each, ask: *What place is this?* (a. a hospital; b. a school)
- Read the directions. Play Track 46 again.
- Ask: *Where does Miriam work?* (at a school)

Ⓓ 💿 **Listen to the whole conversation....**

- Ask students to read the sentences and answer choices silently.
- Read the directions. Play CD 1, Track 47.
- Students compare answers with a partner.
- Say each sentence and call on students to complete it (for example, T: *Pierre is a . . .* Ss: *student.*).

Ⓔ **CLASS. Read and discuss.**

- Read the directions and the question.
- Ask students to raise their hands if they think Miriam is right. Then ask them to raise their hands if they think Pierre is right.
- Call on students to explain their choice (for example, S: *A student isn't a job because you don't get paid.*).

■ **Expansion: Graphic Organizer Practice for 2E**

- On the board, create a two-column chart with the following headings: *Student = job* and *Student = not a job.* Call on students to give you reasons to support either position and write them in the appropriate column (for example, *Student = job: difficult, lots of time; Student = not a job: no pay, no boss*). Ask students to copy the chart into their notebooks.

3 CONVERSATION

 Listen and read the conversation. Then...

- Note: This conversation is the same one students heard in Exercise 2B on page 40.
- Play CD 1, Track 48. Students listen and read along silently.
- Resume playing Track 48. Students listen and repeat.

Controlled Practice   15 minutes

4 PRACTICE

A PAIRS. Practice the conversation. Then make...

- Pair students and tell them to practice the conversation in Exercise 3.
- Then, in Exercise 4A, point to each picture and ask students to say both the job and the place. As needed, explain unfamiliar vocabulary (for example, a construction site: *a place where people make buildings*). Ask students for examples of these places near school or in their neighborhoods.
- Read the directions.
- Copy the conversation onto the board with blanks. Read through the conversation. When you come to a blank, fill it in with information from the first picture. (*a carpenter* and *a construction site*).
- Ask a pair of on-level students to practice the conversation in front of the class. Remind students to say both a job and its workplace.
- Tell pairs to take turns playing each role and to use the information from a picture to fill in the blanks.
- Walk around and check that students are clearly pronouncing the jobs and workplaces.
- Tell students to stand, mingle, and practice the conversation with several new partners.
- Call on pairs to perform for the class.

▬▬ MULTILEVEL INSTRUCTION for 4A

Cross-ability The higher-level partner plays B a few times to model how to select vocabulary.

▬▬ Expansion: Vocabulary Practice for 4A

- Pair students and ask them to turn back to the jobs on pages 26–27 and, in their notebooks, to write a workplace for as many jobs listed there as they can.
- Then students take turns calling out a workplace and the job(s) at that place (for example, A: *A hospital.* B: *A nurse. A doctor.*).

Communicative Practice   20 minutes

B MAKE IT PERSONAL. PAIRS. Make your own...

- Read the directions. With a student, practice the example conversation.
- Pair students and tell them to take turns playing A and B. Say: *You can change the words in the conversation. Just make sure you talk about each other's jobs and where you work.*
- Tell students to stand, mingle, and practice with other partners.
- Call on pairs to perform for the class.

▬▬ MULTILEVEL INSTRUCTION for 4B

Pre-level Allow students to stick fairly closely to the example conversation, but tell them to substitute new job and workplace information.
Above-level Tell students to use expressions not in the conversation. Practice such expressions with them (for example, A: *So, where do you work?* B: *Oh, I work at a school. I'm a teacher's aide.* A: *Oh, really? Wow, that's great.*).

C NETWORK. Find classmates with the same job...

- Read the directions.
- Ask students to stand and mingle. Tell students to ask one another: *What do you do?*
- When students form their groups, remind them to ask one another: *Where do you work?*
- To wrap up, call on students to say their jobs and to identify other students with the same or similar job (for example, *I'm a cashier. Lucia also works at a store. She's a cashier, too.*).

Extra Practice

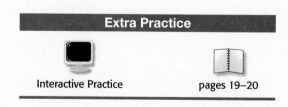

Interactive Practice   pages 19–20

3 CONVERSATION

CD1 T48

Listen and read the conversation. Then listen and repeat.

Dora: What do you do?

Miriam: I'm a nurse.

Dora: Really? Where do you work?

Miriam: I work at a school on Main Street. I'm a school nurse.

Dora: Oh. That's interesting.

4 PRACTICE

A PAIRS. Practice the conversation.
Then make new conversations.
Use the information in the boxes.

A: What do you do?

B: I'm   .

A: Really? Where do you work?

B: I work at   on Main Street.

A: Oh. That's interesting.

B MAKE IT PERSONAL. PAIRS.
Make your own conversations.
Talk about your jobs and workplaces.

A: *Where do you work?*
B: *I work at a store. I'm a cashier.*
A: *Oh. That's nice.*

C NETWORK. Find classmates with
the same job as you. Form a group.
Ask the people in your group,
Where do you work?

a carpenter

a construction site

a caregiver

a nursing home

an assembly line
worker

a factory

a stock clerk

a store

Talk about where you work

Grammar

Simple present affirmative: *Work* **and** *live*

| I
You
We
They | **work** | at a school. |
| | **live** | in Texas. |

| He
She
Miriam | **works** | at a school. |
| | **lives** | in California. |

Grammar Watch

- With *he, she,* and the name of a person, the simple present verb ends in **-s**: work**s**, live**s**

- For spelling rules for the simple present tense with *he, she,* and *it,* see page 273.

PRACTICE

A Alex is talking about himself and some friends. Underline the correct word.

1. That's my friend George. He **work** / <u>**works**</u> at a store.

2. George **live** / <u>**lives**</u> in New York. My wife and I <u>**live**</u> / **lives** in New York, too.

3. I <u>**work**</u> / **works** at a store, too! I'm a cashier.

4. This is Gloria. She **live** / <u>**lives**</u> in Florida. She **work** / <u>**works**</u> at a hospital.

5. Olga and Marcos <u>**work**</u> / **works** at a hospital, too. They're security guards.

B Look at the ID cards. Complete the sentences. Use the verbs in parentheses.

1. Helen Lam (be) _____*is*_____ a nurse.

   She (live) _____*lives*_____ in Los Angeles.

   She (work) _____*works*_____ at General Hospital.

2. Luis Mendoza and Nadif Fall (be) _____*are*_____

   accountants. They (live) _____*live*_____ in Tampa.

   They (work) _____*work*_____ for Andrews Accounting.

C GROUPS OF 5. Play the Memory Game. Talk about what you do and where you work. Use true or made-up information.

Tal: *I'm a cook. I work at a restaurant.*
Sahra: *Tal is a cook. He works at a restaurant. I'm a sales assistant. I work at a store.*

Getting Started 5 minutes

- Say: *We're going to study the simple present of* work *and* live. *In the conversation on page 41, Miriam used this grammar.*
- Play CD 1, Track 48. Students listen. Write on the board: *I work at a school.* Underline *I work.*

Presentation 5 minutes

Simple present affirmative: *Work* and *live*

- Copy the grammar charts onto the board or show the charts on Transparency 2.5 and cover the exercise.
- Point to the subject pronoun in each sentence (*I, you, we, they, he, she*) and circle it. Say each subject and ask the class to repeat.
- As needed, review what each subject pronoun refers to by pointing to yourself and students.
- Point to and underline the verb in each sentence (*work, live; works, lives*). Explain: Work *and* live *are verbs. Nouns are things. Verbs are actions.*
- Say sentences from the left chart. The class repeats.
- Do the same with the right chart. Ask, *When do we add* -s *to the verb?* (with *he, she,* or the name of one person)
- Read the Grammar Watch note. Circle *works* and *lives* in the chart. Write: *He works at a hospital.* Make the *-s* very large for emphasis. Read the sentence and ask the class to repeat. Say: *With* he, she, it, *and singular names like* George *or* Miriam, *add an* -s *to the verb.*
- Write several new sentences with a variety of subjects, but leave the verb out (for example, *John _____ at a hospital*). Say, *work or works? (live or lives?).* Ask students to fill in the blank.
- If you are using the transparency, do the exercise with the class.

Controlled Practice 10 minutes

> **PRACTICE**

A Alex is talking about himself and some friends....

- Read the directions and the example. Ask: *Why do we underline* works? (because the subject is *He*) Ask: *Who is in the picture?* (George) *Where does he work?* (at a store)

- Say: *Look back at the grammar charts for help.*
- Call on students to write the completed sentences on the board. Correct as needed.

B Look at the ID cards. Complete the sentences....

- Ask students to look at the pictures of the ID cards.
- Ask: *Is Helen Lam the same subject as* you, I, they, *or* she? (she) As needed, review the *be* grammar chart on page 14.
- Read the directions. Students compare answers with a partner.
- Call on students to read the completed sentences.

> ### Expansion: Speaking and Vocabulary Practice for B

- On the board, make a list of jobs and workplaces. Call on students to identify jobs and workplaces for the list.
- Pair students and ask them to copy the information into their notebooks and to draw lines to match jobs to workplaces. Some jobs may have more than one workplace (for example, *security guards*).
- Call on pairs to say sentences about jobs and workplaces (*Accountants work in offices. Security guards can work in offices, too.*).

Communicative Practice 10 minutes

C GROUPS OF 5. Play the Memory Game. Talk...

- On the board, write two true statements about yourself: *I'm a teacher. I work at a school.*
- Ask four students to join you in front of the class. Play the game with them to model for the class.
- Form groups of 5.
- Walk around and check that students are able to recall their partners' information. As needed, sit with groups and provide model answers.
- To wrap up, play the game as a class or divide the class in two and tell each half to replay the game.

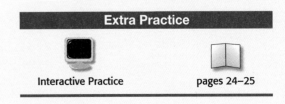

Extra Practice

Interactive Practice   pages 24–25

Show what you know!

1 GRAMMAR

Complete the conversation. Use the words in the box.

- Read the directions. Say the words in the box, omitting the duplicates, and ask the class to repeat.
- Read the example.
- Tell students to refer back to the grammar charts on pages 30 (*a/an*), 31 (singular and plural nouns), 36 (*be*), and 42 (simple present) as needed.
- Remind students to cross out each item they use in the box.
- Walk around and check students' word choice and spelling.
- To check answers, call on a pair of students to perform for the class. Correct as needed.
- *Optional:* Pair students and ask them to practice the conversation. Call on pairs to perform the completed conversation for the class.

2 WRITING

STEP 1. Read the information about Helena Peres....

- Read the directions. Tell students to look at the information about Helena Peres. Call on a student to read it.
- Tell students to write complete sentences, making sure to end with a period.
- Walk around and check that students' writing is accurate and complete.
- Call on three individual students to write one complete sentence on the board (choose students whose writing is correct). If there are mistakes on the board, ask the class to call out corrections as you fix the sentence(s).

STEP 2. Answer the questions about yourself....

- Read the directions and questions. Model the answers by talking about yourself (*I'm a teacher. I work . . .*). Call on a few students to say answers to the questions. Write their responses on the board as a model.
- Walk around and check that students are writing in complete sentences with proper punctuation and capitalization.
- Students compare answers with a partner.
- Call on a few students to read their answers.

 Expansion: Writing and Speaking Practice for STEP 2

- Ask students to interview three other classmates by asking the questions in Step 2.
- *Optional:* Interviewers can write down their partner's responses and then read them to the class when called on.

CD-ROM Practice

Go to the CD-ROM for more practice.

If your students need more practice with the vocabulary, grammar, and competencies in Unit 2, encourage them to review the activities on the CD-ROM. This review can also help students prepare for the final role play on the following Expand page.

Extra Practice

pages 20–21

1 GRAMMAR

Complete the conversation. Use the words in the box.

a   an   waiters   is   Is   ~~Is~~   work   work   works

A: _____Is_____ that Raul?

B: No. That's Pablo Gomez. He _____works_____ with Maria and Helena Peres. They _____work_____ at Rico's Diner.

A: Oh. What do they do?

B: They're _____waiters_____.

A: Really? I _____work_____ at a restaurant, too. I'm _____a_____ cook at Paul's Restaurant. What about you? What do you do?

B: I'm _____an_____ electrician.

A: How's your job? _____Is_____ it hard?

B: Yes, it _____is_____. But it's interesting, too.

2 WRITING

STEP 1. **Read the information about Helena Peres. Answer these questions: What does Helena do? Where does she work? Where does she live?**

Helena _is a waitress._

She _lives in Queens, New York._

She _works at Rico's Diner._

Name: Helena Peres
Job: Waitress
Place of work: Rico's Diner
Home: Queens, New York

STEP 2. **Answer the questions about yourself. What do you do? Where do you work? Where do you live?**

Write complete sentences.

Answers will vary.

_____

_____

_____

3 ACT IT OUT — What do you say?

CD1 T49

STEP 1. 🔘 **Listen to the conversation.**

STEP 2. **PAIRS. You are at school. Student A, introduce Students B and C. Students B and C, continue the conversation. Talk about your jobs and workplaces.**

4 READ AND REACT — Problem-solving

STEP 1. **Read about Karine's problem.**

Karine lives in Riverside. She is a nurse's assistant. She works at Riverside General Hospital. She works days. At night, Karine takes English classes at the Learning Center. She wants to be a nurse.

One day, Karine goes to work. Her manager says, "Karine, I need you to work nights." But Karine has classes at night.

STEP 2. **PAIRS. Talk about it. What is Karine's problem? What can Karine do? Here are some ideas.**

- She can say, "I can't work nights."
- She can find another English class.
- She can call her teacher.
- She can _____.

5 CONNECT

For your Goal-setting Activity, go to page 246.
For your Team Project, go to page 266.

Which goals can you check off? Go back to page 25.

3 ACT IT OUT

STEP 1. Listen to the conversation.

- Play CD 1, Track 49. Students listen.
- As needed, play Track 49 again to aid comprehension.

STEP 2. PAIRS. You are at school. Student A,...

- Read the directions. With two above-level students, practice introducing the two students to each other. Then ask one of the students to introduce you to the other student.
- As needed, ask the class to review the introductions conversation on pages 28–29.
- Form groups of 3 and assign roles.
- Walk around and observe students interacting. Check that one student is introducing the other two and that the two who were introduced continue to talk about what they do and where they work.
- Call on all groups to perform for the class. While groups are performing, use the scoring rubric on page Txiv to evaluate each student's vocabulary, grammar, fluency, and how well he or she completes the task.
- *Optional:* After each group finishes, discuss the strengths and weaknesses of each performance either in front of the class or privately.

4 READ AND REACT

STEP 1. Read about Karine's problem.

- Say: *We are going to read about a student's problem, and then we need to think about a solution.*
- Read the directions.
- Read the story while students follow along silently. Pause after each sentence to allow time for students to comprehend. Periodically stop and ask simple *Wh-* questions to check comprehension (for example, *Where does Karine live? What does she do? When does she work? Does she take English classes? When? Where? What is Karine's problem?*).

STEP 2. PAIRS. Talk about Karine's problem....

- Pair students. Read the directions and the question.
- Read the ideas in the box. Give pairs a couple of minutes to discuss possible solutions for Karine.
- Ask: *Which ideas are good?* Call on students to say their opinion about the ideas in the box (for example, S: *I think she can find another English class because there are many classes.*).
- Now tell students to think of one new idea not in the list (for example, *She can find a new job.*) and to write it in the blank. Encourage students to think of more than one idea and to write them in their notebooks.
- Call on pairs to say their additional solutions. Write any particularly good ones on the board and ask: *Do you think this is a good idea? Why or why not?*

MULTILEVEL INSTRUCTION for STEP 2

Pre-level Students work in groups of 4 to come up with an idea.

Above-level Ask pairs to write at least three new solutions.

5 CONNECT

Turn to page 246 for the Goal-setting Activity and page 266 for the Team Project. See pages Txi–Txii for general notes about teaching these activities.

Progress Check

Which goals can you check off? Go back to page 25.
Ask students to turn to page 25 and check off any remaining goals they have reached. Call on students to say which goals they will practice outside of class.

3 Time for Class

Unit Overview

Goals

- See the list of goals on the facing page.

Grammar

- Imperatives: Affirmative and negative
- *This, that, these, those*: Statements
- *This, that, these, those*: Questions and answers
- Subject and object pronouns

Pronunciation

- The voiced *th* sound
- Word stress

Reading

- Read about good study habits

Writing

- Write sentences about things in your classroom

Life Skills Writing

- Complete a school registration form

Preview

- Set the context of the unit by asking questions about school (for example, *Do you have children in school? Do you like school?*).
- Hold up page 45 or show Transparency 3.1. Read the unit title and ask the class to repeat.
- Explain: Time for class *means that it is time to go to school.*
- Say: *Look at the picture.* Ask the Preview questions: *Where are the people?* (They are at a school.) *Does this place look like your (our) school?* Ask above-level students: *Why/Why not?*
- Write the word *class* on the board and check that students understand (for example, T: *Are you in class now?* Ss: *Yes.* T: *Is it time for class now?* Ss: *Yes.*).

Unit Goals

- Point to the Unit Goals. Explain that this list shows what the class will be studying in this unit.
- Tell students to read the goals silently.
- Say each goal and ask the class to repeat. Explain unfamiliar vocabulary as needed:

    School registration form: *A paper you complete to take a class*

- Tell students to circle one goal that is very important to them. Call on several students to say the goal they circled.
- Write a checkmark (✓) on the board. Say: *We will come back to this page again. You will write a checkmark next to the goals you learned in this unit.*

Time for Class

Preview

Look at the picture.
Where are the people?
Does this place look like
your school?

UNIT GOALS

☐ Give and follow
classroom
instructions

☐ Complete a
school registration
form

☐ Talk about things
in the classroom

☐ Use numbers
10–100

☐ Talk about places
at school

☐ Talk about people
and places at
school

1 WHAT DO YOU KNOW?

A **CLASS.** Look at the pictures. Which things do you know?

> Number 7 is *chalk*.

CD1 T50

B Listen and point to the pictures. Then listen and repeat.

2 PRACTICE

A **PAIRS.** Look at the pictures. Student A, choose one thing. Say, "Point to the _____." Student B, point to the correct picture.

> Point to the notebook.

B **WORD PLAY.** Look at the list of things in the classroom on page 47. Complete the chart with the correct words.

Things you write with	Things you can read	Furniture
chalk	book	desk
marker	dictionary	chair

C **PAIRS.** Compare answers.

1

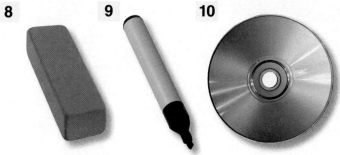

4 5

LONGMAN
Study Dictionary
of American English

Understand more.
Achieve more.

NEW

8 9 10

15 16

Lesson 1 Vocabulary

Getting Started   5 minutes

1 WHAT DO YOU KNOW?

A CLASS. Look at the pictures. Which things...

- Show Transparency 3.2 or hold up the book. Tell students to cover the list of words on page 47.
- Read the directions. Point to picture 7 and read the example. Ask: *Which things in the classroom do you know?*
- Students call out answers as in the example. Help students pronounce classroom objects if they have difficulty.
- If students call out an incorrect classroom object, change the student's answer into a question for the class (for example, *Number 9 is a pen?*). If nobody can identify the correct classroom object, tell students they will now listen to a CD and practice the names of the things in the classroom.

Presentation   5 minutes

B Listen and point to the pictures. Then...

- Read the directions. Play CD 1, Track 50. Pause after number 16 (*cell phone*).
- Walk around and check that students are pointing.
- To check comprehension, say each classroom object in random order and ask students to point to the appropriate picture.
- Resume playing Track 50. Students listen and repeat.

Controlled Practice   15 minutes

2 PRACTICE

A PAIRS. Look at the pictures. Student A, choose...

- Read the directions. Play A and model the example with a student.
- Say: *If your partner points to the wrong thing, say, "No, try again."* Model this with another student.
- Pair students. Walk around and check that A is speaking and B is pointing. Check that A is politely asking B to try again if B points to the wrong thing.

Teaching Tip
Check that students understand that A only speaks and does not point; it is B's job to find and point to the picture. It is important to model pair activities clearly so that partners perform the activity as designed.

MULTILEVEL INSTRUCTION for 2A
Cross-ability Ask the higher-level partner to play Student A a few times to make sure that Student B understands the vocabulary before they switch.

Community Building
Model the activity and how students should correct each other's mistakes. Ask an above-level student to play B and make a mistake. Play A as follows:

A: *Point to the backpack.*
B: (Points to book)
A: *No. Guess (or try) again.*
B: (Points to backpack)
A: *Yes. Good!*

B WORD PLAY. Look at the list of things...

- Read the directions.
- Read the titles in the chart. Pick up a piece of chalk and act like you are writing on the board. Say: *I write with chalk.* Pick up a book and act like you're reading it. Say: *I read a book.* Point to a chair and say: *This is a chair. It is furniture.*
- Walk around and check that students are writing things from the list on page 47.
- Copy the chart onto the board. Call on students to write in answers.
- To wrap up, ask the class to call out items under each heading. Correct any mistakes on the board.

Communicative Practice   10 minutes

C PAIRS. Compare answers.

- Students compare answers with a partner by looking at each other's charts.
- Walk around and spot-check students' answers. Correct as needed.

Lesson 1 Vocabulary

Learning Strategy: Use pictures

- Provide each student with four index cards or tell students to cut up notebook paper into four pieces.
- Read the directions.
- Walk around as students work. If misspellings occur, tell them to check the list on page 47.
- Say: *You can make cards with pictures to remember new words.* Remind students to use this strategy to remember other new vocabulary.

Expansion: Vocabulary Practice

- Form groups of 5. One student is the leader and collects all the flashcards from the Learning Strategy activity and then shows the picture side of one card to the group. Students take turns guessing.
- When a student guesses correctly, the next student guesses at a new card. If a student makes a mistake, the leader can tell the student to guess again or the group can correct the student.
- Students can take turns leading the group.

Communicative Practice   15 minutes

Show what you know!

GROUPS OF 5. Look at the list of things...

- Form groups of 5.
- Read the directions and the example.
- If possible, ask students in each group to put all their classroom items (for example, pencils and books) on their desks to make counting easier.
- After five minutes, tell students to stop. Call on a representative from each group to report what things their group has (T: *Rosa, what did you count in your group?* Rosa: *5 pencils. 4 books. 5 notebooks. . . .*).

Expansion: Listening Practice

- Ask one group to share their list with you.
- Tell the class to close their books and to take out a sheet of blank paper. Dictate the list to students while they copy it (T: *3 dictionaries. 4 backpacks. . . .*).
- Walk around and check for accuracy.

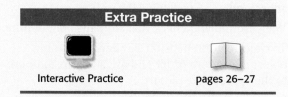

Extra Practice	
Interactive Practice	pages 26–27

2

3

Things in the Classroom

1. desk	**9.** marker
2. chair	**10.** CD
3. computer	**11.** notebook
4. book	**12.** piece of paper
5. dictionary	**13.** folder
6. board	**14.** three-ring binder
7. chalk	**15.** backpack
8. eraser	**16.** cell phone

Learning Strategy

Use pictures

Look at the list of things in the classroom. Make cards for three or four words. On one side, write the word in English. On the other side, draw a picture of the word.

6

7

11

12

13

14

Show what you know!

GROUPS OF 5. Look at the list of things in the classroom. What things do you have with you today? Make a list.

___3___ _____dictionaries_____   Answers will vary.

Listening and Speaking

1 BEFORE YOU LISTEN

A **READ.** Ramiro and Kamila go to English class after work. Read the sentences.

1. Ramiro and Kamila try to bring their books and notebooks to class.
2. Sometimes they borrow some paper.
3. When Ramiro and Kamila are late, they don't interrupt the class.
4. They sit down and turn off their cell phones.

B Look at the pictures. Read the sentences again. Match.

2 LISTEN

A CD1 T51 Look at the picture. Emily Reed is the teacher. She is giving a test today.

Listen to the conversation. What is she saying?

a. Put away your books.
b. Open your dictionaries.
c. Please bring your notebooks.

B CD1 T51 Listen again. Read the sentences. Circle *True* or *False*.

1. Ms. Reed says, "Take out a pencil." **True** (**False**)

2. Aram says, "Can I borrow a pencil?" (**True**) **False**

C CD1 T52 Listen to the whole conversation. Complete the sentence.

_____Ms. Reed's_____ cell phone is ringing.

a. Aram's   b. Chan's   c. Ms. Reed's

Getting Started   10 minutes

Culture Connection

• If time permits, review the vocabulary on page 47.
• Say: *In the United States, most students bring a backpack, a notebook, and other things to class.*
• Ask: *In your home country, what are some things that students bring to school?* Write a list of answers on the board. Point out any similarities or differences with what is on the board and what is considered usual for the U.S. (for example, *It looks like electronic dictionaries are common in the United States and Korea.*).

1 BEFORE YOU LISTEN

A READ. **Ramiro and Kamila go to English class...**

• Read the directions.
• Read each sentence and ask the class to repeat.
• Explain any unfamiliar vocabulary through modeling, if possible. For example, to demonstrate *borrow*, ask a student: *May I borrow your pencil?* Take the pencil, write with it for a second, and then return it while saying *Thank you.*

Teaching Tip

When reading directions, ask comprehension questions to check that the class understands all the information. In this case, ask: *When do Ramiro and Kamila go to English class?* (after work) *What do you do with the sentences?* (read them)

B **Look at the pictures. Read the sentences again....**

• Read the directions. Allow a few moments for students to reread the sentences to themselves.
• Then say: *Look at the first picture.* Hold up your book and point to it. Ask: *Which picture matches sentence 1?* (the second)
• Say: *Match the other pictures.*
• To check answers, walk around and check that students matched the sentences correctly. Then ask the class: *Which sentence matches the first picture?* (4) *Which sentence matches the third picture?* (3) and so on while the class calls out the matching sentence number.

Presentation   15 minutes

2 LISTEN

A **Look at the picture. Emily Reed is...**

• Read the directions and the answer choices.
• Play CD 1, Track 51.
• Ask: *What is she saying?*

Teaching Tip

Optional: Remember that if students need additional support, tell them to read the Audio Script on page 282 as they listen to the conversations.

B **Listen again. Read the sentences....**

• Play Track 51 again.
• To check answers, ask: *Is number 1 true or false?* (false) Make it true by saying: *Ms. Reed says, "Take out a . . . ,"* and tell the class to call out *"a piece of paper."* Ask: *Is number 2 true or false?* (true)

C **Listen to the whole conversation....**

• Read the directions. Play CD 1, Track 52.
• Call on a student to read the completed sentence.

Controlled Practice   10 minutes

3   CONVERSATION

 Listen and read the conversation. Then...

- Note: This conversation is the same one students heard in Exercise 2A on page 48.
- Play CD 1, Track 53. Students listen and read along.
- Check comprehension by asking: *What do the students do?* (put away the books, take out a piece of paper) *What does Aram borrow?* (a pencil)
- Resume playing Track 53. Students listen and repeat. Note that there is an extra pause in Ms. Reed's first line (after *Are you ready for the test?*) to give students time to repeat.

Communicative Practice   25 minutes

4   PRACTICE

A **GROUPS OF 3. Practice the conversation. Then...**

- Form groups of 3 and tell students to practice the conversation in Exercise 3.
- Then, in Exercise 4A, point to each picture and ask students to say what it is. Read the note about *a* and *an*. Tell students to write *a* or *an* and the word for each object next to each picture. Students can refer to page 47 to check spelling.
- Read the directions.
- Copy the conversation onto the board with blanks. Read through the conversation. When you come to a blank, fill it in with information from the first pair of pictures (*notebooks* and *pen*).
- Point out the article *a* before the second blank. Say: *Here we must use a word that goes with* a *or* an. *Which words can we use here?* (pen, piece of paper, pencil, eraser) For *eraser*, change *a* to *an* on the board. Also point out that B's line can use *a* or *an* with a singular noun (for example, *Can I borrow a pencil?*).
- Ask three on-level students to practice the conversation in front of the class.
- Tell groups to take turns playing each role and to use the pictures to fill in the blanks.
- Tell students to stand, mingle, and practice the conversation with several new partners.
- Call on groups to perform for the class.

■■■ **MULTILEVEL INSTRUCTION for 4A**

Cross-ability Assign one pre-level, one on-level, and one above-level student to each group.

First, the pre-level student is A, the on-level student is B, and the above-level student is C. The above-level student serves as a coach or monitor for A. Student C models correct choices.

When they switch roles, the on-level student becomes C, the pre-level student becomes B, and the above-level student becomes A. Now the on-level student can help the pre-level student.

Teaching Tip

Add greater authenticity to role-play practice by telling groups to act out the role play complete with gestures and other movements (for example, in Exercise 4A, B and C actually do what A instructs). This enhances the communicative aspect of the exercise.

B **ROLE PLAY. GROUPS OF 3. Make your own...**

- Read the directions.
- Tell students to write the words for several classroom things from page 47 and any additional ones they know. Call on students (especially above-level) to say additional things they know. Write them on the board and explain any unfamiliar words.
- Form groups of 3 and tell them to practice the conversation.
- Walk around and check that students say singular or plural nouns clearly and are placing them in the conversation correctly.
- Call on groups to perform for the class.

■■■ **MULTILEVEL INSTRUCTION for 4B**

Pre-level To ensure comprehension, tell the "teacher" (A) to say at least one command that B and C carry out.

Above-level Ask the "teacher" (A) in each group to say three commands instead of two. B and C then each ask each other to borrow something.

Extra Practice

Interactive Practice

3 CONVERSATION

CD1 T53

Listen and read the conversation. Then listen and repeat.

Ms. Reed: OK, everyone. Are you ready for the test?
Put away your books. Take out a piece of paper.
Aram: Chan, can I borrow a pencil?
Chan: Sure, Aram.

4 PRACTICE

A GROUPS OF 3. Practice the conversation. Then make new conversations.
Use the pictures.

A: Are you ready for the test?

Put away your   . Take out a   .

B: Can I borrow   ?

C: Sure.

Remember:
a piece of paper
an eraser

B ROLE PLAY. GROUPS OF 3. Make your own conversations.
Student A, you are the teacher. Students B and C, you are the students.

Give and follow classroom instructions

Grammar

Imperatives		
Affirmative		
Take out **Use**	your notebooks. a pencil.	

Negative		
Don't	**look at** **open**	your books. your dictionaries.

Grammar Watch

Use *please* to be polite: ***Please*** *turn off your cell phones.*

1 PRACTICE

Match the sentences and the pictures.

___d___ 1. Turn off the computer.

___f___ 2. Don't open your dictionary.

___e___ 3. Write in your book.

___h___ 4. Don't take out your notebook.

___g___ 5. Don't turn off the computer.

___a___ 6. Open your dictionary.

___b___ 7. Take out your notebook.

___c___ 8. Don't write in your book.

a.

b.

c.

d.
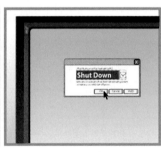

e.

f.

g.

h.

2 LIFE SKILLS WRITING

Complete a school registration form. See page 255.

Lesson 3 Give and follow classroom instructions

Getting Started
5 minutes

- Say: *We're going to study imperatives. In the conversation on page 49, Ms. Reed used this grammar.*
- Play CD 1, Track 53. Students listen. Write on the board: *Take out a piece of paper.* Underline *Take out.*

Presentation
10 minutes

Imperatives

- Copy the grammar charts onto the board or show the charts on Transparency 3.3 and cover the exercise. Say: *You use* imperatives *when you tell someone to do something. Imperatives are also called* commands.
- Read the affirmative imperative statements in the left chart and tell the class to repeat. Say: *We don't say* you *with commands. Also, the verb does not have* -s.
- Read the Grammar Watch note and ask the class to read along silently.
- Say: *Tell me more affirmative commands.* Write them on the board as students call them out, correcting word choice and grammar as needed. Add *Please* to the beginning of each command and say: *Remember to use* please *to be polite.*
- If students run out of ideas, write commands that you commonly use in your class (for example, *Please close the door. Please close your books.*). After you write them, say them, ask the class to repeat, and tell the class to follow the command to demonstrate comprehension.
- Say: *You also use commands when you tell someone not to do something.* Read the negative imperative statements in the right chart and ask the class to repeat.
- Explain: *Negative commands begin with* Don't, *which is a contraction of* Do not. On the board, write a command with *Do not* and then erase *Do not* and replace with *Don't.*
- Point to various affirmative commands on the board. For each one, point and tell the class: *Make it negative.* As students call out the negative form, write it on the board (for example, *Take out your notebooks.* → *Don't take out your notebooks.*). Repeat this for several commands on the board.
- If you are using the transparency, do the exercise with the class.

Controlled Practice
20 minutes

1 PRACTICE

Match the sentences and the pictures.

- Read the directions and the example.
- Say: *Some pictures have an* X *over them.* Ask: *What does the* X *mean?* (Don't)
- Students compare answers with a partner.
- Call on several students to read answers. Correct as needed.

Expansion: Speaking Practice for 1

- Form groups of 5. Play a "polite" Simon Says-style game where the leader issues commands that the others must follow, but only when the leader first says *please* (for example, *Please take out your notebook.*).
- If the leader doesn't say *please*, students should not perform the action. If students do, they are out of the game.

Expansion: Grammar Practice for 1

- Ask students to change each command to affirmative or negative (for example, 1. *Don't turn off the computer.*) and to write the new commands in their notebooks.
- Students can then choose new answers for the new commands.

2 LIFE SKILLS WRITING

Turn to page 255 and ask students to complete the school registration form. See pages Txi–Txii for general notes about the Life Skills Writing activities.

3 PRACTICE

A Read the test directions. Underline...

- Read the directions. Remind students that a picture with an X over it means *Don't*.
- Do item 1 together. Ask: *Use or Don't use?*
- Students compare answers with a partner.
- Call on students to say answers.

B Complete the sentences about classroom rules....

- Read the directions and examples. For item 2, explain: *We say* Don't *because eating in class is not good. The rule is* Don't eat in class!
- Remind students to cross out the words they use.
- Walk around and spot-check to see if students are correctly creating affirmative and negative commands.
- If students write an affirmative command that is incorrect (for example, *Answer your cell phone in class.*), read it to the student and ask: *Is this correct? We answer our cell phones in class?*
- Students compare answers with a partner.
- Call on students to say answers. Correct as needed.

Communicative Practice   20 minutes

Show what you know!

GROUPS OF 3. Make a list of *Dos* and *Don'ts*...

- As a warm-up, add to the rules in Exercises A and B by brainstorming with the class more rules that apply to your classroom. Write them on the board.
- Form groups of 3 and tell students to write at least five *Do* rules and five *Don't* rules.
- Walk around and help as needed.
- Call on several groups to share their list with the class.

MULTILEVEL INSTRUCTION

Cross-ability Ask the higher-level student to contribute at least one new rule not already listed in Exercise 3B or on the board. The lower-level student is responsible for copying classroom rules already on the board or rules featured in Exercise 3B.

Expansion: Graphic Organizer and Writing Practice

- Brainstorm rules that students follow at home (for example, *Lock the door at night. Go to bed at 10:30 P.M.*).
- Ask students to draw a chart in their notebooks with the following headings: *Rules at School* and *Rules at Home*. For *Rules at School*, explain: *Write three rules that you follow in school.* For *Rules at Home*, explain: *Write three rules that you follow at home.* Pair students if pre-level or on-level students need help. Call on students to present their chart to the class.
- As a follow-up, ask: *Are classroom rules and home rules similar? Are they different?*

Progress Check

Can you . . . give and follow classroom instructions?

Say: *We have practiced giving and following classroom instructions. Now, look at the question at the bottom of the page. Can you give and follow classroom instructions?* Tell students to write a checkmark in the box.

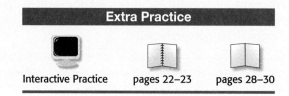

Extra Practice		
Interactive Practice	pages 22–23	pages 28–30

A Read the test directions. Underline the correct words.

1.

Use / Don't use a Number 2 pencil.

2.

Use / **Don't use** a pen.

3.

Right
Ⓐ ⒷⒸⒹ

Wrong
Ⓐ ⓍⒸⒹ
Ⓐ ⓑⒸⒹ

Make / Don't make dark marks in the circles.

4.

Look / **Don't look** at your classmate's test.

B Complete the sentences about classroom rules. Use the words in the box. Use capital letters and add *don't* when necessary.

> answer   ~~bring~~   ~~eat~~   interrupt   listen   try to

1. _____Bring_____ a notebook and pencil.

2. __Don't eat__ in class.

3. _Don't interrupt_ the class when you are late.

4. _____Listen_____ to your classmates.

5. _Don't answer_ your cell phone in class.

6. _____Try to_____ come on time.

Show what you know!   Give and follow classroom instructions

GROUPS OF 3. Make a list of *Dos* and *Don'ts* for your class in your notebook. Use the sentences in Exercise B as a model.

Can you...give and follow classroom instructions? ☐

Reading

1 BEFORE YOU READ

A CLASS. What are your *study habits*? For example, when do you usually study? At lunch? At night? Where do you usually study? At home? At school?

B PAIRS. Match the sentences about study habits with the pictures. Write one sentence from the box under each picture.

> Set study goals.
> Study for a short time.
> Throw out papers you don't need.
> ~~Turn off your cell phone.~~

1. _Turn off your cell phone._

2. _Throw out papers you don't need._

3. _Set study goals._

4. _Study for a short time._

Getting Ready   20 minutes

1 BEFORE YOU READ

A CLASS. What are your *study habits*? For example,...

- Say: *Look at the picture.* Ask: *What is he doing?* (studying)
- Read the directions. Explain: Study habits *are the ways that you study.*
- Call on several students to answer the questions in the directions. Write the questions *When do you usually study?* and *Where do you usually study?* on the board and write students' answers under them so there are several answer choices for each question.

B PAIRS. Match the sentences about study habits...

- Read the directions. Pair students.
- Read the study habits in the box and ask the class to repeat.
- Explain: Set study goals *means to make new goals.*
- Call on a few students to say answers.

MULTILEVEL INSTRUCTION for 1B

Cross-ability The higher-level partner first points to each picture and asks the lower-level partner to read the matching sentence.

Expansion: Speaking Practice for 1B

- Ask: *Which goals do you like? Which one is your favorite?*

Expansion: Critical Thinking Practice for 1B

- Ask: *Can you think of more study habits?*
- Form groups of 3. Ask each group to write at least three additional study habits not listed in Exercise 1B.
- Call on groups to share their study habits with the class. Write any particularly good ones on the board for the class to copy into their notebooks.

Lesson 4 Read about good study habits

Presentation 10 minutes

2 READ

 Ally Einstein is not a good student....

- Explain: *Ally wrote a letter to an advice columnist, someone who works for a newspaper and who helps people with their problems.*
- Read the directions.
- Ask: *What is the title of the article?* (Ask the Professor) *Who is in the picture?* (the professor)
- Play CD 1, Track 54. Students listen and read along silently.
- Review each idea in the letter with students and write the first sentence of each idea on the board. Discuss each one with the class (for example, *Can you set study goals for each week?*).

Controlled Practice 10 minutes

3 CHECK YOUR UNDERSTANDING

A Read the sentences. There is one mistake in each...

- Read the directions and the example.
- Say: *In each sentence, one or two words are wrong. Find the sentences in the article to help you fix the sentences here.*
- To demonstrate, point out that item 1 is the first idea from the article. Further point out that the article states, *Set study goals each **week**.* Say: *That's how we know that* year *in number 1 is wrong.*
- Optional: Say: *Find each sentence in the article and underline it. Then compare the sentences and fix the mistake.*
- Call on students to read the corrected sentences.

B Read the letter again. What is the main idea?...

- Read the directions. Allow time for students to read the letter again.
- Remind students: *The main idea is the most important point in the article.*
- Students compare answers with a partner.
- Call on a few students to say their answer. Some answers may vary slightly.

Communicative Practice 20 minutes

Show what you know!

STEP 1. Choose one language skill you want to...

- On the board, write *listening, speaking, reading, writing, vocabulary,* and *grammar.* Under each one, ask students for their ideas about goals they can set for themselves. If students have difficulty thinking of goals, refer them to the study goals in the pictures on page 52.
- Tell students to choose one of the above areas (for example, *listening*) and to write one goal for it.

Expansion: Speaking Practice for STEP 1

- In one week's time, review students' goals with them and ask them if they achieved their goals.

STEP 2. NETWORK. Who wants to practice...

- Read the directions. Tell students who picked *listening* to stand in one part of the room. Continue for all other skill areas until all students are assigned to stand near other students with the same skill choice.
- Within each group, tell students to mingle, and ask: *What is your study goal?* Check that students understand each other's goals.
- To wrap up, ask several students in each group to share their goals for their skill. On the board, categorize the goals students say under various skill headings (for example, *Listening: Listen to the radio for 20 minutes every day. Talk on the phone to my neighbor once a week.*).

Expansion: Goal-setting Practice for STEP 2

- Encourage students with similar skill goals to form study groups. Allow time in class for them to discuss a plan. For example, a group of students who want to read more might be able to meet at the library after class.

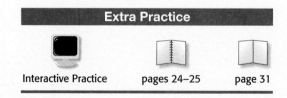

Extra Practice

Interactive Practice   pages 24–25   page 31

CD1 T54

Ally Einstein is not a good student. Her study habits are terrible. Listen. Read Professor Studywell's letter of advice to Ms. Einstein.

Ask the Professor

Dear Ms. Einstein,

Don't worry! You can be a good student. Good study habits help. Here are some ideas.

1) **Set study goals each week.** Write your goals in your notebook. Be sure your goals are small. For example, "Listening: Watch TV in English for ten minutes."

2) **Look at your list of goals every day.** Check off each goal when you finish.

3) **Study in a quiet place.** Sit at a table. Turn off your TV, radio, and cell phone.

4) **Be organized.** Keep important papers. Throw out other papers. Put your important papers in one binder.

5) **Plan your study time.** Try to study for fifteen minutes. Then review for five minutes.

3 CHECK YOUR UNDERSTANDING

A Read the sentences. There is one mistake in each sentence. Correct the mistake.

1. Set study goals each ~~year~~. *week*

2. Be sure your goals are ~~big~~. *small*

3. Turn off your ~~computer~~. *TV, radio, and cell phone*

4. ~~Throw~~ out important papers. *Keep*

5. Put your papers in a ~~notebook~~. *binder*

6. Review for ~~fifteen~~ minutes. *five*

B Read the letter again. What is the main idea? Complete the sentence.

Good _____*study habits*_____ can help you be a good student.

Show what you know!

STEP 1. Choose one language skill you want to practice (for example, listening, speaking, or vocabulary). In your notebook, write one goal for that skill.

STEP 2. NETWORK. Who wants to practice the same skill as you? Find those classmates. Form a group. Ask the people in your group, *What is your study goal?*

Listening and Speaking

1 BEFORE YOU LISTEN

PAIRS. Look at the picture. Write the words from the box on the lines.

keyboard
~~CD~~
mouse
monitor
DVD

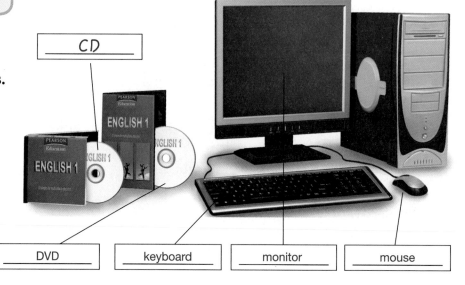

CD

_____ DVD _____   _____ keyboard _____   _____ monitor _____   _____ mouse _____

2 LISTEN

A Look at the picture. Carlos and Kamaria are learning new words in English.

Guess: What is Carlos's question? What is Kamaria's answer?

CD1 T55

B Listen to the conversation. Was your guess in Exercise A correct?

Listen again. What is Carlos asking about? Check (✓) all the correct answers.

☑ a mouse   ☐ a keyboard

☐ DVDs   ☑ CDs

CD1 T56

C Listen to the whole conversation. Complete the sentence.

Carlos says, "This is a ____picture____ of a ____mouse____,

and that's a ____picture____ of ____CDs____."

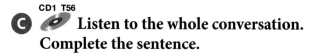

Getting Started   5 minutes

1   BEFORE YOU LISTEN

PAIRS. Look at the picture. Write the words from...

- As a warm-up, ask the class if they use a computer at home or another place (for example, *the library*). Ask: *What do you do on the computer?* (check e-mail, do homework, find information)
- Direct the class to look at the picture. Read the vocabulary words in the box and ask the class to repeat.
- Pair students. Read the directions and the example.
- Students compare answers with a partner.
- Walk around and spot-check students' written answers.

■ Expansion: Speaking Practice for 1

- If you have computers in your classroom, brainstorm with the class a list of common computer imperatives and write them on the board (for example, *touch the keyboard, move the mouse, look at the monitor, type . . .*). Assign pairs of students to one computer. One partner issues commands (imperatives) that the other student follows.

Presentation   20–25 minutes

2   LISTEN

Ⓐ Look at the picture.... Guess:...

- Read the directions.
- Ask: *What is above Carlos's head?* (a mouse)
- Call on students to answer the questions in the directions. Write their guesses on the board.
- Tell students they will listen for the answer in Exercise B.

Ⓑ Listen to the conversation. Was...

- Read the directions. Play CD 1, Track 55.
- Ask: *Was your guess in Exercise A correct?* Circle the correct answers on the board. (Carlos: *What's this called in English?* Kamaria: *It's a mouse.*)

Teaching Tip

Optional: Remember that if students need additional support, tell them to read the Audio Script on page 282 as they listen to the conversations.

Listen again. What is Carlos asking about?...

- Read the directions. Play Track 55 again.
- Students compare answers with a partner.
- Call on a couple of students to say answers.

Ⓒ Listen to the whole conversation....

- Read the directions. Play CD 1, Track 56.
- Students compare answers with a partner.
- Read the completed sentence.
- Ask: *Is Carlos funny? Why or why not?*

3 CONVERSATION

A 💿 **Listen. Then listen and repeat.**

- Ask students to look at the picture at the right. Read the Pronunciation Watch note.
- Demonstrate how to pronounce *th* as in *this* and *these*.
- Explain: *When I say* this, *there is a buzzing sound.* Touch your throat while pronouncing to illustrate.
- Read the directions. Play CD 1, Track 57.
- Resume playing Track 57. Students listen and repeat.
- Play Track 57 a few more times if students have difficulty clearly pronouncing *th*.
- Call on several students to repeat the sentences after you.

Controlled Practice   15 minutes

B 💿 **Listen and read the conversation....**

- Note: This conversation is the same one students heard in Exercise 2B on page 54.
- Read the directions. Play CD 1, Track 58. Students listen and read along silently.
- Resume playing Track 58. Students listen and repeat.
- As students repeat, listen carefully for their production of the voiced *th* in *this*, *these*, and *They're*.

> **Language Note**
>
> When reading from a script, students often pronounce contractions as the full form (for example, *don't* as *do not*). Remind students that contractions have a different pronunciation from the full form. Model pronunciation of *It's* and *They're* and ask the class to repeat.

4 PRACTICE

A PAIRS. Practice the conversation. Then make new...

- Pair students and tell them to practice the conversation in Exercise 3B.

- Then, in Exercise 4A, point to each picture and ask students to say what it is. Tell students to write the name next to each picture. Students can refer to page 47 to check spelling.
- Read the directions.
- Copy the conversation onto the board with blanks. Read through the conversation. When you come to a blank, fill it in with information from the first pair of pictures (*a keyboard* and *DVDs*). Remind students to include *a/an* as needed.
- Ask two on-level students to practice the conversation in front of the class.
- Tell pairs to take turns playing each role and to use the pictures to fill in the blanks.
- Walk around and check that students are clearly pronouncing *th*.
- Tell students to stand, mingle, and practice the conversation with several new partners.
- Call on pairs to perform for the class.

Communicative Practice   15 minutes

B MAKE IT PERSONAL. PAIRS. **Make your own...**

- Read the directions.
- Brainstorm with the class to come up with a list of classroom items in your room. On the board, write singular items under the heading *It's* and plural items under the heading *They're*. Include *a* or *an* for countable singular items.
- Pair students and tell them to practice the conversation, substituting information on the board into the conversation.
- Walk around and tell students to switch roles and practice with vocabulary from the board.
- Call on pairs to perform for the class.

▬▬ MULTILEVEL INSTRUCTION for 4B

Cross-ability Pair on-level and pre-level students. After a few minutes of practice, tell on-level students to practice without a script.

Extra Practice

Interactive Practice

3 CONVERSATION

A Listen. Then listen and repeat.

This	This is a computer.
These	These are CDs.
That's	That's a mouse.

B Listen and read the conversation.
Then listen and repeat.

Carlos: What's this called in English?

Kamaria: It's a mouse.

Carlos: And these? What are these called?

Kamaria: They're CDs.

Pronunciation Watch

To say the *th* sound in *this*, *these*, and *that's*, put your tongue between your teeth.

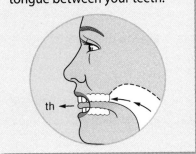

4 PRACTICE

A PAIRS. Practice the conversation. Then make new conversations.
Use the pictures.

A: What's this called in English?

B: It's   .

A: And these? What are these called?

B: They're   .

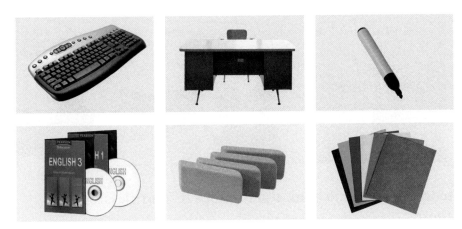

B MAKE IT PERSONAL. PAIRS. Make your own conversations.
Ask about things in your classroom.

Talk about things in the classroom

Grammar

This, that, these, those: Statements

Singular		
This is	a good dictionary.	
That's	a great picture.	

Plural		
These are	good dictionaries.	
Those are	great pictures.	

1 PRACTICE

Grammar Watch

- Use **this** and **these** for people or things near you.
- Use **that** or **those** for people or things <u>not</u> near you.

Contractions
that is = **that's**

A Underline the correct words.

1. <u>**This is**</u> / **These are** a good book.
2. **That's** / <u>**Those are**</u> my classmates.
3. **This is** / <u>**These are**</u> my markers.
4. **That's** / <u>**Those are**</u> my folders.
5. <u>**That's**</u> / **Those are** called a monitor.

B Look at the pictures. Complete the sentences with *This is*, *That's*, *These are*, and *Those are*.

1. <u>These are</u> our books.
2. <u>That's</u> our teacher.
3. <u>Those are</u> good binders.
4. <u>This is</u> my backpack.

C WRITE. Write two sentences in your notebook about things in your classroom. Use *this*, *that*, *these*, or *those*.

> This is my book.

Talk about things in the classroom

Getting Started   5 minutes

- Say: *We're going to study statements with* this, that, these, *and* those. *In the conversation on page 55, Carlos used this grammar.*
- Play CD 1, Track 57. Students listen. Write on the board: *That's a mouse.* Underline *That's.*

Presentation   15 minutes

This, that, these, those: Statements

- Copy the grammar charts onto the board or show the charts on Transparency 3.4 and cover the exercise.
- Hold up a book and say: *This is a book.* Emphasize *this.* The class repeats. Write the sentence on the board and draw a hand holding a book.
- Put a book on a table. Stand a few feet away. Point and say: *That is a book.* Emphasize *that.* The class repeats. Write the sentence on the board and draw a hand pointing to a book far from the hand.
- Read the sentences in the left chart and ask the class to repeat. After each sentence, tell the class to look at the picture that demonstrates the meaning of the sentence.
- Next, hold up two books and say: *These are books.* Emphasize *these.* The class repeats. Write the sentence on the board and draw a hand holding two books.
- Put two books on a table. Stand a few feet away. Point and say: *Those are books.* Emphasize *those.* The class repeats. Write the sentence on the board and draw a hand pointing at two books far from the hand.
- Read the sentences in the right chart and ask the class to repeat. After each sentence, tell the class to look at the picture that shows the meaning of the sentence.
- Now, alternate between holding up one book and holding up two and tell the class to call out *this* or *these.* Repeat several times with different objects.
- Then alternate between pointing to one book and pointing to two books and tell the class to call out *that* or *those.* Repeat several times with different objects.
- To sum up, read the Grammar Watch note.
- If you are using the transparency, do the exercise with the class.

Controlled Practice   15 minutes

1 PRACTICE

Ⓐ Underline the correct words.

- Read the directions. Write the example on the board and point to the answer. Ask: *Why?* (*Book* is singular.)
- Remind students: *That's is a contraction for* that is.
- Say: *Read the sentences before you answer. Remember, say* this *and* that *to talk about one thing, and* these *and* those *for two or more things.*
- Students compare answers with a partner.
- Call on students to read the completed sentences.

Ⓑ Look at the pictures. Complete the sentences...

- Read the directions. Write item 1 on the board and point to the answer. Ask: *Why?* (*Books* is plural and the man is near the books.)
- Say: *Look at the picture before you answer.*
- Students compare answers with a partner.
- Call on students to read the completed sentences.

   Expansion: Grammar Practice for 1B

- Form groups of 3. Have students put their personal classroom objects (books, pencils) on a desk.
- Student A (the presenter) holds up two pencils. Student B calls out *These pencils.* Then A puts the pencils down and points to a nearby dictionary. Student C calls out *That dictionary.* Then B becomes the presenter.

Ⓒ WRITE. Write two sentences in your notebook...

- Read the directions.
- To warm up, point to something in your classroom that is far from you. Ask: *What do I write?* Students should call out *That is/That's a book.* Repeat for objects near and far, singular and plural, so students can see examples of all four expressions.
- Walk around and check that students aren't simply copying what's on the board. Ask students to point to the things they're writing about so you can determine if they used the correct expression (for example, T: [Looking at the sentence *This is a dictionary.*] *Where is your dictionary?* S: [Holding/pointing to the dictionary] *This is my dictionary.*).

Presentation   15 minutes

This, that, these, those: Questions and answers

- Copy the grammar charts onto the board or show the charts on Transparency 3.4 and cover the exercise. Tell the class they will learn how to make and answer questions with *this, that, these,* and *those*.

- Read the singular questions in the left chart using a student's book to illustrate, and ask the class to repeat. Tell the class to reply *Yes, it is.* Repeat with the plural questions, using two books to illustrate, and tell students to reply *Yes, they are.*

- Read the singular questions and answers in the right chart and then the plural ones and ask the class to repeat. Use pens in the classroom to illustrate.

- Copy several questions and answers onto the board with blanks (for example, *Is _____ your book? Yes, _____ is.*). Hold objects in your hand to elicit *this* or *these* from the class. Point to objects to elicit *that* or *those.* Fill in the blanks when students call out the correct answers.

- If you are using the transparency, do the exercise with the class.

Controlled Practice   10 minutes

2 PRACTICE

PAIRS. Look at the pictures. Complete...

- Read the directions and the example. Call on an above-level student to say the answer for item 2. Write it on the board.

- Say: *The picture will help you understand how to complete the conversations. Look at the grammar charts on pages 56 and 57 if you need help.*

- Walk around and listen in on pairs. As needed, tell pairs to look at the picture first to figure out singular or plural and near or far.

- Call on pairs to perform the completed conversations.

■ MULTILEVEL INSTRUCTION for 2

Cross-ability Ask the higher-level partner to act out the actions in each conversation so the lower-level partner can experience it rather than just see it on the page.

Communicative Practice   10 minutes

Show what you know!

PAIRS. Student A, you have ten seconds. Draw...

- Read the directions. Ask students to look at the picture of the notebooks. Say: *I'm Student A. You, the class, are Student B.* Announce: *Ten seconds,* and look at your watch or the classroom clock so students know you're referring to time. In less than ten seconds, draw a picture of a book.

- Stand away from the picture, point to it and ask: *What is that?* Students should call out *Is it a book?*

- Review classroom vocabulary from Lesson 1 (pages 46–47) as needed.

- Pair students. Remind A: *After you draw a picture, ask your partner a* Wh- *question, for example,* What are these? Remind B: *Answer Student A with a* yes/no *question, for example,* Are they pencils?

- Walk around and, as needed, practice with students and demonstrate how to do the activity.

■ MULTILEVEL INSTRUCTION

Pre-level Sit with students and practice with them, playing Student A. Ask above-level volunteers to work with the other pre-level pairs.

Above-level Ask A to draw additional classroom objects that are not listed on page 47 (for example, a globe).

■ Expansion: Pronunciation Practice

- Create flashcards with *this* and *these.* Hold up a card and ask the class to pronounce it. If you cannot hear a difference between *this* and *these,* continue the activity.

Progress Check

Can you . . . talk about things in the classroom?
Say: *We have practiced talking about things in the classroom. Now, look at the question at the bottom of the page. Can you talk about things in the classroom?* Tell students to write a checkmark in the box.

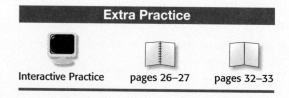

Extra Practice		
Interactive Practice	pages 26–27	pages 32–33

This, that, these, those: Questions and answers

Is	**this** **that**	your book?	Yes, **it** is.

What is	**this**? **that**?	It's a pen.

Are	**these** **those**	your books?	Yes, **they** are.

What are	**these**? **those**?	**They**'re pens.

2 PRACTICE

PAIRS. Look at the picture. Complete the conversations.

What is ___this___ called in English? **1.**

It's an eraser. **2.**

What are those ? **3.**

They're computers. **4.**

Is this a good book? **5.**

Yes, it is. **6.**

Are these markers? **7.**

Yes, they are. **8.**

Pairs
Practice this, that, these, those

Show what you know! Talk about things in the classroom

PAIRS. Student A, you have ten seconds. Draw a picture of one or two things in your classroom. Student B, guess the object or objects.

A: *What are these?*
B: *Are they folders?*
A: *No. They're notebooks.*

Can you… talk about things in the classroom? ☐

Life Skills

1   USE NUMBERS 10–100

CD1 T59

A   Look at the numbers. Listen and point. Then listen and repeat.

10	11	12	13	14
ten	eleven	twelve	thirteen	fourteen

15	16	17	18	19
fifteen	sixteen	seventeen	eighteen	nineteen

B   PAIRS.   Student A, say a number from Exercise A. Student B, write the number. Take turns. Don't repeat a number.

Answers will vary.

_____   _____   _____   _____   _____

CD1 T60

C   Listen and point. Then listen and repeat.

20	21	22	23	30	40
twenty	twenty-one	twenty-two	twenty-three	thirty	forty

50	60	70	80	90	100
fifty	sixty	seventy	eighty	ninety	one hundred

2   PRACTICE

A   Read the words. Write the numbers.

1. twenty-four __24__
2. sixty-one __61__
3. fifty-three __53__
4. ninety-nine __99__
5. forty-seven __47__
6. eighty-six __86__

CD1 T61

B   Listen to the conversations. Circle the number you hear.

1. 9   (19)
2. (12)   20
3. (35)   45
4. (59)   69
5. 14   (40)
6. 13   (30)
7. (17)   70
8. (82)   92

Can you...use numbers 10–100? ☐

Getting Started   2 minutes

- If the number of your classroom is 100 or lower, ask: *What number is our classroom?* As needed, point to the door and ask *Number?* Then write the number on the board, say it, and ask the class to repeat it.

- If the number of your classroom is higher than 100, say the number of another room, for example, the language or computer lab, write it on the board, and ask the class to repeat.

Presentation   15 minutes

1   USE NUMBERS 10–100

A 🔘 **Look at the numbers. Listen and point....**

- Write numbers 10–19 on the board. Say each one and ask the class to repeat them.
- Read the directions. Play CD 1, Track 59. Students listen and point.
- Resume playing Track 59. Students listen and repeat.

B **PAIRS. Student A, say a number from Exercise A....**

- Read the directions. Practice with the class a few times by saying a number between 10 and 19 out loud and having students write it in their notebooks. Students hold up their notebooks to show you their number.
- Pair students and tell them to take turns playing A and B. Remind students not to repeat a number.

■■■ MULTILEVEL INSTRUCTION for 1B

Pre-level Sit with students and dictate numbers to them as they write.

Above-level Student A says two numbers from Exercise 1A. Student B writes both numbers. Students take turns playing A and B.

C 🔘 **Listen and point. Then listen and repeat.**

- Ask students to look at the list of numbers (20–100).
- Read the directions. Play CD 1, Track 60. Students listen and point.
- Resume playing Track 60. Students listen and repeat.

- Begin reading *20, 21, 22, 23,* . . . and ask the class to repeat each one. Continue until 30 while the class repeats. Say: *Thirty. Thirty-* . . . and tell the class to say *one.* Then continue until 40 while the class repeats. Finally, say the numbers 50, 60, 70, 80, 90, and 100 while the class repeats.

Controlled Practice   10 minutes

2   PRACTICE

A **Read the words. Write the numbers.**

- Read the directions. Write the example on the board.
- Write on the board: *thirty-four* _____ and *forty-nine* _____. Ask: *What numbers do I write?* (3 and 4, 4 and 9) Write the numbers in the blanks.
- Students compare answers with a partner.
- Call on students to write answers on the board.

B 🔘 **Listen to the conversations. Circle...**

- Read the directions. Play CD 1, Track 61.
- Call on students to say answers. If many students did not get the correct answers, play Track 61 again.

■■■ Expansion: Listening Practice for 2B

- Many students have difficulty distinguishing between teens and tens (for example, *13* and *30*). Direct students to write the numbers 1 to 10 on a piece of paper. Dictate the following numbers: 1. *15*, 2. *50*, 3. *13*, 4. *30*, 5. *60*, 6. *16*, 7. *80*, 8. *18*, 9. *14*, 10. *40*.

Progress Check

Can you . . . use numbers 10–100?

Say: *We have practiced using numbers 10–100. Now, look at the question at the bottom of the page. Can you use numbers 10–100?* Tell students to write a checkmark in the box.

Controlled Practice 20 minutes

3 TALK ABOUT PLACES AT SCHOOL

A PAIRS. Look at the floor plan. How many...

- Read the words in the vocabulary box and ask the students to repeat. For each, ask the class if you have it at your school (for example, *Do we have a computer lab?*). Students can respond *yes* or *no*.
- Hold up the picture and point to the restrooms. Ask: *What's this?* The class should respond: *The restroom.* Then point to number 2 on the picture and ask: *What's this?* (hall) On the board, write: *2. hall.* Say: *Write hall for number 2.*
- Read the directions. Say: *Look at the things in each room in the school. Write the name of the room.*
- Pair students.
- Walk around and check that students are correctly identifying the places on the floor plan.
- Call on several students to say answers.

Language Note

Students may have difficulty pronouncing words with more than four syllables. Write troublesome words on the board with spaces between syllables: for example, *ca fe te ri a.* Point to each syllable, pronounce the word slowly, and ask the class to repeat it slowly. Then pronounce the word again at regular speed and ask the class to repeat it.

■ MULTILEVEL INSTRUCTION for 3A

Pre-level Students form like-ability groups of 3 or 4 and work together to complete the task.

Above-level Students work with like-ability partners and also draw a simple map of your school with rooms labeled.

B Listen and check your answers. Then...

- Read the directions. Play CD 1, Track 62. Students listen and check their answers. Play the CD as many times as needed.
- Resume playing Track 62. Students listen and repeat.

4 PRACTICE

A Listen. Then listen and repeat.

- Tell students to look at the picture. Use it to explain the meaning of *on the left, on the right, next to,* and *across from.* Show students how to motion and point with their hands when giving directions.
- Read the directions. Play CD 1, Track 63. Students listen.
- Resume playing Track 63. Students listen and repeat. Check that students are using rising/falling intonation correctly.

Communicative Practice 15 minutes

B PAIRS. Practice the conversation. Then look at...

- Read the directions. Copy the conversation from 4A onto the board, but leave blanks where students can insert new information.
- Pair students. Tell A to ask where two places are.
- Tell partners to switch roles and continue practicing with new places. Check that B is giving accurate directions. If B has difficulty, tell him/her to use the picture from Exercise 4A.
- Call on pairs to perform for the class.

■ MULTILEVEL INSTRUCTION for 4B

Pre-level Ask pairs to focus first on the bottom floor before making conversations about places on the top floor.

Above-level Ask pairs to get to different places from various "You are here" points.

Progress Check

Can you . . . talk about places at school?

Say: *We have practiced talking about places at school. Now, look at the question at the bottom of the page. Can you talk about places at school?* Tell students to write a checkmark in the box.

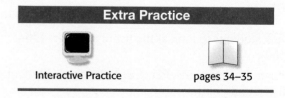

Extra Practice

Interactive Practice   pages 34–35

3 TALK ABOUT PLACES AT SCHOOL

A PAIRS. Look at the floor plan. How many places around school do you know? Write the words from the box on the lines.

> cafeteria   computer lab   elevator   hall
> library   office   ~~restroom~~   stairs

1. _restroom_
2. _hall_
3. _computer lab_
4. _library_
5. _office_
6. _stairs_
7. _elevator_
8. _cafeteria_

CD1 T62

B 💿 Listen and check your answers. Then listen and repeat.

4 PRACTICE

CD1 T63

A 💿 Listen. Then listen and repeat.

A: Which way is Room 230?

B: It's upstairs on the right, next to the elevator.

A: Which way is the cafeteria?

B: It's down the hall, across from Room 102.

B PAIRS. Practice the conversation. Then look at the floor plan. Make new conversations. Ask about different rooms.

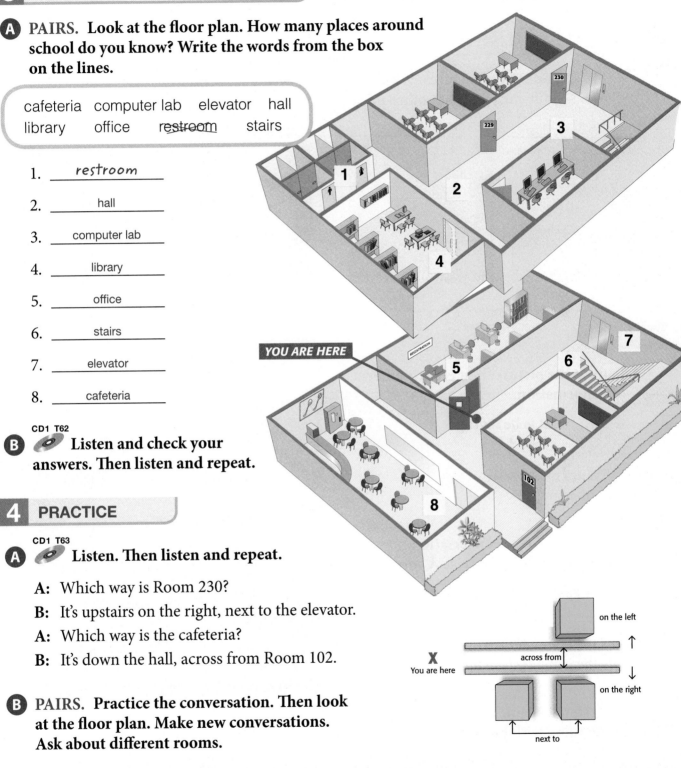

Can you...talk about places at school? ☐

Listening and Speaking

1 BEFORE YOU LISTEN

CLASS. **Look at the pictures. Which people work at your school? Check (✓) the people. What other people work at your school?**

custodian

principal

librarian

computer lab assistant

2 LISTEN

A Look at the picture. Ken is asking Berta for information.

Guess: What is he saying?

a. Help me.
b. Excuse me.
c. Look at me.

CD1 T64

B Listen to the conversation. Was your guess in Exercise A correct?

Listen again. What is Ken's question?

a. Where is the computer lab?
b. Is the computer lab open?
c. Is the computer lab upstairs?

CD1 T65

C Listen again. Who is the man in the room with Ken and Berta?

a. a teacher   b. an office assistant   c. the computer lab assistant

Getting Started — 10 minutes

1 BEFORE YOU LISTEN

CLASS. Look at the pictures. Which people work...

- Point to each picture, say the job title, and ask the class to repeat.
- Ask the following questions after writing all the answers in a scrambled list on the board. As you ask each question, students choose an answer from the board:

    What is a custodian? (a person who cleans the school)

    What is a principal? (the director or leader of a school)

    What is a librarian? (a person who works in the library and organizes all the books)

    What is a computer lab assistant? (a person who helps you in the lab)

- Ask: *Which people work at our school?* Say: *Check the people.*

    Expansion: Vocabulary Practice for 1

- Ask: *What other people work in our school?*
- Write answers on the board with simple definitions (for example, *child-care assistant—the person who takes care of the children*).

> **Culture Connection**
>
> • Say: *Many people work in schools in the U.S.* Point to the pictures of the jobs on page 60 and ask: *Do these people work at schools in your home country?*

2 LISTEN

A Look at the picture.... Guess:...

- Read the directions.
- Ask: *What do you see in the picture? What is happening?* (Ken and Berta are in the lounge. A man is getting a soda.)
- Ask: *What is Ken saying?* Write the answer choices on the board and read them. Call on students to guess.

Presentation — 20 minutes

B Listen to the conversation. Was your...

- Read the directions. Play CD 1, Track 64.
- Circle the correct answer on the board. Ask: *Was your guess correct?*

Listen again. What is Ken's question?

- Read the directions.
- Read each of the three options and ask the class to repeat. For each question, ask: *What kind of question is this?* (a. a *Wh-* question; b. a *yes/no* question; c. a *yes/no* question)
- Play Track 64 again.
- Call on a student to say the answer.

C Listen again. Who is the man....

- Read the directions and the answer choices.
- Play CD 1, Track 65.
- Call on a student to say the answer.

    Expansion: Writing Practice for 2C

- Brainstorm with the class to generate a list of school jobs (for example, *custodian, principal, librarian*). Write them on the board as column headings.
- Ask: *Which jobs do you like?* Tell students to write the jobs in their notebooks. Say: *Circle your favorite job.*
- Students stand and mingle to find other students who circled the same job. When students have found each other, they work together in a group to think of reasons the job they circled is a good job (for example, *computer lab assistant—computers are fun, students are nice, I like to type.*).
- One representative from each group writes the reasons on the board under the job title.

3 CONVERSATION

A 🎧 **Listen. Then listen and repeat.**

- Write some of the words on the board with space between the syllables (for example, *of fice*). Point to a syllable in one of the words and read the Pronunciation Watch note.
- Read the words, saying the stressed syllable more slowly and more loudly. Tell students these syllables are stressed.
- Play CD 1, Track 66. Students listen.
- Resume playing Track 66. Students listen and repeat. For each word, ask: *Which syllable is stressed? First, second, third, . . .?*

B 🎧 **Listen to the words. Mark the stressed...**

- Read the directions. Write the example (*o pen*) on the board. Ask: *Which syllable is stressed?* (the first one) Draw a large dot over *o*.
- Play CD 1, Track 67. Walk around and check that students are marking one syllable.
- Call on students to read the words out loud. Write answers on the board.

C 🎧 **Listen and read the conversation....**

- Note: This conversation is the same one students heard in Exercise 2B on page 60.
- Play CD 1, Track 68. Students listen and read along silently. Explain: Excuse me *is a polite way to get help.* Sorry *is a polite way to say you cannot help.*
- Ask students to look at the pictures. Say: Ask him *is an imperative. It means to ask a man.* Ask her *is an imperative. It means to ask a woman.* Check comprehension by pointing to male and female students while the class calls out *Ask him* or *Ask her.*
- Resume playing Track 68. Students listen and repeat.

Controlled Practice   10 minutes

4 PRACTICE

A PAIRS. **Practice the conversation. Then...**

- Pair students and tell them to practice the conversation in Exercise 3C.

- Then, in Exercise 4A, point to each word in the boxes, say it, and ask the class to repeat. As needed, tell students to look back at pages 59–60 for pictures of these words.
- Read the directions. Copy the conversation onto the board with blanks. Read through the conversation. When you come to a blank, fill it in with information from the boxes (*cafeteria* and *him*). Remind students to match the subject and object pronouns (for example, *he/him*). Also draw students' attention to the *Ask him/her* pictures.
- Ask two on-level students to practice the conversation for the class. Tell students in pairs to take turns playing each role and to use the words in the boxes to fill in the blanks.
- Tell students to stand, mingle, and practice the conversation with several new partners.
- Call on pairs to perform for the class.

MULTILEVEL INSTRUCTION for 4A

Pre-level Sit with students (or assign an above-level student to sit with them) to make sure they can properly substitute information into the conversation.

Above-level Tell pairs to continue the conversation by asking where another place is.

Communicative Practice   20 minutes

B ROLE PLAY. PAIRS. **Make your own...**

- Read the directions. Play A and make up a conversation with an above-level student.
- Pair students and tell them to take turns playing A and B.
- Tell students to write several places to use in the conversation. Students can use places on page 59 and any additional places in their school that they know. Call on students (especially above-level) to say additional places. Write them on the board and explain any unfamiliar ones.
- Walk around and check that students are stressing the correct syllable and correctly pairing subject and object pronouns.
- Call on groups to role-play for the class.

Extra Practice

Interactive Practice   pages 28–29

3 CONVERSATION

CD1 T66

A 🔘 **Listen. Then listen and repeat.**

office   ex**cuse**   **li**brary   li**brar**ian   cafe**te**ria

> **Pronunciation Watch**
>
> A syllable is part of a word. One syllable in each word is stressed.

CD1 T67

B 🔘 **Listen to the words. Mark (●) the stressed syllable.**

1. o pen   2. com pu ter   3. as sist ant   4. prin ci pal   5. cus to di an

CD1 T68

C 🔘 **Listen and read the conversation. Then listen and repeat.**

Ken: Excuse me. Is the computer lab open?

Berta: Sorry. I don't know. Ask him.

Ken: Oh, OK. But . . . Who is he?

Berta: He's the computer lab assistant!

4 PRACTICE

A **PAIRS.** **Practice the conversation. Then make new conversations. Use the words in the boxes.**

A: Excuse me. Is the ▭ open?

B: Sorry. I don't know. Ask ▭ .

A: Oh, OK. But . . . Who is ▭ ?

B: ▭'s the ▭ .

Ask him.   Ask her.

cafeteria	him	he	custodian
office	her	she	office assistant
library	him	he	librarian
principal's office	her	she	principal

B **ROLE PLAY. PAIRS.** **Make your own conversations. Talk about places at your school.**

Talk about people and places at school

Grammar

Object pronouns

Subject pronouns			Object pronouns	
I	am			**me.**
He	is			**him.**
She	is	new here.	Please help	**her.**
We	are			**us.**
They	are			**them.**

Grammar Watch

Subject Pronoun	Object Pronoun	
you	**you**	Are you the librarian? Can I ask **you** a question?
it	**it**	It's interesting. Read **it**.

PRACTICE

A Underline the correct word.

Where's the cafeteria?

Ask him.

1. **A:** Where's the cafeteria?
   B: Sorry. I don't know. Ask **he** / <u>**him**</u>.

2. **A:** Are these the answers?
   B: Yes, but don't look at **they** / <u>**them**</u>.

3. **A:** Please show **we** / <u>**us**</u> your new pictures.
   B: Sure. Here they are.

4. **A:** What's the word for this in English?
   B: Sorry. I don't know. Ask **she** / <u>**her**</u>.

B Read Ms. Reed's instructions to her class. Replace the underlined words. Use *him, her, it, us,* or *them.*

1. Take out your book. Open ~~the book~~ to page 10.
   it

2. Please close ~~your notebooks~~. Thanks.
   them

3. Please don't use your cell phone in class. Use ~~your cell phone~~ in the cafeteria.
   it

4. Ask ~~Ms. Thomas~~ about the computer lab hours. She's the computer lab assistant.
   her

5. Mr. and Mrs. Lin are new here. Please show ~~Mr. and Mrs. Lin~~ the library.
   them

6. Mr. Tran doesn't understand. Please help ~~Mr. Tran~~.
   him

7. Ask ~~Mr. Benson and me~~ your English questions. We're both level 1 teachers.
   us

Getting Started   5 minutes

- Say: *We're going to study subject and object pronouns. In the conversation on page 61, Berta used this grammar.*
- Play CD 1, Track 68. Students listen. Write on the board: *Ask him.* Underline *him*.

Presentation   10 minutes

Object pronouns

- Copy the grammar charts onto the board or show the charts on Transparency 3.5 and cover the exercise.
- Tell students that a *pronoun* is a word we use when we don't use a person's name.
- Read each sentence in the left chart and ask the class to repeat. While reading each sentence, point to a student (or students) to make the meaning of the subject pronouns clear.
- On the board, write several short sentences using subject pronouns (for example, *I am a new student. He is my friend. She is a doctor.*) and ask the class to repeat them. Ask students to tell you more sentences. Write them on the board, correcting grammar as needed.
- Read each sentence in the right chart and ask the class to repeat. While reading each sentence, point to a student (or students) to make the meaning of the object pronouns clear.
- On the board, write several sentences with object pronouns (for example, *Ask him. Please help us.*) and circle the pronouns. Remind students that they just practiced *him* and *her* in Lesson 8 on pages 60–61.
- Point to subject pronouns in sentences on the board and ask students to call out the object pronoun (for example, point to *he* and students should call out *him*). Repeat for object pronouns.
- Read the Grammar Watch note.
- If you are using the transparency, do the exercise with the class.

Controlled Practice   15 minutes

> **PRACTICE**

A **Underline the correct word.**

- Read the directions and the example.
- Students compare answers by practicing the conversations with a partner.
- Call on students to say answers.

B **Read Ms. Reed's instructions to her class....**

- Read the directions and item 1.
- Remind students to use *him* for one man, *her* for one woman, *it* for one thing, and *them* for two or more people or things.
- Students may mistake *your* for *you* in items 2 and 3. Say: Your *is not* you. *Look at the noun to see if it is singular or plural.*
- Call on students to write answers on the board.

Expansion: Writing and Grammar Practice for B

- Pair students.
- Student A writes three classroom instructions (for example, *Please listen to the CD.*). Student B rewrites each sentence with a subject or object pronoun (for example, *Please listen to it.*).

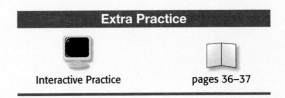

Extra Practice	
Interactive Practice	pages 36–37

REVIEW   Show what you know!

1 GRAMMAR

Complete Ms. Reed's instructions to her class....

- Read the directions. Tell students to refer back to the grammar charts on pages 50 (imperatives), 56–57 (*this, that, these, those*), and 62 (object pronouns) as needed.
- Students compare answers with a partner.
- When reviewing answers, point out how the sentence reveals the correct answer (for example, *2. The answer is* This *because we're talking about one story.*).

2 WRITING

STEP 1. Complete the sentences. Use words from...

- Read the directions. Ask students to look at the vocabulary in the box.
- Remind students to write *Don't* to make negative imperatives. Explain that *your language* (number 2) means the students' first language. Also remind students to begin with a capital letter.
- Students complete the task and compare answers with a partner.
- Call on students to say answers. More than one answer for each item is possible.

STEP 2. Write four more tips for learning English....

- Read the directions.
- Brainstorm additional tips with the class using words from the box. Write a few on the board (for example, *Listen to the radio in English.*).
- Students can copy what's on the board but must also write their own tips.
- Say: *Use a capital letter at the beginning of a sentence and use a period at the end of a sentence.*
- Students compare answers with a partner.
- Call on students to read their tips out loud. Write any particularly good ones on the board and ask students to copy them.

▬▬ **Expansion: Writing Practice for STEP 2**

- Choose a place (not your classroom) at your school where students visit (for example, a computer lab). Ask groups of 4 or 5 to create a list of rules for that place (for example, *Don't eat or drink. Don't check e-mail. Use the microphone to speak.*).

CD-ROM Practice

 Go to the CD-ROM for more practice.

If your students need more practice with the vocabulary, grammar, and competencies in Unit 3, encourage them to review the activities on the CD-ROM. This review can also help students prepare for the final role play on the following Expand page.

Extra Practice
pages 30–31

1 GRAMMAR

Complete Ms. Reed's instructions to her class. Write the correct words.

OK, class. ____Open____ your books to page 10. ____This____ is a picture story.
1. (Open / Close)   2. (This / These)

Now, work with a partner. ____Look____ at the picture. Ask questions. For example,
3. (Look / Don't look)

"Is ____that____ a DVD? Are ____those____ CDs?" Now look at the picture on page 11.
4. (that / those)   5. (that / those)

____Talk____ about ____it____ with your partner. Tell ____him____ or
6. (Talk / Don't talk)   7. (it / them)   8. (he / him)

____her____ about the picture. ____Write____ four sentences about it.
9. (she / her)   10. (Write / Don't write)

Show ____them____ to your partner.
11. (they / them)

2 WRITING

STEP 1. Complete the sentences. Use words from the box. Choose affirmative or negative. There may be more than one correct answer. Answers will vary, but possible answers include:

Tips for Learning English

1. ____Speak____ English in class as much as possible!
2. ____Don't use____ your language in class.
3. ____Read____ English books at home.
4. ____Watch____ TV in English.
5. ____Write____ new words in a notebook.

ask
listen
practice
read
speak
use
study
watch
write

STEP 2. Write four more tips for learning English. Use words from the box in Step 1.

Answers will vary.

_____

_____

_____

_____

■ **Go to the CD-ROM for more practice.**

3 ACT IT OUT — What do you say?

CD1 T69

STEP 1. Listen to the conversation.

STEP 2. PAIRS. You are in the office at school. Student A, you are a new student. Student B, you are an office assistant.

> **Student A:** Ask the office assistant for the location of different places around school.

> **Student B:** The new student needs information about your school. Answer the student's questions.

4 READ AND REACT — Problem-solving

STEP 1. Read about Ali's problem.

Ali is a student at the Greenville Adult School. He is in a level 1 class. Ali has good study habits. He practices English every day.

Today Ali's teacher is giving a test. The teacher says, "Please don't talk. Don't look at your classmates' test papers." Ali is not happy. A classmate is looking at his test paper.

STEP 2. PAIRS. Talk about it. What is Ali's problem? What can Ali do? Here are some ideas.

- He can say, "Please don't look at my paper."
- He can move his paper.
- He can talk to his teacher.
- He can _____.

5 CONNECT

For your Study Skills Activity, go to page 247.
For your Team Project, go to page 267.

Which goals can you check off? Go back to page 45.

3 ACT IT OUT

STEP 1. 💿 Listen to the conversation.

- Play CD 1, Track 69. Students listen.
- As needed, play Track 69 again to aid comprehension.

STEP 2. PAIRS. You are in the office at school....

- Read the directions and the guidelines for Students A and B.
- Pair students. Tell pairs to use real information about your school. Remind students to pretend they are in the office when the conversation begins.
- Walk around and observe partners interacting. Check that A is asking for the location of various places in the school while B is replying with clear directions.
- Call on pairs to perform for the class.
- While pairs are performing, use the scoring rubric on page Txiv to evaluate each student's vocabulary, grammar, fluency, and how well they complete the task.
- *Optional:* After each pair finishes, discuss the strengths and weakness of each performance either in front of the class or privately.

4 READ AND REACT

STEP 1. Read about Ali's problem.

- Say: *We are going to read about a student's problem, and then we need to think about a solution.*
- Read the directions.
- Read the story while students follow along silently. Pause after each sentence to allow time for students to comprehend. Periodically stop and ask simple *Wh-* questions to check comprehension (for example, *Where does Ali go to school? What level is his class? What does the teacher say? Why is Ali not happy?*).

STEP 2. PAIRS. Talk about Ali's problem. What is...

- Pair students. Read the directions and the question.
- Read the ideas in the list. Give pairs a couple of minutes to discuss possible solutions for Ali.
- Ask: *Which ideas are good?* Call on students to say their opinion about the ideas in the list (for example, S: *I think he can talk to his teacher. This is a good idea.*).
- Now tell students to think of one new idea not in the box (for example, *He can move to a new desk.*) and to write it in the blank. Encourage students to think of more than one idea and to write their ideas in their notebooks.
- Call on pairs to say their additional solutions. Write any particularly good ones on the board and ask: *Do you think this is a good idea? Why or why not?*

▬▬ MULTILEVEL INSTRUCTION for STEP 2

Pre-level Ask pairs to agree on one good idea.

Above-level Ask pairs to rank the ideas in the list (including their new idea) on a scale of 1–4 (1 = the best).

5 CONNECT

Turn to page 247 for the Study Skills Activity and page 268 for the Team Project. See pages Txi–Txii for general notes about teaching these activities.

Progress Check

Which goals can you check off? Go back to page 45.

Ask students to turn to page 45 and check off any remaining goals they have reached. Call on students to say which goals they will practice outside of class.

Family Ties

Classroom Materials/Extra Practice

CD 2
Tracks 2–22

Transparencies 4.1–4.6
Vocabulary Cards Unit 4

MCA
Unit 4

Workbook
Unit 4

Interactive Practice
Unit 4

Unit Overview

Goals
- See the list of goals on the facing page.

Grammar
- Possessive adjectives
- Possessive nouns
- Descriptions with *have*
- Descriptions with *be* and *have*

Pronunciation
- Pronunciation of possessive *'s*
- Linking words together: Consonant to vowel

Reading
- Read an article about blended families

Writing
- Write sentences about yourself and your family

Life Skills Writing
- Complete an emergency contact form

Preview
- Set the context of the unit by asking questions about family (for example, *Do you have a big family?*).
- Hold up page 65 or show Transparency 4.1. Read the unit title and ask the class to repeat.
- Explain: Family Ties *means that family members are close to each other. They love and care about each other. Optional:* Explain: *There was also a popular television show in the United States called* Family Ties *in the 1980s, so it's a funny title, too.*
- Say: *Look at the picture.* Ask the Preview questions: *Who are the people?* (family members) *Where are they?* (a birthday party)
- If possible, ask students to bring in a picture of their family for Lesson 1.

Unit Goals
- Point to the Unit Goals. Explain that this list shows what the class will be studying in this unit.
- Tell students to read the goals silently.
- Say each goal and ask the class to repeat. Explain unfamiliar vocabulary as needed:

  Emergency contact form: *A form with the name, address, and phone number of a person to call during an emergency*
- Tell students to circle one goal that is very important to them.
- Call on students to say the goal they circled.

Family Ties

Preview

Look at the picture.
Who are the people?
Where are they?

UNIT GOALS

☐ Talk about family

☐ Describe people

☐ Talk about months and dates

☐ Write dates in numbers and words

☐ Give your birthday and date of birth

☐ Give a child's age and grade in school

☐ Complete an emergency contact form

1 WHAT DO YOU KNOW?

A CLASS. Look at the pictures of Susan's family. What words for family members do you know?

Susan

> Number 6 is her husband.

CD2 T2

B 💿 Listen and point to the people. Then listen and repeat.

2 PRACTICE

A PAIRS. Student A, point to a person and ask, "Who's this?" Student B, answer.

A: *Who's this?*
B: *Susan's mother. Who's this?*
A: *Susan's . . .*

B WORD PLAY. PAIRS. Student A, look at the list of family members on page 67. Say a family member. Student B, say the matching male or female word.

A: *Brother.*
B: *Sister.*

C GROUPS OF 3. Look at Susan's family tree. Talk about the people.

A: *David is Susan's husband.*
B: *Right. And Carol is Susan's mother.*

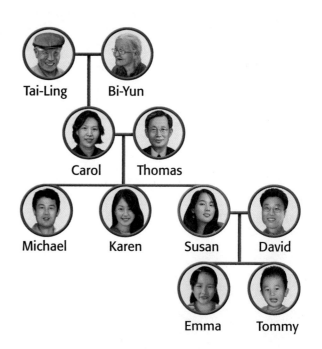

Lesson 1 Vocabulary

Getting Started 5 minutes

1 WHAT DO YOU KNOW?

A CLASS. Look at the pictures of Susan's family...

- Show Transparency 4.2 or hold up the book. Tell students to cover the list of words on page 67.
- Read the directions. Point to number 6 and ask: *Who is this?* Read the example with the class.
- Ask: *Which family members do you know?*
- If students call out an incorrect family member, give students two options (for example, ask: *Is number 7 a wife or a husband?*). Tell the class they will now listen to a CD and practice the names of the family members.

Presentation 10 minutes

B 💿 Listen and point to the people. Then...

- Read the directions. Play CD 2, Track 2. Pause after number 12 (*grandfather*).
- Explain: *The word* children *is plural. The singular form is* child.
- Resume playing Track 2. Students listen and repeat.

Controlled Practice 15 minutes

2 PRACTICE

A PAIRS. Student A, point to a person and ask...

- Read the directions. Read each line in the example and ask the class to repeat. Model correct intonation.
- Play A and model the activity with an above-level student. Explain: *When you answer, always say* Susan's . . . *because this is Susan's family.*
- Explain: Who's *is a contraction of* Who *and* is. Ask: *Why do we say* this, *as in* Who's this? (Because we are pointing to the picture of one person.)
- Pair students. Walk around and, as needed, practice the conversation with pairs by pointing to pictures and asking: *Who's this?*
- To check comprehension, show Transparency 4.2, point to various pictures, and ask individual students: *Who's this?* (Susan's _____)

▬ MULTILEVEL INSTRUCTION for 2A

Pre-level Form groups of 4. When Student A asks *Who's this?* anyone in the group may answer.

Above-level Students make up information about the family members' jobs, for example: A: *Who's this?* B: *Susan's mother. She's a doctor. . . .*

B WORD PLAY. PAIRS. Student A, look at the list...

- Read the directions and the example. Ask: *Who is the match for* husband? (wife)
- Pair students. Walk around and practice with them. After a few minutes, tell students to stand, mingle, and practice the conversation with several other partners.
- To check comprehension, say a word and call on individual students to tell you the matching word.

▬ Expansion: Graphic Organizer Practice for 2B

- Tell students to make a two-column chart with the headings *Male* and *Female* in their notebooks. Students write matching male and female family words in the same row (for example, *brother, sister*). Students can use this table as a reference.

C GROUPS OF 3. Look at Susan's family tree. Talk...

- Explain how the family tree works: *Two people connected by a line (like Tai-Ling and Bi-Yun) are married to each other—they are husband and wife. Lines that go down under married couples are for their children. Michael, Karen, and Susan are the children of Carol and Thomas.*
- Form groups of 3. Read the directions.
- Say: *Student A, say something about a family member, for example,* David is Susan's husband. *Then, Student B, say something more, for example,* Right. And Carol is Susan's mother.
- Walk around and if students have difficulty, use the chart to help them understand the relationships.
- To wrap up, perform the activity as a class.

Teaching Tip

Point, Pause, Repeat, Ask. *Point* to the tree to help illustrate what you explain. *Pause* after short statements so students can process what you just said. *Repeat* the short statement(s) you just said. *Ask* simple comprehension questions to confirm understanding.

Learning Strategy: Write personal sentences

- Read the directions and the example.

- Say: *To remember the word* brothers, *I will write a sentence about my brothers.* Read the example sentence again.

- Tell students to circle four family words in the vocabulary list at the top of the page. Say: *For each word, write a sentence about your real family members.*

- Ask a student: *What is your mother's first name?* (Ana) Write on the board: *Ana is my mother.* Tell students to write sentences like this for the four words they circled.

- Walk around as students work. If misspellings occur, tell them to check the list on page 67. Check that students are capitalizing sentences and using periods. Also check for *subject-verb* agreement.

- Call on students to read their sentences.

- Say: *You can remember new vocabulary when you write sentences that are important to you.* Remind students to use this strategy to remember other new vocabulary.

Communicative Practice   25 minutes

Show what you know!

STEP 1. Draw your family tree in your notebook....

- Read the directions. Copy the sample family tree onto the board.

- Point to the family tree and say: *Put a dotted line between people who have children together. Children go under the parents.*

- Point to the family tree and say: *You are "Me."* Point to names (for example, Bruno) and ask: *Who's this?* (Bruno is my brother.)

- Draw your own family tree on the board. Keep it simple and include, for example, blanks for one set of grandparents, your parents, your siblings (include yourself), and your children and your siblings' children. Point to names on the tree and state their relationship to you (for example, *Steve is my father.*). To give students additional support, write each person's relation to you under his or her name (for example, *Steve—my father*).

- Walk around and help students as they draw their family trees. Point to people in students' trees and ask: *Who's this?*

STEP 2. PAIRS. Show your partner your family tree....

- Read the directions.

- Ask an above-level student to point to someone in your family tree on the board and ask: *Who's this?* (She's my sister.)

- Pair students. Say: *Ask your partner questions about his or her family. Take turns playing A and B.*

- Walk around and check that students are using their family trees and are asking and answering correctly. Point to people in students' trees and ask: *Who's this?*

▬▬ MULTILEVEL INSTRUCTION for STEP 2

Cross-ability The higher-level partner plays A first, asks questions, and also models answers if B has difficulty or responds incorrectly.

▬▬ Expansion: Speaking Practice for STEP 2

- Ask students to present their family trees to the class. Students in the audience ask questions (for example, *Who's your father?*). For an added challenge, presenters can also say what jobs their family members have (for example, *This is my father. He's a teacher.*).

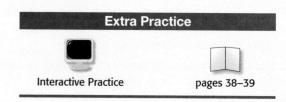

Extra Practice	
Interactive Practice	pages 38–39

Family Members

1. sister
2. brother
3. mother
4. father
5. parents
6. husband
7. wife
8. daughter
9. son
10. children
11. grandmother
12. grandfather

Learning Strategy

Write personal sentences

Write three sentences in your notebook about your family.

Pedro and Carlos are my brothers.

Show what you know!

STEP 1. Draw your family tree in your notebook. Don't use pictures. Use names.

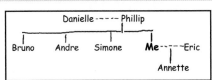

STEP 2. PAIRS. Show your partner your family tree. Ask and answer questions about your family.

A: *Who's Bruno?*
B: *He's my brother.*

Talk about family

Listening and Speaking

1 BEFORE YOU LISTEN

A READ. Read the sentences.

This is Justin Timberlake.
He is a singer.

This is my brother.
He **looks like** Justin Timberlake.

B CLASS. Who do people in your family look like?

 My sister looks like me.

2 LISTEN

A Look at the picture. Dora is showing a photo to Sen.

Guess: Who is the man in the photo?

a. Dora's brother   b. Dora's husband   (c.) Dora's father

B CD2 T3 Listen to the conversation. Was your guess in Exercise A correct?

Listen again. Complete the sentences.

1. Sen says the photo is _____great_____.
   (a.) great   b. interesting   c. nice

2. Sen says the man looks _____nice_____.
   a. great   b. interesting   (c.) nice

C CD2 T4 Listen to the whole conversation.
Read the sentences. Circle *True* or *False*.

1. Sen thinks Dora looks like the woman in the photo.   (True)   False

2. The woman is Dora's sister.   True   (False)

Lesson 2 Talk about family

Getting Started
5 minutes

BEFORE YOU LISTEN

A READ. **Read the sentences.**

- Say: *Look at the first picture. Who's this?* (Justin Timberlake) *Is he famous?* (Yes.) *Why?* (He's a singer.)
- Say: *Look at the next picture. Who's this?* (my brother) *Is he famous?* (No.) *He's not famous, but he looks like Justin Timberlake.*
- Say: Looks like *means that someone looks almost the same as another person. Sometimes people we know look like famous people.*

▬▬ **Expansion: Critical Thinking Practice for 1A**

- Ask: *Is it good to look like a famous person? Why or why not?* List pros and cons on the board (for example, *Pro: People are nice to you. Con: Some people are rude.*).

B CLASS. **Who do people in your family look like?**

- Ask: *Who do people in your family look like?* Write answers on the board (for example, *My sister looks like Jennifer Lopez.*).

Presentation
25 minutes

2 **LISTEN**

A **Look at the picture.... Guess:...**

- Read the directions.
- Ask: *What do you see in the picture?* (two women; a woman holding a photo)
- Ask: *Who is the man in the photo?* Write the answer choices on the board and read them. Call on a few students to guess.

B 🔘 **Listen to the conversation. Was...**

- Read the directions. Play CD 2, Track 3.
- Circle the correct answer on the board. Ask: *Was your guess correct?*

> **Teaching Tip**
>
> *Optional:* Remember that if students need additional support, tell them to read the Audio Script on page 282 as they listen to the conversations.

Listen again. Complete the sentences.

- Read the directions.
- Read each sentence and the answer choices.
- Play Track 3 again. Students listen and complete the sentences.
- Call on students to say answers.

C 🔘 **Listen to the whole conversation....**

- Read the directions. Play CD 2, Track 4.
- Students compare answers with a partner.
- Call on students to say answers.

▬▬ **Expansion: Vocabulary Practice for 2C**

- On the board, write *Nice.* Near it, write the sentence *He looks* <u>nice</u>. Ask: *What other words mean* nice?
- Write answers on the board. (*Possible answers:* kind, friendly, helpful, caring) Students write these words in their notebooks.

▬▬ **Expansion: Listening and Speaking Practice for 2C**

- Play Track 4 again, but pause it after each line. Tell the class to repeat each line.
- After a few times through, tell half the class to play Sen and the other half to play Dora. Without the CD, cue each side to say their lines (for example, Ss [Sen]: *That's a great photo. Who's that?* Other Ss [Dora]: *My father.*).

Controlled Practice   15 minutes

3 CONVERSATION

Listen and read the conversation. Then...

- Note: This conversation is the same one students heard in Exercise 2B on page 68.
- Read the directions.
- Play CD 2, Track 5. Students listen and read along silently.
- Resume playing Track 5. Students listen and repeat.

Language Note

On the board, write *Oh, he looks nice.* Draw an arrow pointing to the comma and label it. Explain: *We pause, or stop, after* Oh. *This is why we use a comma.* Repeat the expression a few times, pausing after *Oh* while pointing to the comma on the board. Call on students to repeat this line after you.

4 PRACTICE

A PAIRS. **Practice the conversation. Then make new...**

- Pair students and tell them to practice the conversation in Exercise 3.
- Then, in Exercise 4A, ask students to look at the family tree and the note. Go over the meaning of *uncle*, *aunt*, and *cousin* using the family tree and your own family as examples.
- Read the directions.
- Copy the conversation onto the board with blanks. Read through the conversation. When you come to a blank, fill it in with information from the family tree.
- Ask two on-level students to practice the conversation in front of the class.
- Tell pairs to take turns playing each role and to use the words in the family tree to try to fill in the blanks.
- Walk around and check that students are using the correct pronoun in *Oh, _____ looks nice.*
- Tell students to stand, mingle, and practice the conversation with several new partners.
- Call on pairs to perform for the class.

MULTILEVEL INSTRUCTION for 4A

Cross-ability The lower-level partner should play A first a few times. The higher-level partner, playing B, can correct A if A says the wrong pronoun in *Oh, _____ looks nice.*

Communicative Practice   15 minutes

B MAKE IT PERSONAL. PAIRS. **Make your own...**

- Read the directions.
- Ask students to take out a family photo. Students who don't have a photo can draw a picture of a family member.
- With an above-level student, make up a new conversation and practice in front of the class. Base the conversation on Exercise 4A.
- Pair students. Say: *Student A, show your picture to your partner. Student B, say something nice about the picture and ask who the people are.*
- Walk around and check that students are using contractions correctly and are asking and answering questions properly.
- Call on individual students to come to the front of the class with their picture. Ask students questions about their pictures (for example, *Who's that?*).

MULTILEVEL INSTRUCTION for 4B

Cross-ability Tell the lower-level students to first present their photos to their partners. The higher-level students are responsible for asking more questions. Tell higher-level students to repeat their questions or ask them in different ways if their partner doesn't understand.

Expansion: Speaking Practice for 4B

- Bring in magazines with pictures of celebrities. Tell students to cut out pictures and create a made-up family tree with celebrities' pictures.
- Students then practice asking and answering questions about their trees with their partners. They base their conversations on Exercise 4A.

Extra Practice

Interactive Practice

CD2 T5

Listen and read the conversation. Then listen and repeat.

Sen: That's a great photo. Who's that?
Dora: My father.
Sen: Oh, he looks nice.
Dora: Thanks.

4 PRACTICE

A PAIRS. Practice the conversation. Then make new conversations.
Use the family tree.

A: That's a great photo. Who's that?

B: My _____.
     (family member)

A: Oh, _____ looks nice.
     (he / she)

B: Thanks.

> Notice three new words:
> uncle, aunt, cousin

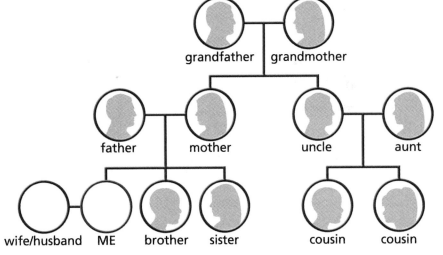

B MAKE IT PERSONAL. PAIRS. Make your own conversations. Bring a family photo to class or draw a picture of a person in your family. Talk about that person.

Grammar

Possessive adjectives

Subject pronouns			Possessive adjectives	
I	am		My	
You	are		Your	
He	is	in the U.S.	His	family is in Peru.
She	is		Her	
We	are		Our	
They	are		Their	

1 PRACTICE

A Maria is showing family photos to a friend. Complete the sentences. Underline the correct word.

1. This is **his** / <u>**my**</u> husband and me.

   Their / <u>**Our**</u> two children aren't in the picture.

2. This is **our** / <u>**your**</u> daughter.

   His / <u>**Her**</u> name is Sara.

3. This is **his** / <u>**our**</u> son.

   <u>**His**</u> / **Her** name is Antonio.

4. These are <u>**my**</u> / **our** parents.

   Her / <u>**Their**</u> names are Liana and Luis.

B Maria is showing more photos to her friend. Complete their conversation with *my, your, his, her,* and *their.*

Maria: This is __m y__ daughter with __h e r__ friend from school.

   This is __m y__ son with __h i s__ cousin.

   And here are the children with __t h e i r__ classmates.

Friend: Nice. __Y o u r__ son looks like you.

Maria: I know. And __m y__ daughter looks like my husband.

CD2 T6

C Listen and check your answers.

Getting Started   5 minutes

- Say: *We're going to study possessive adjectives. In the conversation on page 69, Dora used this grammar.*
- Play CD 2, Track 5. Students listen. Write *My father* on the board. Underline *My*.

Presentation   10 minutes

Possessive adjectives

- Copy the grammar charts onto the board or show the charts on Transparency 4.3 and cover the exercise.
- Read the first sentence in the left chart (*I am in the U.S.*) and ask the class to repeat. Then read its complement sentence in the right chart (*My family is in Peru.*). As you read *I* and *My*, point to yourself. Repeat with other subject pronoun and possessive adjective pairs in the chart and point to students to indicate the match between *You/Your*, *He/His*, *She/Her*, *We/Our*, and *They/Their*.
- To confirm understanding, say: *I am in the U.S. My family is in Peru.* Ask: *Whose family?* (My family) Say: *You are in the U.S. Your family is in Peru.* Ask: *Whose family is in Peru?* (Your family)
- If you are using the transparency, do the exercise with the class.

Teaching Tip

Finding alternative ways to present grammar provides multiple opportunities for students to acquire new language. To reinforce the above presentation, point to your book and say *My book*. Point to a student's book, look at the student, and say *Your book*. Then point to another student's book, look at the class, and say: *His/Her book*. Repeat with other examples for *my*, *your*, *his*, *her*, *our*, and *their*. To check comprehension, perform the same actions but do not say anything. Tell the class to call out the correct expression.

Controlled Practice   15 minutes

1 PRACTICE

A **Maria is showing family photos to a friend....**

- Read the directions and the example. Ask students to look at picture 1.
- Say: *Look carefully at the pictures before you answer.* Do the second sentence in item 1 with the class.
- Call on students to say answers.

B **Maria is showing more photos to her friend....**

- Read the directions. Read the example and ask the class to fill in the second blank. Ask: *Which word in the sentence tells you the answer is* her? (daughter)
- Tell students to read each sentence before answering.
- Walk around and check that students are basing their answers on information in the sentences.

C **Listen and check your answers.**

- Play CD 2, Track 6. Students listen and check their answers.
- *Optional:* Play Track 6 again, pausing after each item to allow students to repeat. Students then practice the conversation in pairs.

Expansion: Writing Practice for 1C

- Pair students who each have a family photo. Students write sentences about the people in their own photo (for example, *This is my husband.*) and then they write sentences about their partner's photo (for example, *That is her son.*).
- Students should try to write at least three sentences each (two about their own photo and one about their partner's).

Presentation   10 minutes

Possessive nouns

- Copy the grammar charts onto the board or show the charts on Transparency 4.3 and cover the exercise. Tell the class they will learn how to use possessive nouns.

- Read the first sentence in the left chart and ask the class to repeat. Read its counterpart in the right chart. Read the Grammar Watch note.

- Pronounce *Luis's* and ask the class to repeat. Explain: *There is an extra syllable because* Luis *ends in* -s. Read the Pronunciation Watch note.

- Hold up various classroom objects that belong to students (for example, a textbook) and call on the class to say to whom it belongs (Ss: *That's Ramon's book.*). Call on students to write each sentence on the board after the class calls it out.

- If you are using the transparency, do the exercise with the class.

Teaching Tip

Use drawings to reinforce grammar concepts. On the board, draw an outline of the U.S. and stick figures for Dora and Luis. Then draw Peru and several family members. (See page 6 for the shapes of the U.S. and Peru.) As you read the sentences in the chart, point to the figures.

Controlled Practice   10 minutes

2   PRACTICE

A Look at the family tree. Complete the sentences.

- Read the directions. Hold up the book and point to Ryan and Eva. Read the example.

- Read the other names and ask the class to repeat.

- Say: *Use possessive nouns to complete the sentences. Look at the family tree first.*

- Students compare answers with a partner. Those who finish early write a sentence on the board.

B Listen and check your answers. Then...

- Read the directions. Play CD 2, Track 7. Students listen and check their answers.

- Resume playing Track 7. Students listen and repeat.

Communicative Practice   10 minutes

Show what you know!

GROUPS OF 3. Talk about the people in the picture....

- Ask students to look at the picture. Say: *The names of the people are under the picture.*

- Play A and read the example conversation with two on-level students.

- Form groups of 3. Say: *A, begin by asking who somebody is. B and C, listen to A and answer the question. Say* I think *to make a guess. Use* looks like *in your answers.*

- Walk around and check that students are using possessive adjectives, possessive nouns, and the expressions *I think* and *looks like*.

■ MULTILEVEL INSTRUCTION

Cross-ability Ask higher-level partners to prompt lower-level partners with questions (for example, [Pointing to someone in the photo] *Who's this?*).

■ Expansion: Speaking Practice

- Form groups of 4. One student shows his or her family photo to the group and writes the names of the people in the photo on a piece of paper, but does not say anything more about it. The other students talk about the photo and try to guess what relationship the people in the photo have with the student who owns it.

Progress Check

Can you . . . talk about family?

Say: *We have practiced talking about family. Now, look at the question at the bottom of the page. Can you talk about family?* Tell students to write a checkmark in the box.

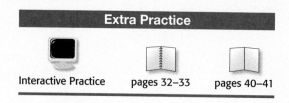

Extra Practice		
Interactive Practice	pages 32–33	pages 40–41

Possessive nouns

Dora Luis	is in the U.S.	Dora's Luis's Dora and Luis's	family is in Peru.

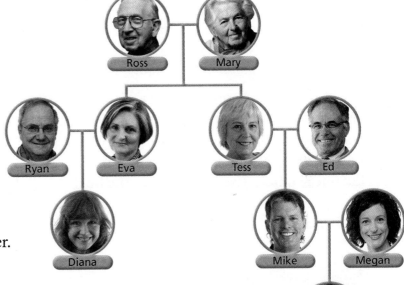

Grammar Watch

Add **'s** to names to show possession.

2 PRACTICE

A Look at the family tree. Complete the sentences.

1. Ryan is ___*Eva's*___ husband.

2. Megan is ___Mike's___ wife.

3. Eva is Ross and ___Mary's___ daughter.

4. Tess is ___Jake's___ grandmother.

5. Ed is ___Tess's___ husband.

6. Diana is Mary and ___Ross's___ granddaughter.

CD2 T7

B 🖸 Listen and check your answers. Then listen and repeat.

Pronunciation Watch

The **'s** adds an extra syllable after the sounds *s, z, sh,* and *ch* (*Luis's, Alex's, Liz's, Josh's,* and *Mitch's*).

Show what you know!   Talk about family

GROUPS OF 3. Talk about the people in the picture. Who are they? Guess.

A: *Who's Ramiro?*
B: *I think he's Rosa's husband.*
C: *Oh. I think he's Rosa's brother. He looks like her.*

Omar, Rosa, Pancho, Ramiro, Lila, Adriana, Miranda

Can you... talk about family? ☐

Read about blended families

Reading

1 BEFORE YOU READ

A CLASS. **Read the information. Then answer the questions.**

In the United States, 48% of married couples get divorced. And 75% of divorced people get married again.

Do many people in your country get divorced? Do they get married again?

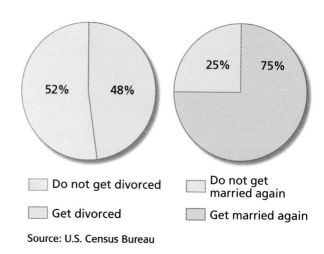

- ☐ Do not get divorced
- ☐ Get divorced
- ☐ Do not get married again
- ☐ Get married again

Source: U.S. Census Bureau

B **Look at the pictures and dates. Complete the information. Use the words in the box.**

divorced   ~~married~~   parents   son   step-mother   step-sister

1 1997

Ann and Bob Peterson get ___married___

2 1998

Ann and Bob with their ___son___, Jimmy

3 2005

Jimmy with his ___parents___

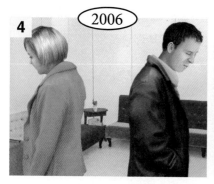
4 2006

Ann and Bob get ___divorced___

5 2008

Jimmy with his mother, step-father, and ___step-sister___

6 2008

Jimmy with his father, ___step-mother___, and step-brothers

Getting Started 10 minutes

 BEFORE YOU READ

A CLASS. Read the information. Then answer...

- Read the directions and the paragraph. Ask: *What does* get divorced *mean?* (to end a marriage)
- Tell the class to look at the first pie chart. Ask: *What do 52% of the people do?* (They don't get divorced.) *What do 48% of the people do?* (They get divorced.)
- Tell the class to look at the second pie chart. Ask: *What do 75% of the people do?* (They get married again.) *What do 25% of the people do?* (They don't get married again.)
- Ask the questions in the exercise: *Do many people in your country get divorced? Do they get married again?*

Teaching Tip

Many students have difficulty understanding graphs and charts. Ask many comprehension questions when presenting a chart or graph to ensure that students understand, for example, *Which piece is bigger, 52% or 48%? Why are there different colors?* (to see the different groups) *What does 48% mean?* (48 out of 100 people)

   To illustrate and reinforce understanding, poll the class with a simple *yes/no* question (for example, *Do you want a new TV?*). Tally the results on the board (for example, *Yes: 9; No: 14*). Add the results (*23*) and write the sum on the board. Calculate the percentage of the *Yes* votes by dividing the number of *Yes* votes by the total number of votes (9/23 = 0.39, approximately 40%, which means the *No* votes were approximately 60%). Draw a pie chart with corresponding pieces. Students copy the pie chart into their notebooks and write the percentages over the pieces.

Expansion: Math and Graphic Organizer Practice for 1A

- After doing the above Teaching Tip activity, poll the class with another simple question (*Who has children?*), tally the results on the board under *Yes* and *No* headings, and ask students to create their own pie chart.
- As a visual aid, draw some sample pie piece sizes on the board to represent basic percentage amounts (for example, a quarter of a circle for 25%, half-circle for 50%, and three-quarters of a circle for 75%).
- Walk around and check that students are creating pieces that are correctly proportioned.

Controlled Practice 10 minutes

B Look at the pictures and dates. Complete the...

- Read the directions and the words in the box. Ask students to repeat the words.
- Explain: *A step-mother is the woman who marries a divorced father with children. A step-sister is the daughter of the step-mother.*
- Do item 1 with the class. Point to the picture and ask: *What year is it?* (1997) Read the incomplete sentence and tell the class to call out the answer (T: *Ann and Bob Peterson get . . .* Ss: *married.*).
- Walk around and check that students are using the illustrations and the word box to write answers.
- Draw a simple time line (a line with the six years from the exercise on it) on the board and call on six students to write the answers under each year on the time line.
- On the board, write *blended family.* Explain: *This family is a blended family. This means that there was a divorce and a remarriage. Step-family members are part of a blended family.*

Read about blended families

Presentation
10 minutes

 2 READ

Listen. Read the article.

- Ask: *What's the title?* (The American Family Today)
- Tell students to look at the picture. Read the caption.
- Play CD 2, Track 8. Students listen and read along silently.
- Explain that special phrases (*blended families,* second paragraph) are put in quotation marks because they are words used in an unusual way.
- *Optional:* Play Track 8 again. Pause the CD after each of the following paragraphs and ask these questions:

  First paragraph: *When did Jimmy's parents get divorced?* (2006)

  Second paragraph: *How many families does Jimmy have?* (two)

  Third paragraph: *Is Jimmy's story common?* (Yes.)

Controlled Practice
15 minutes

3 CHECK YOUR UNDERSTANDING

A PAIRS. Read the article again. Look at the days...

- Read the directions.
- Tell students to look back at the article to find the answers to the questions.
- Walk around and if pairs have difficulty, point to the second paragraph where they can find the answer to each question.
- Call on students to say answers.

B What is the main idea of the article?...

- Remind students: *The main idea is the most important idea of the article.*
- Ask students to read the article again silently.
- Students compare answers with a partner.
- Call on a student to write the completed sentence on the board.
- To wrap up, point to the sentence on the board and ask: *What is this?* (the main idea of the article)

■■■ MULTILEVEL INSTRUCTION for 3B

Cross-ability The higher-level partner points to the part of the article where answers can be found. The lower-level partner reads the passage with the answer and then writes the answer.

■■■ Expansion: Speaking Practice for 3B

- Form like-ability groups of 4 or 5 students. Groups discuss the following questions for at least five minutes: *Does Jimmy have a good life? Why or why not? What are the pros and cons of having a blended family?* You may have to explain that *pros* are good things and *cons* are bad things, or problems. Everyone in each group must share an opinion.
- Call on representatives from each group to discuss the answers to the questions.

Communicative Practice
15 minutes

Show what you know!

Culture Connection
- Say: *Blended families are common in the U.S.*
- Ask: *What about in your country?*

PAIRS. Talk about it. Do you know someone...

- Say: *Think of a person you know who is in a blended family. In your notebook, make a list of all that person's step- or half-family members. Write their names and their relationship to the person you know (for example,* Jorge—Juana's step-brother). *If you don't know anyone in a blended family, make up information.*
- Pair students. Say: *Student A, explain your list to your partner. Say all the people in the list and what their relationship is to the person you know. Student B, listen to Student A. Then show Student A your list and explain all the people in it.*
- Walk around and check that students are discussing step- or half-relatives.

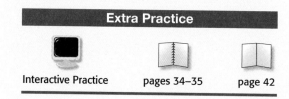

Extra Practice		
Interactive Practice	pages 34–35	page 42

CD2 T8

Listen. Read the article.

The American Family Today

In 2005, Jimmy had a small family. He had a mother and a father. He had no brothers or sisters. Then, in 2006, his parents got divorced.

In 2008, Jimmy's parents both got married again. Jimmy now lives with two "blended families." From Monday to Friday, Jimmy lives with his mother, his step-father, and his step-sister. On Saturdays and Sundays, he lives with his father, his step-mother and his two step-brothers. Jimmy says, "It's a little crazy. But I like my big family."

Jimmy's life isn't simple, but his story is common. Today, one out of three people in the United States is part of a blended family.

10-year-old Jimmy with his new family

3 CHECK YOUR UNDERSTANDING

A PAIRS. Read the article again. Look at the days of the week.
<u>Underline</u> the days Jimmy lives with his mother, his step-father, and his step-sister.
(Circle) the days Jimmy lives with his father, his step-mother, and his two step-brothers.

(Sunday) <u>Monday</u> <u>Tuesday</u> <u>Wednesday</u> <u>Thursday</u> <u>Friday</u> (Saturday)

B What is the main idea of the article? Complete the sentence.

___Blended families___ are common in the U.S. today.

Show what you know!

PAIRS. Talk about it. Do you know someone in a blended family? Who?
How many brothers and sisters does that person have?

Describe people

Listening and Speaking

1 BEFORE YOU LISTEN

CD2 T9

READ. Look at the picture of Zofia's parents and brother. Listen and read the description. Answer the questions.

Zofia's father is *average height* and *heavy*. He has *a mustache*. Her mother is *short* and *average weight*. She has *long hair*. Her brother is *tall* and *thin*. He has *a beard*.

1. Who has a mustache? _____Zofia's father_____

2. Who has a beard? _____Her brother_____

3. Who is average weight? _____Her mother_____

2 LISTEN

CD2 T10

A Look at the picture. Ernesto is showing Zofia a photo. Listen to their conversation. Who are they talking about?

a. Ernesto's father   b. Ernesto's mother   c. Ernesto's brother

CD2 T10

B Listen again. Check (✓) all the things that are true.

Ernesto's brother is _____.

☐ a painter   ✓ a carpenter

✓ great   ☐ interesting   ✓ fun   ☐ smart

☐ short   ✓ tall   ☐ heavy   ✓ thin

CD2 T11

C Listen to the whole conversation. Answer the questions.

1. Which picture shows Ernesto's brother?

a.   (b.)   c.

2. Is Ernesto's brother married?

(a.) yes   b. no

Getting Started 15 minutes

1 BEFORE YOU LISTEN

 READ. Look at the picture of Zofia's...

- Read the directions. Play CD 2, Track 9.
- Say: *Someone who is* average height *is not tall and not short. Someone who is* average weight *is not thin and not heavy.*
- Draw stick figures of a short person, an average height (in the middle) person, and a tall person. Label each *Short, Average Height,* and *Tall.*
- As needed, draw pictures of faces with a mustache and a beard to explain these words. Also draw heads with varying lengths of hair to differentiate between short and long hair.
- Tell students to look carefully at the picture before answering the questions.
- Call on students to say answers.

Presentation 15 minutes

2 LISTEN

Ⓐ **Look at the picture. Ernesto is...**

- Ask: *What do you see in the picture? What is happening?*
- Read the directions.
- Ask: *Who are they talking about?* Write the answer choices on the board and read them.
- Play CD 2, Track 10. Circle the correct answer on the board. Tell students to raise their hands if their guess was correct.

Teaching Tip

Optional: Remember that if students need additional support, tell them to read the Audio Script on page 283 as they listen to the conversations.

Ⓑ **Listen again. Check (✓) all the things...**

- Read the directions. Play Track 10 again. Students listen and check all the things that are true.
- Call on a student to say answers.

Ⓒ **Listen to the whole conversation....**

- Read the directions. Ask students to look at the pictures. For each one, call on students to describe the person in the picture (for example, a. *He has long hair. He has a mustache.*).
- Play CD 2, Track 11.
- Call on students to say answers.

Expansion: Vocabulary Practice for 2C

- With the class, brainstorm additional physical characteristics for hair (for example, *short hair, long hair, curly hair, straight hair*). Write several terms on the board and draw stick figures to illustrate.
- Tell students to write at least three characteristics that describe themselves (for example, *short, average weight, short hair*) in their notebooks.
- Call on students to share their answers with the class. Repeat after students, modeling complete sentences. For example: S: *Short hair.* T: *Yes, you have short hair.* Note: Do not ask students to produce complete sentences, since they have not yet learned the grammar.

Controlled Practice   20 minutes

3 CONVERSATION

 Listen and read the conversation....

- Note: This conversation is the same one students heard in Exercises 2A and B on page 74.
- Play CD 2, Track 12. Students listen and read along silently.
- Ask: *What's a carpenter?* (a person who builds things from wood, such as a house or a boat) As needed, explain *wood* by pointing to something made of wood, such as a bookshelf.
- Explain: *What's he like?* means *Tell me about this person.*
- Resume playing Track 12. Students listen and repeat.

Expansion: Grammar Practice for 3

- Pair students. Student A points to the first line and asks: *What is the possessive adjective?* Student B answers (*your*). Then Student B points to the second line and asks the same question. Pairs continue for the whole conversation.
- Then students circle all the possessive adjectives in the conversation. Tell students to look back at the grammar chart on page 70.

4 PRACTICE

A PAIRS. Practice the conversation. Then make...

- Pair students and tell them to practice the conversation in Exercise 3.
- Ask students to look at the family photo. Say: *Imagine that this is your family.* On the board, draw three stick figures to represent the three people in the picture. Label them *uncle*, *cousin*, and *aunt*.
- Ask students to call out the physical characteristics for each person's height (*short*, *average*, or *tall*), weight (*thin*, *heavy*), and hair (*short*, *long*). Write the correct description near each drawing on the board (for example, *uncle: average height, thin, short hair*). Tell students to write this information under each person in the picture on the page.
- Read the directions. Copy the conversation onto the board with blanks. Read through the conversation. When you come to a blank, fill it in with one of the choices.

- Ask on-level students to practice the conversation in front of the class.
- Tell pairs to take turns playing each role.
- Walk around and check that students are using pronouns and physical characteristics correctly.
- Tell students to stand, mingle, and practice the conversation with several new partners.
- Call on pairs to perform for the class.

Communicative Practice   10 minutes

B MAKE IT PERSONAL. PAIRS. Make your own...

- Read the directions. Student B talks about one person because students haven't studied the plural form *have* yet.
- With an above-level student, make up a new conversation and practice in front of the class. Base the conversation on Exercise 3.
- Pair students. Tell students they can talk about a friend if they want to.
- Walk around and check that students are using contractions correctly and are asking and answering questions properly.
- Call on pairs to perform for the class.

MULTILEVEL INSTRUCTION for 4B

Pre-level Tell students to use the vocabulary on page 74 as much as possible. Teach students to say *no* before a characteristic (for example, *no beard*) in order to give students greater opportunity to use all the vocabulary.

Above-level Student B discusses two people (for example, B: *My brother and my sister are here.* A: *Oh. What's your brother like?*). A can ask about each person separately. For added challenge, ask B to talk about one person they look like and one person they don't.

Extra Practice
Interactive Practice

3 CONVERSATION

CD2 T12

Listen and read the conversation. Then listen and repeat.

Zofia: Is your family here in this country?

Ernesto: My brother is here. He's a carpenter.

Zofia: Oh. What's he like?

Ernesto: He's great. He's a lot of fun.

Zofia: Does he look like you?

Ernesto: No. He's tall and thin and he has long hair.

4 PRACTICE

A PAIRS. Practice the conversation. Then make new conversations. Look at the picture. Imagine these are your uncle, cousin, and aunt.

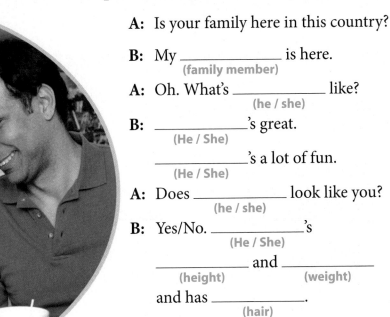

A: Is your family here in this country?

B: My _____ is here.
(family member)

A: Oh. What's _____ like?
(he / she)

B: _____'s great.
(He / She)

_____'s a lot of fun.
(He / She)

A: Does _____ look like you?
(he / she)

B: Yes/No. _____'s
(He / She)

_____ and _____
(height)   (weight)

and has _____.
(hair)

B MAKE IT PERSONAL. PAIRS. Make your own conversations. Student A, ask about your partner's family. Student B, talk about one person. Use true or made-up information.

Describe people

Grammar

Descriptions with *have*

| I
You
We
They | **have** | long hair. | He
She
Ernesto | **has** | short hair. |

1 PRACTICE

A Look at the picture. Underline the correct word.

1. My name is Paul. I **have** / **has** short hair.

2. My parents both **have** / **has** short hair, too.

3. My brother and I both **have** / **has** mustaches.
   But I also **have** / **has** a beard.

4. Our sister looks like our mother. But she
   have / **has** long hair.

B PAIRS. Look at the picture again. Circle Paul.

C PAIRS. Look at the pictures. Describe the people. Use *have* or *has*. Use periods. Answers will vary but could include:

1. Elias _has a mustache._

2. Ayantu _has short hair._

3. Sue and Edna _have long hair._

4. Feng _has long hair._

5. Jim and Bob _have mustaches._

6. Rafael _has short hair, a beard, and a mustache._

Describe people

Getting Started   5 minutes

- Say: *We're going to practice describing people with have. In the conversation on page 75, Ernesto used this grammar.*
- Play CD 2, Track 12. Students listen. Write on the board: *He has long hair.* Underline *He has.*

Presentation   5 minutes

Descriptions with *have*

- Copy the grammar charts onto the board or show the charts on Transparency 4.4 and cover the exercise.
- Read the sentences in the left chart and ask the class to repeat. Strongly pronounce *have* in isolation so that students notice the /v/ sound.
- Read the sentences in the right chart and ask the class to repeat. Since *have* and *has* sound similar, clearly differentiate *has* from *have* when you say them. To make sure students can discriminate between *have* and *has* when they hear them, ask the class to write *has* on one scrap of paper and *have* on another. Say each word randomly and ask the class to hold up the word they hear.
- Using students with varying hair lengths as examples, point to students and tell the class to call out sentences to describe them. Provide practice with examples from both charts so that students can correctly identify when to use *have* or *has*.
- Ask students to close their books. Remove any visual aids for the charts. On the board, write several incomplete sentences:

  We _____ short hair. You _____ a mustache.

  He _____ a beard. Maria _____ long hair.

  Call on students to come to the board and complete the sentences with *have/has.*
- If you are using the transparency, do the exercise with the class.

Controlled Practice   10 minutes

1 PRACTICE

Ⓐ **Look at the picture. Underline the correct word.**

- Read the directions and the example. Write the example on the board and ask: *What's the subject?* (I) Ask: *Do you use* have *or* has *with* I? (have)

- Say: *The sentences are about people in the picture. Find the people in the picture when you answer.*
- Remind students to look at the subject of the sentence before answering and to look at the grammar chart for help.
- Students compare answers with a partner.
- Call on students to say answers.

Ⓑ **PAIRS. Look at the picture again. Circle Paul.**

- Read the directions.
- Hold up the picture and ask: *Where is Paul in the picture?* Tell students to answer using *on the left/right* or *next to*, which they learned in Unit 3. (*Possible answers:* Paul is on the right. Paul is next to his sister.)

Communicative Practice   5 minutes

Ⓒ **PAIRS. Look at the pictures. Describe the people....**

- Ask students to look at the pictures.
- Read the directions and the example.
- Walk around and check that students are using *have/has* correctly and are adding periods.
- Tell students to take turns reading their answers to each other.

▬▬▬ **MULTILEVEL INSTRUCTION for 1C**

Cross-ability Ask higher-level students to check their partners' answers. Higher-level students can also ask their partners to come up with one more descriptive sentence for each picture (for example, *1. Elias has short hair.*) and to write it on a piece of paper. If the lower-level partner has difficulty, the higher-level partner can help.

▬▬▬ **Expansion: Writing Practice for 1C**

- Form groups of 5. Each student writes three sentences to describe one person in the group (for example, *He has short hair. He has a beard. He looks like Marc Anthony.*).
- Each student reads his or her sentences out loud, and the rest of the group guesses the person (Ss: *Is it Hugo?* S: *Yes!*).

Presentation   10 minutes

Descriptions with *be* and *have*

- Copy the grammar charts onto the board or show the charts on Transparency 4.4 and cover the exercise. Tell the class they will learn how to describe people using *be* and *have*.
- Read sentences from the left chart and ask the class to repeat.
- On the board, write several example sentences with blanks for *be*. Use names of your students for third-person singular. Call on students to complete the sentences. Write in the correct form of *be*.
- Do the same for the right chart. Call on students to complete the sentences. Write in the correct form of *have*.
- Say: *Use* be *to talk about height and weight. Use* have *to talk about hair.*
- If you are using the transparency, do the exercise with the class.

Controlled Practice   10 minutes

2 PRACTICE

Ⓐ Read about Donna's family. Underline...

- Read the directions. Say: *Remember, use* be *for height and weight. Use* have *for hair.*
- Walk around and check that students are choosing answers based on whether the physical characteristic is related to hair (*have*) or weight (*be*).
- To check answers, read the paragraph and tell the class to call out answers.

Communicative Practice   20 minutes

Ⓑ PAIRS. Look at the pictures of Donna and...

- Read A in the example conversation with an on-level student reading B and finishing the line.
- Ask: *What are the differences in the pictures?* (In picture A, Donna has short hair. She is thin. In picture B she has long hair. She is heavy. In picture A, Donna's husband is heavy. He has long hair and no beard. In picture B, he is average weight. He has short hair and a beard.)
- Pair students. Call on pairs to perform for the class.

Show what you know!

GROUPS OF 3. Look at your classmates. Complete...

- Copy the chart onto the board. Play A and read the example conversation with an on-level student.
- Ask: *Who has a beard?* (Carlos, Chen, and Viktor) Write *3* in the chart. Read the directions.
- Pair students. Say: *Now, Student A, ask* Who has . . .? *or* Who is . . .? *for every box. Student B, answer the questions.* Write the question starters for A on the board and point to them as you speak.
- Walk around and check that students are summarizing the information (for example, *So, three women have . . .*).
- To wrap up, call out questions to the whole class for every element in the chart (for example, *Who has a beard?*) and call on students to answer.

▬▬ MULTILEVEL INSTRUCTION

Cross-ability Assign a higher-level student to be a group leader. The group leader is responsible for asking questions (for example, *Who has long hair?*). The lower-level students must answer the questions, and the leader records the information in the chart and summarizes it.

▬▬ Expansion: Vocabulary Practice

- Redo "Show what you know!" with new categories: *curly hair, wavy hair, straight hair, thin hair,* and *bald.* As needed, explain each term by drawing a stick figure with each hair style.

Progress Check

Can you . . . describe people?

Say: *We have practiced describing people. Now, look at the question at the bottom of the page. Can you describe people?* Tell students to write a checkmark in the box.

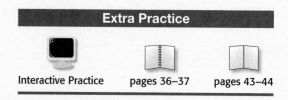

Extra Practice		
Interactive Practice	pages 36–37	pages 43–44

Descriptions with *be* and *have*

	Be	
I	**am**	short.
She	**is**	tall.
We	**are**	average height.
They	**are**	heavy.

	Have	
I	**have**	a mustache.
She	**has**	long hair.
We	**have**	short hair.
They	**have**	beards.

2 PRACTICE

A **Read about Donna's family. Underline the correct words.**

Donna's mother **is** / **has** average height and weight, but her sister **is** / **are** short and heavy. Her sister and her mother both **has** / **have** short hair. Donna's father **is** / **has** a beard, and her brother **is** / **has** a mustache. Her father and her brother both **are** / **have** short hair. Her father **is** / **has** thin, but her brother **is** / **has** heavy.

B **PAIRS. Look at the pictures of Donna and her husband. Talk about the differences.**

A: *In Picture A, Donna is average weight. In Picture B, she's heavy.*
B: *In Picture A, she has . . .*

May 2001

April 2007

Show what you know! Describe people

GROUPS OF 3. Look at your classmates. Complete the chart. Write the number of students.

Beard	Mustache	Long hair	Short hair	Tall	Short

A: *Who has a beard?*
B: *Carlos and Chen have beards.*
A: *Viktor has a beard, too.*
B: *OK. So, three men have beards. What about mustaches?*

Can you...describe people? ☐

Life Skills

1   TALK ABOUT MONTHS AND DATES

A   **CLASS.** What are some important dates in your family?

CD2 T13

B   Look at the calendar pages. Listen and point. Then listen and repeat.

Sunday	Monday	Tuesday	Wednesday	Thursday	Friday	Saturday
1	2	3	4	5	6	7
8	9	10	11	12	13	14
15	16	17	18	19	20	21
22	23	24	25	26	27	28
29	30	31				

January
February
March
April
May
June
July
August
September
October
November
December

2   PRACTICE

A   **GROUPS OF 3.** Student A, say a month.
Student B, repeat the month and say the next month.
Student C, keep going. Then Student B, say a new month.

A: *March.*
B: *March, April.*
C: *March, April, May.*
B: *August.*
C: *August, . . .*

CD2 T14

B   Look at the numbers. Listen and point. Then listen and repeat.

1st	2nd	3rd	4th	5th	6th
first	second	third	fourth	fifth	sixth

7th	8th	9th	10th	11th	12th
seventh	eighth	ninth	tenth	eleventh	twelfth

13th	14th	15th	16th	17th	18th
thirteenth	fourteenth	fifteenth	sixteenth	seventeenth	eighteenth

19th	20th	30th	31st
nineteenth	twentieth	thirtieth	thirty-first

For dates we say *first, second, third,* but we write 1, 2, 3. For example, we say *January fifteenth,* but we write *January 15.*

CD2 T15

C   Look at the calendar above for January. Listen and point to the dates.

Can you…talk about months and dates? ☐

Getting Started   5 minutes

1 TALK ABOUT MONTHS AND DATES

A CLASS. What are some important dates in...

- Write today's date on the board.
- Hold up your book and point to the calendar. Ask: *What is this?* (a calendar) *How many months do you see?* (12) *What is today?* ([today's date]) Point to the date on the board if students need a visual aid to answer the question. Clearly pronounce today's date and ask the class to repeat.
- Ask the question in the directions. If students don't understand, name some important dates on the board, explaining the significance of each as needed (for example, *My birthday is February 10. My son's birthday is . . .*).

Presentation   5 minutes

B Look at the calendar pages. Listen...

- Read the directions.
- Play CD 2, Track 13. Students listen and point.
- Resume playing Track 13. Students listen and repeat.

Controlled Practice   30 minutes

2 PRACTICE

A GROUPS OF 3. Student A, say a month....

- Read the directions.
- Play A and read the example with two on-level students.
- Form groups and assign roles. Tell students to look at the calendar pages if they need help with the names of the months.
- Walk around and check that students are saying months in order.

B Look at the numbers. Listen and...

- Read the directions.
- Play CD 2, Track 14. Students listen and point.
- Resume playing Track 14. Students listen and repeat. Pause the track after *4th*, pronounce *4th* (voiceless *th*), and ask the class to repeat. Model how to pronounce voiceless *th* and make sure that the class can do it. Say: *Put your tongue between your teeth and breathe out* [demonstrate].
- Read the note about writing and saying dates.

C Look at the calendar above...

- Read the directions. Say a few dates and ask the class to repeat.
- Play CD 2, Track 15. Walk around and check that students are pointing to the dates in the calendar for January.
- If students have difficulty, play Track 15 again.
- To check comprehension, copy the January calendar onto the board. Call on individual students to come to the front of the class. Say dates in random order (for example, *January 22nd*) and tell the student to point to them.

Expansion: Listening Practice for 2C

- Pair students.
- Student A dictates three important dates in his or her family (for example, A: *March 16th, May 20th, August 1st*). Student B writes them down and shows them to Student A for confirmation.
- Then, Student B asks the significance of each date (for example, B: *Why is March 16th important?* A: *It's my daughter's birthday.*). Partners switch roles and repeat.

Progress Check

Can you . . . talk about months and dates?

Say: *We have practiced talking about months and dates. Now, look at the question at the bottom of the page. Can you talk about months and dates?* Tell students to write a checkmark in the box.

D Look at the calendars. Write the dates. Use...

- Read the directions and the Writing Watch note.
- As a warm-up, ask: *What is today's date?* Point to the date on the board and tell students to copy it into their notebooks. Say: *Write yesterday's date in your notebook. Write tomorrow's date in your notebook.* Look around the room to see that students are writing the correct dates and capitalizing the months. Then write these dates on the board. Point to them as you say them and allow students to check their own work.
- As students complete the exercise, walk around and check that they are writing dates in month/day/year order.
- Call on students to say the dates. Correct students who say, for example, *twenty-four* instead of *twenty-fourth*. To wrap up, write the dates on the board so students can check that they wrote them the same way.

E Look at the calendars again. Write the dates...

- Read the directions. On the board, write today's date in numbers as in the example. Say: *Each of the 12 months has a number. January is 1. February is 2, and so on.*
- Walk around and check that students are writing dates in the correct order and using dashes.
- Call on students to write answers on the board.

F 🔊 Listen to the conversations. Which...

- Read the directions. Play CD 2, Track 16.
- To check answers, play Track 16 again and write answers on the board as the track plays.
- To reinforce the differences between the answer choices, read each one and ask the class to repeat.

3 GIVE YOUR BIRTHDAY

🔊 Listen and read the conversation. Then...

- Play CD 2, Track 17. Students listen and read along silently.
- Write *July 29* on the board. Point to it and say: *When you read this date, remember to say* th—twenty-ninth.
- Resume playing Track 17. Students listen and repeat.

Communicative Practice   20 minutes

4 PRACTICE

A Walk around the room. Practice the conversation...

- Write the conversation in Exercise 3 on the board with blanks for the name and birthday date.
- Practice the conversation with an on-level student. Fill in the blanks.
- Pair students. Say: *Use your own names and birthdays. Take turns playing A and B.*
- Walk around and check that students are pronouncing ordinal numbers correctly.
- Call on pairs to perform for the class.

B NETWORK. Find classmates with the same...

- Read the directions. Ask several students: *What is your birthday month?* Write your own birthday month on the board and ask if anyone has a birthday in that month. Write each student's name whose birthday falls on a day in your birthday month next to the day of his or her birthday.
- Say: *Walk around and ask other students when their birthday is. When you find another student with the same birthday month, stay with them.*
- Once all the groups are formed, tell each group to make a calendar page for their month and to include their names on the dates of their birthdays.

▬▬ Expansion: Speaking Practice for 4B

- When all the calendar pages are finished, ask one representative from each group to present the calendar to the class by reading the birthday dates and names (*Rosa's birthday is May 22. Rafael's . . .*).

Progress Check

Can you . . . give your birthday and date of birth?
Say: *We have practiced giving birthdays and dates of birth. Now, look at the question at the bottom of the page. Can you give your birthday and date of birth?* Tell students to write a checkmark in the box.

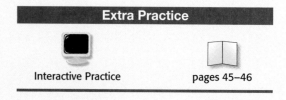

Extra Practice

Interactive Practice   pages 45–46

• For dates, we write the month first, then the day, then the year. Example: *April 5, 2010.*

• Start months with a capital letter.

D Look at the calendars. Write the dates. Use this year.

vers
ary in
cises
d E
ending
he
nt year.

February						
SUN	MON	TUES	WED	THUR	FRI	SAT
1	2	3	4	5	6	7
8	9	10	11	12	13	14
15	16	17	18	19	20	21
22	23	㉔	25	26	27	28

May						
SUN	MON	TUES	WED	THUR	FRI	SAT
1	2	③	4	5	6	7
8	9	10	11	12	13	14
15	16	17	18	19	20	21
22	23	24	25	26	27	28
29	30	31				

July						
SUN	MON	TUES	WED	THUR	FRI	SAT
1	2	3	4	5	6	7
8	9	10	11	12	13	14
15	16	⑰	18	19	20	21
22	23	24	25	26	27	28
29	30	31				

November						
SUN	MON	TUES	WED	THUR	FRI	SAT
1	2	3	4	5	6	7
8	9	10	11	12	13	14
15	16	17	18	19	20	21
22	23	24	25	26	27	28
29	㉚					

February 24, 20_ _   May 3, 20_ _   July 17, 20_ _   November 30, 20_ _

E Look at the calendars again. Write the dates in numbers.

1. ___2-24-10___   2. ___5-3-_ ____   3. ___7-17-_ ____   4. ___11-30-_ ____

CD2 T16

F 🔘 Listen to the conversations. Which date do you hear?

1. a. 3–4–77   ⓑ 3–14–77   4. a. 8–30–95   ⓑ 8–31–95
2. ⓐ 10–2–01   b. 2–10–01   5. ⓐ 12–17–59   b. 12–7–59
3. a. 6–28–88   ⓑ 5–28–88   6. ⓐ 9–2–62   b. 9–22–52

3 GIVE YOUR BIRTHDAY

CD2 T17

🔘 Listen and read the conversation. Then listen and repeat.

A: Yu-Ping, when is your birthday?

B: My birthday is July 29. When is your birthday?

4 PRACTICE

A Walk around the room. Practice the conversation above. Use your own names and birthdays.

B NETWORK. Find classmates with the same birthday month as you. Form a group. Then create a calendar page for your birthday month. Write your names on the dates of your birthdays.

Can you...give your birthday and date of birth? ☐

Listening and Speaking

1 BEFORE YOU LISTEN

A Look at picture 1. Label the people in the picture. Use the words in the box.

> boys   girls   children (kids)

children

girls

boys

B CLASS. Look at picture 2. Read the conversation. Then read the information.

In the U.S., it's OK to ask children their age. We usually do not ask adults their age. What about in your country?

How old are you?

I'm ten. I'm in the fourth grade.

2 LISTEN

A Look at the picture. Zofia is babysitting for her friend's children.

Guess: How old are the children?

CD2 T18

B Listen to Zofia's phone conversation with Assefa. Was your guess in Exercise A correct?

Listen again. Complete the sentences.

1. The boy is in the _____fifth_____ grade.
   a. fourth   (b.) fifth   c. sixth

2. The girl is in the _____first_____ grade.
   (a.) first   b. third   c. fourth

CD2 T19

C Listen to the whole conversation. Answer the questions.

1. Who says Terry is friendly?
   (a.) Zofia   b. Zofia's friend   c. Kevin

2. Who calls Terry "Terry the Terrible"?
   a. Zofia   (b.) Zofia's friend   c. Kevin

Give a child's age and grade in school

Getting Started   5 minutes

Culture Connection

• Say: *In the United States, children go to elementary school. Elementary school starts with kindergarten. Children begin kindergarten when they are four or five years old. Then there is first grade, second grade, ...*

• Ask: *In your country, do you have elementary school? How old are children when they go to school?*

• Say: *Every school district in the United States has different laws or rules about going to school. It is important to know when your child needs to go to school.*

• Ask: *Do you have a child in elementary school?* Call on students to answer and explain more if possible (for example, *Yes, I have a daughter. She is seven years old. She is in second grade.*).

1 BEFORE YOU LISTEN

A **Look at picture 1. Label the people in the picture....**

• Read the directions.

• Say: Boys *is the plural form of* boy. Girls *is the plural form of* girls. Children *means* boys, girls, or both.

• Say: *You can also say* kids *instead of* children. *Just remember that* kids *is informal—you use it in conversation.*

• Students compare answers with a partner.

• Call on students to say answers by prompting them, for example, *Who is first?* (children)

B CLASS. **Look at picture 2. Read the conversation....**

• Read the directions and information while students read along silently.

• Ask: *What about in your country?* Ask on-level and above-level students to explain why in their country asking adults about their age is OK or not. (*Possible answers*: In my country, it is rude to talk about age. In my country, only close family members talk about age. In my country, we say our age in a job interview. All people talk about age.)

Presentation   25 minutes

2 LISTEN

A **Look at the picture.... Guess:...**

• Read the directions. Ask: *What do you see in the picture? What is happening?* As needed, explain that *babysitting* is when you watch children for a few hours when their parents are not home.

• Ask: *How old are the children?* Write *Boy* and *Girl* on the board. Call on students to guess. Write their guesses on the board.

• Tell students they will listen for the answer in Exercise B.

B **Listen to Zofia's phone conversation...**

• Read the directions. Play CD 2, Track 18.

• Circle the correct answer on the board. (The boy is 11, and the girl is 6.) Ask: *Was your guess correct?*

Teaching Tip

Optional: Remember that if students need additional support, tell them to read the Audio Script on page 283 as they listen to the conversations.

Listen again. Complete the sentences.

• Read the directions and the sentences and answer choices. Play Track 18 again.

• Students compare answers with a partner.

• Call on students to say answers.

C **Listen to the whole conversation....**

• Read the directions and the questions and answer choices. Play CD 2, Track 19.

• Students compare answers with a partner.

• Call on students to say answers.

• Ask: *Why does Zofia's friend (Terry's mother) call Terry "Terry the Terrible"?* Hint: *Look at the picture. What is Terry doing?* (She's drawing on the wall.) *Does Zofia see Terry drawing on the wall?* (No.)

3 CONVERSATION

A Listen. Then listen and repeat.

- Read the directions and the Pronunciation Watch note.
- Ask students to name the letters that are vowels. Write them on the board. Ask: *What are consonants?* (all the other letters)
- Read the sentences. Write the sentences with the links on the board.
- Say each sentence slowly and ask the class to repeat. Then say them at normal speed (with connected sounds) and ask the class to repeat. Next, slow down the connected sound speech and ask the class to repeat so that they notice that the consonant sound is merging with the vowel sound in the following word.
- Play CD 2, Track 20. Students listen.
- Resume playing Track 20. Students listen and repeat.

B Listen and read the conversation....

- Note: This conversation is the same one students heard in Exercise 2B on page 80.
- Play CD 2, Track 21. Students listen and read along silently.
- Resume playing Track 21. Students listen and repeat. There is an extra pause in Zofia's last line (after *fifth grade*) to give students time to repeat.

Controlled Practice   20 minutes

4 PRACTICE

A PAIRS. Practice the conversation. Then make new...

- Read the conversation in Exercise 3B to the class and ask students to repeat the places where the consonant sound of a word links to the vowel sound of the next word:

      A: Where are

      B: I'm at

      A: How old, old are

      B: son is, He's in, daughter is, she's in

- Pair students and tell them to practice the conversation in Exercise 3B.

- Then, in Exercise 4A, point to each picture and ask: *How old are the students? What grade are they in?*
- Read the directions.
- Copy the conversation in Exercise 4A onto the board with blanks. Read through the conversation. When you come to a blank, fill it in with the correct words from the boxes.
- Tell pairs to take turns playing each role and to use different ages and grades to fill in the blanks.
- Tell students to stand, mingle, and practice the conversation with several new partners. Call on pairs to perform for the class.

Communicative Practice   10 minutes

B MAKE IT PERSONAL. PAIRS. Make your own...

- With an above-level student, make up a new conversation and practice in front of the class. Base the conversation on Exercise 3B. Play A. Continue the conversation for three or four exchanges.
- Pair students. Walk around and check that students are asking and answering questions about age.

■ MULTILEVEL INSTRUCTION for 4B

Cross-ability The lower-level student in each pair should play A. The higher-level student is responsible for asking more questions (for example, *How old are they? When are their birthdays? What grade are they in?*).

■ Expansion: Speaking Practice for 4B

- Tell students to include information about physical characteristics (for example, hair length, height) while talking about children they know.

5 LIFE SKILLS WRITING

Turn to page 256 and ask students to complete the emergency contact form. See pages Txi–Txii for general notes about Life Skills Writing activities.

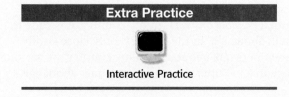

Extra Practice

Interactive Practice

3 CONVERSATION

CD2 T20

A 🔘 **Listen. Then listen and repeat.**

Her son is eleven.

He's in the fifth grade.

Where are you?

CD2 T21

B 🔘 **Listen and read the conversation. Then listen and repeat.**

Assefa: Hi, Zofia. Where are you?

Zofia: I'm at my friend's house. I'm babysitting for her kids.

Assefa: Oh. How old are they?

Zofia: Well, her son is eleven. He's in the fifth grade.
And her daughter is six. She's in the first grade.

4 PRACTICE

A **PAIRS. Practice the conversation. Then make new conversations. Use the information in the boxes.**

A: Hi! Where are you?

B: I'm at my friend's house. I'm babysitting for her kids.

A: Oh. How old are they?

B: Well, her son is _____ . He's in the _____ .
And her daughter is _____ . She's in the
_____ .

12 (years old)
6th grade

8 (years old)
3rd grade

16 (years old)
11th grade

15 (years old)
10th grade

B **MAKE IT PERSONAL. PAIRS. Make your own conversations. Talk about children you know. Use true or made-up information.**

A: *My sister has two children.*
B: *Oh, really? How old are they?*

7 (years old)
2nd grade

10 (years old)
4th grade

5 LIFE SKILLS WRITING

Complete an emergency contact form. See page 256.

Grammar

Questions with *How old*

How old	are	you? they? your friend's children?

How old	is	he? she? Terry?

PRACTICE

A Complete the conversations. Ask about age. Use capital letters when necessary.

Date of birth:
Jan. 4, 1975

Date of birth:
May 6, 2003

Date of birth:
Oct. 4, 1987

Answers will vary depending on the current year.

1. **A:** How old _____is_____ Ya-Wen's son?

   B: He's _____.

2. **A:** How old _____are_____ Eric's cousins?

   B: They're _____.

3. **A:** _____How old are_____ Diego's sisters?

   B: _____They're [   ]._____.

Date of birth:
Aug. 11, 1926

Date of birth:
June 2, 2000

Date of birth:
Sept. 30, 2003

You
Date of birth:

4. **A:** _____How old is_____ Soo-Jin's grandmother?

   B: _____She's [   ]._____.

5. **A:** _How old are_ Eva's kids?

   B: Her son _____is [   ]_____ and her daughter _____is [   ]_____.

6. **A:** How old _____are_____ you?

   B: I'd rather not say!

B PAIRS. Look at these photos of famous people. Guess. How old are they?

Zhang Ziyi

George Clooney

Diego Maradona

Oprah Winfrey

A: *How old is Zhang Ziyi?*
B: *I don't know. I think she's (around) twenty-five.*
A: *Oh, no. I think she's (around) thirty-five.*

Getting Started   5 minutes

- Say: *We're going to study questions with* How old. *In the conversation on page 81, Assefa used this grammar.*
- Play CD 2, Track 21. Students listen. Write *How old are they?* on the board. Underline *How old.*

Presentation   5 minutes

Questions with *How old*

- Copy the grammar charts onto the board or show the charts on Transparency 4.5 and cover the exercise.
- Read the questions in the left chart and ask the class to repeat.
- Read the questions in the right chart and ask the class to repeat.
- Ask students to close their books. Remove any visual aids for the chart. On the board, write: *How old _____ you? How old _____ he?*
- Call on students to tell you whether to put *is* or *are* in the blanks.
- Then ask the question with *you* and call on a few students to answer. After a student answers, ask the rest of the class: *How old is he/she?* Find two students who are the same age and ask the class: *How old are they?*
- If you are using the transparency, do the exercise with the class.

Controlled Practice   10 minutes

PRACTICE

A **Complete the conversations. Ask about age. Use...**

- Read the directions and the example.
- Write the son's date of birth on the board. Calculate his current age based on today's date. Write his age on the board and ask the class to complete B's line.
- Tell students to look at the pictures before they answer.
- Remind students to use subject pronouns for B's line in items 3 and 4.

- Walk around and, as needed, help students with the subtraction calculation to determine the age of the people in the exercise.
- Students compare answers with a partner.
- Call on students to perform for the class.

Community Building
Pair or group students so they can help one another do the calculations.

Communicative Practice   10 minutes

B **PAIRS. Look at these photos of famous people....**

- Read the directions. Say each name, ask the class to repeat, and say why each person is famous (*Zhang Ziyi is an actress. George Clooney is an actor. Diego Maradona is an athlete; he plays soccer. Oprah Winfrey is a talk-show host; she is on TV.*).
- Play A and read the example conversation with an on-level student.
- Pair students. Tell students to use *I don't know* and *I think* when they talk with their partner. Explain that here *around* means *close to* or *about*.
- Walk around and check that each partner is guessing the ages of the famous people.

▬▬ MULTILEVEL INSTRUCTION for B
Cross-ability The higher-level partner plays A and initiates the conversation.

▬▬ Expansion: Speaking Practice for B
- Pairs students and tell them to cut out pictures of people from magazines and guess how old the people are.
- Then call on students to present their pictures to the class while the class guesses how old they are. Above-level students can offer why they think a person is a particular age (for example, *I think he's 50 because he has gray hair.*).

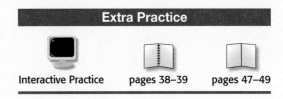

Extra Practice		
Interactive Practice	pages 38–39	pages 47–49

REVIEW Show what you know!

1 GRAMMAR

Look at the picture. Who is Tina? Complete...

- Read the directions and the example. Explain: *The picture is Tina's family. When you read, look at the picture to guess who is who.*
- Tell students to refer back to the grammar charts on pages 70 (possessive adjectives) and 76–77 (descriptions with *be* and *have*) as needed.
- Say: *Read the sentence before you answer and remember to look at the picture.*
- Students compare answers with a partner.
- Read the paragraph and call on individual students to say answers. When reviewing answers, point out how the sentence before reveals the correct answer (for example, *For number 2, the answer is* My *because Tina is speaking in number 1.*).
- Ask: *Who is Tina?* (the tall woman in the back row with a white blouse)

2 WRITING

STEP 1. Look at the picture again. Who is Morris?...

- Read the directions and the example.
- Remind students that they are writing about Morris.
- Students compare answers with a partner.
- Read the paragraph and call on individual students to say answers. Ask: *Who is Morris?* (the man in the middle of the back row)

STEP 2. Look at the picture and read the paragraph...

- Read the directions. Go back to the picture again and find ask: *Where is Mike?* (He is next to Tina. He has a green shirt.)
- Say: *You are Mike. Write about your family. Write at least five sentences.*
- Read the first sentence and ask the class to repeat. Ask: *Is Mike tall?* (Yes.) Write on the board: *I am _____.* Call on students to complete the sentence. (I am tall.)
- Walk around and check that students are writing sentences similar to the ones in Step 1.
- Students compare answers with a partner.
- Call on some students to write sentences on the board.

 Expansion: Speaking Practice for STEP 2

- Review questions with *How old* from page 82.
- Pair students and tell them to read their writing from Step 2 to each other. The partner asks questions about the writing (for example, *How old are your daughters?*).

CD-ROM Practice

■ Go to the CD-ROM for more practice.

If your students need more practice with the vocabulary, grammar, and competencies in Unit 4, encourage them to review the activities on the CD-ROM. This review can also help students prepare for the final role play on the following Expand page.

Extra Practice

pages 40–41

1 GRAMMAR

Look at the picture. Who is Tina? Complete the paragraph about her. Choose the correct words.

Back: Mike, Tina, Morris, Anna, Cindy, and Ben
Front: Laurel, Chris, Jennie, and Amanda

_____My_____ name is Tina. _____My_____
1. (Our / My)   **2.** (My / Her)
husband's name is Mike. We _____are_____
3. (are / have)
both 53 years old, and we're both tall and thin.

_____We_____ have two children. _____Our_____
4. (Our / We)   **5.** (Your / Our)
son's name is Chris, and our daughter's name is

Laurel. Chris is married. _____His_____ wife's name is Jennie. Chris and Jennie have a
6. (His / Her)

daughter. _____Her_____ name is Amanda. She _____is_____ ten years old. Amanda is
7. (Their / Her)   **8.** (has / is)

_____our_____ first granddaughter! She _____is_____ tall, and she _____has_____ long
9. (our / their)   **10.** (is / has)   **11.** (is / has)

hair. Amanda looks just like _____her_____ Aunt Laurel!
12. (my / her)

2 WRITING

STEP 1. Look at the picture again. Who is Morris? Complete the sentences about him. Use *my*, *their*, or the correct form of *be* or *have*. Use capital letters when necessary.

_____My_____ name is Morris. I _____am_____ 75 years old. I _____am_____ tall

and I _____have_____ a beard. _____My_____ wife's name is Anna. She _____is_____

tall, too, and she _____has_____ short hair. We _____have_____ two daughters.

_____Their_____ names _____are_____ Tina and Cindy.

STEP 2. Look at the picture and read the paragraph about Tina. Imagine you are Mike. Write about yourself and your family. Use the paragraph about Morris as an example.

Answers will vary but could include:

My name is Mike. I... am 53 years old. I am tall and I have a mustache. My wife's name is Tina. She is tall,

too, and she has short hair. We have two children. Their names are Chris and Laurel.

_____

_____

3 ACT IT OUT — What do you say?

CD2 T22
STEP 1. 🔘 **Listen to the conversation.**

STEP 2. **PAIRS. You are co-workers.**

> **Student A:** Ask about your friend's family.
> - Ask who is in your friend's family.
> - Choose a family member. Ask, "What is he/she like?"
> - Are there children in your friend's family? Ask about their ages and grades in school.
> - Ask about the children's birthdays.

> **Student B:** Answer your friend's questions about your family. Use your own information, or choose a picture to talk about.

4 READ AND REACT — Problem-solving

STEP 1. **Read about Hae-Jin's problem.**

Hae-Jin lives in Los Angeles with her family. Her grandfather lives in a different part of L.A. He lives alone.

Hae-Jin works at a bank. Her grandfather calls her at work every day. He just wants to talk. But Hae-Jin can't talk on the phone at work.

STEP 2. **PAIRS. Talk about it. What is Hae-Jin's problem? What can Hae-Jin do? Here are some ideas.**

- She can turn her phone off.
- She can say, "Please don't call me at work."
- She can talk to her manager.
- She can _____.

5 CONNECT

For your Goal-setting Activity, go to page 247.
For your Team Project, go to page 267.

3 ACT IT OUT

STEP 1. 💿 Listen to the conversation.

- Play CD 2, Track 22. Students listen.
- As needed, play Track 22 again to aid comprehension.

STEP 2. PAIRS. You are co-workers.

- Read the directions and the guidelines for Students A and B.
- Talk about each picture. Ask students to call out information they see in each picture.
- Pair students. Students practice at their desk with their partner. If possible, tell Student B to use a picture of his or her family to show Student A. Student B may also use one of the pictures on the page.
- Walk around and check that Student A is asking about what Student B's family member is like.
- Call on pairs to perform for the class. While pairs are performing, use the scoring rubric on page Txiv to evaluate each student's vocabulary, grammar, fluency, and how well they complete the task.
- *Optional:* After each pair finishes, discuss the strengths and weakness of each performance either in front of the class or privately.

4 READ AND REACT

STEP 1. Read about Hae-Jin's problem.

- Say: *We are going to read about a student's problem, and then we need to think about a solution.*
- Read the directions.
- Read the story while students follow along silently. Pause after each sentence to allow time for students to comprehend. Periodically stop and ask simple *Wh-* questions to check comprehension, for example, *Who lives with her family?* (Hae-Jin) *Does her grandfather live alone?* (Yes.) *Where does Hae-Jin work?* (at a bank)

STEP 2. PAIRS. Talk about it. What is Hae-Jin's....

- Pair students. Read the directions and the question.
- Read the ideas in the list. Give pairs a couple of minutes to discuss possible solutions for Hae-Jin.
- Ask: *Which ideas are good?* Call on students to say their opinion about the ideas in the list (for example, *I don't think she can turn her phone off because her grandfather will be sad.*).
- Now tell students to think of one new idea not in the box (for example, *She can call him after work.*) and to write it in the blank. Encourage students to think of more than one idea and to write them in their notebooks.
- Call on pairs to say their additional solutions. Write any particularly good ones on the board and ask students if they think it is a good idea, too (*Do you think this is a good idea? Why or why not?*).

▄▄ MULTILEVEL INSTRUCTION for STEP 2

Pre-level For additional support, students work in groups of 3.

Above-level Tell pairs to cover the list of ideas and to come up with three or four of their own solutions first. Then they can look at the list in the book to compare.

5 CONNECT

Turn to page 247 for the Goal-setting Activity and page 267 for guidelines for the Team Project. See pages Txi–Txii for general notes about teaching these activities.

Progress Check

Which goals can you check off? Go back to page 65.
Ask students to turn to page 65 and check off any remaining goals they have reached. Call on students to say which goals they will practice outside of class.

Shop, Shop, Shop

Classroom Materials/Extra Practice

CD 2
Tracks 23–42

Transparencies 5.1–5.6
Vocabulary Cards Unit 5

MCA
Unit 5

Workbook
Unit 5

Interactive Practice
Unit 5

Unit Overview

Goals
- See the list of goals on the facing page.

Grammar
- Simple present affirmative statements
- Simple present *yes/no* questions and short answers; contractions
- Simple present negative statements; contractions

Pronunciation
- Sentence rhythm: stress on important words

Reading
- Read an article about U.S. dollar coins

Writing
- Write sentences about problems with clothing
- Write sentences about things people need, want, or have

Life Skills Writing
- Write a personal check

Preview
- Set the context of the unit by asking questions about shopping (for example, *Do you like to shop? Where do you shop?*).
- Hold up page 85 or show Transparency 5.1. Read the unit title and ask the class to repeat.
- Explain: *Many people like to shop.* Shop, shop, shop *means that people shop a lot.*
- Say: *Look at the picture.* Ask the Preview question: *What do you see?* If students call out various types of clothing, tell them they will learn more words for clothes in this unit.

Unit Goals
- Point to the Unit Goals. Explain that this list shows what the class will be studying in this unit.
- Tell students to read the goals silently.
- Say each goal and ask the class to repeat. To explain any unfamiliar vocabulary, bring in the following items or show them from the book: receipts (page 93), price tags (page 93), and personal checks (page 257) to illustrate. Explain the following term:

    Return something: *To take something that you do not want back to the store and get your money back*
- Tell students to circle one goal that is very important to them.
- Call on students to say the goal they circled.

Shop, Shop, Shop

Preview

**Look at the picture.
What do you see?**

UNIT GOALS

- ☐ Talk about colors
- ☐ Talk about clothes
- ☐ Talk about things you need, want, or have
- ☐ Use U.S. money
- ☐ Talk about prices
- ☐ Read price tags
- ☐ Read a receipt
- ☐ Write a personal check
- ☐ Ask about sizes and colors
- ☐ Return something to a store

1 WHAT DO YOU KNOW?

A CLASS. Look at the pictures. Which clothes do you know? Which colors do you know?

> Number 1 is a dress.
> Number 5 is orange.

CD2 T23

B Listen and point to the pictures. Then listen and repeat.

2 PRACTICE

A WORD PLAY. Look at the pictures and the list of clothes on page 87. Which clothes come in pairs? Write the words.

_____pants_____

_____sneakers_____

_____jeans_____

_____socks_____

_____shoes_____

> These clothes are plural.
> Example: *The pants are black.*

B PAIRS. Ask and answer questions about the pictures.

A: *What's number 12?*
B: *Shoes.*
A: *What color are they?*
B: *Brown. What's number 3?*
A: *A skirt.*
B: *What color is it?*
A: *Red.*

C NETWORK. What is your favorite color? Find classmates with the same favorite color as you. Form a group. Ask the people in your group, *What clothes do you have in that color?*

1

2

5

6

9

10

11

12

Lesson 1 Vocabulary

Getting Started   5 minutes

1 WHAT DO YOU KNOW?

A CLASS. Look at the pictures. Which clothes...

- Show Transparency 5.2 or hold up the book. Tell students to cover the list of words on page 87.
- Read the directions. Point to picture 1 and ask: *What is this?* Read the example with the class.
- Say: *Look at the other pictures.* Ask: *Which clothes do you know?* Students call out answers as in the example.
- Point to picture 5 and ask: *What color is this?* Read the example with the class.
- Say: *Look at the other pictures.* Ask: *Which colors do you know?* Students call out answers.
- If students call out an incorrect article of clothing, change the student's answer into a question for the class (for example, *Is number 3 a blue shirt?*). If nobody can identify the correct item, tell students they will now listen to a CD and practice the names of the colors and clothes.

Presentation   5 minutes

B **Listen and point to the pictures....**

- Read the directions. Play CD 2, Track 23. Pause after number 12 (*brown shoes*).
- To check comprehension, say each article of clothing in random order and ask students to point to the appropriate picture.
- Resume playing Track 23. Students listen and repeat.

Controlled Practice   10 minutes

2 PRACTICE

A WORD PLAY. Look at the pictures and the list...

- Read the directions and the note. Say: Pair *means two parts.* Write on the board: *Pair = 2 parts.*
- Ask: *Are my shoes a pair?* (Yes.) *Why?* (Because there are two of them.) Ask: *Is my shirt a pair?* (No.) Say: *Remember:* A pair *means two parts.*
- Say: *People also say a pair of pants. Why?* (Because each leg is one part.) Call on students to answer.

Expansion: Speaking Practice for 2A

- Bring in several clothing catalogs.
- Form groups of 4. Each group gets at least one catalog. Each student finds clothing he or she likes and writes it down. Students tell each other what clothes they like. Call on students to say the clothing they like (for example, A: [Holds up the catalog picture] *I like this white shirt.*).

B PAIRS. Ask and answer questions about the pictures.

- Read the directions. Read each line in the example and ask the class to repeat.
- Play A and model the example with an above-level student. Change roles and repeat.
- Pair students and tell them to take turns playing A and B.
- To check comprehension, ask individual students: *What's number _____? What color is it/are they?*

MULTILEVEL INSTRUCTION for 2B
Cross-ability The higher-level partner points to the item when asking *What's number _____?*

C NETWORK. What is your favorite color? Find...

- Read the directions, including the questions.
- Ask a few above-level or on-level students both questions. To the class, say: *Think of your favorite color.* Ask a few students to say their favorite color.
- Tell students to stand, mingle, and ask as many students as possible about their favorite color. Say: *Stand with the students who have the same favorite color as you.*
- Walk around and check that students are grouping themselves according to favorite color.
- Then say: *Now ask the students in your group,* What clothes do you have in that color? Provide a model by asking a few students to tell you the clothes they have in their favorite color (for example, S: *I have a blue jacket. I have blue jeans. I have a blue shirt.*).
- Visit each group to check that students are discussing clothing items they have in their group's favorite color.

Lesson 1   Vocabulary

Learning Strategy: Make word groups

- Read the directions, including the questions.
- Draw a chart on the board with the headings *Men* and *Women*. Ask: *Which clothes do men wear?* Write a sample answer under *Men* on the board (for example, *sneakers*). Repeat for *Women* (for example, *a dress*). Tell students to copy the chart.
- Walk around and check that students are using all the vocabulary on page 87. If misspellings occur, tell students to check the list. (*Men:* everything on the page except dress, skirt, and blouse; *Women:* everything on the page)
- Say: *You can remember new words by putting them into groups.* Remind students to use this strategy to remember other new vocabulary.

Communicative Practice   30 minutes

Show what you know!

STEP 1. PAIRS. Describe your clothes.

- On the board, write *I'm wearing . . .* and ask the class to repeat. Say: *When you talk about clothes on your body right now, say* I'm wearing. Point to your clothes and describe them (for example, *I'm wearing brown pants and a white shirt.*).
- Read the directions. Read A's line from the example and ask the class to repeat it.
- Call on an above-level student to say what he or she is wearing (T: *What are you wearing?* S: *I'm wearing a red blouse and beige pants.*).
- Pair students. Say: *Take turns saying what you're wearing.* Walk around and help students identify their own clothing. Correct *a/an* errors you hear.
- Write on the board any new vocabulary students used during the activity. Say each word and ask the class to repeat. To check comprehension, call on a few students to say what they're wearing.

Expansion: Speaking Practice for STEP 1

- Form groups of 4 or 5. Tell each group to plan a fashion show.
- Students take turns being the announcer. The announcer describes what each student in the group is wearing, for example, *Today John is wearing black pants and a white shirt. He's wearing a (new) gray sweater.*

Expansion: Writing and Speaking Practice for STEP 1

- Write on the board: *Who's wearing _____?* Tell students to write at least one question to ask the class.
- Ask each student to come to the front of the class and read his or her question. The student should call on a classmate to answer the question.

STEP 2. NEW PAIRS. What are your classmates...

- Read the directions.
- Play A and read the example conversation with an on-level student. Write the question on the board with a blank (*Who's wearing _____?*).
- Tell the class to look around to see what people are wearing. Read the question on the board and call on students to complete it with different articles of clothing (for example, T: *Who's wearing . . .* S: *a red shirt?*). Tell the class to answer with a student's name. Repeat a few times.
- Pair students and tell them to take turns playing A and B. Walk around and model the conversation as needed.
- To check comprehension, call on a few students to come to the front of the class and ask: *Who's wearing . . . ?* while the class calls out answers.
- To wrap up, use some of the new vocabulary generated by Steps 1 and 2 and ask the class questions, for example, *Who's wearing brown boots?*

MULTILEVEL INSTRUCTION for STEP 2

Pre-level Student A can start by asking who's wearing one article of clothing (for example, A: *Who's wearing gray pants?*), instead of two as in the example conversation.

Above-level Student A asks negative questions also (for example, *Who's not wearing a white shirt?*). B names a few students who aren't wearing the article of clothing.

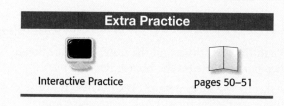

Extra Practice	
Interactive Practice	pages 50–51

3

4

7

8

Learning Strategy

Make word groups

Look at the list of clothes. Which clothes do men wear? Which clothes do women wear? Which clothes do both men and women wear? Make three lists in your notebook.

Show what you know!

STEP 1. PAIRS. Describe your clothes.

A: *I'm wearing a green T-shirt, blue jeans, and black sneakers.*
B: *And I'm wearing . . .*

STEP 2. NEW PAIRS. What are your classmates wearing? Look around the room.

Student A, ask: "Who's wearing _____?"
Student B, name the student.

A: *Who's wearing gray pants and a red sweater?*
B: *Roberto.*
A: *Right!*
B: *Who's wearing . . . ?*

Listening and Speaking

1 **BEFORE YOU LISTEN**

CD2 T24

🔊 **READ. Look at the picture. Listen and read about Mr. Monro's birthday. Then complete the sentences. Underline the correct word.**

It's Mr. Monro's birthday next week. His wife always gives him a gift for his birthday. This year, she asks him, "What do you want for your birthday?"

"How about a jacket?" Mr. Monro says.

"Well," his wife says, "I know you *need* a jacket. Your green jacket is old. But what do you *want*?"

"Oh," Mr. Monro says. "I need a jacket *and* I want a jacket. I want a black jacket!"

1. Mr. Monro needs a **gift** / <u>**jacket**</u>.

2. Mr. Monro wants a <u>**black**</u> / **green** jacket.

2 **LISTEN**

CD2 T25

A 🔊 **Look at the picture. Zofia and Carlos are friends. Listen to their conversation. Who is Robert?**

  (a.) Zofia's brother   b. Zofia's friend   c. Zofia's father

CD2 T25

B 🔊 **Listen again. Read the sentences. Circle *True* or *False*.**

1. Zofia's birthday is next week.   **True**   (**False**)

2. Robert needs clothes.   (**True**)   **False**

3. Robert wants clothes.   **True**   (**False**)

CD2 T26

C 🔊 **Listen to the whole conversation. Complete the sentence.**

Carlos wants a _____backpack_____.

a.    (b.)   c.

Getting Started   10 minutes

1 | BEFORE YOU LISTEN

 READ. Look at the picture. Listen and...

- Read the directions.
- Tell students to look at the picture. Say: *This is Mr. Monro.* Ask: *What is he thinking?* (He needs/wants a new jacket.)
- Play CD 2, Track 24. Students listen and read along silently.
- *Optional:* Play Track 24 again. Pause the CD after the following paragraphs and ask these questions:

  First paragraph: *When is Mr. Monro's birthday?* (next week) *What does his wife ask him?* (What do you want for your birthday?)

  Third paragraph: *What's wrong with his green jacket?* (It's old.)

  Fourth paragraph: *What does Mr. Monro say?* (Oh, I need a jacket *and* I want a jacket. I want a black jacket!)

- Call on two students to say the completed sentences.

Expansion: Writing and Speaking Practice for 1

- Say: *You need clothes, but you want a special color. Think of the clothes you need. Write a list of three things you need (for example, a pair of pants, a dress, and a shirt). On the board, write the heading Clothes I Need with the examples under it.*
- Say: *Look at pages 86–87 for more clothes. In your notebooks, write a list of three things you need. On the board, create a new list with the heading Things I Want. Under it, write a black pair of pants, a red dress, and a green shirt.*
- Say: *Now write a list of the colors you want.*
- Pair students. Tell Student A to ask: *What do you need/want?* Tell Student B to answer: *I need a pair of pants*, or *I want a pair of black pants.* Tell them to take turns asking and answering the questions.
- Walk around and check that students are identifying articles of clothing they need and specific colors they want.

Presentation   20 minutes

2 | LISTEN

A **Look at the picture. Zofia and Carlos...**

- Read the first line of the directions (*Look . . . friends.*). Ask: *What do you see in the picture?* (A man and a woman are talking to each other.)
- Read the rest of the directions and ask: *Who is Robert?* Write the answer choices on the board and read them.
- Play CD 2, Track 25. Students listen and circle the answer.
- Call on a student to circle the answer on the board.

> **Teaching Tip**
>
> *Optional:* Remember that if students need additional support, tell them to read the Audio Script on page 284 as they listen to the conversations.

B **Listen again. Read the sentences....**

- Read each sentence and answer choice.
- Play Track 25 again. Students listen, read, and circle *True* or *False*.
- Call on students to say answers.

C **Listen to the whole conversation...**

- Ask: *What is A? What is B? What is C?* Write the answers on the board to help with spelling.
- Play CD 2, Track 26. Students listen and write the answer in their book.
- Say the sentence and tell the class to call out the answer (*Carlos wants a . . .*).
- *Optional:* Ask: *Why is Carlos funny?* (Because he wants a backpack, too.)

Expansion: Vocabulary Practice for 2C

- On the board, write *I buy gifts for . . .* and tell students to copy this partial sentence.
- Say: *In your notebook, write a list of family members you buy gifts for (for example, my father, my sister).*
- Pair students and say: *Share your list with your partner.*
- Call on students to read their list out loud.

Controlled Practice   20 minutes

3   CONVERSATION

Listen and read the conversation. Then...

- Note: This conversation is the same one students heard in Exercise 2A on page 88.
- Explain: *How about . . . is a common way to make a suggestion.*
- Play CD 2, Track 27. Students listen and read along silently.
- Resume playing Track 27. Students listen and repeat.

4   PRACTICE

A PAIRS. Practice the conversation. Then...

- Pair students and tell them to practice the conversation in Exercise 3.
- Then, in Exercise 4A, ask students to look at the pictures and say what they are. *Wallet* and *handbag* are new, so hold up these items or point to the pictures, say them, and ask the class to repeat.
- Read the directions.
- Copy the conversation onto the board with blanks. Read through the conversation. When you come to a blank, fill it in with information from the pictures (*friend* and *wallet*). Remind students they need to use the correct subject pronoun and possessive adjective for the person.
- Ask two on-level students to practice the conversation in front of the class.
- Tell pairs to take turns playing each role and to use the pictures to fill in the blanks.
- Walk around and check that Student A is using the correct pronouns and possessive adjectives.
- Tell students to stand, mingle, and practice the conversation with several new partners.
- Call on pairs to perform for the class.

▬ MULTILEVEL INSTRUCTION for 4A

Pre-level To build students' confidence, first tell pairs to read the conversation together before taking A and B roles.

Above-level Tell students to cover the conversation and practice only by looking at the information in the boxes.

Communicative Practice   10 minutes

B ROLE PLAY. PAIRS. Make your own...

- Read the directions.
- With an above-level student, make up a new conversation and practice in front of the class. Base the conversation on Exercise 3.
- Remind students that they can use the family vocabulary on pages 67 and 69 and the classroom vocabulary on pages 47 and 55. With the class, brainstorm additional gifts and write new vocabulary on the board (additional clothing, sports equipment, electronics).
- Pair students. Say: *Student A, say you need a gift for someone. Student B, suggest a gift. Use words on the board or new words. Use the words* need *and* want *in your conversation. Take turns playing A and B.*
- Walk around and check that students are using pronouns and possessive adjectives correctly.
- Call on pairs to perform for the class.
- To wrap up, on the board write some of the errors you heard during the role plays. Ask students to correct the mistakes. Go over the corrections by saying the words or sentences correctly and asking the class to repeat.

▬ MULTILEVEL INSTRUCTION for 4B

Cross-ability Tell the higher-level student to write out each sentence of the conversation on strips of paper (one strip per line). If the lower-level partner has difficulty, the higher-level student can hand his or her partner a strip with the appropriate line to read from.

▬ Expansion: Listening and Speaking Practice for 4B

- After a pair performs for the class, call on a student from the audience to report on who wants/needs what (for example, S: *Yolanda needs a gift for her mother. Her mother needs a handbag, but she wants an iPod.*).

Extra Practice

Interactive Practice

3 CONVERSATION

Listen and read the conversation. Then listen and repeat.

Zofia: I need a gift for my brother, Robert. It's his birthday next week.

Carlos: How about clothes?

Zofia: Well, he needs clothes, but he wants a backpack!

4 PRACTICE

A **PAIRS. Practice the conversation. Then make new conversations. Use the information in the boxes.**

A: I need a gift for my _____ . It's _____ birthday next week.
(his / her)

B: How about clothes?

A: Well, _____ needs clothes, but _____ wants _____ !
(he / she)   (he / she)

friend

mother

father

a wallet

a handbag

a watch

B **ROLE PLAY. PAIRS. Make your own conversations. Use different people and gifts.**

Talk about things you need, want, or have

Grammar

Simple present affirmative

I You We They	**need** **want** **have**	new clothes.

He She Robert	**needs** **wants** **has**	new clothes.

Grammar Watch

- With **he**, **she**, or **it**, the simple present verb ends in –**s**.

- Remember: The verb **have** is irregular. Use **has** with **he**, **she**, or **it**.

1 PRACTICE

A Underline the correct word.

1. Mr. Garcia **have** / <u>**has**</u> a blue shirt.

2. He **want** / <u>**wants**</u> a green shirt.

3. Amy and Jeff <u>**have**</u> / **has** black sneakers.

4. I <u>**want**</u> / **wants** black sneakers, too.

5. Our teacher **need** / <u>**needs**</u> a new jacket.

6. He **need** / <u>**needs**</u> new pants, too.

B Complete the sentences.
Use the verbs in parentheses.

1. My sister ____*needs*____ a skirt.
   (need)

2. She ____wants____ a red skirt.
   (want)

3. My brothers ____have____ new shoes.
   (have)

4. Now they ____need____ new socks.
   (need)

5. Allen ____has____ brown jeans.
   (have)

6. We ____want____ brown jeans, too.
   (want)

7. You ____have____ a nice new wallet.
   (have)

8. I ____want____ a new wallet, too.
   (want)

Getting Started   5 minutes

- Say: *We're going to study* want, need, *and* have. *In the conversation on page 89, Zofia used this grammar.*
- Play CD 2, Track 27. Students listen. Write *He needs new clothes, but he wants a backpack!* on the board. Underline *He needs* and *he wants*.

Presentation   10 minutes

Simple present affirmative

- Copy the grammar charts onto the board or show the charts on Transparency 5.3 and cover the exercise.
- Read the sentences in the left chart and ask the class to repeat.
- Read the sentences in the right chart and ask the class to repeat.
- Read the first point in the Grammar Watch note. Circle *wants* and *needs* in the chart. Then write: *He wants a new shirt.* Make the *-s* large for emphasis. Read the sentence and ask the class to repeat.
- Read the second point in the Grammar Watch note.
- Ask students to close their books. Remove any visual aids for the chart. On the board, write the following incomplete sentences:

  You _____ *new clothes.* (want)

  He _____ *new clothes.* (need)

  We _____ *new clothes.* (have)

  She _____ *new clothes.* (have)

- Students call out answers. Write answers on the board.
- If you are using the transparency, do the exercise with the class.

> **Language Note**
>
> Students often do not hear the final *-s* on third-person singular present affirmative verbs. Pronounce it clearly when modeling sentences. Further, provide a variety of examples so that students begin to recognize subjects that fall within the third-person singular category (for example, *The teacher* _____ *new clothes.* *Christina* _____ *new clothes.*).

Controlled Practice   30 minutes

1 PRACTICE

A Underline the correct word.

- Read the directions.
- Ask students to look at the picture of Mr. Garcia. Point to the blue shirt he is wearing and say the example item with emphasis on *has*.
- Say: *Look at the subject of the sentence before answering. Also, look at the grammar chart to help you answer.*
- Walk around as needed to help students make connections between the subjects in the exercise items and the subjects in the chart (for example, *Amy and Jeff = They*).
- Students compare answers with a partner.
- Call on students to say answers.

B Complete the sentences. Use the verbs in parentheses.

- Read the directions and tell students to look at the picture of the woman. Read the example and ask the class to repeat it. Write it on the board.
- Ask: *Why is the answer* needs *and not* need? (Because *My sister* is the same as *she.*) Point to the example on the board and circle *My sister*. Write *she* under it, saying: *They are the same. Remember—look at the subject of the sentence before answering.*
- Students compare answers with a partner.
- Call on students to write answers on the board.

▬▬ Expansion: Vocabulary and Graphic Organizer Practice for 1B

- To provide extra practice with *need*, *want*, and *have*, tell students to make three lists with the headings *Need*, *Want*, and *Have* in their notebooks. Students then write three clothing items they need, three they want, and three they have.
- Students compare lists with a partner by reading the items they listed (for example, *I want new shoes. I need a new jacket.*).
- To practice ordinal numbers, students can also list their items in order of importance (for example, *First, I want new shoes. Second, I want . . .*) and share these with their partner.

2 PRACTICE

Ⓐ PAIRS. Look at the picture of Joe and Ellen...

- Read the directions. Hold up the book, point to the clothing items, and ask: *What is this?* Students call out answers. (a watch, a red shirt, a red blouse)

- Say: *Look at Joe. He has a problem.* (Point to the hole in Joe's jacket and his tattered sneakers.) *What does Joe need?* (a jacket, a pair of shoes) Write students' answers on the board in complete sentences (for example, *He needs a new jacket.*) and ask the class to repeat.

- Say: *Practice with a partner. Student A, ask What does Joe need? Student B, Look at the picture of Joe and answer. Student A, say another thing that Joe needs. Do it again for Ellen.*

- Call on pairs to perform the conversations about Joe and about Ellen for the class.

- To wrap up, write student errors with the simple present affirmative on the board. Ask students to come up and make corrections. Say the correct answers and ask the class to repeat.

▬ MULTILEVEL INSTRUCTION for 2A

Pre-level Tell students to look first at Joe and talk about him, then look at and discuss Ellen.

Above-level Tell students to add a line about what Joe and Ellen already have (for example, A: *What does Joe need?* B: *Well, he has old shoes. So, he needs new shoes.*).

Ⓑ Complete the sentences.

- Point to the thought bubbles above Joe's head and say: *Joe wants the things above his head. He is thinking about what he wants.*

- Read the directions and example. Ask: *Why does Joe need new shoes?* (Because his shoes are old.)

- Remind students to write *new* before the words.

- Students compare answers with a partner.

- Call on students to say answers.

Ⓒ WRITE. Look at the picture again. What do...

- Read the directions. Explain: Both *means you are writing about Joe **and** Ellen.*

- Students compare answers with a partner.

- Call on students to read the answers. Write the sentences on the board, correcting as needed.

Communicative Practice   15 minutes

Show what you know!

STEP 1. Complete the sentence with true...

- On the board, write *I want a red dress* (or *I want a red shirt.*). Ask the class to repeat. Ask individual students: *What do you want?* Write a couple of student responses on the board.

- Read the directions. Say: *Write the things you want.*

- Call on several students to say what they want.

STEP 2. GROUPS OF 5. Play the Memory Game....

- Say: *Listen and remember what your classmates want.*

- Play Agnes and ask two on-level students to play Pedro and Maury. Model the activity.

- Form groups of 5. Walk around and practice with individual groups. As needed, model correct pronunciation and ask students to repeat.

- *Optional:* Ask individual groups to play the Memory Game for the class.

▬ Expansion: Writing Practice for STEP 2

- Tell students to write the five sentences from their group's Memory Game.

- Collect the students' papers and provide feedback.

Progress Check

Can you . . . talk about things you need, want, or have?

Say: *We have practiced talking about things we need, want, or have. Now, look at the question at the bottom of the page. Can you talk about things you need, want, or have?* Tell students to write a checkmark in the box.

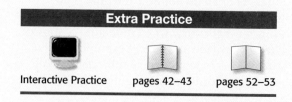

Extra Practice

Interactive Practice   pages 42–43   pages 52–53

2 PRACTICE

A PAIRS. Look at the picture of Joe and Ellen. What do they need? What do they want? Decide together. There is more than one correct answer. Answers will vary.

A: *What does Joe need?*
B: *He needs new shoes.*
A: *Right. He also needs . . .*

B Complete the sentences. Answers will vary but could include:

Joe needs _____new shoes_____.

He wants _____a new watch_____.

Ellen needs _____a new jacket_____.

She wants _____a new blouse_____.

Joe

Ellen

C WRITE. Look at the picture again. What do Joe and Ellen both need? What do they both want? Write sentences. Use capital letters and periods.

Joe and Ellen need _____new jackets. They want new watches._____

Show what you know! Talk about things you need, want, or have

STEP 1. Complete the sentence with true information.

I want _____a red dress_____.

I want _____.

STEP 2. GROUPS OF 5. Play the Memory Game. Talk about clothes you want.

Agnes: *I want a red dress.*
Pedro: *Agnes wants a red dress. I want new jeans.*
Maury: *Agnes wants a red dress. Pedro wants new jeans. I want a green shirt.*

Can you...talk about things you need, want, or have? ☐

Use U.S. money

Life Skills

1 USE U.S. MONEY

A CLASS. **Where do you shop for clothes? Do you pay with cash?**

CD2 T28

B Look at the U.S. money. Listen and point. Then listen and repeat.

1. one dollar ($1.00)

2. five dollars ($5.00)

3. ten dollars ($10.00)

4. twenty dollars ($20.00)

CD2 T29

C Look at the coins. Listen and point. Then listen and repeat.

1. a penny (1¢) 2. a nickel (5¢) 3. a dime (10¢) 4. a quarter (25¢)

2 PRACTICE

A Count the money. Write the amount.

1. _____65¢_____

2. _____94¢_____

3. _____$12.27_____

4. _____$5.11_____

CD2 T30

B Listen and check your answers. Then listen and repeat.

Getting Started   5 minutes

Culture Connection

• On the board, write the heading *Money Around the World*.

• Say: *The money we use in the U.S. is the* dollar. Ask: *What money is used in your home country?* Call on students to say their country and unit of currency (for example, *Mexico—the peso*). Write countries and their currencies on the board.

• Write a $ symbol on the board and ask: *What is this?* (the symbol for dollars) Ask volunteers to write the symbols of their home country's currency in the chart on the board.

Presentation   10 minutes

1 USE U.S. MONEY

A CLASS. **Where do you shop for clothes?...**

• Read the directions. Write the names of stores that students say on the board. As needed, point to the pictures and explain: Cash *is dollar bills or coins.*

B **Look at the U.S. money. Listen and...**

• Play CD 2, Track 28. Students listen and point to the money.

• Resume playing Track 28. Students listen and repeat.

• Say each amount in random order and tell students to point to the appropriate bill.

Expansion: Speaking Practice for 1B

• Point to Washington's face on the $1 bill and ask: *Who's this?* Repeat for the other bills. Write answers on the board:

> *$1—George Washington, 1st president of the U.S.*
>
> *$5—Abraham Lincoln, 16th president of the U.S.*
>
> *$10—Alexander Hamilton, 1st secretary of the treasury (finance/money)*
>
> *$20—Andrew Jackson, 7th president of the U.S.*

Culture Connection

• Say: *In the U.S., famous presidents and important politicians from history are on our bills.*
• Ask: *Who is on the money in your country?*

C **Look at the coins. Listen and point....**

• Play CD 2, Track 29. Students listen and point to the coins.

• Resume playing Track 29. Students listen and repeat. Explain and write on the board: *A penny is also called a* cent. *The symbol* ¢ *means* cents.

• Ask: *How many cents are in a dollar?* (100) *How many cents are in a nickel?* (5) *How many cents are in a dime?* (10) *How many cents are in a quarter?* (25)

Expansion: Speaking Practice for 1C

• Point to the penny and ask: *Who's on the penny?* Repeat for the other coins. Write answers on the board:

> *1¢—Abraham Lincoln, 16th president of the U.S.*
>
> *5¢—Thomas Jefferson, 3rd president of the U.S.*
>
> *10¢—Franklin D. Roosevelt, 32nd president of the U.S.*
>
> *25¢—George Washington, 1st president of the U.S.*

Controlled Practice   30 minutes

2 PRACTICE

A **Count the money. Write the amount.**

• Read the directions.

• Say: *Number 1 is 65 cents. There is one quarter, three dimes, and two nickels.* Write on the board: $25¢ + 10¢ + 10¢ + 10¢ + 5¢ + 5¢ = 65¢$. Ask the class to repeat the equation.

• Review numbers 1–99 on pages 32 and 58.

• Ask students to look at the pictures and write the amount on the line.

B **Listen and check your answers. Then...**

• Read the directions. Play CD 2, Track 30.

• Ask students to recalculate each amount on the board to illustrate the steps to add money (for example, 2. $10¢ + 10¢ + 5¢ + 5¢ + \cdots$).

• Resume playing Track 30. Students listen and repeat.

Lesson 4 Use U.S. money

3 TALK ABOUT PRICES

 Listen. A customer in a clothing store...

- Tell students to look at the pictures. Ask: *What do you see?* (a skirt and a pair of jeans) Say: *Look at the price tags.* Ask: *How much is the skirt?* ($15.99) *How much are the jeans?* ($17.99) *Is the skirt a lot of money? Are the jeans a lot of money?*
- Say: *When you are in a store, you can ask* How much . . . ? *to learn the price.*
- Read the first line of the directions.
- Play CD 2, Track 31. Students listen and repeat.
- Say: *Remember, say* How much is this . . . ? *for singular items and* How much are these . . . ? *for plural items.* Write these two questions as headings on the board. Ask students for clothing items for each one and write them on the board.
- Resume playing Track 31. Students listen and repeat.
- Pair students and tell them to take turns playing the customer and the assistant.
- Call on pairs to perform for the class.

4 PRACTICE

A **Listen. Fill in the price tags.**

- Read the directions. Write the first answer on the board as an example so students remember to write a dollar sign and a decimal point.
- Play CD 2, Track 32. Students listen and write.
- Call on students to write answers on the board.

Communicative Practice   15 minutes

B PAIRS. **Practice the conversation above. Use...**

- On the board, rewrite the conversation from Exercise 3 with blanks for the prices and items.
- Read the directions. Play the assistant and practice the conversation with an above-level student.
- Pair students. Say: *Practice the conversation with the clothes and prices from Exercise 4A.*
- Ask: *Which things are singular?* (blouse, watch) *Which things are plural?* (shoes, jeans) Say: *Take turns playing the customer and the assistant.*
- Call on pairs to perform for the class.

■■■ **MULTILEVEL INSTRUCTION for 4B**

Cross-ability Tell above-level students to play the customer so they control the flow of the conversation.

C Look at the receipt. Answer the questions.

- Read the directions. Ask the question in item 1. Tell students to point to the date on the receipt. Quickly scan the room and check that students are able to find the date. Say: *Ask the student next to you for help if you can't find it.*
- On the board, write *sales tax.* Say: *In most states in the United States, we pay sales tax on clothes and other things we buy.* Ask: *What is the sales tax here?* Write it on the board.
- Explain: Change *is money you get back when you pay for something. For example, if the total is $18.00 and I pay with a $20 bill, then the change is $2.00.*
- Read the directions.
- Walk around and spot-check students' answers. Students compare answers with a partner.
- Call on students to say answers.

5 LIFE SKILLS WRITING

Turn to page 257 and ask students to complete the personal check. See pages Txi–Txii for general notes about the Life Skills Writing activities.

Progress Check

Can you . . . talk about prices and read price tags and receipts?

Say: *We have practiced talking about prices and reading price tags and receipts. Now, look at the question at the bottom of the page. Can you talk about prices and read price tags and receipts?* Tell students to write a checkmark in the box.

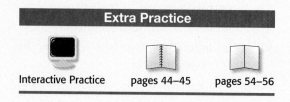

Extra Practice		
Interactive Practice	pages 44–45	pages 54–56

3 TALK ABOUT PRICES

CD2 T31

Listen. A customer in a clothing store is asking about prices. Listen and repeat the conversation. Then practice with a partner.

Customer: Excuse me. How much is this **skirt**?

Assistant: It's **$15.99**.

Customer: And how much are these **jeans**?

Assistant: They're **$17.99**.

4 PRACTICE

CD2 T32

A Listen. Fill in the price tags.

1.  $11.95

2.  $34.99

3.  $23.50

4.  $13.49

B PAIRS. Practice the conversation above. Use the pictures in Exercise A.

C Look at the receipt. Answer the questions.

```
            IMAGINE
     Los Angeles, CA 90027
        (213) 555-6111

08-06-10                2:25 P.M.

  WOMEN'S JEANS           11.99
  WOMEN'S SWEATERS         8.99
  WOMEN'S T-SHIRTS         5.99

  SUBTOTAL                26.97
  TAX 8% ON 26.97          2.16

  TOTAL                   29.13

  CASH AMOUNT PAID        30.00
  CHANGE DUE                .87

Please keep receipt for returns.
  Thank you for shopping at
          IMAGINE.
```

1. What is the date on the receipt?

   Write it in words. _____August 6, 2010_____

2. How much are the jeans? ___$11.99___

3. How much is the tax? ___$2.16___

4. How much are the clothes before tax? ___$26.97___

5. How much are the clothes after tax? ___$29.13___

6. How much is the change? ___87¢___

5 LIFE SKILLS WRITING

Write a personal check. See page 257.

Can you...talk about prices and read price tags and receipts? ☐

Listening and Speaking

1 BEFORE YOU LISTEN

CLASS. Read the information. Answer the question.

Some clothes come in sizes with letters: XS (extra small), S (small), M (medium), L (large), or XL (extra large). What clothes come in sizes with numbers?

2 LISTEN

Ⓐ Look at the picture. Assefa is shopping.

Guess: What is he asking the sales assistant about?

a. the price   b. the color   ⓒ the size

CD2 T33

**Ⓑ 💿 Listen to the conversation.
Was your guess in Exercise A correct?**

Listen again. Complete the sentences.

1. Assefa wants a ____sweater____ for his sister.

   b.      c.

ⓐ

2. Assefa's sister needs a ____large____.

   b.   ⓒ
a.

CD2 T34

Ⓒ 💿 Listen to the whole conversation. Which sweater does the store have?

a.   b.   ⓒ

Getting Started
5 minutes

1 BEFORE YOU LISTEN

CLASS. Read the information. Answer the question.

- Tell students to look at the picture. Ask: *What sizes do you see?* Point to each tag and ask: *What size is this?* Write answers on the board.
- Read the directions and the information. Ask: *What clothes come in sizes with numbers?* (*Some possible answers:* pants, dresses, shoes) Write several clothes that students say on the board.

Presentation
30 minutes

2 LISTEN

A Look at the picture.... Guess:...

- Read the directions.
- Ask: *What do you see in the picture?* (a customer and an assistant, a department store, a red sweater) *What is happening?* (The customer is asking a question about the sweater.)
- Ask: *What is he asking about?* Write the answer choices on the board and read them. Call on students to guess.
- Tell students they will listen for the answer in Exercise B.

B Listen to the conversation. Was your...

- Read the directions. Play CD 2, Track 33.
- Circle the correct answer on the board. Ask: *Was your guess correct?*

> **Teaching Tip**
>
> *Optional:* Remember that if students need additional support, tell them to read the Audio Script on page 284 as they listen to the conversations.

Listen again. Complete the sentences.

- Ask students to look at the pictures and identify the articles of clothing and the sizes.
- Play Track 33 again. Students listen and complete the sentences.

- Call on students to say answers. Write them on the board.

C Listen to the whole conversation...

- Read the directions. Ask students to look at the pictures. For each one, call on students to say the color of the sweater (for example, *This is a green sweater.*).
- Play CD 2, Track 34. Students listen and answer the question.

Expansion: Vocabulary Practice for 2C

- In their notebooks, students make a three-column table with the following headings: *Price, Color, Size.* For each heading, dictate several examples (for example, *Price—$8.75, $15.35, $19.95; Color—blue, orange, yellow; Size—XS, M, XL*). Students copy this information into their table.
- Pair students. Student A randomly says a price, color, or size. Student B must identify what it is:

  A: *$15.35.*
  B: *A price.*
  A: *Good! Orange.*
  B: *A color.*
  A: *Yes!*

- After a few tries, students switch roles and repeat.

Expansion: Speaking Practice for 2C

- Play a *Price Is Right* style activity with the class. If possible, cut out clothing items from a department store catalog. On a separate sheet of paper, tape one cutout picture and write two prices below—one real and one made up. Next to the picture, write the name of the item (for example, *a green blouse*). Repeat this for all the items.
- Hold up one item and say: *How much is this green blouse?* Call on individual students to guess the correct price (for example, *I think it's $19.95.*).
- Students can work as a class or in groups to take turns asking a price and guessing the correct price. Note: Whoever is leading the activity must know the answers.

3 CONVERSATION

A Listen. Then listen and repeat.

- Read the Pronunciation Watch note. On the board, write *important = stressed* and *not important = unstressed (short and weak)*.
- Say: *Listen for the stressed word.* Ask: *What time is it?* and say: *The word* time *is stressed.*
- Say: *Listen for the unstressed words.* Ask: *What time is it?* and say: *What, is,* and *it* are unstressed.
- Write *What time is it?* making *time* bigger than the rest of the words.
- Play CD 2, Track 35. Students listen.
- Resume playing Track 35. Students listen and repeat.
- Play Track 35 again. Students listen and repeat. If students have difficulty with the pronunciation, break each question into chunks and ask the class to repeat.

B Listen. Underline the stressed words.

- Play CD 2, Track 36. Pause after item 1. Ask: *What are the unstressed words?* (*do, you*)
- Resume playing Track 36. Students underline the stressed words.
- Call on students to write answers on the board and say the sentences.

Controlled Practice   15 minutes

C Listen and read the conversation....

- Explain: *You say* too bad *when you are unhappy about something and you can't change it.*
- Say: *Listen to the stressed words.* Play CD 2, Track 37. Students listen.
- Resume playing Track 37. Students listen and repeat.
- Ask students to point out the important words.

4 PRACTICE

A PAIRS. Practice the conversation. Then make new...

- Pair students and tell them to practice the conversation in Exercise 3C.

- Then, in Exercise 4A, ask students to look at the pictures and identify the clothing items and sizes.
- Read the directions and the note.
- Copy the conversation onto the board with blanks. Read through the conversation. When you come to a blank, fill it in with information from the pictures.
- Ask two on-level students to practice the conversation in front of the class. Tell pairs to take turns playing each role and to use the pictures to fill in the blanks.
- Tell students to stand, mingle, and practice the conversation with several new partners.
- Call on pairs to perform for the class.

Communicative Practice   10 minutes

B ROLE PLAY. PAIRS. Make your own...

- Read the directions.
- On the board, begin listing clothing and sizes for students to use in their conversations. Call on students to suggest more clothing and sizes.
- Play A and, with an above-level student, make up a new conversation and practice in front of the class. Use information from the board. Base the conversation on the one in Exercise 3C. Continue the conversation for three or four exchanges (for example, B: *Well, we have a different color in a large.* A: *Which color?* B: *Green.* A: *Hmm. OK. Can I see it?* B: *Sure. I'll be right back.*).
- Pair students. Check that students are asking and answering questions about clothing and size.
- Call on pairs to perform for the class.

■■■ MULTILEVEL INSTRUCTION for 4B

Cross-ability The higher-level partners play A so they control the flow of the conversation. After a few times, students switch roles.

■■■ Expansion: Speaking Practice for 4B

- Ask Student A to also ask about available colors (for example, A: *Do you have this skirt in an extra small in green?*).

Extra Practice

Interactive Practice

3 CONVERSATION

CD2 T35

A Listen. Then listen and repeat.

Do you **have** this **sweater** in a **large**?

It's **for** my **sister**.

Does she **like blue**?

> **Pronunciation Watch**
>
> Important words in a sentence are stressed. Other words are often unstressed. Unstressed words sound short and weak.

CD2 T36

B Listen. Underline the stressed words.

1. Do you <u>like</u> <u>green</u>?

2. Do you <u>need</u> a <u>small</u>?

3. He <u>wants</u> a <u>watch</u>.

CD2 T37

C Listen and read the conversation. Then listen and repeat.

Assefa:	Do you have this sweater in a large?
Assistant:	No, I'm sorry. We don't.
Assefa:	Too bad. It's for my sister and she needs a large.

> a large
> an extra small

4 PRACTICE

A PAIRS. Practice the conversation. Then make new conversations. Use the pictures.

A: Do you have this _____ in _____ ?

B: No, I'm sorry. We don't.

A: Too bad. It's for my sister and she

needs _____ .

B ROLE PLAY. PAIRS. Make your own conversations. Use different clothes and sizes.

Ask about sizes and colors

Grammar

Simple present: *Yes/no* questions and short answers

Do	I we you they	**need** new shoes?	**Yes,**	you we I they	**do.**	**No,**	you we I they	**don't.**
Does	he she			he she	**does.**		he she	**doesn't.**

1 PRACTICE

Grammar Watch

Use the base form of the verb in questions with *do* or *does*. In the chart, *need* is in the base form.

Contractions
don't = *do not*
doesn't = *does not*

A Match the questions with the short answers.

1. Do you have these shoes in a size 9? __d__   a. Yes, he does.

2. Does your son like his new sneakers? __a__   b. No, she doesn't.

3. Does Ms. Cho have a backpack? __b__   c. Yes, they do.

4. Do your sisters want new clothes? __c__   d. Yes, we do.

B Complete the conversations. Use *do, does, don't,* or *doesn't*.
Use capital letters when necessary.

1. **A:** _____Do_____ you have this jacket in black?

   B: Yes, we _____do_____. Here you go.

2. **A:** _____Does_____ Cindy want a new watch?

   B: No, she ____doesn't____. She likes her old watch.

3. **A:** _____Do_____ you need these jeans in a size 14?

   B: No, I ____don't____. I need a size 12.

4. **A:** _____Do_____ you have this shirt in an extra small?

   B: No, we ____don't____. But we have it in a small.

5. **A:** _____Does_____ Mr. Miller like this green sweater?

   B: No, he ____doesn't____. He likes the blue sweater.

C PAIRS. Practice the conversations in Exercise B.

Getting Started 5 minutes

- Say: *We're going to study simple present yes/no questions and short answers. In the conversation on page 95, Assefa used this grammar.*
- Play CD 2, Track 37. Students listen. Write *Do you have this sweater in a large?* on the board. Underline *Do you have.*

Presentation 15 minutes

Simple present: *Yes/no* questions and short answers

- Copy the grammar charts onto the board or show the charts on Transparency 5.4 and cover the exercise.
- Read the first part of the Grammar Watch note while students read along silently. Underline the base form *need* in the grammar chart.
- Read the questions in the left chart and ask the class to repeat. Remind students to use rising intonation with the *yes/no* questions.
- Say: *Use* Do *with I, we, you,* and *they. Use* Does *with* he *and* she.
- Ask students to close their books. Remove any visual aids for the charts. On the board, write the following incomplete sentences:

    1. _____ he need new shoes?
    2. _____ we need new shoes?
    3. _____ she need new shoes?
    4. _____ I need new shoes?

    Call on students to say *Do* or *Does* for each question.
- Ask students to go back to page 91 and look at the picture of Joe and Ellen. Ask: *Does Joe need new shoes?* (Yes, he does.) Write the short answer on the board and ask the class to repeat.
- Read the affirmative and negative short answers from the right chart. Ask the class to repeat. Remind students to use falling intonation with the short answer.
- Say: *When answering* no, *use* don't *or* doesn't. Write *do not* and *does not* on the board and make the contractions. Say: *Don't is a contraction of* do *and* not. *Doesn't is a contraction of* does *and* not.
- If you are using the transparency, do the exercise with the class.

Expansion: Grammar Practice

- Ask other questions about Joe and Ellen and tell students to call out a short answer, for example:

    Does Joe need a new watch? (No, he doesn't.) [He *wants* a new watch.]

    Does Ellen need a new purse? (Yes, she does.)

    Do Joe and Ellen need a new watch? (No, they don't.) [They *want* a new watch.]

Controlled Practice 20 minutes

 PRACTICE

Ⓐ Match the questions with the short answers.

- Read the directions and the example. Ask the class to repeat the example question and answer. When you get to item *d,* say: *It is normal for an assistant in a store to use* we *because* we *means the store.*
- Remind students to match the subject and pronoun in the answer choices (for example, in item 2, *your son = he*).
- Call on students to say answers.

Ⓑ Complete the conversations. Use *do, does, don't,...*

- Read the directions. Play A and read the example with a student.
- Ask: *Why is the answer* Do *in A's line?* (Because *Do* goes with *you.*) *Why is the answer* do *for B's line?* (Because *do* goes with *we.*) Remind students to begin a question with a capital letter.
- Students compare answers with a partner.
- Call on students to say answers.

Ⓒ PAIRS. Practice the conversations in Exercise B.

- Pair students and tell them to take turns playing A and B.
- Walk around and check that students are stressing words correctly. Model the conversation as needed.

MULTILEVEL INSTRUCTION for 1C

Pre-level Pairs first read each line of the conversation out loud before playing A or B.

Above-level After practicing the conversations as they are written, Student B creatively reverses the answer for each conversation (for example, for item 1, B: *No, we don't. I'm sorry.*).

2 PRACTICE

Complete the questions. Use *do* or *does* and the verbs...

- Read the directions. Read the example question, pausing after *Does Ben*. Ask the class: *Why Does?* (Because it goes with Ben.) Continue reading the question and then ask: *Why have?* (Because we use the base form of the verb with *does* or *do*.)
- Then say: *Look at Ben's clothes in the picture.* Ask: *Does Ben have an extra-large white T-shirt?* (Yes, he does.) Read the answer. Write it on the board and point to the capital letter, the comma, and the period.
- Walk around and check that students are using the comma and period in the short answer.
- Students compare answers with a partner and practice the conversations.
- To check answers, call on students to perform the conversations for the class.

Communicative Practice   20 minutes

Show what you know!

STEP 1. Write *yes/no* questions. Use *you*.

- Tell students to look at the picture. Ask: *Does this man like red ties?* (Yes, he does.)
- Read the directions and the example.
- Say: *Remember to use* Do *with you and to end each question with a question mark.*
- Walk around and check that students are using question marks.
- Students compare answers with a partner.
- Call on students to say answers.

STEP 2. PAIRS. Ask and answer the questions...

- Read the directions and the example.
- Pair students. Students take turns asking and answering the questions in Step 1.
- Say: *Remember to use* Do.

STEP 3. NEW PAIRS. Ask your new partner...

- Read the directions and the example.
- Ask students to find a new partner and to tell their new partner the name of their old partner (for example, *My first partner was Pat.*).
- Say: *Remember to use* Does.
- Walk around and check that students are talking about their old partner.
- To check comprehension, ask individual students about themselves (*Do you want new jeans?*) and their old partner (*Does Pat want new jeans?*).

▬▬ MULTILEVEL INSTRUCTION for STEP 3

Cross-ability The lower-level partner starts the conversation and the higher-level partner corrects by providing a model as needed (for example, A: *Do you like red ties?* B: *No, ask about my first partner like this: Does Ed like red ties?* A: *Does Ed like red ties?* B: *Yes, he does.*). Partners switch roles after four questions.

▬▬ Expansion: Grammar Practice for STEP 3

- Tell each student to write what they are wearing in today's class (for example, *a gray T-shirt, blue jeans, and white shoes*). Each student should write at least three articles of clothing.
- Pair students. Students take turns reading their list to their partner (for example, *I have a gray shirt. I have . . .*). Then students can ask each other if they like their clothing (for example, A: [Pointing to his own shirt] *Do you like this shirt?* B: *Yes, I do.* A: *Do you like these pants?* B: *Yes, I do.*).

Progress Check

Can you . . . ask about sizes and colors?

Say: *We have practiced asking about sizes and colors. Now, look at the question at the bottom of the page. Can you ask about sizes and colors?* Tell students to write a checkmark in the box.

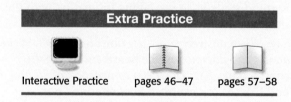

Extra Practice		
Interactive Practice	pages 46–47	pages 57–58

PRACTICE

Complete the questions. Use *do* or *does* and the verbs in parentheses. Use capital letters when necessary. Then look at the pictures. Answer the questions.

1. **A:** _____Does_____ Ben _____have_____ an extra-large white T-shirt?
   (have)
   B: Yes, he does. _____

2. **A:** _____Do_____ Ben and Tina _____have_____ blue shirts?
   (have)
   B: _____Yes, they do._____

3. **A:** _____Does_____ Tina _____need_____ a large red jacket?
   (need)
   B: _____No, she doesn't._____

4. **A:** _____Do_____ Ben and Tina _____need_____ red sweaters?
   (need)
   B: _____No, they don't._____

5. **A:** _____Does_____ Tina _____have_____ a small green sweater?
   (have)
   B: _____No, she doesn't._____

Show what you know! Ask about sizes and colors

STEP 1. Write *yes/no* questions. Use *you*.

1. like / red ties   _Do you like red ties?_

2. have / a favorite color   Do you have a favorite color?

3. need / new clothes   Do you need new clothes?

4. want / new jeans   Do you want new jeans?

STEP 2. PAIRS. Ask and answer the questions in Step 1.

Paula: *Do you like red ties?*
Ed: *Yes, I do.*

STEP 3. NEW PAIRS. Ask your new partner about his or her old partner.

Dan: *Does Ed like red ties?*
Paula: *Yes, he does.*

Can you...ask about sizes and colors? ☐

Read about U.S. dollar coins

Reading

1 BEFORE YOU READ

A CLASS. Look at the $5 bill. Who is the man in the picture?

Abraham Lincoln

B Look at other bills you have. Who are the people on the bills?

C Look at the U.S. presidents on the coins. Which presidents do you know?

1    **2**    **3**    **4**

D GROUPS OF 3. Look at the coins again. Answer the questions in the chart.

	Which president is on the coin?	When was he president?	Which president was he?
1	George Washington	1789–1797	first
2	John Adams	1797–1801	second
3	Thomas Jefferson	1801–1809	third
4	James Madison	1809–1817	fourth

Getting Started 10 minutes

1 BEFORE YOU READ

A CLASS. **Look at the $5 bill. Who is the...**

• Ask: *Who is the man in the picture?* (Abraham Lincoln, 16th president of the U.S.) Ask: *Why is he famous?* (He freed the slaves.)

• Ask: *How many dollars are in a five-dollar bill?* (5)

B CLASS. **Look at other bills you have. Who...**

• Read the directions.

• Write the following on the board for students to copy into their notebooks if they don't already know this information.

> *$1—George Washington, 1st president of the U.S.*
>
> *$5—Abraham Lincoln, 16th president of the U.S.*
>
> *$10—Alexander Hamilton, 1st secretary of the treasury (finance/money)*
>
> *$20—Andrew Jackson, 7th president of the U.S.*

■ **Expansion: Listening Practice for 1B**

• Form groups of 4 or 5. Explain: *I will ask a question. If you know the answer, raise your hand. I will call on you. Say the answer. If you are correct, your group gets one point. The group with the most points after all the questions wins.*

• On the board, write a list of all the groups (*Group 1, Group 2, . . .*) so you can write points next to each one.

• Ask: *Who was the first president of the United States?* Call on the first group member to raise his or her hand. If the student is correct (George Washington), award one point. Ask similar questions (for example, *Who was the seventh/ sixteenth president? Who was the first secretary of the treasury?*). Recycle questions to reinforce the answers. After ten questions, stop and declare the winning group.

C **Look at the U.S. presidents on the coins. Which...**

• Read the directions.

• Say: *These coins are new $1 coins.*

• For each coin, ask: *Who is on the coin? Which president was he? When was he president?* Point out that the answers are on the coins. Read the information on the first coin: *George Washington— 1st president 1789–1797.*

• To check comprehension, ask a few questions and call on students to say the answer (for example, T: *Who was the third president?* S: *Thomas Jefferson.*).

D GROUPS OF 3. **Look at the coins again....**

• Read the directions. Then ask an above-level student to read the questions and example answers. Ask the class to repeat.

• Form groups of 3. Each member can focus on one question in the chart and tell the other members in the group the answer. Group members can practice asking and answering questions to share the answers with the group (for example, A: *George Washington is on coin 1. When was he president?* B: *1789–1797. Which president was he?* C: *First.*).

• Call on students to say answers. Write answers on the board to confirm.

Community Building

If your school or program offers U.S. citizenship preparation classes, now might be a good time to mention them to your class since this lesson is closely connected to American history topics.

Presentation   20 minutes

2   READ

 Listen. Read the article.

- Ask: *What's the title?* (The New One-Dollar Coin)
- Ask students to look at the pictures. Point out the Statue of Liberty and ask if anyone knows where and what it is. (in New York, symbol of U.S., gift from France)
- Play CD 2, Track 38. Students listen and read along silently.
- *Optional:* Play Track 38 again. Pause the CD after each of the following paragraphs and ask these questions:

  First paragraph: *Who is on the new coins?* (U.S. presidents)

  Second paragraph: *What information is on the front of each coin?* (the president's picture, his name, the dates he was president, and which president he was)

  Third paragraph: *What's on the back of the coin?* (the Statue of Liberty)

  Fourth paragraph: *Are the coins popular?* (We'll have to wait and see.)

Controlled Practice   15 minutes

3   CHECK YOUR UNDERSTANDING

A Read the article again. What is the main idea?...

- Remind students: *The main idea is the most important idea of the article.*
- Ask students to read the title and the first paragraph and then to complete the sentence.
- Students compare answers with a partner.
- Call on a student to write the completed sentence on the board.
- To wrap up, point to the sentence on the board and ask: *What is this?* (the main idea of the article)

B Read the sentences. Circle *True* or *False*.

- Read the directions and the example.
- Walk around and if you see incorrect answers, point to where that information is discussed in the article and tell students to read the article again.
- Students compare answers with a partner.
- Call on students to say answers and ask: *Where in the reading did you find the answer?*

Communicative Practice   15 minutes

Show what you know!

PAIRS. Talk about it. Do you have any $1 coins?...

- Read the directions. Pair students.
- Practice with an above-level student. Ask all the questions and have the student say answers.
- Walk around and check that partners are asking and answering the questions.
- Call on students to say answers to the questions.

■■■■ **Expansion: Speaking Practice**

- Pair students and tell them to discuss the following questions: *Do you like coins? Why or why not? Do you like bills? Why or why not?*
- Call on students to say answers. Write several responses on the board, explaining or demonstrating unfamiliar vocabulary as needed. (*Some possible answers:* I like coins because they are small. I don't like bills because they can tear.)

■■■■ **Expansion: Graphic Organizer Practice**

- As a follow-up to the above activity, create a pro/con chart on the board. Write *Bills* above it.
- Call on students to say why they like (pro) bills and why they don't like (con) bills. Repeat for coins.
- Students can copy the charts into their notebooks.

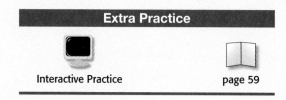

Extra Practice
Interactive Practice   page 59

🎧 Listen. Read the article.

The New One-Dollar Coin

Many Americans don't know the names of the U.S. presidents. But now people can learn their names. How? With money! The U.S. government is making four new $1 coins every year. Each coin shows a different U.S. president.

The front of each coin has a lot of information about the president. It has the president's picture, his name, the dates he was president, and which president he was. For example, the George Washington coin says that he

The new George Washington $1 coin

was the president from 1789 to 1797. It also says he was the first president.

The back of the coin shows the Statue of Liberty. The date of the coin is on the edge.

Some people like the new coins. But other people don't like them. In the past, the U.S. government made other $1 coins. Those coins were not popular. Will the U.S. president $1 coins be popular? We'll have to wait and see.

3 CHECK YOUR UNDERSTANDING

A Read the article again. What is the main idea? Complete the sentence.

The U.S. government is making new _____$1 coins_____.

B Read the sentences. Circle *True* or *False*.

1. Most Americans know all the U.S. presidents.   True   (False)

2. The new $1 coins show different U.S. presidents.   (True)   False

3. On the front of the coin, you see the Statue of Liberty.   True   (False)

4. The old $1 coins were not popular   (True)   False

Show what you know!

PAIRS. Talk about it. Do you have any $1 coins? What is on them? Do you use them? Do you like them?

Return something to a store

Listening and Speaking

1 BEFORE YOU LISTEN

CLASS. **Read the information. Answer the question.**

Sometimes people return clothes to stores. You usually need your receipt to get your money back. Do you ever return clothes?

2 LISTEN

A Look at the pictures. Why do people return clothes? Read the reasons.

ON THE AIR

Four Reasons People Return Clothes

3 They don't fit. They're too big.

1 It doesn't look good. I don't like it.

2 They don't match. The colors don't look good together.

4 The zipper doesn't work. It's broken.

CD1 T39

B 🎵 Matt Spencer is interviewing people on a radio show. He's at the customer service desk in a clothing store. Listen. Who is Matt interviewing?

a. cashiers   b. customer service assistants   c. customers

CD2 T39

C 🎵 Listen again. Number the reasons in Exercise A in the order you hear them.

Return something to a store

Getting Started 5 minutes

1 BEFORE YOU LISTEN

CLASS. Read the information. Answer the question.

- Say: *Look at the picture.* Ask: *What is happening?* (The woman is returning clothes.)
- Say: *Remember that* return *means to take something that you do not want back to the store to get your money back.*
- Read the directions and the paragraph. Ask: *Do you ever return clothes?*

Expansion: Speaking Practice for 1

- If possible, ask students to tell stories about what they returned. Ask: *What did you return? Why?*

Culture Connection

- Say: *In the United States, many stores allow you to make returns.*
- Ask: *What about in your country?*

Presentation 20 minutes

2 LISTEN

A Look at the pictures. Why do people return...

- Read the directions.
- Hold up the book. Point to each picture, and ask about the article of clothing: *What is it? What's the problem?* Students identify the clothing (for example, *pants*) and read the reason (*They don't fit. They're too big.*).
- On the board, write the singular and plural forms of each reason (for example, *It's too big. They're too big.*). Tell students to copy them into their notebooks.

- Finally, hold the book up and point to the circle next to the title of the art, which says *On the air.* Say: On the air *means that a show is on the radio. We will now listen to a radio show.*

B Matt Spencer is interviewing people...

- Read the directions. Point to the picture on page 101 and explain: Customer service employees *are the people in a store who answer your questions and help you when you have a problem.*
- Read the question and the answer choices.
- Play CD 2, Track 39. Students listen.
- Call on the class to say the answer.

Teaching Tip

Optional: If pre-level students need additional support, tell them to read the Audio Script on page 284 as they listen to the conversations.

C Listen again. Number the reasons...

- Read the directions.
- Play CD 2, Track 39. Pause after the first reason (*My husband doesn't like it.*) and ask: *Which reason did you hear?* Students put a *1* in the circle next to *It doesn't look good. I don't like it.*
- Resume playing Track 39. Students number the remaining reasons.
- Students compare answers with a partner, using *first, second, third,* and *fourth.*
- Call on students to read the reasons in order. Ask: *Which one is first/second/third/fourth?*

Return something to a store

Controlled Practice 20 minutes

3 CONVERSATION

A Look at the picture.... Guess:...

- Read the directions.
- Ask: *What is she looking for?* Write the answer choices on the board and ask a student to read them. Call on students to guess.

B Listen to the conversation. Was...

- Read the directions. Play CD 2, Track 40.
- Circle the correct answer on the board. Ask: *Was your guess correct?*

C Listen and read the conversation....

- Play CD 2, Track 41. Students listen and read along silently.
- Resume playing Track 41. Students listen and repeat.

4 PRACTICE

A PAIRS. Practice the conversation. Then make new...

- Pair students and tell them to practice the conversation in Exercise 3C.
- Then, in Exercise 4A, tell students to look at the clothes and reasons on page 100. Write the clothing items and return reasons on the board.
- Read the directions.
- Copy the conversation onto the board with blanks. Read through it. When you come to a blank, fill it in with information from page 100 or the board (*this pair of pants* and *They don't fit. They're too big.*). Ask: *When do we use* this? (for singular items) *When do we use* these? (for plural items)
- Ask two on-level students to practice the conversation in front of the class. Tell pairs to take turns playing each role and to use the pictures to fill in the blanks.
- Walk around and check that students are stressing important words.
- Tell students to stand, mingle, and practice the conversation with several new partners.
- Call on pairs to perform for the class.

MULTILEVEL INSTRUCTION for 4A

Cross-ability Higher-level partners first practice as the assistant and ask questions to help the customer explain (Assistant: *Excuse me? What do you need to return?*).

Communicative Practice 15 minutes

B CLASS. What are other reasons people return things?

- Ask: *What are other reasons people return things?* Write students' answers on the board. (*Possible answers:* 1. It's too expensive. 2. I changed my mind. 3. It's a gift I don't want. 4. I don't like the color. 5. It's too small.)
- Keep all the reasons on the board to refer to in Exercise 4C.

C ROLE PLAY. PAIRS. Make your own...

- Play the customer and model a new conversation based on Exercise 3C with an above-level student. Use new clothing and a new reason.
- If possible, continue the conversation to inspire creativity and humor:
  Assistant: *I need the receipt.*
  Customer: *Yes, I know. I need it, too!*
  Assistant: *Do you have it?*
  Customer: *No, but I want my money back.*
  Assistant: *I'm sorry. I need the receipt.*
- Pair students and ask them to create a new conversation.
- Check that students are stressing important words and using *this/these* correctly. Also check that the reasons for making a return are realistic.

Community Building

As you model the activity, also show students how to prompt each other by pointing to the reasons on the board.

Extra Practice

Interactive Practice

---

3 CONVERSATION

A Look at the picture on the right. A customer is returning a shirt.
Guess: What is she looking for?

a. her money   b. her receipt   c. her credit card

CD2 T40

B Listen to the conversation. Was your guess in
Exercise A correct?

CD2 T41

C Listen and read the conversation.
Then listen and repeat.

Assistant:	Hello. May I help you?
Customer:	Yes. Hi. I need to return this shirt.
Assistant:	What's the problem?
Customer:	It doesn't fit.
Assistant:	Do you have your receipt?
Customer:	Yes, I do. It's here somewhere!

4 PRACTICE

A PAIRS. Practice the conversation. Then make new conversations.
Use different clothes and reasons from page 100.

B CLASS. What are other reasons people return things?

C ROLE PLAY. PAIRS. Make your own conversations.
Use different clothes and problems.

Grammar

Simple present negative

| I
You
We | **don't** | need
want
have
like | this color. |
| They | | **fit.** | |

| He
She
The customer | **doesn't** | need
want
have
like | this color. |
| It | | **fit.** | |

PRACTICE

Grammar Watch

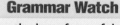

Use the base form of the verb after *don't* or *doesn't*.

A Underline the correct word.

1. The zipper on my jacket **don't** / **doesn't** work.

2. Your new jeans **don't** / **doesn't** fit.

3. I **don't** / **doesn't** have my receipt.

4. They **don't** / **doesn't** like their new shoes.

5. Ms. Wong **don't** / **doesn't** like her new skirt.

6. My husband **don't** / **doesn't** need a tie.

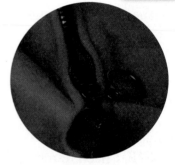

B PAIRS. Look at the picture. Find the problems with the clothes. Tell your partner. There is more than one correct answer.

Answers will vary.

A: *What's the problem in A?*
B: *The jeans don't fit.*
A: *Right.*
B: *What's the problem . . . ?*

C WRITE. Write three problems from Exercise B. Answers will vary but could include:

1. ___A. The jeans don't fit.___

2. ___B. The zipper is broken.___

3. ___C. She doesn't like the shirt.___

Lesson 9 Talk about problems with clothes

Getting Started   5 minutes

- Say: *We're going to study statements with* don't *and* doesn't. *In the conversation on page 101, the customer used this grammar.*
- Play CD 2, Track 41. Students listen. Write on the board: *It doesn't fit.* Underline *It doesn't.*

Presentation   10 minutes

Simple present negative

- Copy the grammar charts onto the board or show the charts on Transparency 5.5 and cover the exercise.
- Say sentences from the left chart and ask the class to repeat.
- Read the Grammar Watch note. On the board, write *needs* and *need.* Ask: *Which one is the base form?* (need)
- Say sentences from the right chart and ask the class to repeat. On the board, write *do + not = don't* and *does + not = doesn't.* Remind students: Don't *is a contraction between* do *and* not. Doesn't *is a contraction between* does *and* not.
- Ask students to close their books. Remove any visual aids for the chart. On the board, write several incomplete sentences:

    I _____ want this   *She _____ like this*
    color.   *color.*
    We _____ have this   *It _____ fit.*
    color.

    Call on students to say *don't* or *doesn't.*
- If you are using the transparency, do the exercise with the class.

Controlled Practice   5 minutes

 PRACTICE

Ⓐ Underline the correct word.

- Read the directions and the example. Say: *Zipper matches the subject pronoun* it *in the grammar chart, so I know that* doesn't *is the correct answer. Match the subject in each sentence with a subject in the chart to know if* don't *or* doesn't *is the answer.*
- Do item 2 with the class. Ask: *What's the subject?* (jeans) *What's the matching pronoun in the grammar chart?* (they) *What's the answer?* (don't)

- Walk around and, as needed, ask students to write the matching subject pronoun to the left of the sentence (for example, *It 1. The zipper . . .*).
- Students compare answers with a partner.
- Call on students to say answers.

Communicative Practice   10 minutes

Ⓑ PAIRS. Look at the picture. Find the problems...

- Read the directions.
- Play A and read the example conversation with an on-level student. Point to the woman's waistline in A and say: *See? The jeans are too big. They don't fit.* Ask: *Where is the woman?* (in a dressing room)
- Pair students and tell them to take turns playing A and B. Walk around and ask students what is wrong with the pictures (for example, *What's the problem in D?*). (*Possible answers:* A: The jeans don't fit. B: The zipper is broken. C: She doesn't like it/the color. D: It doesn't match. E: It's too small.)
- Call on pairs to perform for the class.

■■■ MULTILEVEL INSTRUCTION for B

Pre-level Write all the return reasons on the board as a visual aid for students while they practice. Students can later copy these reasons when they do Exercise C.

Above-level Ask students to name two logical problems per dressing room (for example, Room E: *It doesn't fit. She doesn't like the color.*).

Ⓒ WRITE. Write three problems from Exercise B.

- Read the directions. Say: *Write in complete sentences. Use a capital letter and a period.*
- As an example, point to the conversation in Exercise B where it states, *The new jeans don't fit.* Say: *This is a complete sentence.*
- Say: *Write three different problems.*
- Walk around and check that students are writing problems from the picture in Exercise B and are writing complete sentences.
- Call on students to say answers.

Extra Practice

Interactive Practice   pages 48–49   pages 60–61

1 GRAMMAR

Complete the sentences. Use the verbs in parentheses.

- Read the directions and the example.
- Say: *Read the sentence before you answer and look at the subject.*
- Walk around and, as needed, tell students to refer back to the grammar charts on pages 90 (simple present affirmative), 96 (simple present *yes/no* questions and short answers), and 102 (simple present negative). Say: *Remember to use the base form of the verb with* do *or* don't *and* does *or* doesn't.
- Students compare answers with a partner.
- Read the conversation and call on individual students to say answers. When reviewing answers, point out how the sentence reveals the correct answer (for example, *In the first line, we know the answer is* need *because* need *goes with* I.).
- *Optional:* Pair students and ask them to practice the conversation. Call on pairs to perform the completed conversation for the class.

2 WRITING

STEP 1. Complete the questions. Use words from...

- Read the directions and the example.
- As a warm-up, write *Do you have _____?* on the board. Next to it, write *blue* and *jeans*. Say the question and tell the class to complete it (*Do you have . . .* Ss: *. . . blue jeans?*).
- Erase *blue* and *jeans* and replace with *a black* and *jacket*. Say the question and tell the class to complete it (*Do you have a black jacket?*). Point to *a* and ask: *When do we use* a *or* an? (for singular things)
- Tell students that more than one answer for each item is possible.
- Students compare answers with a partner.
- Call on students to say answers.

STEP 2. PAIRS. Take turns. Student A, ask...

- Read the directions and write the example conversation on the board. Call on a student to finish the question as you write.
- Say: *Use* but *after you say* No, I don't. But *comes after a negative statement and before an affirmative one.*
- To illustrate, write on the board: *No, I don't.* Put a negative sign (–) over it. Then write: *But I have pink shoes.* Put an affirmative sign (+) over it.
- Pair students and tell them to take turns playing A and B. Walk around and check that students are asking and answering questions using *like, need, want,* and *have.*
- As students practice, tell them to use words from the box in Step 1. They can also turn back to the vocabulary list on page 87.

STEP 3. Write sentences about your partner.

- Read the directions and the example.
- Ask a student: *Do you have pink shoes?* On the board, change the student's response to the third person (*Eugenia doesn't have pink shoes.*).
- Walk around and check that students are writing complete sentences and using their partner's name as the subject.
- Tell students to exchange books with a classmate and check each other's answers.
- To wrap up, ask students to share sentences about their partners. Correct as needed and ask the student to repeat the corrected sentence.

CD-ROM Practice

 Go to the CD-ROM for more practice.

If your students need more practice with the vocabulary, grammar, and competencies in Unit 5, encourage them to review the activities on the CD-ROM. This review can also help students prepare for the final role play on the following Expand page.

Extra Practice

pages 50–51

---

1 GRAMMAR

Complete the sentences. Use the verbs in parentheses.

A: Hi. I ___need___ a gift for my friend.
    (need)

  ___Do___ you ___have___ this shirt in white?
          (have)

B: No, we ___don't___. But we ___have___ it in yellow.
                (have)

A: Hmm. My friend ___doesn't like___ yellow.
            (not like)

B: ___Does___ your friend ___like___ blue?
               (like)

A: Yes, he ___does___. He ___needs___ a large.
               (need)

B: OK. Here you go.

2 WRITING

**STEP 1. Complete the questions. Use words from the box or your own ideas.
Add *a* or *an* when necessary.**   Answers will vary. Possible answers include:

   Do you have ___red shoes___?

1. Do you have ___a blue sweater___?

2. Do you want ___a pink shirt___?

3. Do you need ___black shoes___?

4. Do you like ___white pants___?

red	white	sweater	jacket
yellow	pink	jeans	shoes
blue	orange	pants	shirt
beige	purple		
black			

**STEP 2. PAIRS. Take turns. Student A, ask a question from Step 1.
Student B, give true answers. Then add information.**

Eric: *Do you have red shoes?*
Mai: *No, I don't. But I have pink shoes. Do you have . . . ?*

STEP 3. Write sentences about your partner.   Answers will vary.

   Mai has pink shoes.

1. _____

2. _____

3. _____

3 ACT IT OUT — What do you say?

CD2 T42

STEP 1. 🔘 **Listen to the conversation.**

STEP 2. **You are in a clothing store. Student A, you are a customer. Student B, you are an assistant.**

> **Student A:** You need a gift. You want a red sweater.
> • Don't look at the picture.
> • Ask the assistant for a sweater.
> • Ask for the size you need.
> • Ask the price.
> • Thank the assistant.

> **Student B:** The customer wants a sweater.
> • Look at the sweaters.
> • Answer the customer's questions.

STEP 3. **Review the conversation on page 101 (CD 2 Track 40).**

STEP 4. **It's the next day.**

> **Student A:** You want to return the sweater.
> • The zipper doesn't work.
> • You have the receipt.

> **Student B:** The customer wants to return the sweater.
> • Ask why.
> • Ask for the receipt.

ON SALE!
$19.99

XS S M L XL

4 READ AND REACT — Problem-solving

STEP 1. **Read about Luis's problem.**

Luis's birthday is today! His friends give him some gifts. His friend Paula gives him a CD. His friend Solomon gives him a T-shirt. His friend Ayantu gives him a tie.

The tie is nice, but Luis doesn't need a tie. He wants a new wallet. He doesn't have the receipt, but the box has the name of the store on it.

STEP 2. **PAIRS. Talk about it. What is Luis's problem? What can Luis do? Here are some ideas.**

- He can return the tie and buy a wallet.
- He can give the tie to another friend.
- He can keep the tie.
- He can _____.

5 CONNECT

For your Community-building Activity, go to page 248.
For your Team Project, go to page 268.

Which goals can you check off? Go back to page 85.

Show what you know!

3 ACT IT OUT

STEP 1. Listen to the conversation.

- Play CD 2, Track 42. Students listen.
- As needed, play Track 42 again to aid comprehension.

STEP 2. You are in a clothing store. Student A,...

- Read the directions and the guidelines for Students A and B.
- Pair students. Students practice at their desk with their partner.
- Walk around and check that Student A is correctly asking *yes/no* questions in the simple present and that Student B is giving correct short answers.
- Call on pairs to perform for the class. While pairs are performing, use the scoring rubric on page Txiv to evaluate each student's vocabulary, grammar, fluency, and how well they complete the task.
- *Optional:* After each pair finishes, discuss the strengths and weakness of each performance either in front of the class or privately.

STEP 3. Review the conversation...

- Tell students to review the conversation on page 101.
- Play CD 2, Track 40. Students listen.
- As needed, play Track 40 again to aid comprehension.

STEP 4. It's the next day.

- Read the directions and the guidelines for Students A and B.
- Pair students. Students practice at their desk with their partner.
- Walk around and check that Student A is correctly using the negative of *be* and that Student B is asking about the reason for returning the sweater.
- Call on pairs to practice for the class.
- While pairs are performing, use the scoring rubric on page Txiv to evaluate each student's vocabulary, grammar, fluency, and how well they complete the task.
- *Optional:* After each pair finishes, discuss the strengths and weakness of each performance, either in front of the class or privately.

4 READ AND REACT

STEP 1. Read about Luis's problem.

- Say: *We are going to read about a student's problem, and then we need to think about a solution.*
- Read the directions.
- Read the story while students follow along silently. Pause after each sentence to allow time for students to comprehend. Periodically stop and ask simple *Wh-* questions to check comprehension (for example, *When is Luis's birthday? What does Paula give him?*).

STEP 2. PAIRS. Talk about it. What is Luis's...

- Pair students. Read the directions and the question.
- Read the ideas in the list. Give pairs a couple of minutes to discuss possible solutions for Luis.
- Ask: *Which ideas are good?* Call on students to say their opinion about the ideas in the list (for example, S: *I don't think he can keep the tie because he doesn't need it.*).
- Now tell students to think of one new idea not in the box (for example, *He can sell it on the Internet.*).

MULTILEVEL INSTRUCTION for STEP 2

Pre-level For more support, students work in groups of 3.

Above-level Ask pairs to discuss the pros and cons of each idea. Call on pairs to say the pros and cons of each (for example, *He can return the tie and buy a wallet.* Pro: *This is an easy way to get a wallet.* Con: *Maybe the wallets at the store are all expensive. He will pay more money for it.*).

5 CONNECT

Turn to page 248 for the Community-building Activity and page 268 for the Team Project. See pages Txi–Txii for general notes about teaching these activities.

Progress Check

Which goals can you check off? Go back to page 85.

Ask students to turn to page 85 and check off any remaining goals they have reached. Call on students to say which goals they will practice outside of class.

Home, Sweet Home

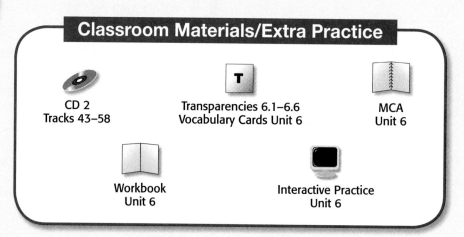

CD 2
Tracks 43–58

Transparencies 6.1–6.6
Vocabulary Cards Unit 6

MCA
Unit 6

Workbook
Unit 6

Interactive Practice
Unit 6

Unit Overview

Goals

• See the list of goals on the facing page.

Grammar

• *There is/There are*; contractions
• *Is there/Are there*; short answers; contractions
• Prepositions *at, from, in, on, to*

Pronunciation

• Stress in compound nouns

Reading

• Read an article about smoke alarms

Writing

• Write sentences about houses and things in them
• Write directions to a place

Life Skills Writing

• Address an envelope

Preview

• Set the context of the unit by saying: *There are different types of homes—a house is one. What else?* (*Possible answers:* an apartment, a condo/townhouse)

• Hold up page 105 or show Transparency 6.1. Read the unit title and explain: *This is the title of an old American song. It means your home is important to you and a place where you feel good.*

• Say: *Look at the picture.* Ask the Preview questions: *Where are the people?* (They are in a new home.) *Why are they there?* (They want a new home.)

Unit Goals

• Point to the Unit Goals. Explain that this list shows what the class will be studying in this unit.

• Tell students to read the goals silently.

• Say each goal and ask students to repeat. Explain unfamiliar vocabulary as needed:

  Rent: *To pay money to use a house or apartment*

  Address: *The number and street of a place*

  Directions: *A list of streets and turns that tells you how to go from one place to another place*

• Show an envelope. Explain: Address *can be a verb also.* To address *an envelope means to write the address on the envelope.* Draw an envelope on the board and write an address on it. As you write, say: *I am addressing this envelope. I am writing the address.*

• Tell students to circle one goal that is very important to them. Call on several students to say the goal they circled.

Home, Sweet Home

Preview

**Look at the picture.
Where are the people?
Why are they there?**

UNIT GOALS

- ☐ Describe a house
- ☐ Ask about an apartment for rent
- ☐ Ask about things in a house
- ☐ Read addresses
- ☐ Give your address
- ☐ Address an envelope
- ☐ Read apartment ads
- ☐ Give directions

1   WHAT DO YOU KNOW?

A **CLASS.** Look at the pictures. Which rooms do you know? Which things in the rooms do you know?

> D is a bedroom.
> Number 13 is a bathtub.

CD2 T43

B Listen and point to the pictures. Then listen and repeat.

2   PRACTICE

A **PAIRS.** Student A, look at the pictures. Name the things in a room. Student B, guess the room.

A: *A table and chairs.*
B: *Is it the living room?*
A: *No.*
B: *The dining room?*
A: *Right.*

B **WORD PLAY. GROUPS OF 3.** Student A, look at the list of things in a house on page 107. Draw a picture of one thing. Students B and C, guess the thing.

B: *A dresser.*
A: *No.*
C: *A refrigerator.*
A: *Right.*

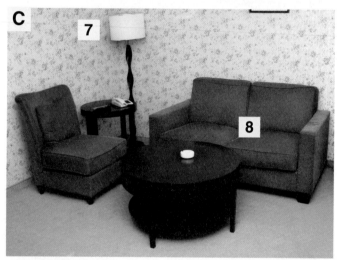

Getting Started 5 minutes

Culture Connection

• Ask: *Do people rent apartments in your country? Are houses expensive in your country?*

• Say: *Apartments are very popular in the United States. Houses can be very expensive. So, many people start in an apartment and then buy a house later.*

1 WHAT DO YOU KNOW?

A CLASS. Look at the pictures. Which rooms...

• Show Transparency 6.2 or hold up the book.

• Tell students to cover the list of words on page 107.

• Point to picture D and read the first sentence in the example. Ask: *Which things in this room do you know?*

• Students call out answers (for example, *Number 10 is a bed.*). Point to the other rooms (A–E). For each, ask: *What room is this? Which things in this room do you know?* Students call out answers.

• If students call out an incorrect room or item, change the answer into a question for the class (for example, *Number 13 is a shower?*). If nobody can identify the correct item, tell students they will now listen to a CD and practice the names of the rooms of the house and things in the rooms.

Presentation 10 minutes

B 💿 Listen and point to the pictures....

• Play CD 2, Track 43. Pause after number 14 (*toilet*).

• Walk around and check that students are pointing.

• To check comprehension, say each room and each item in random order and ask students to point to the appropriate picture.

• Resume playing CD 2, Track 43. Students listen and repeat. Explain: *The things in the living room, bedroom, and living room are called* furniture. *The things in the kitchen are called* appliances. On the board, write these as headings and then write the furniture and appliances under them for students to copy into their notebooks.

Controlled Practice 10 minutes

2 PRACTICE

A PAIRS. Student A, look at the pictures. Name...

• Read the directions. Read each line in the example and ask the class to repeat. Model correct intonation.

• Play A and model the example with an above-level student. Pair students and tell them to take turns playing A and B. Say: *Student A, don't point to the pictures.*

• Walk around and, as needed, remind students not to point to the pictures. To check comprehension, say things in one room and call on individual students to say the room (for example, T: *Table, chair.* S: *Dining room?* T: *Yes!*).

▇ MULTILEVEL INSTRUCTION for 2A

Pre-level Students first label the rooms and the things in them for easy reference.

Above-level For each room, ask Student A to say an additional item not in the pictures (for example, A: *A TV.* B: *Is it the living room?* A: *Yes.*) Partners take turns playing A and B.

B WORD PLAY. GROUPS OF 3. Student A,...

• Ask students to look at the picture. Ask: *What's the student drawing?* (a refrigerator)

• Read the directions. To practice, draw a picture of an item (for example, a microwave) on the board. Call on students to guess it.

• Form groups of 3 and tell students to take turns playing each role.

• Call on a few individual students to draw one item on the board. Students call out answers.

▇ Expansion: Vocabulary Practice for 2B

• Tell students to create flashcards for the vocabulary on page 107, with the word on one side of the card and a drawing or (if catalogs or magazines are available) a photo on the other.

• Pair students. Student A holds up the picture side of one card while Student B guesses what it is. When Student B guesses correctly, B then holds up another card while A guesses the item.

Learning Strategy: Make labels

- Read the directions.

- In class, tell students to make three or four cards to label things in the classroom (for example, *a desk, a chair*). Ask students to tape their cards to nearby things in the classroom.

- Tell students to make three or four cards for things in their house.

- Walk around as students work. If misspellings occur, tell them to check the vocabulary list on page 107.

- Say: *Put your cards on things in your home. Practice saying the words.* Remind students to use this strategy to remember other new vocabulary.

Communicative Practice   25 minutes

Show what you know!

STEP 1. Think about your dream house....

- Read the directions.

- Ask students to look at the list. Say: *This dream house has a living room, a dining room, . . .*

- Explain: *A laundry room has a washing machine and a dryer.*

- Ask: *What does your dream house have?*

> **Teaching Tip**
>
> Expose students to authentic materials to inspire creative thinking and genuine opportunities to practice English. Bring in real estate magazines or home ads with pictures from your local newspaper to pass around to give students ideas about what can be in their dream house. Write any new vocabulary on the board and explain as needed (for example, *a two-car garage, a balcony, a guest room*).

STEP 2. PAIRS. Talk about your dream house.

- Read the directions and the example.

- On the board, write, *My dream house has _____ rooms.* Ask: *How many rooms are in your dream house? What rooms does it have?* Call on students to answer in complete sentences (*It has . . .*).

- Say: *Use* and *before your last room.* Read the example again and emphasize *and*.

- Pair students. Say: *Take turns talking about your dream house. Say how many rooms it has, and then name all the different rooms.*

- Walk around and check that students are saying *My dream house has _____ rooms* and *It has. . . .* As you walk around, ask individual students: *What's in your dream house?* (four bedrooms, two kitchens)

- Call on students to talk about their dream house.

▬▬▬ MULTILEVEL INSTRUCTION for STEP 2

Pre-level Walk around and ask *Wh-* questions to help students start talking (for example, *How many bedrooms do you want?*).

Above-level Encourage students to use vocabulary they know that is not listed on page 107.

▬▬▬ Expansion: Speaking Practice for STEP 2

- Pair students. Tell A to say a room and B to say as many things as possible that go in that room:

  A: *Kitchen.*

  B: *A refrigerator, a stove, . . .*

- If B doesn't name all the things listed for that room on page 107, A can prompt B to say more items (for example, *What else is in a kitchen?*). Students then switch roles and continue.

▬▬▬ Expansion: Speaking Practice for STEP 2

- Pair students and tell them to take turns discussing what things they need or want (for example, A: *I need a new dresser. Do you? B: No, I don't. I need a new bed, and I want a new stove.*).

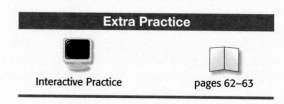

Extra Practice

Interactive Practice   pages 62–63

B

Rooms and Things in a House

A. kitchen
1. sink
2. stove
3. microwave
4. refrigerator

B. dining room
5. table
6. chair

C. living room
7. lamp
8. sofa

D. bedroom
9. dresser
10. bed
11. closet

E. bathroom
12. shower
13. bathtub
14. toilet

Learning Strategy

Make labels

Look at the list of things in a house. Choose three or four words. Write each word on a card. Put the cards on the things in your house. For example, write the word *chair* on a card. Tape the card to a chair in your living room.

D

Show what you know!

STEP 1. **Think about your dream house. Which rooms are in the house? Make a list in your notebook.**

STEP 2. PAIRS. **Talk about your dream house.**

A: *My dream house has nine rooms. It has a living room, a dining room, a kitchen, three bedrooms, two bathrooms, and a laundry room.*
B: *My dream house . . .*

> living room
> dining room
> kitchen
> 3 bedrooms
> 2 bathrooms
> laundry room

Listening and Speaking

1 BEFORE YOU LISTEN

PAIRS. Label the pictures. Use the words in the box.

> cheap   dark   expensive   large   old   new   small   sunny

a __new__ kitchen   an __old__ kitchen   a __large__ bathroom   a __small__ bathroom

a __sunny__ bedroom   a __dark__ bedroom   an __expensive__ place   a __cheap__ place

2 LISTEN

A Dan and Emily Reed are looking for a house. Look at the computer monitor. What can you say about the house?

Answers will vary.

CD2 T44

B Listen to the conversation. Check (✓) the correct answer.

1. Dan says the house looks _____.
   ☐ cheap   ☑ great   ☐ large

2. The house has _____. (Check (✓) two answers.)
   ☑ two bedrooms   ☐ three bedrooms
   ☑ a large kitchen   ☐ a dining room

CD2 T45

C 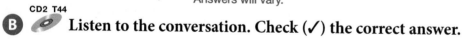 Listen to the whole conversation. What's wrong with the house?

a. It's old.   b. It's very expensive.   (c.) It's not in the United States.

Lesson 2 Talk about a house for rent

Getting Started — 5 minutes

1 BEFORE YOU LISTEN

PAIRS. Label the pictures. Use the words in the box.

- Read the directions.
- Read each word in the box and ask the class to repeat. Write one pair of opposites on the board (for example, *cheap/expensive*). Tell students these are opposites. To clarify, write additional examples on the board: *black/white*, *off/on*, and *up/down*.
- For the remaining pairs, say a word and ask the class to call out its opposite (for example, T: *What is the opposite of* dark? Ss: *Sunny.* T: *Good!*).
- If possible, demonstrate the meaning of these adjectives by using what's available in your classroom For example, to demonstrate *sunny*, open the blinds to allow sunlight into your room. To demonstrate *dark*, close the blinds and turn off the classroom lights momentarily.
- Pair students. Remind them to cross out the words they use in the box.
- Call on students to say answers. Hold up the book, point to a picture, and ask: *What is this?*
- To wrap up, pronounce $2,000 (two thousand dollars) vs. $200 (two hundred dollars) and ask the class to repeat.

MULTILEVEL INSTRUCTION for 1
Pre-level Tell students to look at all the pictures first and guess the answer before they write.
Above-level Tell pairs to discuss why each room has a certain label (for example, A: *Why is this a new kitchen?* B: *Because it has new appliances.*).

Expansion: Vocabulary Practice for 1
- Pair students. Student A says a word (for example, *expensive*). Student B says the opposite word (for example, *cheap*).
- Each pair writes a list of opposites in their notebooks.

Presentation — 15 minutes

2 LISTEN

A Dan and Emily Reed are looking for a house....

- Read the directions and have students look at the picture. Ask: *How many people are in Dan and Emily's family?* (three—Dan, Emily, and their baby)
- Ask students to describe the house. (Possible answers: *It's small but new. It's sunny. It's cheap/not expensive.*)

Expansion: Critical Thinking Practice for 2A
- Ask the class: *What do you think? Does the Reed family need a house? Why or why not?* (*Possible answer:* Yes, because they have a baby.)

B Listen to the conversation. Check...

- Read each question and the answer choices. Ask the class to repeat. Tell students that number 2 has two answers.
- Play CD 2, Track 44. Students listen and check the correct answer.
- Students compare answers with a partner.
- Say each sentence and call on the class to say the answer.

Teaching Tip
Optional: Remember, if students need additional support, tell them to read the Audio Script on page 284 as they listen to the conversations.

C Listen to the whole conversation....

- Play CD 2, Track 45. Students listen and circle the correct answer.
- Call on the class to say the answer.

Talk about a house for rent

Controlled Practice   15 minutes

3 CONVERSATION

 Listen and read the conversation....

- Note: This conversation is the same one students heard in Exercise 2B on page 108.
- Play CD 2, Track 46. Students listen and read along silently.
- Explain: Wow! *is a common expression to show that you are excited and* Really? *is an expression to show that you are interested in something.*
- Resume playing Track 46. Students listen and repeat.

4 PRACTICE

A PAIRS. **Practice the conversation. Then make new...**

- Pair students and tell them to practice the conversation in Exercise 3.
- Then, in Exercise 4A, ask students to look at the pictures and the words in the boxes. Say *garage, laundry room,* and *yard* and ask the class to repeat.
- Point to the pictures and explain the new vocabulary as needed: *A garage is where you put your vehicles or cars. A laundry room is where you clean your dirty clothes or laundry. A yard is outside. Yards sometimes have grass.*
- Read the directions.
- Copy the conversation onto the board with blanks. Read through it. When you come to a blank, fill it in with information from the boxes (*new bathroom* and *garage*). As you fill in the blanks, remind A to repeat the last thing that B says.
- Ask two on-level students to practice the conversation in front of the class.
- Tell pairs to take turns playing each role and to use information from the boxes to fill in the blanks.
- Tell students to stand, mingle, and practice the conversation with several new partners.

MULTILEVEL INSTRUCTION for 4A

Pre-level Play Track 46 again and allow students to listen and repeat a few more times.

Above-level Tell students to continue the conversation by asking about two more rooms.

Communicative Practice   10 minutes

B ROLE PLAY. PAIRS. **Make your own...**

- With an above-level student, make up a new conversation and practice for the class. Base the conversation on Exercise 3.
- Tell students to copy the vocabulary words for rooms from pages 107 and 109 into their notebooks and direct them to use these words in their conversations.
- Pair students and tell them to take turns playing A and B.
- Walk around and check that students are using correct intonation for statements and questions and are using appropriate adjectives (for example, *sunny, nice, large*) for each room or place.
- Call on pairs to perform for the class.
- To wrap up, on the board write some of the errors you heard during the role plays. Ask students to correct the mistakes. Go over the corrections by saying the words or sentences correctly and asking the class to repeat.

MULTILEVEL INSTRUCTION for 4B

Pre-level Tell students to use the same conversation as in Exercise 4A and to just change one or two lines (for example, A: *Oh, wow! This house looks wonderful!*).

Above-level Tell students to close their books and create a new conversation without looking at the conversation. Students may first copy important vocabulary (for example, *new bathroom, garage*) into their notebooks before they close their books.

Expansion: Vocabulary Practice for 4B

- Bring a local real estate magazine to class and write new vocabulary on the board (for example, *walk-in closet, eat-in kitchen*) from the ads. Explain unfamiliar vocabulary as needed.
- Tell students to practice the conversation in Exercise 4A using the new vocabulary on the board.

Extra Practice

Interactive Practice

3 CONVERSATION

CD2 T46

Listen and read the conversation. Then listen and repeat.

Dan: Oh, wow! This house looks great!

Emily: Really?

Dan: Yes. There are two bedrooms and a large kitchen.

Emily: What about a dining room?

Dan: Well, no. There's no dining room.

4 PRACTICE

A PAIRS. **Practice the conversation. Then make new conversations. Use the information in the boxes.**

A: Oh, wow! This house looks great!

B: Really?

A: Yes. There are two bedrooms and a   .

B: What about a   ?

A: Well, no. There's no   .

new bathroom

garage

sunny kitchen

laundry room

nice living room

yard

B ROLE PLAY. PAIRS. **Make your own conversations. Use different rooms.**

Grammar

There is/There are

There is	a	living room.
There's	one	bathroom.
There are	two	bedrooms.

There is		dining room.
There's	no	bathtub.
There are		closets.

····· **Grammar Watch**

Contractions
There's = *There is*

1 PRACTICE

A Look at the apartment ad. Read the sentences. Check (✓) *True* or *False*. Correct the false sentences.

FOR RENT

Large one-bedroom apartment with dining room, new bathroom, and new kitchen. Five closets! Garage. $700/month.

Call 213-555-4892

		True	False
	There's one bedroom.		
1.	~~There are two bedrooms.~~	☐	✓
2.	There's one bathroom.	✓	☐
	There's a dining room.		
3.	There's no dining room.	☐	✓
4.	There's a new kitchen.	✓	☐
	There are five closets.		
5.	There's one closet.	☐	✓
	There's a garage.		
6.	There's no garage.	☐	✓

B Look at the picture on page 111. Complete the conversation. Use the words in the box. You will use some words more than once. Use capital letters when necessary.

> there's a   there are two   there's no

A: So, tell me about your new house!

B: Well, _____*there are two*_____ sunny bedrooms.

A: Nice! What about bathrooms?

B: _____There are two_____ bathrooms.

A: Great. And a dining room?

B: _____There's no_____ dining room, but _____there's a_____ table and chairs in the kitchen. _____There's a_____ large yard, too. We love it!

Lesson 3 Describe a house

Getting Started   5 minutes

- Say: *We're going to study* There is *and* There are. *In the conversation on page 109, Dan used this grammar.*
- Play CD 2, Track 46 again. Students listen. Write on the board: *There are two bedrooms.* Underline *There are* and the final *-s* in *bedrooms.*

Presentation   10 minutes

There is/There are

- Copy the grammar charts onto the board or show the charts on Transparency 6.3 and cover the exercise.
- Read the Grammar Watch note while students read along silently. Write it on the board.
- Say sentences from the left chart and ask the class to repeat. Ask: *When do I use* There is? (for singular nouns) *When do I use* There are? (for plural nouns)
- Write on the board: _____ *one bathroom.* Ask: *Do I write* There's *or* There are? *How do you know which one to use?* (You look at the noun—*bathroom* is singular.) Repeat with other examples from the chart.
- Point to items in your classroom and make statements with *there is/are* (for example, *There are two books on my desk.*). Call on students to say other examples.
- Read the sentences from the right chart and ask the class to repeat. Explain: *Use* no *after* there's *or* there are *to make a negative statement.* Again, use your classroom as an example and say negative statements (for example, *There are no computers in this room.*). Call on students to say other examples.
- If you are using the transparency, do the exercise with the class.

Controlled Practice   15 minutes

1 PRACTICE

A Look at the apartment ad. Read the sentences....

- Read the directions, ad, and example. Remind students that *there is* is singular and *there are* is plural and to look at the noun to decide which to use.
- Walk around and check that students are correcting the false sentences.
- Students compare answers with a partner.
- Call on students to say answers. For the false items, call on the class to say the correction.

B Look at the picture on page 111. Complete...

- Read the directions and the example.
- Remind students that *there is* is singular and *there are* is plural and to look at the noun before answering.
- Tell the class to look at the picture on page 111. To warm up, discuss the house with the class (for example, T: *How many rooms are in the house? What do you see?*).
- Walk around and if students have difficulty, point out the noun in each sentence (singular or plural) and also use the picture on page 111 to confirm if the answer should be affirmative or negative.
- Also check that students are using capital letters as needed.
- Students check answers with a partner by role-playing the completed conversation.
- Call on a pair to perform the conversation for the class. Another student can copy the conversation onto the board for added reinforcement.

▬▬ Expansion: Writing and Speaking Practice for 1B

- Tell students to create an apartment ad for their own home or one they make up.
- Pair students and tell them to exchange ads. Students can take turns telling their partner what's in the apartment using *there is, there are, there's no,* and *there are no.*

Communicative Practice   30 minutes

2   PRACTICE

WRITE. Look at the picture of the house. What's in...

- Read the directions and the example.
- Copy the example sentence on the board and point out the possessive nouns that help to identify each room (for example, *parents' bedroom*). Point to the word *bedroom* and ask the class: *Whose bedroom?* (the parents' bedroom)
- Help students identify each room. Hold up your book, point to a room, and ask: *What room is this? Optional:* Ask students to label each room in the picture using the words from the directions (for example, *upstairs bathroom, downstairs bathroom, . . .*).
- As students call out the name of each room, write it on the board and tell the class to come up with at least one example sentence that you copy onto the board under the room name.
- For every example sentence on the board, point to the punctuation and ask the class: *What is this?* (an apostrophe/a comma/a period) Label the punctuation marks and remind students about their meaning, as needed: *The apostrophe makes the noun possessive. The comma separates the two parts of the sentence. The period ends the sentence.*
- As needed, explain *upstairs* and *downstairs* by drawing an example of a two-story house on the board with arrows pointing to each floor or by using the existing picture to illustrate.
- Walk around and check that students are using the three sentence beginnings (*There is . . .* , *There's no . . .* , and *There are no . . .*).
- Students take turns reading their writing to a partner and pointing to the rooms in the picture on page 111 to illustrate what they say.
- To wrap up, choose each room in turn and call on as many students as possible to say the sentences they wrote about it.

Teaching Tip

Ask students to first write their sentences on a sheet of notebook paper before transferring them to the textbook page. This way, if students make mistakes or you spot errors in their writing, they can correct them and then write a clean version in the textbook page.

Show what you know!

GROUPS OF 3. **Talk about things in the rooms...**

- Read the directions.
- Play A and read the example conversation with two above-level students.
- First, talk about the things and rooms in your home and call on two above-level students to ask you questions, as in the example.
- Form groups of 3 and tell them to take turns playing each role.
- Walk around and check that students are using *there is/are* in the affirmative and negative.
- As you walk around, participate briefly in each group to ensure that all members are actively listening, asking relevant questions, and describing their own homes relative to what others in the group are saying, as in the example.

▬▬ MULTILEVEL INSTRUCTION

Pre-level Sit with groups and prompt them to help get them started (for example, T: *What things are in your living room?*). If available, ask above-level students to sit in with groups and prompt students with similar questions.

Above-level Groups of students talk about things they want or need for each room of their home (for example, A: *In my kitchen, there's an old green table. I want a new table.*).

Progress Check

Can you . . . describe a house?

Say: *We have practiced describing houses. Now, look at the question at the bottom of the page. Can you describe a house?* Tell students to write a checkmark in the box.

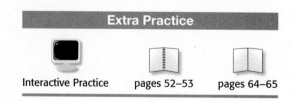

Extra Practice		
Interactive Practice	pages 52–53	pages 64–65

WRITE. Look at the picture of the house. What's in each room? What's *not* in each room? Write sentences about the upstairs bathroom, the downstairs bathroom, the parents' bedroom, the children's bedroom, the living room, and the kitchen. Use *there is*, *there are*, *there's no*, and *there are no*.

In the parents' bedroom, there's a lamp. In the children's bedroom, there's no lamp.

Answers will vary.

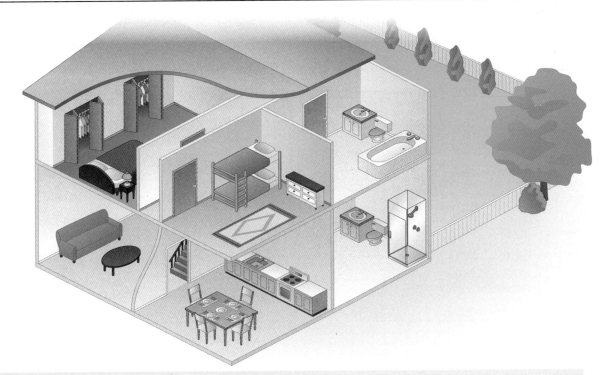

Show what you know! Describe a house

GROUPS OF 3. Talk about things in the rooms of your house.

A: *In my bedroom, there's a bed and a dresser.*
B: *What about closets?*
A: *No, there are no closets.*
C: *In my bathroom . . .*

Can you...describe a house? ☐

Reading

1 BEFORE YOU READ

A Look at the pictures. Complete the sentences. Use the words in the box.

> ~~fire~~   neighbor   smoke   smoke alarm

1. There's a ___fire___ in the apartment.

2. There's a lot of ___smoke___.

3. The ___smoke alarm___ goes off.

4. A ___neighbor___ sees the smoke and calls 911.

B CLASS. Talk about it. What do smoke alarms do?

C Look at the pie chart. How many people get hurt every year from fires at home? How many people get killed every year? 16,000 people are hurt every year from fires. 3,200 people are killed every year from fires.

D Do you have smoke alarms in your home? Where are they? For example, are they near the kitchen? The living room? The bedroom?

Number of people hurt or killed every year because of fires at home

■ Number of people killed
▨ Number of people hurt

3,200   16,000

Source: U.S. Fire Administration

Getting Started   25 minutes

1   BEFORE YOU READ

A **Look at the pictures. Complete the sentences....**

- Read the directions and the example.
- Use the pictures to explain the vocabulary in the box. If there is a smoke alarm in your classroom, point to it and say: *There's the smoke alarm. If there is smoke, it will go off.* Go off *means to make a sound like beep, beep! beep!* On the board, write *go off = make a sound (beep! beep! beep!).* Explain *smoke* by pointing to the smoke rising up from the trash can in the pictures. As needed, explain: *A neighbor is a person who lives next to (or near) you.*
- Students compare answers with a partner.
- Call on students to write answers on the board. Call on other students to read each answer on the board.

B CLASS. **Talk about it. What do smoke alarms do?**

- Read the directions.
- Call on several students to say what smoke alarms do (*Possible answers:* They go off when there is smoke. They detect smoke. They make a loud noise when there is smoke. They tell people when there is a fire.)

C **Look at the pie chart. How many people...**

- Read the first sentence of the directions. Then ask: *What is the title of the chart?* (Number of people hurt or killed every year because of fires at home)
- Read the questions in the directions and tell the class to call out answers.

Expansion: Math Practice for 1C

- Ask pairs to use the pie chart to calculate the percentage of people killed and the percentage of people hurt because of fires at home. Ask: *What percentage of people are killed?* (17%) *What percentage of people are hurt?* (83%) To figure out these amounts divide the number of people hurt or killed by the total number of people (3,200 ÷ 19,200 × 100 = % of people killed).
- Students copy the pie chart into their notebooks and write the percentages on each piece.

D **Do you have smoke alarms in your home? Where...**

- Read the questions. Tell the class your answers to the questions as an example.
- *Optional:* Before calling on individuals, ask pairs or groups of 3 to discuss the questions.
- Call on several students to answer the questions. Then, to check listening comprehension, ask the rest of the class questions about what the student just reported (for example, T: *How many smoke alarms are in Lupe's home? Where are they? Does she have a smoke alarm in her bedroom?*).

Community Building

When asking the class the questions, focus your attention on different groups of students to ensure that all students get a chance to speak. Make eye contact with all students and encourage students who do not often speak to answer at least one question.

Expansion: Speaking Practice for 1D

- Ask the class: *Where can you buy a smoke alarm?* Call on several students to share information about which stores have smoke alarms and how much they cost.
- Write this information on the board for students to copy into their notebooks.

Presentation   15 minutes

2 READ

🔊 **Listen. Read the article.**

- Ask: *What's the title?* (Smoke Alarms—A Life-Saver!) Ask: *What does* Life-Saver *mean?* (something that can save your life)
- Ask students to look at the pictures.
- Play CD 2, Track 47. Students listen and read along silently.
- *Optional:* Play Track 47 again. Pause the CD after each of the following four parts:

   Title and introductory sentence: *How many people get hurt?* (16,000) *How many people get killed?* (3,200)

   First column: *Should you put an alarm in the kitchen?* (No.) As needed, use the drawing to explain the meaning of *hallway* (for example, T: *In this picture, the smoke alarm is in the hallway.*).

   Second column: *How do you test your alarm?* (Push the test button and listen for the sound.)

   Third column: *What does the "chirp" sound mean?* (It's time to replace the battery.)

Controlled Practice   5 minutes

3 CHECK YOUR UNDERSTANDING

Ⓐ Read the article again. What is the main idea?...

- Remind students: *The main idea is the most important idea of the article.*
- Ask students to read the article again silently and complete the sentence.
- Students compare answers with a partner.
- Call on a student to write the completed sentence on the board.
- To wrap up, point to the sentence on the board and ask: *What is this?* (the main idea of the article)

Ⓑ Read the sentences. Underline the correct words.

- Do item 1 with the class.
- Call on students to read the completed sentences.

▬▬ Expansion: Writing Practice for 3B

- Students make a safety poster for display in their home or in the classroom. Using available materials (construction paper, markers), students copy the completed sentences from Exercise 3B and add information from the article (for example, *In the U.S., about 3,200 people get killed every year . . .*).

▬▬ Expansion: Grammar Practice for 3B

- Students rewrite items 2–4 of Exercise 3B in the imperative form (for example, *2. Put a smoke alarm . . .*). Call on students to say the imperatives.

Communicative Practice   15 minutes

Show what you know!

Draw a floor plan of your home. Put smoke alarms...

- Read the directions.
- To warm up, draw a simple floor plan of your own home, indicating where smoke alarms are.
- Create a symbol to represent the smoke alarm (for example, a circle) for students to use in their own drawings.
- If students don't know where the smoke alarms are in their house, ask them to draw them where they think they should go. Students should follow the advice in the article.
- Call on students to present their drawing to the class and to say where the smoke alarms are (for example, S: *Here is my home. There's a smoke alarm in the hallway next to my bedroom.*).

▬▬ Expansion: Critical Thinking Practice

- Pairs discuss the following questions: *Why should you check the alarm every month?* (to make sure the battery isn't dead and that the alarm works) *What are other ways to stay safe in your home?* (*Possible answer:* Keep a fire extinguisher nearby, unplug appliances not in use, keep home clean and organized.)
- Discuss answers to the questions as a class.

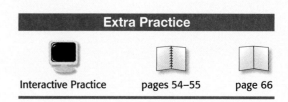

Extra Practice		
Interactive Practice	pages 54–55	page 66

CD2 T47

Listen. Read the article.

SMOKE ALARMS – A Life-Saver!

Every year in the U.S., about 16,000 people get hurt because of fires in their homes. And about 3,200 people get killed. Smoke alarms can keep you safe.

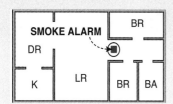

Where should you put your smoke alarms?

Put one smoke alarm near the bedroom area. You can also put smoke alarms in the living room or other rooms. But don't put an alarm in your kitchen. It will go off when you cook!

When should you check the smoke alarms?

Does your smoke alarm work? How do you know? Check the alarm every month. To check an alarm, push the test button and listen for the alarm sound.

When should you change the batteries?

Change the batteries every year. But if your alarm makes a "chirp" sound, put in a new battery right away. Your smoke alarms can't help you if they don't work!

3 **CHECK YOUR UNDERSTANDING**

A Read the article again. What is the main idea? Complete the sentence.

_____Smoke alarms_____ can keep you safe from fires.

B Read the sentences. Underline the correct words.

1. In the U.S., about 16,000 people **get hurt** / **get killed** every year from fires in their homes.

2. You should put a smoke alarm near your **kitchen** / **bedroom**.

3. Check your smoke alarms every **month** / **year**.

4. Change the batteries every **month** / **year**.

Show what you know!

Draw a floor plan of your home. Put smoke alarms in the correct places.

Listening and Speaking

1 BEFORE YOU LISTEN

A READ. **Read about Amy and Lei Sun.**

Amy and Lei Sun are looking for an apartment. They want a furnished apartment because they don't have furniture. They also want an apartment with appliances, like a refrigerator.

Studio apartments for rent!

B CLASS. **Look at the pictures. Which apartment is furnished? Which apartment is unfurnished?**

2 LISTEN

A **Look at the picture. Amy and Lei are talking to a building manager.**

Guess: What is Amy asking about?

CD2 T48

B 💿 **Listen to the conversation. Was your guess in Exercise A correct?**

Listen again. Underline the correct words.

1. The apartment is on the **second** / **seventh** floor.

2. The apartment has **beds** / **a dresser**.

3. The apartment has a **stove** / **refrigerator**.

CD2 T49

C 💿 **Listen to the whole conversation. Answer the questions.**

1. The building manager asks Amy and Lei: "Are you interested?"

   Who says "Yes"? _____Amy_____   Who says "No"? _____Lei_____

2. Do you think Amy and Lei want the apartment? Why?

   Answers will vary.
   _____

Getting Started 10 minutes

BEFORE YOU LISTEN

A READ. Read about Amy and Lei Sun.

- Ask students to look at the pictures of the studio apartments. Ask: *What's a studio apartment?* (An apartment with one room that is both the living room and the bedroom. Studios also have a bathroom and usually a very small kitchen.)
- Ask: *What's in the picture on the left?* Students call out things in the room using *There's* or *There are* (for example, *There's a sofa.*).
- Ask: *What about the picture on the right? What's not there?* Students call out things not in the room using *There's no* or *There are no* (for example, *There's no sofa.*).
- Read the directions and the information while students read along silently.
- On the board, write *furnished* and *unfurnished*. Say each word and ask the class to repeat. Point to *un-* and say: *-un means no; furnished means with furniture; unfurnished means no furniture.*
- On the board, write the heading *Appliances*. Say: *A refrigerator is an appliance. What are some others?* As students call out answers, write them on the board under the heading. Before you write an answer, ask the class to spell the word (for example, T: *A stove? How do you spell* stove? Ss: *S-T-O-V-E.*).

B CLASS. Look at the pictures. Which apartment...

- Tell students to look at the pictures. Ask: *Which apartment is furnished?* (the one on the left)
- Ask: *What about your apartment? Was it furnished or unfurnished?* Call on students to say answers. Ask students who reply *unfurnished*: *Did it have appliances? What appliances?*

Presentation 15 minutes

LISTEN

A Look at the picture.... Guess:...

- Read the directions.
- Ask: *What is Amy asking about?* Call on students to guess. Write their guesses on the board.

B Listen to the conversation. Was...

- Read the directions. Play CD 2, Track 48.
- Circle the correct answer on the board. Ask: *Was your guess correct?* (Answer: *an apartment*)

> **Teaching Tip**
>
> *Optional:* Remember that if students need additional support, tell them to read the Audio Script on page 285 as they listen to the conversations.

Listen again. Underline the correct words.

- Read the directions. Play Track 48 again. Students listen and underline the correct word to complete each sentence.
- Students compare answers with a partner.
- Call on students to say answers.

C Listen to the whole conversation....

- Read the directions and questions. Say: *For each question in number 1, you must write* Amy *or* Lei.
- Play CD 2, Track 49. Students listen and answer the questions. Say: Yes and no *is a common expression that means that part of the answer to a question is yes and part is no.*
- Students compare answers with a partner.
- Call on students to say answers. For number 2, ask students to explain why they think Amy and Lei want or don't want the apartment. (Yes: Because it has some appliances and furniture. No: Because it doesn't have some appliances and furniture.) List the students' reasons on the board.

Expansion: Graphic Organizer Practice for 2C

- Tell students to make a two-column pro and con chart in their notebooks about having a furnished apartment. Write *Pro* and *Con* on the board and say: Pros *are good things.* Cons *are problems.*
- Ask: *What's good about a furnished apartment?* (You don't have to buy furniture.) *What's bad about a furnished apartment?* (It's probably more expensive.)
- Students can work with a partner or in small groups to get more ideas. Higher-level students in pairs or groups can help their partners phrase answers correctly. Call on students to read their charts out loud.

3   CONVERSATION

A 💿 **Listen. Then listen and repeat.**

- Read the directions and Pronunciation Watch note. Say: *A two-word noun is a noun that has two words, like* floor lamp *or* dining room.
- Write the two-word nouns on the board. Add *living room* and *table lamp* as additional examples. Say: *The first word is stressed.*
- Draw circles above the words on the board and point to them. Ask students if they remember what a syllable is (a part of a word). Say: *Some of the first words in these two-word nouns have two syllables:* table, living, dining. *In these words, the first syllable is stressed.*
- Play CD 2, Track 50. Students listen.
- Play Track 50 again. Students listen and repeat.

B 💿 **Listen to the sentences. Mark (•)...**

- Read the directions. Play CD 2, Track 51.
- Students compare answers with a partner. Call on a couple of students to write answers on the board.

Controlled Practice   20 minutes

C 💿 **Listen and read the conversation....**

- Note: This conversation is the same one students heard in Exercise 2B on page 114.
- Say: *There are two people talking—a building manager and a customer.*
- Play CD 2, Track 52. Students listen and read along silently.
- Resume playing Track 52. Students listen and repeat.
- Ask: *How many bedrooms are in a one-bedroom apartment?* (one) *What are appliances?* (things in the kitchen, such as a stove, or a refrigerator)

4   PRACTICE

A **PAIRS. Practice the conversation. Then make new...**

- Form groups of 3 and tell students to practice the conversation in Exercise 3C.

- Then, in Exercise 4A, point to the words in the boxes, say them, and ask the class to repeat. As needed, tell students to look back at pages 106–107 for pictures of these words.
- Read the directions.
- Copy the conversation onto the board with blanks. Read through the conversation. When you come to a blank, fill it in with information from the boxes (*studio*, *sofa*, and *coffee table*).
- Ask two on-level students to practice the conversation in front of the class.
- Pair students and tell them to take turns playing each role and to use the words in the boxes to fill in the blanks.
- Walk around and check that students are stressing two-word nouns correctly.
- Tell students to stand, mingle, and practice the conversation with several new partners.

Communicative Practice   10 minutes

B **ROLE PLAY. PAIRS. Make your own...**

- On the board, write: *A—looking for an apartment* and *B—building manager.* Under each one, write things that the person can say. Use expressions from the conversations on page 115.
- With an above-level student, play A and make up a new conversation and practice for the class. Use information from the board. Base the conversation on Exercise 3C. Continue the conversation for three or four exchanges.
- Pair students. Walk around and check for appropriate stress on two-word nouns.
- Call on pairs to role-play for the class.

▬▬ MULTILEVEL INSTRUCTION for 4B

Cross-ability Ask above-level students to sit in with pairs and take the role of B, the rental manager. The pre-level pair can be a couple or friends looking for an apartment for rent. B's job is to make sure that each pre-level partner asks at least one question.

Extra Practice

Interactive Practice

---

3 CONVERSATION

CD2 T50

A **Listen. Then listen and repeat.**

•
floor lamp   There's a floor lamp.

•
dining room   It's in the dining room.

CD2 T51

B **Listen to the sentences. Mark (•) the stress on the underlined words.**

1. There's a <u>coffee table</u>.

2. There are two <u>desk lamps</u>.

CD2 T52

C **Listen and read the conversation. Then listen and repeat.**

Amy: Excuse me. Is there an apartment for rent in this building?

Manager: Yes, there is. There's a one-bedroom apartment on the second floor.

Amy: Oh, great. Is it furnished?

Manager: Well, yes and no. There's a dresser, but no beds.

Lei: Oh. Well, are there appliances?

Manager: Uh, yes and no. There's a stove, but no refrigerator.

4 PRACTICE

A **PAIRS. Practice the conversation. Then make new conversations. Use the words in the boxes.**

A: Excuse me. Is there an apartment for rent in this building?

B: Yes, there is. There's a ⬜⬜⬜ apartment on the second floor.

A: Oh, great. Is it furnished?

B: Well, yes and no. There's a ⬜⬜⬜ , but no ⬜⬜⬜ .

B **ROLE PLAY. PAIRS. Make your own conversations. Student A, you are looking for an apartment. Student B, you are the building manager.**

> studio
> two-bedroom
> three-bedroom

> sofa
> desk
> table

> coffee table
> lamp
> chairs

Grammar

Is there/Are there

Is there	a table?		Yes,	there is.	No,	there isn't.
Are there	lamps?			there are.		there aren't.

1 PRACTICE

A   **Complete the conversations. Underline the correct words.**

1. **A:** <u>Is there</u> / **Are there** a bathtub in the bathroom?

   B: No, **there is** / <u>there isn't</u>. There's a shower.

2. **A:** **Is there** / <u>Are there</u> closets in the bedrooms?

   B: Yes, **there is** / <u>there are</u>. There's a closet in each bedroom.

3. **A:** **Is there** / <u>Are there</u> table lamps in the living room?

   B: No, **there are** / <u>there aren't</u>. There are floor lamps.

4. **A:** <u>Is there</u> / **Are there** a coffee table in the living room?

   B: Yes, <u>there is</u> / **there isn't**. There's a small coffee table and a sofa.

5. **A:** <u>Is there</u> / **Are there** a dining room in the apartment?

   B: No, <u>there isn't</u> / **there aren't**.

6. **A:** <u>Is there</u> / **Are there** a sunny kitchen?

   B: Yes, <u>there is</u> / **there are**. The kitchen is very sunny.

7. **A:** <u>Is there</u> / **Are there** a table in the kitchen?

   B: Yes, <u>there is</u> / **there are**. There's a table and four chairs.

CD2 T53

B   **Listen and check your answers.**

C   **PAIRS. Practice the conversations in Exercise A.**

Getting Started 5 minutes

- Say: *We're going to study questions with* Is there/Are there. *In the conversation on page 115, Amy used this grammar.*
- Play CD 2, Track 52. Students listen. Write *Is there an apartment for rent in this building?* on the board. Underline *Is there an apartment.*

Presentation 10 minutes

Is there/Are there

- Copy the grammar charts onto the board or show the charts on Transparency 6.4 and cover the exercise.
- Read the questions in the left chart and ask the class to repeat. Then read the possible answers from the right chart and ask the class to repeat.
- Write on the board: *There is a table.* Point to it and say: *This is a statement.* Point to a table in your classroom and say: *There is a table.* Erase *There is* and replace with *Is there.* Also change the period into a question mark. Point to the question and say: *This is a question.*
- Ask: *Is there a table?* (Make it true for your classroom.) Students call out *Yes, there is.*
- Ask: *Are there tables?* (Make it true for your classroom.) Students call out *Yes, there are.*
- Use the top picture and bottom picture to ask the class questions about things in the pictures (for example, [top picture] T: *Are there chairs?* Ss: *Yes, there are.*).
- Call on individual students to make up a question about one of the pictures. Call on other students to say answers. Write the questions and answers on the board for reinforcement of the grammar points.
- Ask students more questions about singular and plural things in your classroom. Give students the opportunity to answer in the affirmative and negative (for example, T: *Is there a refrigerator?* Ss: *No, there isn't.*).
- If you are using the transparency, do the exercise with the class.

Controlled Practice 25 minutes

1 PRACTICE

A Complete the conversations. Underline...

- Read the directions and the example.
- Remind students to look at the subject (the thing) in each line. Say: *Use* is *with singular nouns and* are *with plural nouns.* Ask: *What is the subject in number 1?* (a bathtub) *Is it singular or plural?* (singular)
- Walk around and if students are having difficulty, ask them to circle the subject in line A of each conversation. Then ask them to write *singular* or *plural* next to it before they answer.

B Listen and check your answers.

- Play CD 2, Track 53. Students listen and check their answers.
- Call on students to say answers.

C PAIRS. Practice the conversations in Exercise A.

- Pair students and tell them to take turns playing A and B.
- Walk around and check that students are pronouncing *isn't* and *aren't* correctly. Model as needed.

MULTILEVEL INSTRUCTION for 1C
Cross-ability The above-level students play A. Ask the above-level students to help their partners with pronunciation.

Expansion: Writing and Speaking Practice for 1C

- Students write three sentences about things in the classroom (for example, *There's a whiteboard.*) and three sentences about things not in the classroom (for example, *There's no refrigerator.*).
- Then, after each sentence, students rewrite their sentences as questions (for example, *Is there a whiteboard?*).
- Pair students and tell them to ask each other their questions. Students must answer *Yes, there is/are* or *No, there isn't/aren't.*

2 PRACTICE

WRITE. Write questions. Use the words in parentheses....

- Read the directions and the example question. Students call out *Yes, there are.*
- Copy the example question and answer onto the board. Read the note about capitalization and punctuation and use the example to illustrate the points in the note.
- Tell students to look back at the grammar chart on page 116 if they need help in writing a question.
- Say: *Remember, look at the picture before you answer.* Walk around and check for correct word order, capitalization, and punctuation.
- *Optional:* Pair students and ask them to practice the conversation. Call on pairs to perform for the class.

Communicative Practice   20 minutes

Show what you know!

STEP 1. Complete this picture of a kitchen.

- Ask: *What appliances are in a kitchen?* As students call out answers, write words on the board (for example, *a refrigerator, a stove*).
- Ask: *What furniture is in a kitchen?* (for example, *a table, chairs*) Again, write words on the board as students call out answers.
- Read the directions. Walk around, point to things in students' pictures and ask: *What's this?*

STEP 2. PAIRS. Don't look at your partner's picture!...

- Ask an above-level student: *Is there a table in your picture?* (S: *Yes, there is. It's across from the stove.*)
- Tell students to use *next to* and *across from* in their answers. As needed, refer to page 59 to review these prepositions with the class or demonstrate by using things in the classroom. Demonstrate *next to* by holding up two books next to each other and saying: *This book is next to the other book.* Demonstrate *across from* by stating, for example, *I'm across from the window.*
- Pair students and tell them to take turns playing A and B. Tell A to ask questions. Remind students not to look at their partner's picture.

- Walk around and check that pairs are accurately describing their pictures. If not, ask the student where things are located in their picture and model an answer for the student to repeat.
- To check comprehension, ask individual students what things are in their picture. Check students' pictures to confirm their description.

▅▅ MULTILEVEL INSTRUCTION for STEP 2

Pre-level Students draw lines connecting furniture and appliances and label each line with *across from* or *next to* (for example, a line—labeled *next to*—connecting the stove and a refrigerator on the same wall).

Above-level Student B says two pieces of information about the location of each thing (for example, *It's across from the stove, and it's next to the refrigerator.*).

STEP 3. SAME PAIRS. Look at your partner's...

- On the board, draw a sample kitchen picture.
- Look at an above-level student's picture. Ask: *What is different?* (S: *In my picture, the refrigerator is next to the stove. In your picture, the refrigerator is across from the stove.*) *What is the same?* (S: *In our pictures, the sink is next to the stove.*) Write these answers on the board as examples of what to say.
- Read the directions. Point to the example sentences on the board and tell the class to talk about what is the same and what is different about their pictures.
- Check that students are discussing similarities and differences while using *across from* and *next to* accurately. Model corrections.

▅▅ Expansion: Speaking Practice

- Tell students to repeat the "Show what you know!" exercises with a different room.

Progress Check

Can you . . . ask about things in a house?

Say: *We have practiced asking about things in a house. Now, look at the question at the bottom of the page. Can you ask about things in a house?* Tell students to write a checkmark in the box.

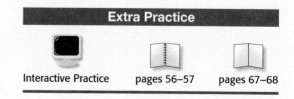

Extra Practice
Interactive Practice   pages 56–57   pages 67–68

WRITE. **Write questions. Use the words in parentheses. Then look at the picture and write short answers.**

1. (there / two / are / tables)

   A: _Are there two tables?_

   B: _Yes, there are._

2. (lamps / are / on the tables / there)

   A: _Are there lamps on the tables?_

   B: _Yes, there are._

3. (a sofa / in the room / there / is)

   A: _Is there a sofa in the room?_

   B: _Yes, there is._

4. (book / on the sofa / is / there / a)

   A: _Is there a book on the sofa?_

   B: _No, there isn't._

5. (pictures / there / are / in the room)

   A: _Are there pictures in the room?_

   B: _No, there aren't._

Show what you know!   Ask about things in a house

STEP 1. **Complete this picture of a kitchen.**

STEP 2. **PAIRS. Don't look at your partner's picture! Ask questions about your partner's picture. Draw the picture on a piece of paper.**

A: *Is there a refrigerator?*
B: *Yes, there is. It's across from the stove.*

STEP 3. **SAME PAIRS. Look at your partner's picture. Is the picture on your paper the same?**

Can you...ask about things in a house? ☐

Life Skills

1 READ ADDRESSES

CD2 T54

A Listen and read the addresses. Then listen and repeat.

6103 Lake Drive, Apartment 27

98 East High Street

45720 Foothill Road

3095 Sunset Boulevard

1463 2nd Avenue, Apartment 10

852 Mission Street, Apartment 903

B PAIRS. Listen to your teacher. Repeat the conversation. Then practice with a partner.

A: *What's the address, please?*
B: *It's 6103 Lake Drive, Apartment 27.*

2 PRACTICE

A PAIRS. Make new conversations. Use the addresses above.

B Look at the addresses again. Write the words for each abbreviation.

1. St. _Street_
2. Ave. _Avenue_
3. Dr. _Drive_
4. Rd. _Road_
5. Blvd. _Boulevard_
6. Apt. _Apartment_

> **Writing Watch**
>
> Use periods in abbreviations in addresses.
> Example: *St.*

C Write your street address. Use abbreviations. _Answers will vary._

D CLASS. Walk around the room. Ask three classmates for their addresses. Use true or made-up information. Write the addresses in your notebook.

A: *What's your address?*
B: *1451 Pine Street, Apartment 3.*

E NETWORK. Who lives in your neighborhood (area)? Find those classmates. Form a group. Ask the people in your group, *What street do you live on?*

3 LIFE SKILLS WRITING   Address an envelope. See page 258.

Can you...read addresses and give your address? ☐

Getting Started 5 minutes

Culture Connection

• Tell students to write an address from their home country in their notebooks. Ask: *What information do you need in this address?* (for example, street number, street name).

• Say: *In the United States, an address needs the street number and the name of the street.*

Presentation 5 minutes

1 READ ADDRESSES

A Listen and read the addresses. Then...

• Play CD 2, Track 54. Students listen and read along.

• Resume playing Track 54. Students listen and repeat.

Controlled Practice 15 minutes

B PAIRS. Listen to your teacher. Repeat...

• Read the example conversation. The class repeats.

• Pair students. Pairs take turns playing A and B.

• Walk around and help with pronunciation.

• Call on pairs to perform for the class.

2 PRACTICE

A PAIRS. Make new conversations. Use the...

• Play A and practice the conversation given in Exercise 1B with an on-level student.

• Say each address given in Exercise 1A and ask the class to repeat.

• Pair students. Tell them to take turns playing A and B and to use all the addresses.

• Walk around and help with pronunciation.

• Call on pairs to perform for the class.

B Look at the addresses again. Write the words...

• Tell students to write the words they know.

• For each abbreviation, ask: *What's the word for . . . ?* Tell the class to call out the spelling as you write the word on the board.

• Tell students to fill in any words they left blank.

C Write your street address. Use abbreviations.

• Read the directions and the note.

• Remind students to write the street number, street name, and if applicable, a comma plus an apartment number.

Communicative Practice 10 minutes

D CLASS. Walk around the room. Ask three...

• Play A and model the conversation with an on-level student. After B says the address, ask: *Can you spell the street, please?*

• Say: *Take your notebook, stand up, and ask three students for their address. Write the addresses. Also ask,* Can you spell that, please? Remind students that they can make up an address.

E NETWORK. Who lives in your neighborhood...

• Read the directions. Ask an above-level student: *What are your cross streets?* When the student answers, draw a simple picture of the cross streets and a dot to represent the student's home. Use the drawing on the board to illustrate *cross street*.

• Students stand, mingle, and ask one another for cross streets to determine who lives in similar neighborhoods. After students have divided themselves into groups, say: *Ask people in your group,* What street do you live on?

• Ask a few students to state the street they live on.

3 LIFE SKILLS WRITING

Turn to page 258 and ask students to fill out the envelope. See pages Txi–Txii for general notes about the Life Skills Writing activities.

Progress Check

Can you . . . read addresses and give your address?

Say: *We have practiced reading and giving addresses. Now, look at the question at the bottom of the page. Can you read addresses and give your address?* Tell students to write a checkmark in the box.

Controlled Practice   10 minutes

4   READ APARTMENT ADS

PAIRS. Look at the words. Find their abbreviations...

- Read the directions and each ad. Say each abbreviation as its full word when you read.
- Read the note about utilities.
- Say: *Look at number 1. Air conditioning is A/C. Read the ads until you find an abbreviation that could mean air conditioning.* (Ad B. It says A/C.)
- Do item 2 with the students in the same way.
- Walk around and if students are having difficulty, point out which ad to read.
- Students compare answers with a partner.
- Call on students to write answers on the board.

■■■ MULTILEVEL INSTRUCTION for 4

Pre-level Form groups of 3 to complete the exercise.

Above-level When students finish, ask them to copy each ad into their notebooks but to use the full words and not abbreviations.

5   PRACTICE

Ⓐ Look at the ads again. Answer the questions....

- Read the directions. Ask the example question: *Which apartment or house has three bedrooms?* Students call out *D*. Repeat for item 2.
- Students compare answers with a partner.
- Call on students to say answers.

Communicative Practice   10 minutes

Ⓑ PAIRS. Talk about it. Which apartment or house...

- Read the directions.
- Play A and model the conversation with an on-level student. Then practice again using true information.
- Pair students. Say: *Student B, use* need *and* have *when you answer why you like the apartment or house.*
- Walk around and check that students are using *need* and *have* and are clearly pronouncing plural nouns (for example, ... *because it has three bedrooms*).

■■■ MULTILEVEL INSTRUCTION for 5B

Pre-level Students first write out the reasons they like one of the apartments before they talk about it.

Above-level Students give at least three reasons why they like a house or apartment.

■■■ Expansion: Speaking Practice for 5B

- Ask students to write three important things they need when they look for an apartment or house (for example, *a yard, a laundry room, and a large kitchen*).
- Students compare answers with a partner and then tell the class what their partner needs (for example, *José needs a yard, a laundry room, and a large kitchen.*).

Progress Check

Can you ... read apartment ads?

Say: *We have practiced reading apartment ads. Now, look at the question at the bottom of the page. Can you read apartment ads?* Tell students to write a checkmark in the box.

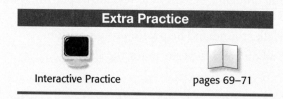

Extra Practice

Interactive Practice   pages 69–71

4 READ APARTMENT ADS

PAIRS. Look at the words. Find their abbreviations in the apartment ads below. Write the abbreviations.

1. air conditioning __A/C__
2. bathroom __BA__
3. bedroom __BR__
4. building __Bldg.__

5. dining room __DR__
6. included __incl.__
7. kitchen __Kit__
8. large __Lg__

9. laundry __Lndry__
10. living room __LR__
11. parking __Pkg__
12. utilities __Utils.__

A. | BR/1BA Apt. in New Bldg. $975 Utils. incl. 259 Water St. Citywide Rentals (213) 555-4488

B. 2 BR/1BA Apt. $1,300 New Kit, A/C 4177 Los Feliz Blvd. (323) 555-3276

utilities = gas, electricity, water

C. 2 BR/2BA House $1,850 Lndry, Pkg 561 Franklin Ave. (818) 555-0200

D. 3 BR/ 2 BA House $2,100 Lg DR & LR 2319 Greenleaf Ave. (562) 555-9264

5 PRACTICE

A Look at the ads again. Answer the questions. Write the letter of the ad.

Which apartment or house . . .

1. __D__ has three bedrooms?
2. __D__ has a large dining room?
3. __B__ has air conditioning?
4. __C__ is $1,850 a month?

5. __C__ has laundry and parking?
6. __B__ has a new kitchen?
7. __A__ has utilities included in the rent?
8. __A__ is new?

B PAIRS. Talk about it. Which apartment or house do you like?

A: *Which apartment or house do you like?*
B: *I like B.*
A: *Why?*
B: *Because I need two bedrooms, and it has a new kitchen.*

Can you...read apartment ads? ☐

Give directions

Listening and Speaking

1 **BEFORE YOU LISTEN**

CLASS. **Look at these words: *north, south, east, west*. Where can you see these words?**

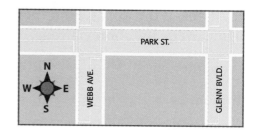

2 **LISTEN**

A **Look at the picture. Lei and Amy need a new sofa. Lei is calling Joe's Furniture Store.**

Guess: Why is he calling?

a. for directions
b. for the store hours
c. for prices

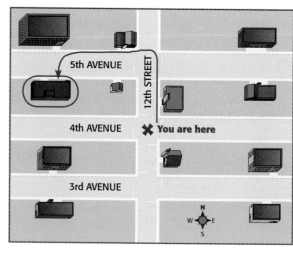

CD2 T55

B **Listen to the phone call. Was your guess in Exercise A correct?**

Listen again. Answer the questions.

1. Which number do you press for store hours? ___1___

2. Which number do you press for directions to the store? ___2___

3. Which number do you press for directions from the north? ___1___

4. Which number do you press for directions from the south? ___2___

CD2 T56

C **Listen to the whole phone call. Complete the directions to Joe's Furniture Store. Listen again and draw the route.**

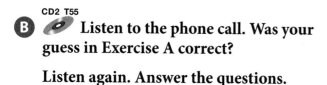

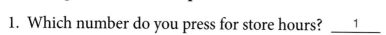

To Joe's Furniture Store

Go ____north____ on 12th Street.
Turn ____left____ on Fifth Avenue.
Continue on Fifth Avenue for
___1___ block.
It's across from the ____hospital____.

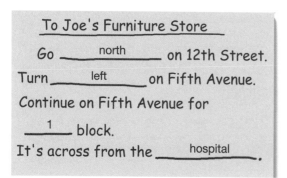

Getting Started   5 minutes

1 **BEFORE YOU LISTEN**

CLASS: Look at these words: *north, south, east,...*

- Ask the class to look at the picture. Ask: *What's N?* (north) Repeat for the other directions.
- Ask: *Where do you see these words?* (on a map, on the highway, in street names, in city names)
- Draw a simple four-way direction cross on the board. Label each direction with a single letter. Point to each letter and ask: *What direction is this?*
- Point to directions in a random order and call on individual students to say the direction.
- Bring in a local map and use it to practice *north, south, east,* and *west* with the class (for example, T: *We are here* [pointing]. *The mall is north of our school. The highway is . . .*).

Presentation   15 minutes

2 **LISTEN**

A **Look at the picture.... Guess:...**

- Read the directions.
- Ask: *Why is Lei calling?* Write the answer choices on the board and read them.
- As needed, remind students that *directions* are a list of instructions on how to go from one place to another place. Explain: Store hours *are the days and times the store is open.*
- Call on students to guess.

B   **Listen to the phone call. Was...**

- Read the directions. Play CD 2, Track 55.
- Circle the correct answer on the board. Ask: *Was your guess correct?*

Teaching Tip

Optional: Remember that if students need additional support, tell them to read the Audio Script on page 285 as they listen to the conversations.

Listen again. Answer the questions.

- Read the directions. Say: *Listen for the numbers to press.* Read the questions. Explain *from the north/ south* by using a local map and explaining the directions to your school from the north and then the directions to your school from the south.
- Play Track 55 again. Students listen and answer the questions.
- Students compare answers with a partner.
- Call on students to say answers.

Controlled Practice   25 minutes

C   **Listen to the whole phone call....**

- Copy the map onto the board and draw arrows to explain *turn left* and *turn right.*
- Play CD 2, Track 56. Students listen and fill in the blanks.
- Explain: Once again *means one more time.*
- Play Track 56 again if students need more time.
- Students read the completed directions to a partner.

Listen again and draw the route.

- Read the last line of the directions. Say: Route *means the streets you take to go from one place to another place.*
- Look at the street map with the students. Point out the "You are here" symbol (or draw it on the map on the board) and ask students to find the direction symbol (or draw it on the board). Say: *Start here.*
- Play Track 56 again. Students listen and draw the route.
- Walk around and check for accuracy and completeness.
- Students compare completed routes with a partner.

▦ Expansion: Listening Practice for 2C

- Think of directions to a local store. Say the directions, using *north, south, east,* and *west* while students copy into their notebooks (for example, *Go north on Main. Turn left on 17th. Then turn south on Broadway.*).

3 CONVERSATION

Two friends are talking. Listen and read...

- Read the directions.
- Play CD 2, Track 57. Students listen and read along silently.
- Explain: *How do you get to . . . is a very common way to ask for directions. Uh-huh is a quick way of saying* Yes, that's right *in conversation.* You can't miss it *means that it is easy to see.*
- Resume playing Track 57. Students listen and repeat. Note that there is an extra pause in B's last line (after *Continue for one block*) to give students time to repeat.

4 PRACTICE

Ⓐ PAIRS. Practice the conversation. Then make new...

- Pair students and tell them to practice the conversation in Exercise 3.
- Then, in Exercise 4A, point to each word in the boxes, say it, and ask the class to repeat.
- Read the directions.
- Copy the conversation onto the board with blanks. Read through the conversation. When you come to a blank, fill it in with information from the boxes (*Sam's Appliances, south,* and *computer store*).
- Ask two on-level students to practice the conversation in front of the class.
- Tell pairs to take turns playing each role and to use the words in the boxes to fill in the blanks.
- Walk around and check that students are stressing important words such as direction words and names and saying the directions clearly.
- Tell students to stand, mingle, and practice the conversation with several new partners.
- Call on pairs to perform for the class.

▮▮ MULTILEVEL INSTRUCTION for 4A

Pre-level Partners read through all the lines together before taking roles and practicing.

Above-level Ask A to draw out the directions that B says after each practice.

Communicative Practice 15 minutes

Ⓑ MAKE IT PERSONAL. PAIRS. Make your own...

- Read the directions. Brainstorm for places students can ask about, for example, their favorite restaurant/movie theater/mall and write them on the board. Draw a simple map and sketch the directions from here (school) to various destinations. As you do so, say the directions and ask the class to repeat.
- Play B and model the conversation with an on-level student.

▮▮ MULTILEVEL INSTRUCTION for 4B

Pre-level Tell A and B to write in the key directions on their map before practicing (for example, *go east, turn right, continue for 3 miles*).

Above-level Tell students they can try to give directions without using a map. Also, to confirm the directions, tell A to repeat the directions that B says (A: *OK, so I go north on Bristol.*).

▮▮ Expansion: Speaking Practice for 4B

- Form groups of 4 or 5. Each student says their favorite store and how to get there from school.
- Then one person in the group draws a map that includes everyone's stores.
- Students can then practice asking and answering how to get from one store to another on the map.

Extra Practice
Interactive Practice

3 CONVERSATION

CD2 T57

Two friends are talking. Listen and read the conversation. Then listen and repeat.

A: How do you get to Joe's Furniture Store?

B: Joe's Furniture Store? Let's see . . . First, go north on 12th Street.

A: North?

B: Uh-huh. Then turn left on Fifth Avenue. Continue for one block. It's on the left across from the hospital. You can't miss it.

A: Thanks.

4 PRACTICE

A PAIRS. Practice the conversation. Then make new conversations. Use the words in the boxes.

A: How do you get to   ?

B: ? Let's see . . . First, go   on 12th Street.

A: ?

B: Uh-huh. Then turn left on Fifth Avenue.

Continue for one block. It's on the left across from

the   . You can't miss it.

A: Thanks.

| Sam's Appliances |
| Ali's Air Conditioners |
| Kitty's Kitchen |

| south |
| east |
| west |

| computer store |
| bookstore |
| hotel |

B MAKE IT PERSONAL. PAIRS. Make your own conversations. Ask for directions from your school to a store your partner likes.

A: *What's your favorite department store?*
B: *I like Kale's.*
A: *How do you get there from here?*
B: *Go north on . . .*

Give directions

Grammar

Prepositions

You're coming	**from**	home.
You're going	**to**	Joe's Furniture Store.

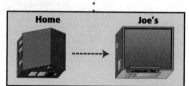

The store is	**in**	Riverside.
Turn left	**at**	the second light.
The store is	**on**	Fifth Avenue.
It's	**at**	231 Fifth Avenue.

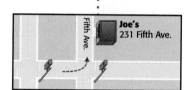

PRACTICE

A Complete the directions. Underline the correct words.

Directions to Our New Apartment

• Our apartment is **on** / in Tenth Avenue **in** / at Greenville.

• If you're coming **from** / to the school, go from / **to** the first light.

• Turn right **at** /on the light. You're now **on** / in Tenth Avenue.

• Our apartment is **on** / to the corner of Tenth Avenue and Elm Street. It's in / **at** 3245 Tenth Avenue.

B Complete the conversation. Use the words in the box.

~~at~~   at   from   in   on   to

A: Where is Eric's office?

B: It's _____at_____ 649 Second Avenue _____in_____ Riverside.

A: OK. How do I get there _____from_____ here?

B: It's easy. Go _____to_____ First Street and turn right _____at_____ the light. Continue for three blocks. Eric's office is on the right.

A: Is there a coffee shop near his office?

B: Yes. There's a nice coffee shop _____on_____ Second Avenue.

Getting Started   5 minutes

- Say: *We're going to study prepositions. In the conversation on page 121, B used this grammar.*
- Play CD 2, Track 57. Students listen. Write on the board: *It's on the left.* Underline *on*.

Presentation   5 minutes

Prepositions

- Copy the grammar charts onto the board or show the charts on Transparency 6.5 and cover the exercise. Say: *Prepositions help us understand where things are.*
- Elicit the prepositions students already know (*across from* and *next to*) by placing classroom objects (for example, books and pencils) next to each other or across from each other and asking *Where is the book?* (next to the pencil) Repeat with more examples.
- Use common classroom objects to demonstrate *on* by placing a pencil on a book. Point to the pencil and ask the class: *Where is the pencil?* (on the book)
- Read the two sentences in the left chart while pointing to the picture under it. Say: *Use* from *for where you start. Use* to *for where you want to go.*
- Read the sentences in the right chart. Say: *Use* at *for a specific place. Use* in *for cities. Use* on *for streets.* Read the sentences again and point to the map to illustrate. Write the headings *In*, *At*, and *On* on the board. Ask students to come up with more examples using *in*, *at*, and *on*. Write them on the board.
- If you are using the transparency, do the exercise with the class.

Controlled Practice   20 minutes

PRACTICE

A Complete the directions. Underline the correct words.

- Read the directions.
- Remind students: Use *at* for a specific place. Use *in* for cities. Use *on* for streets.
- Students compare answers with a partner.
- Call on students to read the completed sentences.

B Complete the conversation. Use the words in the box.

- Read the directions and the example. Ask: *Why do we say* at? (Because *649 Second Avenue* is an address—a specific place)
- Students compare answers with a partner.
- Copy the conversation onto the board with blanks. Call on students to write in the answers. Read the completed conversation while the class repeats.
- *Optional:* Pair students and ask them to practice the conversation. Call on pairs to perform the completed conversation for the class.

Expansion: Writing Practice for A

- Tell students to write directions from their home to school using *in*, *at*, *on*, *from*, and *to*.

Expansion: Grammar Practice for A

- Create flashcards that each have one preposition from the grammar chart. Create other flashcards that each have a street name, a city, a light location (for example, *the second light*), a street address, or the name of a store.
- Form groups of 5. Each group receives a batch of mixed-up flashcards and must make pairs that match a preposition with an appropriate word (for example, *at* and *555 Main St.*).
- Groups lay out the paired cards on their desks while you walk around and check.

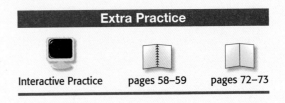

Extra Practice

Interactive Practice   pages 58–59   pages 72–73

Show what you know!

1 GRAMMAR

Complete the conversation between Ana and...

- Read the directions and the example.
- Tell students to refer back to the grammar charts on pages 110 (*there is/there are*) and 116 (*is there/ are there*) as needed.
- Explain: A good sale *means that things in the store have a special low price.*
- Students compare answers with a partner.
- Read the conversation and call on individual students to say answers.
- *Optional:* Pair students and ask them to practice the conversation. Call on pairs to perform the completed conversation for the class.

2 WRITING

STEP 1. Look at the map. Complete the directions...

- Tell students to look carefully at the map before they complete the directions and to read each sentence completely before answering.
- Tell students to refer back to the grammar chart on page 122 (prepositions) as needed.
- Students compare answers with a partner.
- Call on students to come to the board and write each line of the completed directions.

STEP 2. Now write directions from Ted's Furniture...

- Read the directions.
- On the board, write *second street*. Ask: *What's the problem?* (no capital letters) Remind students to use a capital letter for street names. Rewrite as *Second Street*.
- Tell students to trace the directions with their finger and say them. Hold up your book and demonstrate the following example: T: [While tracing up 2nd St.] *Go north on 2nd Street, and turn left on 3rd Avenue . . .*
- Walk around and spot-check students' writing for accuracy, proper capitalization, and use of periods.

 Expansion: Writing Practice for STEP 2

- Ask students to write the reverse directions:
    1. From Al's Appliance Store to Ted's Furniture Store
    2. From Ted's Furniture Store to Ana's apartment

CD-ROM Practice

 Go to the CD-ROM for more practice.

If your students need more practice with the vocabulary, grammar, and competencies in Unit 6, encourage them to review the activities on the CD-ROM. This review can also help students prepare for the final role play on the following Expand page.

Extra Practice

pages 60–61

1 GRAMMAR

**Complete the conversation between Ana and a building manager. Use *is there*, *there's*,
there's no, and *there are no*. Use capital letters when necessary.**

Ana: This apartment is very nice. __Is there__ a laundry room in the building?

Manager: Yes, __there's__ a laundry room on the second floor.

Ana: Good. __Is there__ a garage?

Manager: Yes, __there's__ a garage, too.

Ana: OK. One more thing. What about furniture? There's a table in the living room,

but __there's no__ sofa, and __there are no__ chairs in the dining room.

Manager: Well, __there's__ a furniture store in Smithfield. Their furniture is good,

and it's not expensive. And __there's__ a good sale on now.

2 WRITING

**STEP 1. Look at the map. Complete the directions from Ana's apartment
to the furniture store.**

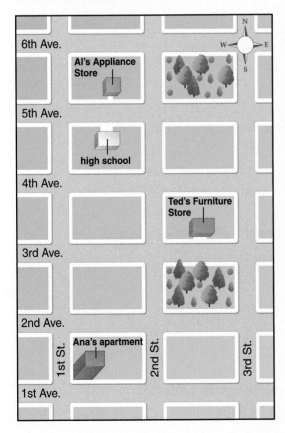

Directions __from__ **Ana's apartment**

__to__ **Ted's Furniture Store:**

Go __east__ on 1st Avenue __to__

2nd Street. Turn __left__ on 2nd Street.

Go __to__ 3rd Avenue. Turn

__right__ on 3rd Avenue. The store is

__on__ 3rd Avenue between 2nd and

3rd Streets across from a small park.

**STEP 2. Now write directions from Ted's
Furniture Store to Al's Appliance Store.**

Go west on 3rd Avenue to 2nd Street. Turn right on 2nd

Street. Go to 5th Avenue. Turn left on 5th Avenue. The

appliance store is on 5th Avenue between 1st and 2nd

Streets across from a high school.

3 ACT IT OUT   What do you say?

CD2 T58

STEP 1. 💿 **Listen to the conversation.**

STEP 2. PAIRS. Student A, you want to rent an apartment. Student B, you are an apartment manager.

Student A: You are calling about an apartment.
- Ask the manager about the rooms in the apartment.
- Ask about the furniture and the appliances.
- Ask for directions to the apartment.

APARTMENT FOR RENT

2 Bedrooms
Call 310-555-8927

Student B: Someone calls you to ask about an apartment you manage.
- Answer the questions about the apartment.
- Give directions to the apartment.

4 READ AND REACT   Problem-solving

STEP 1. **Read about Silvia's problem.**

Silvia lives in a two-bedroom apartment. She lives with her mother, her husband, and their daughter. The apartment is small, but it's nice. The living room is sunny. The kitchen is new. The appliances are good. The rent is $800. But now the building manager wants to raise the rent. He wants $900.

STEP 2. **PAIRS. Talk about it. What is Silvia's problem? What can Silvia do? Here are some ideas.**

- She can get a second job.
- She can find another apartment.
- She can talk to the building manager.
- She can _____.

5 CONNECT

For your Goal-setting Activity, go to page 248.
For your Team Project, go to page 269.

Which goals can you check off? Go back to page 105.

3 ACT IT OUT

STEP 1. 🎧 Listen to the conversation.

- Play CD 2, Track 58. Students listen and read along silently.
- As needed, play Track 58 again to aid comprehension.

STEP 2. PAIRS. Student A, you want to rent...

- Read the directions and the guidelines for Students A and B.
- Pair students. Students practice at their desk with their partner.
- Walk around and check that Student A is asking about the apartment and for directions to it. Student B can make up directions. Student A needs to listen carefully and remember them.
- Call on pairs to perform for the class. While pairs are performing, use the scoring rubric on page Txiv to evaluate each student's vocabulary, grammar, fluency, and how well they complete the task.
- *Optional:* After each pair finishes, discuss the strengths and weakness of each performance either in front of the class or privately.

4 READ AND REACT

STEP 1. Read about Silvia's problem.

- Say: *We are going to read about a student's problem, and then we need to think about a solution.*
- Read the directions.
- Read the story while students follow along silently. Pause after each sentence to allow time for students to comprehend.
- Periodically stop and ask simple *Wh-* questions to check comprehension (for example, *How many bedrooms are there in Silvia's apartment? How much is the rent?*).

STEP 2. PAIRS. Talk about it. What is....

- Pair students. Read the directions and the question.
- Tell pairs to cover the list before reading it. Give pairs a couple of minutes to discuss possible solutions for Silvia.
- Call on pairs to say their ideas.
- Then tell the class to uncover the list. Read each solution and discuss if anyone already suggested that solution (for example, *Julia said she can get a second job.*).
- Give pairs a couple of minutes to discuss their opinion about each idea in the list.
- Call on students to say their opinion about the ideas in the list (for example, S: *She doesn't need to get a second job. She just needs to save more money for rent.*).
- Now tell students to think of one new idea not in the box (for example, *She can spend less money at restaurants.*) and to write it in the blank. Encourage students to think of more than one idea and to write them in their notebooks.

■ MULTILEVEL INSTRUCTION for STEP 2

Cross-ability The higher-level partner says an idea from the list and the lower-level partner states an opinion about it (for example, A: *She can get a second job.* B: *Yes, this is a good idea.*).

5 CONNECT

Turn to page 248 for the Goal-setting Activity and page 268 for the Team Project. See pages Txi–Txii for general notes about teaching these activities.

Progress Check

Which goals can you check off? Go back to page 105.

Ask students to turn to page 105 and check off any remaining goals they have reached. Call on students to say which goals they will practice outside of class.

7 Day After Day

Classroom Materials/Extra Practice

CD 3
Tracks 2–17

Transparencies 7.1–7.5
Vocabulary Cards Unit 7

MCA
Unit 7

Workbook
Unit 7

Interactive Practice
Unit 7

Unit Overview

Goals

- See the list of goals on the facing page.

Grammar

- Simple present: Questions with *When* and *What time*; Prepositions of time
- Adverbs of frequency: *always, usually, sometimes, never*
- Questions with *How often*; Expressions of frequency

Pronunciation

- Reduced pronunciation of *do you*
- Third-person *-es* ending

Reading

- Read an article about free time in the U.S.

Writing

- Write sentences about your schedule and free-time activities

Life Skills Writing

- Complete a timesheet
- Write a note to request time off

Preview

- Set the context of the unit by asking questions about daily activities in your class (for example, *What do we do every day in class?* Possible answers: We read our book. We speak to a partner. We write in our notebooks.). Say: *In this unit we will learn about activities you do every day.*
- Hold up page 125 or show Transparency 7.1. Read the unit title and ask the class to repeat.
- Explain: Day After Day *means* every day.
- Say: *Look at the picture.* Ask the Preview question: *What do you see?* (people talking, children drawing)
- If students begin to call out daily activities, explain: *In this unit we will learn more about daily activities or things you do every day.*

Unit Goals

- Point to the Unit Goals. Explain that this list shows what the class will be studying in this unit.
- Tell students to read the goals silently.
- Say each goal and ask the class to repeat. If possible, bring in a daily planner or a printed schedule of your daily activities. Display them as you explain the following vocabulary as needed:

    Daily routine: *things you do every day*

    Work schedule: *a plan of the days and hours you work*

    Time off: *time that you do not work*

    How often: *how many times; how frequently*

- Tell students to circle one goal that is very important to them. Call on several students to say the goal they circled.

Day After Day

Preview

Look at the picture.
What do you see?

1 WHAT DO YOU KNOW?

A **CLASS.** Look at the pictures. Which activities do you know?

> Number 4 is "eat breakfast."

B  **CD3 T2** Listen and point to the pictures. Then listen and repeat.

2 PRACTICE

A **WORD PLAY. PAIRS.** Student A, look at the list of daily activities on page 127. Act out an activity. Student B, guess the activity.

B: *Wash the dishes?*
A: *No.*
B: *Cook dinner?*
A: *Right!*

B **CD3 T3** Look at the time in each picture. Listen and point. Then listen and repeat.

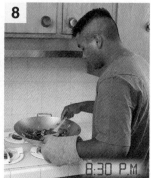

C **PAIRS.** Look at the pictures. Student A, ask about an activity. Student B, say the time.

A: *What time does he go to work?*
B: *At nine.*
A: A.M. *or* P.M.?
B: A.M.
A: *Right!*
B: *What time does he . . . ?*

> A.M. = *in the morning*
> P.M. = *in the afternoon,*
> *in the evening, or*
> *at night*

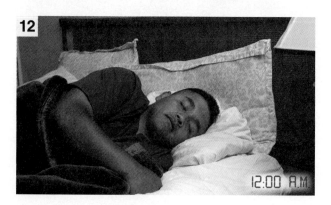

Lesson 1   Vocabulary

Getting Started   10 minutes

1 WHAT DO YOU KNOW?

A CLASS. Look at the pictures. Which...

- Show Transparency 7.2 or hold up the book. Tell students to cover the list of words on page 127.
- Write on the board: *Number _____ is _____.*
- Point to picture 4 and ask: *What is this?* Read the example with the class.
- Say: *Look at the other pictures.* Ask: *Which activities do you know?* Students call out answers as in the example. Point to the board if a student needs help forming the sentence.
- If students call out an incorrect activity, change the answer into a question for the class (for example, *Number 2 is eat dinner?*). If nobody can identify the correct activity, tell students they will now listen to a CD and practice the names of the activities.

Presentation   5 minutes

B 🔘 Listen and point to the pictures. Then...

- Read the directions. Play CD 3, Track 2. Pause after number 12 (*go to sleep*).
- To check comprehension, say each activity in random order and ask students to point to the appropriate picture.
- Resume playing Track 2. Students listen and repeat.

Controlled Practice   30 minutes

2 PRACTICE

A WORD PLAY. PAIRS. Student A, look at the list...

- Read the directions. Read each line in the example and ask the class to repeat. Model correct intonation.
- Play A and model the example with an above-level student.
- Pair students and tell them to take turns playing A and B.
- Walk around and help students correct each other's mistakes.

▬ Expansion: Vocabulary Practice for 2A

- Call on individual students to act out an activity while the other students guess the activity. Show the actor which activity to do by pointing to it in the book or writing it on a slip of paper.
- Whoever guesses correctly becomes the new actor.

B 🔘 Look at the time in each picture....

- Read the directions. Play CD 3, Track 3. Pause after number 12 (*twelve o'clock*).
- Walk around and make sure students are pointing.
- To check comprehension, say each time in random order and ask students to point to the appropriate picture.
- Resume playing Track 3. Students listen and repeat.

C PAIRS. Look at the pictures. Student A, ask...

- Read the directions and the note. Ask: *What time is it right now? Is it A.M. or P.M.?*
- Read each line in the example and ask the class to repeat. Model correct intonation.
- Point to student B's first line, *At nine,* and say: *Use at for times.*
- Play A and model the example with an above-level student.
- Pair students and tell them to take turns playing A and B.
- Walk around and help students correct each other's mistakes.
- To check comprehension, ask individual students: *What time does he (get home, cook dinner, . . .)?*

▬ MULTILEVEL INSTRUCTION for 2C

Cross-ability Before pairs practice the conversation, the higher-level partner reads each line of the example conversation while the lower-level partner listens and repeats.

▬ Expansion: Speaking Practice for 2C

- Reverse Exercise 2C and tell Student A to ask: *What does he do at . . . ?* For example:

  A: *What does he do at 10:00 P.M.?*
  B: *He watches TV.*
  A: *Right!*

- Say: *Use -s or -es at the end of the verb.*
- To wrap up, ask pairs to perform for the class.

Learning Strategy: Write personal sentences

- Provide each student with four index cards or tell them to cut up notebook paper into four pieces.
- Read the directions.
- On the board, draw two rectangles. In one rectangle, write *I _____ at 7:00 A.M.* In the other, write *get up.* Say: *On one side, I wrote a sentence with a blank. On the other side, I wrote the activity I do at 7:00 A.M.*
- Walk around as students work. If misspellings occur, tell them to check the list on page 127. Check that students are capitalizing sentences and using periods.
- Call on students to read their sentences.
- Say: *You can remember new vocabulary when you write sentences that are important to you.* Remind students to use this strategy to remember other new vocabulary.

Show what you know!

STEP 1. What do you do every day? Complete...

- Ask: *What activities do you do every day?* (get up, eat breakfast, . . .) When students call out answers, ask: *What time do you . . . ?*
- Write a few responses on the board (for example, *I cook dinner at 6:30 P.M.*). Say each one and ask the class to repeat.
- Read the directions and the example. Tell students that they will use their answers in the conversation in Step 2.
- Walk around and help as needed. Remind students to write *A.M.* or *P.M.* correctly.
- Call on a few students to read their answers out loud. As needed, model correct pronunciation and ask students to repeat.

Communicative Practice   15 minutes

STEP 2. GROUPS OF 3. Ask about your classmates'...

- Read the directions.
- Play A and model the example with an above-level student. Use some of the Step 1 responses on the board.
- Say: *The question* What's your schedule like? *means* Please tell me your schedule.

- Pair students and tell them to take turns playing A and B.
- Walk around and, as needed, model correct pronunciation and ask students to repeat. To check comprehension, ask individual students: *What's your schedule like?*

▆ MULTILEVEL INSTRUCTION for STEP 2

Pre-level Practice with students first by asking them what their schedule is like before they practice with their partner.

Above-level Students practice with books closed. Additionally, Student A can ask: *What's your schedule like during the week? What's your schedule like on weekends?*

STEP 3. Report to the class.

- Remind students: *When the subject is a person's name, add* -s *or* -es *to the verb.* To show this, write a true statement about yourself on the board: *I get up at 7:00 A.M.* Cross out *I*, and above it write your name and add -s to the verb: *Danny gets up at 7:00 A.M.* Say it and ask the class to repeat.
- Read the verb transformations in the note (*go → goes*) and ask the class to repeat.
- Call on an above-level student to report about one or more students (for example, *Carlos goes to work at 8:30 A.M. He . . .*). Then call on the other students to report on at least one classmate.
- As needed, model correct pronunciation of verbs with -s or -es and ask students to repeat.

▆ Expansion: Speaking Practice for STEP 3

- Call on students to report what their classmates do in the morning, in the afternoon, and in the evening (for example, T: *What does Carolina do in the morning?* S: *She gets up at six. She goes to work at . . .*).

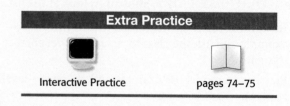

Extra Practice
Interactive Practice pages 74–75

3 8:30 A.M.

4 8:45 A.M.

5 9:00 A.M.

6 7:15 P.M.

9 9:15 P.M.

10 9:30 P.M.

Daily Activities

1. get up
2. take a shower
3. get dressed
4. eat breakfast
5. go to work
6. get home
7. exercise
8. cook dinner
9. eat dinner
10. wash the dishes
11. watch TV
12. go to sleep

Learning Strategy

Write personal sentences

Look at the list of daily activities. Make cards for three or four activities. On one side, write a sentence with a blank about your daily schedule. On the other side, write the activity you do at that time.

Show what you know!

STEP 1. What do you do every day? Complete the sentences. Write activities and times.

I ___go to work___ at ___7:00 A.M.___ .   I _____ at _____ .

I _____ at _____ .   I _____ at _____ .

STEP 2. GROUPS OF 3. Ask about your classmates' daily activities.

A: *What's your schedule like?*
B: *I go to work at seven. I eat lunch at. . . .*

STEP 3. Report to the class.

Carolina goes to work at seven.

go → goes
wash → washes
watch → watches

Listening and Speaking

1 BEFORE YOU LISTEN

A CLASS. Look at Gloria's schedule. Which days is she busy? Which day is she free?

Sunday	Monday	Tuesday	Wednesday	Thursday	Friday	Saturday
Work	Class	Work	Class	Work		Work

B PAIRS. When are you free? What do you do in your free time? Check (✓) the activities. What other activities do you do?

☐ see a movie

☐ go to the mall

☐ play soccer

☐ go to the park

2 LISTEN

A Look at the picture. Gloria and Sen are classmates.

Guess: What are they talking about?

a. homework (b.) plans for Saturday   c. directions to the mall

B CD3 T4 Listen to the conversation.
Was your guess in Exercise A correct?

Listen again. Complete the sentences.

1. On Saturdays Sen ___works___.
   (a.) works   b. goes to school   c. babysits for her cousin

2. Sen gets home at ___8:00___ on Saturdays.
   a. 6:00   b. 7:00   (c.) 8:00

C CD3 T5 Listen to the whole conversation. What does Gloria want to do on Saturday?

a.

(b.)

Getting Started   5 minutes

1 BEFORE YOU LISTEN

Ⓐ CLASS. Look at Gloria's schedule. Which days...

- Ask: *What day is today?*
- Read the directions and ask: *What does* busy *mean?* As needed, explain: Busy *means that you are doing an activity. For example, when people are at work, they are busy.*
- Ask: *Which days is Gloria busy?* (Sunday, Monday, Tuesday, Wednesday, Thursday, and Saturday) *Which day is she free?* (Friday)
- Ask: *What is free time?* As needed, say: Free time *is when you do something fun.* When are you free? *means* When do you have free time?

▰ **Expansion: Vocabulary and Writing Practice for 1A**

- Say: *Gloria is free on Fridays. She has free time. What does Gloria do in her free time? Guess.* Call on students to say free-time activities (go to the park, play with her kids, . . .). Write several on the board.
- Tell students to copy Gloria's schedule into their notebooks and write in free-time activities for her day off.

Ⓑ PAIRS. When are you free? What do you do...

- Ask two or three above-level students: *When are you free? What do you do in your free time?* Write their responses on the board (for example, *Vincent likes to watch movies.*).
- Read the rest of the directions (*Check the . . .*). Point to each picture, say the activity, and ask the class to repeat (*see a movie, . . .*). After each picture, ask students if they do this activity (*Do you see movies in your free time?*).
- Pair students. Partners ask each other the questions.
- Walk around and check that students are discussing free-time activities.
- Call on students to report to the class about their free-time activities.
- Using students' responses (for example, *read a book, listen to music*), write a list of additional activities on the board and tell students to copy it into their notebooks. Explain unfamiliar vocabulary as needed.

▰ **MULTILEVEL INSTRUCTION for 1B**

Cross-ability As a first step, the higher-level partners ask their partner if they do any of the activities listed in Exercise 1B (for example, *Do you go to the mall?*).

Presentation   35 minutes

2 LISTEN

Ⓐ Look at the picture.... Guess:...

- Read the directions.
- Write the answer choices on the board.
- Call on students to guess. Tell them they will listen for the answer in Exercise B.

Ⓑ 💿 **Listen to the conversation. Was your...**

- Read the directions. Play CD 3, Track 4.
- Explain: How about a movie? *is a common way to ask* Do you want to see a movie?
- Circle the correct answer on the board. Ask: *Was your guess correct?*

> **Teaching Tip**
>
> *Optional:* Remember that if students need additional support, tell them to read the Audio Script on page 285 as they listen to the conversation.

Listen again. Complete the sentences.

- Read the directions.
- Read each sentence and the answer choices.
- Play Track 4 again. Students listen and complete the sentences.
- Call on students to say answers.

Ⓒ 💿 **Listen to the whole conversation....**

- Ask: *What activity is picture* a? (see a movie at the theater) *What about picture* b? (see a movie at home)
- Play CD 3, Track 5. Students listen.
- Ask: *What does Gloria want to do on Saturday?* (watch a DVD)
- Play Track 5 as many times as needed.

3   CONVERSATION

A   Listen. Then listen and repeat.

- Read the directions and the Pronunciation Watch note about *do you*.
- Play CD 3, Track 6. Students listen.
- Resume playing Track 6. Students listen and repeat.
- *Optional:* Copy the questions onto the board and underline *do you* in each one. Above it, write *d'ya*. Point to the board as you alternate saying each question in full form (*do you*) and shortened/modified (*d'ya*) form. Students listen and repeat.

▨ Expansion: Speaking Practice for 3A

- Pair students and tell them to ask each other the questions in Exercise A. Walk around and model pronunciation of *d'ya* if students have difficulty.

B   Listen. Complete the sentences.

- Read the directions. Play CD 3, Track 7 as many times as necessary to aid comprehension.
- Call on a few students to write the completed questions on the board.

Controlled Practice   20 minutes

C   Listen and read the conversation....

- Note: This conversation is the same one students heard in Exercise 2B on page 128.
- Read the directions. Play CD 3, Track 8. Students listen and read along silently.
- Resume playing Track 8. Students listen and repeat.

4   PRACTICE

A   PAIRS. Practice the conversation. Then make...

- Pair students and tell them to practice the conversation in Exercise 3C.
- Then, in Exercise 4A, point to each picture, say the activity, day, or time. Ask the class to repeat.
- Copy the conversation onto the board with blanks and read it. When you come to a blank, fill it in with information from the boxes.

- Ask two on-level students to practice the conversation on the board for the class. Erase the words in the blanks and ask two above-level students to make up a conversation for the class.
- Pair students and tell them to take turns playing A and B and to use the information in the boxes to fill in the blanks.
- Walk around and check that students are pronouncing *do you* like "*d'ya*." Tell students to stand, mingle, and practice the conversation with several new partners.
- Call on pairs to perform for the class.

▨ MULTILEVEL INSTRUCTION for 4A

Pre-level Before they practice in pairs, say each line and ask students to repeat after you. While pairs practice, listen closely to their pronunciation. As needed, interrupt, model, and ask students to repeat after you.

Above-level After students practice a couple of times, ask them to cover all but the first words of each line as they continue.

Communicative Practice   10 minutes

B   MAKE IT PERSONAL. PAIRS. Make your own...

- Read the directions. On the board, list some activities, days, and times for students to use in their conversations. Call on students to suggest additional ones.
- With an above-level student, use information from the board and make up a new conversation. Play A and practice for the class.
- Pair students. Walk around and check that students are using information on the board or other vocabulary from the unit.
- Call on pairs to perform for the class.

▨ MULTILEVEL INSTRUCTION for 4B

Pre-level Students substitute information on the board into the conversation in Exercise 4A.

Above-level Ask students to include pickup or drop-off location information (for example, *Pick me up at my home. I live at . . .*).

Extra Practice

Interactive Practice

3 CONVERSATION

CD3 T6

A Listen. Then listen and repeat.

When do you get home?
What do you mean?

CD3 T7

B Listen. Complete the sentences.

1. _____*What do you*_____ do in your free time?

2. _____When do you_____ have English class?

3. _____What time do you_____ go to work?

CD3 T8

C Listen and read the conversation. Then listen and repeat.

Gloria: Are you free tomorrow? How about a movie?

Sen: Sorry, I'm busy. I work on Saturdays.

Gloria: Oh. Well, when do you get home?

Sen: At 8:00.

> **Pronunciation Watch**
>
> In informal conversation, *do you* often sounds like "d'ya."

---

4 PRACTICE

A PAIRS. Practice the conversation. Then make new conversations. Use the information in the boxes.

A: Are you free tomorrow? How about a movie?

B: Sorry, I'm busy. I ▨▨▨▨▨ on ▨▨▨▨▨ .

A: Oh. Well, when do you get home?

B: At ▨▨▨▨▨ .

B MAKE IT PERSONAL. PAIRS. Make your own conversations. Use different activities, days, and times.

take a computer class

babysit

visit my grandparents

Fridays

Thursdays

Sundays

Grammar

Simple present: Questions with *When* and *What time*				Prepositions of time
When	**does**	Sen	**work?**	**On** Saturdays.
		she	**get home?**	**At** 8:00.
	do	you	**have class?**	**From** Monday **to** Friday.
What time	**does**	the movie it	**start?**	**At** 6:00.
	do	they	**have dinner?**	**From** 7:00 **to** 8:00.

1 PRACTICE

Grammar Watch

- Use *from...to...* with days and times. This shows when an activity starts and ends.
- *on Mondays* = *every Monday*
- For more prepositions of time, see page 273.

A Complete the sentences about Alicia's schedule. Use *on*, *at*, *from*, or *to*.

1. Alicia starts work ___at___ 8:00 ___on___ Mondays.

2. She works ___from___ Monday ___to___ Friday.

3. ___On___ Fridays she has dinner with her father.

   They eat ___at___ 7:00.

4. Alicia has English class ___from___ 10:00 ___to___ 12:00

   ___on___ Saturdays.

5. She meets her friends at the mall ___at___ 3:00.

6. ___On___ Sundays she plays soccer ___at___ 11:00.

7. She watches TV ___from___ 9:00 ___to___ 11:00. She goes to sleep ___at___ 11:30.

B Complete the conversation. Read the answers. Then complete the questions.

1. **A:** When ___do___ Paul and Elise ___go___ to work?

   B: They go to work at 9:00. They work from Monday to Friday.

2. **A:** What time ___do___ they ___get home___?

   B: Paul gets home at six. Elise gets home at 6:30.

3. **A:** And when ___does___ Paul ___cook dinner___?

   B: He cooks dinner at 7:00. They eat together from 7:30 to 8:30.

Lesson 3 Talk about daily activities

Getting Started 5 minutes

- Say: *We're going to study simple present questions with* when *and what time. In the conversation on page 129, Gloria and Sen used this grammar.*
- Play CD 3, Track 8. Students listen. Write *When do you get home?* on the board. Underline *When do.*

Presentation 10 minutes

Simple present: Questions with *When* and *What time*; Prepositions of time

- Copy the grammar charts onto the board or show Transparency 7.3 and cover the exercise.
- Read the questions in the left chart and ask the class to repeat. Then read the answers in the right chart and ask the class to repeat.
- Read the first Grammar Watch note. Say: *In Unit 6, you used the prepositions* on, at, from, *and* to *to give directions. Now you will learn how to use them to talk about time.*
- Read the second Grammar Watch note. Explain: *We say* Mondays *with an -s because we are talking about every Monday—all Mondays.*
- Ask students to close their books. Remove any visual aids for the chart. On the board, write the following incomplete sentences:
    1. When _____ Brian work? _____ Fridays.
    2. When _____ you have class? _____ Tuesday _____ Thursday.
    3. When _____ he get home? _____ 6:00.
  Call on students to say answers.
- Read the third Grammar Watch note. Tell students to use the chart on page 273 when they need to review prepositions of time.
- If you are using the transparency, do the exercise with the class.

Teaching Tip

Conduct "pop" reviews/quizzes throughout the day's lesson by recycling the content learned in this grammar presentation. For example, later in the class, find time to ask individual students: *When do you have class? What time do you have dinner?* It keeps students "on their toes" and can help keep the energy level high in the classroom while reinforcing grammar and communication.

Controlled Practice 25 minutes

1 PRACTICE

Ⓐ Complete the sentences about Alicia's schedule....

- Read the directions and the example. Ask the class to repeat the example.
- Do item 2 with the class. Read the sentence. Say: *I see* Monday *and* Friday. *What prepositions do we need?* (*from* and *to*) Point to the area of the grammar chart that shows the short answer *From Monday to Friday.*
- Say: *Read each sentence before you answer.*
- Walk around and spot-check for errors. Circle incorrect answers and ask students to read their sentence again and to check the grammar charts and/or the Grammar Watch note.
- Students compare answers with a partner.
- Call on students to say answers.

Ⓑ Complete the conversation. Read the answers....

- Read the directions and the example. For the example, read line B (the answer) first. Ask: *What is the activity?* (go to work) Say: *OK. Now, let's read the question.*
- Read the example question (line A). Ask: *Why is the first answer* do? (Because the subject is Paul and Elise and that's the same as *they.*) Ask: *Why is the second answer* go? (Because the verb in the answer is *go.*)
- Students compare answers with a partner and role-play the completed conversations. Call on pairs to perform for the class.

▬ Expansion: Grammar and Speaking Practice for 1B

- Pair students. Ask each pair to rewrite the conversations with different names, times, and days.
- Pairs role-play the new conversations.
- Call on pairs to perform for the class.

2 PRACTICE

A Look at Claude's schedule. Write questions about...

- Say: *Look at Claude's schedule.* Ask: *What does he do on Fridays? On Saturdays? On Sundays?*
- Write the example on the board. Call on a student to fill in the words and read the full question.
- Remind students to write *do* or *does* after *When* or *What time.* Also tell students to look back at the grammar charts on page 130 if they need help.
- Walk around and check that students are using correct word order and question marks.
- Call on students to write answers on the board.

B PAIRS. Ask and answer the questions in Exercise A.

- Read the directions. Ask the class the example question from Exercise A: *What time does Claude start work on Fridays?* (at 8:00)
- Pair students and tell them to take turns asking and answering all the questions.
- Walk around and check that students are asking and answering questions, pronouncing *do you* like *d'ya,* and using the correct prepositions.
- To check answers, ask individual students questions from Exercise A.

■■■ MULTILEVEL INSTRUCTION for 2B

Pre-level To build students' confidence, first practice the activity with them.

Above-level After they complete the exercise, tell students to ask their partner when Claude has free time (A: *When does Claude have free time?* B: *On Saturdays in the morning.* A: *What about Sundays?* B: *He has free time then, too. He exercises and has dinner with his mom.*).

Communicative Practice   20 minutes

Show what you know!

STEP 1. When do you do each activity? Fill in...

- Say: *Write the times you do each activity. Don't write in the "Partner" spaces.*
- If students need more room to write, tell them to copy the chart into their notebook.

- Walk around and make sure students are writing times correctly.

STEP 2. PAIRS. When does your partner do each...

- Read the directions and the example conversation.
- Ask a student: *When do you get up on Fridays?* Write the student's answer on the board.
- Pair students. Tell them to take turns asking and answering questions. Say: *Write your partner's answers in the "Partner" spaces in the chart in Step 1.*
- Walk around and make sure students are saying *Fridays* and *Saturdays.* As needed, remind students: *We say* Fridays *with an -s because we are talking about every Friday—all Fridays.*

STEP 3. WRITE. In your notebook, write about...

- Read the directions and the example.
- Say: *Look at your chart and your partner's chart. Circle the times you and your partner do an activity at the same time.*
- Walk around and help as needed. If students do not do any activities at the same time, tell them to write one sentence about themselves and another sentence about their partner.
- Call on several students to say what they and their partner do at the same time.

■■■ Expansion: Speaking Practice for STEPS 2 and 3

- Students stand up and mingle and repeat Step 2 with at least three new partners.
- They then report to the class (as in Step 3) about activities they do at the same time as any of their partners.

Progress Check

Can you . . . talk about daily activities?

Say: *We have practiced talking about daily activities. Now, look at the question at the bottom of the page. Can you talk about daily activities?* Tell students to write a checkmark in the box.

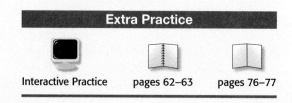

Extra Practice		
Interactive Practice	pages 62–63	pages 76–77

Friday	Saturday	Sunday
work—8:00	soccer game—9:00	exercise—2:00
	study with Maria—1:00	dinner with Mom—6:00

2 PRACTICE

A Look at Claude's schedule. Write questions about his activities. Use the words in parentheses.

1. What time does Claude start work on Fridays?
   (What time / Claude / start work on Fridays)

2. What time does Claude play soccer on Saturdays?
   (What time / Claude / play soccer on Saturdays)

3. What time do Claude and Maria study on Saturdays?
   (What time / Claude and Maria / study on Saturdays)

4. When does Claude exercise?
   (When / Claude / exercise)

5. When do Claude and his mother have dinner?
   (When / Claude and his mother / have dinner)

B PAIRS. Ask and answer the questions in Exercise A.

Show what you know! Talk about daily activities

STEP 1. **When do you do each activity? Fill in the "You" columns.**

	You		Partner	
	Friday	Saturday	Friday	Saturday
get up				
eat dinner				
watch TV				

STEP 2. PAIRS. **When does your partner do each activity? Ask questions. Complete the chart.**

You: *Ana, when do you get up on Fridays?*
Ana: *I get up at 7:00.*

STEP 3. WRITE. **In your notebook, write about activities you and your partner do at the same time.**

Ana and I both watch TV from 6:00 to 7:00 on Fridays.

Can you… talk about daily activities? ☐

Life Skills

1 TALK ABOUT WORK SCHEDULES

CLASS. Look at the calendar. Say the days of the week.

DECEMBER

Sun.	Mon.	Tues.	Wed.	Thurs.	Fri.	Sat.

Writing Watch

Start days of the week with capital letters. Example: *Sunday*

End abbreviations for days of the week with a period. Example: *Sun.*

2 PRACTICE

PAIRS. Student A, look at the work schedule on the left. Student B, look at the schedule on the right. Don't look at your partner's schedule. Ask and answer questions. Complete the information.

A: *When does Ming work?*
B: *She works Tuesday to Saturday, from 11:00 to 5:00.*

- For Mon.–Fri., we say Monday to Friday or from Monday to Friday.
- For Mon., Wed., Fri., we say Monday, Wednesday, and Friday.
- For 11:00–5:00, we say eleven to five or from eleven to five.

Student A

The Computer Store

Work Schedule: December 9–15

Ming Chu	Tues.–Sat., 11:00 A.M.–5:00 P.M.
Pedro Molina	Mon.–Fri., 2:30 P.M.–8:30 P.M.
Maya Kabir	Tues., Thurs., Sat., 7:00 A.M.–4:00 P.M.
Danny Wu	Wed., Thurs., Fri., 6:30 A.M.–10:30 A.M.
Bruno Duval	Wed.–Sun., 3:00 P.M.–10:00 P.M.

Student B

The Computer Store

Work Schedule: December 9–15

Ming Chu	Tues.–Sat., 11:00 A.M.–5:00 P.M.
Pedro Molina	Mon.–Fri., 2:30 P.M.–8:30 P.M.
Maya Kabir	Tues., Thurs., Sat., 7:00 A.M.–4:00 P.M.
Danny Wu	Wed., Thurs., Fri., 6:30 A.M.–10:30 A.M.
Bruno Duval	Wed.–Sun., 3:00 P.M.–10:00 P.M.

Can you...talk about work schedules? ☐

Lesson 4 Talk about work schedules and time sheets

Getting Started 5 minutes

- Say: *A work schedule is a list of the times you work in a week.*
- Ask: *Do you have a work schedule? Which days do you work?* Call on a couple of students to answer.

Teaching Tip

When presenting a new lesson, repeat key words from the lesson title to keep students focused on the topic. Write the words *work schedule* and *time sheets* on the board as a reminder of some of the key elements in this lesson.

Presentation 10 minutes

1 TALK ABOUT WORK SCHEDULES

CLASS. Look at the calendar. Say the days of the week.

- Read the directions and the Writing Watch note. Ask: *What's the month on this calendar?* (December)
- Point to *Sun.* on the calendar and tell the class: *This is an abbreviation. It's a short form of the word.* Ask: *What day is this?* (Sunday) *How do you spell Sunday?* (S-U-N- · · ·) Write *Sunday* on the board. Next to it write the abbreviation *Sun.*
- Point to each abbreviation and first ask: *What day is this?* Say the day and ask the class to repeat.
- To check comprehension, point to days in random order and call on students to say the day.

Controlled Practice 30 minutes

2 PRACTICE

PAIRS. Student A, look at the work schedule...

- Read the directions and the note.
- On the board, write: *Wed.–Sat.* Ask: *How do you say this?* (Wednesday to Saturday or from Wednesday to Saturday) Point to the dash and say: *This is a dash—it connects days.*
- Under *Wed.–Sat.*, write: *Wed., Fri., Sun.* Ask: *How do I say this?* (Wednesday, Friday, and Sunday) Point to a comma and say: *This is a comma—it separates days.*

- Point to *Wed.–Sat.* and ask: *Is Thursday included?* (Yes.) Point to *Wed., Fri., Sun.* Ask: *Is Thursday included?* (No.)
- Play A and model the example conversation with an on-level student.
- Walk around and check that students are using abbreviations, commas, and dashes correctly. Also listen for correct use of *from* and *to*.
- Call on students to write answers on the board.

■ MULTILEVEL INSTRUCTION for 2
Cross-ability Tell the higher-level student to repeat the schedule several times to help the lower-level student write it correctly.

■ Expansion: Listening Practice for 2

- Tell students to open their notebooks. Say: *Number your paper from 1 to 5 and write what I dictate. First, I will say a student's name. Write it. Then I will say a work schedule. Write it next to the name. Use abbreviations for the days.*
- Use real students' names.
    1. (*name*) Thurs.–Sun., 7:00–11:00 P.M.
    2. (*name*) Mon., Wed., Sat., 10:00 A.M.–3:00 P.M.
    3. (*name*) Fri.–Wed., 8:30 A.M.–12:00 P.M.
    4. (*name*) Sun., Wed., Fri., 1:00–8:30 P.M.
    5. (*name*) Mon.–Fri., 9:00 A.M.–6:00 P.M.

■ Expansion: Vocabulary Practice for 2

- Introduce the word *shift*. Say: *A shift is the time of day when you work.* Write a chart on the board:

Shift	Example
morning shift	6:00 A.M.–11:00 A.M.
afternoon shift	12:30 P.M.–5:00 P.M.
evening shift	6:00 P.M.–10:00 P.M.

- Say: *Working past midnight is called the* graveyard shift *(for example, 11:30–4:30 A.M.).* Explain: *It's called the* graveyard shift *because after midnight everything is quiet like a graveyard.*
- Pairs then ask each other: *What shift do you work?* Tell students to include the time they work in their answer (for example, *I work the morning shift at the restaurant. I work from 5:00 to 10:00 A.M.*).

Progress Check

Can you . . . talk about work schedules?

Say: *We have practiced talking about work schedules. Now, look at the question at the bottom of the page. Can you talk about work schedules?* Tell students to write a checkmark in the box.

Talk about work schedules and time sheets

3 READ A TIME SHEET

Look at Mariam's time sheet. Complete the sentences.

- Tell students to look at Mariam's time sheet. Explain: *A time sheet is a list of the days and hours you worked. You fill out a time sheet after you work.*
- Read the notes for the time sheet.
- Explain: Off *means you do not work at that time.*
- Read the directions and the example. Point to the times next to the days on the time sheet to show where the answers come from.
- Students compare answers with a partner.
- Call on a few students to write answers on the board.

Teaching Tip

When presenting forms or charts to the class, group students who may have trouble following along without assistance.

▬ Expansion: Speaking Practice for 3

- Write the following questions on the board. Ask students to discuss them with a partner and write answers in their notebooks:

  1. *Which day does Mariam work from 8:30 A.M. to 1:00 P.M.?* (Monday)
  2. *How many days does she work?* (Four)
  3. *What day does she start work at 12:00 P.M.?* (Saturday)
  4. *When does she finish work at 5:00 P.M.?* (Tuesday and Saturday)

Communicative Practice   10 minutes

4 PRACTICE

Read the information. Complete your time sheet...

- Read the directions. Say: *Write your name on the time sheet.*
- Read the paragraph. Ask: *What time do you work?* (From 7:00 A.M. to 3:00 P.M.) Say: *Use the information in the paragraph to fill out the time sheet.*

- Students compare answers with a partner.
- Walk around and check that students have filled out the time sheet accurately. Circle any mistakes and ask students to read the paragraph again carefully.

▬ Expansion: Listening Practice for 4

- Students copy the days and time in/out portion of the time sheet from page 133 into their notebooks.
- Dictate the following schedule that students copy into their charts:

  You work from 8:00 A.M. to 2:30 P.M. at City Center Hospital. You are off on Wednesdays and Fridays.

- Walk around and check that students wrote the correct schedule. Repeat the dictation as many times as necessary.

5 LIFE SKILLS WRITING

Turn to page 259 and ask students to complete the note. See pages Txi–Txiii for general notes about the Life Skills Writing activities.

Progress Check

Can you . . . read and complete a time sheet?

Say: *We have practiced reading and completing time sheets. Now, look at the question at the bottom of the page. Can you read and complete a time sheet?* Tell students to write a checkmark in the box.

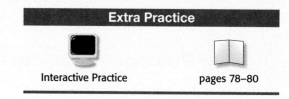

Extra Practice

Interactive Practice   pages 78–80

3 READ A TIME SHEET

Look at Mariam's time sheet. Complete the sentences.

❶ employee = worker

❸ Time In = the time you start work

TIME SHEET

❶ EMPLOYEE NAME
Last — Said,
First — Mariam

❷ EMPLOYEE I.D. # 987-65-4321

Week ending 7/15

DAY	**❸ TIME IN**	**❹ TIME OUT**	HOURS
Mon.	8:30 A.M.	1:00 P.M.	4.5
Tues.	9:00 A.M.	5:00 P.M.	8
Wed.	8:30 A.M.	3:30 P.M.	7
Thurs.	off		
Fri.	off		
Sat.	12:00 P.M.	5:00 P.M.	5
Sun.	off		

Employee Signature — _Mariam Said_

TOTAL HOURS 24.5

❷ I.D. # = Identification Number
Some companies use Social Security numbers (SSNs) for employee I.D. numbers.

❹ Time Out = the time you finish work

1. Mariam worked on _Monday, Tuesday, Wednesday, and Saturday_.

2. On Tuesday she started work at _9:00 A.M._.

3. On _Wednesday_ she finished work at 3:30.

4. She was off on _Thursday, Friday, and Sunday_.

5. She worked _4.5_ hours on Monday.

4 PRACTICE

Read the information. Complete your time sheet for the week.

You work from 7:00 A.M. to 3:00 P.M. at City Center Hospital. You are off on Tuesdays and Thursdays. Your employee I.D. number is 00312. Today is Saturday, March 11.

5 LIFE SKILLS WRITING

Write a note to your manager. Ask for time off. See page 259.

TIME SHEET

EMPLOYEE NAME
First ____ Last ____

EMPLOYEE I.D. # 00312

Week ending _3/11_

	TIME IN	TIME OUT	HOURS
Sun.	7:00 A.M.	3:00 P.M.	8
Mon.	7:00 A.M.	3:00 P.M.	8
Tues.	off		
Wed.	7:00 A.M.	3:00 P.M.	8
Thurs.	off		
Fri.	7:00 A.M.	3:00 P.M.	8
Sat.	7:00 A.M.	3:00 P.M.	8
Employee Signature		**TOTAL HOURS** 40	

Can you...read and complete a time sheet? ☐

Talk about weekend activities

Listening and Speaking

1 BEFORE YOU LISTEN

A READ. **Read the information.**

In the U.S. and Canada, many people work from Monday to Friday.
They are free on the weekend (Saturday and Sunday).

B CLASS. **Are you free on the weekend? What do you do? Check (✓) the activities. What other activities do you do?**

☐ clean

☐ spend time with my family

☐ shop for food

2 LISTEN

A **Look at the picture. Mei-Yu and Ernesto are leaving work.**

Guess: What day is it? Friday

CD3 T9

B 🔵 **Listen to the conversation. Was your guess in Exercise A correct?**
Listen again. Complete the schedules.

Mei-Yu

Saturday	Sunday
Clean the house	Spend time with family

Ernesto

Saturday	Sunday
Shop for food	Go to the park

CD3 T10

C 🔵 **Listen to the whole conversation. In Ernesto's house, what do they call Sunday?**

a. "work day"   b. "play day"   c. "fun day"

Talk about weekend activities

Getting Started   5 minutes

1   BEFORE YOU LISTEN

A READ. Read the information.

- Read the short paragraph while students read along silently.
- Ask: *What days are the weekend?* (Saturday and Sunday)

B CLASS. Are you free on the weekend? What...

- Read the directions.
- Say each activity and ask the class to repeat.
- Say: *These are free-time activities.* Ask: *Are they fun? Is it fun to clean / to spend time with your family / to shop for food?*
- Ask: *Are you free on the weekend? What do you do?* Say: *Check the activities you do.*
- Ask individual students if they do each activity: *Do you clean / spend time with your family / shop for food? What other activities do you do?*

Culture Connection

- Ask: *Is your free time in the United States different from your free time in your home country?* For students who answer *yes*, ask: *What do you do here that is different?* For students who answer *no*, ask: *What do you do that is the same?*
- Ask: *Do people in your country have a lot of free time? Do you think Americans have a lot of free time?* Call on students to explain if they can (for example, *I think Americans work too much. They don't have enough free time.*).

Presentation   20 minutes

2   LISTEN

A Look at the picture.... Guess:...

- Read the directions. Say: Leave work *means stop work and go home or somewhere else.*
- Ask: *What does Mei-Yu want to do?* (She wants to spend time with her family.) *What does Ernesto want to do?* (He wants to play soccer.)

- Ask: *What day is it?* (Friday) Call on students to answer the question. Write answers on the board.

B Listen to the conversation. Was...

- Read the directions. Play CD 3, Track 9.
- Ask: *Was your guess in Exercise A correct?* Circle the correct day on the board.

Teaching Tip

Optional: Remember that if students need additional support, tell them to read the Audio Script on page 285 as they listen to the conversation.

Listen again. Complete the schedules.

- Say: *Mei-Yu and Ernesto are talking about what they do on the weekend. Look at the schedules. Read the directions.*
- Play Track 9 again. Students listen and complete the schedules.
- Students compare answers with a partner.
- Call on students to say answers.

C Listen to the whole conversation...

- Read the directions. Write the answer choices on the board and read them.
- Play CD 3, Track 10. Students listen and circle the answer.
- Call on the class to say the answer.

▬ Expansion: Graphic Organizer Practice for 2C

- Tell students to make a two-column chart in their notebooks with the headings *Mon.–Fri.* and *Sat.–Sun.*
- Say: *Write activities you do from Monday to Friday in the first column (for example, go to work). Write activities you do on Saturdays or Sundays in the second column (for example, go shopping).*
- Students share answers with a partner and then share with the class (for example, *On Mondays, I go shopping. On Saturdays, I clean.*).

Controlled Practice   20 minutes

3   CONVERSATION

 Listen and read the conversation. Then...

- Note: This conversation is the same one students heard in Exercise 2B on page 134.
- Play CD 3, Track 11. Students listen and read along silently.
- Explain: Gee *is a common word people use during informal conversation when they are excited.* Always *means* every time, *in this case, every Saturday.*
- Resume playing Track 11. Students listen and repeat.

■■ MULTILEVEL INSTRUCTION for 3

Pre-level Demonstrate to students how to trace words you read out loud with your finger. Tell students to trace with their fingers while they read.

Above-level Ask students to speak more quickly to imitate the rhythm of the speakers on the CD.

4   PRACTICE

A **PAIRS. Practice the conversation. Then make new...**

- Pair students and tell them to practice the conversation in Exercise 3.
- Then, in Exercise 4A, point to each picture, say the activity, and ask the class to repeat.
- Copy the conversation onto the board with blanks and read it. When you come to a blank, fill it in with information from the pictures (A: *cook, ride my bike*; B: *do the laundry, go to the beach*).
- Ask two on-level students to practice the conversation in front of the class.
- Pair students and tell them to take turns playing each role and to use the words in the boxes to fill in the blanks.
- Walk around and check that students are pronouncing *do you* as *d'ya* and are clearly pronouncing the various activities.
- Tell students to stand, mingle, and practice the conversation with several new partners.

■■ MULTILEVEL INSTRUCTION for 4A

Pre-level Tell students to first read each activity in the pictures out loud together before making new conversations.

Above-level Encourage students to brainstorm activities not already listed on page 135 to use in their conversations (for example, *go jogging*).

Communicative Practice   15 minutes

B **MAKE IT PERSONAL. PAIRS. Make your own...**

- With an above-level student, play A and make up a new conversation and practice for the class. Use the vocabulary from Exercise 4A or any other activities learned during this unit. Continue the conversation for three or four exchanges.
- Pair students. Tell them to stress activity words (for example, *I always do my **homework** on Saturdays.*).
- Walk around and check that students are each discussing what they always do on Saturdays and Sundays.
- Call on pairs to perform for the class.
- To wrap up, on the board write some of the errors you heard during the role plays. Ask the class to call out corrections. Go over the corrections by saying the words or sentences correctly and having students repeat.

■■ MULTILEVEL INSTRUCTION for 4B

Pre-level Sit with students (or assign above-level students) and practice with them.

Above-level Tell students to discuss what activities they do in the morning, afternoon, and evening (for example, *Well, on Saturdays I always work on my car in the morning, play basketball in the afternoon, and play video games in the evening.*).

Extra Practice

Interactive Practice

CONVERSATION

CD3 T11

Listen and read the conversation. Then listen and repeat.

Mei-Yu: Gee, I'm so glad it's Friday!

Ernesto: Me, too. What do you usually do on the weekend?

Mei-Yu: Well, I always clean the house on Saturdays, and I always spend time with my family on Sundays. What about you?

Ernesto: I usually shop for food on Saturdays, and I sometimes go to the park on Sundays.

4 PRACTICE

A PAIRS. **Practice the conversation. Then make new conversations. Use the pictures.**

A: Gee, I'm so glad it's Friday!

B: Me, too. What do you usually do on the weekend?

A: Well, I always _____ on Saturdays, and I always _____ on Sundays. What about you?

B: I usually _____ on Saturdays, and I sometimes _____ on Sundays.

cook

ride my bike

do my homework

play basketball

read the paper

go dancing

do the laundry

go to the beach

work on my car

play cards

play video games

go swimming

B MAKE IT PERSONAL. PAIRS. **Make your own conversations. Talk about your weekend activities.**

Grammar

Adverbs of frequency

I You We They	always usually sometimes never	clean	on Saturdays.
He She		cleans	

Grammar Watch

always	100%
usually	
sometimes	
never	0%

Adverbs of frequency go before all verbs except *be*.

PRACTICE

A Marcos is a student at Greenville Adult School. Look at his schedule. Complete the e-mail with *always, usually, sometimes,* or *never* and the correct form of the verb.

	Mon.	Tue.	Wed.	Th.	Fri.	Sat.	Sun.
7:00	exercise	exercise	exercise	exercise	exercise		
8:00–12:00	class	work	class	work	class		
12:30	lunch	lunch	lunch	lunch	lunch	lunch	lunch
1:00–5:00	work		work		work	work	soccer?

Hi Cristina,

How are you? I'm fine. My new job is great. I ___usually___ ___work___ in the
                                                1. (work)

afternoon, but I ___sometimes___ ___work___ in the morning. In my free time, I do a lot of
                             2. (work)

things. I ___always___ ___exercise___ at 7:00 A.M. Then, on Mondays, Wednesdays, and
                        3. (exercise)

Fridays, I ___always___ ___have___ class. I ___always___ ___have___ lunch at
               4. (have)   **5. (have)**

12:30. I ___never___ ___work___ on Sundays. It's my only day off! I ___sometimes___
               6. (work)

___play___ soccer in the afternoon with my brothers. I love Sundays!
     7. (play)

Write soon,

Marcos

Getting Started   5 minutes

- Say: *We're going to study adverbs of frequency. In the conversation on page 135, Ernesto and Mei-Yu used this grammar.*
- Play CD 3, Track 11. Students listen. On the board, write: *I always clean the house on Saturdays and I usually shop for food.* Underline *always* and *usually.*

Teaching Tip

Before presenting the grammar chart, spend some time thinking about the frequency of certain activities in your class (for example, *Juana always comes to class on time.*) and use these as examples that students can relate to when presenting the grammar point of the lesson.

Presentation   10 minutes

Adverbs of frequency

- Copy the grammar chart onto the board or show Transparency 7.4 and cover the exercise. Say: *Adverbs of frequency help us to understand how often (or how many times) we do activities.*
- First, review subject/verb agreement. Circle the top group of subject pronouns (*I, You, We, They*) and circle the verb *cook.* Ask: *What is the verb?* (clean) Remind students: *If the subject is* I, you, we, *or* they, *don't put an -s on the verb.* Say each subject with the verb and ask the class to repeat.
- Circle the bottom group of subject pronouns (*He, She*). Ask: *What is the verb?* (cleans) Remind students: *If the subject is* he *or* she, *put an -s on the verb.* Say each subject with the verb and ask the class to repeat.
- Now, point to and underline the adverb of frequency in each sentence in the grammar chart. Say: *Adverbs of frequency usually go before the verb.* Read sentences and point to each word as you read. Ask the class to repeat.

- Read the Grammar Watch note. Write the following sentences on the board:
    1. *Carlos <u>always</u> eats breakfast.*
    2. *Anya <u>usually</u> eats breakfast.*
    3. *Rodrigo <u>sometimes</u> eats breakfast.*
    4. *Abebe <u>never</u> eats breakfast.*
  In a separate column, write the following:
    a. *3 days a week*
    b. *5 days a week*
    c. *0 days a week*
    d. *7 days a week.*
  Explain: X days a week *means how many days in a week. Ask students to match 1–4 with a–d and to write answers in their notebooks. Call on students to say answers. (1. d, 2. b, 3. a, 4. c)
- If you are using the transparency, do the exercise with the class.

Controlled Practice   20 minutes

PRACTICE

 Marcos is a student at Greenville Adult School....

- Read the directions and the example.
- Ask: *Why is* usually *the answer?* (Because Marcos works from 1:00 to 5:00 four days a week.) *Why is* work *the answer?* (Because the subject is I.)
- Say: *Read each sentence first before you answer. Look at the schedule to see how many days Marcos does the activity.*
- Walk around and check that students are checking the schedule before they write an adverb of frequency. Also check that the verb agrees with *I.*
- Students compare answers with a partner.
- Call on students to say answers.

■■ **Expansion: Graphic Organizer and Writing Practice for A**

- Ask students to make a weekly schedule in the same style as Marcos's schedule. Students can compare schedules and write sentences (at least five) about their partner's schedule (for example, *She sometimes eats lunch at 1:00.*).

B Look at Marcos and his family's Sunday activities....

- Read the directions.
- Point to the picture for item 1 and ask: *What is the activity?* (visit my family) Say: *Look at the words in blue (I/always/on Sundays).* Say: *I always . . .* Ask the class to complete the answer (Ss: *. . . visit my family on Sundays.*). Say the complete answer and ask the class to repeat.
- Point to each picture and ask: *What is the activity?* (2. eat lunch, 3. play soccer, 4. play cards, 5. read, 6. wash the dishes)
- Say: *Look at the activity and look at the words in blue. Write a complete sentence.*
- Walk around and check that students are writing complete sentences and spelling activities correctly.
- As needed, tell students to look back at pages 127, 134, and 135 to check their spelling for the activities.
- Students compare answers with a partner.
- Call on students to say answers.

Communicative Practice 20 minutes

Show what you know!

STEP 1. Complete the sentences with true or false...

- Read the directions. Ask a student: *What do you usually do at night?* (watch TV) On the board, write: *I usually <u>watch TV</u> at night.*
- Say: *Write an activity for number 1 and number 2. For number 3, write something you never do. For number 4, write something you always, usually, sometimes, or never do. Make sure that at least one item has false (made-up) information. You will use these sentences in Step 2.*
- Walk around and check that students are completing each sentence with an acceptable answer.

STEP 2. PAIRS. Student A, read a sentence....

- Pair students. Read the directions.
- Read the example conversation with an on-level student. Play A. Emphasize *never* in the follow-up statement.

- Say: *After your partner guesses true or false, answer Yes or No. If your answer is Yes, repeat your original sentence. If your answer is No, make your original sentence true (for example,* I never watch TV at night.*). To make your original sentence true, you need to change the adverb of frequency.*
- Call on a pair to make up a conversation in which B guesses incorrectly as in the example.
- To check answers, call on pairs to perform for the class.

MULTILEVEL INSTRUCTION for STEP 2

Pre-level Sit with students and, as needed, help them correct false sentences as in the example.

Above-level Tell students to follow up B's guess with as much information as possible (for example, A: *I usually watch TV at night.* B: *True.* A: *No. I never watch TV at night. I work nights! I sometimes exercise after work.*).

Expansion: Writing and Speaking Practice for STEP 2

- On the board, write the following sentences:
  1. *I sometimes _____ after English class.*
  2. *I always go to English class _____.*
  3. *I never go to English class _____.*
  4. *I _____ study English _____.*
- Say: *Copy the sentences into your notebook and complete them. Make two true and make two false.*
- Pair students and tell them to take turns reading their sentences to each other as in Step 2.
- Student B guesses *True* or *False*, and Student A says *Yes* or *No*.

Progress Check

Can you . . . talk about weekend activities?

Say: *We have practiced talking about weekend activities. Now, look at the question at the bottom of the page. Can you talk about weekend activities?* Tell students to write a checkmark in the box.

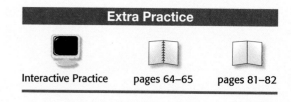

Extra Practice		
Interactive Practice	pages 64–65	pages 81–82

B Look at Marcos and his family's Sunday activities. Imagine that you are Marcos. Write sentences about your activities. Use the words in parentheses.

1. I always visit my family on Sundays.
   (I / always / on Sundays)

2. We always have lunch at 12:30.
   (We / always / at 12:30)

3. My brothers and I sometimes play soccer in the park.
   (My brothers and I / sometimes / in the park)

4. My father and sister usually play cards.
   (My father and sister / usually)

5. My mother usually reads after lunch.
   (My mother / usually / after lunch)

6. My mother never does the dishes on Sundays.
   (My mother / never / on Sundays)

Show what you know! Talk about weekend activities

STEP 1. Complete the sentences with true or false information.

1. I usually _____ at night.   3. I never _____.

2. I always _____ on Sundays.   4. I _____.

STEP 2. PAIRS. Student A, read a sentence. Student B, guess *True* or *False*.

A: *I usually watch TV at night.*
B: *True.*
A: *No. I never watch TV at night. I work nights!*

Can you...talk about weekend activities?   ☐

Reading

1 BEFORE YOU READ

PAIRS. Talk about it. How much free time do you have a day? What do you do in your free time?

2 READ

CD3 T12

Listen. Read the article.

How much free time do Americans have? American men have about 5 hours and 37 minutes of free time a day. American women have about 5 hours.

What do Americans do with their free time? These are three common activities.

They watch TV. Men watch 2 hours and 48 minutes of TV a day. Women watch less TV. They watch 2 hours and 22 minutes.

They exercise. Men exercise or play sports for about 23 minutes a day. Women exercise only 12 minutes a day.

They spend time with family and friends. Men talk on the phone or spend time with family and friends for about 50 minutes a day. Women talk on the phone or spend time with family and friends for about an hour a day.

What's one reason American men have more free time than American women? Men cook and clean for only 30 minutes a day. Women cook and clean for 1 hour and 43 minutes a day!

Source: American Time Use Survey. U.S. Department of Labor, Bureau of Labor Statistics, 2005

3 CHECK YOUR UNDERSTANDING

A Read the article again. Circle *True* or *False*.

1. Women have more free time than men.   True   (False)
2. Men watch more TV than women.   (True)   False
3. Women play more sports than men.   True   (False)
4. Men spend more time with family and friends than women do.   True   (False)
5. Women cook and clean more than men.   (True)   False

Getting Started   10 minutes

1 BEFORE YOU READ

A PAIRS. Talk about it. How much free time...

- Ask the class the questions in the directions. Call on a couple of students to answer (for example, *I have free time in the evening. I like to watch TV.*).
- Pair students. Partners ask each other the questions in the directions.
- Call on students to report on their partner (for example, *Pablo has free time in the morning. He likes to read the newspaper.*).

Community Building

Include regular periods of free time during class to allow students to work on collaborative projects or play games requiring them to practice English.

Presentation   10 minutes

2 READ

📀 **Listen. Read the article.**

- Ask: *What is the title?* (Time Out) Say: *Look at the pictures. What is the article about? Guess.* Call on students to say what they think the article is about (for example, *I think it's about free time.*).
- Play CD 3, Track 12. Students listen and read along silently.
- If students have difficulty following along, play Track 12 again and pause at various points.

- *Optional:* Play Track 12 again. Pause the CD after the following paragraphs and ask these questions:

  First paragraph: *How much free time do American men/women have?* (men: 5 hours and 37 minutes a day; women: 5 hours)

  Second paragraph: *How much TV do men/ women watch?* (men: 2 hours and 48 minutes; women: 2 hours and 22 minutes)

  Third paragraph: *How much time do men/women exercise?* (men: 23 minutes a day; women: 12 minutes a day)

  Fourth paragraph: *How much time do men/ women spend with their family and friends?* (men: 50 minutes per day; women: 1 hour per day)

Controlled Practice   10 minutes

3 CHECK YOUR UNDERSTANDING

A Read the article again. Circle *True* or *False*.

- Read the directions. Explain that *more . . . than* is a way to compare two things.
- To illustrate *more than*, hold up three pencils and ask a student to hold up two. Say: *I have more pencils than (Student).*
- Students compare answers with a partner.
- Walk around and help as needed. Tell students to check their answers by looking back at the article.
- Call on students to say answers and to make false statements true (for example, *3. Men play more sports than women.*).

Communicative Practice   30 minutes

B PAIRS. **Talk about it. Are the sentences...**

Culture Connection

• Read the directions. Ask: *Is number 1 true in your home country?* Ask students to explain (for example, *No, because in my country men spend more time with family and friends.*).

• Pair students.

• Walk around and check that students are giving reasons why or why not each sentence is true in their home country.

• Call on several students to say if each item is true or false in their home country.

▄▄ MULTILEVEL INSTRUCTION for 3B

Pre-level Before they begin speaking with a partner, ask students to think about their home country and write *true* or *false* next to each item in Exercise 3A.

Above-level Ask students to wrap up by making one or two statements comparing their home country and their partner's home country (for example, *In my home country, men have more free time than women. But in Julia's home country, women have more free time than men.*).

C Look at the bar graphs. How do Americans...

• Read the directions. Read the title of the first bar graph. Say: *There is a bar for men and a bar for women.*

• Draw the first bar graph on the board. Ask: *Where is the label for the activity?* (underneath the bottom line of the graph) *Where is the amount of time measured?* (at the left side of the graph) *In the first two graphs, what is the time measured in—hours or minutes?* (hours) *In the last two graphs?* (minutes)

• Read the first item and let students call out the correct answer for the blank (5). Point out that the bar for *men* is just under the 6 hour marker on the line labeled *Hours* (the vertical axis). This means we know the bar is less than 6. Additionally, explain: *The* vertical axis *is called the* y-axis (label on board). *The* horizontal axis *is called the* x-axis (label on board).

• Walk around and check that students are referring to the correct bar graph before they write answers.

◯ Show what you know!

CLASS. How much free time do you have? Take...

• Say: *In your notebook, write how much free time you have for every day of the week. Then add all the hours together. This is your total free time.*

• On the board, create a simple bar graph, similar to those in Exercise 3C. Label the y-axis *Hours* and mark the intervals 0, 5, 10, 15, 20, 25, 30, 35, and 40. Label the x-axis *Hours of free time a week.* Ask a few students: *How much free time do you have?* Draw bars that represent their total amounts and write their names at the top of the bars.

• Say: *Ask every student in the class how much free time he or she has.* Draw a bar for each student. You can make the bars thin as long as it's clear what name goes with each bar.

• Walk around and check that students have created bar graphs large enough to fit all students. Use the graph on the board to correct any labeling errors.

• Ask the class to call out the free time for each student. Complete the graph on the board. Ask: *Who has the most free time? The least?* To explain these terms, point to the bar of the student with the most time and to the bar of the student with the least time.

▄▄ Expansion: Graphic Organizer Practice

• Ask: *What do you do when you have free time?* Draw the axes of a graph on the board and label one side *Hours a Week* and the other side *Activities.*

• Say: *Draw a graph like this in your notebooks. Choose four free-time activities and draw a bar on the graph for each activity. Label the bar with the name of the activity. Each bar shows the number of hours you spend per week on that activity.*

• After the graphs are completed, call on students to report to the class (for example, *I have about X hours of free time a week. I _____ for about _____ hours every week.*).

Extra Practice

Interactive Practice	pages 66–67	page 83

B PAIRS. Talk about it. Are the sentences in Exercise A true or false in your country?

C Look at the bar graphs. How do Americans spend their free time?
Complete the sentences.

a.

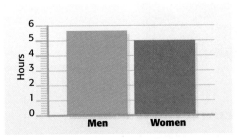

Hours of free time a day

Men have about __5__ hours and
37 minutes of free time every day.
Women have about __5__ hours
of free time every day.

c.

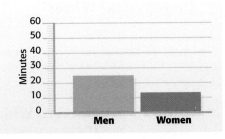

Minutes of exercise a day

Men exercise for about __23__ minutes
every day.
Women exercise about __12__ minutes
every day.

b.

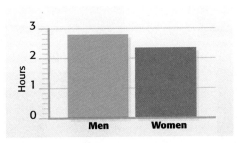

Hours of TV a day

Men watch about __2__ hours and
48 minutes of TV every day.
Women watch about __2__ hours and
22 minutes of TV every day.

d.

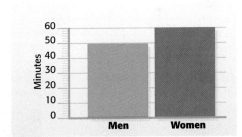

Minutes with family and friends a day

Men spend about __50__ minutes
every day with family and friends.
Women spend about __60__ minutes
every day with family and friends.

Show what you know!

CLASS. How much free time do you have? Take a survey. Make a bar graph
for your class. Use the bar graphs above as a model.

Listening and Speaking

1 **BEFORE YOU LISTEN**

CLASS. Do you relax? When?

2 **LISTEN**

A Look at some ways people relax. Which of these activities do you do?

ON THE AIR **Ways to Relax**

☑ take a hot bath   ☐ do puzzles   ☑ go running

☐ knit   ☑ listen to music   ☑ take a long walk

CD3 T13

B Listen to the radio show. The host, Sue Miller, talks about relaxing. Look at the pictures in Exercise A. Check (✓) the four activities Sue Miller talks about.

CD3 T13

C Listen again. Complete the sentence. Check (✓) all the correct answers.

Sue Miller says, "You need to relax every day. It helps you _____."

☑ study better   ☑ work better   ☐ be a better friend   ☑ be a better parent

Talk about how often you do something

Getting Started 5 minutes

 1 BEFORE YOU LISTEN

CLASS. Do you relax? When?

- Say: *Look at the picture of the woman.* Ask: *What is she doing?* (reading the newspaper) *Is she relaxed?* (Yes.)
- Remind students that *relax* means to have fun, be calm, and not work.
- Ask: *Do you relax? When?* (*Some possible answers:* in my free time, after work, on the weekend)
- Write several responses on the board.
- Ask: *How do you relax? What do you do?* Write students' responses on the board. Say: *We are going to learn about ways that people relax.*

Presentation 15 minutes

2 LISTEN

A Look at some ways people relax. Which of these...

- Read the directions. Say each activity and ask the class to repeat.
- Ask: *Which of these activities do you do? When?* Students call out answers (for example, *I take a hot bath on Sundays.*).

B Listen to the radio show. The host,...

- Read the directions. Play CD 3, Track 13. Students listen.
- If students have difficulty following along, play Track 13 again and pause at various points.
- Students compare answers with a partner.
- Call on students to say answers.

Expansion: Vocabulary Practice for 2B

- Ask students to say additional ways to relax. They can say new activities or activities from the unit (for example, *go swimming, play video games, take a nap*).
- Make a list on the board. Explain any unfamiliar vocabulary.
- Ask students to write their three favorite ways to relax.
- Call on students to say their favorite ways to relax.

C Listen again. Complete the sentence....

- Read the directions. Play Track 13 again. Students listen and check the answers.
- Call on a student to say the answers.

Expansion: Graphic Organizer Practice for 2C

- Group students according to one free-time activity they like to do (for example, *Group 1: listen to music, Group 2: take a long walk*). Divide your class into four or five groups. Each group has one activity focus.
- Each group creates a bar graph that shows how much time each group member spends doing that activity (for example, *Group 1: listen to music*: Julio: 6 hours per week; Alejandra: 7 hours per week; Bao: 5 hours per week). The *x*-axis has student's names and the *y*-axis tracks how many total hours per week they spend doing the activity.
- Call on a representative from each group to share their group's graph with the class and report on the results (for example, *Julio listens to music for 7 hours a week.*).

Lesson 8 Talk about how often you do something

3 CONVERSATION

A Listen. Then listen and repeat.

- Read the Pronunciation Watch note.
- Say the ending sound for *wash* (/ʃ/) and read the example. Emphasize the extra syllable when *-es* is added. Do the same for *relax* (/ks/).
- Play CD 3, Track 14. Students listen.
- Resume playing Track 14. Students listen and repeat.

Controlled Practice   25 minutes

B Look at the pictures. Listen to your teacher....

- Point to each picture, say each emotion, and ask the class to repeat. Say the word, and then say it in a sentence (for example, *Happy—He's happy.*).
- Ask: *What is the opposite of happy?* (sad) Repeat for *relaxed* (stressed) and *excited* (bored).

C Cover the conversation in Exercise D....

- Read the directions. Say: *Look at the picture. This is Brenda.*
- Ask: *How does Brenda feel?* Write students' answers on the board.
- Play CD 3, Track 15. Students listen.

D Listen again. Read the conversation....

- Play CD 3, Track 15 again. Students listen.
- Ask: *Was your answer in Exercise C correct?* Circle the correct answer on the board.

E Listen and repeat the conversation.

- Play CD 3, Track 16. Students listen and repeat.
- Make sure students are pronouncing *do you* as *d'ya*.

4 PRACTICE

A PAIRS. Practice the conversation. Then make new...

- Pair students and tell them to practice the conversation in Exercise 3D.
- Then, in Exercise 4A, point to the activities on page 140, say them, and ask the class to repeat.

- Copy the conversation onto the board with blanks and read it. When you come to a blank, fill it in with information from page 140 (*take a hot bath*).
- Ask two on-level students to practice the conversation in front of the class.
- Pair students and tell them to take turns playing each role and to use the activities on page 140 to fill in the blanks.

MULTILEVEL INSTRUCTION for 4A
Cross-ability The higher-level partner first plays Alan a couple of times. Then partners switch roles. If needed, higher-level students can point to an activity on page 140.

Communicative Practice   15 minutes

B ROLE PLAY. PAIRS. Make your own...

- On the board, begin listing activities, days, and times for students to use in their conversations. Call on students to suggest more of each.
- With an above-level student, make up a new conversation and practice for the class. Use information from the board, for example:
  - T: *You don't look happy.*
  - S: *I know. I'm not happy. I'm stressed. I need to relax.*
  - T: *Well, I go swimming to relax.*
  - S: *That's a good idea. How often do you swim?*
  - T: *Every night! I have a pool in my backyard. Come over!*
- Pair students. Call on pairs to perform for the class.

Expansion: Pronunciation Practice for 4B

- Pair students and tell to them to ask each other: *What do you do to relax?*
- Students then write a sentence about their partner (for example, *She knits.*).
- Call on students to say their sentence.

Extra Practice

Interactive Practice

3 CONVERSATION

Pronunciation Watch

The *-es* ending on verbs adds an extra syllable after some sounds, for example, *'s', 'z', 'sh',* and *'ch'*.

A CD3 T14 **Listen. Then listen and repeat.**

wash   I **wash** the dishes after dinner.
washes   He **washes** the dishes in the morning.

relax   We **relax** at night.
relaxes She **relaxes** on Sundays.

B **Look at the pictures. Listen to your teacher. Repeat the words.**

happy   relaxed   excited   bored   sad   stressed

C CD3 T15 **Cover the conversation in Exercise D. Listen. How does the woman feel?**   stressed

D CD3 T15 **Listen again. Read the conversation. Was your answer in Exercise C correct?**

Alan: You look stressed.
Brenda: I know. I *am* stressed. I really need to relax.
Alan: Well, I **play soccer** to relax.
Brenda: That's a good idea. How often do you **play soccer**?
Alan: Every **weekend**!

E CD3 T16 **Listen and repeat the conversation.**

4 PRACTICE

A PAIRS. Practice the conversation. Then make new conversations. Use the activities from page 140.

B ROLE PLAY. PAIRS. Make your own conversations. Use different ways of relaxing and different times.

Talk about how often you do something

Grammar

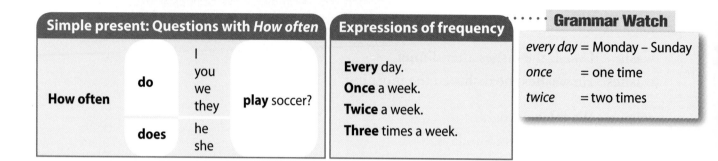

Simple present: Questions with *How often*			
How often	**do**	I you we they	**play** soccer?
	does	he she	

Expressions of frequency

Every day.

Once a week.

Twice a week.

Three times a week.

····· **Grammar Watch**

every day = Monday – Sunday

once = one time

twice = two times

PRACTICE

A **WRITE.** Artur is a student at Greenville Adult School. Look at his schedule.

Write questions. Use *How often* and the activities in the schedule.

Sun.	Mon.	Tues.	Wed.	Thurs.	Fri.	Sat.
ride my bike	have class	ride my bike	have class	ride my bike	have class	ride my bike
play soccer	ride my bike	see friends	ride my bike	see friends	ride my bike	play soccer
		go food shopping		do laundry		

1. _How often does Artur ride his bike?_

2. _How often does he ...?_

3. _How often does he have class?_

4. _How often does he ride his bike?_

5. _How often does he see friends?_

6. _How often does he go food shopping?_

B **PAIRS.** Ask and answer the questions in Exercise A. Give two answers for every question.

A: *How often does Artur play soccer?*
B: *Twice a week. Every Saturday and Sunday.*
A: *Right.*
B: *How often does Artur . . . ?*

Lesson 9 Talk about how often you do something

Getting Started   5 minutes

- Say: *We're going to study questions with* How often *and expressions of frequency. In the conversation on page 141, Brenda and Alan used this grammar.*
- Play CD 3, Track 15. Students listen. Write *How often do you play soccer?* on the board. Underline *How often*.

Presentation   10 minutes

Questions with *How often*; Expressions of frequency

- Copy the grammar charts onto the board or show Transparency 7.5 and cover the exercise.
- Say questions from the left chart and ask the class to repeat. Say: How often . . . ? *means* How many times *a week or a day? (or in any other period of time).*
- Read the Grammar Watch note while students read along silently.
- Remove all visual aids to the chart. Write on the board:

    1. *How often _____ you play basketball?*
    2. *How often _____ Javier play basketball?*
    3. *How often _____ she play basketball?*

  Call on students to say *do* or *does* to complete each question.
- Write the seven days of the week on the board in a list. Place a checkmark by each day and ask: *How often?* (every day) Erase the checkmarks and continue to ask *How often?* to elicit *once a week*, *twice a week*, and *three times a week*.
- Wrap up by checking a certain number of days on the board and then asking one of the questions on the board (for example, T: *How often do you play basketball?* [T checks Monday, Tuesday, and Wednesday.] Ss: *Three times a week.*).
- If you are using the transparency, do the exercise with the class.

Controlled Practice   15 minutes

  PRACTICE

A WRITE. **Artur is a student at Greenville...**

- Say: *Look at the activities in Artur's schedule. Artur has* ride my bike *in his schedule. So, we can write the question:* How often does Artur ride his bike?
- Say: *Remember to start your question with* How often does he . . . ? *Use a question mark.*
- Walk around and check that students are writing questions for all the different activities in the schedule. Check for and correct missing questions marks.

B PAIRS. **Ask and answer the questions in Exercise...**

- Read the example conversation with an on-level student. Play A, and then switch roles and have the student ask a new question (for example, A: *How often does Artur ride his bike?* B: *Every day.*).
- Pair students and tell them to take turns asking and answering the questions in Exercise A.
- Walk around and help as needed. Allow students to give short answers (for example, *Twice a week.*) or complete sentences (for example, *He exercises every day.*).

MULTILEVEL INSTRUCTION for B

Pre-level Form groups of 4. One pair asks a question and the other pair answers.

Above-level Partners also ask each other where Artur does his activities (for example, A: *Where does he ride his bike?* B: *In the park.*). Students can make up answers.

Expansion: Speaking Practice for B

- Pair students and ask them to write a list of at least five activities they each do once a week or more.
- Ask students to ask each other how often they do these activities (for example, *How often do you exercise?*).

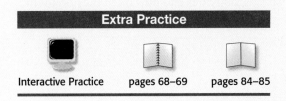

Extra Practice		
Interactive Practice	pages 68–69	pages 84–85

1 GRAMMAR

A DICTATION. Listen. Complete...

- Tell students they will listen to a conversation twice. The first time they will just listen. The second time they will listen and fill in the blanks.
- Play CD 3, Track 17. Students listen.
- Play Track 17 again. Students listen and fill in the blanks. If students cannot keep up, pause the CD to allow more time.
- Now tell students they will listen to the conversation again and check their answers. Play Track 17 again.

B PAIRS. Practice the conversation.

- Pair students and tell them to take turns playing A and B.
- Walk around and model pronunciation as needed.

MULTILEVEL INSTRUCTION for 1B

Cross-ability Ask an above-level student who has finished the activity to monitor pairs of pre-level students and to model pronunciation as needed.

2 WRITING

STEP 1. PAIRS. Talk about a free-time activity.

- Read the directions.
- Tell students to review the grammar charts on pages 130 (prepositions of time) and 142 (simple present questions with *How often* and expressions of frequency).
- Play A and read the example conversation with an on-level student.
- Pair students. Say: *Ask your partner about one free-time activity and how often your partner does the activity.*
- Walk around and check that students are naming specific activities and how often they do them.

STEP 2. Write three sentences about your partner's...

- Read the directions and the example sentences. Say: *Use these sentences as a model. Write true sentences about your partner.*
- Walk around and check that students are adding *-s* or *-es* to the verb as needed.
- Call on several students to write their sentences on the board. Correct as needed.

Expansion: Writing Practice for STEP 2

- Ask students to write four sentences about their own free-time activities. Give students the following prompts: *1. I always . . . 2. I usually . . . 3. I sometimes . . . . 4. I never. . . .*

STEP 3. NETWORK. Find classmates with the same...

- Read the directions. Say: *Think of one activity you like to do. Ask other students if they do the same activity (for example,* Do you play soccer?*).*
- Call on a few students to say their activity to make sure there is some variety in the classroom and to give other students ideas about who to find.
- Students stand, mingle, and find other students with the same free-time activity. Students can find others by asking *Do you (play soccer)?*
- After students have assembled into same-activity groups, say: *Now ask the people in your group,* How often do you _____?

Expansion: Speaking Practice for STEP 3

- Call on a representative from each group to report on how often each group member does the activity (for example, *Su-Chen plays soccer three times a week. Pedro plays soccer every day. Amy. . . .*).

CD-ROM Practice

Go to the CD-ROM for more practice.

If your students need more practice with the vocabulary, grammar, and competencies in Unit 7, encourage them to review the activities on the CD-ROM. This review can also help students prepare for the final role play on the following Expand page.

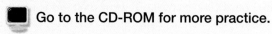

Extra Practice

pages 70–71

1 GRAMMAR

CD3 T17

A 💿 DICTATION. **Listen. Complete the conversation.**

A: Hey, Brenda. You look great.

B: Thanks, Alan. I feel great! I think it's my bike rides in the park.

A: Oh? _____How_____ often _____do_____ you ride your bike?

B: Three _____times_____ a week.

A: Really? _____When_____?

B: I _____always_____ ride my bike before work, _____from_____ 6:00 to 7:00,

and I _____usually_____ ride on Saturdays from 9:00 to 10:00.

A: Good for you!

B PAIRS. **Practice the conversation.**

2 WRITING

STEP 1. PAIRS. Talk about a free-time activity.

A: *What do you do in your free time?*
B: *I play soccer.*
A: *Oh. How often do you play?*
B: *Once a week. I play on Thursdays from five to seven.*

STEP 2. Write three sentences about your partner's free-time activity.

David plays soccer once a week. He plays on Thursdays. He plays from 5:00 to 7:00.

_____

_____

_____

_____

STEP 3. NETWORK. Find classmates with the same free-time activity as you. Form a group. Ask the people in your group, *How often do you_____?*

Go to the CD-ROM for more practice.

3 ACT IT OUT — What do you say?

STEP 1. Review the Lesson 2 conversation between Gloria and Sen (CD 3 Track 4).

STEP 2. Imagine you are making plans to do something together this week. Use your weekly schedule. Decide on an activity, a day, and a time.

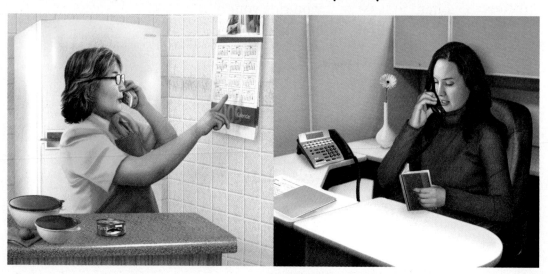

4 READ AND REACT — Problem-solving

STEP 1. Read about Diran's problem.

Diran has a busy life. He is a construction worker, and he works from Monday to Saturday. He also takes English classes at night from Monday to Thursday. On Sundays, he spends time with his family. He also goes food shopping, and he pays the bills. Life at home is not relaxing. Diran is always tired and stressed. He needs to relax, but he doesn't have time.

STEP 2. PAIRS. Talk about it. What is Diran's problem? What can Diran do? Here are some ideas.

- He can listen to music on the way to work.
- He can read on his lunch break.
- He can go out with friends on Friday nights.
- He can _____.

5 CONNECT

For your Study Skills Activity, go to page 249.
For your Team Project, go to page 269.

Which goals can you check off? Go back to page 125.

3 ACT IT OUT

STEP 1. Review the Lesson 2 conversation...

- Play CD 3, Track 4. Students listen.
- As needed, play Track 4 again to aid comprehension.

STEP 2. Imagine you are making plans to...

- Pair students and tell them to make a weekly schedule with activities and times for each day of the week or use one they already made in the unit.
- Walk around and check that students are using their weekly schedule to discuss plans to do something together. Call on pairs to perform for the class.
- While pairs are performing, use the scoring rubric on page Txiv to evaluate each student's vocabulary, grammar, fluency, and how well they complete the task.
- *Optional:* After each pair finishes, discuss the strengths and weaknesses of each performance either in front of the class or privately.

4 READ AND REACT

STEP 1. Read about Diran's problem.

- Say: *We are going to read about a student's problem, and then we need to think about a solution.*
- Read the story while students follow along silently. Pause after each sentence to allow time for students to comprehend. Periodically stop and ask simple *Wh-* questions to check comprehension; for example, *What does Diran do?* (He's a construction worker.) *When does he take English classes?* (from Monday to Thursday).

STEP 2. PAIRS. Talk about it. What is Diran's...?

- Pair students. Ask: *What is Diran's problem?* (He needs to relax, but he doesn't have time.) *What can Diran do?*
- Read the ideas in the list. Give pairs a couple of minutes to discuss possible solutions for Diran.
- Tell students to cover the list of ideas before reading them. Ask: *What can Diran do?* Call on students to say answers. Write some on the board. Tell students to uncover the list of ideas. Point out any ideas on the board that are the same or similar.

- Read the list of ideas. Ask: *Which ideas are good?* Call on students to say their opinion about the ideas in the box (for example, S: *I think Diran can listen to music on the way to work. I listen to music on the way to work.*).
- Pair students. Tell them to think of one new idea not in the box (for example, *He can take a long walk in the morning.*) and to write it in the blank. Encourage students to think of more than one idea and to write them in their notebooks.
- Call on pairs to say their additional solutions. Write any particularly good ones on the board and ask students if they think it is a good idea, too (*Do you think this is a good idea? Why or why not?*).

Teaching Tip

Encourage students who have difficulty discussing solutions to Diran's problem to just say whatever they can and not worry about making a mistake. As needed, help them form their answers into complete sentences that they can repeat back to you (for example, S: *Music . . . no good . . . relax . . .* T: *Music is not relaxing. Now repeat after me. Music . . .* S: *Music . . .*). Finally, write the complete sentences on the board. Students can copy them and refer to them during class.

MULTILEVEL INSTRUCTION for STEP 2

Pre-level Sit with pairs and read each idea. After each idea, ask both students: *Do you like this idea? Why or why not?*

Above-level Pairs come up with three additional ideas. Then pairs rank their new ideas and the ideas on page 144 on a scale of 1–7 (with 7 being worst). Call on students to say why they ranked the way they did.

5 CONNECT

Turn to page 249 for the Study Skills Activity and page 269 for the Team Project. See pages Txi–Txii for general notes about teaching these activities.

Progress Check

Which goals can you check off? Go back to page 125.

Ask students to turn to page 125 and check off the goals they have reached. Call on students to say which goals they will practice outside of class.

From Soup to Nuts

Classroom Materials/Extra Practice

CD 3
Tracks 18–33

Transparencies 8.1–8.6
Vocabulary Cards Unit 8

MCA
Unit 8

Workbook
Unit 8

Interactive Practice
Unit 8

Unit Overview

Goals

- See the list of goals on the facing page.

Grammar

- Count nouns and non-count nouns
- Choice questions with *or*
- Simple present: Questions with *How many* and *How much*

Pronunciation

- *I like* and *I'd like*

Reading

- Read an article about expiration dates on foods

Writing

- Write a shopping list
- Write a sentence about the nutritional value of foods
- Write sentences about food your classmates want

Life Skills Writing

- Write a note about things you need at the store

Preview

- Set the context of the unit by asking: *Where do you buy food?* (*Possible answers:* local grocery stores, farmer's market, local restaurants)

- Hold up page 145 or show Transparency 8.1. Read the unit title and explain: From Soup to Nuts *means* from beginning to end. *Soup is sometimes the first part of a meal, and nuts are sometimes the end of a meal. So, in this unit you will learn all kinds of foods.*

- Say: *Look at the picture.* Ask the Preview questions: *Where are the people?* (at the check-out counter / in a supermarket or grocery store) *What are they doing?* (shopping / buying groceries / checking out)

Unit Goals

- Point to the Unit Goals. Explain that this list shows what the class will be studying in this unit.

- Tell students to read the goals silently.

- Say each goal and ask students to repeat. To explain *food label*, show a box or can of food and point to the label. To explain *menu*, show a restaurant menu or pass menus around the room. (Many restaurants have menus available for printing on their website.)

- Explain additional unfamiliar vocabulary as needed:

    Meal: *food that you eat at a certain time; breakfast, lunch, and dinner are meals*

    Nutritional value: *how good a certain food is for you*

- Tell students to circle one goal that is very important to them. Call on several students to say the goal they circled.

From Soup to Nuts

Preview

Look at the picture.
Where are the people?
What are they doing?

UNIT GOALS

- [ ] Talk about common foods
- [ ] Write a note about things you need at the store
- [ ] Read a menu
- [ ] Order a meal in a restaurant
- [ ] Use food measurements
- [ ] Compare food prices
- [ ] Read food labels
- [ ] Talk about the nutritional value of foods
- [ ] Plan a healthy meal

1 WHAT DO YOU KNOW?

A **CLASS.** Look at the pictures. Which foods do you know?

> Number 19 is eggs.

CD3 T18

B Listen and point to the pictures. Then listen and repeat.

2 PRACTICE

A **PAIRS.** Student A, name a food group. Student B, name two foods in the group.

A: *Vegetables.*
B: *Cabbage and lettuce.*

B **WORD PLAY. GROUPS OF 4.** Student A, look at the list of foods on page 147. Choose a food, but don't say it. Students B, C, and D, ask *yes/no* questions and guess the food.

B: *Do you eat it for breakfast?*
A: *Sometimes.*
C: *Is it in the "fruit" group?*
A: *Yes.*
D: *Is it red?*
A: *No.*
B: *Bananas?*
A: *Yes!*

C **PAIRS.** Look at the food pyramid. The colors show the amount of food you need from each food group. Match the colors in the pyramid to the food groups.

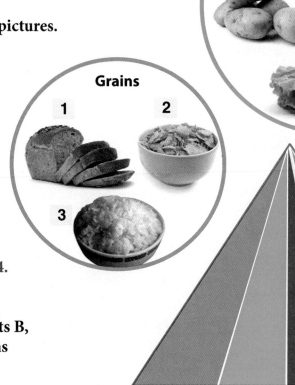

Source: www.MyPyramid.gov

Getting Started 5 minutes

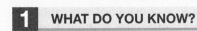

1 WHAT DO YOU KNOW?

Ⓐ CLASS. Look at the pictures. Which foods...

- Show Transparency 8.2 or tell students to cover the list of words on page 147.
- Point to picture 19 and read the example. Ask: *Which foods do you know?*
- Students call out answers (for example, *Number 10 is bananas.*).
- If students call out an incorrect food, change the answer into a question for the class (for example, *Number 3 is cereal?*). If nobody can identify the correct item, tell students they will now listen to a CD and practice the names of the food.

Presentation 5 minutes

Ⓑ 💿 Listen and point to the pictures....

- Play CD 3, Track 18. Pause after number 20 (*beans*).
- Walk around and check that students are pointing.
- To check comprehension, say each food in random order and ask students to point to the appropriate picture.
- Resume playing Track 18. Students listen and repeat. Say: *Each food is in a food group. Remember the foods in each group.*

Controlled Practice 20 minutes

2 PRACTICE

Ⓐ PAIRS. Student A, name a food group. Student B,...

- Read the directions. Read each line in the example and ask the class to repeat.
- Play A and model the example with an above-level student. Pair students and tell them to take turns playing A and B. Say: *Student A, don't point to the pictures.*
- Walk around and, as needed, remind students not to point to the pictures. To check comprehension, say a food group and call on individual students to say two foods in the group (for example, T: *Fruit.* S: *Apples and oranges.* T: *Yes!*).

▮▮ MULTILEVEL INSTRUCTION for 2A

Cross-ability Tell the higher-level student to play A. When saying the name of the food group, A also points to the picture to aid B's comprehension.

▮▮ Expansion: Vocabulary Practice for 2A

- Say words at random (foods and groups) from the list on page 147 and the pictures. Tell students to call out whether it is a food or a group (for example, T: *Fruits.* Ss: *Group.* T: *Good! Butter.* Ss: *Food.* T: *Excellent!*).

Ⓑ WORD PLAY. GROUPS OF 4. Student A, look at...

- On the board, write the following headings: *Meal, Group,* and *Color.* Ask: *What meals do you have?* (breakfast, lunch, . . .) *What colors are the foods?* (red, orange, . . .) *What are the food groups?* (vegetables, grains, . . .) Write the answers.
- Read the directions. Remind students that a *yes/no* question begins with *Do, Is,* or *Are.*
- Read each line in the example conversation and ask the class to repeat. Model correct intonation.
- Form groups of 4 and tell students to take turns playing A. Tell students to make questions using the colors, meals, and food groups on the board.

▮▮ MULTILEVEL INSTRUCTION for 2B

Pre-level Assign roles. B always asks a meal question (*Do you eat it for breakfast?*). C always asks the food group question (*Is it a kind of fruit?*). D always asks a color question (*Is it red?*). Students practice a few times in one role before switching.

Above-level Ask A to also think about foods not listed on page 147.

Ⓒ PAIRS. Look at the food pyramid. The colors show...

- Say: *This is a food pyramid. It shows us the different food groups.*
- Explain: Amount *means* how much.
- As an example, hold up your book (or use Transparency 8.2) and draw a line to match the vegetable group to the green bar in the pyramid.
- Walk around and check that students are matching each group to a bar in the pyramid.

Learning Strategy: Make word groups

- Read the directions. Ask: *Which foods from the list do you eat for breakfast?* Students call out answers (*cereal, yogurt, . . .*). Write a few answers on the board.
- Tell students to write a three-column chart in their notebooks with *Breakfast, Lunch,* and *Dinner* as the headings.
- Walk around as students work. If misspellings occur, tell them to check the vocabulary list on page 147.
- Say: *You can remember new words by putting them into groups.* Remind students to use this strategy to remember other new vocabulary.

Communicative Practice   25 minutes

Show what you know!

STEP 1. Which foods do you eat? Fill in the "You"...

- Copy the chart onto the board. Read the directions.
- Ask a couple of students: *What vegetables do you eat?* Write responses in the chart on the board (for example, *potatoes, carrots, onions*). Then ask them how often they eat that food. Write responses in the chart (for example, *onions—once a week*).
- Tell students they can write *once a week, twice a week, three times a week, four times a week, five times a week,* or *every day* in the *How often?* column. Write these expressions on the board for easy reference.

STEP 2. PAIRS. Talk about the foods you eat....

- Read the directions.
- Play Marcus and model the example with an above-level student.
- On the board, write: *What _____ do you eat?* Under the blank write *vegetables, fruit,* and *meat and beans.* Ask several students: *What kind of vegetables/fruit/meat and beans do you eat?* and write responses on the board. Follow this question with *How often?* and write students' responses in the chart on the board.
- Pair students.
- Walk around and check that students are talking about foods from the correct groups and filling in the chart.

MULTILEVEL INSTRUCTION for STEP 2

Pre-level To help build confidence, practice with students (or ask an above-level student to assist) until they are comfortable making new conversations on their own.

Above-level Tell students to also ask their partner what kind of oils, dairy, and meat and beans they eat. Students can write this additional information on the side of the chart or in their notebooks.

STEP 3. Report to the class.

- Read the directions and the example.
- Call on students to report. Say: *Tell us about your partner.* As needed, prompt them by asking: *What vegetable/fruit/meat and beans does your partner eat? How often?*
- Correct pronunciation as needed.

Expansion: Graphic Organizer Practice for STEP 3

- Identify a food that most of the class eats (for example, *bread*).
- On the board, create a bar chart whose horizontal axis (*x*-axis) contains space to write ten students names and whose vertical axis (*y*-axis) contains the following: *never, once a week, twice a week, three times a week, four times a week, five times a week, six times a week, every day.*
- Call on a few students to say how often they eat bread. Write their names along the x-axis and also draw a bar to represent how often they eat it.
- Tell students to copy the chart into their notebooks. Students stand, mingle, and ask ten other students how often they eat bread. While mingling, students jot down other students' names and how often they eat bread.
- Students then return to their seats and finish their chart.
- Call on students to report on what they found (for example, S: *Maria eats bread five times a week. Pascual eats bread three times . . .*).

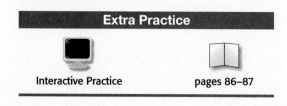

Extra Practice

Interactive Practice   pages 86–87

Common Foods

1. bread	**6.** cabbage	**11.** vegetable oil	**16.** chicken
2. cereal	**7.** lettuce	**12.** butter	**17.** fish
3. rice	**8.** apples	**13.** milk	**18.** beef
4. potatoes	**9.** oranges	**14.** cheese	**19.** eggs
5. onions	**10.** bananas	**15.** yogurt	**20.** beans

Fruit

8

9

10

Oils

11

12

Learning Strategy

Make word groups

Look at the list of foods. Make a chart of foods you eat. At the top of the chart, write *breakfast*, *lunch*, and *dinner*. In each column, write one or two foods.

Show what you know!

STEP 1. Which foods do you eat? Fill in the "You" columns in the chart. Write one food from each food group. Write how often you eat each food.

Food Groups	You		Your Partner	
	What?	**How often?**	**What?**	**How often?**
Vegetables	potatoes	twice a week		
Fruit				
Meat and beans				

STEP 2. PAIRS. Talk about the foods you eat. Talk about how often. Complete the chart with your partner's information.

Marcus: *What vegetables do you eat?*
Agnes: *Potatoes.*
Marcus: *How often do you eat potatoes?*
Agnes: *Twice a week. What kind of vegetables…?*

STEP 3. Report to the class. Agnes eats potatoes twice a week.

Listening and Speaking

1 BEFORE YOU LISTEN

CD3 T19

💿 **READ. Look at the pictures. Listen and read about Jason's lunch. Answer the questions.**

It's 12:00. It's time for lunch. Jason is hungry. He is at the mall. Jason likes hamburgers, so he eats a hamburger. But he is still hungry, so he eats a piece of pizza. But he is *still* hungry, so he eats a taco. It's now 12:30. It's time for dessert!

1. Where is Jason? _____ at the mall _____

2. How does he feel? _____ hungry _____

3. What does he eat for lunch? _a hamburger, pizza, and a taco_

2 LISTEN

A **Look at the picture. Marius and Gabriela are friends.**

Guess: What are they talking about?

CD3 T20

B 💿 **Listen to the conversation. Was your guess in Exercise A correct?**

Listen again. Answer the questions.

1. Who is hungry?
   a. Marius   b. Gabriela   (c.) Marius and Gabriela

2. What does Marius want for lunch?
   (a.) pizza   b. tacos   c. a hamburger

3. What does Gabriela want for lunch?
   a. pizza   (b.) tacos   c. a hamburger

CD3 T21

C 💿 **Listen to the whole conversation. Complete the sentence.**

Gabriela says, "Let's have pizza and tacos for _____."
(a.) breakfast   b. lunch   c. dinner

Getting Started 10 minutes

Culture Connection

• Say: *Fast-food restaurants are very popular in the United States.*

• On the board, write several popular fast-food chains in your area (for example, *McDonald's, Wendy's, Taco Bell*). Ask students to call out more names as you write. Ask: *What kinds of food can you get there?* (hamburgers, french fries, soda, tacos, salad, . . .)

• Ask: *Are fast-food restaurants popular in your country? What fast-food restaurants are there in your country? Is the food different from U.S. restaurants?* List some foods that students name on the board.

• Ask above-level students: *Why are U.S. fast-food restaurants popular?* (Because people don't make time to cook at home.)

• Ask: *Is the food at fast-food restaurants healthy?* (Possible answers: Some of the food is healthy, for example, salad and yogurt. A lot of the food is not healthy.)

1 BEFORE YOU LISTEN

 READ. **Look at the pictures. Listen and read....**

• Read the directions. Play CD 3, Track 19. Students listen and read along silently.

• To check comprehension, ask the following and point to the correct picture: *What does Jason eat at 12:00?* (a hamburger) *What does he eat at 12:10* (a piece of pizza) *What does he eat at 12:20?* (a taco) *What does he want at 12:30?* (ice cream)

• Call on students to say answers to the questions.

Expansion: Speaking Practice for 1

• Pair students. Ask: *Do you eat pizza? Hamburgers? Tacos? Desserts?* Tell students to use adverbs of frequency (*never, sometimes, usually, always*) in their answers (for example, *I sometimes eat hamburgers.*).

• To wrap up, ask the class the questions and call on students to answer.

Presentation 20 minutes

2 LISTEN

A **Look at the picture.... Guess:...**

• Read the directions. Point to the people in the picture. Ask: *What are they talking about?*

• Call on students to answer. Write answers on the board.

B **Listen to the conversation. Was...**

• Read the directions. Play CD 3, Track 20.

• Explain expressions as needed:

> *What do you want for lunch?* is a common way to ask, *What food do you want to eat for lunch?*
>
> *Yeah, me too* is a common way to say you feel the same as the person talking.
>
> *I love* as in *I love pizza* is a common way to say you enjoy something very much.

• Ask: *Was your guess in Exercise A correct?* Circle the correct answers on the board. (Answer: what to eat for lunch)

Teaching Tip

Optional: Remember that if students need additional support, tell them to read the Audio Script on page 286 as they listen to the conversation.

Listen again. Answer the questions.

• Read the directions. Play Track 20 again. Students listen and answer the questions.

• Students compare answers with a partner.

• Call on students to say answers.

C **Listen to the whole conversation....**

• Read the directions. Play CD 3, Track 21.

• Explain: *Marius says only in It's only 10:30 to stress that he thinks it's not time for lunch.*

• Call on students to say the answers.

Controlled Practice   20 minutes

3   CONVERSATION

Listen and read the conversation. Then...

- Note: This conversation is the same one students heard in Exercise 2B on page 148.
- Play CD 3, Track 22. Students listen and read along silently.
- Resume playing Track 22. Students listen and repeat.

4   PRACTICE

A PAIRS. Practice the conversation. Then make new...

- Pair students and tell them to practice the conversation in Exercise 3.
- Then, in Exercise 4A, ask students to look at the pictures and the words in the boxes. Say each one and ask the class to repeat.
- Copy the conversation onto the board with blanks and read it. When you come to a blank, fill it in with information from the boxes (*breakfast, scrambled eggs,* and *pancakes*). As you fill in the blanks, remind Student A to say another food for the same meal.
- Ask two on-level students to practice the conversation in front of the class.
- Tell pairs to take turns playing each role and to use different information from the boxes to fill in the blanks.
- Tell students to stand, mingle, and practice the conversation with several new partners.

MULTILEVEL INSTRUCTION for 4A

Pre-level Play Track 22 again and allow students to listen and repeat a few more times.

Above-level Ask students to include how often they eat some food (for example, *I love scrambled eggs! I always eat scrambled eggs for breakfast.*).

Communicative Practice   10 minutes

B MAKE IT PERSONAL. PAIRS. Make your own...

- With an above-level student, make up a new conversation and practice for the class. Base the conversation on Exercise 3.
- Tell students to copy the vocabulary words for food from pages 146, 147, and 149 into their notebooks and direct them to use these words in their conversations.
- Pair students and tell them to take turns playing A and B.
- Walk around and check that students are using correct falling intonation for statements and rising intonation for questions.
- Call on pairs to perform for the class.
- To wrap up, on the board write some of the errors you heard during the role plays. Ask students to correct the mistakes. Go over the corrections by saying the words or sentences correctly and asking the class to repeat.

Language Note

To help pairs sound more realistic, practice with them. Model personal expression and emotion in your speaking parts (such as *enthusiasm* in the conversation in Exercises 3 and 4) and encourage students to do the same.

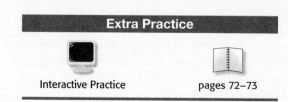

Extra Practice

Interactive Practice   pages 72–73

3 CONVERSATION

CD3 T22

Listen and read the conversation. Then listen and repeat.

Marius: Wow, I'm hungry!

Gabriela: Yeah, me too. What do you want for lunch?

Marius: Pizza. I love pizza! What about you?

Gabriela: I don't really like pizza, but I love tacos!

4 PRACTICE

A **PAIRS.** Practice the conversation. Then make new conversations. Use the information in the boxes.

A: What do you want for _____?

B: _____. I love _____! What about you?

A: I don't really like _____, but I love _____!

breakfast — scrambled eggs — pancakes

dinner — steak — pasta

dessert — cake — cookies

B **MAKE IT PERSONAL. PAIRS.** Make your own conversations. Use different meals and foods.

UNIT 8   **149**

Talk about common foods

Grammar

Count nouns		Non-count nouns	
Gabriela wants	**a taco.**	I want	**pasta.**
She loves	**tacos.**	I love	**pasta.**

Grammar Watch

- You can count some nouns. They are called **count nouns:** *one taco, two tacos*
- You can't count some nouns. They are called **non-count nouns:** ~~*one pasta, two pastas*~~
- For a list of more non-count nouns, see page 274.
- For spelling rules for plural count nouns, see page 274.

1 PRACTICE

Complete the shopping list.

TO BUY

4 oranges

6 eggs

black beans

apple juice

2 large onions

banana yogurt

3 bananas

5 green apples

2 LIFE SKILLS WRITING

Write a note about things you need at the store. See page 260.

Getting Started   5 minutes

- Say: *We're going to study count and non-count nouns. In the conversation on page 149, Gabriela used this grammar.*
- Play CD 3, Track 22. Students listen. Write *I don't really like pizza, but I love tacos!* on the board. Underline *pizza* and *tacos*.

Presentation   10 minutes

Count nouns and Non-count nouns

- Copy the grammar charts onto the board or show Transparency 8.3 and cover the exercise.
- Read the Grammar Watch note while students read along silently. Write it on the board.
- Say sentences from the count nouns chart and ask the class to repeat.
- Say sentences from the non-count nouns chart and ask the class to repeat.
- On the board, make a two-column chart with *Count nouns* and *Non-count nouns* as the headings. Write several foods from pages 146, 147, and 149 on the board (not in the chart). Include count and non-count foods (for example, *milk*, *potatoes*, *apples*, *rice*). Point to each word and ask the class if it is a count or non-count noun. After the class correctly identifies each food as count or non-count, write it under the appropriate heading.
- If you are using the transparency, do the exercise with the class.

▄▄▄ Expansion: Writing and Speaking Practice

- Using foods on the board, students write three simple sentences with *want* and three simple sentences with *like*. For *want*, students use the singular form of count nouns (for example, *I want an apple.*). For *like*, students use the plural form of count nouns (for example, *I like apples.*). Students can use non-count nouns for either *like* or *want*.
- Students then turn their statements into questions and ask a partner (for example, A: *Do you like apples?* B: *Yes, I do. Do you like bread?* A: *No, I don't.*).

Controlled Practice   30 minutes

1 PRACTICE

Culture Connection

- Say: *Look at the picture. What place is this?* (a market, a grocery store) *In the United States, most people buy their food at a grocery store. Large grocery stores are called supermarkets.* Write *supermarket* on the board.
- Ask: *In your country, are supermarkets popular? Here in the United States, do you shop at a supermarket?* Call on students to say answers.

Complete the shopping list.

- Say: *Look at the shopping list.* Ask: *Do you use a shopping list when you go to the store?*
- Say: *Look at the food in the picture.* Ask: *How many oranges do you see?* (four) Say: *Look at the shopping list. It says 4 oranges.*
- Read the directions. Say: *Look at the word or number in the list. Then try to find the food in the picture.*
- Walk around and check that students are completing the prompts on the shopping list.
- Students compare answers with a partner.
- Say each prompt on the list and call on students to complete each one (for example, T: *We need to buy 6 . . .* S: *Eggs.* T: *Good!*).

Teaching Tip

Bring in some actual food items to illustrate the difference between count and non-count nouns.

2 LIFE SKILLS WRITING

Turn to page 260 and ask students to complete the note. See pages Txi–Txii for general notes about the Life Skills Writing activities.

3 PRACTICE

Look at the pictures. Complete the conversations....

- Ask students to call out what food is in each picture. Students can write the name of the food next to the picture. Say: *Remember, some foods are count nouns and some are non-count.*
- Walk around and check for accurate spelling. Tell students to review the words on pages 146–147 if errors occur.
- *Optional:* Tell students to practice the completed conversations with a partner.
- To check answers, call on pairs to role-play the individual conversations. After each one, ask students if the food in question is a count noun or a non-count noun.

Communicative Practice   15 minutes

Show what you know!

STEP 1. WRITE. You have five minutes. Write foods...

- Read the directions and the Writing Watch note.
- Play A and read the example conversation with a student. Tell students to write *cheese* next to bananas. Ask: *Is cheese a count or non-count noun?* (non-count)
- Say: *Use the plural form for count nouns. Don't change non-count nouns.*
- Pair students and tell them to use foods from pages 146–147 and 150–151.
- Walk around and check for accuracy. If a student writes the wrong food, change the student's answer to a question and ask, for example: *Are apples white?*

▮ MULTILEVEL INSTRUCTION for STEP 1

Cross-ability Assign higher-level students to sit with lower-level students and suggest one food for each color to get them started (*white: eggs; red: apples; green: broccoli*).

STEP 2. GROUPS of 3. Compare answers.

- Form groups of 3 and tell them to take turns asking and answering the questions.
- Call on students to write answers on the board.
- Brainstorm with the class to generate more foods for each color.

▮ Expansion: Graphic Organizer and Speaking Practice

- Ask students to make a two-column chart in their notebooks with *Foods I love* and *Foods I like* as the headings.
- Say: *Foods you love are your favorite foods. Foods you like are foods that you enjoy, but they are not your favorite.*
- Ask students to write food under each heading. Pair students and tell them to compare answers:

  A: *What foods do you love?*
  B: *I love bread. I love cheese . . . What foods do you love?*
  A: *I love pizza. I love beans. What foods do you like?*
  B: *I like rice.*

Community Building

Divide the class into groups of four or five. Tell each group to make a list of food they want to take for an imaginary three-day camping trip with the students in their group (for example, *We want lots of fruit. We need 20 apples, 15 bananas.*). Each group can appoint a secretary to write the list. Each group must choose foods from all six food groups.

Progress Check

Can you . . . talk about common foods?

Say: *We have practiced talking about common foods. Now, look at the question at the bottom of the page. Can you talk about common foods?* Tell students to write a checkmark in the box.

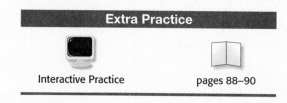

Extra Practice
Interactive Practice   pages 88–90

Look at the pictures. Complete the conversations. Write the correct form of the word.

1.

   A: ____Apples____ are good for you.

   B: I know. I eat an ____apple____ every day.

2.

   A: I love ____eggs____ .

   B: Me too! I often have two ____eggs____ for breakfast.

3.

   A: Do you have any ____butter____ ?

   B: Of course! I always have ____butter____ in the house. It's in the refrigerator.

4.

   A: I eat ____rice____ every day.

   B: Me too. I love ____rice____ !

Show what you know!   Talk about common foods

STEP 1. WRITE. You have five minutes. Write foods for each color.

Answers may vary but could include:

yellow: ____bananas, cheese, eggs (yolk), rice, butter____

white: ____rice, milk, eggs (shell), cheese, bread, onions (inside)____

red: ____apples____

green: ____apples, cabbage, lettuce____

> **Writing Watch**
>
> Use commas (,) between things in a list. Example: *bananas, cheese, . . .*

STEP 2. GROUPS OF 3. Compare answers.

A: *What foods are yellow?*
B: *Bananas.*
C: *Cheese.*

Can you...talk about common foods? ☐

Reading

1 BEFORE YOU READ

A Look at the pictures. Where do you keep each food? Write each food in the box for the place you keep it. Answers may vary but could include:

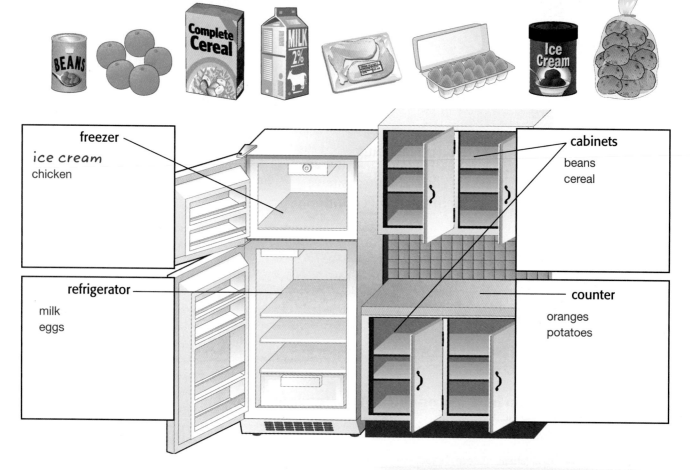

freezer
ice cream
chicken

refrigerator
milk
eggs

cabinets
beans
cereal

counter
oranges
potatoes

B Sometimes there's a date on food. Why? Read the information and the label.

C CLASS. Look at the label again. Can a store sell this milk on October 15? Can you drink this milk on October 15?

Stores cannot sell food after a sell-by date. If you have food at home with an old sell-by date, it's usually OK to eat it a short time after the date.

Getting Started   15 minutes

1 BEFORE YOU READ

Ⓐ Look at the pictures. Where do you keep...

- Read the directions. Say each storage area (for example, *freezer*) and ask the class to repeat.
- Ask: *Where do oranges go?* (on the counter or in the refrigerator) *Where does cereal go?* (in the cabinets or on the counter)
- Walk around and check that students are writing foods in the boxes. Note that students may keep things in different places.
- Students compare answers with a partner. Encourage students to talk about why they keep each food item in a particular place. (For example, *I keep potatoes in my cabinets because I don't have counter space.*)
- Call on students to say answers.

Community Building

Divide the class into four groups for *freezer, cabinets, refrigerator,* and *counter.* Ask each group to make a list of foods that is kept in that place (for example, the freezer group makes a list of freezer foods). The interaction among group members will help build class community.

Expansion: Vocabulary Practice for 1A

- Ask: *What's in your freezer/refrigerator/cabinets?* Ask students to make a list in their notebooks of all the food they can remember in each storage place at home.
- Pair students. Students ask each other the questions and share answers.

Ⓑ Sometimes there's a date on food. Why? Read...

- Say: *Sometimes there's a date on food.* Ask: *Why?* (Because stores cannot sell food after that date.) Call on a couple of students to guess.
- Tell students to look at the picture. Slowly read the explanation under the picture. Ask: *What is the sell-by date for the milk in the picture?* (October 14)

Expansion: Critical Thinking Practice for 1B

- Ask: *What other foods have a sell-by date?* (meat, chicken, milk products, . . .) Write responses on the board.

Ⓒ CLASS. Look at the label again. Can a store sell...

- Read the directions. Ask: *Can a store sell this milk on October 15?* (No.) *Why not?* (Because the sell-by date is October 14.) *Can you drink this milk on October 15?* (Yes.)

Expansion: Vocabulary and Critical Thinking Practice for 1C

- Say: *You will see a* use-by *date on some foods. The* use-by *date is when the food is too old to eat. The* use-by *date is also called the* expiration *date.*
- Write the above terms on the board for students to copy into their notebooks.
- Ask: *Which date is later, the sell-by or the use-by date?* (the use-by date)

Presentation 15 minutes

2 **READ**

Listen. Read the article.

- Tell students to look at the picture. Ask: *What is this person (shopper) doing?* (checking the sell-by date on a bottle of milk)
- Ask: *What is the title of the article? What does* Eat Fresh *mean?* (It means to eat new food.)
- Play CD 3, Track 23. Students listen and read along silently.
- If students have difficulty following along, play Track 23 again and pause at various points.
- Ask if there are words they do not understand and explain them (for example, Fresh food *is new food.*).
- *Optional:* Play Track 23 again.

Controlled Practice 15 minutes

3 **CHECK YOUR UNDERSTANDING**

A Read the article again. What is the main idea?

- Read the directions. Allow time for students to read the article again.
- Remind students: *The main idea is the most important point in the article.*
- By a show of hands, poll the class and ask who thinks the answer is *a* and who thinks it is *b*.
- Explain that *b* is true, but it is just a detail, not the main point. Say that *a* is the answer.

B Read the sentences. Circle *True* **or** *False.*

- Read the directions.
- Walk around and help as needed. Tell students to check their answers by looking back at the article.
- Call on students to say answers. For false items, call on students to correct the statement to make it true. (3. Keep eggs in the refrigerator. 4. Cook or freeze chicken a day or two after you buy it.)

Communicative Practice 15 minutes

Show what you know!

PAIRS. Talk about it. How can you use...

- Read the directions and the example.
- On the board, write *I want to look at the dates on the* _____ *in my* _____ *.* Tell students they can use this sentence when talking to their partner.
- Pair students. Walk around and check that students are talking about the information in the article and the food in their homes.
- Call on individual students to say the foods they will check when they go home.

MULTILEVEL INSTRUCTION

Pre-level If students have difficulty saying original sentences, provide them with the following prompt: *I want to look at the dates on the (food) in my refrigerator/freezer/cabinet.*

Above-level Ask students to also discuss how often (*always, usually, sometimes,* or *never*) they buy food that is very close to the sell-by or use-by date (for example, *I never buy milk that's old. Sometimes I buy bread that's old.*).

Expansion: Writing and Speaking Practice

- Form groups of 5. Each group makes a poster that contains tips related to *sell-by* dates.
- One student can copy tips from the article onto notebook paper and list them in order from most important to least important. Another student can write the tips on poster paper. A third student can present the poster and read the tips to the class.
- All students can contribute to the poster by drawing pictures of food or affixing clippings of food pictures from magazines or advertisements.
- If possible, groups can add tips of their own (for example, *Put bread in the freezer to keep it fresh.*).
- Students create a poster that can be displayed in the classroom or taken home.

Extra Practice

Interactive Practice   pages 74–75   page 91

CD3 T23

Listen. Read the article.

Eat Fresh!

Do you buy fresh food? Are you sure? Be careful! Stores sometimes sell old food. Check the dates.

How long can you keep your food at home? Here are some tips.

Milk is good for two to ten days after its sell-by date.

This careful shopper always checks the date on food.

Eggs are good for three to five weeks after their sell-by dates. Just keep them in the refrigerator!

Chicken is different. The sell-by date on chicken is information for the store. The refrigerators in stores are very cold. But your home refrigerator isn't as cold. Cook or freeze chicken a day or two after you buy it. You can keep chicken in the freezer for twelve months.

Some food, like **canned food**, doesn't have a sell-by date. But it isn't good forever. Try to use your canned food in twelve months.

3 CHECK YOUR UNDERSTANDING

A Read the article again. What is the main idea?

a. Make sure your food is fresh. Check the dates.

b. Put your food in the right place. Keep milk in the refrigerator.

B Read the sentences. Circle *True* or *False*.

1. Stores sometimes sell old food. — (True) False

2. It's OK to use milk two days after its sell-by date. — (True) False

3. It's OK to keep eggs on the counter for three weeks. — True (False)

4. It's OK to keep chicken in the refrigerator for a week. — True (False)

5. Canned food is good for one year. — (True) False

Show what you know!

PAIRS. Talk about it. How can you use the information from the article at home?
What other foods have expiration dates?

> I want to check the dates on the chicken in my refrigerator.

Listening and Speaking

1   BEFORE YOU LISTEN

CLASS. Look at the pictures. Which foods do you eat or drink?

| tomato soup | coffee | turkey sandwich | fries ✓ | soda ✓ | baked potato |

| hamburger ✓ | iced tea | green salad | fruit cup | apple pie | ice cream |

2   LISTEN

A   Look at the picture. Greg and his wife are ordering lunch. Greg says, "I'd like a hamburger." What does this mean?

   a. He likes hamburgers.

   (b.) He wants a hamburger.

CD3 T24

B   Listen to the conversation. Was your answer in Exercise A correct?

Listen again. What does Greg order? Check (✓) the pictures in Before You Listen.

CD3 T25

C   Listen to the whole conversation. Answer the questions.

   1. What does Greg's wife think? ___Greg's lunch isn't very healthy.___

   2. What does Greg order for dessert? ___apple pie___

Getting Started   10 minutes

Culture Connection

• Say: *In the United States, it is very common to see a menu on the wall at fast-food restaurants.*
• Ask: *In your country, do all fast-food restaurants have menus on the wall? Are the prices on the menu?*

 1 BEFORE YOU LISTEN

CLASS. Look at the pictures. Which foods do you eat...

• Read the directions. Ask: *Who eats tomato soup?* Ask students to raise their hands if they eat tomato soup. Note that students should not mark the checkboxes, because they will use the checkboxes in Exercise 2B.
• Go through each featured food in the same way (for example, T: *Who drinks coffee?* [Students raise their hands.]).
• As needed, say each food and ask the class to repeat.

Language Note

Encourage students to keep a personal dictionary in their notebooks. As they learn new vocabulary (such as food items here), they can copy the words into their notebooks and write a translation in their native language next to it.

Presentation   30 minutes

 2 LISTEN

Ⓐ Look at the picture. Greg and his wife are ordering...

• Tell students to look at the picture.
• Ask: *What do you see in the picture? What is happening?* (Greg and his wife are ordering lunch.)
• Write the answer choices on the board and read them. Say: *Greg says, "I'd like a hamburger." What does this mean?* Call on students to answer.

Ⓑ 🔘 Listen to the conversation. Was your...

• Read the directions. Play CD 3, Track 24.
• Explain: *I'd like is a polite way of saying I want.*
• Ask: *Was your answer correct?*
• On the board, write: *I'd like a _____.* and *I'd like _____.* Remind students: *Say I'd like + a or an to ask for food that is a singular count noun, for example,* I'd like a green salad. *If you are asking for a food that is a plural count noun or a non-count noun, say* I'd like *without a or an, for example,* I'd like fries. I'd like ice cream.
• Circle the correct answer on the board. Ask: *Was your answer correct?*

Teaching Tip

Optional: Remember that if students need additional support, tell them to read the Audio Script on page 286 as they listen to the conversation.

Listen again. What does Greg order? Check (✓)...

• Read the directions. Play Track 24 again.
• Call on students to say the answers.

Ⓒ 🔘 Listen to the whole conversation....

• Read the directions. Say: *Listen for the food that Greg orders.*
• Play CD 3, Track 25.
• Ask: *Does Greg make a healthy choice?* (No, because apple pie is not healthy.)
• Call on students to ask and answer the questions.
• Play Track 25 as many times as needed to aid comprehension.

3 CONVERSATION

A 🔘 **Listen. Notice the pronunciation of...**

- Read the directions. Play CD 3, Track 26. Students listen.
- Say: *I'd* is a contraction for *I would*. On the board, write: *I'd = I would*. Remind students that *I'd like* is a polite way to say *I want*.
- Ask: *What is the difference between* I like *and* I'd like? (*I like* means that you enjoy that food, but *I'd like* means you want to eat that food now.)
- As needed, provide isolated repetition practice of *I* vs. *I'd*. Emphasize the /d/ in *I'd* and ask students to repeat in isolation and in full sentences.
- Resume playing Track 26. Students listen and repeat.

Controlled Practice   20 minutes

B 🔘 **Listen and read the conversation. Then...**

- Note: This conversation is the same one students heard in Exercise 2B on page 154.
- Tell students to listen for *I'd*. Play CD 3, Track 27. Students listen and read along silently.
- Resume playing Track 27. Students listen and repeat.

4 PRACTICE

A **PAIRS. Practice the conversation. Then make...**

- Pair students and tell them to practice the conversation in Exercise 3B. Say: *Say* please *to be polite when ordering.*
- Then, in Exercise 4A, point to the menu, say the items, and ask the class to repeat.
- Copy the conversation onto the board with blanks. Read through it. When you come to a blank, fill it in with the name of a food or drink from the menu (for example, *a cup of tomato soup, soda,* and *a green salad*). Tell students: *Say* a cup of *or* a bowl of *tomato soup.*
- Ask two on-level students to practice the conversation in front of the class. Tell the class that A is the waitress and B is the customer. Tell pairs to take turns playing each role and to use the menu to fill in the blanks.

- Walk around and check that students are clearly pronouncing *I'd like*. Tell students to stand, mingle, and practice the conversation with new partners.

◼︎ **MULTILEVEL INSTRUCTION for 4A**

Pre-level Say each line and ask students to repeat after you before they practice in pairs. Monitor pronunciation carefully.

Above-level After pairs practice a couple of times, ask them to cover all but the first words of each line as they speak.

Communicative Practice   10 minutes

B **ROLE PLAY. PAIRS. Make your own....**

- Play A and, with an above-level student, use information from the menu and make up a new conversation.
- Pair students and tell them to take turns playing A and B.
- Walk around and check that students are using information from the menu.
- Call on pairs to role-play for the class.

◼︎ **MULTILEVEL INSTRUCTION for 4B**

Pre-level To help build confidence, practice with students until they are comfortable making new conversations on their own.

Above-level Ask students to order something and then change their mind (for example, *I'd like pepperoni pizza. No, wait, I'm sorry. I'd like a green salad.*).

◼︎ **Expansion: Speaking Practice for 4B**

- At the end of the conversation, tell A to offer a special price for one or two items that are "on sale" when B is ordering (for example, A: *Hamburgers are only $3.00 today.* B: *Really? OK. I'd like one.*).

Extra Practice

Interactive Practice

CD3 T26

A 🔘 Listen. Notice the pronunciation of *I like* and *I'd like*.
Then listen and repeat.

(I like) coffee.   (I'd like) coffee.   (I like) yogurt.   (I'd like) yogurt.

CD3 T27

B 🔘 Listen and read the conversation. Then listen and repeat.

Waitress: Can I help you?

Greg: Yes. I'd like a hamburger and a soda.

Waitress: Is that a large soda or a small soda?

Greg: Large, please.

Waitress: OK, a large soda. . . . Anything else?

Greg: Yes. A small order of fries.

4 PRACTICE

A PAIRS. Practice the conversation. Then make new conversations.
Use the menu.

A: Can I help you?

B: Yes. I'd like _____
                      (food)

and _____.
    (drink)

A: Is that a large _____
                         (drink)

or a small _____ ?
              (drink)

B: Large, please.

A: OK, a large _____ . . . .
                      (drink)

Anything else?

B: Yes. _____ .
              (food)

B ROLE PLAY. PAIRS. Make
your own conversations.
Use the menu.

Starters	Sides	Desserts
tomato soup..cup $1.00 bowl $1.25	baked potato $1.85	apple pie $1.75
	fries ..... small $1.25 large $1.75	ice cream $2.25
green salad $1.00		fruit cup $2.00

Sandwiches	Drinks
hamburger $3.25	soda ...... small $1.00 large $1.25
chicken sandwich $3.75	iced tea .... small $1.00 large $1.25
	coffee ..... small $1.00 large $1.25

Order a meal in a restaurant

Grammar

···· **Grammar Watch**

Choice questions with *or*			
Would you like **coffee**	**or**	**tea?**	**Tea**, please.
Do you want **a large soda**		**a small soda?**	I want **a large soda**.

Grammar Watch

Some questions with *or* are choice questions.
Answer with your choice.
Do not say *yes* or *no*.

PRACTICE

A **Complete the questions. Use the words in parentheses.**

1. Do you want ___chicken soup or a salad___ ?
   (chicken soup / salad)

2. Would you like ___a fish sandwich or a hamburger___ ?
   (a fish sandwich / a hamburger)

3. Do you want ___fries or a baked potato___ ?
   (fries / a baked potato)

4. Do you want ___soda or juice___ ?
   (soda / juice)

5. Would you like ___ice cream or apple pie___ ?
   (ice cream / apple pie)

CD3 T28

B **Listen and check your answers.**
Then listen and repeat.

In *choice questions with or*, the voice goes up ↗ on the first choice and down ↘ on the last choice.

Do you want soup or salad?

Show what you know! Order a meal in a restaurant

STEP 1. PAIRS. Student A, you are a waiter. Student B, you are a customer. Student A, ask Student B the questions in Exercise A. Write Student B's answers on the order pad.

STEP 2. Report to the class.

Maria wants chicken soup, a ...

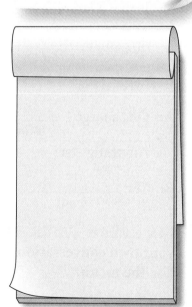

Can you... order a meal in a restaurant? ☐

Order a meal in a restaurant

Getting Started 5 minutes

- Say: *We're going to study choice questions with or. In the conversation on page 155, the waitress used this grammar.*
- Play CD 3, Track 27. Students listen. Write *Is that a large soda or a small soda?* on the board. Underline *a large soda or a small soda.*

Presentation 5 minutes

Choice questions with *or*

- Copy the grammar charts onto the board or show Transparency 8.4 and cover the exercise.
- Read the questions and answers from the charts and ask the class to repeat.
- Read the Grammar Watch note.
- If you are using the transparency, do the exercise with the class.

Controlled Practice 10 minutes

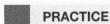

PRACTICE

A Complete the questions. Use the words...

- Read the directions and do the first item with the class. Write it on the board.
- Read the pronunciation note. To demonstrate, ask the example question in item 1. Make your voice go up on *chicken soup* and down on *salad*. Ask the class to repeat.
- Tell students they will know if the question is a choice question because the person asking the question will stress the choices and will pause slightly after the first example (for example, *Do you want* coffee *or* tea? The answer could be *Tea, please* or it could be *Coffee, please.*).
- Walk around and check that students are writing *or* between the choices.

B 🔘 **Listen and check your answers. Then...**

- Play CD 3, Track 28. Students listen and check their answers.
- Resume playing Track 28. Students listen and repeat.

Communicative Practice 10 minutes

Show what you know!

STEP 1. PAIRS. Student A, you are a waiter....

- Read the directions.
- Play the waiter and practice with an above-level student. Write the customer's choices on the board.
- Pair students and tell them to take turns as the waiter and the customer.
- Walk around and check that the customer is answering as in the grammar chart (for example, *A hamburger, please.*).

> **◼ MULTILEVEL INSTRUCTION for STEP 1**
> **Cross-ability** Ask the lower-level student to play the waiter (A) first. The higher-level student can be the customer and repeat the answers as needed until A can write them correctly.

STEP 2. Report to the class.

- Read the directions and the example.
- Call on individual students to say what their partner wants (for example, *Maria wants . . .*).
- *Optional:* Introduce *Maria would like. . . .*

Progress Check

Can you . . . order a meal in a restaurant?
Say: *We have practiced ordering a meal in a restaurant. Now, look at the question at the bottom of the page. Can you order a meal in a restaurant?* Tell students to write a checkmark in the box.

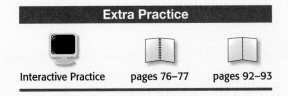

Extra Practice

Interactive Practice   pages 76–77   pages 92–93

Lesson 7 Compare food prices; Read food labels

Getting Started 10 minutes

- Say: *It is common to receive advertisements from food stores in the mail or see them in the newspaper. Many stores try to offer the cheapest prices. You can compare one ad to another. Let's look at some ads.*
- *Optional:* Bring in food ads to show the class.

Presentation 5 minutes

1 COMPARE FOOD PRICES

A Look at the ad for Farmer Tom's....

- Read the note. Ask students what *lb.* is the abbreviation for (*pound*). Point to various foods to provide examples for the points in the note. Ask: *Which food's price depends on weight?* (chicken, bananas, apples, and onions)
- Play CD 3, Track 29. Students listen and repeat.

Controlled Practice 25 minutes

B Look at the ad for Country Market....

- Read the directions. Play CD 3, Track 30. Students listen and fill in the amounts.
- Play Track 30 again as needed.
- To check answers, write the foods on the board and call on five students to write the price for each.

2 PRACTICE

A Look at the prices in the ads again. Where is each...

- Read the directions. To demonstrate, ask: *Where is chicken cheaper?* (Students circle the price at Farmer Tom's.)
- Ask where each food is cheaper. (*Answers:* Farmer Tom's—chicken, bananas, yogurt, apples, and onions; Country Market—bread.)

Expansion: Speaking Practice for 2A

- Ask students to continue the conversation by discussing the price difference between the two stores (for example, A: *Where is chicken cheaper?* B: *At Farmer Tom's.* A: *How much cheaper is it?* B: *Let's see.* [Calculates $3.29 – $2.99 = $0.30] *It's 30 cents cheaper.*).

B Two friends are comparing prices at...

- Read the directions. Play CD 3, Track 31. Students listen.
- Resume playing Track 31. Students listen and repeat.
- Pair students and tell them to take turns playing A and B.
- Walk around and check that in A's question students' voices go up for the first choice and down for the second.

C PAIRS. Practice the conversations. Then make...

- Pair students and tell them to practice the conversation in Exercise 2B.
- Write the conversation on the board, leaving blanks where students can substitute new information. Explain that students must choose a count noun for the first food choice and a non-count noun for the second choice.
- Ask a pair of on-level students to practice the conversation in front of the class.
- Tell pairs to take turns playing each role and to use information from the ads in the blanks.
- Tell students to stand, mingle, and practice the conversation with several new partners.

D NETWORK. Talk to your classmates. Ask, *Where...*

- Read the directions. Ask an above-level student the questions.
- Brainstorm with the class reasons why a store is a good place to shop (for example, *low prices, wide selection, good service, short lines, fresh produce*).

Progress Check

Can you . . . use measurements and compare food prices?

Say: *We have practiced using measurements and comparing food prices. Now, look at the question at the bottom of the page. Can you use measurements and compare food prices?* Tell students to write a checkmark in the box.

Compare food prices; Read food labels

Life Skills

69¢/lb. = sixty-nine cents a pound
or
sixty-nine cents per pound

1 COMPARE FOOD PRICES

CD3 T29

A Look at the ad for Farmer Tom's. Listen and repeat the prices and amounts.

CD3 T30

B Look at the ad for Country Market. Listen and fill in the prices.

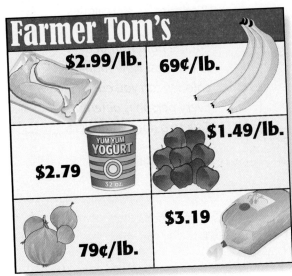

2 PRACTICE

A Look at the prices in the ads again. Where is each food cheaper?
Circle the cheaper price.

CD3 T31

B Two friends are comparing prices at the two stores. Listen to the
conversation. Then listen and repeat.

A: Where are **onions** cheaper, Farmer
Tom's or Country Market?

B: Farmer Tom's. They're **79 cents a pound**.

A: Where is **bread** cheaper, Farmer
Tom's or Country Market?

B: Country Market. It's **$2.59**.

C PAIRS. Practice the conversations. Then make new conversations.
Use different foods from the ads.

D NETWORK. Talk to your classmates. Ask, *Where do you shop for food?*
Then ask, *Is that a good place to shop? Why?*

Can you...use measurements and compare food prices? ☐

How do you stay healthy? Here are some tips.

Tips to Stay Healthy

- Don't eat a lot of fat.
- Don't eat a lot of sodium.
- Don't eat a lot of sugar.

12 calories   300 calories

Eat the right number of calories. How many calories can you eat? Every person is different. Talk to a doctor or nurse.

4 | PRACTICE

A **Look at the pictures. Check (✓) the foods that are healthy.**

Answers will vary but could include:

☐    ☐   ☐   ✓

✓   ☐    ✓    ✓

B **PAIRS.** Talk about your answers in Exercise A.

A: Green beans are good for you.
B: Why?
A: Because they don't have fat.

A: Ice cream isn't good for you.
B: Why not?
A: Because it has a lot of fat and sugar.

C **GROUPS OF 3.** Which healthy foods do you usually eat?

A: *I eat a lot of beans.*
B: *Really? Well, I eat rice every day. What about you, Li?*
C: *I eat . . .*

Presentation   10 minutes

3 TALK ABOUT NUTRITION

How do you stay healthy? Here are some tips.

- Ask: *What is the title of the box?* Explain: *A tip is advice or helpful information.*
- Point to the pictures and ask students to identify the food they see (*meat, butter, salt, chips, sugar, cake*).
- Read the tips. Students read along.
- Use the pictures to help explain unfamiliar vocabulary as needed:

  Fat *is oily and is in beef. What other foods have a lot of fat?* (butter, ice cream, some cheese, . . .)

  Sodium *is in salt. We often put it on foods like french fries.*

  Sugar *makes food taste sweet. One food with a lot of sugar is cake. What other foods have a lot of sugar?* (cookies, ice cream, pie, . . .)

  A calorie *tells you how much energy a food can produce. People need a certain amount of calories every day to stay healthy. We burn calories through exercise and everyday activities.*

Controlled Practice   5 minutes

4 PRACTICE

A Look at the pictures. Check (✓) the foods that...

- Read the directions.
- Ask: *Do healthy foods have a lot of fat or a little fat?* (a little fat) *Do healthy foods have a lot of sodium or a little sodium?* (a little) *What about sugar?* (Healthy foods have a little sugar.)
- Poll the class on each item. If students disagree, ask them to explain their position (for example, *I think ice cream is good for you if it is low fat.*).

Communicative Practice   15 minutes

B PAIRS. Talk about your answers in Exercise A.

- Play A and read the example conversations with a student.

- Say: *When food is healthy, we say it is good for you. When food is not healthy, we say it isn't good for you.*
- Call on a few students to explain their position about a couple of foods from Exercise A as in the example conversations (for example, *Are pancakes good for you?*).
- Pair students and tell them to practice each conversation using the foods in the pictures. Tell them to take turns playing A and B.
- Walk around and check that students are discussing whether each food is healthy or not healthy.

■■■ MULTILEVEL INSTRUCTION for 4B

Cross-ability Tell the higher-level student in each pair to first ask the lower-level student a question to get the conversation started (for example, A: *Are pancakes good for you?* B: *No.* A: *Why?* B: *Because . . .*).

C GROUPS OF 3. Which healthy foods do you...

- Form groups of 3 and tell them to discuss the question: *Which healthy foods do you usually eat?* Tell them to say how often they eat healthy foods (for example, *I like apples. I usually eat an apple every day at lunch.*).
- Walk around and help students who are having difficulty by asking them first to write two or three healthy foods they eat and how often they eat them.
- Call on several students to say what healthy foods they usually eat.

■■■ Expansion: Graphic Organizer and Writing Practice for 4C

- Form groups of 3. Ask students to make a weekly meal planner that includes as much healthy food as possible.
- First, students write a list of healthy food they have in their kitchen or that they plan to buy.
- Then students list meals they will serve their family (or themselves) for each day of the coming week (for example, *Friday—dinner—chicken and salad*). They can use true or made-up information.
- In a week, ask students to take out their meal plans. Ask students if they actually made those meals.

Controlled Practice   10 minutes

D Food labels give you important...

- As a warm-up, bring in examples of food labels if possible. Pass around packages or cans of food with labels for students to see.

- Point to the bread label. Ask: *What information do you see?* (serving size, servings per container, . . .)

- Read the notes. Copy them on the board and allow adequate time for students to digest the information in each one.

- Read the example question and ask the class to call out the answer. To explain *slice*, point to the picture of a slice of bread.

- Walk around and check that students are referring to the food label as they answer the questions.

- To check answers, read each question and call on individual students to say answers.

Communicative Practice   5 minutes

E WRITE. Look at the labels. Which drink is better...

- Read the directions. Ask: *What is* oz. *the abbreviation for?* (ounce or ounces) Remind students that healthy foods have little fat, sodium, and sugar.

- Ask students to compare both labels and complete the sentence.

- Walk around and help students write complete sentences if they have difficulty.

- Students compare their answer with a partner. Tell students that they each may give different reasons.

Expansion: Life Skills Speaking Practice for 4E

- Pair students. Partners take turns asking each other the questions in Exercise D for the soda and iced tea in the pictures in Exercise E (for example, Soda, A: *How much is one serving?* B: Twelve ounces. *How many servings are in the can?* A: *One. How many . . .*).

- To wrap up, call on several individual students to answer questions about either food (for example, T: *How many calories are in the iced tea?*).

Progress Check

Can you . . . talk about the nutritional value of foods?

Say: *We have practiced talking about the nutritional value of foods. Now, look at the question at the bottom of the page. Can you talk about the nutritional value of foods?* Tell students to write a checkmark in the box.

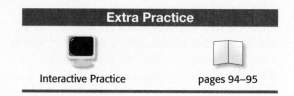

Extra Practice	
Interactive Practice	pages 94–95

D Food labels give you important information about the food. Look at this label for bread. Then answer the questions.

g = gram or grams
mg = milligram or milligrams

Nutrition Facts	Calories 90
Serving Size: 1 slice	Total Fat.................... 1 g
Servings per	Sodium .... 180 mg
Container: 18	Sugars .... 3 g
	Net Wt. = ... 1 lb. 8 oz.

Serving Size = the amount you eat at one time

Net Wt. = Net Weight = how much food is in the container

1. How much is one serving? __1 slice__

2. How many servings are in the package? __18__

3. How many calories are in one serving? __90__

4. How much fat is in one serving? __1 gram__

5. How much sodium is in one serving? __180 milligrams__

6. How much sugar is in one serving? __3 grams__

E WRITE. Look at the labels. Which drink is better for your health? Why?

Nutrition Facts	
Serving Size: 12 oz.	
Servings per Container: 1	
Calories 140	
Total Fat..................... 0 g	
Sodium .... 50 mg	
Sugar .... 33 g	

Nutrition Facts	
Serving Size: 12 oz.	
Servings per Container: 1	
Calories 75	
Total Fat..................... 0 g	
Sodium .... 0 mg	
Sugar .... 16 g	

Answers will vary but could include:

__Iced tea__ is better for your health because __it doesn't have fat,__

__and it doesn't have a lot of calories__ .

Can you...talk about the nutritional value of foods? ☐

Listening and Speaking

1   BEFORE YOU LISTEN

CLASS. Look at the pictures. Which other foods are steamed, grilled, or fried?

steamed vegetables   grilled chicken   fried fish

2   LISTEN

CD3 T32

A **CLASS.** Listen to the radio talk show. Answer the questions.   Answers will vary but could include:

1. What is the talk show about?   food / healthy foods / nutrition

2. What information does the caller want?   The caller wants information about healthy foods.

3. Does he get the information?   Yes, he gets the information.

CD3 T32

B Listen again. Answer the questions in the chart about each food.

ON THE AIR   How Healthy Is It?

	How many calories?	How much fat? (in grams)
Fried chicken	250	12
Grilled chicken	100	3
French fries (small)	290	15
Baked potato	130	0

C **GROUPS OF 3.** Look at the pictures. Plan a healthy dinner for Greg. Choose from the pictures.

A: *How about salad, a baked potato, and fruit?*
B: *No, he needs meat. How about . . . ?*

Getting Started   5 minutes

1 BEFORE YOU LISTEN

CLASS. Look at the pictures. Which other foods...

- Tell students to look at the pictures. Say: *There are many ways to cook food.*
- Point to each of the pictures in turn and explain:

  These vegetables are steamed. When water is very hot, it changes to steam.

  The chicken is grilled. In a grill, the heat is under the food.

  The fish is fried. To fry means to cook something in hot oil.

- On the board, write the following headings: *steamed, grilled,* and *fried.* Under each, ask students to call out additional foods from pages 146–149, 154, and 158.

▬▬ **Expansion: Speaking Practice for 1**

- Choose three foods (for example, *chicken, potatoes,* and *broccoli*) and ask students to discuss which way (*grilled, steamed,* or *fried*) is the healthiest (for example, *I think grilled chicken is healthy because there is only a little fat.*). Students can discuss in pairs or small groups.

Presentation   15 minutes

2 LISTEN

A 🔘 **CLASS. Listen to the radio talk show....**

- Read the directions, including the questions. Play CD 3, Track 32. Students listen.
- Call on students to answer the questions.

B 🔘 **Listen again. Answer the questions...**

- Tell students to look at the chart. Say each question and point out the areas that students must fill in (for example, *Listen for how many calories are in fried chicken.*).
- Play Track 32 again. Students listen and fill in the chart.
- Play Track 32 again if students had difficulty understanding all the information.
- Call on students to write answers on the board.

C **GROUPS OF 3. Look at the pictures. Plan...**

- Read the directions.
- Pair students. To help students organize a meal, ask them to choose a *main course,* a *drink,* a *side dish,* and a *dessert.* Write these headings on the board and review the menu on page 155.
- Walk around and help as needed. Check that students aren't including unhealthy foods (for example, *chocolate cake*).
- Call on pairs to say their dinner plan for Greg. Partners can take turns discussing different foods they chose.

Controlled Practice   25 minutes

3 CONVERSATION

A CLASS. **Look at the pictures. Which of these...**

- Point to each picture, say the food, and ask the class to repeat.
- Ask: *Which of these foods do you like?* Call on several students to say answers.

Expansion: Vocabulary Practice for 3A

- Pair students and tell them to ask each other which food group each of the foods belongs to (for example, A: *Which food group do shrimp belong to?* B: *Meat and beans.*).

B 💿 **Greg and Liz are planning dinner....**

- Read the directions. Play CD 3, Track 33. Students listen and read along silently.
- Explain: *Let's is a contraction for* Let us. *It is common in conversation to say* Let's have _____ for dinner.
- Resume playing Track 33. Students listen and repeat.

4 PRACTICE

A PAIRS. **Practice the conversation. Then make...**

- Pair students and tell them to practice the conversation in Exercise 3B.
- Then point to the words in the boxes, say them, and ask the class to repeat.
- Copy the conversation onto the board with blanks and read it. When you come to a blank, fill it in with information from the boxes (*turkey, tomatoes*).
- Ask two on-level students to practice the conversation in front of the class.
- Pair students and tell them to take turns playing each role and to use the words in the boxes to fill in the blanks.
- Walk around and check that students are stressing two-word nouns correctly.
- Tell students to stand, mingle, and practice the conversation with several new partners.

MULTILEVEL INSTRUCTION for 4A

Pre-level Say each line and ask students to repeat after you before they practice in pairs. While pairs practice, listen closely to their pronunciation.

Above-level After pairs practice a couple of times, ask them to cover all but the first words of each line as they speak.

Communicative Practice   10 minutes

B MAKE IT PERSONAL. PAIRS. **Plan an...**

- Read the directions.
- Ask two students to role-play the sample conversation. Model pronunciation as needed.
- Review ways of making suggestions as in the example conversation (*Let's put . . . And how about . . . ? I'd like . . .*). Write these expressions on the board and ask students to call out several suggestions before pairs complete the task.
- Pair students.
- Walk around and check that students are agreeing, disagreeing, and making further suggestions about food to put in the salad.

MULTILEVEL INSTRUCTION for 4B

Pre-level Form groups of 4. Each student suggests at least one ingredient.

Above-level Ask students to name their salad and to create a menu with two or three salad options if time permits.

C CLASS. **Tell your classmates about the salad.**

- Read the directions and the example line. To warm up, ask students to call out additional ingredients (for example, T: *Tell me what to put in the salad.* Ss: *Tomatoes. Onions. Avocado.*). Repeat the ingredients students say.
- Call on students to report to the class about their salad as in the example.

Extra Practice

Interactive Practice

3 CONVERSATION

A CLASS. Look at the pictures. Which of these foods do you like?

B 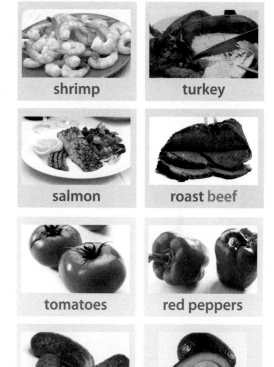 Greg and Liz are planning dinner. Listen and read their conversation. Then listen and repeat.

CD3 T33

shrimp

turkey

salmon

roast beef

tomatoes

red peppers

cucumbers

avocados

Liz: Let's have **chicken** for dinner.

Greg: OK. How much **chicken** do we need?

Liz: Two pounds.

Greg: OK. And let's have salad with it.

Liz: Good idea. We have lettuce, but we need **onions**.

Greg: How many **onions** do we need?

Liz: Just one.

4 PRACTICE

A PAIRS. Practice the conversation. Then make new conversations. Use the pictures.

B MAKE IT PERSONAL. PAIRS. Plan an interesting salad.

Maria: *Let's put nuts in the salad.*
Roberto: *OK. And how about avocados?*
Maria: *Oh, I don't like avocados. Let's put a mango in it.*

C CLASS. Tell your classmates about the salad.

Roberto: *Our salad has nuts, mango, . . .*

Plan a healthy meal

Grammar

Simple present: Questions with *How many* and *How much*

How many	eggs	do we have? are there?	A lot. 	Not many.
How much	milk	do we have? is there?	A lot.	Not much.

Grammar Watch

- Use *how many* with plural count nouns.
- Use *how much* with non-count nouns.

PRACTICE

A Look at the picture. Read the answers. Complete the questions with *How many* or *How much* and a noun.

1. **A:** _How many oranges_ are there?

   B: Not many. We only have three.

2. **A:** _How much milk_ do we have?

   B: Not much. Let's get more milk!

3. **A:** _How many eggs_ are there?

   B: Twelve. We don't need more.

4. **A:** _How much cheese_ is there?

   B: There is no cheese! Put it on the shopping list.

5. **A:** _How many potatoes_ are there?

   B: Six. And they're big!

   A: Great. Let's have baked potatoes tonight.

B PAIRS. Look at the picture again. Continue the conversation in Exercise A. Ask about other food in the refrigerator.

A: *How much orange juice is there?*
B: *There's a lot. We don't need orange juice.*
A: *How many apples…?*

Getting Started   5 minutes

- Say: *We're going to study questions with* How many *and* How much. *In the conversation on page 155, Greg used this grammar.*
- Play CD 3, Track 33. Students listen. Write *How much chicken do we need?* and *How many onions do we need?* on the board. Underline *How much chicken* and *How many onions*.

Presentation   10 minutes

Simple present: Questions with *How many* and *How much*

- Copy the grammar charts onto the board or show Transparency 8.5 and cover the exercise. Read the Grammar Watch note.
- Read questions and answers from the charts and ask students to repeat.
- Ask students for examples of count nouns. Say: *We use* many *with plural count nouns. For example, I can say* many apples *or* many bananas.
- Point to *are* in *How many eggs are there?* in the grammar chart and say: *Remember to use* are *with plural nouns.*
- Ask students for examples of non-count nouns. Say: *We use* much *with non-count nouns. For example, I can ask* How much milk is there? *or* How much water is there? *Point to* is *in* How much milk is there? *and say: Remember to use* is *with non-count nouns.*
- Tell students they can also say *A little* to express *Not much.* Both expressions (*Not much* and *A little*) are common in everyday conversation.
- On the board, write (but do not label) a plural count noun form, for example, *tomatoes*. Point to *tomatoes* and ask students if they should use *How much* or *How many* with this word (*How many,* because *tomatoes* is a plural count noun).
- On the board, write (but do not label) a non-count noun, for example, *rice*. Point to *rice* and ask students if they should use *How much* or *How many* with this word (*How much,* because *rice* is a non-count noun).
- If you are using the transparency, do the exercise with the class.

Controlled Practice   10 minutes

> **PRACTICE**

A **Look at the picture. Read the answers. Complete...**

- Read the directions and the example.
- Tell students to look at the picture of the refrigerator. Say: *The conversations are about the food in the refrigerator.*
- Explain: *Do you see the three oranges? Use the picture to help you understand the conversations and how to complete the question. Also, read the answer carefully and decide if the food is a count or non-count noun.*
- Students role-play the completed conversations with a partner to check answers.
- *Optional:* Call on pairs to perform the completed conversations for the class.

Communicative Practice   10 minutes

B **PAIRS. Look at the picture again. Continue...**

- Read the directions.
- Play A and read the example conversation with a student. Continue the conversation as directed for one or two more exchanges.
- Pair students. Tell A to look at the food in the refrigerator and ask B a question.
- Walk around and check that B is expanding on the conversation after saying how much food there is (for example, *There's a lot. We don't need orange juice.*).
- To wrap up, pair students and ask them to ask and answer at least two questions about how much food there is in the refrigerator.

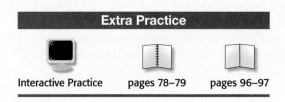

Extra Practice		
Interactive Practice	pages 78–79	pages 96–97

1 GRAMMAR

 DICTATION. Two friends are talking...

- Read the directions. Ask: *What is an* omelet? If no one can answer correctly, say: *To make an omelet, you mix eggs together and cook them. Many people put cheese and other foods in the omelet.*
- Tell students they will listen to the conversation twice. The first time they will just listen. The second time they will listen and fill in the blanks.
- Play CD 3, Track 34. Students listen.
- Play Track 34 again. Students listen and fill in the blanks. If students cannot keep up, pause the CD to allow more time.
- Now tell students they will listen to the conversation again and check their answers. Play Track 34 again.
- Pair students and tell them to role-play the completed conversation.
- Ask one pair to role-play the completed conversation for the class. Correct as needed.

2 WRITING

STEP 1. You are planning a meal. Which foods...

- Read the directions.
- Students circle one food in each pair.

STEP 2. GROUPS OF 5. Ask your classmates...

- Read the directions. Form groups of 5.
- Tell students to ask choice questions with *or* (for example, *Do you want soup or salad?*).
- As needed, review how to make choice questions with *or* on page 156.
- Tell students to count how many people choose each food and fill in the blanks in their book just like the example.
- Walk around and listen for students correctly asking and answering choice questions with *or*.

STEP 3. Write six sentences in your notebook about...

- Read the directions and the example sentence.
- On the board, write: (*Number*) *students want* (*choice 1*), and (*Number*) *students want* (*choice 2*). Ask students for information to complete the sentence (for example, *Three students want rice, and three students want potatoes.*). Work through another example with them.
- Tell students to use the model on the board to help them write their sentences. Say: *Begin the sentence with the word for a number. For example, write* Four, *not* 4. Remember to use a capital letter and a period.
- Walk around and check that students are writing complete sentences with proper capitalization and punctuation. Also check that students are writing numbers in words (for example, *Four*, not *4*).

STEP 4. Tell the class about your group's meal.

- Read the directions and the example. First, call on an above-level student from a group to tell the class about their group's meal.
- Call on other groups to share.

CD-ROM Practice

 Go to the CD-ROM for more practice.

If your students need more practice with the vocabulary, grammar, and competencies in Unit 8, encourage them to review the activities on the CD-ROM. This review can also help students prepare for the final role play on the following Expand page.

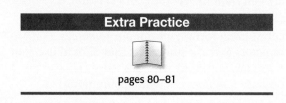

Extra Practice

pages 80–81

1 GRAMMAR

CD3 T34

DICTATION. Two friends are talking about a recipe for a cheese omelet. **Listen and complete the conversation.**

A: This omelet is really good. What's in it?

B: _Eggs_ and cheese. Oh, and there's ____salt____, but not much.

A: Eggs? How ____many____ eggs?

B: Three.

A: And how ____much____ cheese?

B: Just one slice.

A: What do you cook it in? Do you use butter ____or____ oil?

B: I use ____oil____, but it's good with ____butter____, too.

2 WRITING

STEP 1. You are planning a meal. Which foods do you want? Circle one thing in each pair. Answers will vary.

1. soup or salad   3. rice or potatoes   5. coffee or tea

2. meat or fish   4. carrots or green beans   6. ice cream or cake

STEP 2. GROUPS OF 5. Ask your classmates about their choices. Count the students. Write the number next to each food. Answers will vary.

> How many people want soup?

soup _2_ salad _3_

1. soup ____   salad ____   4. carrots ____   green beans ____

2. meat ____   fish ____   5. coffee ____   tea ____

3. rice ____   potatoes ____   6. ice cream ____   cake ____

STEP 3. Write six sentences in your notebook about your group's choices.

> Two students want soup, and three students want salad.

STEP 4. Tell the class about your group's meal.

> Our group wants salad, fish, ...

 Go to the CD-ROM for more practice.

3 ACT IT OUT — What do you say?

STEP 1. Review the Lesson 5 conversation between Greg and the waitress (CD 3 Track 24).

STEP 2. PAIRS. You are at a small restaurant. Student A, you are a waiter or waitress. Student B, you are a customer.

Student A: Take the customer's order. Ask about the size of the drink.

Student B: Order something to eat and drink.

Kitty's Kitchen — MENU

Sandwiches ... $5.95 *chicken, fish, turkey*	Soda: cola, orange *Small* .... $1.00 *Large* $1.50
Hamburger $4.50	
Tacos (2) $4.95	Juice: orange, apple, tomato *Small* .... $1.95 *Large* $2.75
Pizza .... $7.25 *Today's special:* *Vegetable* $8.25	Coffee *Small* .... $1.00 *Large* $1.60
Salads: *Green* .... $3.95 *Fruit* $4.75	Tea *Small* .... $.85
French fries ... $2.95	*Large* $1.50

4 READ AND REACT — Problem-solving

STEP 1. Read about Eduardo's problem.

Eduardo is 45 years old. He is heavy. Eduardo's doctor tells him, "Be careful. You need to eat healthy foods. Don't eat foods with a lot of calories and fat." Eduardo usually has lunch at a fast-food restaurant. He has a big cheeseburger, fries, and a large soda every day. He eats dinner at home with his family. His wife is a great cook, and the children love her food. But she cooks a lot of fried food.

STEP 2. PAIRS. Talk about it. What is Eduardo's problem? What can Eduardo do? Here are some ideas.

- He can bring a sandwich from home for lunch.
- He can eat small servings.
- He can ask his wife to cook different food for him.
- He can _____.

5 CONNECT

For your Community-building Activity, go to page 249.
For your Team Project, go to page 270.

Which goals can you check off? Go back to page 145.

Show what you know!

3 ACT IT OUT

STEP 1. Review the Lesson 5...

- Tell students to review the conversation in Exercise 3B on page 155.
- Tell them to first read the conversation silently and then practice it with a partner.
- Play CD 3, Track 24. Students listen.
- As needed, play Track 24 again to aid comprehension.

STEP 2. PAIRS. You are at a small restaurant....

- Read the directions and the guidelines for A and B.
- Pair students and tell them to study the menu before they begin practicing.
- Review foods that come in sizes. Point out various menu items (for example, *soda, juice, coffee,* and *tea*).
- The waiter or waitress (Student A) can begin the conversation with *Can I help you?* as on page 155.
- Walk around and check that Student A is taking the customer's order and asking about size.
- Call on pairs to practice for the class.
- While pairs are performing, use the scoring rubric on page Txiv to evaluate each student's vocabulary, grammar, fluency and how well they complete the task.
- *Optional:* After each pair finishes, discuss the strengths and weakness of each performance either in front of the class or privately.

4 READ AND REACT

STEP 1. Read about Eduardo's problem.

- Say: *We are going to read about a student's problem, and then we need to think about a solution.*
- Read the directions.
- Read the story while students follow along silently. Pause after each sentence to allow time for students to comprehend. Periodically stop and ask simple *Wh-* questions to check comprehension (for example, *How old is Eduardo? What does Eduardo's doctor say? Where does Eduardo like to eat?*).

STEP 2. PAIRS. Talk about it. What is Eduardo's...

- Pair students. Ask: *What is Eduardo's problem?* (He is heavy.) *What can Eduardo do?*
- Read the ideas in the list. Give pairs a couple of minutes to discuss possible solutions for Eduardo.
- Ask: *Which ideas are good?* Call on students to say their opinion about the ideas in the list (for example, S: *I think he can bring a sandwich from home. He can save money, too.*).
- Now tell students to think of one new idea not in the box (for example, *He can exercise more.*) and to write it in the blank. Encourage students to think of more than one idea and to write them in their notebooks.
- Call on pairs to say their additional solutions. Write any particularly good ones on the board and ask students if they think it is a good idea, too (*Do you think this is a good idea? Why or why not?*).

■ MULTILEVEL INSTRUCTION for STEP 2

Cross-ability Form groups of 3 pre-level students and assign an above-level student to facilitate discussion by asking each of the pre-level students his or her opinion (*What can Eduardo do?*).

5 CONNECT

Turn to page 249 for the Community-building Activity and page 270 for the Team Project. See pages Txi–Txii for general notes about teaching these activities.

Progress Check

Which goals can you check off? Go back to page 145.

Ask students to turn to page 145 and check off the goals they have reached. Call on students to say which goals they will practice outside of class.

9 Rain or Shine

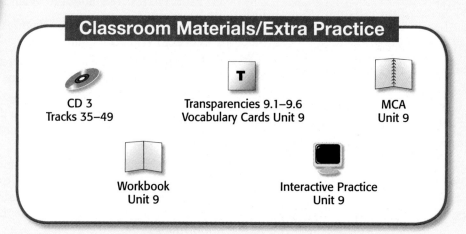
Unit Overview

Goals
- See the list of goals on the facing page.

Grammar
- Present continuous affirmative and negative statements
- Present continuous *yes/no* questions and short answers
- Adverbs of degree: *Very, really, pretty*

Pronunciation
- *-ing* ending

Reading
- Read an article about small talk

Writing
- Write sentences about today's weather

Life Skills Writing
- Write a postcard to a friend

Preview
- Set the context of the unit by asking simple questions about current weather conditions: *Is it hot/warm/cold outside?* If possible, point out a window or let students look outside.
- Hold up page 165 or show Transparency 9.1. Read the unit title and explain: Rain or Shine *means in any weather. Outdoor sports events and music concerts will happen rain or shine. This means they will happen in any weather.*
- Say: *Look at the picture.* Ask the Preview questions: *What do you see?* (Four people beneath an umbrella) *Does it often rain where you live?* (Yes./No.) *What do you do when it rains?* (I stay home. I watch TV. I read. I sleep.)

Goals
- Point to the Unit Goals. Explain that this list shows what the class will be studying in this unit.
- Tell students to read the goals silently.
- Say each goal and ask the class to repeat. Explain unfamiliar vocabulary as needed:

  Weather: *the temperature and conditions outside (rain, sun, wind, snow, . . .)*

  Seasons: *winter, spring, summer, fall*

  Postcard: *a card with a picture that you mail to a friend or family member*
- Tell students to circle one goal that is very important to them. Call on students to say the goal they circled.

Rain or Shine

Preview

Look at the picture. What do you see? Does it often rain where you live? What do you do when it rains?

UNIT GOALS

- [ ] Talk about the weather and seasons
- [ ] Talk about what you are doing now
- [ ] Write a postcard
- [ ] Talk about weather conditions
- [ ] Plan for an emergency
- [ ] Ask what someone is doing now
- [ ] Understand a weather report

1 WHAT DO YOU KNOW?

A CLASS. Look at the pictures. Which seasons do you know? Which words about weather do you know?

> C is spring. Number 8 is sunny.

CD3 T35

B 🔘 Listen and point to the pictures. Then listen and repeat.

2 PRACTICE

A PAIRS. Student A, point to a picture and ask about the weather. Student B, answer.

A: *What's the weather like?*
B: *It's hot and sunny.*

B WORD PLAY. PAIRS. Look at the list of weather words on page 167. Talk about the weather in your home country.

A: *I'm from Colombia. It's usually cool and sunny there.*
B: *Oh, really? In Korea, the winter is . . . .*

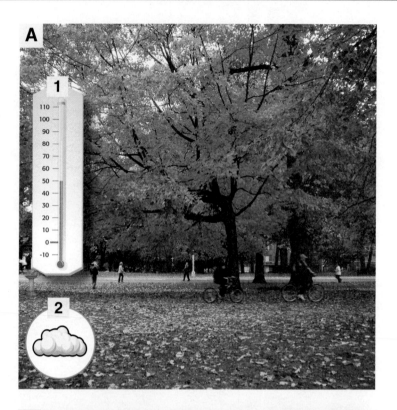

Lesson 1   Vocabulary

Getting Started   5 minutes

1   WHAT DO YOU KNOW?

A CLASS. Look at the pictures. Which seasons do...

- Show Transparency 9.2 or hold up the book. Tell students to cover the list of words on page 167.
- Write on the board: _____ *is* _____. *Number* _____ *is* _____.
- Point to picture C and read the example. Ask: *Which seasons do you know?* Students call out answers as in the example.
- Ask: *Which words about weather do you know?* Point to the board if a student needs help forming the sentences. Students call out words associated with each season (for example, *cool, cloudy*).
- Point to the thermometer in one of the pictures and explain: *This is a thermometer. It tells the temperature so you know how hot or cold it is.*
- If students call out an incorrect season or weather word, change the student's answer to a question for the class (for example, *Number 2 is rainy?*). If nobody can identify the correct item, tell students they will now listen to a CD and practice words for seasons and weather.

Presentation   10 minutes

B 💿 Listen and point to the pictures. Then...

- Read the directions. Play CD 3, Track 35. Pause after number 8 (*sunny*).
- To check comprehension, say each season and weather word in random order and ask students to point to the appropriate picture.
- Resume playing Track 35. Students listen and repeat.

Controlled Practice   10 minutes

2   PRACTICE

A PAIRS. Student A, point to a picture and ask about...

- Read the directions. Play A and model the example with an above-level student.

- Pair students and tell them to take turns playing A and B.
- Walk around and help students correct one other's mistakes.

▬▬ MULTILEVEL INSTRUCTION for 2A

Cross-ability To prepare, the higher-level partner (A) first says a season. The other student (B) looks at the list on page 167 and responds with appropriate weather words (for example, A: *Fall.* B: *Cool. Cloudy.*).

▬▬ Expansion: Vocabulary Practice for 2A

- Pair students and ask them to write colors in their notebooks that are associated with each season (for example, *Fall: red, yellow, brown*).
- Pair students and have them ask each other about the colors they chose (A: *What fall colors do you like?* B: *Red, yellow, and brown. What fall colors do you like?*).

B WORD PLAY. PAIRS. Look at the list of weather...

- Read the directions and the example conversation.
- Say: *Think about your home country.* Ask: *What is the weather like there?* Allow a minute for students to plan their answer.
- Call on a few students to answer. Remind them to use the words in the list on page 167.
- Pair students. Walk around and check that they are asking about each other's home countries and are using the vocabulary on page 167.

▬▬ Expansion: Vocabulary Practice for 2B

- Pair students and ask them to write all the weather words at the bottom of page 167 individually on scraps of paper. Ask pairs to line up the season words on top of their desk. Under each season, students place words that apply for that season (for example, *Fall: cool, cloudy*).
- Form groups of 5. For each group, scramble a set of the vocabulary scraps on a desk. Give the class 30 seconds to reassemble the words under the appropriate season. The first group to do it successfully wins.

Learning Strategy: Listen for new words

- Read the directions.
- Ask: *What is the weather like today?* Write a few answers on the board (for example, *cool, cloudy*).
- If possible, turn on a radio in the classroom and tune to a weather report. When the broadcast is on, tell students to listen carefully for weather words they hear.
- Call on a few students to say words they hear and write them on the board.
- If you don't have access to a radio, bring in a newspaper or print out a local weather forecast from the Internet, provide copies, and read it to the class or have them read it in pairs.
- Ask: *What is the learning strategy?* If students don't guess correctly, write on the board: *You can remember new vocabulary by listening for words on TV or radio.* Remind students they can use this strategy to remember other new vocabulary.

Communicative Practice   25 minutes

Show what you know!

STEP 1. CLASS. Walk around the room. Ask four...

- Tell students that now they will practice talking about their favorite season.
- Read each line in the example conversation and ask the class to repeat. Model correct intonation.
- Ask a few students: *What's your favorite season? Why?* Recast any errors in grammatically correct form (for example, S: *Because like weather.* T: *Because **I** like **the** weather.*), and ask the class to repeat (Ss + T: *Because I like . . .*).
- Read the example conversation and ask the class to repeat a couple more times if many students have difficulty formulating the correct sentences.
- On the board, write a few students' responses in the same format as in the chart (*Name, Favorite Season, Reason*).
- Tell students to use the words that describe each season in the box on page 167 to explain why they like a particular season (for example, *Fall: cool, cloudy: I like fall because it's cool but not rainy.*).
- Read the directions.

- Students stand, mingle, and record their partners' responses in the chart.
- Walk around and check that students are filling out the chart and are asking, *What's your favorite season? Why?*

STEP 2. Report to the class. How many people like...

- On the board, write the four seasons: *Winter, Spring, Summer,* and *Fall.*
- Call on several students to say which partners they had and what they learned (for example, S: *Maria's favorite season is winter. She likes snow.*).
- Write students' names under their favorite season. Call on students to say how many people in their groups like each season.

Teaching Tip

Informally assess students' performances in a variety of ways as they walk around the room to get information from their classmates. For example, be an active participant in some mingling activities and be an observer during others. Alternating between observation and participation will provide you with more knowledge about how your students are progressing or where they may need more instruction.

Expansion: Speaking and Writing Practice for STEP 2

- Tell students to ask four classmates about their least favorite seasons. Students can create a chart in their notebooks similar to the one in "Show what you know!" but with *Least Favorite Season* as a heading.
- Explain: Least favorite *means what you don't like.*

    A: *What's your least favorite season?*
    B: *I don't like spring.*
    A: *Why?*
    B: *Because I don't like the weather. I like cold weather.*

Extra Practice

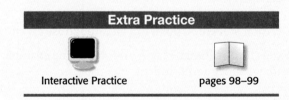

Interactive Practice   pages 98–99

B

3

4

C

5

6

Weather and Seasons

A. fall	**B. winter**	**C. spring**	**D. summer**
1. cool	**3.** cold	**5.** warm	**7.** hot
2. cloudy	**4.** snowy	**6.** rainy	**8.** sunny

Learning Strategy

Listen for new words

Look at the list of weather and season words. Watch the weather report in English on TV or listen to it on the radio. Write three or four weather words you hear.

Show what you know!

STEP 1. CLASS. Walk around the room. Ask four classmates about their favorite seasons. Complete the chart.

Sylvia: *What's your favorite season?*
Paul: *I like spring.*
Sylvia: *Why?*
Paul: *Because I like the weather. It's warm, but not hot.*

Name	Favorite Season	Reason
Paul	spring	warm, not hot

STEP 2. Report to the class. How many people like each season?

Talk about what you are doing now

Listening and Speaking

1 BEFORE YOU LISTEN

READ. Look at the map. Read about Laura and her family. Then complete the sentences. Underline the correct words in each sentence.

Laura lives in Green Bay, Wisconsin. In Green Bay, winter is usually cold and snowy. Laura often visits her family in winter. Her family lives in Tampa, Florida. Winter there is usually nice. It's warm and sunny.

1. Laura usually visits her family in **Green Bay / Tampa** in the winter.
2. Winter in Tampa is usually **cold and snowy / warm and sunny**.

2 LISTEN

A Look at the picture. Laura is in Tampa. She is calling her friend David in Green Bay. Guess: How does Laura feel?

a. happy   b. excited   c.)bored

CD3 T36

B Listen to the conversation. What do you think? Was your guess in Exercise A correct?

CD3 T36

C Listen again. Answer the questions.

1. Who is Laura visiting?
   a. friends   b.) family   c. classmates

2. Where is Laura's family now?
   a. at home   b.) at work   c. at school

3. How is the weather in Tampa?
   a. hot and rainy   b. warm and rainy   c.) cold and rainy

CD3 T37

D Listen to the whole conversation. What does David say about the weather in Green Bay? Complete the sentence.

"It's not ____warm____, but it's ____sunny____."

Getting Started   5 minutes

1   BEFORE YOU LISTEN

READ. Look at the map. Read about Laura and her...

- Read the directions. Say: *Look at the map.* Ask: *What cities do you see?* (Green Bay and Tampa)
- Read the paragraph while the class reads along silently.
- Say: *The answers are in the paragraph. Read it again if you don't know the answers.*
- Call on a couple of students to read answers.
- To wrap up, ask the class to mark where you are on the map. Call on a few students to describe what typical seasons are like. Write answers on the board and ask students to copy them into their notebooks for extra practice (for example, T: *What is summer like here?* S: *Summer is always hot.*).

> **Teaching Tip**
>
> Use the map of the United States to ask students to point to where you are right now. Take advantage of opportunities to use maps to help students strengthen their understanding of geography.

Presentation   25 minutes

2   LISTEN

Ⓐ Look at the picture.... Guess:...

- Read the directions.
- Say: *Look at the pictures of the people.*
- Write the answer choices on the board and read them. Ask: *How does Laura feel?* Call on students to say their choice.
- Tell students they will listen for the answer in Exercise 2B.

Ⓑ Listen to the conversation. What do you...

- Read the directions. Play CD 3, Track 36.
- Circle the correct answer on the board. Ask: *Was your guess correct? How do you know?* If students are not sure, explain: *Laura doesn't say* I'm bored, *but we can hear it in the way she talks.*
- Play Track 36 again as necessary, pointing out the final line in particular.

Ⓒ Listen again. Answer the questions.

- Read the directions.
- Read each question and the answer choices.
- Play CD 3, Track 36. Students listen and answer the questions.
- As needed, play Track 36 again to allow students another opportunity to listen to the conversation while answering the questions.
- Read each question and call on students to say answers.

Ⓓ Listen to the whole conversation. What...

- Read the directions. Play CD 3, Track 37.
- Call on a student to read the completed sentence.

▬ Expansion: Speaking Practice for 2D

- Ask students to redraw the map of the United States with Green Bay and Tampa marked.
- On the board, write common weather symbols for different weather conditions (for example, a sun for *hot*, a cloud for *cloudy*, . . .). Label each picture using words from the list on page 167.
- Pair students and ask them to draw weather symbols near each city (these can be different from the recorded conversation). Students can also include other major cities with weather symbols on their maps (first mark them on your map, which students can then copy).
- Tell pairs to take turns delivering a weather report (for example, A: *It's warm and sunny in Los Angeles. It's cold and rainy in Tampa.*).
- Call on a few students to mark the map on the board and deliver a weather report to the class. Call on students from the audience to ask the "weatherperson" questions (for example, A: *How's the weather in Green Bay?* B: *It's beautiful and sunny.*).

3   CONVERSATION

A   Listen. Notice the pronunciation of...

- Read the directions. Play CD 3, Track 38. Students listen.
- Ask students what *It's* is a contraction for. (*It is*)
- Tell students to circle or underline *-ing* in the sentences.
- Resume playing Track 38. Students listen and repeat.
- Play the CD again as many times as needed until the class is comfortable pronouncing *-ing* clearly.

Expansion: Listening Practice for 3A

- Ask students to call out a city they know. Create sentences such as the ones below.
- Say the following sentences. Ask students to raise their hands for the one that uses present continuous:

  a. It snows in Chicago. b. It's snowing in Chicago.

  a. It's raining in Portland. b. It rains in Portland.

  a. It snows in Kansas City. b. It's snowing in Kansas City.

  a. It's raining in Detroit. b. It rains in Detroit.

Controlled Practice   15 minutes

B   Listen and read the conversation. Then...

- Note: This conversation is the same one students heard in Exercises 2B and C on page 168.
- Tell students to listen for *-ing*. Play CD 3, Track 39. Students listen and read along silently.
- Resume playing Track 39. Students listen and repeat.

4   PRACTICE

A PAIRS. Practice the conversation. Then make new...

- Pair students and tell them to practice the conversation in Exercise 3B.
- Then, in Exercise 4A, tell students to look at the boxes. *Foggy, humid,* and *windy* are new vocabulary. Say each word and ask the class to repeat.

- If possible, hold up or point to a map in the classroom to show students the location of Dallas, San Francisco, and Boston. If a map is not available, draw one on the board.
- Copy the conversation onto the board with blanks and read it. When you come to a blank, fill it in with information from the boxes (for example, *Dallas, friends, hot, humid*).
- Ask a pair of on-level students to practice the conversation in front of the class.
- Tell pairs to take turns playing each role.
- Walk around and check that students are pronouncing *-ing* clearly and stressing the words from the boxes.
- Tell students to stand, mingle, and practice the conversation with several new partners.
- Call on pairs to perform for the class.

MULTILEVEL INSTRUCTION for 4A

Pre-level Ask students to write choices above each blank (in pencil) and to write a choice in each blank before practicing.

Above-level After pairs practice a couple of times, tell them to cover all but the first words of each line as they speak.

Communicative Practice   15 minutes

B ROLE PLAY. PAIRS. Make your own...

- Read the directions. On the board, write *Cities, People,* and *Weather.* Call on students to say various words for each heading. Write several appropriate responses on the board under the correct heading (for example, *Cities: Los Angeles, Santa Ana, Houston*).
- Play A and, with an above-level student, use information from the board and make up a new conversation.
- Pair students and tell them to take turns playing A and B.
- Call on pairs to role-play for the class.

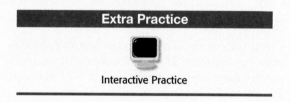

Extra Practice

Interactive Practice

CD3 T38

A 💿 **Listen. Notice the pronunciation of -*ing*. Then listen and repeat.**

It rains in Tampa.   It's rain**ing** in Tampa.
It snows in Green Bay.   It's snow**ing** in Green Bay.

CD3 T39

B 💿 **Listen and read the conversation. Then listen and repeat.**

David: Hello?

Laura: Hi! It's me. How are you?

David: Fine, thanks. Where are you?

Laura: I'm in Tampa. I'm visiting family, but they're at work now.

David: Tampa! That's great! How's the weather there?

Laura: Well, it's cold and rainy.

4 PRACTICE

A PAIRS. Practice the conversation.
Then make new conversations.
Use the information in the boxes.

A: Hello?

B: Hi! It's me. How are you?

A: Fine, thanks. Where are you?

B: I'm in ⬚⬚⬚⬚⬚ . I'm visiting
⬚⬚⬚⬚⬚ , but they're at work now.

A: ⬚⬚⬚⬚⬚ ! That's great! How's
the weather there?

B: Well, it's ⬚⬚⬚⬚⬚ and
⬚⬚⬚⬚⬚ .

Dallas		
San Francisco	hot	humid
Boston		
friends	cool	foggy
my aunt and uncle		
my cousins	warm	windy

B ROLE PLAY. PAIRS. Make your own conversations.
Use different cities, people, and weather.

Talk about what you are doing now

Grammar

Present continuous: Statements

Affirmative				
I	**am**			
You We They	**are**			
		visiting	family.	
He She Laura	**is**			
It	**is**	**raining.**		

Negative				
I	**am**			
You We They	**are**			
		not	**working.**	
He She David	**is**			
It	**is**		**snowing.**	

1 PRACTICE

Amy is calling her cousin Ben in Seattle. Complete the conversation.

Ben: What are you doing?

Amy: I <u>'m watching</u> TV. What are *you* doing?
                 1. (watch)

Ben: I <u>'m talking</u> to you!
          2. (talk)

Amy: Very funny. How's the weather there?

Ben: Well, it <u>'s not raining</u>, but it's cold. How's the weather in Chicago?
              3. (not rain)

Amy: It <u>'s snowing</u> here.
          4. (snow)

Ben: Oh. Is it cold?

Amy: Yes. I <u>'m wearing</u> two sweaters.
           5. (wear)

Ben: Is Jason home?

Amy: Yes. He <u>'s not working</u> today.
          6. (not work)

Ben: What about the kids? What are they doing?

Amy: They're outside. They <u>'re making</u> a snowman!
           7. (make)

Grammar Watch

- Use the present continuous for things that are happening now.
- Remember: We usually use contractions with *be* in conversations.
- *make → making*
  For spelling rules for the present continuous, see page 274.

2 LIFE SKILLS WRITING

Write a postcard. See page 261.

Getting Started   5 minutes

- Say: *We're going to study statements with present continuous. In the conversation on page 169, Laura used this grammar.*
- Play CD 3, Track 39. Students listen. Write *I'm visiting family* on the board. Underline *I'm visiting.*

Presentation   10 minutes

Present continuous: Statements

- Copy the grammar charts onto the board or show Transparency 9.3 and cover the exercise.
- Read the first bullet of the Grammar Watch note. Ask: *What is happening right now?* Say and write some example sentences on the board (for example, *It is raining right now. I am breathing. I am standing.*). Underline *be* and the *-ing* verb in each sentence.
- Remind students about how to use *be* with the subject pronouns in the chart (for example, *I am, You are, . . .*).
- Say: *We form the present continuous with* be *and another verb with* -ing. While explaining this, use one of the sentences in the left chart as an illustration. Read it and ask the class to repeat.
- Read the negative sentences in the right chart and ask the class to repeat.
- Say: *To make a negative sentence, add* not *between* be *and the verb with* -ing. Again, use a sentence in the chart to illustrate these points. Write it on the board.
- Say and write additional sentences that express things happening right now in the classroom (for example, *I am teaching the class.*). Write at least two sentences on the board. Then write negative sentences that complement the affirmative ones (for example, *I am not watching TV.*). Use these sentences to illustrate the use of *be, not,* and *-ing.*
- Read the other bullets of the Grammar Watch note. Say a sentence from the charts (for example, *I am visiting family.*) and ask students to come to the board and rewrite the sentence using a contraction (*I'm visiting family.*).
- If you are using the transparency, do the exercise with the class.

Controlled Practice   25 minutes

1 **PRACTICE**

Amy is calling her cousin Ben in Seattle. Complete...

- Play Ben and read the example with a student.
- Tell students to use contractions as in the example. Say: *Look at the subject first. We know it's I in number 1. Use the correct form of* be *to make the contraction. Look back at the chart for help.*
- Walk around and check that students are using an apostrophe to make an appropriate contraction, adding *-ing* to the verb in parentheses, and using *not* appropriately. Also check that students correctly make the spelling transformation for number 7 (*making*).
- To check answers, call on students to each write one full sentence on the board.
- *Optional:* Pair students and ask them to practice the conversation. Call on pairs to perform the completed conversation for the class.

MULTILEVEL INSTRUCTION for 1

Cross-ability The higher-level student recites each line and the lower-level student repeats it before they take turns practicing the conversation.

Expansion: Vocabulary and Grammar Practice for 1

- Ask students to cut out pictures from magazines of people doing different activities.
- Pair students and ask them to write what the people in the pictures are doing (for example, *He's talking on a cell phone. She's reading a newspaper.*). Tell students they can use pronouns or nouns (for example, *the woman, the man,* or *the family*).
- Call on students to show their picture(s) to the class and say what is happening. Students can paste their picture to a piece of colored paper and write their sentences under the picture. This would make a great product to display in the classroom.

2 **LIFE SKILLS WRITING**

Turn to page 261 and ask students to write a postcard. See pages Txi–Txii for general notes about the Life Skills Writing activities.

3 PRACTICE

PAIRS. Look at the pictures. Find at least 10...

- To warm up, ask: *What's happening in picture 1?* Write a few responses on the board (for example, *Two men are running.*).

- Repeat the above step for picture 2.

- Read the example conversation with a student. Follow these steps:

   1. With the class, find a few differences between the pictures (for example, *In picture 1, a woman is wearing a pink shirt. In picture 2, she is wearing a blue and yellow dress.*). Hold up the book. Circle the differences in the pictures and draw a line connecting the dissimilar parts in each picture.

   2. Practice the conversation for each.

   3. Tell students to mark all the differences they can find in the pictures.

   4. Practice a couple more exchanges with the class before pairing students.

- Pair students and tell them to talk about what is different between the two pictures.

- Walk around and check that students are comparing what the same people are doing in each picture as in the sample conversation.

■■ MULTILEVEL INSTRUCTION for 3

Pre-level Point to various people in each picture and ask students to tell you what the people are doing before pairs complete the task.

Above-level After completing the exercise, Student A calls out something that is happening in one of the pictures (for example, *Two men are jogging.*). Student B identifies the correct picture (for example, *Two men are jogging in picture 1.*).

■■ Expansion: Speaking Practice for 3

- Pair students and ask them to find and discuss the similarities in both pictures (for example, A: *There are three people sitting on benches in picture 1.* B: *There are also three people sitting on benches in picture 2.*).

Communicative Practice   20 minutes

Show what you know!

STEP 1. WRITE. Imagine that you're visiting friends...

- Read the directions.

- To warm up, tell the class that you are imagining you're visiting a friend in another city (for example, *I'm visiting my friend Brian.*). Then say what you are doing (*I'm playing video games with Brian.*) and write the sentence on the board.

- Remind students to use *be* and a verb with *-ing*.

- Students compare answers with a partner.

- Call on students. Ask them who their friend is and where they are. Finally, ask them what they are doing. Write some present continuous sentences on the board (for example, *We're washing his car.*).

STEP 2. GROUPS OF 5. Play the Memory Game....

- Explain that students will use the sentence they wrote in Step 1. With two students, read the example. The student playing Lucy completes the answer.

- To warm up, practice the game with a few students for the class.

- Form groups of 5. Walk around and check that students are taking turns and changing their partners' sentences to the third person (for example, *Ana is . . .*). It's OK for students to use *he* or *she*.

- Call on one student from each group to report what his or her group is doing.

Progress Check

Can you . . . talk about what you are doing now?

Say: We have practiced talking about what we are doing. Now, look at the question at the bottom of the page. Can you talk about what you are doing now? Tell students to write a checkmark in the box.

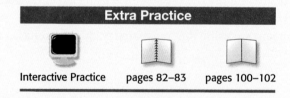

Extra Practice		
Interactive Practice	pages 82–83	pages 100–102

PAIRS. **Look at the pictures. Find at least 10 differences. Talk about them.**

A: *In Picture 1, a woman is eating an apple.*
B: *Right. And in Picture 2, she isn't eating an apple. She's eating a banana.*

Show what you know!   Talk about what you are doing now

STEP 1. WRITE. Imagine that you're visiting friends in another city. It's a beautiful day. What are you doing? Complete the sentence.

I _____ Answers will vary. _____.

STEP 2. GROUPS OF 5. Play the Memory Game. Talk about what you are doing.

Ana: *I'm taking a walk in the park with my family.*
Boris: *Ana is taking a walk. I'm eating lunch outside with my family.*
Lucy: *Ana is taking a walk. Boris is . . . .*

Can you...talk about what you are doing now?   ☐

Life Skills

1 TALK ABOUT WEATHER CONDITIONS

A **PAIRS.** Which words for bad weather and emergencies do you know? Write the correct words from the box under each picture.

an earthquake	a snowstorm
a flood	a thunderstorm
~~a heat wave~~	a tornado
a hurricane	a wild fire

1. *a heat wave*

2. a hurricane

3. a tornado

4. a wild fire

5. a thunderstorm

6. a flood

7. a snowstorm

8. an earthquake

CD3 T40

B Listen and check your answers. Then listen and repeat.

2 PRACTICE

A What do you do in bad weather or an emergency? Check (✓) *Do* or *Don't*.

B **PAIRS.** Compare answers.

	DO	DON'T	DOs and DON'Ts in an Emergency
1.	✓		go downstairs in a tornado
2.		✓	go under a piece of furniture, like a desk, in an earthquake
3.	✓		stay in your house in a flood
4.	✓		cover your windows before a hurricane
5.		✓	go swimming in a thunderstorm
6.	✓		drink a lot of water in a heat wave
7.		✓	go outside for a long time in a snowstorm
8.	✓		leave your house when a wild fire is near

Getting Started 10 minutes

• Ask: *Is there bad weather in your home country? What kind?* If needed, prompt students with *There's a lot of . . . rain/wind/snow. . . .*

• Ask: *Is the weather in your home country different from the weather here in the United States? How is it different?* (*Possible answer:* Yes, in my home country it's very rainy. Here in the United States it's sunny.)

Presentation 10 minutes

1 TALK ABOUT WEATHER CONDITIONS

A PAIRS. Which words for bad weather and...

• Say: *Look at the words in the box. These are words for bad weather and emergencies.* Remind students: *An emergency is a dangerous situation. You must do something immediately.*

• Ask: *Which words for bad weather and emergencies do you know?*

• Say each emergency and ask the class to repeat.

• Pair students and read the rest of the directions to get students started. Tell student to guess if they don't know all the answers for sure.

• Call on students to use words they learned in the unit to explain each weather emergency in the box (for example, *A thunderstorm is windy and rainy.*).

B 🔊 Listen and check your answers. Then...

• Play CD 3, Track 40. Students listen and check their answers.

• Resume playing Track 40. Students listen and repeat.

Expansion: Vocabulary Practice for 1B

• Ask students to identify specific emergencies that affect your part of the country. Ask: *What emergencies happen here?* As students call out answers, list them on the board.

Controlled Practice 15 minutes

2 PRACTICE

A What do you do in bad weather or an emergency?...

• Explain that a *Do* is a good or safe action and a *Don't* is a bad or dangerous action. Write on the board: *DO = good, safe* and *DON'T = bad, dangerous.*

• Say: *We do different things to stay safe during a weather emergency. Sometimes one action is safe for one emergency, but it is not safe for a different emergency.*

• Read each action. Change each one into a question that the class answers (for example, T: *Do you go downstairs in a tornado?* Ss: *Yes!*).

• Explain unfamiliar vocabulary by simple illustration or demonstration (for example, to illustrate *go under a piece of furniture*, kneel down and move as if going under a desk).

B PAIRS. Compare answers.

• Tell students to look at their partner's list and to look for differences between their lists.

• Practice with a student to demonstrate how to compare answers (for example, A: *Do you go downstairs in a tornado?* B: *No, I don't.* A: *Oh, I do.*).

• Walk around and check that students are able to interact as in the above sample conversation.

• To check answers, say each action and ask the class to call out *do* or *don't.*

MULTILEVEL INSTRUCTION for 2B

Pre-level Students work in groups of 4 for more support.

Above-level Pairs discuss why they should or should not do each action (for example, A: *It's important to go downstairs in a tornado because it is safe under the ground.*).

3 PLAN FOR AN EMERGENCY

A CLASS. Look at the Garcia family's...

- To warm up, tell students there is a plan if there is an emergency at your school. Explain what will happen in the event of a fire or other emergency.
- Read the emergency family plan and the note while students read along silently. Explain: Long distance *refers to phone numbers outside your area code.* Give some examples.
- Ask: *What information is important to include in an emergency plan?* As students call out information, write responses on the board (*places to meet, emergency phone numbers*). Ask students to copy them into their notebooks as headings.

Communicative Practice   10 minutes

B Make an emergency plan for your family. Write...

- Read the directions. Tell students to use the headings on the board.
- Walk around and check that students are writing places to meet and emergency phone numbers. Remind students to include area codes.

▬ Expansion: Writing Practice for 3B

- Ask students to draw a map that shows directions from their home to a place to go in the event of an emergency (for example, say: *Draw a map showing the roads to a meeting place near your home*). Be sure that students label the places where they can go to meet.
- Pair students and tell them to take turns asking and answering questions about their plans.

Presentation   15 minutes

4 PRACTICE

A GROUPS OF 3. What do you need in an...

- Say each item in the word box and ask the class to repeat. Explain: First aid *is emergency medical help you give someone before other help arrives. Some things in a first aid kit are a book to tell you what to do, bandages, tape, scissors, something to clean cuts with, and plastic gloves.*

- Form groups of 3 and tell students to match the words and pictures.
- Walk around and check that students are interacting with their partners to match the words and pictures.

B 🔘 Listen and check your answers. Then...

- Play CD 3, Track 41. Students listen and check their answers.
- Resume playing Track 41. Students listen and repeat.

C WRITE. Make a list in your notebook of things...

- Read the directions. Say: *Think of things you have in your home.*
- To help students get started, call on a few students to say what things they have in their home for an emergency, such as the things in Exercise 4A.
- Write some responses on the board. Explain any new vocabulary as needed.

▬ Expansion: Speaking Practice for 4C

- Ask students to explain what we use each thing for (for example, *You need water to drink. You need a radio to listen to the news. You need batteries for the radio.*).
- Write student-generated definitions on the board (correct as needed) and tell students to copy the definitions into their notebooks.

Progress Check

Can you . . . plan for an emergency?

Say: *We have practiced planning for an emergency. Now, look at the question at the bottom of the page. Can you plan for an emergency?* Tell students to write a checkmark in the box.

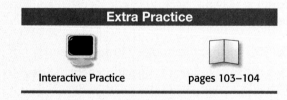

Extra Practice	
Interactive Practice	pages 103–104

3 PLAN FOR AN EMERGENCY

A **CLASS.** Look at the Garcia family's emergency plan. What information is important to include in an emergency plan?

B Make an emergency plan for your family. Write the emergency plan in your notebook.

> **Emergency Family Plan**
>
> **Places to meet**
> 1. Outside our apartment building
> 2. Main post office: 2209 7th Street
>
> **Emergency phone numbers**
> **Carla**
>   Work (510) 555-8317
>   Cell (510) 555-1194
> **Luis**
>   Work (510) 555-7835
>   Cell (510) 555-7834
> **Maria**
>   School (510) 555-4965
> **Uncle Alex** (312) 555-0552

> In an emergency, you can't always call someone in your area code. Include a long distance number.

4 PRACTICE

A **GROUPS OF 3.** What do you need in an emergency? Match the words and pictures.

batteries	candles	a first aid kit	a flashlight
matches	medicine	a radio	~~water~~

1. _water_ 2. _radio_ 3. _batteries_ 4. _medicine_

5. _a first aid kit_ 6. _matches_ 7. _candles_ 8. _a flashlight_

CD3 T41

B Listen and check your answers. Then listen and repeat.

C **WRITE.** Make a list in your notebook of things you have for an emergency.

Can you...plan for an emergency? ☐

Ask what someone is doing now

Listening and Speaking

1 BEFORE YOU LISTEN

**CLASS. Look at the picture and read.
Where are the people? What are they doing?**

**Do you watch the weather report on
TV? What channel do you watch?**

Can you turn on the TV? I want to check the weather.

2 LISTEN

**A Look at the picture of Dan Reed.
Where is he? What is he buying?
Guess: Why is he buying these things?**

CD3 T42

**B Listen to Dan's conversation with Emily.
Was your guess in Exercise A correct?
Listen again. Answer the questions.**

1. What is Emily doing?
   a. She's shopping.
   b. She's watching TV.
   c.(circled) She's reading a magazine.

2. Why is Dan going home early?
   a.(circled) A storm is coming.
   b. The supermarket is closing.
   c. He wants to watch the news on TV.

CD3 T43

**C Listen to the whole conversation. Complete the sentences.
Check (✓) the correct answers.**

1. Dan is buying _____. (Check more than one answer.)
   ☑ water   ☑ food   ☐ a flashlight   ☑ batteries   ☐ clothes

2. Emily says, "Get _____, too."
   ☐ candles   ☑ matches   ☐ a first aid kit

3. Emily says, "We need _____!"
   ☐ good friends   ☐ a good TV   ☑ good weather

Getting Started

1 BEFORE YOU LISTEN

> **Culture Connection**
>
> • Ask: *How do people prepare for emergencies in your home country? Do they buy things in a store?*
>
> • Say: *It is common in the United States for people to buy kits that already have everything they need.*
>
> • Ask: *How do you hear about an emergency in your home country—emergency broadcasts on TV and the radio as in the U.S.? Horns sounded outside?*

CLASS: Look at the picture and read. Where...

• Say: *Look at the picture.* Ask: *Where are the man and the woman?* (at home / in their living room)

• Ask: *What is the man doing?* (reading a magazine) *What is the woman doing?* (walking into the room / talking to the man)

• Ask: *Do you watch the weather report on TV? Which channel do you watch?* On the board, list common stations in your area if students are unfamiliar with channel listings. If possible, ask students what times the news is on and include this on the board.

Presentation

2 LISTEN

Ⓐ Look at the picture.... Guess:...

• Say: *Look at the picture of Dan Reed.* Ask: *Where is he? What is he buying? What is he holding? What is he doing?*

• Ask: *Why is he buying these things?* Call on students to answer. Write their answers on the board.

Ⓑ Listen to Dan's conversation with...

• Read the directions. Play CD 3, Track 42.

• Ask: *Was your guess in Exercise A correct?* Circle the correct answers on the board. (Dan is at a supermarket. He is buying water. A storm is coming, so he is getting prepared.)

> **Teaching Tip**
>
> *Optional:* Remember that if students need additional support, tell them to read the Audio Script on page 287 as they listen to the conversation.

Listen again. Answer the questions.

• Read the directions and the questions and answer choices.

• Play Track 42 again.

• Explain: In fact *is an expression we use to add information. The new information is that Dan is coming home early. He is coming home before he usually does.*

• Students compare answers with a partner.

• Call on students to say answers.

Ⓒ Listen to the whole conversation...

• Read the directions. Play CD 3, Track 43.

• Students compare answers with a partner.

• Call on students to read the completed sentences.

▬▬ Expansion: Speaking Practice for 2C

• Call on students to say how much various emergency items cost and where to shop to get the best price (for example, *Batteries are cheap at Shop-For-Less on Warner and Grand.*).

Ask what someone is doing now

Controlled Practice 20 minutes

3 CONVERSATION

 Listen and read the conversation. Then...

- Note: This conversation is the same one students heard in Exercise 2B on page 174.
- Say: *Listen to the words with* -ing. Play CD 3, Track 44. Students listen and read along silently.
- Resume playing Track 44. Students listen and repeat.
- Say each sentence and ask students to point out the words that end with *-ing* (*watching, reading,* and *coming*).

4 PRACTICE

A PAIRS. Practice the conversation....

- Pair students and tell them to practice the conversation in Exercise 3.
- Then, in Exercise 4A, ask students to look at the information in the boxes. Say each new activity, weather word, and location and ask the class to repeat.
- Copy the conversation with blanks onto the board and read it. When you come to a blank, fill it in with information from the boxes (for example, *checking e-mail, hurricane, gas station*).
- Ask two on-level students to practice the conversation in front of the class.
- Tell pairs to take turns playing each role and to use the pictures to fill in the blanks.
- Walk around and check that students are pronouncing *-ing* clearly.
- Tell students to stand, mingle, and practice the conversation with several new partners.
- Call on pairs to perform for the class.

MULTILEVEL INSTRUCTION for 4A

Pre-level Ask students to write choices above each blank (in pencil) and to write a choice in each blank before practicing.

Above-level After pairs practice a few times, tell them to cover the conversation and practice only by looking at the information in the boxes.

Expansion: Speaking Practice for 4A

- Ask pairs to cover all but the first word in each line of the conversation and attempt to recall the lines as they practice.

Communicative Practice 15 minutes

B ROLE PLAY. PAIRS. Make your own...

- Read the directions.
- On the board, write *Activities, Locations,* and *Emergencies* as headings. Call on students to say different activities (for example, *vacuuming, making dinner, watching a movie*), locations (for example, *post office, department store, restaurant*), and emergencies (for example, *earthquake, wild fire*). Write them under the appropriate heading.
- With an above-level student, use information from the board and make up a new conversation. Play A and practice for the class.
- Pair students and tell them to take turns playing A and B.
- Walk around and check that students are using information on the board or recycling other vocabulary from the unit.
- Call on pairs to role-play for the class.
- To wrap up, on the board write some of the errors you heard during the role plays. Ask students to correct the mistakes. Go over the corrections by saying the words or sentences correctly and asking the class to repeat.

Extra Practice

Interactive Practice

---

3 CONVERSATION

CD3 T44

🔘 **Listen and read the conversation. Then listen and repeat.**

Dan: Are you watching the news?

Emily: No, I'm not. I'm reading a magazine.

Dan: Well, turn on the TV. A big storm is coming.

Emily: Really?

Dan: Yes. In fact, I'm coming home early. I'm at the supermarket now.

4 PRACTICE

Ⓐ **PAIRS. Practice the conversation. Then make new conversations. Use the information in the boxes.**

A: Are you watching the news?

B: No, I'm not. I'm _____.

A: Well, turn on the TV. A _____ is coming.

A: Really?

B: Yes. In fact, I'm coming home early. I'm at the _____ now.

checking e-mail	making lunch	cleaning the apartment
hurricane	thunderstorm	snowstorm

| gas station | grocery store | drugstore |

Ⓑ **ROLE PLAY. PAIRS. Make your own conversations. Use different activities and locations.**

Grammar

Present continuous: *Yes/no* questions and short answers

Are	you they you		
	he	**watching**	the news?
Is	she Emily		
	it	**raining**?	

			Yes,			**No,**		
I **am**.						I'm **not**.		
they **are**.						they'**re not** OR they **aren't**.		
we **are**.						we'**re not** OR we **aren't**.		
he **is**.						he'**s not** OR he **isn't**.		
she **is**.						she'**s not** OR she **isn't**.		
it **is**.						it'**s not** OR it **isn't**.		

Grammar Watch

shop → shopping
See page 274 for spelling rules.

1 PRACTICE

Look at the picture. Daron and Lena are on vacation. Answer the questions. Use short answers.

1. **A:** Are Lena and Daron working?

   B: *No, they're not.*

2. **A:** Is it raining?

   B: No, it's not.

3. **A:** Is Lena wearing a T-shirt?

   B: Yes, she is.

4. **A:** Are they shopping for food?

   B: No, they're not.

5. **A:** Is Daron talking to a man?

   B: Yes, he is.

6. **A:** Is Lena looking at Daron?

   B: No, she's not.

Getting Started   5 minutes

- Say: *We're going to study yes/no questions and short answers with the present continuous. In the conversation on page 175, Dan and Emily used this grammar.*
- Play CD 3, Track 44. Students listen. On the board, write: *Are you watching the news? No, I'm not.*

Presentation   10 minutes

Present progressive: *Yes/no* questions and short answers

- Copy the questions from the left grammar chart onto the board or show Transparency 9.4 and cover the exercises.
- Read each question from the chart and ask the class to repeat.
- Ask: *Why are there two* you's? (*You* can be either singular or plural. We use *you* to talk to one person, who would answer *I . . . ,* and we use it to talk to more than one person, who would answer *We . . .*) Address one student and ask: *Are you watching the news?* (No, . . .) Then address the whole class and ask: *Are you watching the news?* (No, . . .)
- On the board, write: *Are you working?* Point to each element in the question and say: *To make a question, first use a form of* be (are), *a subject pronoun* (you), *and finally a verb +* ing (working) *for the activity.*
- If it's not already displayed, copy the right chart onto the board.
- Ask a question from the left chart and call on students to say a correct affirmative short answer (for example, T: *Is it raining?* S: *Yes, it is.*). Remind students not to use contractions for affirmative short answers.
- Next, continue asking individual students questions from the left chart and ask them to answer with an appropriate negative short answer. Say the alternative negative contraction answer to remind students that there is an alternative answer for first-person plural and second- and third-person responses.
- Ask students to call out other verbs. Write them on the board, and then tell students to ask and answer questions with them.
- If you are using the transparency, do the exercise with the class.

Controlled Practice   25 minutes

1   **PRACTICE**

Look at the picture. Daron and Lena are on vacation....

- Say: *Look at the picture.* Ask: *What are Daron and Lena doing?* (They're on vacation.)
- Read the Grammar Watch note.
- Read the example and ask the class to repeat. Ask: *Why does the answer have* they're? (Because it's two people—Lena and Daron.)
- Remind students to check the grammar chart if they don't remember how to answer a question. Remind students that *Lena* is the same as *she* and *Daron* is the same as *he.*
- Walk around and check that students are writing short answers with the appropriate subject pronoun.
- Students compare answers with a partner.
- Say each question and call on students to say the answers.
- *Optional:* Pair students and ask them to practice the conversations. Call on pairs to perform the completed conversations for the class.

▪▪▪ Expansion: Speaking and Writing Practice for 1

- Pair students and ask them to cut out a picture from a magazine of a person or people doing something.
- Ask each pair to write at least five questions about what the person or people in the picture are doing (as in Exercise 1). Tell students they must write questions that have *yes* and *no* answers.
- Students then switch partners and ask their new partner questions about his or her picture.

Teaching Tip

Use the picture to script a dialogue between the salesperson and Lena and Daron. Using art in novel ways to create new role-play situations is a way to provide opportunities for practical English practice.

Ask what someone is doing now

2 PRACTICE

A WRITE. Write *yes/no* questions. Use the words in...

- Read the example. Remind students to look back at the grammar chart to find the correct form of *be* to start the question. Also tell students to add *-ing* to the verb in parentheses.
- Students compare answers with a partner.
- Call on students to write the questions on the board. Correct as needed and read each one while the class repeats.

B PAIRS. Look at the picture on page 176. Ask and...

- Play A and practice the sample conversation with a student.
- Pair students and tell them to take turns playing A and B.
- Walk around and check that students are pronouncing *-ing* clearly.
- Call on pairs to practice the questions and answers for the class.

▬▬ MULTILEVEL INSTRUCTION for 2B

Cross-ability The higher-level partner first models the correct short answer. The higher-level student can use the illustration of Daron and Lena on page 176 to confirm which answers are correct.

C NETWORK. You have the day off from work...

- Read the directions. Ask: *Where do you go?* Call on several students to answer. Read the rest of the directions. Call on the rest of the class to share an answer. Tell students to stand and find other people with the same answer (for example, *the beach, the mall, at home*) and to sit with them.
- Tell students to ask others in their group: *What do you do there?* Walk around and observe each group.
- To wrap up, call on students to say what they do when they have the day off. Write popular locations on the board and write what students do under each location (for example, *the beach: swim*).

Communicative Practice   20 minutes

Show what you know!

STEP 1. WRITE. It's raining. You're at home. What...

- On the board, write *Activities at home.* Call on several students to say common activities they do at home (for example, *cooking, cleaning, relaxing, sleeping, working, . . .*). Write student responses on the board.
- Remind students to write in a complete sentence as in the example, *I'm studying.*
- Call on several students to share what they wrote.

STEP 2. GROUPS OF 3. Student A, act out your...

- Read the directions. Form groups of 3.
- Play A and practice with two other students. Pretend you are reading and tell Students B and C to say their lines.
- Walk around and check that students are guessing by asking *yes/no* present continuous questions.
- Spend time sitting with groups and guessing along with the students. Model pronunciation as needed.
- Call on several students to act out activities for the class while other students guess the activity.

▬▬ Expansion: Speaking Practice for STEP 2

- Ask students what they do in different weather conditions (for example, T: *It's sunny and you're outside. What are you doing?* S: *I'm riding my bicycle.*).

Progress Check

Can you . . . ask what someone is doing now?

Say: *We have practiced asking what someone is doing. Look at the question at the bottom of the page. Can you ask what someone is doing now?* Tell students to write a checkmark in the box.

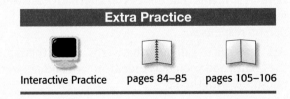

Extra Practice		
Interactive Practice	pages 84–85	pages 105–106

A **WRITE.** Write *yes/no* questions. Use the words in parentheses. Use capital letters and question marks.

1. (Lena and Daron / shop) _Are Lena and Daron shopping?_

2. (they / eat) _Are they eating?_

3. (Lena / wear a skirt) _Is Lena wearing a skirt?_

4. (Daron / wear a jacket) _Is Daron wearing a jacket?_

5. (he / listen to music) _Is he listening to music?_

6. (they / buy / CDs) _Are they buying CDs?_

B **PAIRS.** Look at the picture on page 176. Ask and answer the questions in Exercise A.

A: *Are Lena and Daron shopping?*
B: *Yes, they are. Are they . . . ?*

C **NETWORK.** You have the day off from work and school. Where do you go? Find classmates with the same answer as you. Then ask, *What do you do there?*

Show what you know! Ask what someone is doing now

STEP 1. WRITE. It's raining. You're at home. What are you doing? Write the activity.

I'm studying.

_____

STEP 2. GROUPS OF 3. Student A, act out your activity from Step 1. Students B and C, guess the activity.

B: *Are you reading a magazine?*
A: *No, I'm not.*
C: *Are you studying?*
A: *Yes, I am.*

Can you...ask what someone is doing now? ☐

Read about small talk

Reading

1 BEFORE YOU READ

CLASS. **Talk about it. Look at the cartoons.**
Answer the questions.

1. Where are the people in each cartoon?
   What are they doing?

2. The people in the cartoons are strangers. What are they talking about?

a.

b.

c.

d.

e.

Getting Started   15 minutes

1 BEFORE YOU READ

CLASS. Talk about it. Look at the cartoons. Answer...

- Look at picture *a* with the class. Ask the questions and call on students to say answers. Write answers on the board. (They're in a park. They're relaxing. They're talking about the weather.) If necessary, explain that *strangers* do not know each other.

- For picture *a*, explain: I hear *means that you saw the news or someone told you*. For picture *b*, explain: *The Lakers are a professional basketball team in Los Angeles.*

- Pair students and tell them to ask and answer the questions.

- Walk around and check that students are answering the questions for each picture.

- For each picture, call on students to share their answers with the class. Encourage other students to say alternative answers (for example, additional activities).

- Possible answers:
  a. The people are in a park. They're relaxing on a bench. They're talking about the weather.
  b. The people are in a deli/market/convenience store. They're watching a basketball game on TV. They're talking about the game/the winning team.
  c. The people are at the bus stop. They're waiting for a bus. They're talking about the bus because it's late.
  d. The people are in a clothing store/department store. They're shopping. They're talking about the sale at the store.
  e. The people are at a party. They're getting food. They're talking about the food.

- *Optional:* Pair students and ask them to practice the conversations in the cartoons. Call on pairs to perform the conversations for the class.

Expansion: Speaking Practice for 1

- Ask pairs to repeat this task by using pictures or comic strips from newspapers.

Language Note

Provide opportunities for your students to authentically practice small talk. At the beginning of class or at other times, engage your students in light casual conversation. A routine of repetitive and predictable questions should precede any new materials. Students at this level need to become comfortable using a limited range of small talk expressions.

Presentation   15 minutes

2 READ

 Listen. Read the article.

- Tell students to look at the picture. Ask: *Where are these people?* (at a bus stop) *What are they doing?* (talking) *Are the people friends?* (Maybe *or* No, they aren't.) *Or are they strangers?* (Probably *or* Yes, they are.) *Why are they talking to each other?* (Because they're friendly.)
- Ask: *What's the title of the article? What does* Small Talk *mean?* (to talk about everyday things, such as the weather)
- Play CD 3, Track 45. Students listen and read along silently.
- *Optional:* Pause the CD after each paragraph and ask the following questions:

  First paragraph: *Do you make small talk?*

  Second paragraph: *What topics do you like for small talk?*

  Third paragraph: *Why don't we talk about personal things for small talk?*

  Fourth paragraph: *How do you answer in a friendly way? Do you smile, nod, or repeat what you hear?*

Controlled Practice   15 minutes

3 CHECK YOUR UNDERSTANDING

🅐 **Read the article again. What is the main idea?**

- Remind students: *The main idea is the most important idea of the article.*
- Ask students to read the article again silently and choose the correct answer.
- Poll the class and ask students to raise their hand for either *a* or *b.* Say: b *is the answer.* Ask: *Why?* (Because it's about the whole article.)

🅑 **Read these sentences. Are they OK for small talk?...**

- Read the directions and the example.
- Ask: *Is it OK to talk about the weather? Why or why not?* (Yes, because the weather is not personal.). Remind students to check the article.
- Call on students to say answers.

Communicative Practice   15 minutes

Show what you know!

PAIRS. Imagine you are at work. You see a co-worker...

- Read the directions. First, with an above-level student, make up a conversation. Try to discuss the weather, sports, or other topics from the reading. Write it on the board.
- Pair students. Walk around and check that students are writing a complete role play that uses small talk for appropriate topics.
- Call on pairs to practice for the class. Encourage humor by praising groups that are funny; model clear pronunciation as needed.

Community Building

Inspire creativity by giving groups time to role-play at their desks before calling them to perform for the class.

To ensure that one or two students don't dominate the conversations, tell groups to create lines of equal length for all speakers.

▮▮ MULTILEVEL INSTRUCTION

Pre-level Ask pairs to focus on the weather. Monitor and assist as needed.

Above-level Ask pairs to include the following details: food they ate that day, the weather, something humorous about the workplace, and a current event.

▮▮ Expansion: Writing and Speaking Practice

- Students choose one small talk topic from the reading.
- Students write three sentences about their topic that they would say to a person they meet at work or at school (for example, *weather: It's nice today.*).
- Pair students and tell them to practice using their small talk expressions with each other.

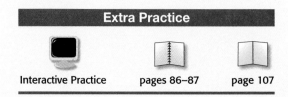

Extra Practice		
Interactive Practice	pages 86–87	page 107

CD3 T45

Listen. Read the article.

Small Talk Is Big!

We tell children, "Don't talk to strangers." But we do it all the time. We talk to strangers at the supermarket, at the bus stop, and at the coffee shop. We make small talk every day.

What do we talk about? Only a few topics are OK. The weather is a good topic. Everyone talks about the weather. We say, "What a nice day!" or "It's so hot!" Some other good topics for small talk are sports, food, transportation, and shopping.

Two strangers make small talk at a bus stop.

We don't talk about personal things. In the United States, we don't make small talk about money, love, or health problems.

Answer a person's small talk in a friendly way. Smile and say something more about the topic. For example, when someone says, "This is such great weather!" you can say, "I know. It's so beautiful out! I love the spring."

In the U.S., small talk is a big part of our culture. We think it's a way to be friendly!

3   **CHECK YOUR UNDERSTANDING**

A **Read the article again. What is the main idea?**

a. The weather is a good topic for small talk.

b. We make small talk with strangers, but only a few topics are OK.

B **Read these sentences. Are they OK for small talk? Write *OK* or *Not OK* next to each one.**

1. Look at all this rain!   OK
2. The food looks so good!   OK
3. What's your address?   Not OK
4. Are you married?   Not OK

5. How much money do you make?   Not OK
6. Great game last night, right?   OK
7. Oh, no! The bus is late again!   OK
8. I have a problem with my foot.   Not OK

Show what you know!

PAIRS. Imagine you are at work. You see a co-worker. You don't know the person. Try to make small talk. Write a short conversation. Role play your conversation.

Listening and Speaking

1 **BEFORE YOU LISTEN**

PAIRS. **Do you know these words? Label the pictures. Use the words in the box.**

boots	ear muffs	gloves	a hat	~~light clothes~~	a raincoat
a scarf	shorts	sunblock	sunglasses	an umbrella	a bottle of water

ON THE AIR **Weather!** Do you have the right clothes, accessories, and supplies?

1. light clothes

2. _____ shorts _____

3. a bottle of water

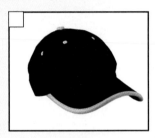

4. _____ a hat _____

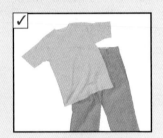

5. _____ sunblock _____

6. _____ sunglasses _____

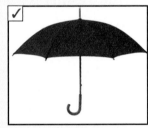

7. _____ a raincoat _____

8. _____ an umbrella _____

9. _____ boots _____

10. _____ gloves _____

11. _____ a scarf _____

12. _____ ear muffs _____

Understand a weather report

Getting Started
10 minutes

1 BEFORE YOU LISTEN

PAIRS. Do you know these words? Label the pictures....

- Read the directions.
- Say each word and ask the class to repeat.
- Read the title: *Weather! Do you have the right clothes, accessories, and supplies?*
- Ask: *What is number 1?* (light clothes) *What about number 2?* (shorts)
- Pair students. Say: *Help each other label the pictures. Cross out the words you use.*
- Walk around and spot-check students' answers. If there are mistakes, point to them and ask students to guess another answer.
- To check answers, ask the class to call out each item as you say its number.

Language Note

Write the vocabulary words on index cards or flashcards and have pairs or groups practice pronouncing the words when flashing the cards to one another.

■■■ **Expansion: Vocabulary Practice for 1**

- For each item, ask if it is an article of clothing, an accessory, or a supply (for example, T: *Are shorts clothes, accessories, or supplies?* Ss: *Clothes.*).

Lesson 8 Understand a weather report

2 LISTEN

A Listen to the weather report...

- Tell students they are going to listen to a weather report. Use the map to point out four cities they will hear: Los Angeles, Atlanta, New York City, Chicago.
- Read the directions.
- Play CD 3, Track 46. Students check the things they hear.
- Students compare answers with a partner.
- Play Track 46 again. Students check their answers.
- To check answers, call out each item on page 180 and ask: *Did you check . . . ?*

B Listen again. Write the temperature...

- Tell students to look at the map. Ask students to describe the weather in Los Angeles, Atlanta, New York City, and Chicago. Tell students to use the words *rainy, cloudy, windy,* and *sunny.*
- Read the note about temperatures.
- Play Track 46 again. Tell students to listen for the temperatures and to write them in the spaces provided on the map.
- Call on students to say the temperatures.

Expansion: Listening Practice for 2B

- Have the class listen to a real national weather report that mentions several cities and their temperatures. Ask students to write the cities and temperatures. Check answers by asking questions about the broadcast (for example, *What is the temperature in Denver?*).

Controlled Practice   20 minutes

3 CONVERSATION

A Look at the picture.... Guess:...

- Read the directions. Ask: *How is the weather?* Students call out answers (cold). Ask: *How do you know the weather is cold?* (Because Marta is wearing a jacket, a hat, and gloves.)

B Listen to the conversation....

- Play CD 3, Track 47. Students listen.
- Ask: *Was your guess correct?*

C Listen and read the conversation....

- Play CD 3, Track 48. Students listen and read along silently. If needed, explain: Really *and* pretty *mean* very, *as in very cold and very windy.* Then resume playing Track 48. Students listen and repeat.
- Say each sentence and ask the class to repeat.

4 PRACTICE

A PAIRS. Practice the conversation. Then make new...

- Pair students and tell them to practice the conversation in Exercise 3C. Tell them to take turns playing each role.
- Then copy the conversation onto the board with blanks. Read through the conversation. When you come to a blank, fill it in with information from the legend on the map (for example, *sunny, windy*).
- Ask a pair of on-level students to practice the conversation in front of the class.
- Pair students and tell them to take turns playing each role and to use weather words from the map to fill in the blanks.
- Call on pairs to perform for the class.

Communicative Practice   20 minutes

B ROLE PLAY. PAIRS. Make your own...

- Play A and, with an above-level student, use information about today's weather. Then pair students. Tell them to take turns playing A and B.
- Call on pairs to role-play for the class.

Extra Practice

Interactive Practice

CD3 T46

2 LISTEN

CD3 T46

A 💿 Listen to the weather report. What clothes, accessories, and supplies do you hear? Check (✓) the pictures on page 180.

CD3 T46

B 💿 Listen again. Write the temperature for each city on the map.

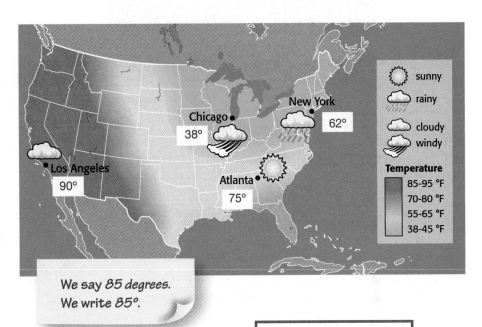

We say *85 degrees.*
We write *85°.*

3 CONVERSATION

A Look at the picture. Marta is ready to go outside.

Guess: How is the weather?

CD3 T47

B 💿 Listen to the conversation. Marta is talking to her husband, Joel.

Was your guess in Exercise A correct?

CD3 T48

C 💿 Listen and read the conversation. Then listen and repeat.

Joel: Are you going out?
Marta: Yes. Why?
Joel: Well, it's really cold, and it's pretty windy.
Marta: That's OK. I have a scarf and gloves!

4 PRACTICE

A PAIRS. Practice the conversation. Then make new conversations. Use different weather words and clothes, accessories, or supplies from page 180.

B ROLE PLAY. PAIRS. Make your own conversations. Talk about today's weather.

Talk about the weather

Grammar

Adverbs of degree: *Very, really, pretty*

	Adverb	Adjective
It's	**very** **really** **pretty**	hot. cold. windy.

	Adverb	Adjective
He's	**very** **really** **pretty**	happy. hungry. tired.

... **Grammar Watch**

Use *very*, *really*, or *pretty* before an adjective to make it stronger.

PRACTICE

A WRITE. Write sentences with the words in parentheses. Use capital letters and periods. Then match the sentences with the pictures.

1. _____It's really cold._____ D
   (really / it's / cold)

2. ____It's pretty hot out here.____ B
   (out here / pretty / it's / hot)

3. _____It's very windy._____ A
   (very / it's / windy)

4. _____It's really foggy._____ C
   (foggy / really / it's)

A

B

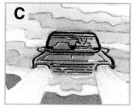
C

D

B PAIRS. Read the conversation. Find the three adjectives in blue. Add the word *very*, *really*, or *pretty* before each adjective. Use each word only once.

A: How's the weather?   Answers will vary but could include:
                                                really
B: It's ^nice.

A: Then let's take a walk!
                              very
B: OK. But I'm ^hungry. Let's eat first.
                          pretty
A: Well, there's a ^good restaurant on Main Street.

B: OK. Let's go there.

C SAME PAIRS. Perform your conversation for the class.

D WRITE. Write sentences in your notebook about today's weather.

Getting Started 5 minutes

- Say: *We're going to study the adverbs of degree:* very, really, *and* pretty. *In the conversation on page 181, Joel used this grammar.*
- Play CD 3, Track 48. Students listen. Write on the board: *Well, it's really cold, and it's pretty windy.* Underline *really* and *pretty*.

Presentation 5 minutes

Adverbs of degree: *Very, really, pretty*

- Copy the grammar charts onto the board or show Transparency 9.5 and cover the exercise.
- Read the Grammar Watch note. Say: *In this lesson, adjectives describe the weather or a person.*
- Read a sentence from the left chart (for example, *It's pretty hot.*). Say the grammatical function of each word (for example, *It's* = *subject + verb*; *pretty* = *adverb*; *hot* = *adjective.*). Ask: *What does it mean?* (the weather)
- Say: Very, really, *and* pretty *mean the same thing. They all make the adjective stronger. Pretty hot is stronger than just* hot.
- Read sentences from the right chart.
- Write a few sentences from the charts on the board with a blank for the adverb (for example, *It's _____ hot.*). Call on students to come up to the front and tell them to write an adverb (*very, really,* or *pretty*). Read the completed sentence out loud and have the class repeat.
- If you are using the transparency, do the exercise with the class.

Controlled Practice 15 minutes

PRACTICE

Ⓐ Write sentences with the words in parentheses...

- Read the directions and the example.
- Ask: *What's the weather like in each picture?*
- Walk around and check that students are matching the correct pictures and correctly unscrambling the sentences.
- Students compare answers with a partner.
- Call on students to say answers.

Ⓑ PAIRS. Read the conversation. Find the three...

- Read the directions.
- Play A and practice the conversation with a student.
- Reread each line and ask students to call out the adjectives (*nice, hungry, good*). Tell students to underline the adjectives to remember them.
- Pair students and tell them to take turns playing A and B. Remind students to add *really, very,* or *pretty* before each adjective and to use each word only once.

    Expansion: Speaking Practice for B

- Ask pairs to add *very, really,* or *pretty* to the conversation in Exercise 3B on page 169.

Ⓒ SAME PAIRS. Perform your conversation...

- Call on pairs to practice their new conversations. Ask students to stress each adverb because they are important words.

    MULTILEVEL INSTRUCTION for C
    Pre-level Partners first rehearse each line of their conversation together to improve rhythm.
    Above-level After pairs practice a few times, ask them to write and perform a new role play about the weather with *really, very,* and *pretty*. The conversation can begin with *How's the weather?*

Communicative Practice 5 minutes

Ⓓ WRITE. Write sentences in your notebook...

- Read the directions. To warm up, ask: *How's the weather today?* Call on a student to say an answer (for example, *It's windy.*) and write it on the board. Encourage students to use adverbs from the grammar charts if appropriate.
- Walk around and read students' sentences. Write any particularly well written ones on the board as models.
- Call on students to read their sentences.

Extra Practice

Interactive Practice   pages 88–89   pages 108–109

1   GRAMMAR

 DICTATION. Listen. Complete...

- Tell students they will listen to a conversation twice. The first time they will just listen. The second time they will listen and fill in the blanks.
- Play CD 3, Track 49. Students listen.
- Play Track 49 again. Students listen and fill in the blanks. If students cannot keep up, pause the CD to allow more time.
- Now tell students they will listen to the conversation again and check their answers. Play Track 49 again.
- To check answers, call on a pair of students to practice the completed conversation. Write answers on the board to allow students to confirm their spelling.
- *Optional:* Pair students and ask them to practice the conversation. Call on pairs to perform the completed conversation for the class.

2   WRITING

STEP 1. PAIRS. Look at the picture....

- Read the directions and the example.
- Tell students to look at each apartment and think about what is happening. Pair students and tell them to take turns saying what is happening in each window as in the example conversation.
- Walk around and check that students are able to discuss what is happening in each window.

MULTILEVEL INSTRUCTION for STEP 1

Pre-level Pair students with a higher-level student who can say what the people are doing in each picture as a model for the pre-level student.

Above-level Pairs can also discuss what the people are not doing in each picture (for example, A: *In Apartment 1, the man is not watching TV.*).

STEP 2. Choose six apartments. Write sentences...

- Ask students to choose six apartments and to write one sentence about each one. Read the example.
- Walk around and check that students are using a capital letter and proper punctuation in each sentence. Also check that students are writing the present continuous form correctly.
- Call on several students to read their sentences out loud.

Expansion: Listening Practice for STEP 2

- Form groups of 5.
- One student silently chooses an apartment and then says what's happening in it (for example, A: *A woman is reading.*). The other students guess the apartment (B: *Is it Apartment 5?* A: *Yes!*).
- Whoever guesses correctly takes over and describes another apartment.

CD-ROM Practice

 Go to the CD-ROM for more practice.

If your students need more practice with the vocabulary, grammar, and competencies in Unit 9, encourage them to review the activities on the CD-ROM. This review can also help students prepare for the final role play on the following Expand page.

Extra Practice

pages 90–91

1 GRAMMAR

CD3 T49

DICTATION. **Listen. Complete the sentences.**

A: Hi, Sandy. It's me, Gail. Are you at work?

B: _____No_____ , I __'m not_____ . I'm home. There's a ____really____ bad snowstorm here. Schools are closed again.

A: Wow! So, what _____are_____ the kids ____doing____ ?

B: Well, Tony and Dino are outside in the snow. They __'re taking_____ pictures.

A: That's nice. What about Maria? _____Is_____ she ____playing____ in the snow?

B: ____No____ , she _____isn't_____ . She __'s playing_____ computer games with my dad.

A: And you?

B: Well, I __'m cooking_____ . And my mom and I ____are doing____ laundry. I'm not at work, but I'm ____pretty____ busy. And I'm ____very____ tired.

2 WRITING

STEP 1. PAIRS. Look at the picture. What are the people doing?

A: *In Apartment 1, the man is sleeping.*
B: *Right. And in Apartment 2 . . . .*

STEP 2. Choose six apartments. Write sentences about the people. Answers will vary but could include:

In Apartment 1, the man is sleeping.

In Apartment 2, the woman is eating.

In Apartment 3, the people are watching TV.

In Apartment 4, the man is cleaning.

In Apartment 8, the girl is writing.

In Apartment 9, the man is checking e-mail.

Go to the CD-ROM for more practice.

3 ACT IT OUT — What do you say?

STEP 1. Review the Lesson 2 conversation between Laura and David (CD 3 Track 36).

STEP 2. PAIRS. You are friends. You are talking on the phone.

Student A: You're on vacation. Choose a place.
- Call your friend at home.
- Talk about the weather.
- Talk about what you are doing.

Student B: You're at home. Your friend calls you.
- Ask "Where are you?"
- Ask about the weather.
- Ask "What are you doing?"
  Continue the conversation.

4 READ AND REACT — Problem-solving

STEP 1. Read about Danielle's problem.

Danielle is at home one morning with her mother and her baby. Her husband is out of the country. He is visiting his sick father. There is a big storm, and there is no electricity. The power is out in the whole neighborhood. Danielle is very worried. There are no candles in the house, and there are no batteries for the flashlight. She doesn't have any canned food.

STEP 2. PAIRS. Talk about it. What is Danielle's problem? What can Danielle do? Here are some ideas.

- She can call a neighbor to ask for supplies.
- She can go get supplies.
- She can wait for the power to come back on.
- She can _____.

5 CONNECT

For your Community-building Activity, go to page 250.
For your Team Project, go to page 270.

Go back to page 165. Which goals can you check off?

3 ACT IT OUT

STEP 1. Review the Lesson 2 conversation between...

- Tell students to review the conversation in Exercise 3B on page 169.
- Tell them to first read the conversation silently and then practice it with a partner.
- Play CD 3, Track 39. Students listen.
- As needed, play Track 39 again to aid comprehension.

STEP 2. PAIRS. You are friends. You are talking...

- Pair students. Read the directions and the guidelines for A and B.
- Tell students playing A to prepare their information first by writing a list with their location, activities, and what the weather is like.
- Tell students playing B to begin the conversation with *Hello?* as on page 169.
- As pairs prepare, tell them to switch roles to practice both positions.
- While pairs are performing, use the scoring rubric on page Txiv to evaluate each student's vocabulary, grammar, fluency, and how well they complete the task. If time permits, ask pairs to switch roles and do a second performance.
- *Optional:* After each pair finishes, discuss the strengths and weaknesses of each performance either in front of the class or privately.

4 READ AND REACT

STEP 1. Read about Danielle's problem.

- Say: *We are going to read about a student's problem, and then we need to think about a solution.*
- Read the directions.
- Read the story while students follow along silently. Pause after each sentence to allow time for students to comprehend. Periodically stop and ask simple *Wh-* questions to check comprehension, for example, *Where is Danielle's husband?* (out of the country) *How does Danielle feel?* (worried).

STEP 2. PAIRS. Talk about it. What is Danielle's...

- Pair students. Ask: *What is Danielle's problem?* (There is a big storm, and there is no electricity.) *What can Danielle do?*
- Read the ideas in the list. Ask: *Which ideas are good?* Call on students to say their opinion about the ideas in the box (for example, S: *I think she can call a neighbor for supplies because neighbors always help.*).
- Pair students. Tell them to think of one new idea not in the box (for example, *She can go to a hotel with her mother and baby.*) and to write it in the blank. Encourage students to think of more than one idea and to write them in their notebooks.
- Call on pairs to say their additional solutions. Write any particularly good ones on the board and ask students if they think it is a good idea, too (*Do you think this is a good idea? Why or why not?*).

▮▮▮ **MULTILEVEL INSTRUCTION for STEP 2**
Pre-level Sit with students, say each idea in the list and ask students to explain why they like or don't like each solution (for example, A: *She can't get supplies because she can't see.*).
Above-level Pairs discuss the problems with each idea (for example, A: *If she goes to get supplies, maybe she will get hurt.*).

5 CONNECT

Turn to page 250 for the Community-building Activity and page 270 for the Team Project. See pages Txi–Txii for general notes about teaching these activities.

Progress Check

Which goals can you check off? Go back to page 165.

Ask students to turn to page 165 and check off the goals they have reached. Call on students to say which goals they will practice outside of class.

10

Around Town

Classroom Materials/Extra Practice

CD 4
Tracks 2–18

T
Transparencies 10.1–10.6
Vocabulary Cards Unit 10

MCA
Unit 10

Workbook
Unit 10

Interactive Practice
Unit 10

Unit Overview

Goals
• See the list of goals on the facing page.

Grammar
• Prepositions of place
• Simple present: Questions with *How, How much,* and *Where*
• Present continuous for future

Pronunciation
• Word stress: /ə/ in unstressed syllables
• Sentence stress: /ə/ in unstressed words

Reading
• Read an article about public libraries

Writing
• Write about weekend plans

Life Skills Writing
• Write directions to your home

Preview

• Set the context of the unit by asking questions about things in the neighborhood around the school—for example, *What is next to our school? What is across the street?* (*Possible answers:* houses/homes, stores)

• Hold up page 185 or show Transparency 10.1. Read the unit title and ask the class to repeat.

• Explain: Around Town *means to go to many places in a town or city.*

• Say: *Look at the picture.* Ask the Preview question: *What do you see?* (A man and a woman are looking at a map.)

• Explain: *In this unit we will learn more about places in the community.*

Unit Goals

• Point to the Unit Goals. Explain that this list shows what the class will be studying in this unit.

• Tell students to read the goals silently.

• Say each goal and ask the class to repeat. Explain unfamiliar vocabulary as needed:

Traffic sign: *Explain by showing the traffic signs on page 192.*

Bus route: *the streets or highways the bus usually travels*

• Tell students to circle one goal that is very important to them. Call on several students to say the goal they circled.

Around Town

Preview

**Look at the picture.
What do you see?**

UNIT GOALS

- ☐ Give locations of places in the community
- ☐ Talk about forms of transportation
- ☐ Read traffic signs
- ☐ Read bus signs and schedules
- ☐ Ask about bus routes and costs
- ☐ Write directions to your home
- ☐ Ask about places in the community
- ☐ Talk about future plans

1 WHAT DO YOU KNOW?

A **CLASS.** Look at the pictures. Which places do you know?

> Number 3 is a post office.

CD4 T2

B Listen and point to the pictures. Then listen and repeat.

2 PRACTICE

A **PAIRS.** Look at the pictures. Student A, choose a place. Say something you do there. Student B, name the place.

A: *I buy stamps there.*
B: *The post office.*
A: *Right.*

B **WORD PLAY.** Look at the list of places on page 187. Which places have the word *station*? Which places have the word *store*? Which place has the word *shop*? Make three lists.

Words with *station*

fire station

police station

gas station

Words with *store*

drugstore

department store

Word with *shop*

coffee shop

C Do you know other words with *station*, *store*, or *shop*? Write other words you know. Answers will vary but could include:

train station   clothing store   flower shop

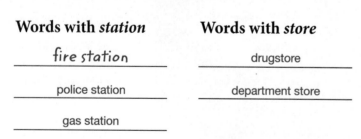

Getting Started   5 minutes

1 WHAT DO YOU KNOW?

A CLASS. Look at the pictures. Which places...

- Show Transparency 10.2 or tell students to cover the list of words on page 187.
- Point to picture 3 and read the example with the class.
- Say: *Look at the other pictures.* Ask: *Which places do you know?* Students call out answers as in the example.
- If a student calls out an incorrect place, change the answer to a question for the class (for example, *Number 14 is a drugstore?*). If nobody can identify the correct place, tell students they will now listen to a CD and practice the names of places.

Presentation   5 minutes

B 🔘 Listen and point to the pictures. Then...

- Read the directions. Play CD 4, Track 2. Pause after number 15 (*a hair salon*).
- To check comprehension, say each job in random order and ask students to point to the appropriate picture.
- Resume playing Track 2. Students listen and repeat.

▪▪▪ **Expansion: Vocabulary Practice for 1B**

- With the class, brainstorm other places that they know and write them on the board (for example, *office building, library, bookstore, restaurant, hospital, store/clothing store, hotel,* and *school*).

Controlled Practice   25 minutes

2 PRACTICE

A PAIRS. Look at the pictures. Student A, choose...

- Brainstorm with the class things you do at each place pictured on pages 186–187. Ask: *What do you do at the _____?* for several places. Write some answers on the board (for example, *I buy medicine at the drugstore.*).

- Read each line in the example and ask the class to repeat. Model correct intonation.
- Play A and practice the conversation with an above-level student. Pair students and tell them to take turns playing A and B.

B WORD PLAY. Look at the list of places on page...

- Read the directions.
- Say: *There are three kinds of places in the list:* stations, stores, *and* shops. Explain: Stores *and* shops *are places where you can buy things. A store is usually larger than a shop. A station is where you receive a service, such as transportation services in a gas station or a train station.*
- Walk around and check that students are writing words under the appropriate heading.
- Call on students to say answers.

Culture Connection

- Say: Coffee shop *can mean different things in different parts of the United States. In some areas, a coffee shop is a small diner (an inexpensive restaurant). In other areas, a coffee shop is just that—a place that serves only coffee.*
- Ask: *Are there words for places that mean different things in different parts of your home country?* Call on students to give examples.
- Say: *Coffee shops are very popular in the United States. Some, like Starbucks, are very trendy, or popular, especially with young people.* Ask: *Are coffee shops popular in your home country, or are there similar places that are popular with teenagers and young adults?*

C Do you know other words with *station, store,* **or...**

- Ask: *Do you know other words with* station, store, *or* shop? Write answers on the board (*some possible answers:* subway station, train station, service station, bookstore, card store, flower shop, ice cream shop). Explain vocabulary as needed.
- Tell students to write in the spaces on the page.

▪▪▪ **Expansion: Vocabulary Practice for 2C**

- In their notebooks, ask students to write the names of actual places (and street names, if possible) of the stations, stores, and shops in their community (for example, *a hair salon: Judy's Styles on Paso Doble Blvd.*). Pair students if individual students have difficulty thinking of names of places.

Learning Strategy: Use your language

- Provide each student with four index cards or tell students to cut up notebook paper into four pieces.

- Read the directions. If you have students with low first-language literacy skills, pair them with more capable peers if possible.

- Walk around as students work. If misspellings occur, tell them to check the list on page 187.

- Say: *You can use your language to help you remember new words in English.* Remind students to use this strategy to remember other new vocabulary.

Community Building

As groups, have students from the same first language teach a few words from their first language for places in the community to the class. Each group can deliver a 3–5 minute presentation where they can first say a word in English (for example, *a fire station*), and then again in their first language before the class repeats it.

Communicative Practice   25 minutes

Show what you know!

STEP 1. GROUPS of 3. **Draw a map of the streets...**

- Read the directions. Draw a sample map on the board of the neighborhood around the school. Include your school. Ask students to call out a few places around the neighborhood on those streets (for example, *a gas station, a supermarket*). Include them on the map.

- Play A and practice the conversation with two students. Then create a new conversation by asking students about places on the map (for example, A: *Is there a post office around here?* B: *Yes . . .*).

- On the board, write: *Is there a _____ around here?* Tell students to ask one another this question when figuring out what to put on the map. Tell students to ask about all the places on page 187.

- Remind students how to use *across from*, *on*, and *next to*. Add a house on both sides of a street on the map on the board. Say that one house is **across from** the other one. Label the street with the houses (for example, *Walnut*) and say: *The houses are on Walnut Street.* Finally, draw another on the same side of the street as one of the houses and say: *This house is **next to** that house.*

- Form groups of 3. Tell students to first talk about what places are near your school and then to begin drawing a map. One student may want to be the official artist, or all three students may draw individual maps.

- Walk around and check that students are discussing what is in the area around the school. Also check that students are labeling all relevant streets and locations on the map.

STEP 2. **Show your map to another group....**

- Read the directions. Ask each group to share their map with another group (for example, G1: *Do you have the supermarket?* G2: *Yes, we do. Do you have the post office?* G1: *No, we don't.*). Tell students to find out what is the same and what is different.

- Tell one student in each group to make a list of the places that are the same and those that are different on the two maps.

- Ask individual groups to explain to the class what is the same and what is different on their map compared to another group's map (G1: *We have the drugstore on our map. The other group does not.*).

Expansion: Vocabulary Practice for STEP 2

- After Step 2, ask each group to add places to their map that other groups have. Groups continue comparing their maps to other groups' maps until all groups have all the sample places on their maps.

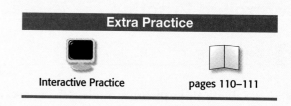

Extra Practice	
Interactive Practice	pages 110–111

3

4

5

6

9

10

24 HOUR ATM

Places in the Community

1. a fire station
2. a police station
3. a post office
4. a bus stop
5. a park
6. a drugstore
7. a gas station
8. a supermarket

9. a bank
10. an ATM
11. a laundromat
12. a parking lot
13. a department store
14. a coffee shop
15. a hair salon

13

14

Show what you know!

STEP 1. GROUPS OF 3. Draw a map of the streets near your school. Talk about the places around your school. Put the places on the map.

A: *Is there a drugstore around here?*
B: *Yes. It's across the street.*
C: *Right. And there's a bank on Fifth Street, next to the supermarket.*

STEP 2. Show your map to another group. Are your maps the same?

Listening and Speaking

1 BEFORE YOU LISTEN

A **READ. Look at the flyer. Read the information.**
Foodsmart, a new supermarket, is opening
on Saturday, October 8.

The supermarket is **near** the library.
It's **around the corner from** the bank.
It's **down the block from** the post office.

B **CLASS. What is near your school? What is
around the corner from your school?
What is down the block from your school?**

2 LISTEN

A **Look at the picture. Berta is asking a
mail carrier for directions.**

Where does she want to go?
Foodsmart

CD4 T3
B   **Listen to the conversation.
Was your answer in Exercise A correct?**

Listen again. Where is the new supermarket?

a.
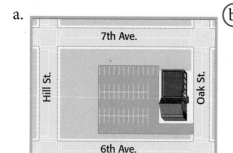

(b.)
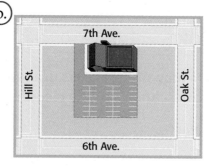

c.
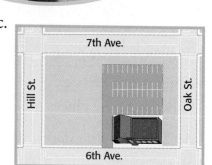

CD4 T4
C   **Listen to the whole conversation. Answer the questions.**

1. Are there many people at the supermarket?   (a.) no   b. yes

2. When is the grand opening?   a. today   (b.) tomorrow

Getting Started   5 minutes

1 BEFORE YOU LISTEN

A READ. Look at the flyer. Read the information.

- Ask: *What is a flyer?* (A flyer is a one-page advertisement.)
- Tell students to look at the Grand Opening picture. Ask: *What does* Grand Opening *mean?* If students don't know, say: *It means that a store is new and its first open day will be special.*
- Ask: *What day is the Grand Opening for the supermarket?* (Saturday, October 8)
- Read the three lines (*The supermarket . . . post office*). Stress the words in bold.
- Redraw the Grand Opening picture on the board. Use arrows to review *near* and to explain *around the corner from* and *down the block from*.

B CLASS. What is near your school? What is around...

- Ask: *What's near our school? What's around the corner from our school? What's down the block?*
- As students answer, draw a simple map and include the places they say. Again, draw arrows to illustrate the prepositional phrases.

▬ Expansion: Writing Practice for 1B

- Form groups of 3. Tell students to imagine that they are preparing to open a store or restaurant and they are planning for a grand opening.
- Ask each group to decide the name for their store or restaurant and to create a flyer that advertises something to attract customers, such as special sales prices on certain items.
- Call on each group to present their flyer.

Presentation   25 minutes

2 LISTEN

A Look at the picture. Berta is asking a mail carrier...

- Read the directions.
- Ask: *Where does she want to go?* (to Foodsmart) Call on students to guess. Write their answers on the board.
- Tell students they will listen for the answer in Exercise B.

B 🖸 Listen to the conversation. Was your...

- Read the directions. Play CD 4, Track 3.
- Explain: *Asking* Sorry? *is a common way to ask someone to repeat something.* Model the rising intonation of *Sorry?* and tell the class to repeat.
- Ask: *Was your answer in Exercise A correct?* Circle the correct answers on the board.

> **Teaching Tip**
>
> *Optional:* Remember that if students need additional support, tell them to read the Audio Script on page 288 as they listen to the conversation.

Listen again. Where is the new supermarket?

- Ask: *Where is the new supermarket?*
- Before playing the CD, ask students to call out the location of the store in each picture (for example, *In picture a, the store is on Oak Street between 6th and 7th Avenues.*).
- As needed, model correct pronunciation of ordinal numbers (*6th, 7th*). As needed, review other ordinals.
- Play Track 3 again. Students circle the letter of the map that shows the correct location.
- Call on students to say the answer (*b. The supermarket is on 7th Avenue between Hill Street and Oak Street*).

C 🖸 Listen to the whole conversation....

- Read the directions. Play CD 4, Track 4.
- Call on students to say the answers.
- Ask: *Why is the conversation funny at the end?* (Because the grand opening is tomorrow, not today.)

▬ Expansion: Speaking Practice for 2C

- Pair students. Student A describes the location of the supermarket in one of the pictures in Exercise 2B while Student B guesses (for example, A: *It's on Oak Street between 7th Avenue and 6th Avenue.* B: *Picture b?* A: *Right.*). Partners switch roles after each try.

3 CONVERSATION

A 💿 **Listen. Then listen and repeat.**

- Read the directions.
- Say: *The word* food *has one syllable.* (Say it and ask the class to repeat.) *The words* around *and* open *have two syllables.* (Say them and ask the class to repeat.)
- Write *around* and *open* on the board and put the circle above the stressed syllables. Read the Pronunciation Watch note.
- Point to the circle above *around* and tell students this symbol means the syllable is stressed.
- Play CD 4, Track 5. Students listen.
- Resume playing Track 5. Students listen and repeat.

Controlled Practice   15 minutes

B 💿 **Listen and read the conversation....**

- Note: This conversation is the same one students heard in Exercise 2B on page 188.
- Read the directions. Say: *Listen for stressed and unstressed syllables.*
- Play CD 4, Track 6. Students listen and read along silently.
- Resume playing Track 6. Students listen and repeat.

4 PRACTICE

A **PAIRS. Practice the conversation. Then make new...**

- Pair students and tell them to practice the conversation in Exercise 3B.
- Then, in Exercise 4A, ask students to look at the information in the map. Say each place and its location and ask the class to repeat. Explain: *The DMV is where you get a driver's license. A courthouse is where you see a judge.*
- Copy the conversation onto the board with blanks and read it. When you come to a blank, fill it in with information from the map and pictures (for example, *the DMV, 6th Ave., Elm St., Pine St.*).
- Ask two on-level students to practice the conversation in front of the class.
- Tell pairs to take turns playing each role and to use the pictures to fill in the blanks.

- Walk around and check that students are pronouncing two-syllable words correctly (*ExCUSE, LOOKing, beTWEEN,* and *SORry*).
- Tell students to stand, mingle, and practice the conversation with several new partners.
- Call on pairs to perform for the class.

▮▮ **MULTILEVEL INSTRUCTION for 4A**
Pre-level Ask students to write choices above each blank (in pencil) and to write in a choice in each blank before practicing.
Above-level After pairs practice a few times, tell them to cover the conversation and practice only by looking at the information in the boxes.

Communicative Practice   15 minutes

B MAKE IT PERSONAL. PAIRS. **Make your own...**

- Read the directions. On the board, write *Place, On,* and *Between.* Call on students to say various places near your school. Write the street where each place is located and the streets it is between (for example, Place: *Supermarket,* On: *Bristol Ave.,* Between: *1st St. and Grand Blvd.*).
- Play A and, with an above-level student, use information from the board and make up a new conversation.
- Pair students and tell them to take turns playing A and B.
- Call on pairs to perform for the class.

▮▮ **Expansion: Speaking Practice for 4B**
- Form groups of 4 or 5. Provide available materials such as construction paper, and ask each group to create a simple map of the neighborhood around the school that includes all major cross streets.
- Ask students to cut out small shapes that represent places in the neighborhood. Students label each piece and place them at various points on the map.
- They use these locations to make conversations about asking for directions. For added challenge and practice, students can move places around.

▮▮▮▮▮▮▮ **Extra Practice** ▮▮▮▮▮▮▮

Interactive Practice

3 CONVERSATION

CD4 T5

A 🔘 **Listen. Then listen and repeat.**

a **round**   **o** pen   to **day**   po **lice**   **sta** tion

CD4 T6

B 🔘 **Listen and read the conversation. Then listen and repeat.**

Berta: Excuse me. Can you help me?
I'm looking for Foodsmart.

Mail Carrier: Sure. It's on Seventh between Hill and Oak.

Berta: Sorry?

Mail Carrier: It's on Seventh Avenue between Hill Street
and Oak Street.

Berta: Thanks.

> **Pronunciation Watch**
>
> In a two-syllable word, one syllable is stressed. The other syllable is unstressed. The vowel in the unstressed syllable often has a very short, quiet sound.

4 PRACTICE

A **PAIRS.** Practice the conversation. Then make new conversations. Use the pictures and map.

A: Excuse me. Can you help me?

I'm looking for _____.
                              (place)

B: Sure. It's on _____ between
                     (Avenue)
_____ and _____.
   (Street)   **(Street)**

A: Sorry?

B: It's on _____ between _____
           (Avenue)   **(Street)**
and _____.
     (Street)

A: Thanks.

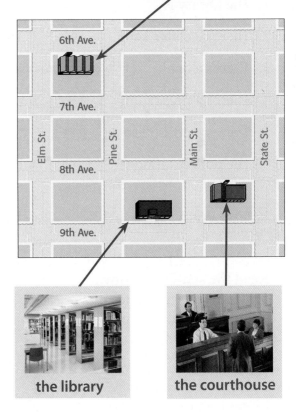

the DMV

the library   the courthouse

B **MAKE IT PERSONAL. PAIRS.** Make your own conversations. Use places and streets near your school.

Grammar

· · · · · **Grammar Watch**

For more prepositions of place, see page 274.

Prepositions of place

The supermarket is	**around**	the corner from the bank.
	down	the block / the street.
	between	Hill and Oak Streets.
	on	the corner of 10th Street and Pine Street.
	near	the library.

PRACTICE

Complete the sentences about the location of some places in Riverside. Use *around*, *down*, *between*, *on*, or *near*.

1. The library is _____*on*_____ the corner of Oak and Elm Streets.

2. There's a coffee shop _____*on*_____ the corner of 9th and Elm Streets.

3. There's a bank _____*around*_____ the corner from the police station.

4. There's a fire station _____*down*_____ the street from the police station.

5. There's a post office _____*near*_____ the library.

6. The police station is _____*on*_____ Park Street _____*between*_____ 9th and 10th Streets.

Show what you know!   Give locations of places in the community

Read the sentences above again. Write the names of the places on the map.

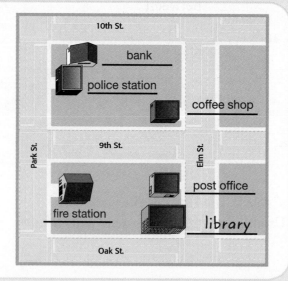

Can you...give locations of places in the community? ☐

Getting Started   5 minutes

- Say: *We're going to study prepositions of place. In the conversation on page 189, the mail carrier used this grammar.*
- Play CD 4, Track 6. Students listen. Write on the board: *It's on Seventh between Hill and Oak.* Underline *on* and *between*.

Presentation   15 minutes

Prepositions of place

- Copy the grammar chart onto the board or show Transparency 10.3 and cover the exercise.
- Remind students: *A preposition helps us understand where something is.* To illustrate, ask about an item in the room: *Where's my dictionary? Oh, it's on the table.* Explain: *The preposition is on.*
- Read sentences from the chart and ask the class to repeat. Draw a simple map of four cross streets and draw in various places to illustrate each preposition.
- On the map you made, draw various configurations to illustrate the meaning of each preposition (for example, draw a box next to a vertical line. Label the box *store*. Label the line *5th St.* Say: *The store is on 5th Street.* Then draw one horizontal line above the "store" and one below it. Give street names to the horizontal lines and say: *The store is between _____ and _____.*).
- Finally, add more streets and more places to your "map" on the board. Point to a random place on the map, prompt the class with a preposition (for example, *near*), and call on individual students to use that preposition to describe the location (for example, *The store is near the restaurant.*).
- If you are using the transparency, do the exercise with the class.

Language Note

To provide students with additional visual references to practice prepositions of place, use Velcro patches, blocks, or any available manipulatives to simulate the position of places in the community. Be sure that your places are clearly labeled so that students can call out where places are relative to one another as you move them around.

Controlled Practice   15 minutes

PRACTICE

Complete the sentences about the location of some...

- Read the directions and the example.
- Tell students to look back at the grammar chart to see patterns for when certain prepositions are used (for example, _____ *the corner* could possibly take *around* or *on*).
- Walk around and check that students are locating places on the map before they write.
- Call on students to say answers.

Show what you know!

Read the sentences above again. Write the names...

- Read the directions.
- Tell students to read their answers from the Practice exercise so they know where each place is located.
- Walk around and check that students are labeling the places accurately.
- Copy the map onto the board.
- If possible, for each answer, call up students to point out where the places are on the map relative to one another (for example, a student points to both the post office and the library to show their close proximity to each other while saying: *5. There's a post office near the library.*).

Progress Check

Can you . . . give locations of places in the community?

Say: *We have practiced giving locations of places in the community. Now, look at the question at the bottom of the page. Can you give locations of places in the community?* Tell students to write a checkmark in the box.

Extra Practice

Interactive Practice   pages 92–93   pages 112–113

Talk about transportation

Getting Started   10 minutes

Culture Connection

• Write *Public Transportation* as a heading on the board. Ask students what kinds of transportation are popular in their country. Write several responses under the heading on the board. Point to them and say: *These are forms of public transportation.*

•Talk about public transportation in your area (for example, *Here in Surf City, people can take the bus to work or school.*). Ask students if they use the public transportation in your area (for example, *Do you take the bus?*).

Presentation   5 minutes

1 TALK ABOUT FORMS OF TRANSPORTATION

 Look at the kinds of transportation....

• Read the first sentence of the directions (*Look at . . .*). Read the note.
• Say each form of transportation and ask the class if they use it (for example, T: *A bus. Do you take the bus?* Ss: *Yes./No.*).
• Play CD 4, Track 7. Students listen and point.
• Resume playing Track 7. Students listen and repeat.
• To wrap up, ask: *What kind of transportation do you usually take?* Call on students to answer.

Controlled Practice   5 minutes

2 PRACTICE

A GROUPS OF 5. **Ask your classmates how they...**

• Ask a few students how they get to school. As needed, prompt them to use *take, drive, ride,* or *walk* in their responses.
• Copy the chart onto the board and include students' responses. If students get to school more than one way, check all possible ways.
• Form groups of 5. Tell students to take turns asking one another, *How do you get to school?* and to write all their group members' names in the chart.

• Say: *If someone in your group uses transportation that is not in the chart, write it where it says* Other.
• Walk around and check that students are using the correct article or possessive and correct verb to describe their mode of transportation.
• As they finish, tell each group: *Choose one person to report to the class.*

■ **Expansion: Speaking Practice for 2A**

• Tell students to find out how often their partner uses certain forms of transportation (for example, A: *How often do you take the bus?* B: *Twice a week.*).

B **Report to the class.**

• Read the directions and the example.
• Call on the designee in each group to report about the students in their group as in the example.
• When students answer, emphasize the *-s* ending in third-person singular verbs and asking them to repeat.

Communicative Practice   15 minutes

C NETWORK. **Who gets to school the same way as...**

• Tell students to stand, mingle, and ask each other: *How do you get to school?* Say: *Stand with students who use the same kind of transportation as you.*
• After students have grouped themselves, say: *Now, what problems do you have?* To get groups started, call on a student in a group who can say a problem (for example, *The bus is sometimes late.*).
• To wrap up, call on a representative from each group to restate the problems discussed (*The bus is sometimes late. Sometimes it's crowded.*).

Progress Check

Can you . . . talk about forms of transportation?
Say: *We have practiced talking about forms of transportation. Now, look at the question at the bottom of the page. Can you talk about forms of transportation?* Tell students to write a checkmark in the box.

Life Skills

1   TALK ABOUT FORMS OF TRANSPORTATION

CD4 T7

Look at the kinds of transportation. Listen and point. Then listen and repeat.

a bus

a subway

a train

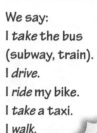

> We say:
> I *take* the bus
> (subway, train).
> I *drive*.
> I *ride* my bike.
> I *take* a taxi.
> I *walk*.

a car

a bike

a taxi

2   PRACTICE

A   GROUPS OF 5. Ask your classmates how they get to school. Write their names in the chart.

A: *How do you get to school?*
B: *I take the bus.*

B   Report to the class.

Susan takes the bus to school.

Names	Take the bus	Take the train	Walk	Drive	Other
Susan	✓				

C   NETWORK. Who gets to school the same way as you?
Find classmates who get to school the same way. Form a group.
Talk about problems with transportation.

Can you...talk about forms of transportation? ☐

PAIRS. Look at the signs. Match the signs to their meanings. Write the meaning under each sign.

Don't turn left.	~~Stop.~~	Two-way traffic. Drive on the right.

☐ **STOP**

☐

☑

1. _Stop._

2. Two-way traffic. Drive on the right.

3. Don't turn left.

Drive slowly. Children often cross the street here.	Drive slowly. Wait for other cars.	Right lane ends ahead. Stay to the left.

☐

☐ YIELD

☑

4. Right lane ends ahead. Stay to the left.

5. Drive slowly. Wait for other cars.

6. Drive slowly. Children often cross the street here.

Be ready to stop for trains.	Don't drive here.	Drive slowly. People often cross the street here.

☑ R X R

☐

☐ DO NOT ENTER

7. Be ready to stop for trains.

8. Drive slowly. People often cross the street here.

9. Don't drive here.

4 PRACTICE

CD4 T8

Listen to the conversations. Which signs are the people talking about? Check (✓) the correct signs above.

Can you...read traffic signs? ☐

Presentation 5 minutes

3 **READ TRAFFIC SIGNS**

PAIRS. Look at the signs. Match the signs to their...

- Read the directions. Point to each sign and ask: *What does this mean?* Elicit responses from as many students as possible.

- Ask students: *Where do you see these signs?* (on the street) Prompt students with the correct preposition to get them started (for example, T: *Where do you see a stop sign? On . . .* Ss: *On a street corner.*).

- Tell students to read each meaning and look quickly at all the signs to choose the correct one.

- Walk around and point to a student's incorrect response and ask him or her to check again.

- To check answers, call on students to say answers. Use the artwork to explain vocabulary as needed (for example, *The two arrows in different directions means* two-way traffic.).

Expansion: Writing Practice for 3

- Pair students and ask them to create a new type of traffic sign that doesn't yet exist (or a sign that isn't pictured on page 192). Ask pairs to draw their sign and write a sentence explaining its meaning.

- Call on pairs to present their sign to the class (*Our sign means drive slowly and turn right.*).

Controlled Practice 40 minutes

4 **PRACTICE**

 Listen to the conversations. Which signs...

- Read the directions. Play CD 4, Track 8. Students listen and check the correct signs in Exercise 3.

- Play Track 8 as many times as necessary.

- Call on students to say which signs are checked.

Progress Check

Can you . . . read traffic signs?

Say: *We have practiced reading traffic signs. Now, look at the question at the bottom of the page. Can you read traffic signs?* Tell students to write a checkmark in the box.

5 READ BUS SIGNS AND SCHEDULES

PAIRS. Student A, look at the buses on the left....

- Read the directions.
- Play A and practice the conversation with a student.
- Pair students and tell them to take turns playing A and B.
- Walk around and check that students are asking and answering questions about their buses. As needed, model correct pronunciation of ordinal numbers (*fourth, second*). As needed, review other ordinals.
- To check answers, play A and ask the class which bus goes to Pine St. and which one goes to 2nd Ave. Then switch roles and ask students which bus goes to Green St. and which one goes to Elm St.

Language Note

If people in your part of the U.S. talk about buses in a different way (for example, *the Number 29* vs. *the 29*), tell students the way that is preferred in your area and to use it in the conversation.

▪ MULTILEVEL INSTRUCTION for 5

Cross-ability The higher-level student plays A first and then partners switch roles.

6 PRACTICE

A Look at the bus schedules. Listen and...

- Read the directions. Explain: *There are three buses: Bus 36, Bus 47, and Bus 51. Each bus stops at four streets.* As you speak, hold up the picture and point.
- To warm up, ask the class to call out the times for a couple of buses listed on the schedule (for example, T: *What time does Bus 36 leave River Road?* Ss: *8:16.*).
- Play CD 4, Track 9. Students listen and fill in the missing items.
- Play Track 9 as many times as necessary.
- To check answers, ask the class: *What times does Bus 36 leave 39th Avenue? What time does Bus 47 leave Park Avenue? What time does Bus 51 leave Pine Street?*

B PAIRS. **Look at the schedules again. Answer...**

- Read the directions and the example.
- Pair students.
- Students compare answers with a partner.

▪ MULTILEVEL INSTRUCTION for 6B

Pre-level Tell students to first circle the answers in the schedule in 6A.

Above-level In addition to comparing answers for each item, students should look at the bus schedule and ask one another: *Which bus leaves at _____?* (for example, A: *Which bus leaves at 8:23?* B: *Bus 47.*).

Teaching Tip

The activities on this page can be enhanced with *realia*, authentic materials from the real world. In this case, bring in copies of a local bus schedule. Pairs can ask each other questions as in Exercise 6B.

Progress Check

Can you . . . read bus signs and schedules?

Say: *We have practiced reading bus signs and schedules. Now, look at the question at the bottom of the page. Can you read bus signs and schedules?* Tell students to write a checkmark in the box.

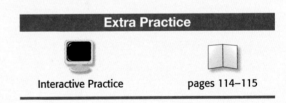

Extra Practice

Interactive Practice pages 114–115

5 READ BUS SIGNS AND SCHEDULES

PAIRS. Student A, look at the buses on the left. Student B, look at the buses on the right. Don't look at your partner's buses. Ask and answer questions. Write the missing numbers on the buses.

A: *Which bus goes to Pine Street?*
B: *The Number 51. Which . . . ?*

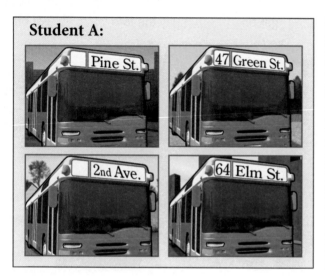

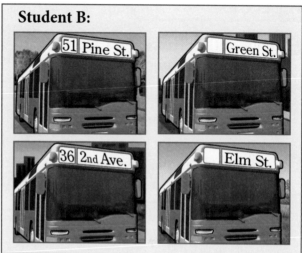

6 PRACTICE

A 🔘 Look at the bus schedules. Listen and fill in the missing times.

GREENVILLE BUS SCHEDULES

BUS 36		BUS 47		BUS 51	
39th Ave.	8:06	39th Ave.	8:14	King Dr.	8:15
River Rd.	8:16	Clay St.	8:23	State St.	8:22
16th Ave.	8:24	Park Ave.	8:34	Oak St.	8:31
2nd Ave.	8:35	Green St.	8:40	Pine St.	8:36

B **PAIRS.** Look at the schedules again. Answer the questions.

1. What time does Bus 36 leave 16th Avenue? ____8:24____

2. What time does Bus 47 leave 39th Avenue? ____8:14____

3. What time does Bus 51 leave State Street? ____8:22____

Can you...read bus signs and schedules? ☐

Ask about bus routes and costs

Listening and Speaking

1 **BEFORE YOU LISTEN**

CLASS. Look at the pictures. Listen to your teacher and repeat.

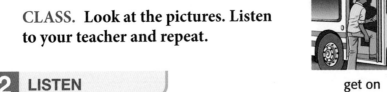

get on   pay the fare   get off

2 **LISTEN**

A Look at the picture. Tara and Matt are going to a concert.

Guess: Why are they talking to the police officer? They need directions.

CD4 T10

B Listen to the conversation. Was your guess in Exercise A correct?

Listen again. Read the sentences. Circle *True* or *False*. Make the false sentences true.

        4
1. They need the Number ~~5~~ bus.   **True**   (**False**)

     off
2. They get ~~on~~ at Second Street.   **True**   (**False**)

3. The fare is $2.00.   (**True**)   **False**

   not
4. It is ˄OK to give the driver a five-dollar bill.   **True**   (**False**)

CD4 T11

C Listen to the second part of the conversation. Tara and Matt are getting off the bus. Answer the questions.

1. Matt asks the woman for _____.
   a. exact change   (b.) directions   c. a map

2. The woman _____ directions to Adams College.
   a. gives   (b.) doesn't give   c. gets

3. The woman says "_____"
   a. It's over there.   b. It's on Second Street.   (c.) Study, study, study!

Getting Started   5 minutes

1   BEFORE YOU LISTEN

CLASS. Look at the pictures. Listen to your teacher...

- Read the directions.
- Say each action and ask the class to repeat.

> **Language Note**
>
> Find opportunities for students to recycle the language of event sequences (for example, *get on, pay the fare,* and *get off*) into their role plays and performances.

Presentation   30 minutes

2   LISTEN

A **Look at the picture.... Guess:...**

- Read the directions.
- Say: *Look at the picture of Tara, Matt, and the police officer.* Ask: *Why are they talking to the police officer?*
- Write students' guesses on the board.

B **Listen to the conversation. Was...**

- Read the directions. Play CD 4, Track 10.
- Explain: Exact change *means you pay the right amount of money.* As needed, write this definition on the board.
- Ask: *Was your guess in Exercise A correct?* Circle the correct answers on the board.

> **Teaching Tip**
>
> *Optional:* Remember that if students need additional support, tell them to read the Audio Script on page 288 as they listen to the conversation.

Listen again. Read the sentences. Circle *True* or...

- Read the directions. Play Track 10 again.
- Call on students to say the answers.

C **Listen to the second part of...**

- Read the directions. Play CD 4, Track 11.
- Ask students why Matt says *Now what?* (They got off the bus and Matt needs more directions.)
- Call on students to say the answers.
- Ask: *Why is the woman funny?* (Because she thinks that Matt is asking about attending the college and not just finding it.)

Expansion: Speaking Practice for 2C

- Ask students to create a role play in which the bus driver argues with the customer about not having exact change:

Customer:	*Here is a five dollar bill.*
Driver:	*I'm sorry, ma'am. I can't take that.*
Customer:	*Why?*
Driver:	*I need exact change.*
Customer:	*But I don't have it!*
Driver:	*You can go to the bank on the corner of Fourth and Pine and get change!*

Lesson 5 Ask about bus routes and costs

3 CONVERSATION

A Listen. Then listen and repeat.

- Read the directions and the Pronunciation Watch note.
- Play CD 4, Track 12. Students listen.
- Resume playing Track 12. Students listen and repeat.
- To wrap up, first say each sentence slowly and pronounce each distinct vowel sound (/du/, not /də/). Then repeat each sentence at regular speaking speed to show students how vowel sounds change when speaking at a normal rate.

Controlled Practice   15 minutes

B Listen and read the conversation. Then...

- Note: This conversation is the same one students heard in Exercise 2B on page 194.
- Say: *Listen for the unstressed words. Optional:* Tell students to also listen for the stressed words.
- Play CD 4, Track 13. Students listen and read along silently.
- Resume playing Track 13. Students listen and repeat.
- Say each sentence and ask students to point out the unstressed words (*do, you, to, the, and, at, from, does*).

4 PRACTICE

A PAIRS. Practice the conversation. Then...

- Pair students and tell them to practice the conversation in Exercise 3B.
- Then, in Exercise 4A, tell students to look at the information in the pictures. Say each place, bus number, and change amount and ask the class to repeat.
- Read the directions.
- Copy the conversation onto the board with blanks. Read through the conversation. When you come to a blank, fill it in with information from the boxes (for example, *Pine Hill Park, Number 15 bus, $1.00*).
- Ask two on-level students to practice the conversation in front of the class.

- Tell pairs to take turns playing each role and to use the pictures to fill in the blanks.
- Walk around and check that students are choosing information from the boxes, pronouncing unstressed words correctly, and stressing important words.
- Tell students to stand, mingle, and practice the conversation with several new partners.
- Call on pairs to perform for the class.

MULTILEVEL INSTRUCTION for 4A

Pre-level Ask students to write choices above each blank (in pencil) and to write in a choice in each blank before practicing.

Above-level After pairs practice a few times, tell them to cover the conversation and practice only by looking at the information in the boxes.

Communicative Practice   10 minutes

B MAKE IT PERSONAL. PAIRS. Make your own...

- Read the directions.
- On the board, write the headings *Places, Transportation,* and *Cost.* Call on students to say different places near the school, modes of transportation (*bus, subway, train*), and typical costs. Write them under the appropriate heading.
- Play A and, with an above-level student, use information from the board to make up a new conversation.
- Pair students and tell them to take turns playing A and B.
- Walk around and check that students are using information from the board or other vocabulary from the unit.
- Call on pairs to perform for the class.

Expansion: Speaking Practice for 4B

- Ask pairs to discuss how often they take the bus (for example, A: *How often do you take the 57?* B: *Oh, sometimes. I usually take the 60.*).

Extra Practice

Interactive Practice

3 CONVERSATION

CD4 T12

A Listen. Then listen and repeat.

How do you get to Adams College?

Take the bus, and get off at Second Street.

CD4 T13

B Listen and read the conversation. Then listen and repeat.

Tara: Excuse me. How do you get to Adams College?
Officer: Take the Number 4 bus, and get off at Second Street.
    It's not far from there.
Tara: Thanks. Oh, and how much does the bus cost?
Officer: Two dollars, but you need exact change.

4 PRACTICE

A PAIRS. Practice the conversation.
Then make new conversations.
Use the pictures.

A: Excuse me. How do you get to
    ?

B: Take the   , and get off at
    Second Street. It's not far from there.

A: Thanks. Oh, and how much does
    the bus cost?

B: , but you need exact
    change.

B MAKE IT PERSONAL. PAIRS.
Make your own conversations.
Ask for directions from school to
places in town.

Pine Hill Park

Green's

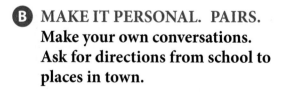

the main
post office

Grammar

Simple present: Questions with *How*, *How much*, and *Where*

How	do you get to Adams College?	Take the Number 4 bus.
How much	does it cost?	$2.00.
Where	do you get off?	Second Street.

····· **Grammar Watch**

Remember: For questions in the simple present, use ***does*** with *he*, *she* and *it*.

1 PRACTICE

A Maria is going shopping. Put the pictures in the correct order (1–4).

B Unscramble the words to ask questions about Maria. Use capital letters and question marks.

1. (Maria / does / shop for food / where) _Where does Maria shop for food?_

2. (get there / how / she / does) _How does she get there?_

3. (does / cost / how much / the milk) _How much does the milk cost?_

4. (she / does / get home / how) _How does she get home?_

5. (the bus / where / she / does / wait for) _Where does she wait for the bus?_

C PAIRS. Ask and answer the questions in Exercise B.

A: *Where does Maria shop for food?*
B: *At Bob's supermarket. How . . . ?*

Getting Started   5 minutes

- Say: *We're going to study simple present questions with* How, How much, *and* Where. *In the conversation on page 195, Tara used this grammar.*
- Play CD 4, Track 13. Students listen. Write *How do you get to Adams College?* on the board. Underline *How do you get.*

Presentation   10 minutes

Simple present: Questions with *How, How much,* and *Where*

- Copy the grammar charts onto the board or show Transparency 10.4 and cover the exercise.
- Explain: *The answer to* How . . . ? *is a way that something happens, in this case a kind of transportation. The answer to* How much . . . ? *is an amount of money. The answer to* Where . . . ? *is a place.*
- Read the questions and answers in the charts and ask the class to repeat.
- Tell students to close their books or cover whatever visual aid allows them to see the chart.
- On the board, write several answers in the same style as the right chart: *Take the Number 5 bus. $3.50. Fourth Street.* Point to each answer on the board and ask students to call out whether *How, How much,* or *Where* is the appropriate question word for this type of answer (for example, T: [Points to $3.50.] Ss: *How much?* T: *Good!*).
- Read the Grammar Watch note.
- Ask students to make up a whole question for each answer on the board (for example, *How much does it cost to get to Adams College?*).
- Call on students to say their questions.
- If you are using the transparency, do the exercise with the class.

Controlled Practice   20 minutes

1 PRACTICE

ⓐ Maria is going shopping. Put the pictures in...

- Point to each picture and ask: *What's happening in this picture?* As students describe each picture, write key vocabulary on the board (for example, *shopping list, grocery bags, milk containers*).

- Use the words on the board to say sentences about what Maria is doing (for example, *Maria has a shopping list. She is at the store.*) and ask the class to repeat.
- Read the directions. Students write the number of each picture in the box.
- Call on students to say answers. Ask: *What is first? What is second? . . .*

ⓑ Unscramble the words to ask questions about...

- Read the directions and the example.
- Write the example item on the board and ask a student to come up and demonstrate how to write the question. Point to it and remind students to write the question word (*How, How much,* or *Where*) first, followed by *do/does,* followed by the subject pronoun (*you/it*).
- Walk around and check that students are using capital letters and punctuation correctly.
- Students compare answers with a partner.
- Call on students to write answers on the board.

ⓒ PAIRS. Ask and answer the questions...

- Read the directions and the example conversation.
- Pair students and tell them to take turns asking and answering questions. Tell students to look carefully at the pictures in Exercise 1A to answer the questions their partner asks.
- *Answers:*
    1. A: *Where does Maria shop for food?*
       B: *At Bob's supermarket.*
    2. A: *How does she get there?*
       B: *She walks.*
    3. A: *How much does the milk cost?*
       B: *$3.00 (a gallon).*
    4. A: *How does she get home?*
       B: *She takes the bus.*
    5. A: *Where does she wait for the bus?*
       B: *On Elm Street.*

▬▬ MULTILEVEL INSTRUCTION for 1C

Pre-level Practice asking and answering questions with students before they work with their partner.

Above-level Ask students to cover their unscrambled answers from Exercise 1B and to ask their partner the questions.

Ask about places in the community

2 PRACTICE

A **Pilar is new in town. She is asking a woman for...**

- Tell students to look at the picture. Read the directions and the example.
- Remind students to use a capital letter when starting a sentence.
- Walk around and check that students are properly forming questions. If students have trouble with *do/does*, refer them to the grammar chart on page 196.

B 🔘 **Listen and check your answers.**

- Play CD 4, Track 14. Students listen and check answers.
- Play Track 14 again to aid comprehension.
- Call on students to write the questions on the board. Correct as needed.
- *Optional:* Play Track 14 again, pausing after each line to allow students to repeat. Students then practice the conversation in pairs. Call on pairs to perform for the class.

Communicative Practice   25 minutes

3 LIFE SKILLS WRITING

Turn to page 262 and ask students to complete the note giving directions to their home. See pages Txi–Txii for general notes about the Life Skills Writing activities.

Show what you know!

STEP 1. Look at the pictures. Where do you buy...

- Read the directions.
- Say each thing out loud and ask: *Where do you buy _____?* As needed, review store vocabulary on page 187 (*drugstore*, *supermarket*, and *department store*).
- Call on students to name their favorite stores in the above categories. Write them on the board.
- Walk around and check that students are writing answers in a format similar to the example.

STEP 2. PAIRS. Talk about your answers in Step 1.

- Read the directions. Play B and practice the example conversation with a student. Make up a price for the milk (for example, B: *$2.99.*).
- Pair students and tell them to take turns playing A and B.
- Walk around and check that students are interacting as in the example conversation. If students have difficulty, prompt them by asking *Where do you buy _____?* and practicing with them until they can comfortably say where they buy the item and how much it costs.

▨ **MULTILEVEL INSTRUCTION for STEP 2**

Pre-level For an additional prompt, ask students to write the price of the items in Step 1 (for example, *milk—DVS Drugstore—$2.99*).

Above-level Ask students to expand the conversation to include the question *How do you get there?*

▨ **Expansion: Speaking Practice for STEP 2**

- Bring in ads from local drugstores and supermarkets.
- Form groups of 4 and give each group a flyer or ad. Each group then breaks up into pairs. Each pair uses the flyer to practice the conversation in Step 2.

Progress Check

Can you . . . ask about places in the community?

Say: *We have practiced asking about places in the community. Now, look at the question at the bottom of the page. Can you ask about places in the community?* Tell students to write a checkmark in the box.

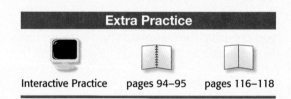

Extra Practice		
Interactive Practice	pages 94–95	pages 116–118

A Pilar is new in town. She is asking a woman for directions. Complete the questions with *How, How much,* or *Where.* Use the words in parentheses and add *do* or *does.*

Pilar: Excuse me. __How do you get to__ Pine Hill Park?
　　　　　　　　　1. (you / get to)

Woman: Take the Number 4 train.

Pilar: OK. ___Where do you get___ the train?
　　　　　　2. (you / get)

Woman: The train station is down the block. Do you see it?

Pilar: Oh, yes. And ___where do you buy___ a ticket?
　　　　　　　　　3. (you / buy)

Woman: In the station.

Pilar: ___How much does it cost___ ?
　　　　4. (it / cost)

Woman: $2.00.

Pilar: OK. Sorry, one more question. ___Where do you get off___ for the park?
　　　　　　　　　　　5. (you / get off)

Woman: Park Avenue. There's a big sign for the park. You can't miss it.

CD4 T14
B Listen and check your answers.

---

3 LIFE SKILLS WRITING Write directions to your home. See page 262.

Show what you know! Ask about places in the community

STEP 1. Look at the pictures. Where do you buy these things? Write the places.

milk— DVS Drugstore _____

_____ _____

STEP 2. PAIRS. Talk about your answers in Step 1.

A: *Where do you buy milk?*
B: *At DVS Drugstore.*
A: *Oh? How much does it cost there?*

chocolate

tissues

milk　　pens

Can you...ask about places in the community? ☐

Read about public libraries

Reading

1 **BEFORE YOU READ**

Match the sentences and pictures. Write one sentence from the box under each picture.

> Mr. Park goes to the library with his children every Saturday.
> The librarian scans the books.
> They bring the books to the librarian at the front desk.
> They choose books to **borrow**.
> They **return** the books by the **due date**.
> They give the librarian their **library cards**.

1. _Mr. Park goes to the library with_
   his children every Saturday.

2. They choose books to borrow.
   _____

3. They bring the books to the librarian at

   the front desk.

4. They give the librarian their library cards.
   _____

5. The librarian scans the books.
   _____

6. They return the books by the due date.
   _____

Lesson 7 Read about public libraries

Getting Started   20 minutes

Culture Connection

• Ask: *Do you go to the library? What about in your home country?*

• Say: *In the U.S., many people like to go to the library. They can find information, study, and learn many things. Library cards are free.*

• If possible, bring in information to share with your class about getting a library card from the local library.

1 BEFORE YOU READ

Match the sentences and pictures. Write one...

• Read the directions and the example. Explain: *Look at the picture. You can see that Mr. Park is going to the library with his children.*

• Read each sentence in the box and ask the class to repeat.

• Tell students to look carefully at each picture and to find a sentence in the box that shows the action in the picture. Walk around and help as needed.

• Call on students to say answers.

Teaching Tip

Act out the event sequence with a group of students. Then ask groups to create their own role plays for the event sequence.

Expansion: Writing and Vocabulary Practice for 1

• Pair students. Ask them to write alternative sentences to describe the action in each picture (for example, for picture 1, *Mr. Park likes to visit the library with his kids.*).

• Call on students to write their sentences on the board and say them to the class. Correct as needed.

Lesson 7 Read about public libraries

Presentation
15 minutes

2 READ

 Listen. Read the article.

- Tell students to look at the picture. Ask: *What place is this?* (a public library) *What are the children doing?* (listening to a story)

- Say: *I want you to predict or guess what the article is about. Look at the picture and the title. What is this article about?* (*Possible answer:* things to do at the library) Call on students to guess and write different guesses on the board.

- Say: *Before you read an article, try to guess what it is about by looking at the title and picture(s). They can help you understand the article before you start reading.*

- Play CD 4, Track 15. Students listen and read along silently.

- *Optional:* Pause the CD after each paragraph and ask the following questions:

    First paragraph: *Can you borrow CDs or DVDs from the library?*

    Second paragraph: *Can you do homework at the library?*

    Third paragraph: *Can children use the library?*

    Fourth paragraph: *Can the library help you find a job?*

    Fifth paragraph: *How can you find out more?*

Controlled Practice
10 minutes

3 CHECK YOUR UNDERSTANDING

Read the article again. Answer the questions. Check...

- Read the directions. Say: *You can check more than one item.*

- As needed, explain: Look up *means to search or to find.*

- Walk around and help as needed. Tell students to check their answers by looking back at the article.

- Call on students to say answers. Also, ask students if there are other things they can do at the library. On the board, write any additional things that students say or that you can think of that are applicable in your area (for example, *join a reading club, get tutoring, get income tax forms*).

Communicative Practice
15 minutes

Show what you know!

Go to your public library. Get a library card. What...

- Read the directions, including the questions. Call on students to answer the questions (for example, *I like to read books with my child. I can study at the library and practice English.*).

- On the board, draw a simple map of the area around your school and include the closest library. While drawing the map, call on students to tell you where various places and streets are located (for example, *There's a library on Broadway and Harbor. It's across the street from a fast-food restaurant.*).

- Ask students to copy the map into their notebooks. If possible, visit the library's website to obtain the hours of operation and what students will need to obtain a library card. Discuss what students will need.

- *Optional:* Ask students to go to the library, check out a book, and bring it to class. The book can be for themselves or for their children. As an incentive, reward students who follow through with this by giving them time to read in class.

▬ Expansion: Writing and Speaking Practice

- Form groups of 4. Ask each group to make a list (or a poster, if possible) of things *not* to do at the library (for example, *Don't eat. Don't talk on your cell phone. Don't listen to loud music.*).

- Ask each group to present their list to the class.

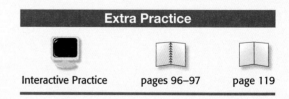

Extra Practice		
Interactive Practice	pages 96–97	page 119

CD4 T15

🔊 **Listen. Read the article.**

At the Library

Do you go to your public library? What can you do there? You can borrow books and magazines or read newspapers. What other things can you do at the library?

Story time at the Greenville Public Library

Most libraries have CDs and DVDs. Do you want to see a movie? Borrow it from the library. Do you like a song on the radio? Borrow the CD.

Most libraries also have computers. You can look up information on the Internet or check e-mail. You can also do your homework.

Many libraries have activities for children. Librarians read stories to young children. And there are often after-school programs or summer programs for older children.

The library can help you find a job. Libraries often have information about jobs in the area. And some libraries have classes to help you get a job or start a small business.

These are just some of the things you can do at the library. Go to your public library or check their website to find out more.

What's the best thing about the library? Everything there is free!

3 CHECK YOUR UNDERSTANDING

Read the article again. Answer the questions. Check (✓) all the correct answers.

1. What can you borrow from the library?

   ☑ books   ☑ CDs   ☐ computers

   ☑ DVDs   ☑ magazines   ☐ radios

2. What can you do at the library?

   ☐ see a movie   ☑ look up information online

   ☑ listen to children's stories   ☑ find job information

Show what you know!

Go to your public library. Get a library card. What activities do you want to do at your library? How can your library help you learn English?

Talk about weekend plans

Listening and Speaking

1 BEFORE YOU LISTEN

CLASS. Look at the pictures. Do you go to events like these in your community?

Where do you get information about events in your community? For example, do you look in the newspaper? Do you watch TV?

grand opening

concert

2 LISTEN

CD4 T16

(A)  Look at the Greenville Weekend Community Schedule. Listen to the radio show and complete the information.

baseball game

yard sale

ON THE AIR

The Greenville Weekend Community Schedule

Grand Opening

Place: Foodsmart

Day: _____Saturday, October 8_____

Time: _____3:00 P.M._____

Concert

Place: Greenville Community College

Day: _____Saturday (night)_____

Time: _____8:00 P.M._____

Baseball Game

Place: Greenville _____Park_____

Day: _____Sunday (afternoon)_____

Time: 1:00 P.M.

Yard Sale

Place: the Community Center across

from the _____fire_____ station

Day: _____Sunday_____

Time: 10:00 A.M. to _____4:00 P.M._____

Getting Started 5 minutes

1 BEFORE YOU LISTEN

CLASS. Look at the pictures. Do you go to events...

- Point to each picture and ask: *What is a concert?* (It's musicians playing music or singing for other people.) *What is a yard sale?* (An event where people sell their old things in their front yard.)
- Ask the questions.
- Write students' responses on the board. *Some possible answers:* TV, radio, the Internet, friends, flyers, posters, billboards (a large sign above a street or on a building), and classified ads.

Culture Connection

- Ask: *Do you have events like these in your home country? Are they different from the events in the United States? How are they different?*

Presentation 20 minutes

2 LISTEN

A **Look at the Greenville Weekend...**

- Read the directions. Say: *There are four events. What are they?* (grand opening for Foodsmart, a baseball game, a concert, and a yard sale)

- Say: *For each event, you need to know the place, the day, and the time. Listen for the missing information.*
- Play CD 4, Track 16. Students listen and complete the missing information.
- Play Track 16 again to allow students to check their answers. As needed, explain unfamiliar expressions, such as *It doesn't cost just to look.* To explain, say: *This means that you don't have to pay to look.*
- Students compare answers with a partner by asking: *What day is the Foodsmart Supermarket grand opening? What time is the . . . ?*
- To wrap up, ask several students the same questions about place, day, and time.

Expansion: Speaking Practice for 2A

- Form like-ability pairs and tell them to take turns asking each other: *What time is the _____?* and *Where is the _____?* As an added challenge, ask above-level students to make up information about which bus to take and on what street to catch it.

B 💿 **Listen again. Which events are free?...**

- Read the directions. Play Track 16 again. Students listen and check the correct answers.
- Ask: *Which events are free?* Call on students to answer.

C **CLASS. Are there free events in your...**

- Read the directions and the example. Call on students and write responses on the board.
- If possible, bring in a free local magazine (or newspaper insert) that lists free community activities. Pass it around to students or use it for ideas of activities to list on the board. Tell students where they can pick up free community magazines.

Controlled Practice   20 minutes

3 CONVERSATION

A **Look at the picture.... Guess:...**

- Read the directions. Ask: *What are they talking about?* (what they are doing this weekend / going to a concert)
- Call on students to guess. Write their guesses on the board.

B 💿 **Listen to the conversation. Was your...**

- Read the directions. Play CD 4, Track 17.
- Ask: *Was your guess in Exercise A correct?* Circle the correct answers on the board.

> **Teaching Tip**
>
> *Optional:* If students need additional support, tell them to read the conversation in Exercise 3C.

C 💿 **Listen and read the conversation....**

- Read the Pronunciation Watch note. Ask: *Why does* want to *sound like* wanna *in conversation?* (Because the unstressed *to* combines with *want*.)
- Read the directions. Play CD 4, Track 18. Students listen and read along silently.
- Resume playing Track 18. Students listen and repeat.
- Check that students are pronouncing *want to* as *wanna*.

4 PRACTICE

A 💿 **PAIRS. Practice the conversation...**

- Pair students and tell them to practice the conversation in Exercise 3C.
- Tell students to look at the events in the Greenville Weekend Community Schedule on page 200.
- Copy the conversation onto the board with blanks. Read through the conversation. When you come to a blank, fill it in with an event and a place from page 200 (for example, *grand opening, Foodsmart*).
- Ask two on-level students to practice the conversation in front of the class.
- Tell pairs to take turns playing each role and to use the information from the Greenville Weekend Community Schedule on page 200.
- Walk around and check that students are pronouncing *wanna* correctly.
- Tell students to stand, mingle, and practice the conversation with several new partners.
- Call on pairs to perform for the class.

Communicative Practice   15 minutes

B **MAKE IT PERSONAL. PAIRS. Make your...**

- Play A and, with an above-level student, use information about events in your community.
- On the board, write several events based on what students call out or you find in a community guide (see Exercise 2C). Tell students they can use these events in their conversations or they can use other events they know about.
- Pair students and tell them to take turns playing A and B.
- Call on pairs to perform for the class.

■ **Expansion: Speaking Practice for 4B**

- Ask pairs to continue their conversations to include when the event occurs, how much it costs, and how to get there.

Extra Practice

Interactive Practice

B Listen again. Which events are free? Check (✓) all the correct answers.

☑ the grand opening   ☑ the baseball game

☐ the concert   ☑ the yard sale

C CLASS. Are there free events in your community? What are some examples?

> There are free movies at the library.

3 CONVERSATION

A Look at the picture. Sufia and Viet are classmates.

Guess: What are they talking about?
Weekend plans

B Listen to the conversation. Was your guess in Exercise A correct?

C Listen and read the conversation. Then listen and repeat.

Viet: What are you doing this weekend?

Sufia: I'm going to **a concert**.

Viet: Oh? Where's **the concert**?

Sufia: At **the community college**. Do you want to go?

Viet: Sounds great.

Pronunciation Watch

In informal conversation, *want to* often sounds like "wanna."

4 PRACTICE

A PAIRS. Practice the conversation. Then make new conversations. Use the events in the Greenville Weekend Community Schedule on page 200.

B MAKE IT PERSONAL. PAIRS. Make your own conversations. Give true information.

Talk about future plans

Grammar

Present continuous for future

What	**are** you **doing**	next weekend?	**I'm going**		to a concert.
How	**are** you **getting**	there?	**I'm taking**		the bus.
Who	**are** you **going**	with?	My sister. She**'s meeting**		me there.

PRACTICE

A Ms. Reed's students are talking about their activities. Read each sentence.
Is the person talking about the present or the future? Check (✓) the correct box.

		Present	Future
1. **Ernesto:**	I'm working next weekend.	☐	✓
2. **Mei-Yu:**	I'm doing my English homework now.	✓	☐
3. **Carlos:**	Are you coming with us to the movie tomorrow?	☐	✓
4. **Assefa:**	When are you visiting your grandparents?	☐	✓
5. **Dora:**	I'm sorry, but I can't talk now. I'm cooking dinner.	✓	☐

B Complete the conversations. Use the present continuous
form of the verbs in parentheses.

1. **A:** What ____are____ you ____doing____ tomorrow?
   (do)

   B: I __'m meeting_____ my friends at the mall.
   (meet)

   A: How ____are____ you ____getting____ there?
   (get)

   B: I __'m taking_____ the bus.
   (take)

2. **A:** Where ____is____ Sam ____going____ this weekend?
   (go)

   B: He __'s going_____ to Riverside for a concert.
   (go)

3. **A:** When ____are____ your children ____visiting____ you?
   (visit)

   B: They __'re coming_____ for dinner next Sunday.
   (come)

Getting Started 5 minutes

- Say: *We're going to study present continuous for future plans. In the conversation on page 201, Viet and Sufia used this grammar.*
- Play CD 4, Track 18. Students listen. Write on the board: *What are you doing this weekend?* and *I'm going to a concert.* Underline *are you doing* and *I'm going.*

Presentation 10 minutes

Present continuous for future

- Copy the grammar charts onto the board or show Transparency 10.5 and cover the exercise.
- Read the questions and answers in the charts. Tell the class that these questions are about what is happening tomorrow and not what is happening right now.
- Ask: *I'm is a contraction for what two words?* (*I + am*) Remind students that contractions are usually used in conversation.
- Ask students to close their books. Remove or cover any visual aids that show the charts.
- Copy the questions onto the board but leave blanks for the words in bold (the verbs), for example, *What _____ you _____ tomorrow?* Call on students to complete the sentences.
- Call on students to write responses in the blanks. Correct as needed.
- If you are using the transparency, do the exercise with the class.

Controlled Practice 15 minutes

> **PRACTICE**

A Ms. Reed's students are talking about their...

- Read the directions and the example. Ask: *How do you know Ernesto is talking about the future?* (Because he says *next weekend.*)
- Say: *Check only one box for each line.*
- Walk around and help as needed. If students make a mistake, point to any clues in the question that reveal if the person is talking about the present or the future (for example, in item 2, the answer is *Present* because the question has *now* in it).
- Students compare answers with a partner.
- To check answers, ask the class to call out *present* or *future* for each item.

B Complete the conversations. Use the present...

- Read the directions and the example.
- Do the example with the class by copying it onto the board and calling on students to tell you what to write.
- Walk around and check that students are writing the correct form of *be* and are adding *-ing* to the verb in parentheses.
- Students compare answers with a partner.
- Read the conversations and call on individual students to say answers.
- *Optional:* Pair students and ask them to practice the conversations. Call on pairs to perform the completed conversations for the class.

Extra Practice

Interactive Practice   pages 98–99   pages 120–121

1 GRAMMAR

Complete the conversation. Underline the correct...

- Tell students to refer back to the grammar charts on pages 190 (prepositions of place), 196 (simple present questions), and 202 (present continuous for future).
- Read the example. Ask: *Why is* present continuous *the answer?* (Because the question is about the future.) Do the next item with the class. Ask: *Why is* simple present *the answer?* (Because B goes every Friday.)
- Walk around and help as needed.
- Students compare answers with a partner.
- Call on students to say answers. Correct as needed.
- *Optional:* Pair students and ask them to practice the conversation. Call on pairs to perform the completed conversation for the class.

2 WRITING

STEP 1. Think about your weekend plans. Fill in...

- Read the directions and the example.
- Copy the chart onto the board. Fill in the "You" rows with made-up information.
- Explain: *Fill in only the "You" rows.*
- Walk around and help as needed. If students have trouble thinking of activities to write, refer them to the activities on page 200.

STEP 2. PAIRS. Talk about your plans. Complete...

- Practice the example conversation with a student. Fill in the "Your Partner" rows on the board.
- Walk around and check that students are writing their partner's responses in the proper places in the chart.

STEP 3. Write two sentences about your plans and...

- Read the directions and the example sentence. On the board, write two sentences about your plans and two sentences about your partner's plans from the information in the chart on the board.
- Tell students that their sentences should include *when, what,* and *who* for each plan.
- Walk around and help as needed. Check students' use of capitalization and punctuation and correct as needed.

Expansion: Writing Practice for STEP 3

- Students change all their sentences in future tense to simple present (for example, *I am going to a concert on Saturday afternoon. ➤ I go to concerts on Saturday afternoons.*).

Expansion: Speaking Practice for STEP 3

- Pair students. Students make up a conversation using both their simple present and future tense sentences from the above Expansion and Step 3 (for example, A: *What are you doing this weekend?* B: *I'm going to a concert in the park.* A: *Do you like concerts?* B: *Oh, yes. I always go to concerts in the park on Saturdays. What about you?*).

CD-ROM Practice

 Go to the CD-ROM for more practice.

If your students need more practice with the vocabulary, grammar, and competencies in Unit 10, encourage them to review the activities on the CD-ROM. This review can also help students prepare for the final role play on the following Expand page.

Extra Practice
pages 100–101

1 GRAMMAR

Complete the conversation. Underline the correct words.

A: What **do you do** / <u>**are you doing**</u> tomorrow?

B: I **go** / <u>**'m going**</u> to the library in Greenville. I **go** / **'m going** every Friday.

A: Every Friday! <u>**How**</u> / **Where** do you get there?

B: Well, I always <u>**take**</u> / **am taking** the Number 2 bus. The library is on Oak **near** / <u>**between**</u> 7th and 8th Avenues. The bus stops <u>**down**</u> / **near** the block from the library.

A: Oh, really? **What** / <u>**When**</u> are you going?

B: At noon. Why?

A: I **go** / <u>**'m going**</u> to the DMV. It's right <u>**around**</u> / **between** the corner from the library. We can go together!

2 WRITING

STEP 1. Think about your weekend plans. Fill in the "You" rows. Write two activities.

	What?	When?	Who?
You	concert	Sat. afternoon	me, Amy, Joe
Your Partner			

STEP 2. PAIRS. Talk about your plans. Complete the chart.

Laura: *What are you doing this weekend?*
Antonio: *I'm going to a concert in the park.*
Laura: *Oh. When . . .*

STEP 3. Write two sentences about your plans and two sentences about your partner's plans.

I am going to a concert on Saturday afternoon. I am going with . . .

Go to the CD-ROM for more practice.

Show what you know!

3 ACT IT OUT — What do you say?

STEP 1. Review the Lessons 2 and 5 conversations (CD 4 Tracks 3 and 10).

STEP 2. PAIRS. Student A, you are a visitor to Riverside. Student B, you live in Riverside.

Student A: You need directions to a place.
- Look at the pictures. Choose a place.
- Ask where the place is.
- Ask how to get to the place.

Student B: Help the visitor.
- Find the place on the map.
- Say where the place is.
- Give the visitor directions.

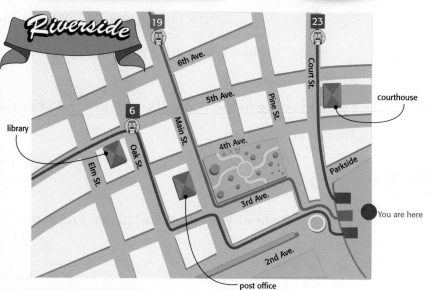

4 READ AND REACT — Problem-solving

STEP 1. Read about Minh's problem.

Minh takes the bus to work every day. He often reads the newspaper on the bus. Today, he gets off the bus at his usual stop. He gets to work and puts his coat away. But something is wrong. Where are his reading glasses? Are they still on the bus? He is worried. He can work without his glasses, but they are expensive. He doesn't want to lose them.

STEP 2. PAIRS. Talk about it. What is Minh's problem? What can Minh do? Here are some ideas.

- He can call the bus company's Lost and Found department.
- He can buy new glasses.
- He can ask the bus driver the next day.
- He can _____.

5 CONNECT

For your Goal-setting Activity, go to page 251.
For your Team Project, go to page 271.

Which goals can you check off? Go back to page 185.

Show what you know!

3 ACT IT OUT

STEP 1. Review the Lessons 2 and 5 conversations...

- Tell students to review the conversations in Exercise 3B on page 189 and Exercise 3B on page 195.
- Tell them to read the conversations silently and then practice them with a partner.
- Play CD 4, Tracks 6 and 13. Students listen.
- As needed, play Tracks 6 and 13 again to aid comprehension.

STEP 2. PAIRS. Student A, you are a visitor to...

- Point to the pictures and say each place and ask the class to repeat.
- Pair students. Read the directions and the guidelines for A and B. Ask the class where the places are located. Call on a couple of students to say answers (for example, *The library is on 5th Avenue between Oak Street and Elm Street.*).
- Tell pairs to use the "You are here" point on the map as the starting point.
- Walk around and check that A is asking appropriate questions and B is using prepositions clearly to give accurate directions from the chosen starting point.
- Call on pairs to perform for the class.
- While pairs are performing, use the scoring rubric on page Txiv to evaluate each student's vocabulary, grammar, fluency, and how well they complete the task.
- *Optional:* After each pair finishes, discuss the strengths and weaknesses of each performance either in front of the class or privately.

4 READ AND REACT

STEP 1. Read about Minh's problem.

- Say: *We are going to read about a student's problem, and then we need to think about a solution.*
- Read the directions.
- Read the story while students follow along silently. Pause after each sentence to allow time for students to comprehend. Periodically stop and ask simple *Wh-* questions to check comprehension (for example, T: *How often does Minh take the bus?* S: *Every day.* T: *Can he find his glasses?* S: *No.*).

STEP 2. PAIRS. Talk about it. What is Minh's...

- Pair students. Ask: *What is Minh's problem?* (He can't find his glasses.) *What can Minh do?*
- Read the list of ideas. Ask: *Which ideas are good?* Call on students to say their opinion about the ideas in the box (for example, S: *I think he can buy new glasses because they are cheap at the drugstore.*).
- Pair students. Tell them to think of one new idea not in the box (for example, *He can look for his glasses at home.*) and to write it in the blank. Encourage students to think of more than one idea and to write them in their notebooks.
- Call on pairs to say their additional solutions. Write any particularly good ones on the board and ask students if they think it is a good idea, too (*Do you think this is a good idea? Why or why not?*).

MULTILEVEL INSTRUCTION for STEP 2

Pre-level Sit with students, say each idea in the list, and ask students to explain why they like or don't like each solution (for example, A: *He can't call the Lost and Found department. They're closed.*).

Above-level Pairs discuss the problems with each idea (for example, A: *If he calls Lost and Found, maybe they won't know because the glasses are still on the bus.*).

5 CONNECT

Turn to page 251 for the Goal-setting Activity and page 271 for guidelines for the Team Project. See pages Txi–Txii for general notes about teaching these activities.

Progress Check

Which goals can you check off? Go back to page 185.

Ask students to turn to page 185 and check off any remaining goals they have reached. Call on students to say which goals they will practice outside of class.

11 Health Matters

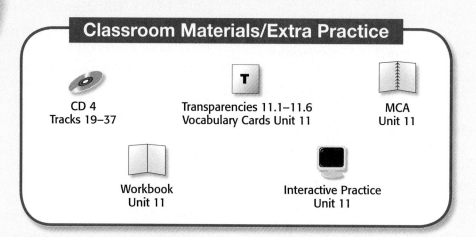

Classroom Materials/Extra Practice

CD 4
Tracks 19–37

Transparencies 11.1–11.6
Vocabulary Cards Unit 11

MCA
Unit 11

Workbook
Unit 11

Interactive Practice
Unit 11

Unit Overview

Goals

- See the list of goals on the facing page.

Grammar

- Review: Simple present: Information and *Yes/no* questions and answers
- Past of *be:* Statements
- *Should/Shouldn't*

Pronunciation

- Reduced forms *wasn't/weren't*

Reading

- Read an article about walking for your health

Writing

- Write suggestions for health problems

Life Skills Writing

- Complete a medical history form

Preview

- Set the context of the unit by taking the roll and asking questions about students who are absent (*Where is Maria? Is she sick? Is she at the doctor?*). Follow-up questions (or if no one is absent): *Do you speak English when you go to the doctor?* (Yes./No.) *How often?* (always/sometimes/never)

- Hold up page 205 or show Transparency 11.1. Read the unit title and ask the class to repeat.

- Say: *The word* matter *can be a verb; it means to be important. And it can be a noun; it means topics. Therefore, the title* Health Matters *means two things. It means that health is important, and it means topics about health.* Ask: *What do you think this unit is about?* (important topics about health)

- Say: *Look at the picture.* Ask the Preview question: *What do you see?* (doctor, patient, scale)

- Ask: *What is the doctor doing?* On the board, write: *He is weighing the patient.* Remind students that this is present continuous.

GOALS

- Point to the Unit Goals. Explain that this list shows what the class will be studying in this unit.

- Tell students to read the goals silently.

- Say each goal and ask the class to repeat. Explain unfamiliar vocabulary as needed:

    Absence: *when you cannot go to work or school*

- Tell students to circle one goal that is very important to them. Call on several students to say the goal they circled.

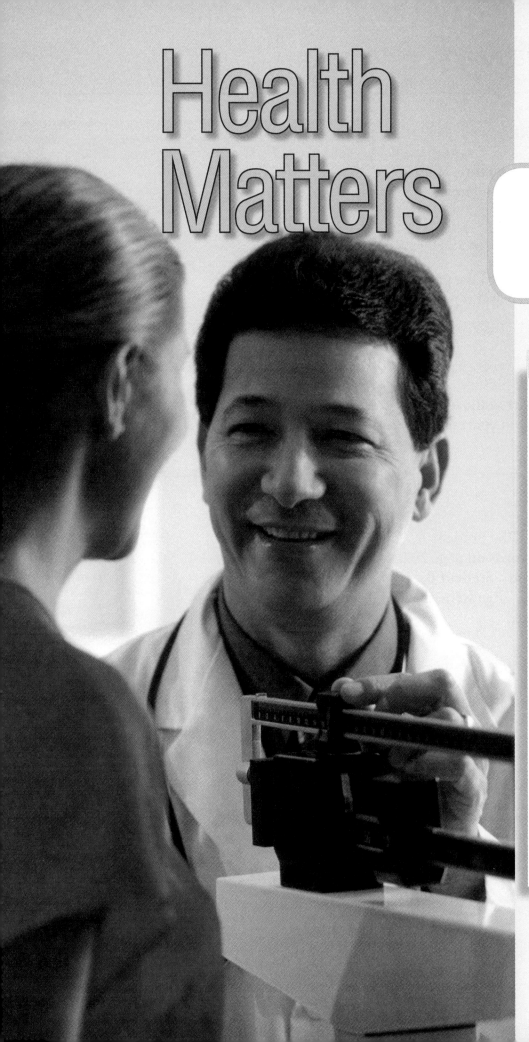

Health Matters

Preview

**Look at the picture.
What do you see?**

UNIT GOALS

- ☐ Name parts of the body
- ☐ Call to explain an absence
- ☐ Talk about health problems
- ☐ Make a doctor's appointment
- ☐ Complete a medical history form
- ☐ Follow instructions during a medical exam
- ☐ Read medicine labels
- ☐ Talk about the past
- ☐ Give advice

1   WHAT DO YOU KNOW?

A CLASS. Look at the picture. Which parts of the body do you know?

> Number 3 is her leg.

CD4 T19

B Listen and point to the parts of the body. Then listen and repeat.

2   PRACTICE

A PAIRS. Look at the picture. Student A, say a part of the body. Student B, point to the part of the body.

> Ankle.

B WORD PLAY. PAIRS. Student A, look at the list of words on page 207. Say a part of the body. Student B, ask for the spelling. Then write the word on the picture.

A: *Stomach.*
B: *How do you spell that?*
A: *S-T-O-M-A-C-H.*
B: *Thanks.*

C Match the pictures and words. Write the correct letter.

a. shake   b. touch   c. nod   d. clap

1. __b__   2. __d__   3. __c__   4. __a__

Lesson 1 Vocabulary

Getting Started   5 minutes

1 WHAT DO YOU KNOW?

A CLASS. Look at the picture. Which parts...

- Show Transparency 11.2 or hold up the book. Tell students to cover the list of words at the bottom of page 207.
- Ask: *Where are the people?* (at a park) *What are they doing?* (exercising, doing *tai chi*)
- Ask students if they know what *tai chi* is (a kind of exercise) or where it is from (China).
- Tell students to look at the picture and ask: *Which parts of the body do you know?* Help guide students by prompting them with numbers (for example, *What is number 1?*).
- Students call out parts of the body that they recognize. Correct pronunciation as needed.
- If students call out an incorrect part of the body, change the student's answer to a question for the class (for example, *Number 3 is her knee?*). If nobody can identify the correct item, tell students to listen for it when you play the CD.

Presentation   5 minutes

B 🔘 Listen and point to the parts of...

- Read the directions. Play CD 4, Track 19. Pause after number 20 (*foot/feet*). Explain: *Number 10 and number 20 have irregular plural forms.* Write *tooth/teeth* and *foot/feet* on the board.
- Walk around and check that students are pointing.
- To check comprehension, say each part of the body in random order and ask students to point to the appropriate number on the picture.
- Resume playing Track 19. Students listen and repeat.

Controlled Practice   35 minutes

2 PRACTICE

A PAIRS. Look at the picture. Student A, say a part...

- Read the directions.
- Play A and model the task with an above-level student.
- Pair students and tell them to take turns playing A and B.
- Walk around and help students correct each other's mistakes.

MULTILEVEL INSTRUCTION for 2A

Pre-level Form groups of 3. A points to a part of the body, and B and C both identify the part of the body.

Above-level For added challenge, Student A can describe the location of a part of the body and ask B to identify it (for example, A: *It's under his nose. What is it?* B: *His mouth?* A: *Yes, that's right.*).

B WORD PLAY. PAIRS. Student A, look at the list...

- Read the directions. Read each line in the example and ask the class to repeat. Model correct intonation.
- Play A and practice with an above-level student.
- Pair students and tell them to take turns playing A and B.
- Walk around and help students correct each other's mistakes.

MULTILEVEL INSTRUCTION for 2B

Cross-ability The higher-level student plays B and helps the lower-level student by first pointing to a part of the body that A must say and spell.

C Match the pictures and words. Write the correct...

- On the board, write *shake, touch, nod,* and *clap.* Point to each word and tell the class to do the action (for example, *Shake your head.*). Model actions students do not know. Say each word and ask the class to repeat.
- Read the directions.
- Call on students to say answers.

Learning Strategy: Make labels

- On the board, write a word (for example, *chest*) and say it. "Study" the word by slowly pointing to each letter and saying them (*C-H-E-* · · ·).
- Cover or erase the word, and rewrite the word slowly as if recalling from memory to demonstrate to students that you are trying to recall the word.
- Read the directions.
- Walk around and if misspellings occur, tell students to check the list on page 207.
- Call on a few students to say what words they wrote. Ask students to spell their words.
- Say: *You can remember new words by making labels and putting them on the objects.* Remind students to use this strategy to remember other new vocabulary.

Expansion: Vocabulary Practice

- Pair students. Distribute adhesive notes or tape and scraps of paper, and tell students to write a part of the body on each note and affix it to their bodies.
- Student A calls out a part of the body, and Student B removes that note from his or her own body.

Show what you know!

STEP 1. Listen and follow the commands.

- Play CD 4, Track 20. Students listen and follow the commands.
- Write the six actions on the board (*touch, clap, close, shake, point to,* and *nod*). Say each one and perform the action (for example, *I am pointing to my desk.*).
- If necessary, play Track 20 again to make sure the class can follow the commands.

Communicative Practice   15 minutes

STEP 2. GROUPS OF 5. Student A, you are...

- Read the directions.
- Play A and perform the example with a group of 4 students.
- Read the Simon Says note. Ask: *Do you play Simon Says? Do you have another name for this game in your country?*
- Form groups of 5 and choose a student in each group to be A. Remind A to only sometimes say *please.*
- Walk around and check each group's performance. Participate with groups as needed. Give A immediate feedback about pronunciation.
- If time permits, choose other students to play A and ask groups to repeat the game.
- To wrap up, perform the game as a class. Ask a student to lead as A.

Community Building

If possible, arrange for a field trip to a local park for some recreational time. Play Simon Says–style games to practice parts of the body vocabulary.

Teaching Tip

Language acquisition is enhanced when students can physically respond to imperatives they are learning. In addition to the physical response activity on this page (Step 2), continue to recycle short common classroom commands that students can respond to (for example, *Please open your books to page _____. Please close the door. Please turn on/off the light.*).

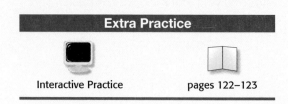

Extra Practice

Interactive Practice   pages 122–123

Parts of the Body

1.	head	**11.**	ear
2.	face	**12.**	chest
3.	leg	**13.**	elbow
4.	ankle	**14.**	wrist
5.	shoulder	**15.**	knee
6.	stomach	**16.**	neck
7.	eye	**17.**	hand
8.	nose	**18.**	back
9.	mouth	**19.**	arm
10.	tooth/teeth	**20.**	foot/feet

Learning Strategy

Make labels

Look at the list of parts of the body. Choose three or four words. Find a picture of a person in a magazine. Write each word in the correct place. For example, write the word *arm* on the person's arm.

Show what you know!

STEP 1. CD4 T20 Listen and follow the commands.

STEP 2. GROUPS OF 5. Student A, you are the leader. Give commands. Say *please* sometimes. Students B, C, D, and E, follow the command only when Student A says *please*. When you make a mistake, sit down.

A: *Clap your hands.*

B, C, D, E:

A: *Clap your hands, please.*

B, C, D, E:

> This game is like "Simon Says."

Call to explain an absence

Listening and Speaking

1 BEFORE YOU LISTEN

CD4 T21

READ. Look at the pictures. Listen and read about the children. Complete the sentences.

These children don't feel well. They feel sick. Barbara has a sore throat. Li has a stomachache. Asad has a toothache. And Rodolfo has a headache.

sore throat   stomachache

1. Barbara's _____ throat _____ hurts.
2. Li's _____ stomach _____ hurts.
3. Asad's _____ tooth _____ hurts.
4. Rodolfo's _____ head _____ hurts.

toothache   headache

2 LISTEN

A Look at the picture. Mrs. Lee is calling her son Alex's school.

Guess: What's the matter with Alex?
He's sick. He has a sore throat and a headache.

CD4 T22

B Listen to Mrs. Lee's conversation with the office assistant. Was your guess in Exercise A correct?

Listen again. Answer the questions.

1. Who is Ms. Wong?
   (a.) a teacher   b. an office assistant

2. Is Alex going to school today?
   a. yes   (b.) no

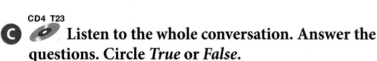

CD4 T23

C Listen to the whole conversation. Answer the questions. Circle *True* or *False*.

1. Mrs. Lee's other children feel well.   True   (False)
2. Mrs. Lee asks to call the school again later.   (True)   False

Getting Started 10 minutes

1 BEFORE YOU LISTEN

 READ. Look at the pictures. Listen and...

- Point to each picture, say the problem, and ask the class to repeat. Say: Ache *means* pain. On the board, write *stomach*. Point to it and say: *This is a part of the body.* Add *ache* to the word on the board. Point to it and say: *This is a problem.*
- Read the directions. Play CD 4, Track 21. Say: *Underline the word* has *in the paragraph.* Explain: *When someone is sick, say* He (*or* She) has a sore throat, stomachache, toothache, *or* headache.
- Read the example. Ask: *Why is* throat *the answer?* (Because the sentence is about Barbara.)
- Call on a few students to write the completed sentences on the board.

■■ **Expansion: Speaking Practice for 1**

- Write the following conversation on the board:
    A: *What's the matter?*
    B: *My _____ hurts. I have a _____.*
- Fill in the blanks with a part of the body and a related problem (for example, *My stomach hurts. I have a stomachache.*). Practice the conversation with a student. Switch roles and practice again.
- Pair students and have them practice the conversation, substituting new words from the pictures on page 208.
- For added challenge, write more parts of the body that use *ache* on the board. Ask students to use these words in their conversation (for example, *earache, backache*).
- Call on pairs to perform for the class.

Language Note

Students may have difficulty pronouncing *ache* correctly. Clearly model correct pronunciation and provide time for sustained practice for words with *ache*.

Presentation 20 minutes

2 LISTEN

Ⓐ **Look at the picture.... Guess:...**

- Read the directions.
- Ask: *What's the matter with Alex?* Explain: *What's the matter?* means *What's the problem?*
- Call on students to answer the question. Write answers on the board.

Ⓑ **Listen to Mrs. Lee's conversation...**

- Read the directions. Play CD 4, Track 22.
- Ask: *Was your guess in Exercise A correct?* Circle the correct answers on the board. (Answer: He's sick. / He has a sore throat and a headache.)

Teaching Tip

Optional: Remember that if students need additional support, tell them to read the Audio Script on page 288 as they listen to the conversation.

Listen again. Answer the questions.

- Read the directions. Play Track 22 again.
- Students compare answers with a partner.
- Call on a couple of students to say answers.

Ⓒ **Listen to the whole conversation....**

- Read the directions. Play CD 4, Track 23.
- Explain: I hope he feels better soon *means* I hope he is well soon. Can I call you back *means* I need to call you again later.
- Ask: *What happens at the end of the conversation?* (The other children say they are sick, too.)
- Call on students to read the statements and answer *true* or *false*.

■■ **Expansion: Vocabulary Practice for 2C**

- Pair students. A acts out a problem (for example, a sore throat, a stomachache, a toothache, a headache). B guesses the problem (for example, A: [Rubs forehead, frowns.] B: *You have a headache!* A: *Yes. I have a headache.*).

3 CONVERSATION

 Listen and read the conversation. Then...

- Note: This conversation is the same one students heard in Exercise 2B on page 208.
- Read the directions. Play CD 4, Track 24. Students listen and read along silently.
- Resume playing Track 24. Students listen and repeat.
- As students repeat, listen carefully for their production of /i/ and /ɪ/ as in *feel* and *sick*.

■ Expansion: Pronunciation Practice for 3

- Say the following pairs of words and have the class repeat: *1. feel, fill; 2. he's, his; 3. feet, fit.*

■ Expansion: Listening Practice for 3

- Tell students to number a sheet of paper from 1 to 6. On the board, write *same* and *different*. Explain: *Listen to the pair of words. If the words are the same, write* same. *If they are different, write* different.
- Say the following pairs of words: *1. feel, fill* (different); *2. he's, his* (different); *3. he's, he's* (same); *4. feet, fit* (different); *5. fit, fit* (same)
- Call on the class to say the answers.

Controlled Practice   15 minutes

4 PRACTICE

Ⓐ PAIRS. Practice the conversation. Then....

- Pair students and tell them to practice the conversation in Exercise 3.
- Then, in Exercise 4A, tell students to look at the information in the boxes. Say each family member and illness and ask the class to repeat. Explain: *Sometimes when you are sick you have a* fever, *which means your body is very hot. The flu is more serious than a cold. A person with the flu has a fever and aches everywhere.*
- Copy the conversation onto the board with blanks and read it. When you come to a blank, fill it in with information from the boxes. Circle *he* where it appears in the conversation and above it write *she*. Remind students to say *he* for a male and *she* for a female.

- Ask two on-level students to practice the conversation in front of the class.
- Tell pairs to take turns playing each role and to use the boxes to fill in the blanks. Remind students to include *a/an* as needed. Tell students to stand, mingle, and practice the conversation with several new partners.
- Call on pairs to perform for the class.

Communicative Practice   15 minutes

Ⓑ ROLE PLAY. PAIRS. Student A, you're sick....

- Read the directions. Play A and make up a conversation with an above-level student.
- Pair students and tell them to take turns playing A and B.
- Walk around and check that Student A is clearly pronouncing a problem. Ask Student B to repeat Student A's problem to demonstrate comprehension (for example, A: *This is Claudia. I can't come to work today. I have a sore throat.* B: *A sore throat? I'm sorry to hear that.*).
- Call on groups to role-play for the class.

■ MULTILEVEL INSTRUCTION for 4B

Pre-level Pairs first write out their conversation and practice from it a few times before practicing without a script.

Above-level Brainstorm additional ways for B to respond to A (for example, *I hope you get better. Take care of yourself. Get some rest.*) and write them on the board.

■ Expansion: Speaking and Vocabulary Practice for 4B

- Pairs make up a new conversation between friends. When making new conversations, ask A to include information about specific parts of the body that hurt. Tell students to refer back to the vocabulary on page 207 (for example, A: *My back hurts a lot.*).

Extra Practice

Interactive Practice

---

3 CONVERSATION

CD4 T24

Listen and read the conversation. Then listen and repeat.

Assistant: Good morning. Greenville Elementary.

Mrs. Lee: Hello. This is Terry Lee. I'm calling about my son Alex.

Assistant: Is that Alex Lee?

Mrs. Lee: Yes. He's sick today. He has a sore throat and a headache.

Assistant: I'm sorry to hear that. What class is he in?

Mrs. Lee: He's in Ms. Wong's class.

4 PRACTICE

A **PAIRS.** Practice the conversation. Then make new conversations. Use the information in the boxes. Change *he* to *she* when necessary.

A: Good morning. Greenville Elementary.

B: Hello. This is Terry Lee. I'm calling about my [   ] Alex.

A: Is that Alex Lee?

B: Yes. **He**'s sick today. **He** has [   ] and [   ].

A: I'm sorry to hear that. What class is **he** in?

B: **He**'s in Ms. Wong's class.

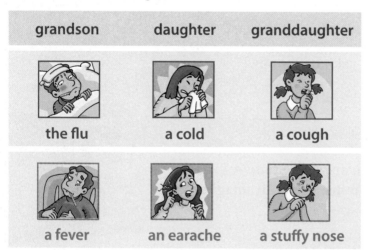

grandson	daughter	granddaughter
the flu	a cold	a cough
a fever	an earache	a stuffy nose

B **ROLE PLAY. PAIRS.** Student A, you're sick. Call work or school.

A: *Hi. This is _____. I can't come to work today. I have a . . . .*

B: *I'm sorry to hear that.*

Grammar

Review: Simple present

Information questions and answers		Yes/no questions and answers	
How do you **feel**? **How does** Alex **feel**?	My throat **hurts**. He **doesn't feel** well.	**Do** you **have** a fever? **Does** he **have** a fever?	**Yes**, I **do**. **No**, he **doesn't**.

PRACTICE

Maria and her mother are in Dr. Philip's office. Complete their conversation. Use the correct form of the verbs in parentheses. Give short answers.

Mom: Dr. Philip, I'm worried about Maria. I think she ___has___ the flu.
(have)

Doctor: How ___do___ you ___feel___, Maria?
(feel)

Maria: Terrible. I ___have___ a cough and a stuffy nose.
(have)

Doctor: What about your throat? ___Does___ it ___hurt___?
(hurt)

Maria: Yes, it ___does___. But just a little. ___Do___ I ___have___ a fever?
(have)

Doctor: Let's see, . . . No, you ___don't___.

Mom: ___Does___ she ___have___ the flu, Dr. Philip?
(have)

Doctor: No. She ___doesn't have___ the flu. It's just a bad cold.
(not have)

Mom: That's good. I ___feel___ a lot better now!
(feel)

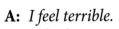 **Show what you know!**   Talk about health problems

PAIRS. You are friends. Student A, you are sick. Student B, ask questions. Find out your friend's symptoms. Use your imagination!

A: *I feel terrible.*
B: *What's wrong?*
A: *My _____ hurts.*
B: *Do you have . . . ?*

Can you. . . talk about health problems?   ☐

Getting Started   5 minutes

- Say: *We're going to review the simple present. In the conversation on page 209, Mrs. Lee used this grammar.*
- Play CD 4, Track 24. Students listen. Write on the board: *He has a sore throat.* Underline *has.*

Presentation   5 minutes

Review: Simple present

- Copy the grammar charts onto the board or show Transparency 11.3 and cover the exercise.
- Read the questions and answers in the left chart and ask the class to repeat. Do the same with the right chart.
- For each chart, ask: *Why does the first question have* do? (Because *do* goes with *you/I.*) *Why does the second question have* does? (Because *does* goes with *Alex/he.*) Explain: *When you use* do *or* does, *use the base form of the next verb, as in* How does he **feel**? *Do not add* -s.
- Ask students to close their books. Remove any visual aids for the charts. On the board, write: *How _____ you feel? My _____ hurts.* Call on students to fill in the blanks. Remind students to use *hurts* when talking about one part of the body and *hurt* when talking about more than one.
- Write on the board: *_____ he _____ a fever? No, he _____.* Again, call on students to fill in the blanks. Erase the answers and change *he* to *you.* Repeat the step.
- If you are using the transparency, do the exercise with the class.

Controlled Practice   5 minutes

 PRACTICE

Maria and her mother are in Dr. Philip's office....

- Read the directions and Mom's first line.
- Say: *Remember, each question will need a form of* do. *Look back at the chart if you don't remember which words to use.*
- If many students have difficulty, write some lines on the board, and as a class figure out the answers.

- If students have difficulty knowing which form of the verb to write, tell students to circle the subject in each sentence and to think about which verb form goes with that subject.
- *Optional:* Pair students and ask them to practice the conversation. Call on pairs to perform the completed conversation for the class.

Communicative Practice   15 minutes

Show what you know!

PAIRS. You are friends. Student A, you are sick....

- Pair students. Read the directions.
- On the board, write the following headings: *Parts of the Body, Symptoms,* and *Questions.* Tell students a *symptom* is a health problem that indicates you are sick, such as *a fever, a cough,* or *a stuffy nose.*
- Call on students to say several parts of the body. List them under the *Parts of the Body* heading. Repeat for *Symptoms.*
- Under the *Questions* heading, write: *Do you have a _____?* Call on students to say several symptoms. For each symptom, write a new question (for example, *Do you have a sore throat?*).
- Practice the example conversation with a student. Use information from the board. Tell students to use words and questions from the board to make up new conversations.
- Walk around and check that students are using a wide range of vocabulary.

Progress Check

Can you . . . talk about health problems?

Say: *We have practiced talking about health problems. Now, look at the question at the bottom of the page. Can you talk about health problems?* Tell students to write a checkmark in the box.

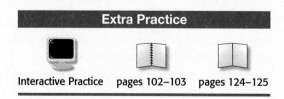

Extra Practice		
Interactive Practice	pages 102–103	pages 124–125

See the doctor and get medicine

Getting Started   10 minutes

Culture Connection

• Ask students if they need to make a doctor's appointment in their home country or if they can just walk in and see the doctor right away.

• As needed, explain: To make an appointment *means to set a certain time to do something, in this case to see a doctor.*

Presentation   5 minutes

 1 SEE THE DOCTOR

 Viktor Petrov is calling City Clinic...

• Read the directions. Play CD 4, Track 25. Students listen and read along silently.

• Resume playing Track 25. Students listen and repeat.

• Remind students: I'd like to *is a polite way to say* I want to. I'd *is a contraction for* I would. Explain: *An opening is a time in the schedule when the doctor can see you.*

Controlled Practice   10 minutes

2 PRACTICE

A **Listen to the conversation again....**

• Read the directions.

• Before playing the CD, ask students to call out any differences between the two cards (for example, *Card* a *says March 2, but card* b *says March 3.*).

• Play CD 4, Track 26. Students listen and circle the letter of the correct appointment card.

B PAIRS. **Practice the conversation. Use your...**

• Pair students and tell them to assign roles to each other (Caller and Assistant). Tell the assistant to suggest the day, date, and time on card *a*.

• Walk around and check that students are using their own names and the information from card *a*. Be sure that the caller confirms the assistant's suggested appointment time.

• Call on pairs to perform for the class. Provide feedback about pronunciation and interaction (for example, *I really like how natural you both sounded.*).

■ MULTILEVEL INSTRUCTION for 2B

Pre-level Form groups of 4. Tell each group to read each line of the conversation together before practicing with a partner.

Above-level Pairs change the conversation so that the caller says OK to the date but is not available at the time suggested by the assistant. The assistant must offer a second time (for example, A: *How about 2:00?* C: *No, 2:00 is no good. I work at 2:00.* A: *How about 4:30?* C: *OK.*).

Communicative Practice   10 minutes

C PAIRS. **Make a new conversation. Use different...**

• Copy the conversation from Exercise 1 onto the board but leave blanks for the caller's name and the elements in blue, red, and purple.

• On the board, write several days, dates, and times. Elicit this information from students as you write.

• Play the caller and ask a student to use information on the board to suggest an appointment time.

• Pair students with a different partner from the one they had in Exercise B. Tell the assistant to fill out the appointment card. Then ask partners to switch roles and make a new conversation. The new assistant can fill out the appointment card with the new caller's appointment information.

• Draw an appointment card on the board. To wrap up, call on a few pairs to make up a new conversation for the class. One student (the assistant) can fill out the card on the board.

3 LIFE SKILLS WRITING

Turn to page 263 and ask students to complete the medical history form. See pages Txi–Txii for general notes about the Life Skills Writing activities.

See the doctor and get medicine

Life Skills

1 SEE THE DOCTOR

CD4 T25

Viktor Petrov is calling City Clinic to make an appointment. Listen and read his conversation with the office assistant. Then listen and repeat.

Assistant:	City Clinic. Can I help you?
Viktor:	This is Viktor Petrov. I'd like to make an appointment for a check-up.
Assistant:	Sure. For what day?
Viktor:	Can I come in tomorrow?
Assistant:	No, I'm sorry. There are no openings this week. How about next **Thursday afternoon** at **2:00**?
Viktor:	Okay. Next **Thursday** at **2:00** is good.
Assistant:	Okay, that's **Thursday**, **March third**, at **2:00** P.M. See you then.

2 PRACTICE

CD4 T26

A Listen to the conversation again. Circle the letter of the correct appointment card.

a.
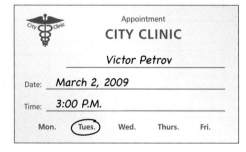

(b.)
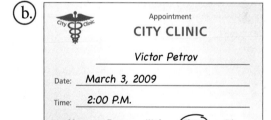

B PAIRS. Practice the conversation. Use your own name.

C PAIRS. Make a new conversation. Use different days, dates, and times. Complete the appointment card with your partner's information.

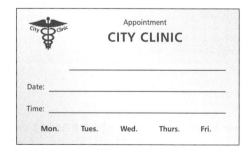

3 LIFE SKILLS WRITING

Complete a medical history form. See page 263.

A PAIRS. Viktor is at City Clinic for his check-up. Look at the pictures.
Write an instruction under each picture. Use the instructions in the box.

Lie down.	Open your mouth and say *Ahh*.	
Look straight ahead.	Roll up your sleeve.	~~Step on the scale.~~
Make a fist.	Sit on the table.	Take a deep breath.

1. _____Step on the scale._____

2. _____Roll up your sleeve._____

3. _____Sit on the table._____

4. _____Open your mouth and say, *Ahh*._____

5. _____Look straight ahead._____

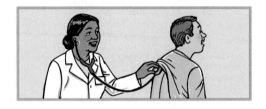

6. _____Take a deep breath._____

7. _____Lie down._____

8. _____Make a fist._____

B PAIRS. Student A, you are a doctor. Student B, you are a patient. Student A,
give Student B instructions. Student B, act out the instructions.

Can you. . .see the doctor? ☐

Controlled Practice   10 minutes

4   PRACTICE

Ⓐ PAIRS. Viktor is at City Clinic for his check-up....

- Read the directions.
- For the first item, point to the picture of the scale and ask: *What is this?* Then ask: *What is the doctor saying?* (Step on the scale.)
- Read each instruction and, as possible, briefly demonstrate them. Ask the class to repeat.
- Pair students.
- Walk around and check that pairs are interacting to choose the correct instructions for each picture.
- Call on students to say answers.

> **Language Note**
>
> If possible, pair students with the same first language when they're practicing a conversation with lots of new vocabulary. The higher-level partner explains any language that the partner doesn't recognize.

Communicative Practice   5 minutes

Ⓑ PAIRS. Student A, you are a doctor. Student B,...

- Read the directions.
- As a class, call out a couple of instructions and ask the class to follow your instructions (for example, *Open your mouth and say ahh.*).
- Pair students.
- Walk around and model clear pronunciation as needed.

▇▇ MULTILEVEL INSTRUCTION for 4B

Pre-level Form groups of 3. One student is the doctor while the two other students are patients who respond to the same instruction from the doctor.

Above-level Ask Student A to deliver two instructions at once.

▇▇ Expansion: Listening Practice

- Play a Simon Says–style game with the class by issuing commands with the word *please* affixed to instructions that you actually want students to carry out. Students who respond to an instruction without the word *please* are out of the game and must sit down.

Progress Check

Can you . . . see the doctor?

Say: *We have practiced seeing the doctor. Now, look at the question at the bottom of the page. Can you see the doctor?* Tell students to write a checkmark in the box.

Lesson 4   See the doctor and get medicine

Presentation   5 minutes

5   READ MEDICINE LABELS

A Match the words and pictures....

- Read the directions and the example. Use the pictures and mime to explain the words in the box.
- *Optional:* Explain any unfamiliar vocabulary in the box:

    Alcoholic beverage: a drink with alcohol, such as beer, wine, or liquor

    Orally: by mouth or in your mouth

    Out of reach: not easy to touch because, for example, it's on a high shelf or in a locked drawer

    Tablet: a small solid pill (refer to the picture)

- Say the words in the box and ask the class to repeat.

B Listen and check your answers.

- Play CD 4, Track 27. Students listen and check their answers.
- To wrap up, ask the class to call out answers.

Controlled Practice   15 minutes

6   PRACTICE

A Listen. Complete the medicine label.

- Read the directions. Ask: *What's the name of the medicine?* (Pain Away!) *What kind of medicine is this?* (pain reliever / fever reducer) Say: *Look at the label to see what kind of medicine it is. Optional:* Explain that *relieve* and *reduce* mean *to go away* or *to go down.*
- Read each direction and say the word *blank* for each empty space.
- Play CD 4, Track 28. Students listen and write.
- Play Track 28 again. Students listen and check their answers.
- Call on students to read the completed warnings.

Expansion: Speaking and Vocabulary Practice for 6A

- Ask students what kind of symptoms this medicine can treat; say: *What problems does this medicine help?* (headache, fever, back pain, . . .).

B Look at the medicine label. Answer the questions.

- Read the directions and the example. Ask: *What's the name of the medicine?* (Max-Profen) *What kind of medicine is this?* (pain reliever / fever reducer).
- Students compare answers with a partner.
- To check answers, call on one student to read a question and another student to answer it.

Expansion: Listening Practice for 6B

- Pair students. Student A creates a new medicine label by changing the numbers used in the directions and warnings (for example, *Take 2 tablets orally every 6–8 hours.*).
- Student B asks A the questions. When Student A responds, Student B copies down the answers without looking at the label. Then Student A shows Student B the label to check the answers.

Teaching Tip

Bring in examples of real medicine labels and repeat Exercise 6B. Using real labels adds authenticity to the experience and can boost students' confidence level.

Progress Check

Can you . . . read medicine labels?

Say: *We have practiced reading medicine labels. Now, look at the question at the bottom of the page. Can you read medicine labels?* Tell students to write a checkmark in the box.

Extra Practice

Interactive Practice   pages 104–105   pages 126–128

5 READ MEDICINE LABELS

A Match the words and pictures. Write the correct words from the box under each picture.

alcoholic beverage	~~orally~~
out of reach	tablet

1. ___orally___   2. ___tablet___   3. ___alcoholic beverage___   4. ___out of reach___

CD4 T27

B 🔘 Listen and check your answers.

6 PRACTICE

CD4 T28

A 🔘 Listen. Complete the medicine label.

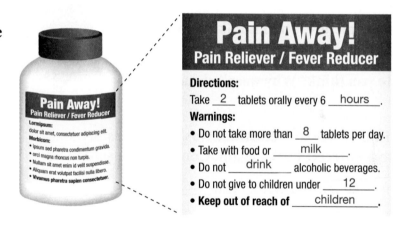

Pain Away!
Pain Reliever / Fever Reducer

Directions:
Take __2__ tablets orally every 6 __hours__ .
Warnings:
- Do not take more than __8__ tablets per day.
- Take with food or ___milk___ .
- Do not ___drink___ alcoholic beverages.
- Do not give to children under __12__ .
- **Keep out of reach of** ___children___ .

B Look at the medicine label. Answer the questions.

MAX-PROFEN
Pain Reliever / Fever Reducer

Directions: Take 1 tablet orally
every 4–6 hours
Warnings:
- Do not take more than 6 tablets
per day.
- Take with food or milk.
- Do not drink alcoholic beverages.
- Do not give to children under 12.
- **Keep out of reach of children.**

1. What is this medicine for? ___pain or fever___

2. How much of the medicine do you take at one time? ___1 tablet___

3. How often do you take this medicine? ___every 4–6 hours___

4. How much of this medicine can you take in one day? ___6 tablets___

5. What do you take this medicine with? ___food or milk___

6. Where should you keep this medicine? ___out of reach of children___

Can you...read medicine labels? ☐

Listening and Speaking

1 BEFORE YOU LISTEN

A Look at the calendar.
Read the information.

		January		
MONDAY	TUESDAY	WEDNESDAY	THURSDAY	FRIDAY
2	3	4	5 Today!	6

Jan. 4 = *yesterday*
Jan. 4 at night = *last night*
Jan. 3 = *the day before yesterday*

B CLASS. Answer the questions.

Where were you yesterday?
Where were you last night?
Where were you the day before yesterday?

2 LISTEN

A Look at the picture. Tuan is talking to
Luisa. Luisa wasn't at work yesterday.

What do you think? Why wasn't she at work?

CD4 T29
B Listen to the conversation. Was your guess in
Exercise A correct? Listen again. Complete the sentences.

1. Luisa's daughter was home with _____a bad cold_____ .

(a.)   b.   c.

2. Her daughter is now _____in school_____ .

a.   (b.)   c.

CD4 T30
C Listen to the whole conversation. Who is sick now? _____Luisa_____

Getting Started   5 minutes

1 BEFORE YOU LISTEN

A Look at the calendar. Read the information.

- Say: *Now, we're going to talk about the past. Look at the picture of the calendar.* Read the note and ask the class to repeat each expression.
- On the board, write today's date. Point to it and say, for example, *Today is May 17.* Say: *Yesterday was May 16. Yesterday means the day before today.* To the left of today's date, write yesterday's date and the word *yesterday*.

B CLASS. Answer the questions.

- Ask the first question (*Where were you yesterday?*). Explain: *Were is a past tense form of* be. *We'll study this grammar in the next lesson.*
- Write students' responses on the board. Students can respond in phrases (for example, *at home*).
- Ask the other questions and call on students to answer. Write students' responses under the dates on the board. Divide responses under yesterday's date into afternoon and night activities by writing them in separate colors or separate labeled spaces.

▬ Expansion: Graphic Organizer Practice for 1B

- Tell students to draw in their notebooks three connected boxes of equal size as in the calendar. The right box is *Today*. Ask students to fill in activities they did for today, yesterday, and the day before yesterday in the spaces for those days. Tell students to write at least three activities for each day, using activity vocabulary from Unit 7.
- Call on students to say what activities they did.

Presentation   30 minutes

2 LISTEN

A Look at the picture.... What do you think?...

- Say: *Look at the picture.* Ask: *Who are the people?* (Luisa and Tuan) *Where are they?* (*Possible answers:* at work, in an office)
- Read the directions.

- Ask: *Why wasn't Luisa at work yesterday?*
- Call on students to answer the question. Write answers on the board.

B   Listen to the conversation. Was...

- Read the directions. Play CD 4, Track 29.
- As needed, explain the following expressions:

  Too bad: Another way of saying *I'm sorry (to hear that)*

  My daughter was home sick: same as *was at home because she was sick*

  A lot better: much less sick; almost well

- Ask: *Was your guess in Exercise A correct?* Circle the correct answers on the board. (Answer: Luisa wasn't at work because her daughter was home sick.)

> **Teaching Tip**
>
> *Optional:* Remember that if students need additional support, tell them to read the Audio Script on page 289 as they listen to the conversation.

Listen again. Complete the sentences.

- Read the directions. Point to each picture in item 1 and ask: *What's her problem?* (a. the flu, b. stomachache, c. sore throat)
- Point to each picture in item 2 and ask: *Where is she?* (a. in bed, b. at school, c. in the hospital)
- Play Track 29 again. Students listen, circle the letter of the correct picture, and complete the sentence.
- Call on students to say answers. Tell students to say the full sentence for each answer.

C Listen to the whole conversation....

- Read the directions. Play CD 4, Track 30.
- Explain: *Take care means to stay well.*
- Ask: *Who is sick now?* (Luisa) *Optional:* Ask *why.* (She has her daughter's cold now.)

Lesson 5　Talk about the past

3　CONVERSATION

A 💿 **Listen. Then listen and repeat.**

- Read the Pronunciation Watch note.
- Play CD 4, Track 31. Students listen.
- Ask students to underline the verb in each sentence.
- Resume playing Track 31. Students listen and repeat.

B 💿 **Listen to the sentences. Check (✓)...**

- Read the directions. Play CD 4, Track 32.
- Call on students to say the word they checked. Pronounce each answer and ask the class to repeat.

Controlled Practice　15 minutes

C 💿 **Listen and read the conversation....**

- Note: This conversation is the same one students heard in Exercise 2B on page 214.
- Play CD 4, Track 33. Students listen and read along silently.
- Ask students to underline all examples of *were*, *weren't*, *was*, and *wasn't* in the first two lines: (Tuan: *weren't*; Luisa: *was*).
- As students repeat, listen carefully for their unstressed pronunciation of *was/were* and stressed pronunciation of *wasn't/weren't*.
- Resume playing Track 33. Students listen and repeat.

4　PRACTICE

A **PAIRS. Practice the conversation. Then....**

- Pair students and tell them to practice the conversation in Exercise 3C.
- Then, in Exercise 4A, tell students to look at the information in the boxes. Say: *There are three types of information: times, people, and health problems.* Say them and ask the class to repeat.
- Copy the conversation onto the board and complete it with words from the boxes. Circle *She* where it appears in the conversation and above it write *He*. Remind students to say *he* for a male and *she* for a female.

- Play A and practice with a student. Switch roles.
- Tell pairs to take turns playing each role and to use the boxes to fill in the blanks.
- Walk around and check that students are choosing information from the boxes and are clearly contrasting the stressed/unstressed pronunciation of the past tense forms of *be*.
- Tell students to stand, mingle, and practice the conversation with several new partners.
- Call on pairs to perform for the class.

■ MULTILEVEL INSTRUCTION for 4A

Pre-level Ask students to underline each use of *she* in the conversation and to write *he* above each one as a reminder to change pronouns as necessary.

Above-level Ask students to talk about two sick people in their conversations (for example, B: *I know. My son and my grandson were home sick. . . .*). Remind them to make all other needed changes in verbs and pronouns.

Communicative Practice　10 minutes

B **ROLE PLAY. PAIRS. Make your own...**

- On the board, write *People*, *Times*, and *Health Problems*. Call on students to say additional vocabulary similar to that in Exercise 4A (for example, *Tuesday*, *yesterday afternoon*, *daughter*, *backache*).
- Play A and, with an above-level student, use information from the board and make up a new conversation.
- Pair students and tell them to take turns playing A and B.
- Call on pairs to role-play for the class.

■ Expansion: Speaking Practice for 4B

- Review asking about immediate future activities. Tell students to end their conversations by adding information about activities in the immediate future (for example, A: *So, are you going to lunch now?* B: *Yes, I am.* A: *Can I go with you?* B: *Sure!*).

■ Extra Practice

Interactive Practice

3 CONVERSATION

Pronunciation Watch

Was and *were* are often unstressed. *Wasn't* and *weren't* are stressed.

CD4 T31

A 🔊 Listen. Then listen and repeat.

She was **sick**.   She **was**n't in s**chool**.

It was the **flu**.   It **was**n't a **cold**.

They were **ab**sent.   They **were**n't **late**.

CD4 T32

B 🔊 Listen to the sentences. Check (✓) the word you hear.

1. ☐ was   ☑ wasn't   2. ☑ were   ☐ weren't

3. ☑ was   ☐ wasn't   4. ☐ were   ☑ weren't

CD4 T33

C 🔊 Listen and read the conversation. Then listen and repeat.

Tuan: You weren't here yesterday.

Luisa: I know. My daughter was home sick. She had a bad cold.

Tuan: Oh, too bad. How is she now?

Luisa: A lot better, thanks. She's back at school.

4 PRACTICE

A **PAIRS.** Practice the conversation. Then make new conversations. Use the words in the boxes. Change *she* to *he* when necessary.

A: You weren't here _____ .

B: I know. My _____ was home sick.

   She had a bad _____ .

A: Oh, too bad. How is **she** now?

B: A lot better, thanks. **She**'s back at school.

B **ROLE PLAY. PAIRS.** Make your own conversations. Use different times, people, and health problems.

> Wednesday
> last night
> the day before yesterday

> son
> grandson
> granddaughter

> headache
> earache
> stomachache

Grammar

Past of be: Statements

Affirmative			Negative		
I He She Luisa's daughter	**was**	sick yesterday.	I He She Luisa	**wasn't**	sick last week.
We You They	**were**		We You They	**weren't**	

Grammar Watch

Contractions

wasn't = was not
weren't = were not

1 PRACTICE

A Some of Ms. Reed's students have the flu. Complete
Ms. Reed's sentences. Underline the correct words.

1. Pierre and Miriam **are** / **were** here today, but they **are** / **were** absent yesterday.

2. Sen **is** / **was** OK now, but she **is** / **was** sick last night.

3. Ilya and Mei-Yu **are** / **were** in school yesterday, but they **aren't** / **weren't** here now.

4. Kamaria **is** / **was** at the doctor's office yesterday. Now she **is** / **was** at home in bed.

5. Assefa **isn't** / **wasn't** here now, but he **is** / **was** here yesterday.

6. I **am** / **was** OK last week, but now I **am** / **was** sick!

B Complete the paragraph about Sonia and her sister. Use *was* or *were*.

Sonia ___was___ home sick the day before yesterday.
1.

Her sister ___was___ sick, too. They ___were___
2.   3.

both in bed all day. Sonia's parents ___were___
4.

worried. Yesterday Sonia ___was___ a lot
5.

better. Her sister ___was___ better, too.
6.

Sonia's parents ___were___ very happy!
7.

Talk about the past

Getting Started   5 minutes

- Say: *We're going to study how to use* be *to talk about the past. In the conversation on page 215, Tuan and Luisa used this grammar.*
- Play CD 4, Track 33. Students listen. Write on the board: *You weren't here yesterday* and *My daughter was home sick.* Underline *weren't* and *was.*

Presentation   10 minutes

Past of *be*: Statements

- Copy the grammar charts onto the board or show Transparency 11.4 and cover the exercise.
- Say: *Use* was *with the subjects* I, he, *and* she. *Use* were *with the subjects* we, you, *and* they.
- Read sentences from the left chart and ask the class to repeat.
- Say: *To make negative statements, use* wasn't *or* weren't. Read the Grammar Watch note.
- Read sentences from the right chart and ask the class to repeat.
- Ask students to close their books. Remove any visual aids for the chart. Write the following on the board:

    1. *He _____ sick the day before yesterday. (was/were)*
    2. *He _____ sick yesterday. (wasn't/weren't)*
    3. *They _____ sick last night. (was/were)*

- Call on students to say the correct answers. Fill in the blanks on the board.
- If you are using the transparency, do the exercise with the class.

Controlled Practice   20 minutes

 PRACTICE

A **Some of Ms. Reed's students have the flu....**

- Read the directions and the first part of item 1. Say: *How do you know that* are *is the answer?* (Because the sentence says *today.*) *Look for* today *or* yesterday *in the sentences as a clue.*

- Copy item 1 onto the board. Use it to illustrate the point below.
- Explain: *In each sentence, a comma separates two parts of the sentence. One part is about the present time, and the other part is about the past. Use* is/are *for present time and* was/were *for past time.*
- Explain: But *means that you are showing a difference.*
- Students compare answers with a partner.
- *Optional:* Ask students to write a + sign above the part of each sentence about the present and a − sign above each part that is about the past.
- Call on students to read the completed items.

B **Complete the paragraph about Sonia and her sister....**

- Read the directions.
- Remind students to look at the subject in each sentence to know if *was* or *were* is the correct answer.
- Tell students to look back at the charts if they can't remember which word to use.
- Call on students to read their answers.

▮▮▮   Expansion: Listening Practice for 1B

- Conduct the following dictation activity. Read the following sentences and ask students to write them in their notebooks. Repeat each sentence only once:

    1. *Maria was sick yesterday.*
    2. *Francisco wasn't sick yesterday.*
    3. *My brothers weren't sick last night.*
    4. *You weren't sick yesterday morning.*
    5. *He and his brother were sick yesterday.*

- If students have difficulty distinguishing between the affirmative and negative forms of the past tense of *be,* provide isolated listening practice by modeling the same sentence with both *were* and *weren't* (for example, *Maria was sick yesterday. Maria wasn't sick yesterday.*). Write the sentences you say on the board. Point to either the affirmative or negative verb and say the sentence so students can notice the pronunciation difference.

2 · PRACTICE

A Look at yesterday's attendance sheet. Complete...

- Tell the class to look at the attendance sheet. Ask: *Who was late?* (Min Jung Lee) *Who was in school?* (Luisa Flores, Min Jung Lee, and Dora Moreno) *Who was absent?* (Carlos Delgado, Eun Young Lim, Sonia Lopez, and Emilio Vargas)
- Read the example. Ask: *How do you know* wasn't *is the correct answer?* (Because the chart shows that Carlos was absent.)
- Explain that *there* in item 3 means *in class.*
- Call on students to say answers.

Communicative Practice · 25 minutes

B WRITE. Look at the pictures. Write two sentences...

- Read the directions.
- Write two headings on the board (*Last week* and *Yesterday*). Call on students to say several things that are happening in each picture and write their answers under the appropriate heading (for example, *Last week: It was 50 degrees.*).
- Write a sentence using information from the lists on the board. Prompt students to call out how to complete the sentence (for example, T: *Last week it was 50 degrees, but yesterday it was . . .* Ss: *70 degrees!* T: [Writes *70 degrees*]). Remind students: But *means that you are showing a difference.*
- Say: *You can move the time expressions* last week / yesterday *to the end of each part of the sentence.* Rewrite the sentence on the board with the time expressions at the end of each clause (*It was 50 degrees last week, but it was 70 degrees yesterday.*). Read the sentences. Ask: *Are both times in the past?* (Yes.)
- Pair students and tell them to use information on the board or things they notice in the pictures.

▪ MULTILEVEL INSTRUCTION for 2B

Pre-level Before pairs practice, point to matching parts of the picture and prompt students to call out the differences (for example, T: [Points to the teacher in the first picture.] *Last week, the teacher was . . .* Ss: *Sick.* T: [Points to the teacher in the second picture.] *Yesterday, the teacher was . . .* Ss: *Fine.*).

Above-level Ask students to write two additional sentences (one for each picture).

Show what you know!

PAIRS. Look at the pictures again. Talk about...

- Read the directions and the example conversation. With the class, brainstorm a list of differences between the pictures. Write them on the board (for example, *Last week: 50 degrees; Yesterday: 70 degrees*).
- Call on students to use a past tense form of be to talk about a difference (for example, *Last week it was 50 degrees, but yesterday it was 70 degrees.*). Write a couple of responses on the board.
- Walk around and check that students are comparing differences and using the past tense of *be* correctly.
- Call on pairs to perform for the class.

▪ Expansion: Speaking Practice

- Brainstorm with students things they remember from the previous class (yesterday or some time earlier), for example, *On Tuesday Maria was absent, but today she is here. She was sick, but now she's OK/better/well.*
- On the board, write two headings: the name of the day of the last class (for example, *Tuesday*) and *Today.*
- Pair students and ask them to talk about differences between the last class and today's class based on information on the board or other things they remember.

Progress Check

Can you . . . talk about the past?

Say: *We have practiced talking about the past. Now, look at the question at the bottom of the page. Can you talk about the past?* Tell students to write a checkmark in the box.

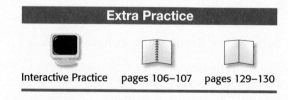

Extra Practice		
Interactive Practice	pages 106–107	pages 129–130

A Look at yesterday's attendance sheet. Complete the sentences with *was*, *were*, *wasn't*, or *weren't*.

	Here	Absent
Carlos Delgado		✓
Luisa Flores	✓	
Min Jung Lee	✓ late	
Eun Young Lim		✓ sick
Sonia Lopez		✓ sick
Dora Moreno	✓	
Emilio Vargas		✓

1. Carlos ___wasn't___ in class yesterday.

2. Luisa and Min Jung ___were___ there, but Min Jung ___was___ late.

3. Eun Young and Sonia ___weren't___ there. They ___were___ both home sick.

4. Dora ___was___ there, but Emilio ___wasn't___ .

B WRITE. Look at the pictures. Write two sentences about each picture. Answers will vary but could include:

Last week

Yesterday

1. _The teacher was sick last week._

2. _The computer was on the desk last week._

3. _The teacher wasn't sick yesterday._

4. _The computer was next to the desk yesterday._

Show what you know! Talk about the past

PAIRS. Look at the pictures again. Talk about the differences.
Use *was*, *were*, *wasn't*, and *weren't*.

A: *Last week the teacher was sick.*
B: *Right. And yesterday she wasn't sick.*

Can you...talk about the past? ☐

Reading

1   BEFORE YOU READ

A   CLASS.   Do you walk every day? Do you walk a lot? Do you think walking is good for you?

B   Look at the pictures. Which words complete the sentence? Circle the correct answers.

When you walk a lot, _____.

a.

you lose weight

b.

you get sick

c.

you have more energy

d.

You're in excellent health. No problems.

you prevent health problems

e.
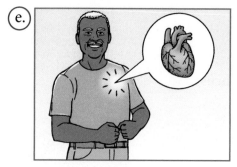
your heart gets strong

f.
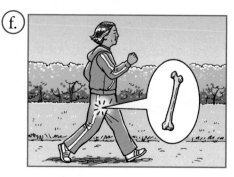
your bones get strong

Getting Started — 10 minutes

1 — BEFORE YOU READ

A CLASS. **Do you walk every day? Do you walk a lot?...**

- Ask the first two questions in the directions. Call on students to answer *yes/no*.
- Ask: *Do you think walking is good for you? Why?* (Because it is exercise.)

Expansion: Writing Practice for 1A

- Tell students to think about where they walk in their neighborhood. Ask them to draw a simple map showing where they walk.
- Tell students to write sentences with directions about where they walk (for example, *I turn left on Maple St., and I walk for three blocks.*).

B **Look at the pictures. Which words complete...**

- Read the directions. Say: *Walking is good for your health.*
- Read each answer choice. Explain any vocabulary as needed (for example, *When* you have more energy, *you can do more things and not get tired.*). Use the pictures to help explain vocabulary.
- Students compare answers with a partner.
- Call on students to say answers.

Presentation   10 minutes

2 READ

Listen. Read the article.

- Ask: *What is the title?*
- Before playing the CD, say: *Look quickly at the article and find three benefits or good effects of walking. You have ten seconds to find the information.*
- Call on students to say benefits they read in the article. Write a few on the board (for example, *You lose weight. You have a lot of energy.*).
- Play CD 4, Track 34. Students listen and read along silently.
- *Optional:* Pause the CD after each list and ask the following questions:

  First bulleted list: *When you walk every day, what happens?* (You lose weight. Your bones get strong. . . .)

  Second bulleted list: *How can you add steps to your daily routine?* (Don't take the elevator. Take the stairs. . . .)

- If students have difficulty following along, play Track 34 again and pause as needed.
- Ask students if there are words they do not understand and explain them.

Controlled Practice   10 minutes

3 CHECK YOUR UNDERSTANDING

Ⓐ Read the article again. What is the main idea?

- Remind students: The main idea is the most important idea of the article.
- Ask students to read the article again silently and choose the correct answer.
- To check the answer, poll the class and ask students to raise their hand for *a* or *b*.

Ⓑ Read the sentences. Circle *True* or *False*.

- Read the directions.
- Call on students to say answers. Ask students to restate false statements as true (2. *Most people walk 4,000 steps a day.* 3. *To walk more, you can add steps to your daily routine.*).

Expansion: Listening and Writing Practice for 3B

- Dictate the following sentences:
  1. *When you walk every day, you don't lose weight.*
  2. *To add steps, take the elevator. Don't take the stairs.*
  3. *Walking prevents heart disease.*
- According to what the article says, ask students to write *True* or *False* next to each sentence. (1. False, 2. False, 3. True)

Communicative Practice   10 minutes

Show what you know!

NETWORK. Do you need to walk more? What can...

- Ask a couple of students the questions and write their answers on the board in complete sentences (for example, *Yes, I need to walk more. I can walk to the post office. I can walk to the grocery store. I can take the stairs at work.*).
- Pair students. Tell each partner to think of at least five things they can do to walk more.
- Walk around and check that partners are making lists, sharing information, and using *can*.
- To wrap up, call on a few students to share what they suggest and what their partner suggests.
- Say: *Remember to check with your partner every week during the break time.* Ask: *Are you meeting your goals?*
- Note: Initiate this follow-up yourself for two weeks or until students begin to do it on their own.

MULTILEVEL INSTRUCTION

Cross-ability The higher-level student prompts the lower-level student by asking *Can* questions (for example, *Can you walk to the store? Can you walk to school?*).

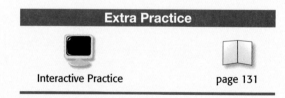

Extra Practice

Interactive Practice   page 131

CD4 T34

Listen. Read the article.

Walk Your Way to Good Health!

It's free. It's easy. It's good for you. And guess what? You already do it every day! What is it? Walking!

Alan and Sue walk a lot. They walk 10,000 steps every day.

When you walk every day:
- You lose weight.
- Your bones get strong.
- Your heart gets strong.
- You prevent health problems like heart disease.
- You have a lot of energy.

For good health, you should walk 10,000 steps a day (about five miles).

Most people walk 4,000 steps a day. These 4,000 steps are part of your daily routine. You walk from the kitchen to the bedroom. You walk to your car or to the bus stop. You walk from the entrance of the school to your classroom. So you only need 6,000 more steps a day. You can add those steps to your daily routine:
- Don't take the elevator. Take the stairs.
- Walk when you talk on the phone.
- Get off the bus one stop early and walk the rest of the way.
- Don't park near the place you're going.

It's easy. So what are you waiting for? Start walking!

3 **CHECK YOUR UNDERSTANDING**

A Read the article again: What is the main idea?

a. Most people walk 4,000 steps a day.   (b.) Walking is good for your health.

B Read the sentences. Circle *True* or *False*.

1. People should walk 10,000 steps a day.   (True)   False
2. Most people walk 6,000 steps a day.   True   (False)
3. To walk more, you need to go to the gym.   True   (False)

Show what you know!

NETWORK. Do you need to walk more? What can you do? Make a list. Find a partner. Look at your partner's goals. Check with your partner every week during your break. Ask, *Are you meeting your goals?*

Give advice

Listening and Speaking

1 BEFORE YOU LISTEN

CLASS. Talk about it. What do you do for a toothache? a backache? the flu?

2 LISTEN

Ⓐ Read the chart. Are your answers from *Before You Listen* in the chart?

ON THE AIR **What Does the Doctor Say?**

Problem	Advice	The doctor says . . .	
		Do	Don't
2 A toothache	Put heat on it.	☐	✓
	Eat a piece of onion.	✓	☐
	Drink lime juice.	✓	☐
1 A backache	Use an ice pack.	✓	☐
	Take a hot shower.	✓	☐
	Use a heating pad.	✓	☐
3 The flu	Stay in bed.	✓	☐
	Drink a lot.	✓	☐
	Take antibiotics.	☐	✓

Important: You should see a doctor or nurse if you don't feel better soon.

Getting Started

10 minutes

1 BEFORE YOU LISTEN

CLASS. Talk about it. What do you do for a...

- Read the directions.
- Call on students to say how they treat these health problems. Write remedies on the board. Categorize remedies as *home remedies* (for example, *drinking herbal tea*) or *medical treatment* (for example, *taking prescribed medicine*).
- Explain that home remedies often use food or simple methods that people can do at home. Medical treatment refers to medicine and doctor-prescribed treatment.

Culture Connection

- Ask: *What home remedies do people use in your home country for a toothache, backache, or sore throat?*
- Call on students to share various home country remedies that may be different from the ones already discussed.

Presentation

20 minutes

2 LISTEN

A Read the chart. Are your answers...

- Read the directions. Say: *Look at the advice.* Read each piece of advice and ask the class to repeat.
- Ask: *Are your answers from* Before You Listen *in the chart?* Call on students to say any advice in the chart (for example, *Stay in bed.*) that is the same as what they discussed in Before You Listen.

Lesson 8 Give advice

B 🔘 **Listen to the radio show. Number...**

- Read the directions. Play CD 4, Track 35. Students write the numbers 1–3 in the boxes at the left of the chart.
- Call on the class to say the order of the problems (T: *What is number 1?* Ss: *A backache.*).

C 🔘 **Listen again. What does the doctor...**

- Read the directions. Play Track 35 again. Students check the appropriate box at the right of each item.
- To check answers, say each piece of advice as a question and ask students to respond appropriately (for example, T: *A toothache—put heat on it?* Ss: *Don't put heat on it.*).

■■■ **Expansion: Vocabulary Practice for 2C**

- Pair students or form small groups. Ask them to brainstorm additional health problems and write them in their notebooks (for example, *a stomachache, a cold, a headache*). Each pair or group then writes suggestions next to each problem. Call on students to share what they wrote and write good suggestions on the board.

Controlled Practice   20 minutes

3 **CONVERSATION**

A **Look at the pictures. Clara has a sore throat....**

- Read the first part of the directions. Ask: *What does her friend Peter suggest?* (tea and honey) Do you think it is a good suggestion? (Yes./No.)
- Say: *Let's listen to see what Clara thinks.*

B 🔘 **Listen and read the conversation. Then...**

- Read the directions. Play CD 4, Track 36. Students listen and read along silently.
- Resume playing Track 36. Students listen and repeat.

4 **PRACTICE**

A **PAIRS. Practice the conversation. Then make new...**

- Pair students and tell them to practice the conversation in Exercise 3B.
- Then, in Exercise 4A, tell students to look at the information in the chart in Exercise 2A on page 220.
- Read the directions.
- Copy the conversation onto the board and fill it in with words from page 220. Play A and practice with a student. Switch roles.
- Tell pairs to take turns playing each role.
- Walk around and check that students are using the information from the chart on page 220.
- Tell students to stand, mingle, and practice the conversation with several new partners.
- Call on pairs to perform for the class.

Communicative Practice   10 minutes

B **ROLE PLAY. GROUPS OF 3. Make your own...**

- Play A and, with an above-level student, use problems and suggestions not found on page 220.
- Brainstorm with the class to come up with additional vocabulary to use.
- Pair students and tell them to take turns playing A and B.
- Walk around and check that students are suggesting logical remedies for symptoms.
- Call on pairs to perform for the class.

■■■ **MULTILEVEL INSTRUCTION for 4B**

Pre-level Form groups of 4 and elicit additional problems and suggestions from them to get them started. Write information on the board.

Above-level While pre- and on-level pairs are still working, ask above-level pairs to present their conversation to the class in order to provide the class with examples of how to make new conversations.

Extra Practice

Interactive Practice

B *CD4 T35* Listen to the radio show. Number the problems in the chart on page 220 in the order you hear them.

C *CD4 T35* Listen again. What does the doctor say? Check (✓) *Do* or *Don't* for each problem on the chart on page 220.

3 CONVERSATION

A Look at the pictures. Clara has a sore throat. What does her friend Peter suggest? Do you think it is a good suggestion?

Peter tells Clara to drink tea and honey.

B *CD4 T36* Listen and read the conversation. Then listen and repeat.

Clara: I have a sore throat.
Peter: I'm sorry to hear that. Maybe you should drink tea and honey.
Clara: That's a good idea.
Peter: But call the doctor if you don't feel better soon. You really shouldn't wait too long.

4 PRACTICE

A PAIRS. Practice the conversation. Then make new conversations. Use the information from the chart on page 220.

B ROLE PLAY. GROUPS OF 3. Make your own conversations. Use different problems and suggestions.

Grammar

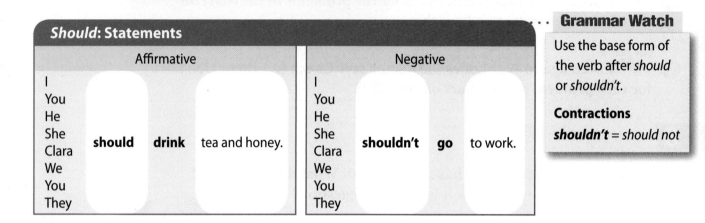

Should: Statements

Affirmative		
I You He She Clara We You They	**should** **drink**	tea and honey.

Negative		
I You He She Clara We You They	**shouldn't** **go**	to work.

Grammar Watch

Use the base form of the verb after *should* or *shouldn't*.

Contractions
shouldn't = *should not*

PRACTICE

A Complete the sentences about some people's problems. Underline the correct word. Choose affirmative for one sentence and negative for the other.

1. Agnes has a bad back. She **should / <u>shouldn't</u>** lift heavy things.

   She **<u>should</u> / shouldn't** ask a nurse about back exercises.

2. Ben has a stomachache. He **<u>should</u> / shouldn't** drink a lot of tea.

   He **should / <u>shouldn't</u>** eat fries.

3. Hassan has a sore throat and a cough. He **should / <u>shouldn't</u>** talk too much.

   He **<u>should</u> /shouldn't** take medicine.

4. Lan's ankle hurts. She **should / <u>shouldn't</u>** walk. She **<u>should</u> / shouldn't** put ice on it.

B GROUPS OF 3. Read the labels. What do they mean? Talk about them.

A: *What does this mean: "Take medication on an empty stomach"?*
B: *It means you shouldn't take it with food.*
C: *Right. You should take it before or after you eat.*

a.

TAKE MEDICATION ON AN **EMPTY STOMACH**

b.

P.M.

c.

DO NOT REFRIGERATE

d.
TAKE MEDICATION **WITH FOOD**

e.

DO NOT DRINK MILK or EAT DAIRY PRODUCTS WHILE TAKING THIS MEDICATION

Getting Started   5 minutes

- Say: *We're going to study* should *and* shouldn't. *In the conversation on page 221, Peter used this grammar.*
- Play CD 4, Track 36. Students listen. Write on the board: *Maybe you should drink tea and honey* and *You really shouldn't wait too long.* Underline *should* and *shouldn't*.

Presentation   5 minutes

Should: **Affirmative and Negative Statements**

- Copy the grammar charts onto the board or show Transparency 11.5 and cover the exercise. Say: *When you give advice, use* should.
- Read sentences from the charts and ask the class to repeat.
- Read the first part of the Grammar Watch note. Write *He rests* on the board. Point out the *-s* and elicit the reason it is there (because with the subject *He*, the verb *rest* ends in *-s*). Then write *He should rest.* Point out that *rest* does not have *-s* because the verb after *should* must be in the base form. Explain that *should* and *shouldn't* do not change. They only have one form no matter what the subject is.
- Read the second part of the Grammar Watch note. Ask students to say a couple of classroom rules using *should* or *shouldn't* (for example, *You should bring your book to class. You shouldn't eat food in class.*). Write them on the board.
- If you are using the transparency, do the exercise with the class.

Controlled Practice   15 minutes

PRACTICE

A **Complete the sentences about some people's...**

- Read the directions and the example.
- Ask: *Why is the answer* shouldn't? (Because Agnes has a bad back and lifting things can hurt it.)
- Walk around and check that students understand the logic in each sentence by asking why they chose their answer, as above.
- Call on students to read the sentences with the correct answers.

B **GROUPS OF 3. Read the labels. What do they...**

- Read the directions.
- With a student, practice the example conversation. Then read each label direction and explain any unfamiliar vocabulary (for example, An empty stomach *means there is no food in your stomach.*).
- Pair students and tell them to take turns playing A and B. Tell B to explain each direction by using *should* and *shouldn't* as in the example.
- Walk around and check that students are using *should* and *shouldn't* in their explanations.
- To wrap up, call on pairs to perform for the class.
- Answers will vary. Possible answers could include:
  a. You should take it on an empty stomach. You shouldn't take it with food.
  b. You should take it at night. You shouldn't take it in the morning.
  c. You shouldn't put it in the refrigerator.
  d. You should take it with food. You shouldn't take it on an empty stomach.
  e. You shouldn't take this medicine with milk or cheese (with dairy products).

▀▀ **MULTILEVEL INSTRUCTION for B**
Cross-ability The lower-level partner plays A for a few times before playing B.

▀▀ **Expansion: Vocabulary Practice for B**

- Form groups of 3 or 4. Ask students to choose three common health problems (for example, *a headache, a sore throat, a cold*) and to list things that people *should* and *shouldn't* do on poster board or notebook paper (for example, *Headache: You shouldn't exercise.*).
- Each pair or group can present their list to the class.

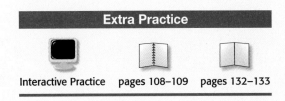

Extra Practice

Interactive Practice   pages 108–109   pages 132–133

Show what you know!

1 GRAMMAR

Complete the conversation between Ernesto and...

- Read the directions and the example. Ask: *Why is* weren't *the right answer? (Because the subject is* You.)

- Tell students to refer back to the grammar charts on pages 210 (simple present), 216 (past of *be*), and 222 (*should/shouldn't*) as needed. Remind students: *Look at the subject of each sentence. This can help you figure out the answer.*

- Students compare answers with a partner.

- Call on students to say answers.

- *Optional:* Pair students and ask them to practice the conversation. Call on pairs to perform the completed conversation for the class.

2 WRITING

STEP 1. GROUPS OF 3. **Read the problems. Make...**

- Read the directions. With two students, practice the example conversation.

- Form groups of 3.

- Walk around and check that students in each group are discussing suggestions for each problem.

- If students need more guidance, tell them to review the suggestions in Exercise 2A on page 220. Additionally, brainstorm with the class to provide groups with a couple of suggestions to discuss.

- Tell students to take notes while they discuss suggestions for the problems.

▬ MULTILEVEL INSTRUCTION for STEP 1

Cross-ability Each group should have one above-level student who facilitates discussion by making sure that the other two group members each say an opinion.

▬ Expansion: Writing Practice for STEP 1

- For each problem in Step 1, ask students to write two sentences about what each person *shouldn't* do.

STEP 2. **Write one suggestion for each problem.**

- Tell students to write one complete suggestion sentence for each problem.

- Tell students to look at their notes from Step 1.

- To wrap up, call on several students to write their sentences on the board. If there are mistakes, ask the class to call out corrections while you rewrite the sentences on the board.

CD-ROM Practice

■ Go to the CD-ROM for more practice.

If your students need more practice with the vocabulary, grammar, and competencies in Unit 11, encourage them to review the activities on the CD-ROM. This review can also help students prepare for the final role play on the following Expand page.

Extra Practice

pages 110–111

1 GRAMMAR

Complete the conversation between Ernesto and Mei-Yu. Use the words in the box. Use capital letters when necessary.

> does   feels   has   have   hurts   should   was   was   ~~weren't~~

Ernesto: You ___weren't___ here last week.

Mei-Yu: No, I ___was___ home. My son ___was___ sick with the flu.

Ernesto: Oh, I'm so sorry to hear that. ___Does___ he feel better now?

Mei-Yu: Not really. He still ___has___ a bad headache, and his throat ___hurts___.

Ernesto: Hmm. Maybe you ___should___ take him to the doctor.

Mei-Yu: We ___have___ an appointment for tomorrow.

Ernesto: Well, I hope he ___feels___ better soon.

Mei-Yu: Thanks.

2 WRITING

STEP 1. GROUPS OF 3. Read the problems. Make suggestions.

Problem 1
Bobby, a 10-year-old boy, has a stomachache every morning before school. What should his parents do?

Problem 2
Sara has a backache. Her friend tells her to exercise. Is this a good suggestion? Sara isn't sure. What should she do?

Problem 3
Ted has a bad sore throat. He wants to go to work. His wife thinks he should stay home. What should he do?

A: *OK, Problem 1. What should Bobby's parents do?*
B: *Hmm. Maybe they should talk to his teacher. Maybe there's a problem at school.*
C: *Or, maybe they should take him to the doctor.*

STEP 2. Write one suggestion for each problem.   Answers may vary but could include:

Problem 1. They should see a doctor. They should ask him about his school and classmates. They should talk to his teacher.

Problem 2. She shouldn't exercise. She should take hot showers. She should see a doctor. She should use a heating pad.

Problem 3. He should listen to his wife. He shouldn't go to work. He should drink a lot of tea and honey. He should see a doctor.

3 ACT IT OUT — What do you say?

CD4 T37
STEP 1. 🔘 **Listen to the conversation.**

STEP 2. PAIRS. **Student A, you are a doctor. Student B, you are a patient.**

Student A:	**Student B:**
• Ask the patient, "What's the matter?" • Give the patient instructions. • Give the patient advice.	• Choose a health problem. Answer the doctor's questions. • Follow the doctor's instructions. • Thank the doctor.

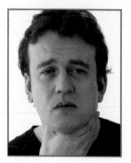  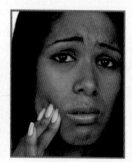 

4 READ AND REACT — Problem-solving

STEP 1. **Read about Genet's problem.**

Genet is a cashier. She works full-time, Monday to Friday. She has a seven-year-old son, Solomon. Solomon is in the second grade. He is usually at school all day from Monday to Friday. Today, Solomon is sick. He doesn't have a fever, but he has a stuffy nose and a sore throat. He has a headache. He feels terrible. He wants to stay home. But who can take care of him? Genet can't miss work.

STEP 2. PAIRS. **Talk about it. What is Genet's problem? What can Genet do? Here are some ideas.**

- She can send her son to school.
- She can stay home with her son.
- She can ask a neighbor to stay with her son.
- She can _____.

5 CONNECT

For your Goal-setting Activity, go to page 252.
For your Team Project, go to page 271.

Which goals can you check off? Go back to page 205.

3   ACT IT OUT

STEP 1. 💿 Listen to the conversation.

- Play CD 4, Track 37. Students listen.
- As needed, play Track 37 again to aid comprehension.

STEP 2. PAIRS. Student A, you are a doctor....

- Read the directions and the guidelines for Student A and B.
- Talk about each picture. Ask students to call out information they see in each picture (for example, *The man has a sore throat. The woman has a stomachache.*).
- Provide a model by asking an above-level student *What's the matter?* and engaging the student in a role play according to the guidelines.
- Pair students. Tell A to begin by asking: *What's the matter?* Students practice at their desk with their partner.
- Walk around and check that A is giving instructions and advice and that B is able to name and describe symptoms or problems.
- Also check that A can offer advice for the problem and give explicit instructions about what B should and shouldn't do.
- Call on pairs to perform for the class. While pairs are performing, use the scoring rubric on page Txiv to evaluate each student's vocabulary, grammar, fluency and how well they complete the task.
- *Optional:* After each pair finishes, discuss the strengths and weakness of each performance either in front of the class or privately.

4   READ AND REACT

STEP 1. Read about Genet's problem.

- Say: *We are going to read about a student's problem, and then we need to think about a solution.*
- Read the directions.
- Read the story while students follow along silently. Pause after each sentence to allow time for students to comprehend. Periodically stop and ask simple *Wh-* questions to check comprehension, for example, *What does Genet do?* (She's a cashier.) *What's the matter with Solomon?* (He has a stuffy nose and a sore throat.)

STEP 2. PAIRS. Talk about it. What is Genet's...

- Pair students. Ask: *What is Genet's problem?* (Her son is sick.) *What can Genet do?*
- Read the ideas in the list. Ask: *Which ideas are good?* Call on students to say their opinion about the ideas in the list (for example, *I don't think she can send her son to school because he is sick.*).
- Now tell students to think of one new idea not in the box (for example, *She can ask a co-worker to switch hours with her so she works on Saturday. Then on Saturday she can get a babysitter.*) and to write it in the blank. Encourage students to think of more than one idea and to write them in their notebooks.
- Call on pairs to say their additional solutions. Write any particularly good ones on the board and ask students if they think it is a good idea, too (*Do you think this is a good idea? Why or why not?*).

■■■ MULTILEVEL INSTRUCTION for STEP 2

Pre-level Sit with students, say each idea in the list, and ask students to explain why they like or don't like each solution (for example, *She can't stay home because she needs to work.*).

Above-level Pairs discuss the problems with each idea (for example, *If she stays home, maybe she will get fired.*).

5   CONNECT

Turn to page 252 for the Goal-setting Activity and page 271 for the Team Project. See pages Txi–Txii for general notes about teaching these activities.

Progress Check

Which goals can you check off? Go back to page 205.

Ask students to turn to page 205 and check off the goals they have reached. Call on students to say which goals they will practice outside of class.

12

Help Wanted

CD 4
Tracks 38–54

Transparencies 12.1–12.6
Vocabulary Cards Unit 12

MCA
Unit 12

Workbook
Unit 12

Interactive Practice
Unit 12

Unit Overview

Goals

- See the list of goals on the facing page.

Grammar

- *Can:* Affirmative and negative statements
- *Can: Yes/no* questions and short answers
- Past of *be:* Questions and answers

Pronunciation

- Unstressed *can,* stressed *can't*
- Stressed *can* and *can't* in short answers

Reading

- Read an article about making a good first impression

Writing

- Write a want ad for a job you want
- Write sentences about your job experience and skills

Life Skills Writing

- Complete a job application

Preview

- Set the context of the unit by asking questions about what jobs they have (for example, *Do you work? Do you have a job? What is your job?*). Additionally, ask questions about *when* students work (for example, *Do you work before/after class?*).
- Hold up page 225 or show Transparency 12.1. Read the unit title. Ask: *What does* Help Wanted *mean?* (A company has a job and is looking for someone to hire.) *Where do you see Help Wanted signs?* (in store windows) *Where do you see help wanted ads?* (in newspapers)
- Say: *Look at the picture.* Ask the Preview question: *What do you see?* (a woman on the phone) Ask: *What is she doing?* (looking at the help wanted ads in the newspaper / trying to get a job / calling about a job)

Unit Goals

- Point to the Unit Goals. Explain that this list shows what the class will be studying in this unit.
- Tell students to read the goals silently.
- Say each goal and ask the class to repeat. Explain unfamiliar vocabulary as needed:

  Want ads: *job advertisements in newspapers*

  Body language: *movements you make with your body that show what you are feeling or thinking*

  Work experience: *your past jobs*

  Job application: *a form you complete to get a job*

- Tell students to circle one goal that is very important to them. Call on several students to say the goal they circled.

Help Wanted

Preview

**Look at the picture.
What do you see?**

UNIT GOALS

- ☐ Respond to a Help Wanted sign
- ☐ Talk about job skills
- ☐ Read want ads
- ☐ Talk about hours you can work
- ☐ Ask about job skills
- ☐ Use correct body language at a job interview
- ☐ Talk about work experience
- ☐ Complete a job application

1 WHAT DO YOU KNOW?

A CLASS. Look at the pictures. Which job duties can you name?

> Number 1 is "answer the phone."

CD4 T38

B Listen and point to the pictures. Then listen and repeat.

2 PRACTICE

A PAIRS. Student A, point to a picture. Ask, "What is he/she doing?" Student B, answer.

A: *What is he doing?*
B: *He's using a computer.*

B WORD PLAY. TWO TEAMS. Play Charades.

- Team 1, go first. Student A on Team 1, act out a job duty.
- Team 1, guess the duty. You have one minute. You get one point for a correct guess.
- Student A on Team 2, you're next.
- Teams take turns. The team with the most points wins.

C WRITE. What do you do at work or at home every day? Write one of your duties. Look at the list on page 227 or use your own ideas.

At work, <u>I drive a truck</u>.

OR

At home, <u>I take care of my children</u>.

At _____, _____.

Lesson 1 Vocabulary

Getting Started   5 minutes

1 **WHAT DO YOU KNOW?**

A **Look at the pictures. Which job duties can...**

- Show Transparency 12.2 or hold up the book. Tell students to cover the list of words on page 227.
- Read the directions. Point to picture 1 and read the example. Ask: *Which job duties do you know?*
- Students call out answers as in the example. Help students pronounce job duties if they have difficulty.
- If students call out an incorrect job duty, change the student's answer into a question for the class (for example, *Number 2 is use a computer?*).
- If nobody can identify the correct job duty, tell students they will now listen to a CD and practice the names of the things in the classroom.

Presentation   5 minutes

B **Listen and point to the pictures....**

- Read the directions. Play CD 4, Track 38. Pause after number 12 (*help people*).
- Walk around and check that students are pointing.
- To check comprehension, say each job duty in random order and ask students to point to the appropriate picture.
- Resume playing Track 38. Students listen and repeat.

Controlled Practice   15 minutes

2 **PRACTICE**

A **PAIRS. Student A, point to a picture. Ask...**

- Read the directions. Play A and model the example with a student.
- Say: *If your partner says the wrong job duty, say, "No, try again."* Model this with another student.
- Pair students. Walk around and check that A is pointing to a picture while asking a question and that B is guessing job duties. Check that A is politely asking B to try again if B names the wrong job duty.

Expansion: Speaking Practice for 2A

- To practice and review vocabulary for places, for each picture, ask: *Where is he/she?*

B **WORD PLAY. TWO TEAMS. Play Charades.**

- Read the directions.
- Model the activity by acting out a job duty (for example, *deliver packages*) while the class guesses the duty.
- Form groups of 4–8. Each group divides itself into two teams. Each team elects a Student A to begin.
- Walk around and check that Student A is able to effectively demonstrate any job duty on page 227.
- Ask each group which team won.
- To wrap up, call on a few individual students to act out a job duty while the class guesses.

MULTILEVEL INSTRUCTION for 2B

Pre-level Limit each actor's choices (for example, duties 1–4) and tell the actor to read all four choices to the guessing team before silently choosing one to act out.

Above-level Form like-ability teams and require the acting student to perform two duties (for example, *pick up packages* and *clean floors*).

Communicative Practice   35 minutes

C **WRITE. What do you do at work or at home...**

- Read the directions and the examples.
- To provide a model, ask a few students what they do at work, at home, and at other locations (for example, *at school, at my grandmother's house, . . .*). Write their responses on the board.
- Walk around and spot-check students' writing to make sure they are following the format of the examples.
- Call on a few students to write their sentence on the board. Ask the class to call out corrections to any errors. Fix them on the board.

Learning Strategy: Make connections

- Provide each student with four index cards or tell students to cut up notebook paper into four pieces.
- Read the directions.
- On the board, write a job duty (for example, *fix things*). Draw a box around it. Say: *Tell me a job where you can fix things.* (a television repair person) Write a response on the board. Draw a box around it.
- *Optional:* Ask students to match the job duties on page 227 to jobs listed in Unit 2.
- Point to the job duty box and say: *A duty.* Point to the other box and say: *Job for the duty.*
- Walk around as students work. If misspellings occur, tell students to check the list on page 227.
- Say: *You can make cards to remember new words.* Remind students to use this strategy to remember other new vocabulary.

■ Expansion: Graphic Organizer and Vocabulary Practice

- Tell students to make a chart in their notebooks with three to five place headings (for example, *At work, At home, At school, At my mother's house*). Ask students to write duties (page 227) they have at each place.
- Brainstorm additional place-related job duties and write them on the board for students to use.
- Students can keep this sheet as a vocabulary reminder as they work through the activities in this unit.

Show what you know!

STEP 1. CLASS. Walk around the room...

- Read the directions. Tell students that *duties* means things they have to do every day.
- With a couple of students, practice the example conversation for the class.
- Tell students to ask their partner for their name if they don't remember it.
- Tell students to stand, mingle, and write their classmates' information in the chart.
- Walk around and check that students are discussing particular places and duties.

STEP 2. Report to the class.

- Call on students to report what they wrote in their charts (*At work, Min-Ji drives a truck. At home, she helps people.*).
- Tell students they can move *at work* and other place expressions to the beginning or end of a statement.

Community Building

Brainstorm with your class a list of classroom jobs or duties that students perform to keep the class running effectively. Write them on the board (for example, *put away the tables*). Review or assign classroom jobs (for example, *materials monitor*) to students and make a list of responsibilities on the board.

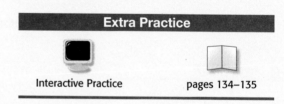

Extra Practice

Interactive Practice   pages 134–135

2

3

4

6

7

8

10

Job Duties

1. answer the phone
2. take messages
3. use a computer
4. make copies
5. drive a truck
6. lift heavy boxes
7. deliver packages
8. supervise workers
9. fix things
10. take care of grounds
11. clean floors
12. help people

Learning Strategy

Make connections

Look at the list of job duties. Make cards for three or four words. On one side, write a job duty. On the other side, write one job that matches the duty.

Show what you know!

STEP 1. CLASS. Walk around the room. Ask about your classmates' duties. Complete the chart.

Paul: *Min-Ji, what do you do every day?*

Min-Ji: *At work, I drive a truck. What about you?*

Paul: *At home, I . . .*

Name	Duty	Place
Min-Ji	drives a truck	at work

STEP 2. Report to the class.

Min-Ji drives a truck at work.

Respond to a Help Wanted sign

Listening and Speaking

1 **BEFORE YOU LISTEN**

CLASS. **Look at the picture of Dino's Diner. What do you see?**

2 **LISTEN**

A **Look at the picture. Assefa is in Dino's Diner. Guess: Why is he there?**

a. He wants a hamburger.
b. He works there.
c. He wants a job.

CD4 T39
B **Listen to the conversation. Was your guess in Exercise A correct? Listen again. Complete the sentences.**

1. Assefa is a _____cook_____.

2. He makes great _____hamburgers_____.

CD4 T40
C **Listen to the whole conversation. Read the sentences. Circle *True* or *False*.**

1. Dino gives Assefa a job. (**True**) **False**

2. Assefa is starting his new job tomorrow. **True** (**False**)

3. Assefa answers Dino's phone. (**True**) **False**

Getting Started   5 minutes

1 BEFORE YOU LISTEN

CLASS. Look at the picture of Dino's Diner....

- Tell students to look at the picture. Ask: *What place is this?* (a restaurant / Dino's Diner)
- Ask: *What do you see?* (A Help Wanted sign)

Presentation   20 minutes

2 LISTEN

Ⓐ Look at the picture.... Guess:...

- Read the directions. Ask: *Why is he there?*
- Write the answer choices on the board and read them.
- Call on students to guess.

Ⓑ 💿 Listen to the conversation. Was...

- Read the first part of the directions. Play CD 4, Track 39.
- Ask: *Was your guess correct?* Circle the correct answer on the board.

Teaching Tip

Optional: Remember that if students need additional support, tell them to read the Audio Script on page 290 as they listen to the conversation.

Listen again. Complete the sentences.

- Read each sentence and the answer choices.
- Play Track 39 again. Students listen and complete the sentences.
- To check answers, call on two students to write the sentences on the board. Correct as needed. Read them and ask the class to repeat.

Ⓒ 💿 Listen to the whole conversation....

- Read the directions. Play CD 4, Track 40.
- Ask: *What does the phone never stops mean?* (The phone rings a lot. / People often call Dino's.)
- Call on students to say answers. Tell students to make false statements true. (2. Assefa is starting his new job now.)
- Ask: *Why is Dino upset about the phone?* (He can't cook because he needs to answer the phone.)
- Ask students if they understand why the end of the conversation is funny. (Because Assefa starts his new job right now.) Elicit an explanation from on-level or above-level students.

Community Building

Create Help Wanted signs for classroom jobs. Post them in your room. Students can read the signs and "apply" for a job!

3 CONVERSATION

A 🎧 **Listen. Then listen and repeat.**

- Read the directions and the Pronunciation Watch note. Play CD 4, Track 41. Students listen.
- On the board, write a few statements with *can* (for example, *I can clean floors. He can make pizza.*). Circle *can* in the sentences you write and pronounce each sentence. Ask the class to repeat.
- Change *can* to *can't* in the sentences on the board and repeat the step above.
- Ask: *Why do we stress* can't? (Because it is difficult to hear the negative contraction if it is unstressed.)
- Resume playing Track 41. Students listen and repeat.

B 🎧 **Listen to the sentences. Check...**

- Read the directions. Play CD 4, Track 42.
- Call on students to say answers.

■ **Expansion: Pronunciation Practice for 3B**

- To reinforce clear pronunciation of *can* and *can't*, call a student to the front of the room. On a piece of paper, write a sentence with *can* or *can't* (for example, *I can clean floors.*). Show it only to the student.
- Ask the student to read the sentence to the class. The class holds up one finger for *can* and two fingers for *can't*. Repeat with other students.
- For more practice, pairs can repeat this activity.

Controlled Practice   20 minutes

C 🎧 **Listen and read the conversation....**

- Note: This conversation is the same one students heard in Exercise 2B on page 228.
- Say: *Listen for the unstressed pronunciation of* can *and the stressed pronunciation of* can't.
- Play CD 4, Track 43. Students listen and read along silently.
- Resume playing Track 43. Students listen and repeat.
- Walk around and check that students are stressing *can/can't* correctly.

4 PRACTICE

A PAIRS. **Practice the conversation. Then make new...**

- Pair students and tell them to practice the conversation in Exercise 3C.
- Then, in Exercise 4A, introduce the new vocabulary in the boxes by saying each job title and asking the class to repeat. Then ask what each person does [for example, *What does a sales assistant do?* (uses a cash register and takes returns)]. As needed, use the pictures and items in the classroom to explain vocabulary.
- To check comprehension, tell students to close their books and, as above, ask what each person does and who does each task [for example, *Who takes inventory?* (an office assistant)].
- Copy the conversation onto the board with blanks and read it. When you come to a blank, fill it in with information from the first row (*a sales assistant, use a cash register, take returns*).
- Ask a pair of on-level students to practice the conversation in front of the class. Remind students to say both a job and its skills.
- Tell pairs to take turns playing each role and to use the boxes to fill in the blanks.
- Walk around and check that students are stressing *can* and *can't* correctly.
- Tell students to stand, mingle, and practice the conversation with several new partners.
- Call on pairs to perform for the class.

Communicative Practice   15 minutes

B ROLE PLAY. PAIRS. **Make your own...**

- Brainstorm additional jobs and skills. Ask: *What jobs did you have in the past? What jobs do you want?* Write them on the board.
- Pair students and tell them to take turns playing A and B.
- Walk around and check that A is clearly pronouncing what he or she can and can't do.

Extra Practice

Interactive Practice

3 CONVERSATION

CD4 T41

A 🔘 **Listen. Then listen and repeat.**

He can **make ham**burgers.　　He **can't** make **piz**za.

CD4 T42

B 🔘 **Listen to the sentences. Check (✓) the word you hear.**

1. ☐ can　☑ can't　　2. ☑ can　☐ can't　　3. ☑ can　☐ can't

CD4 T43

C 🔘 **Listen and read the conversation. Then listen and repeat.**

Assefa: I noticed the Help Wanted sign.
I'd like to apply for a job.

Dino: OK. Which job?

Assefa: Well, I'm a cook. I can make great hamburgers.

Dino: Can you make pizza?

Assefa: No. I can't make pizza, but I can learn.

> **Pronunciation Watch**
>
> **Can** is usually unstressed.
> The vowel is short and quiet.
> **Can't** is stressed. The vowel is
> long and clear.

4 PRACTICE

A **PAIRS.** **Practice the conversation.
Then make new conversations.
Use the information in the boxes.**

A: I noticed the Help Wanted sign.
I'd like to apply for a job.

B: OK. Which job?

A: Well, I'm ＿＿＿＿＿. I can
＿＿＿＿＿ .

B: Can you ＿＿＿＿＿ ?

A: No. I can't ＿＿＿＿＿ , but I can learn.

B **ROLE PLAY. PAIRS. Make your own
conversations. Use different jobs
and skills.**

a sales assistant

use a cash register

take returns

an office assistant

use a computer

take inventory

a carpenter

make cabinets

fix furniture

Grammar

Can: Statements

		Affirmative	
I You He Assefa She We You They	**can**	**make** **use**	hamburgers. a computer.

		Negative	
I You He Assefa She We You They	**can't**	**make** **use**	pizza. a cash register.

Grammar Watch

Use the base form of the verb after *can* or *can't*.

Contractions
can't = *can not*

---

1 **PRACTICE**

A **Read Olga's job skills. Complete the sentences with *can* or *can't*.**

Name: _Olga Popova_

Office Jobs 4U

Check the skills you have.

☐ use a computer	☑ make copies
☑ answer phones	☐ write reports
☑ take messages	☑ organize things

☐ work with numbers
☑ help customers
☐ deliver mail

1. Olga ____can't____ use a computer, but she ____can____ answer phones.

2. She ____can____ take messages, but she ____can't____ write reports.

3. She ____can't____ work with numbers, but she ____can____ organize things.

4. She ____can't____ deliver mail, but she ____can____ make copies.

5. She ____can____ help customers.

B **GROUPS OF 3. Look at the job skills in Exercise A. What can you do? What can't you do? Tell your partner.**

A: *I can use a computer. What about you?*
B: *I can use a computer, too.*
C: *I can't use a computer, but I can . . . .*

A: *I can't write reports.*
B: *I can't write reports, either.*
C: *I can write reports, but I can't . . .*

Getting Started   5 minutes

- Say: *We're going to study statements with* can. *In the conversation on page 229, Assefa used this grammar.*
- Play CD 4, Track 43. Students listen. Write *I can make great hamburgers* and *I can't make pizza* on the board. Underline *can make* and *can't make*.

Presentation   5 minutes

Can: Statements

- Copy the grammar charts onto the board or show Transparency 12.3 and cover the exercise.
- Read the Grammar Watch note. Read sentences from the charts and ask the class to repeat. Remind students that in statements *can* is unstressed and *can't* is stressed.
- Brainstorm with the class a list of skills, which can be a combination of new and existing skills from page 227 (for example, *drive a truck, sing in Italian, type quickly,* and *make pizza*).
- Write them on the board and ask a few students if they can do them. Students should respond in full form (for example, T: *Can you drive a truck?* S: *Yes, I can drive a truck. / No, I can't drive a truck.*).
- If you are using the transparency, do the exercise with the class.

Controlled Practice   5 minutes

1 PRACTICE

Ⓐ Read Olga's job skills. Complete the sentences...

- Say: *This form has a list of many skills.* Ask: *Which skills does Olga have?* Students call out the checked skills.
- Ask: *Can Olga use a computer?* (No.) *Can she answer phones and take messages?* (Yes.)
- Read the example and say *blank* for the blank space. Read the sentence again and prompt the class to call out the answer to fill in the blank (*can*).
- Walk around and spot-check students' work. Students compare answers with a partner.
- Call on students to say answers. Ask students to repeat if they do not clearly pronounce *can* vs. *can't.*

Communicative Practice   20 minutes

Ⓑ GROUPS OF 3. Look at the job skills in Exercise A....

- Read the directions. With two students, practice the first conversation. Say: *If you have the same skill as your partner, say* I can _____, too.
- With two other students, practice the second example. Say: *If you do not have the same skill as your partner, say,* I can't _____ either.
- Model a negative example with a student. Prompt the student to say a skill he or she has that you don't have (for example, S: *I can speak three languages. What about you?* T: *I can't speak three languages.*).
- Form groups of 3. Pre-level and on-level students may need time to write down or think about a few skills they have before they begin practicing.
- Walk around and listen for students using *can . . . too* and *can't . . . either* to agree with their partner. Also listen for appropriate stress of *can* and *can't.*
- To wrap up, ask one student to make one statement about something he or she can do. Then that student turns to the next student and asks, *What about you?* The new student answers and then makes another statement and asks the next student, and so on.

▉ **MULTILEVEL INSTRUCTION for 1B**

Cross-ability Ask the highest-level student in each group to play A first and to help the lower-level partners by modeling affirmative or negative answers as needed.

▉ **Expansion: Writing and Speaking Practice for 1B**

- Ask students to make a chart in their notebooks with two headings: *Can* and *Can't.* Tell students to use all the skills and abilities vocabulary they learned in this unit (see Exercise 1A on page 230 and the skills listed on page 227) and write what they can and can't do in the appropriate column.
- After students have listed what skills they have and do not have, ask them to write affirmative and negative sentences for the skills (for example, *I can make copies. I can't use a computer.*).
- Pairs students and have them discuss their skills. To warm up, write the following example conversation on the board and practice it with a student (A: *I can make copies. Can you?* B: *Yes, I can make copies, too. I can also use a computer. Can you?*).

Controlled Practice   5 minutes

2 PRACTICE

Look at the pictures. Complete the sentences...

- Read the directions. Point to the first picture and ask: *Can he make furniture?* (No.) Say: *That's why the answer is* can't make.
- Check that students are writing the base form of the verbs. Remind students to use the base form of verbs with *can*.
- Students compare answers with a partner.
- Call on students to write answers on the board. Ask the same students to read their answer out loud. Check their pronunciation of *can* and *can't*.

Communicative Practice   20 minutes

Show what you know!

PAIRS. Look at the picture. What can the people...

- Read the directions.
- With a student, read the example. Point to a few additional people and ask the class to call out what they can or can't do (for example, *The woman in the green shirt can't speak Spanish.*).
- Pair students.
- Walk around and if pairs are having difficulty getting started, point to a person and ask: *What can he/she do? What can't he/she do?* (*Some possible answers:* The man in the green shirt can't fix the light. The woman in the blue shirt can talk on the phone. The woman in the red shirt can use a cash register. The woman in the purple shirt can't lift the heavy box. The man in the red shirt can help the customer. The woman in the green shirt can't speak Spanish.)
- To wrap up, identify all the people in the picture and ask the class to tell you what they can and can't do.

▅▅ MULTILEVEL INSTRUCTION

Pre-level Ask pairs to focus on one half of the picture. Provide students with skill vocabulary for people in that side of the picture by writing some skills on the board (for example, *lift heavy boxes, speak Spanish, carry heavy things*).

Above-level Ask pairs to identify two or more people who have (or lack) the same skills (for example, *The woman on the phone and the man at the customer service desk can help customers.*).

▅▅ Expansion: Speaking Practice

- Photocopy and distribute a crowd scene from a magazine or newspaper picture and ask pairs to discuss what the people can and can't do.

Language Note

Students may have difficulty clearly pronouncing the final *-t* in *can't*. Tell students that shaking their head *no* while saying *can't* in conversation is a good way to make sure that they aren't misunderstood.

Progress Check

Can you . . . talk about job skills?

Say: *We have practiced talking about job skills. Now, look at the question at the bottom of the page. Can you talk about job skills?* Tell students to write a checkmark in the box.

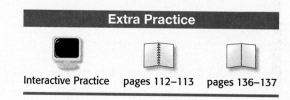

Extra Practice		
Interactive Practice	pages 112–113	pages 136–137

Look at the pictures. Complete the sentences with *can* or *can't* and the verbs in the box.

cook	drive	~~make~~
speak	take	take care of

1.

He ___can't make___ furniture.

2.

She ___can drive___ a taxi.

3.

They ___can speak___ English.

4.

We ___can't cook___ .

5.

I ___can take___ messages.

6.

He ___can't take care of___ children.

Show what you know! Talk about job skills

PAIRS. Look at the picture. What can the people do? What can't they do?

A: *The man in the green shirt can't fix the light.*
B: *Right. The woman in the red shirt can use a cash register.*

Can you... talk about job skills? ☐

Life Skills

1 READ WANT ADS

A   **PAIRS.** Read the information. Talk about it.
Do you work? Do you work full-time or part-time?

A: *I work full-time in a factory. What about you?*
B: *I have two part-time jobs.*

Full-time = 35–40 hours a week
Part-time = less than 35 hours a week

B   Want ads are one way people find out about
job openings. Look at the want ads. Find the
abbreviations for these words. Write the
abbreviations.

1. full-time   ___*FT*___

2. experience   ___exp.___

3. necessary   ___nec.___

4. hour   ___hr.___

5. part-time   ___PT.___

HELP WANTED	
A	**TRUCK DRIVER** FT. Exp. nec. $18/hr. FAX: Hanako (650) 555-2579
B	**CHILD-CARE WORKER** PT. M–F 9–3 $12/hr. Call Jasmine: (650) 555-3328.
C	**COOKS** Bill's Burgers No exp. nec. $7/hr. Evenings. Apply in person. 409 Market St.

2 PRACTICE

A   **PAIRS.** Look at the want ads again. Complete the
sentences. Write the letter of the ad.

1. Job __A__ is full-time.

2. Job __B__ pays $12 an hour.

3. Job __C__ is evenings only.

4. You don't need experience for Job __C__.

5. You need to go to the place to apply for Job __C__.

6. You can call someone at the place for Job __B__.

7. You can send a fax to the place for Job __A__.

B   **GROUPS OF 4.** Talk about it. What are some
other ways people find out about job openings?

Getting Started 3 minutes

- Ask: *What do you read when you look for a job?* (want ads in a newspaper or other source)
- Explain: *When you read information about an available job, you are reading a want ad.*
- Ask: *Where can you find want ads?* (in newspapers, on bulletin boards, in the job placement or employment center at your school, on the Internet, . . .)

Presentation 10 minutes

1 READ WANT ADS

Ⓐ PAIRS. Read the information. Talk about it....

- Read the notes.
- Ask the questions in the directions. Call on a few students to answer. Write students' responses on the board under the headings *Full-time* and *Part-time* (for example, *Full-time: office assistant, 40 hours a week, 8 A.M.–5 P.M.*).
- Pair students. Tell students who have never worked (or haven't worked in a long time) that they can discuss a job they want in the future (for example, *I want to be a mechanic. I want a full-time job.*).
- Call on several students to share their answers with the class.

▬▬ **MULTILEVEL INSTRUCTION for 1A**
Pre-level Form groups of 4. Ask one student to read a question out loud while the others take turns answering. Sit with groups to help.
Above-level Ask students to also discuss the following questions: *Do you want to change your hours? Do you want to change jobs? Why or why not?*

Controlled Practice 15 minutes

Ⓑ Want ads are one way people find out about job...

- Read the directions.
- Ask: *What is a want ad?* (an ad for a job)
- Point out where to find the abbreviation for *full-time* in ad A.
- Call on students to write answers on the board.
- Read the want ads and explain any unfamiliar vocabulary.

▬▬ **Expansion: Critical Thinking Practice for 1B**
- Pair students to discuss the following questions:
  1. *Why do want ads use abbreviations?* (Because it is too expensive to print full words.)
  2. *Why do ads sometimes not include some information, such as a telephone number or the pay rate?* (Because the business doesn't want phone calls. Some businesses prefer to talk about pay in person.)

2 PRACTICE

Ⓐ PAIRS. Look at the want ads again. Complete...

- Read the directions and the example.
- Pair students. For each ad, ask students to identify: (1) part-time or full-time, (2) the pay, and (3) how to apply.
- Call on students to read the completed sentences out loud.

▬▬ **MULTILEVEL INSTRUCTION for 2A**
Pre-level On the board, write each ad without abbreviations. Say: *Look at the full version if you can't remember all the abbreviations.*
Above-level Time students and allow them only three minutes to complete the activity. When they finish, they can help other students or check their work.

Communicative Practice 5 minutes

Ⓑ GROUPS OF 4. Talk about it. What are some...

- Read the directions.
- Brainstorm a couple of additional ways (for example, *word-of-mouth, on the Internet*) and write them on the board.
- Pair students and ask them to think of at least three additional ways to find jobs.
- Call on pairs to share with the class.

Culture Connection

- Ask: *How do people find out about jobs in your home country?* (word-of-mouth, job postings at various places, . . .) *Can you use the same ways in the United States?*

Presentation   5 minutes

⊙ PAIRS. Read the information. Talk about it....

- Read the first sentence of the directions.
- Read the information to the class.
- Ask: *Which shift do you work?* Call on a few students to answer.
- Pair students.
- Walk around and check that students are discussing shifts. For students who do not work, tell them to discuss a shift they would like to work (for example, *I like the afternoon shift. I can go to work after class.*).
- Call on students to say what shift they work.

Controlled Practice   15 minutes

⊙ NETWORK. Find classmates with the same...

- Read the directions and ask a couple of students the questions (T: *Do you like your shift?* S: *Yes, I do.* T: *Why?* S: *Because I can go to class in the morning and work in the afternoon.*).
- Poll the class about which work shift they have. Assign students to sit with others with the same shift. Tell each group to ask the questions in the directions.
- If grouping is not possible because not enough students share the same shift, tell students to stand, mingle, and ask several other students the questions in the directions. Tell students to write down their classmates' answers to help them remember.
- To wrap up, call on students to report about who they talked with (for example, *Maria likes her shift. She works the day shift at a factory. She picks up her kids after work.*).

⊙ 🎵 Two friends are talking about a job...

- Read the directions. Preview the want ads with the class by calling on individual students to read each ad out loud.
- Say: *Circle the want ad they are talking about.* Play CD 4, Track 44. Students listen and circle the ad.
- Ask: *Which ad are they talking about?* (B) *How do we know B is the answer?* (Because no experience is necessary, it's part-time, and the pay is $7 an hour.)

⊙ PAIRS. Look at the ads again. Answer the question.

- Read the directions. Ask: *What information do we need to answer the question?* (the pay rate per hour and the number of hours per week)
- Pair students. Walk around and check that students are calculating the weekly pay using information from the want ad.
- Call on several students to say the answer. Call on a student who says the correct answer to come to the board and do the calculations.

⊙ WRITE. Write a want ad for a job you want....

- Read the directions. On the board, write the headings *Hours, Pay,* and *Experience required.* Call on students to suggest several options for each heading and write them on the board.
- Say: *Use abbreviations in your ads. Look at the ads on pages 232–233 for ideas.*
- Walk around and help with spelling. If students' ads are missing information, suggest what to include (for example, *What about experience?*).

Communicative Practice   10 minutes

⊙ PAIRS. Talk about your want ads. Why do you...

- Read the directions and the example.
- Pair students. Walk around and check that they are giving reasons for wanting the job they created.

⊙ Report to the class.

- Call on students to say the job their partner wants and to say why their partner wants that job.

Progress Check

Can you . . . read want ads?

Say: *We have practiced reading want ads. Now, look at the question at the bottom of the page. Can you read want ads?* Tell students to write a checkmark in the box.

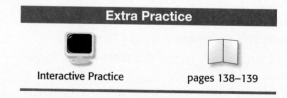

Extra Practice	
Interactive Practice	pages 138–139

C PAIRS. Read the information. Talk about it. Which shift do you work?

The **day shift** is usually from 7:00 A.M. to 3:00 P.M.
The **afternoon shift** is usually from 3:00 P.M. to 11:00 P.M. or 12:00 A.M.
The **night shift** is usually from 11:00 P.M. to 7:00 A.M.

D NETWORK. Find classmates with the same work shift as you. Form a group. Ask the people in your group, *Do you like your shift? Why?*

CD4 T44

E Two friends are talking about a job opening. Look at the want ads. Listen to the conversation. Which ad are they talking about?

HELP WANTED		
SALES ASSISTANT To work afternoon shift in busy store. FT. $10/hr. Call Tom: 323-555-4179	**STOCK CLERKS** PT., all shifts available. No exp. nec. From $7/hr. Fax: 915-555-2286	**NURSE'S ASSISTANT** Greenville General Hospital FT. M-F, 11 P.M. to 7 A.M. $12/hr. Apply in person. 5200 River St.
A	**B**	**C**

F PAIRS. Look at the ads again. Answer the question.

How much money does the nurse's assistant make in one week? _____$480_____

G WRITE. Write a want ad for a job you want. Include the hours, pay, and experience required.

H PAIRS. Talk about your want ads. Why do you want this job?

Antonio: *I want a job as a security guard. The pay is good, and I can work the day or night shift. What about you, Tamar?*

Tamar: *I want a job as . . .*

I Report to the class.

HELP WANTED

Antonio wants a job as a security guard.

Can you...read want ads? ☐

Listening and Speaking

1 BEFORE YOU LISTEN

READ. Look at the picture of the clothing store Imagine. Read the information. Answer the questions.

It's a busy day! It's Wednesday, and there is a big sale at Imagine. There are a lot of customers in the store. All of the salespeople are working hard. They are helping customers, working the cash registers, and taking returns. Right now, the elevator is out of order. People need to take the escalator. So the salespeople are giving directions, too.

1. Why are there a lot of people at Imagine today?
   a. It's the weekend.   (b.) There's a big sale.

2. Why are the salespeople giving directions?
   (a.) The elevator isn't working.   b. The store is very big.

2 LISTEN

A **Look at the picture again. Guess: Who is the woman?**

a. a customer   (b.) an employee

CD4 T45

B 🔘 **Listen to the conversation. Was your guess in Exercise A correct?**

Listen again. Which questions does the woman ask the man? Check (✓) the correct questions.

☑ Can you work this Saturday?   ☐ Can you work this evening?
☐ Can you work from 2:00 to 6:00?   ☑ Can you work from 2:00 to 7:00?

CD4 T46

C 🔘 **Listen to the whole conversation. Answer the questions.**

1. Who is the man?
   a. a new sales assistant   (b.) an elevator repair person

2. Who does the woman think the man is?
   (a.) a new sales assistant   b. an elevator repair person

3. What does the woman want the man to do?
   (a.) work her shift on Saturday   b. fix the elevator on Saturday

Getting Started
5 minutes

1 BEFORE YOU LISTEN

READ. **Look at the picture of the clothing store...**

- Read the directions. Ask lower-level students: *What do you see in the picture?* (a woman, a man, a clothing store)
- Ask higher-level students: *What's happening in the picture?* (A woman is talking to a man about the elevator.)
- Ask: *Is there a problem?* (Yes.) *What's the problem?* (The elevator [is broken].) *What does* out of order *mean?* (broken or not working)
- Read the paragraph while students read along silently. Explain any unfamiliar vocabulary. Then ask students to read it again silently.
- Ask the class to call out answers to the questions.

Presentation
25 minutes

2 LISTEN

Ⓐ Look at the picture again.... Guess:...

- Read the directions. Write the answer choices on the board and read them.
- Ask: *What is a customer?* (a person who buys things) *What is an employee?* (a person who works for someone)
- Ask: *Who is the woman, a customer or an employee?*
- Call on students to guess.

Ⓑ 💿 Listen to the conversation. Was...

- Read the first part of the directions. Play CD 4, Track 45.
- Ask: *Was your guess correct?* Circle the correct answer on the board. (Answer: an employee)

Teaching Tip

Optional: Remember that if students need additional support, tell them to read the Audio Script on page 290 as they listen to the conversation.

Listen again. Which questions does the woman ask...

- Read the directions. Read each choice and ask the class to repeat.
- Play Track 45 again. Students complete the sentences.
- Explain: I need a favor *means that you want someone to help you.*
- Play Track 45 again if many students have difficulty identifying the correct answers.
- Call on two students to say answers.
- To check answers, call on two students to write the sentences on the board. Correct as needed. Read them and ask the class to repeat.

Ⓒ 💿 Listen to the whole conversation....

- Read the directions. Play CD 4, Track 46.
- Call on students to ask and answer the questions.
- As needed, explain: Guy *as in* I'm the elevator repair guy *is an informal word for* man. Elevator repair guy *is an informal title.*
- Ask: *Why is the end of the conversation funny?* (Because Dana thinks Sam is an employee but he is really the elevator repairperson.)

Expansion: Listening Practice for 2C

- Conduct the following dictation activity: Tell students to write the numbers 1–5 on a sheet of paper. Call out the following work hours. Repeat once.

  1. *7:00 to 3:00*
  2. *4:00 to 11:00*
  3. *6:30 to 12:30*
  4. *8:30 to 4:00*
  5. *5:00 to 1:00*

- Call on students to write the answers on the board. Correct as necessary.

Lesson 5 Talk about hours you can work

3 CONVERSATION

Ⓐ 🔘 Listen. Then listen and repeat.

- Read the directions and the Pronunciation Watch note. Play CD 4, Track 47. Students listen.
- Say: *The pronunciation of* can *and* can't *in short answers is different from their pronunciation in questions.* Ask: *How is it different?* (In questions, *can* is unstressed and *can't* is stressed. In short answers, *can* and *can't* are both stressed.)
- Resume playing Track 47. Students listen and repeat.

Controlled Practice   15 minutes

Ⓑ 🔘 Listen and read the conversation....

- Note: This conversation is the same one students heard in Exercise 2B on page 234.
- Say: *Listen for the different ways to pronounce* can *and* can't.
- Play CD 4, Track 48. Students listen and read along silently.
- Resume playing Track 48. Students listen and repeat.
- Walk around and check that students are stressing *can/can't* correctly.

4 PRACTICE

Ⓐ PAIRS. Practice the conversation. Then make new...

- Pair students and tell them to practice the conversation in Exercise 3B.
- Then, in Exercise 4A, tell students to look at the information in the boxes. Say each place, day, and time period and ask the class to repeat.
- Copy the conversation onto the board with blanks and read it. When you come to a blank, fill it in with information from the boxes (for example, *restaurant, tomorrow, 6:00–11:00*).
- Ask two on-level students to practice the conversation for the class. Tell pairs to take turns playing each role and to use the words in the boxes to fill in the blanks.

- Tell students to stand, mingle, and practice the conversation with several new partners.
- Call on pairs to perform for the class.

■ **MULTILEVEL INSTRUCTION for 4A**

Pre-level Tell students to write answers in the blanks before practicing.

Above-level As part of their last line, ask students playing A to give a reason why they can't work (for example, A: *... because I can't. I have a doctor's appointment. Can you work ...?*).

■ **Expansion: Vocabulary and Speaking Practice for 4A**

- Ask who works in each place (for example, *Who works in a restaurant?*) and on the board, write the jobs students say for each place (for example, *restaurant: server, busperson, cook, host/hostess*).
- Tell pairs to continue their conversations to include a misunderstanding where A thinks B is an employee (for example, A: *Aren't you the new server?* B: *No, I'm here to eat lunch. I'm a customer!*).

Communicative Practice   15 minutes

Ⓑ ROLE PLAY. PAIRS. Make your own...

- Read the directions. On the board, write the headings *Places*, *Days*, and *Hours*. Call on students to say additional vocabulary similar to the information in the boxes in Exercise 4A (for example, *post office, gas station, Tuesday, from 7:00 to 4:00*) and write it on the board.
- Play A and, with an above-level student, use information from the board and make up a new conversation.
- Pair students and tell them to take turns playing A and B.
- Walk around and check that students are using information from the board.
- Call on pairs to role-play for the class.

3 CONVERSATION

CD4 T47

A 🔘 **Listen. Then listen and repeat.**

A: Can you start tomorrow?

B: Yes, I **can**.

A: Can you work Saturday?

B: No, I **can't**.

CD4 T48

B 🔘 **Listen and read the conversation. Then listen and repeat.**

Dana: Hi, I'm Dana.

Sam: Hi, I'm Sam. Wow. This store is really busy.

Dana: I know. Listen, I need a favor. Can you work this Saturday?

Sam: Uh, well, yes, I can.

Dana: Oh, great, thanks, because I can't. Can you work from 2:00 to 7:00?

Sam: Um, yes. I guess so.

4 PRACTICE

A PAIRS. **Practice the conversation. Then make new conversations. Use the words in the boxes.**

A: This _____ is really busy.

B: I know. Listen, I need a favor.
Can you work _____ ?

A: Uh, well, yes, I can.

B: Oh, great, thanks, because I can't.
Can you work from _____ ?

A: Um, yes. I guess so.

restaurant	tomorrow	6:00–11:00
hospital	Monday	8:00–3:00
hotel	June 11	4:00–10:00

B ROLE PLAY. PAIRS. **Make your own conversations. Ask someone you work with to change shifts with you.**

A: *Listen, I need a favor. Can you work _____?*

B: *_____? Yes, I can.*

A: *Oh, great. And can you work _____?*

B: *_____? Sure.*

A: *Thanks!*

Grammar

Can: Yes/no questions and short answers

| Can | you
he
she
Sam
they | work
use | this Saturday?
a computer? | | Yes, | I
he
she
he
they | can. | No, | I
he
she
he
they | can't. |

1   **PRACTICE**

> Remember: Use a comma (,) after *Yes* or *No* in short answers.

A   **WRITE. Write questions with *can*.**
Use the words in parentheses. Give short answers.

1. **A:** ___Can you work nights?___
              (you / work nights)
   B: ___Yes, I can.___ I'm free every night.

2. **A:** ___Can you work weekends?___
              (you / work weekends)
   B: ___No, I can't.___ I can only work weekdays. I'm busy on weekends.

3. **A:** ___Can you come to work early tomorrow?___
              (you / come to work early tomorrow)
   B: ___Yes, I can.___ What time should I come in?

4. **A:** ___Can she start tomorrow?___
              (she / start tomorrow)
   B: ___Yes, she can.___ She can be here at 9:00.

5. **A:** ___Can your sister fix the car?___
              (your sister / fix the car)
   B: ___Yes, she can.___ She's good with cars.

6. **A:** ___Can Bill drive a truck?___
              (Bill / drive a truck)
   B: ___No, he can't.___ He doesn't have a driver's license.

CD4 T49

B   **Listen and check your answers.**

C   **PAIRS. Practice the conversations in Exercise A.**

Lesson 6 Ask about job skills

Getting Started   5 minutes

- Say: *We're going to study* can *in yes/no questions and short answers. In the conversation on page 235, Dana and Sam used this grammar.*
- Play CD 4, Track 48. Students listen. Write on the board: *Can you work this Saturday?* and *Yes, I can.* Underline *Can you work* and *Yes, I can.*

Presentation   10 minutes

Can: Yes/no questions and short answers

- Copy the grammar charts onto the board or show Transparency 12.4 and cover the exercise.
- Read a couple of questions from the left chart and ask the class to repeat. Model rising intonation for the questions and falling intonation for the answers.
- Ask: *Why do we use the base form of the verb?* (Because of *can.*)
- Say: *To make a short answer, say* yes *or* no *and then use a subject pronoun and* can *or* can't.
- Read short answers from the right chart and ask the class to repeat.
- Ask students to close their books. Remove any visual aids for the chart. Write the following on the board (don't write the words in parentheses):

    1. *Can you _____ the phone?* (answer) *Yes, I _____.* (can)
    2. *Can she _____ heavy boxes?* (lift) *No, she _____.* (can't)
    3. *_____ they make copies?* (Can) *Yes, _____ _____.* (they can)

- Call on students to say the correct answers. Fill in the blanks on the board.
- If you are using the transparency, do the exercise with the class.

Controlled Practice   15 minutes

1 PRACTICE

A WRITE. Write questions with *can*. Use the words...

- Read the directions and the first item.
- Copy item 1 onto the board. Use it to illustrate the points below.

- Explain: *In the question, put* Can *first. Then put the subject* (you), *then the verb* (work), *and then* nights *because it tells us when he works.*
- Ask: *How do you know the answer is yes?* (Because the next sentence is *I'm free every night.*) Say: *Read and be sure you understand the sentence for line B to know if the answer is* yes *or* no.
- Students compare answers with a partner.

B Listen and check your answers.

- Play CD 4, Track 49 as often as needed.

C PAIRS. Practice the conversation in Exercise A.

- Pair students and tell them to practice all the conversations as A or B and then to switch roles.
- Walk around and check that students are using rising intonation when asking questions and falling intonation when replying.
- To wrap up, call on pairs to perform for the class.

MULTILEVEL INSTRUCTION for 1C
Pre-level Promote fluency by modeling questions and answers and asking students to repeat before they practice in pairs.
Above-level Pairs make up new conversations by improvising new responses to the same questions (for example, 1. A: *Can you work nights?* B: *No, I can't. I take English classes at night.*).

Expansion: Writing and Speaking Practice for 1C

- Ask students to write in their notebooks five work-related things they can do (for example, *I can use a computer.*) and five things they can't do (for example, *I can't lift heavy boxes.*).
- Tell them to write questions for each of their statements (for example, *Can you use a computer?*) on a separate piece of paper.
- Pair students and tell them to practice taking turns reading each other's questions and responding to them.

Communicative Practice   30 minutes

2 PRACTICE

A Look at the want ad. Write job interview questions...

- Read the directions and the want ad.
- As needed, explain *files* (papers you keep in a folder and usually put in a cabinet).
- Say: *Choose information from the ad and ask a question about it. For example, what question can you ask about the work hours?* (Can you work full-time?) Write *Can you work full-time?* on the board.
- Say: *Write questions with* can *for four other pieces of information in the ad.*
- Walk around and check that students are writing *Can you* in front of the ad information.
- Students compare answers with a partner.
- Call on students to write their questions on the board. Tell the class to call out corrections. Correct as needed.

B PAIRS. Student A, ask the questions in Exercise A...

- Read the directions and the example conversation.
- Pair students and tell them to take turns asking the questions they wrote in Exercise A. If students wish, they can answer with made-up information.
- Say: *Student B, to add more information, talk about a skill that is similar to the one Student A asks you about.* To reinforce, review the example conversation and say: *Taking messages and answering the phone go together.*
- To wrap up, call on pairs to perform for the class. Each pair can ask just a couple of questions.

MULTILEVEL INSTRUCTION for 2B

Pre-level First practice with pairs by having them ask you a question (for example, S: *Can you work full-time?* T: *Yes, I can.*).

Above-level Partners being asked give one or two negative responses but then say something else they can do (for example, A: *Can you organize files?* B: *No, I can't. I don't know how to file, but I can use a computer.*).

C WRITE. In your notebook, write five sentences...

- Read the directions. Tell students to write answers to the questions in Exercise A.

- Brainstorm with the class to identify additional skills by asking students to say their various skills. Write some on the board for others to use.
- Walk around and check spelling, grammar, and capitalization.

Show what you know!

STEP 1. Think of a job. Write the name of the job.

- Read the directions. Tell students they can write any job. Review job vocabulary in this unit by asking students to call out the jobs they remember.
- Call on several students to say the job they wrote. Ask students why they chose that job.

STEP 2. GROUPS OF 5. Student A, say, "Guess...

- Read the directions. With four students, practice the example conversation.
- Form groups of 5. Say: *When you think you know the job, ask,* Are you a . . . ? *Wait for your turn to ask.*
- Walk around and participate with the various groups to monitor students' comprehension.
- To wrap up, play the game as a whole class.

Expansion: Writing and Speaking Practice

- Ask students to create their own want ad for a job they want to have. To get them started, ask students to think about exactly what they want (for example, *part-time, 20 hours a week, mornings, M–F, some filing, answering phones*).
- Students then practice interviewing each other for each position.

Progress Check

Can you . . . ask about job skills?

Say: *We have practiced asking about job skills. Now, look at the question at the bottom of the page. Can you ask about job skills?* Tell students to write a checkmark in the box.

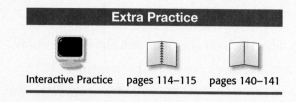

Extra Practice		
Interactive Practice	pages 114–115	pages 140–141

2 PRACTICE

A Look at the want ad. Write job interview questions with *can*.
Ask about a job applicant's skills and work hours.

1. Can you answer phones? _____

2. Can you use a computer? _____

3. Can you organize files? _____

4. Can you write reports? _____

5. Can you work full-time? _____

> **HELP WANTED**
>
> Office assistant. Answer phones, use a computer, organize files, write reports. Full-time.

B PAIRS. Student A, ask the questions in Exercise A. Student B, give true answers and add information.

A: *Can you answer phones?*
B: *Yes, I can. I can take messages, too.*

C WRITE. In your notebook, write five sentences about your skills. Use skills from Exercise A or other skills.

Show what you know! Ask about job skills

STEP 1. Think of a job. Write the name of the job. _____

STEP 2. GROUPS OF 5. Student A, say, "Guess my job." Other students, ask *yes/no* questions with *can* about Student A's job skills. You can ask ten questions.

A: *Guess my job.*
B: *Can you use a cash register?*
A: *No, I can't.*
C: *Can you drive a truck?*
A: *No, I can't.*
D: *Can you make furniture?*
A: *Yes, I can.*
E: *Are you a carpenter?*
A: *Yes, I am.*
B: *OK, my turn. Guess my job.*

Can you... ask about job skills? ☐

Reading

1 BEFORE YOU READ

A **Read the paragraph. Then complete the sentence.**

When you meet someone for the first time, you form an opinion about that person. For example, you think, "This person is helpful" or "This person is fun." This is your *first impression*.

A first impression is your opinion about a person you meet for the ___first___ time.

B **PAIRS.** **Talk about it. Think about someone at work or school. What was your first impression of this person?**

A: *I work with Camilo. My first impression was, "He's really friendly."*
B: *Simone is in my computer class. . . .*

C **A person's *body language* is one thing that helps you form an impression. Your body language is important in a job interview. Look at the pictures. Read the sentences. Then practice the body language.**

a

They're shaking hands firmly.

b

They're making eye contact.

c

She has her hands on her lap.

d

He's leaning forward.

e

She's smiling.

f

He's standing about three feet away.

Getting Started   20 minutes

1   BEFORE YOU READ

Ⓐ Read the paragraph. Then complete the sentence.

- Read the directions.
- Read the paragraph while the class follows along silently.
- Read the final sentence, stop at the blank, and have the class call *first* to complete it.

Ⓑ PAIRS. Talk about it. Think about someone...

- Read the directions and the example.
- Brainstorm various adjectives to describe first impressions (for example, *nice, friendly, funny, serious, smart, . . .*) and write them on the board.
- As a fun warm-up, ask the class to talk about their first impression of you, the teacher.
- Pair students. Tell them to each take turns describing their first impression of someone they know from work or school. Encourage students to use the adjectives on the board.
- Walk around and check that students are using adjectives to describe people. If they have difficulty, model expressions for them to repeat (for example, *He's really smart. He's really funny.*).

Ⓒ A person's *body language* is one thing that helps...

- Read the directions.
- Say: *Body language is part of communication. People learn what you are thinking or feeling from how you are moving your body and your face.*
- Read the sentence in each box, then demonstrate each action for the class.

    Expansion: Listening Practice for 1C

- Call pairs to the front of the class and issue body language commands to them (for example, *Shake hands firmly and smile.*).

> **Teaching Tip**
>
> Demonstrate "bad" body language by not making eye contact, shaking hands weakly, standing too close to someone as examples of what not to do. Students may find it humorous, which may help reinforce good body language habits.

Presentation   10 minutes

2 READ

🔘 **Listen. Read the article.**

- Ask: *What is the title?* Say: *Look at the picture. What is happening in the picture? What does it say under the picture?* (A good job interview . . .)
- Play CD 4, Track 50. Students listen and read along silently.
- *Optional:* Pause the CD after each paragraph and ask the following questions:

    First paragraph: *Why is body language important?* (Because you make an impression with your body language.)

    Second paragraph: *What should you do when you meet the interviewer?* (shake hands firmly, make eye contact, . . .)

    Third paragraph: *How can you be a good listener?* (sit up, lean forward, don't touch your face, . . .)

    Fourth paragraph: *When the interview is over, what should you do?* (shake hands, smile, thank the interviewer, . . .)

- If students have difficulty following along, play Track 50 again and pause as needed.
- Ask students if there are words they do not understand and explain them.

Controlled Practice   10 minutes

3 CHECK YOUR UNDERSTANDING

🅐 **CLASS. Read the article again. What is the main...**

- Read the directions. Allow time for students to read the article again. Remind students: *The main idea is the most important point in the article.*
- Call on a few students to say their answer. Some answers may vary slightly.

🅑 **PAIRS. Give each other tips on good body language...**

- Read the directions and the example conversation.
- Tell students to first look back at the article and to write three tips they like.
- Pair students. Tell them to talk about the tips.
- To wrap up, call on several students to say several tips. Write any good new ones on the board.

🅒 **CLASS. Talk about it. What are some other ways...**

- Ask students to call out other ways to make a good first impression in a job interview. Write them on the board in complete sentences.
- If students have difficulty thinking of ideas, give them examples of ways not to behave and ask them how to correct this behavior (for example, T: *Is it good to wear shorts and a T-shirt?* Ss: *No!* T: *Then what should you wear?* Ss: *Nice/Business clothes.*). Write their suggestions on the board.
- Ask students to copy the list on the board into their notebooks. To wrap up, call on students to read items from the list on the board and to suggest any other ways to make a good first impression.

Communicative Practice   15 minutes

Show what you know!

PAIRS. Role-play a job interview. Use good...

- Read the directions. Pair students and ask them to think of a job.
- Ask each partner to write three tips he or she will use in the interview (for example, *stand three feet away, shake hands, make eye contact*).
- Tell the interviewer to ask questions using *can*. Tell the interviewee to answer the questions and to demonstrate three body language tips.
- Call on pairs to perform for the class. Provide feedback about body language and clarity of speech.

▊▊ MULTILEVEL INSTRUCTION

Pre-level After each pair has thought of a job to interview for, sit with students and help them create appropriate questions for that job.

Above-level Ask students to include information about schedule and availability in their conversations.

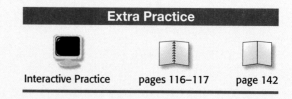

Extra Practice		
Interactive Practice	pages 116–117	page 142

CD4 T50

Listen. Read the article.

MAKING A GOOD FIRST IMPRESSION

You have a job interview. How can you make a good first impression? Your words are important, but your body language is important too. Here are some tips.

When you meet the interviewer, shake hands firmly. Stand about three feet away. Make eye contact and smile. You may feel stressed, but try to look relaxed.

A good job interview starts with good body language.

When you sit down, stay relaxed and look friendly. Sit up in your chair and lean forward a little. This shows you are listening to the interviewer. Put your hands on your lap. Don't touch your face or hair.

When you leave the interview, shake hands with the interviewer again. Smile and make eye contact. And don't forget: Thank the interviewer.

Practice all these tips before you go to your interview. The right body language can help you get the job. Good luck!

3 CHECK YOUR UNDERSTANDING

A CLASS. Read the article again. What is the main idea?

The right body language helps you make a good first impression.

B PAIRS. Give each other tips on good body language for a job interview. Use your own words.

A: *First, you should shake hands and smile.*
B: *Right. And you should also . . .*

C CLASS. Talk about it. What are some other ways to make a good first impression in a job interview?

Show what you know!

PAIRS. Role play a job interview. Use good body language!

Talk about work experience

Listening and Speaking

1 **LISTEN**

A Look at the picture of Bao Tran and Hanh Le in the *Greenville Reporter*.

Guess: Why are they in the newspaper?

They are opening a restaurant in Greenville. or They have a new restaurant.

CD4 T51

B Listen to the Greenville News Radio show *Meet Your Neighbors*. Was your guess in Exercise A correct?

CD4 T51

C Listen again. Complete the sentences. Choose the correct words from the box.

| a hospital | people's homes |
| a restaurant | a hotel |

1. Bao was a cook in _____a restaurant_____ .

2. Hanh was a cook in _____people's homes_____ .

D Complete the newspaper article. Use words from the radio interview with Bao and Hanh.

ON THE AIR

People in the News

Greenville Reporter

Meet Bao Tran and Hanh Le. They are the owners of *Saigon*, Greenville's first Vietnamese ___restaurant___. Many people here know Bao and Hanh. Bao was a ___cashier___, a waiter, and a ___cook___ at the Greenville Café for ___8___ years, and Hanh worked in many people's homes as a cook. Bao and Hanh were also ___students___ at the Greenville Adult School. Their first teacher, Emily Reed, says: "They were very good ___students___, but they were *great* ___cooks___. Our class parties were always wonderful because of Bao and Hanh's ___food___. I'm sure their restaurant will be a big success." Everyone in Greenville wishes the couple lots of luck.

Bao Tran (left) and Hanh Le

E PAIRS. Compare answers.

Talk about work experience

Getting Started   5 minutes

1   LISTEN

A **Look at the picture.... Guess:...**

- Read the directions.
- Ask: *Where are Bao and Hanh? Why are they in the newspaper?*
- Call on students to guess. Write their guesses on the board.

Presentation   5 minutes

B  **Listen to the Greenville News Radio...**

- Read the directions. Play CD 4, Track 51.
- Explain: Is this your first restaurant? *means* Is this the first restaurant that you have owned?
- Ask: *Was your guess correct?* Write the correct answer on the board.
- Ask: *Where is the restaurant?* (Right across from the new Foodsmart Supermarket.)

> **Teaching Tip**
>
> *Optional:* Remember that if students need additional support, tell them to read the Audio Script on page 290 as they listen to the conversation.

Controlled Practice   20 minutes

C **Listen again. Complete the sentences....**

- Read the directions.
- Read the places in the word box while the class repeats.
- Play Track 51 again. Students listen and then complete the sentences.
- Play Track 51 as many times as necessary to aid comprehension.
- To check answers, read each sentence and tell the class to call out the answer.

> **Culture Connection**
>
> - Say: *Many people in the United States like to start their own business.*
> - Ask: *Do you want to start your own business? What kind of business would you like to have?* (restaurant, store, . . .)

D **Complete the newspaper article. Use words from...**

- Read the directions. Read the article with the blanks as students follow along.
- Play Track 51 again and tell students to fill in the blanks with the missing information. Pause the track after the first answer is revealed. Resume playing the CD to allow the class to complete the exercise.

E **PAIRS. Compare answers.**

- Pair students. Students show each other their completed articles.
- To check answers, call on students to take turns reading the completed article.

> **Teaching Tip**
>
> Completion activities such as the one in Exercise 1D are a great opportunity for students to demonstrate their reading comprehension.
>
> If possible, meet with students individually and ask them several comprehension questions about the article to gauge their comprehension —for example, *Who owns the Saigon restaurant?* (Bao Tran and Hanh Le) *Who was their first teacher?* (Emily Reed)
>
> If individual meetings are not possible, send students home with a list of questions about the reading and have them write answers for homework.

Controlled Practice   20 minutes

2 CONVERSATION

Ⓐ When a person is successful at something...

- Write *successful* on the board. Ask: *What does to be successful mean?* (*Some possible answers:* to be happy, to have money, to have a business)
- Read the directions. Ask students to carefully read the conversation silently.
- Ask: *Why does Ayantu say "Congratulations!" to Ivan?* (Because Ivan has his first café.)

Ⓑ 💿 Listen and read the conversation....

- Play CD 4, Track 52. Students listen and read along silently.
- Resume playing Track 52. Students listen and repeat.

3 PRACTICE

Ⓐ PAIRS. Practice the conversation. Then make new...

- Pair students and tell them to practice the conversation in Exercise 2B.
- Then, in Exercise 3A, ask students to look at the pictures and say what they are. *Hair stylist* is new vocabulary, so ask: *What is a hair stylist?* (someone who works in a hair salon who cuts and styles hair)
- Copy the conversation onto the board with blanks and read it. When you come to a blank, fill it in with information from the boxes (for example, *hair salon, hair stylist, three*).
- Ask two on-level students to practice the conversation in front of the class.
- Tell pairs to take turns playing each role and to use the pictures to fill in the blanks.
- Walk around and check that students are stressing important words and using rising intonation for questions.
- Tell students to stand, mingle, and practice the conversation with several new partners.
- Call on pairs to perform for the class.

▰ MULTILEVEL INSTRUCTION for 3A

Pre-level To focus on fluency, model the intonation of each line in the conversation, substituting new information, and ask students to repeat before practicing with a partner.

Above-level Tell the interviewers to ask their partner why he or she started a business (for example, A: *Why did you start your own café?* B: *Because I wanted to be successful and happy.*).

Communicative Practice   10 minutes

Ⓑ ROLE PLAY. PAIRS. Make your own...

- Read the directions. On the board, write the headings *Places, Jobs,* and *Times.* Call on students to say additional vocabulary similar to the information in the boxes in Exercise 3A (for example, *restaurant, cook, two years*) and write it on the board.
- Play A and, with an above-level student, use information from the board and make up a new conversation.
- Pair students and tell them to take turns playing A and B.
- Walk around and check that students are using information from the board.
- Call on pairs to role-play for the class.
- To wrap up, on the board write some of the errors you heard during the role plays. Ask students to correct the mistakes. Go over the corrections by saying the words or sentences correctly and asking the class to repeat.

▰ MULTILEVEL INSTRUCTION for 3B

Cross-ability The lower-level students can read from cue cards with interview questions written on them. Partners work together to write the questions on the cards before practicing.

Extra Practice

Interactive Practice

2 CONVERSATION

A When a person is successful at something, we say "Congratulations!" Read the conversation in Exercise B. Why does Ayantu say "Congratulations!" to Ivan?

CD4 T52

B Listen and read the conversation. Then listen and repeat.

Ayantu: Congratulations! This place looks great!
Ivan: Thanks.
Ayantu: So, is this your first café?
Ivan: Yes, it is. But I worked in a café before.
Ayantu: Oh. What did you do?
Ivan: I was a waiter.
Ayantu: How long were you there?
Ivan: Two years.

3 PRACTICE

A PAIRS. Practice the conversation. Then make new conversations. Use the information in the boxes.

A: Congratulations! This place looks great!
B: Thanks.
A: So, is this your first _____ ?
B: Yes, it is. But I worked in a _____ before.
A: Oh. What did you do?
B: I was a _____ .
A: How long were you there?
B: _____ years.

B ROLE PLAY. PAIRS. Make your own conversations. Use different stores, jobs, and times.

hair salon

hair stylist

three

grocery store

cashier

four

clothing store

sales assistant

five

Grammar

Past of *be*: Questions and answers

Were	you they			I we they	**was.** **were.** **were.**		I we they	**wasn't.** **weren't.** **weren't.**	
Was	he Bao she it	successful?	**Yes,**	he she it	**was.** **was.** **was.**	**No,**	he she it	**wasn't.** **wasn't.** **wasn't.**	
How long were	you	at your last job?		Five years. From 2003 to 2008.					

PRACTICE

A   WRITE. **Write questions. Use *was* or *were*.**

1. What / your last job   <u>What was your last job?</u>

2. the job / full-time   <u>Was the job full-time?</u>

3. How long / you / there   <u>How long were you there?</u>

4. you / happy there   <u>Were you happy there?</u>

CD4 T53

B   💿 **Listen and check your answers.**

C   PAIRS. **Student A, you are a manager. Student B, you are a job applicant. Student A, interview the job applicant. Ask the questions in Exercise A. Student B, look at the job application. Answer the manager's questions.**

A: *What was your last job?*
B: *I was a cashier.*

> **Grammar Watch**
>
> **Contractions**
> ***wasn't*** = was not
> ***weren't*** = were not

JOB HISTORY:

Company: <u>Sam's Department Store</u>   **Address:** <u>3 Main Street</u>

Phone Number: <u>(760) 555-1279</u>   <u>Riverside, California 93501</u>

Job: <u>Cashier (full-time)</u>   **Dates Worked: From** <u>2001</u> **To** <u>2007</u>

Reason for Leaving: <u>store closed</u>

Talk about work experience

Getting Started   5 minutes

- Say: *We're going to study simple past questions and answers with* be. *In the conversation on page 241, Ivan used this grammar.*
- Play CD 4, Track 52. Students listen. Write *How long were you there?* on the board. Underline *How long were.*

Presentation   5 minutes

Past of *be*: Questions and answers

- Copy the grammar charts onto the board or show Transparency 12.5 and cover the exercise.
- Read the questions from the left chart while the class repeats.
- Read the affirmative short answers from the right chart while the class repeats.
- Ask specific questions from the left chart (for example, *Was he successful?*) and call on individual students to give an appropriate affirmative short answer (*Yes, he was.*).
- Read the Grammar Watch note. Say the negative short answers while the class repeats.
- Continue asking individual specific questions but tell students to answer negatively (for example, T: *Was it full-time?* S: *No, it wasn't.*).
- If you are using the transparency, do the exercise with the class.

Controlled Practice   10 minutes

 **PRACTICE**

A WRITE. **Write questions. Use** *was* **or** *were***.**

- Read the directions and the example. Ask: *Where do you put* was? (after *What*)
- Say: *If you see a* Wh- *word, use a form of* be *after it. If there is no* Wh- *word, use the form of* be *first.*

B 🔘 **Listen and check your answers.**

- Play CD 4, Track 53. Students listen and check their answers.
- Call on students to say answers.

Communicative Practice   10 minutes

C PAIRS. **Student A, you are a manager. Student B,...**

- Read the directions and the example. For each field in the application, say the name and ask students to call out the written information (for example, T: *Company. What is the company?* Ss: *Sam's Department Store.*).
- Pair students. Tell A to write a few questions first while B reviews the information in the application.
- Walk around and ask interview-style questions as you visit each pair.
- To wrap up, on the board write some of the errors you heard during the role plays. Ask students to correct the mistakes. Go over the corrections by saying the words or sentences correctly and asking the class to repeat.

■■■ **MULTILEVEL INSTRUCTION for C**

Pre-level Write possible questions for each field on a sheet of paper (for example, *What company did you work for?*) and hand them out as a reference for students to use while they practice.

Above-level In addition to the questions about the information in the application, ask each interviewer to ask one or two questions more.

■■■ **Expansion: Vocabulary and Critical Thinking Practice for C**

- With the class, brainstorm additional reasons for leaving a job and write them on the board (for example, *change in work schedule, conflict with school schedule*).
- Ask students to discuss which reasons are good and which are not good (for example, *bad boss—It's not good to say* bad boss *because it shows that I might not like the new boss.*).

Extra Practice
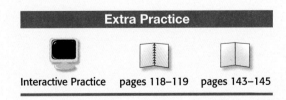
Interactive Practice   pages 118–119   pages 143–145

1 GRAMMAR

Eun-Young Lim is interviewing for a job as a...

- Read the directions and the example.
- Tell students to refer back to the grammar charts on pages 230 and 236 (*can/can't*) and 242 (*were/was*) as needed.
- Students compare answers with a partner.
- Read the conversations and call on individual students to say answers.
- *Optional:* Pair students and ask them to practice the conversations. Call on pairs to perform the completed conversations for the class.

Expansion: Writing and Speaking Practice for 1

- Ask pairs to rewrite the conversation using different information (for example, *Spanish* instead of *Korean*).
- Then ask each pair to perform the new conversation.

2 WRITING

STEP 1. Complete the information about a job...

- Read the directions. Tell students they can make up information if they don't want to use true information.
- Tell students to look back at the application on page 242 for ideas.
- Walk around and check that students are writing appropriate answers. If many students fail to understand some fields in the application, write them on the board and brainstorm various appropriate answers.

STEP 2. Write three sentences about the job in Step 1.

- Read the example sentences.
- Create a couple of sentences from information on the board (if any) from Step 1. Or ask a student to tell you some information from his or her application that you can use to make a sentence.
- Walk around and check that students are capitalizing the first letter of the first word, using the past tense of *be*, and using proper punctuation.
- To wrap up, call on several students to read their sentences out loud. Write them on the board.

Teaching Tip

Students can first practice writing sentences in their notebooks before transferring them to the textbook page.

3 LIFE SKILLS WRITING

Turn to page 264 and ask students to complete the job application. See pages Txi–Txii for general notes about the Life Skills Writing activities.

CD-ROM Practice

 Go to the CD-ROM for more practice.

If your students need more practice with the vocabulary, grammar, and competencies in Unit 12, encourage them to review the activities on the CD-ROM. This review can also help students prepare for the final role play on the following Expand page.

Extra Practice

pages 120–121

1 GRAMMAR

Eun-Young Lim is interviewing for a job as a sales assistant at Imagine.
Complete the parts of the interview with *was*, *were*, *can*, and *can't*.

1. **Manager:**   So, I see you _____ *were* _____ a sales assistant at Creative Clothing

   in Smithfield. How long _____ *were* _____ you there?

   Eun-Young: Three years. I _____ *was* _____ there from 2003 to 2006. Then my family moved.

2. **Manager:**   So, _____ *can* _____ you speak Korean? We have a lot of Korean customers.

   Eun-Young: Yes, I _____ *can* _____ speak Korean, English, and a little Spanish.

   I _____ *was* _____ a cashier in a Mexican restaurant for six months.

3. **Manager:**   Our store is always busy on weekends. _____ *Can* _____ you work weekends?

   Eun-Young: Well, I can work Saturdays, but I _____ *can't* _____ work Sundays.

   Manager: That's OK. When can you start?

   Eun-Young: I _____ *can* _____ start next weekend.

2 WRITING

STEP 1. Complete the information about a job you had. Use true or
made-up information.

Company: _____

Job: _____   Dates Worked: From _____ To _____

Reason for Leaving: _____

STEP 2. Write three sentences about the job in Step 1.

I was a sales assistant at Creative Clothing in Smithfield. I was there for three years.

I left because my family moved. _____

_____

_____

_____

3 LIFE SKILLS WRITING   Complete a job application. See page 264.

4 ACT IT OUT — What do you say?

CD4 T54

STEP 1. Listen to the job interview.

STEP 2. Choose a place and a job. Make a list of the skills you need for this job. Student A, you are the manager. Interview Student B for the job. Ask about Student B's skills and experience. Ask when Student B can work.

HELP WANTED!
Cooks, Waiters

HELP WANTED!
Sales Assistants, Stock Clerks

HELP WANTED!
Office Assistants

5 READ AND REACT — Problem-solving

STEP 1. Read about Jin-Su's problem.

Jin-Su is a supervisor in a large store. He finds new employees for the store. He interviews people for cashier jobs and sales jobs. Jin-Su's manager thinks Jin-Su is a good supervisor, because he always finds good employees.

Jin-Su's younger cousin Min-Ji needs a job. Min-Ji wants to work as a cashier. She asks Jin-Su, "Can I work at your store?" Jin-Su wants to help Min-Ji. But he doesn't think she is a good worker. She is always late, and she isn't very organized.

STEP 2. PAIRS. Talk about it. What is Jin-Su's problem? What can he do? Here are some ideas.

- He can say, "There are no job openings now."
- He can give Min-Ji a job.
- He can help Min-Ji find a different job.
- He can _____.

6 CONNECT

For your Goal-setting Activity, go to page 252.
For your Team Project, go to page 272.

Which goals can you check off? Go back to page 225.

4   ACT IT OUT

STEP 1. 💿 Listen to the job interview.

- Play CD 4, Track 54. Students listen.
- As needed, play Track 54 again to aid comprehension.

STEP 2. Choose a place and a job. Make a list of...

- Pair students. Read the directions and the guidelines for A and B. For each picture, ask: *What is this place?* (restaurant/store/office) *What jobs are available?* (cooks, waiters, sales assistants, . . .). Briefly brainstorm what skills are associated with each job (for example, T: *What skills do you need to be a sales assistant?* S: *You need to help customers.*).
- Tell students playing A to prepare their information first by writing a list of questions to ask. Tell students playing B to write down their skills and experience.
- As pairs prepare, tell them to reverse roles to practice both positions.
- While pairs are performing, use the scoring rubric on page Txiv to evaluate each student's vocabulary, grammar, fluency, and how well they complete the task. If time permits, ask pairs to switch roles and do a second performance.
- *Optional:* After each pair finishes, discuss the strengths and weaknesses of each performance either in front of the class or privately.

5   READ AND REACT

STEP 1. Read about Jin-Su's problem.

- Say: *We are going to read about a student's problem, and then we need to think about a solution.*
- Read the directions.
- Read the story while students follow along silently. Pause after each sentence to allow time for students to comprehend. Periodically stop and ask simple *Wh-* questions to check comprehension—for example, *What is Jin-Su's job?* (He is a supervisor in a large store.) *Who needs a job?* (Jin-Su's cousin)

STEP 2. PAIRS. Talk about it. What is Jin-Su's problem? What...

- Pair students. Ask: *What is Jin-Su's problem?* (His cousin wants a job, but she isn't a good worker.) *What can Jin-Su do?*
- Read the ideas in the list. Ask: *Which ideas are good?* Call on students to say their opinion about the ideas in the box (for example, S: *I think he can give Min-Ji a job because he can train her to get better.*).
- Pairs students. Tell them to think of one new idea not in the box (for example, *He can tell Min-Ji to take a job skills class.*) and to write it in the blank. Encourage students to think of more than one idea and to write them in their notebooks.
- Call on pairs to say their additional solutions. Write any particularly good ones on the board and ask students if they think it is a good idea, too (*Do you think this is a good idea? Why or why not?*).

▬▬ MULTILEVEL INSTRUCTION for STEP 2

Pre-level Sit with students, say each idea in the list, and ask students to explain why they like or don't like each solution (for example, A: *He can't say there are no openings because it is not true.*).

Above-level Pairs discuss the problems with each idea (for example, A: *If he gives her a job, maybe she will do badly.*).

▬▬ CONNECT

Turn to page 252 for guidelines for the Goal-setting Activity and page 272 for the Team Project. See pages Txi–Txii for general notes about teaching these activities.

Progress Check

Which goals can you check off? Go back to page 225.

Ask students to turn to page 225 and check off the goals they have reached. Call on students to say which goals they will practice outside of class.

Persistence Activities

Unit 1   Name Game

GROUPS OF 5. Play the Name Game.

Diana: My name is Diana.

Luis: This is Diana. My name is Luis.

Olga: This is Diana. This is Luis. My name is Olga.

Tran: This is Diana. Excuse me. What's your name again, please?

Luis: Luis.

Tran: OK, thanks. This is Diana. This is Luis. This is Olga. My name is Tran.

Laila: This is Diana. This is Luis. This is Olga. This is Tran. My name is Laila.

Unit 2 Goal Setting: Why Learn English?

A Complete the sentence. Check (✓) all the boxes that are true for you.

I want to learn English to _____.

☐ get a job

☐ get more education

☐ help my children
with school

☐ get a new job

☐ become a U.S. citizen

☐ talk to doctors and my
children's teachers

B PAIRS. Talk about your answers in Exercise A.

A: *I want to learn English to _____.*
B: *That's interesting. I want to . . .*

C CLASS. Tell the class your goals.

Unit 3   School Supplies

A **GROUPS OF 3. What do students bring to class? Make a list of ten things.**

School Supplies

a pencil _____   _____

_____   _____

_____   _____

_____   _____

_____   _____

For help, look at
the pictures of
classroom objects
on pages 46–47.

B **SAME GROUPS. Take turns. Ask,** *Are you ready for school today?*

    A: *Are you ready for school today?*
    B: *Yes. I have a pencil, a . . . .*
        What about you? Are you ready for school today?
    C: *Yes. I have a pencil, a . . . .*

C **Before you come to class next time, check that you have your supplies. Use the list.**

Unit 4   My Friends and Family

A **Think about your classmates, friends, neighbors, co-workers, and family.
In your notebook, write the names of people you want to speak English to.**

Classmates	Friends	Neighbors	Co-workers	Family
Sonia	Bo	Mr. Smith	Alice	Ricardo
Mai		Sally	Joe	Pablo

B **Choose two or three people from your list. In your notebook, write your goals for
speaking to each person in English. Use the ideas below or your own ideas.**

    I want to talk to Sonia in English about my family.
    I want to say hello to Alice in English.
    I want to read to Ricardo in English.

C **Which goals will you do this week? Circle your goals for this week.**

D **PAIRS. Tell your partner your goals for this week. Check with each other next
week. Did you complete your goals?**

This week, I want to talk to . . . . What about you?

Unit 5   Class Jobs

A CLASS. Look at the list of class jobs. These assistants help the teacher.
Are there other jobs in your class? Write them in the list.

Job	Job Duty
Assistant 1	Write today's date on the board.
Assistant 2	Erase the board.
Assistant 3	Give out supplies.
Assistant 4	Take attendance.
Assistant 5	Collect supplies.
Assistant 6	_____

B CLASS. Choose assistants to help your teacher. Write the students' names in
the list. Change assistants every week.

Unit 6   My Vocabulary Learning Strategies

A CLASS. Look at the Learning Strategies on pages 7, 27, 47, 67, 87, and 107.

B Which strategies do you use to learn vocabulary? Check (✓) the strategies.

☐ Write personal sentences   ☐ Use your language

☐ Use pictures   ☐ Make word groups

☐ Make labels   ☐ Other: _____

C GROUPS OF 5. Talk about it. Which strategies do you use?

A: *I use my language, and I use pictures. What about you?*
B: *I . . .*

D Write your vocabulary goal for this week.

I want to learn _____ new words this week.
                    (number)

I will use _____ to help me remember the new words.
              (title of Learning Strategy)

E SAME GROUPS. Tell your group your goal. Check with each other next week.
Did you complete your goals?

Unit 7 Daily Planner

A When do you study or practice English? Write a daily planner. Use the planner below as a model. Make one planner for every day of the week.

Day: Monday	
Activity	Time
Go to English class	8:30 A.M.—11:30 A.M.
Use English at work	1:00 P.M.—5:00 P.M.
Listen to music in English	5:00 P.M.—5:30 P.M.
Do my homework	8:30 P.M.—9:00 P.M.

B GROUPS OF 3. Show your planners to your group.

(Note: For the Unit 8 Activity, you will need to bring tea and cookies or other refreshments.)

Unit 8 Getting-to-Know-You Tea

A CLASS. Bring tea and cookies to class. Take some of the tea and cookies. Sit with a classmate you don't know.

B PAIRS. Take turns. Ask and answer the questions below.

Lin: *What's your name?*
Mario: *My name is Mario. What's your name?*

- What's your name?
- Where are you from?
- Tell me about your family.
- What do you do?
- What do you like to do on the weekend?
- What kind of food do you like?
- What's your favorite holiday?
- What are your interests and special skills?

C Report to the class. Say one new thing you learned about your partner.

On the weekend, Mario cooks for his family.

Unit 9   Important Dates in School

A CLASS. **What dates are important in school from now to the end of the term? Look at the events in the box for some ideas. Make a list of important dates and events in the next month.**

> Tests   School holidays   Last day of class   Registration for next semester

B **Make a calendar. Write the important events on the calendar.**

November

S	M	T	W	T	F	S
		1 Election Day	2	3	4	5 Test	6
7	8	9	10	11 Veterans Day – School closed	12	13
14	15	16	17	18	19	20
21	22 Thanksgiving Party	23	24	25 Thanksgiving – School closed	26	27
28	29	30				

C GROUPS OF 5. **Plan ahead. Are there any events on the calendar you need to prepare for? Are there any events next month you need to prepare for? What do you need to do? Say two or three things for each event.**

A: *We have a test on November fifth.*
B: *Right. We need to study!*
C: *And we need to get a lot of sleep . . .*

Unit 10 Things I Read in English

A CLASS. Think about things you read in English in your community. Read the chart. Can you think of other things you read in English in your community?

Activity	Always	Sometimes	Never
I read signs in English on store windows.			
I read signs in English on doors.			
I read traffic signs in English.			
I read street signs in English.			
I read ads in English.			
I read food labels in English.			
I read menus in English.			
I read signs on buses in English.			

B Which activities do *you* do? How often? For each activity in the chart, check (✓) *always, sometimes,* or *never.*

C GROUPS OF 3. Talk about your answers in Exercise B.

A: *I sometimes read signs in English on store windows. What about you?*
B: *I never read signs in English on store windows. What about you?*
C: *I sometimes read signs in English on store windows. I . . .*

D What do you want to read in English? Write one goal for next week. Check with each other in two weeks. Did you complete your goal?

Next week, I will _____ in English.

E SAME GROUPS. Talk about your goals.

Unit 11 Individual Barriers, Group Support

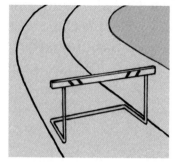

A CLASS. *Barriers* are things that keep you from your goals. Think about your goals for studying English. What are some barriers? Make a list. Use ideas from the box or your own ideas.

> My husband needs the car. The baby-sitter can't come.
> I'm tired after work. The school parking lot isn't safe.

B Copy the list of barriers your class made in Exercise A. Which barriers in Exercise A are true for you? Check (✓) them. Circle one of the barriers you checked.

C NETWORK. Find classmates with the same barrier you circled. Make a group.

D GROUPS. What can you do to overcome your barrier? Make a list of ideas.

Call a classmate. Find out what I missed.

Unit 12   Now I Can

A Look at the first page of each unit. Read the Unit Goals. Which goals did you check off? Choose one goal that you are proud of from each page. Write the goals in a chart in your notebook.

Unit #	Now I Can . . .
1	Now I can talk about school.
2	Now I can introduce someone.

B Report to the class. Tell the class one goal that you can do now.

Now I can write a personal check!

C CLASS. Stand up and clap for everyone. CONGRATULATIONS ON YOUR SUCCESS!

Life Skills Writing

Unit 1

1 BEFORE YOU WRITE

A Read the form. Find *Print*, and *Ink*. What do they mean?

Please print. Use blue or black ink.

Name: _Morena_____ _Elsa_____ _Clara_____
             LAST   FIRST   MIDDLE

☐ Male   ☑ Female

Signature: _Elsa Morena_____

B Read the form again. Match the words with the examples in the box.

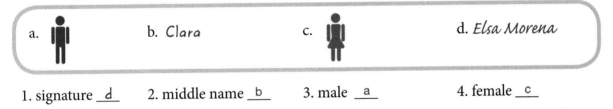

a.   b. *Clara*   c.   d. *Elsa Morena*

1. signature _d_   2. middle name _b_   3. male _a_   4. female _c_

2 WRITE

Complete the form. Use your own information.   Answers will vary.

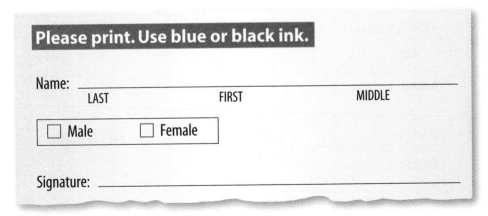

Please print. Use blue or black ink.

Name: _____
      LAST   FIRST   MIDDLE

☐ Male   ☐ Female

Signature: _____

Can you...complete a form with your personal information? ☐

Unit 2

Read the form. Then read the sentences. One word in each sentence is not correct. Find the word and cross it out. Write the correct word.

Title (please check)

☑ Mr.　☐ Ms.　☐ Mrs.　☐ Miss　☐ Dr.

Name (please print)

Nowak　　　　　Alex　　　　　M.

LAST　　　　　　FIRST　　　　　MIDDLE INITIAL

Phone

(312) 555-1313　　(312) 555-8976　　(779) 555-0123

HOME　　　　　　WORK　　　　　　CELL

　　　　　　Mr.
1. Alex's title is ~~Dr.~~
　　　　last
2. Alex's ~~middle~~ name is Nowak.
　　　　　male
3. Alex is a ~~female.~~
　　　　　work
4. Alex's ~~cell~~ phone number is (312) 555-8976.
　　　　　cell
5. Alex's ~~work~~ phone number is (779) 555-0123.

2 WRITE

Complete the form. Use true or made-up information.

Answers will vary.

Title (please check)

☐ Mr.　☐ Ms.　☐ Mrs.　☐ Miss　☐ Dr.

Name (please print)

LAST　　　　　　　　FIRST　　　　　　MIDDLE INITIAL

Phone

HOME　　　　　　　WORK　　　　　　　CELL

Can you...complete a form at work?　☐

Unit 3

A Read the school registration form. Find *M*, *F*, and *Subject*. What do they mean?

LAC Community School | **Registration Form**

Student's Name ___Lee___ ___Jin-Su___
                LAST   FIRST

□ M ☑ F

Phone: ___(779) 555-0123___

Classroom: ___205___ Subject: ___English 1___

Teacher: ___Mr. Myers___

B Read the form again. Then underline the correct words.

1. The student's **first name** / **last name** is Lee.

2. The student's **phone number** / **classroom number** is 205.

3. The student is **a man** / **a woman**.

4. The student is in **English 1** / **English 2**.

5. The teacher's name is **Mr. Myers** / **Mr. Lee**.

Complete the school registration form. Use your own information.   Answers will vary.

LAC Community School | **Registration Form**

Student's Name _____
             LAST   FIRST

□ M □ F

Phone: _____

Classroom: _____ Subject: _____

Teacher: _____

Can you...complete a school registration form? □

Unit 4

A We fill out emergency contact forms at work, at home, and at school. Why is this important?

B Read the emergency contact form. Find *In case of emergency, Relationship, Daytime,* and *Evening.* What do they mean?

EMERGENCY CONTACT INFORMATION

STUDENT'S NAME (LAST, FIRST) _____ Bernard, Annette _____

IN CASE OF EMERGENCY, CALL:				
NAME	RELATIONSHIP	DAYTIME	EVENING	OTHER
Miriam Bernard	mother	(305) 555-1925	(305) 555-8877	Cell (786) 555-4343
Claude Bernard	father	(305) 555-7846	same as above	—

C Read the form again. Then read the sentences. Circle *True* or *False.*

1. The student's name is Bernard Annette. True (False)
2. Her mother is Miriam Bernard. (True) False
3. Her father's evening phone number is (305) 555-8877. (True) False

2 WRITE

Complete the emergency contact form for yourself. Use true or made-up information. Answers will vary.

EMERGENCY CONTACT INFORMATION

STUDENT'S NAME (LAST, FIRST) _____

IN CASE OF EMERGENCY, CALL:				
NAME	RELATIONSHIP	DAYTIME	EVENING	OTHER

Can you...complete an emergency contact form? ☐

Unit 5

A Read the check. Find *Pay to the order of, In the amount of,* and *Memo.*
What do they mean?

Zofia Kowalska   1243
17100 Collins St.
Encino, CA 91316   DATE _6/9/10_

PAY TO THE
ORDER OF _Imagine_ $ [44.50]

IN THE
AMOUNT OF _Forty-Four 50/100_   DOLLARS

FIRST SAVINGS BANK
CA
MEMO _Gift for Ivan_   _Zofia Kowalska_

122213311: 5556665656 1243

B Read the check again. Answer the questions.

1. Who is the check from? _Zofia Kowalska_   4. How much money is the check for? _$44.50_

2. Who is the check to? _Imagine_   5. What does the check pay for? _Gift for Ivan_

3. What is the date on the check? _6/9/10_   6. Find Zofia's signature. Circle it.

You're buying work clothes from the store Clothes World. The total is $39.75.
Write a check. Use today's date.

                                                              101

                                    DATE _Answers will vary._

PAY TO THE
ORDER OF _Clothes World_ $ [39.75]

IN THE
AMOUNT OF _Thirty-nine 75/100_   DOLLARS

FIRST SAVINGS BANK
CA
MEMO _work clothes_   _Answers will vary._

122213311: 5556665656 101

Can you...write a personal check? ☐

Unit 6

Read the envelope. Then read the sentences. Underline the correct words.

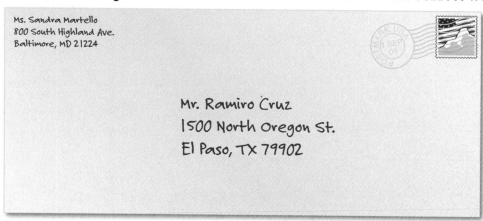

1. The letter is from <u>**Sandra Martello**</u> / **Ramiro Cruz**.
2. The letter is to **Sandra Martello** / <u>**Ramiro Cruz**</u>.
3. Sandra Martello lives on <u>**South Highland Avenue**</u> / **North Oregon Street**.
4. Sandra Martello lives in the city of **Maryland** / <u>**Baltimore**</u>.
5. Ramiro Cruz lives in the state of <u>**Texas**</u> / **Maryland**.
6. Ramiro Cruz's zip code is **El Paso** / <u>**79902**</u>.

2 WRITE

You are writing a letter to a friend or to your teacher at the school address. Address the envelope. Use true or made-up information.   Answers will vary.

Can you...address an envelope?   ☐

Unit 7

Look at the note. Then answer the questions.

> *Memorandum*
>
> To: Cristina Ramos
> From: David Lambert
> Date: June 1, 2010
> Subject: Vacation request
>
> ◇◇
>
> I would like to take my vacation from June 20 to 24.
> Please let me know if this is approved.
>
> Thank you.

1. Who is the note from? _David Lambert_

2. Who is the note to? _Cristina Ramos_

3. Guess: What is their relationship? _Manager and employee_

4. What is the reason for the note? _Vacation request_

5. What do you think? What is going to happen next? _Answers will vary._

Write a note to your manager. Ask for permission to take a vacation or time off from work. Use true or made-up information. Answers will vary.

> *Memorandum*
>
> To:
> From:
> Date:
> Subject:
>
> ◇◇

Can you...write a note to your manager about vacation time? ☐

Unit 8

Look at the note. Then answer the questions.

1. Who is the note from? _Barbara_

2. Who is the note to? _Sam_

3. What do you think their relationship is?

   Answers will vary.

4. How much rice do they need? _2 lbs._

5. How much coffee do they need? _1 lb._

6. How many tomatoes do they need? _4_

10/24

Sam,

Please get these things
from the store:

2 lbs. rice

1 gal. milk

1 lb. coffee

8 apples

4 large tomatoes

Thanks!

Barbara

2 WRITE

**Write a note to someone in your house. Make a list of six things
you need from the store. Use true or made-up information.** Answers will vary.

Can you...write a note about things you need from the store? ☐

Unit 9

1 BEFORE YOU WRITE

Read the postcard. Then answer the questions.

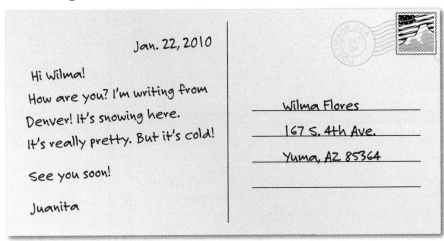

1. Who is the postcard from? _Juanita_

2. Who is the postcard to? _Wilma Flores_

3. Where is Juanita right now? _Denver_

4. How is the weather in Denver? _It's snowing and cold._

5. Where does Wilma live? _Yuma, AZ_

2 WRITE

Write a postcard to a friend. Tell your friend about the weather.

Answers will vary.

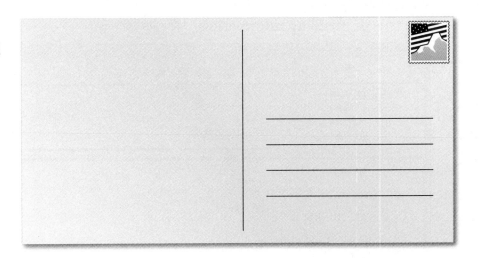

Can you...write a postcard? ☐

Unit 10

1 **BEFORE YOU WRITE**

Read the e-mail. Then answer the questions.

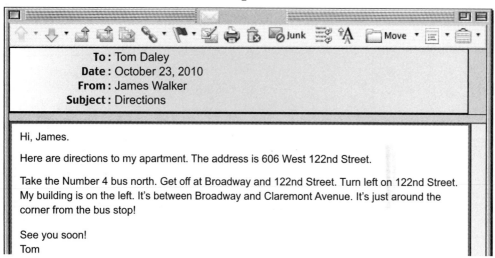

To : Tom Daley
Date : October 23, 2010
From : James Walker
Subject : Directions

Hi, James.

Here are directions to my apartment. The address is 606 West 122nd Street.

Take the Number 4 bus north. Get off at Broadway and 122nd Street. Turn left on 122nd Street. My building is on the left. It's between Broadway and Claremont Avenue. It's just around the corner from the bus stop!

See you soon!
Tom

1. What is Tom's address? _His address is 606 West 122nd Street._

2. What bus does James take? _James takes the Number 4 bus north._

3. Where does he get off? _He gets off at Broadway and 122nd Street._

4. Where is Tom's building? _Tom's building is on 122nd Street, between Broadway and Claremont Avenue._

2 **WRITE**

Write an e-mail to a friend. Give your friend directions to your home. Use true or made-up information. Answers will vary.

To :
Date :
From :
Subject :

Can you…write directions to your home? ☐

Unit 9

1 BEFORE YOU WRITE

Read the postcard. Then answer the questions.

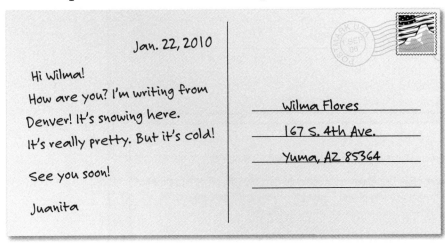

Jan. 22, 2010

Hi Wilma!
How are you? I'm writing from
Denver! It's snowing here.
It's really pretty. But it's cold!

See you soon!

Juanita

Wilma Flores
167 S. 4th Ave.
Yuma, AZ 85364

1. Who is the postcard from? _Juanita_

2. Who is the postcard to? _Wilma Flores_

3. Where is Juanita right now? _Denver_

4. How is the weather in Denver? _It's snowing and cold._

5. Where does Wilma live? _Yuma, AZ_

2 WRITE

Write a postcard to a friend. Tell your friend about the weather.

Answers will vary.

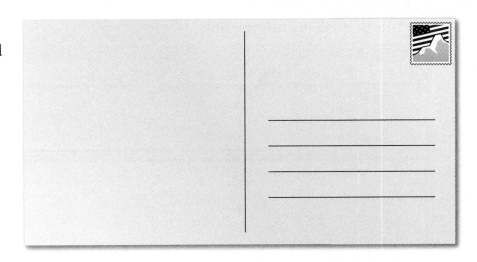

Can you...write a postcard? ☐

Unit 10

Read the e-mail. Then answer the questions.

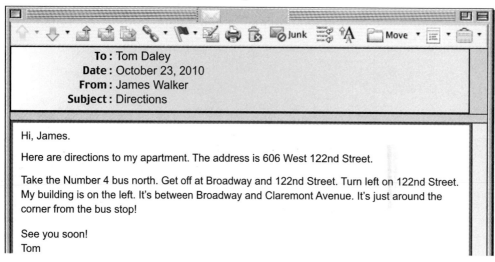

To : Tom Daley
Date : October 23, 2010
From : James Walker
Subject : Directions

Hi, James.

Here are directions to my apartment. The address is 606 West 122nd Street.

Take the Number 4 bus north. Get off at Broadway and 122nd Street. Turn left on 122nd Street. My building is on the left. It's between Broadway and Claremont Avenue. It's just around the corner from the bus stop!

See you soon!
Tom

1. What is Tom's address? _His address is 606 West 122nd Street._

2. What bus does James take? _James takes the Number 4 bus north._

3. Where does he get off? _He gets off at Broadway and 122nd Street._

4. Where is Tom's building? _Tom's building is on 122nd Street, between Broadway and Claremont Avenue._

Write an e-mail to a friend. Give your friend directions to your home. Use true or made-up information. Answers will vary.

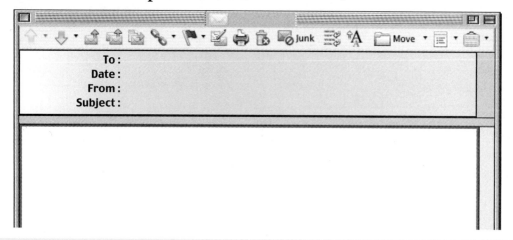

To :
Date :
From :
Subject :

Can you...write directions to your home? ☐

Unit 9

1 BEFORE YOU WRITE

Read the postcard. Then answer the questions.

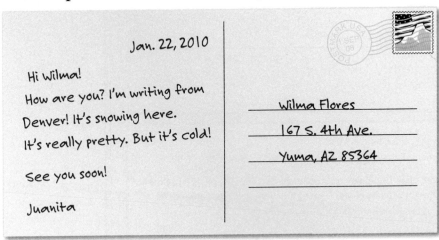

1. Who is the postcard from? _Juanita_____
2. Who is the postcard to? _Wilma Flores_____
3. Where is Juanita right now? _Denver_____
4. How is the weather in Denver? _It's snowing and cold._____
5. Where does Wilma live? _Yuma, AZ_____

2 WRITE

Write a postcard to a friend. Tell your friend about the weather.
Answers will vary.

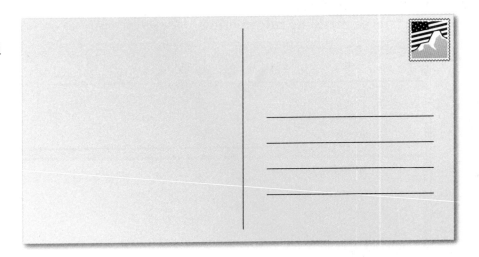

Can you...write a postcard? ☐

Unit 10

1 BEFORE YOU WRITE

Read the e-mail. Then answer the questions.

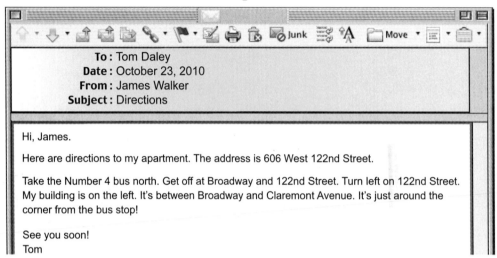

To : Tom Daley
Date : October 23, 2010
From : James Walker
Subject : Directions

Hi, James.

Here are directions to my apartment. The address is 606 West 122nd Street.

Take the Number 4 bus north. Get off at Broadway and 122nd Street. Turn left on 122nd Street. My building is on the left. It's between Broadway and Claremont Avenue. It's just around the corner from the bus stop!

See you soon!
Tom

1. What is Tom's address? _His address is 606 West 122nd Street._

2. What bus does James take? _James takes the Number 4 bus north._

3. Where does he get off? _He gets off at Broadway and 122nd Street._

4. Where is Tom's building? _Tom's building is on 122nd Street, between Broadway and Claremont Avenue._

2 WRITE

Write an e-mail to a friend. Give your friend directions to your home. Use true or made-up information. Answers will vary.

To :
Date :
From :
Subject :

Can you...write directions to your home? ☐

Unit 11

1 BEFORE YOU WRITE

A Read the form. Find the illnesses and conditions. Discuss the meanings.

PATIENT HEALTH QUESTIONNAIRE

Name _Blanca Gomes_   Date of Birth _8/21/69_   ☐ M ☑ F

Address _621 Arizona Ave., El Paso, TX 79902_   Phone _(915) 555-3538_

Please check illnesses or conditions you have now or had in the past	Childhood	☑ Measles ☑ Mumps ☑ Chicken Pox	Adult	☑ Asthma ☐ High Blood Pressure ☐ HIV/AIDS	☐ Diabetes ☐ Tuberculosis ☐ Heart Disease

Are you allergic to any medicine? Please list: _Penicillin_

Are you currently taking any medication? Please list: _Asthma medication_

B Read the form again. Answer the questions.

1. What illnesses did Ms. Gomes have as a child? _measles, mumps, and chicken pox_

2. What illnesses does she have now? _Asthma_

3. What medicine does she take? _Asthma medication_

4. What medicine is she allergic to? _Penicillin_

2 WRITE

Complete the form for yourself. Use true or made-up information. Answers will vary.

PATIENT HEALTH QUESTIONNAIRE

Name _____   Date of Birth _____   ☐ M ☐ F

Address _____   Phone _____

Please check illnesses or conditions you have now or had in the past	Childhood	☐ Measles ☐ Mumps ☐ Chicken Pox	Adult	☐ Asthma ☐ High Blood Pressure ☐ HIV/AIDS	☐ Diabetes ☐ Tuberculosis ☐ Heart Disease

Are you allergic to any medicine? Please list: _____

Are you currently taking any medication? Please list: _____

Can you...complete a medical history form? ☐

Unit 12

Read the job application form. Find *Over 18 years of age*, *Last attended*, and *Most recent*. What do they mean?

Review the job applications on pages 242 and 243. Then complete this job application. Use true or made-up information. Answers will vary.

Green's Department Store

Personal Information

Last Name _____ First Name _____

Home Address _____
City   State   Zip

Home Phone _____ E-mail _____

Job applying for _____ When can you start? _____

Are you over 18 years of age? _____ If not, date of birth _____

Please list all the times you are available to work (from 6 A.M. to 12 A.M.)

SUN _____ M _____ T _____ W _____ TH _____ F _____ SAT _____

Education

Last school attended _____ Date last attended _____
(name of school)

Job History (list most recent first)

Company _____ Phone Number _____

Address _____

Job _____ Dates worked from _____ to _____

Reason for leaving _____

Company _____ Phone Number _____

Address _____

Job _____ Dates worked from _____ to _____

Reason for leaving _____

Can you...complete a job application? ☐

Team Projects

Unit 1   Meet Your Classmates   <u>MAKE A POSTER</u>

Materials
- large paper
- markers
- digital camera or cell phone with camera

TEAM OF 4   Captain, Co-captain, Assistant, Spokesperson

GET READY   **Captain:** Ask your teammates, "Where are you from?"
Assistant: Write your teammates' answers in the chart. Add the Captain's answer
Co-captain: Watch the time. You have five minutes.

First Name	Last Name	Country

CREATE   **Co-captain:** Get the materials. Then watch the time. You have ten minutes.
Team: Create your poster.

REPORT   **Spokesperson:** Tell the class about your poster.

Meet Your Classmates

Dora is from Peru.

Dawit is from Ethiopia.

Sen is from Vietnam.

Arturo is from El Salvador.

Unit 2   Where People Work   <u>MAKE A VENN DIAGRAM</u>

Materials
- large paper
- markers

TEAM OF 4   Captain, Co-captain, Assistant, Spokesperson

GET READY   **Team:** Choose two workplaces from the box.
Captain: Ask your teammates, "What jobs are in these workplaces?"

| a construction site | a hospital | a hotel | an office |
| a restaurant | a school | a service station | a store |

Workplace 1: _____	Workplace 2: _____

CREATE   **Co-captain:** Get the materials. Then watch the time.
You have eight minutes.
Team: Create your Venn diagram.

<u>JOBS IN A HOTEL</u>
housekeeper
driver

<u>JOBS IN BOTH</u>
office assistant
landscaper
security guard
cook

<u>JOBS IN A SCHOOL</u>
teacher
principal
librarian
nurse

REPORT   **Spokesperson:** Tell the class about your Venn diagram.

Unit 3 Our School MAKE A BOOKLET

TEAMS OF 4 Captain, Co-captain, Assistant, Spokesperson

Captain: Ask your teammates, "What do new students need to know about your school?" Ask about the important people and their titles. Ask about the important places and the room numbers.

Assistant: Write your teammates' answers in the charts.

Co-captain: Watch the time. You have five minutes.

Materials
- 3 pieces of white paper
- pen or small marker
- stapler and staples

Important People	Job Titles

Important Places	Room Numbers

CREATE **Co-captain:** Get the materials. Then watch the time. You have ten minutes.
Team: Create your booklet. Draw a map of your school in the booklet.

REPORT **Spokesperson:** Tell the class about your booklet.

Unit 4 Holidays MAKE A CALENDAR

CLASS

GET READY Create a calendar for the year. Use one piece of paper for each month. Put it at the front of the room.

Materials
- 12 pieces of white paper
- markers

CREATE Write holidays on the calendar. Include U.S. holidays and holidays from your countries.

REPORT Take turns. Tell the class about one holiday. Begin with January 1.

Unit 5 **Where We Shop** MAKE A BAR GRAPH

Materials
- large paper
- colored markers

TEAMS OF 4 Captain, Co-captain, Assistant, Spokesperson

GET READY **Captain:** Ask your teammates about places they shop for clothes. Ask *yes/no* questions about the places in the chart. For example, ask, "Do you shop in department stores?" (**Team:** You can answer *yes* for more than one place.)
Co-Captain: Watch the time. You have five minutes.
Assistant: Complete the chart with your teammates' names and *yes* or *no*. Add the Captain's Answer.

Name	In Department Stores	In Small Clothing Stores	In Thrift Stores	On the Internet	In Other Places

CREATE **Co-captain:** Get the materials. Then watch the time. You have ten minutes.
Team: Create your bar graph.

REPORT **Spokesperson:** Tell the class about your bar graph.

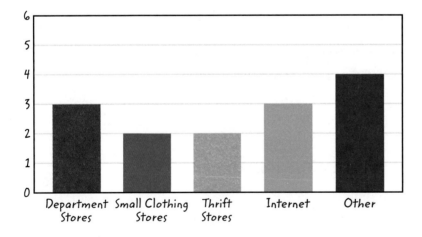

Unit 6: Your Dream House <u>MAKE A FLOOR PLAN</u>

Materials
- large paper
- markers

TEAMS OF 4 Captain, Co-captain, Assistant, Spokesperson

GET READY **Captain:** Ask your teammates, "What does your dream house look like?"
Team: Decide together. How many floors does your dream house have? Which rooms are on each floor?
Assistant: Write your teammates' answers.
Co-captain: Watch the time. You have five minutes.

> *1st floor: kitchen, dining room, living room, laundry room*

CREATE **Co-captain:** Get the materials. Then watch the time. You have ten minutes.
Team: Create the floor plan for your dream house. (Hint: See page 113 for an example of a floor plan.)

REPORT **Spokesperson:** Tell the class about your floor plan.

Unit 7 A Day in the Life of . . . <u>MAKE A MAGAZINE</u>

TEAMS OF 4 Captain, Co-captain, Assistant, Spokesperson

Materials
- 1 piece of white paper
- pen or small marker
- pictures of a famous person (optional)
- stapler and staples

GET READY **Team:** Choose a famous person.
Captain: Ask your teammates, "Imagine: What does this person do all day?"
Assistant: Complete the chart.
Co-captain: Watch the time. You have five minutes.

Person: _____					
Morning		**Afternoon**		**Evening**	
Activity	Time	Activity	Time	Activity	Time

CREATE **Co-captain:** Get the materials. Then watch the time. You have ten minutes.
Team: Create a magazine page for your famous person.

REPORT **Spokesperson:** Tell the class about your famous person's day.

COLLECT **Class:** Collect the magazine pages from each group. Staple them together to make a magazine of *People in the News*.

Unit 8 What's for Lunch or Dinner? <u>MAKE A MENU</u>

TEAMS OF 4 Captain, Co-captain, Assistant, Spokesperson

GET READY You are opening an American restaurant.
Captain: Ask your teammates, "What's the name of your restaurant? What's on the lunch or dinner menu?"
Assistant: Write your teammates' answers in the chart.
Co-captain: Watch the time. You have five minutes.

Materials
- 2 pieces of white paper
- pen or small marker
- stapler and staples

Restaurant Name: _____		Menu for: _____	
Main Courses	**Sides**	**Desserts**	**Drinks**

CREATE **Co-captain:** Get the materials. Then watch the time. You have ten minutes.
Team: Create your menu.

REPORT **Spokesperson:** Tell the class about your menu.

Unit 9 How's the Weather? <u>GIVE A WEATHER REPORT</u>

Materials
- large paper
- markers

TEAMS OF 4 Captain, Co-captain, Assistant, Spokesperson

GET READY Your teacher will give each team a month.
Captain: Ask your teammates, "What's the weather here like in _____?"
(month)
Assistant: Write your teammates' answers in the chart.
Co-captain: Watch the time. You have five minutes.

Month: _____		
	Temperatures	**Kind of Weather**
High		
Low		

CREATE **Co-captain:** Get the materials. Then watch the time. You have ten minutes.
Team: Create your weather report.

REPORT **Spokesperson:** Give your group's weather report. The class guesses the month.

Unit 10 Our Community MAKE A BOOKLET

Materials
- 1 piece of white paper
- pen or small marker
- stapler and staples

TEAMS OF 4 Captain, Co-captain, Assistant, Spokesperson

GET READY **Team:** Choose a kind of place from the box below.
Captain: Ask your teammates, "What _____
(kind of place)
in our city do you like? Where are they? Why do you like them?"
Assistant: Write your teammates' answers in the chart.
Co-captain: Watch the time. You have five minutes.

| famous places | museums | parks | places for children |
| places to relax | places for sports | restaurants | stores |

Kind of Place _____		
Name of Place	**Location**	**Why It's Good**

CREATE **Co-captain:** Get the materials. Then watch the time. You have ten minutes.
Team: Create a booklet page for your places.

REPORT **Spokesperson:** Tell the class about the places on your page.

Unit 11 Staying Healthy MAKE A POSTER

Materials
- large paper
- markers

TEAMS OF 4 Captain, Co-captain, Assistant, Spokesperson

GET READY **Captain:** Ask your teammates, "What habits are good for your health (healthy)? What habits are not good for your health (unhealthy)?"
Assistant: Write your teammates' answers in the chart.
Co-captain: Watch the time. You have five minutes.

Healthy Habits	**Unhealthy Habits**

CREATE **Co-captain:** Get the materials. Then watch the time. You have ten minutes.
Team: Create your poster.

REPORT **Spokesperson:** Tell the class about your poster.

Unit 12 **Skills You Need** MAKE A POSTER

Materials
- large paper
- markers

TEAMS OF 4 Captain, Co-captain, Assistant, Spokesperson

GET READY **Team:** Think of three jobs. Brainstorm with your teammates.
Captain: Ask your teammates, "What skills do you need for those jobs?"
Assistant: Write your teammates' answers in the chart.
Co-captain: Watch the time. You have five minutes.

Job 1: _____
Skills

Job 2: _____
Skills

Job 3: _____
Skills

CREATE **Co-captain:** Get the materials. Then watch the time.
You have ten minutes.
Team: Create your poster.

REPORT **Spokesperson:** Tell the class about your poster.

Grammar Reference

Unit 2, Lesson 3, page 31

Some irregular plural nouns

child	**children**	person	**people**
man	**men**	foot	**feet**
woman	**women**	tooth	**teeth**

Unit 2, Lesson 9, page 42

Spelling rules for simple present tense: Third-person singular (*he, she, it*)

1. Add **-s** for most verbs: *work—work**s**   play—play**s***
2. Add **-es** for words that end in **-ch, -s, -sh, -x,** or **-z** : *watch—watch**es**   relax—relax**es***
3. Change the **y** to **i** and add **-es** when the base form ends in a consonant **+y**: *study—stud**ies***
4. Add **-s** when the base form ends in a **vowel + y**: *play—play**s**   enjoy—enjoy**s***
5. Some verbs have **irregular forms**: *do—**does**   have—**has**   go—**goes***

Unit 7, Lesson 3, page 130

Prepositions of time

at 9:00

before 9:00

after 9:00

Sunday	Monday	Tuesday	Wednesday	Thursday	Friday	Saturday
		1	2	3	4	5
6	7	8	9	10	11	12
13	14	15	16	17	18	19
20	21	22	23	24	25	26
27	28	29	30	31		

May 2012

on Monday

Sunday	Monday	Tuesday	Wednesday	Thursday	Friday	Saturday
		1	2	3	4	5
6	7	8 ←→ 9		10	11	12
13	14	15	16	17	18	19
20	21	22	23	24	25	26
27	28	29	30	31		

May 2012

for two days

(*in* + month)

in May

(*in* + year)

in 2012

(*on* + date)

on May 2

Unit 8, Lesson 3, page 150

Some common non-count nouns

Food: beef, bread, butter, cabbage, cake, cereal, chicken, chocolate, fish, ice cream, lettuce, oil, pizza, rice, salmon, shrimp, soup, yogurt

Drinks: coffee, juice, milk, soda, tea, water

School Subjects: art, English, history, math, music, science

Activities: basketball, homework, laundry, soccer

Others: air-conditioning, chalk, electricity, furniture, hair, information, luggage, money, news, paper, transportation, weather

Remember: Non-count nouns are singular. Example: *Pizza is my favorite food.*

Spelling rules for plural count nouns

Add **-s** to most nouns	book—books	
Add **-es** to most nouns that end in **-ch**, **-s**, **-sh**, **-x**, or a consonant + **o**.	watch—watch**es** guess—guess**es** dish—dish**es**	box—box**es** potato—potato**es**
Change **y** to **i** and add **-es** to nouns that end in a consonant + **y**.	baby—bab**ies**	city—cit**ies**
Change **f** to **v** and add **-s** to nouns that end in **-fe**. Change **f** to **v** and add **-es** to nouns that ends in **-f**.	knife—kni**ves** loaf—loa**ves**	wife—wi**ves** shelf shel**ves**

Unit 9, Lesson 3, page 170

Spelling rules for present continuous

1. Add **-ing** to the base form: *cook—cooking   eat—eating*
2. For verbs that end in *e*, drop the final *e* and add **-ing**: *take—taking   make—making*
3. For one-syllable verbs that end in a consonant, a vowel, and a consonant, double the final consonant and add **-ing**. Do not double the final consonant if it is a *w*, *x*, or *y*: *get—getting play—playing*

Unit 10, Lesson 3, page 190

Prepositions of place

in *Los Angeles*	**across from** *the bank*
on *First Street*	**around** *the corner*
at *231 First Street*	**next to** *the supermarket*
down *the block*	**near** *the corner*
between *First* **and** *Second Streets*	**in/at** *school*

Word List

UNIT 1

Countries

Brazil, 7
Canada, 7
China, 7
El Salvador, 7
England, 7
Ethiopia, 7
Haiti, 7
Korea, 7

Mexico, 7
Peru, 7
Poland, 7
Russia, 7
Somalia, 7
the United States, 7
Vietnam, 7

absent, 12
boring, 18
easy, 18
first name, 10
for work, 16
friendly, 19
good, 18
great, 18
hard, 18

helpful, 19
Interesting, 18
last name, 10
late, 12
shake hands, 8
smart, 19
title, 11
to be safe, 16
to be with family, 16

UNIT 2

accountant, 27
actor, 34
area code, 32
artist, 27
assembly line worker, 41
athlete, 37
bank,
caregiver, 41
carpenter, 41
cashier, 27
child-care center, 32
child-care worker, 27

clean, 38
construction site, 41
cook (n), 27
cook (v), 38
doctor, 27
driver, 27
electrician, 27
factory, 41
gardener, 27
good with children, 39
good with numbers, 39
homemaker, 27

hospital, 32
housekeeper, 27
nurse, 27
nursing home, 41
office, 32
office assistant, 27
organized, 38
painter, 27
pay the bills, 38
phone number, 32
restaurant, 32

sales assistant, 27
security guard, 40
singer, 37
stock clerk, 41
store, 41
take care of
  children, 38
uniform, 40
use a computer, 38
waiter, 27
waitress, 27

UNIT 3

across from, 49
backpack, 47
board, 47
book, 47
borrow, 48
bring, 48
cafeteria, 59
CD, 47
cell phone, 47
chair, 47
computer, 47
computer lab, 59

computer lab assistant, 60
custodian, 60
desk, 47
dictionary, 47
DVD, 54
elevator, 59
eraser, 47
folder, 47
for a short time, 52
hall, 59
interrupt, 51
keyboard, 54

librarian, 60
library, 59
marker, 47
monitor, 54
mouse, 54
next to, 50
notebook, 47
office, 59
on the left, 59
on the right, 59
piece of chalk, 47
piece of paper, 47

principal, 60
set study goals, 52
stairs, 59
study habits, 52
teacher, 48
three-ring binder, 47
throw out, 52
turn off, 50

UNIT 4

aunt, 69
average height, 74
average weight, 74
beard, 74
birthday, 79
blended family, 72
boy, 80
brother, 67
calendar, 78
children, 67
cousin, 69
date, 78
date of birth, 79
daughter, 67
divorced, 72

family tree, 67
father, 67
girl, 80
grandfather, 67
grandmother, 67
half-sister, 72
heavy, 74
husband, 67
kids, 80
long hair, 74
looks like, 70
month, 78
mother, 67
mustache, 74
parents, 67

remarried, 72
short, 74
short hair, 76
sister, 67
son , 67
stepbrother, 72
stepfather, 72
stepmother, 72
stepsister, 72
tall, 74
thin, 74
uncle, 69
wife, 67

Days
Sunday, 78
Monday, 78
Tuesday, 78
Wednesday, 78
Thursday, 78
Friday, 78
Saturday, 78

Months
January, 78
February, 78
March, 78
April, 78
May, 78
June, 78
July, 78
August, 78
September, 78
October, 78
November, 78
December, 78

UNIT 5

beige, 87
bill, 98
black, 87
blouse, 87
blue, 87
broken, 100
brown, 87
cash, 92
change, 93
coin, 92
credit card, 101
dime, 92
dress, 87

extra large, 94
extra small, 94
fit, 100
gift, 88
government, 99
gray, 87
green, 87
handbag, 89
jacket, 87
jeans, 87
large, 94
look good, 100
match, 100

medium, 94
money, 92
need, 88
nickel, 92
orange, 87
pants, 87
penny, 92
personal check, 93
pink, 87
president, 98
price, 93
price tag, 93
purple, 87

quarter, 92
receipt, 93
red, 87
return
   something, 100
shirt, 87
shoes, 87
size, 94
skirt, 87
small, 94
sneakers, 87
socks, 87
sweater, 87

T-shirt, 87
tax, 93
wallet, 89
want, 88
watch, 88
white, 87
work, 100
yellow, 87
zipper, 100

UNIT 6

address, 118
air-conditioning, 119
apartment, 112
appliances, 114
avenue, 118
bathroom, 107
bathtub, 107
bed, 107
bedroom, 107
boulevard, 118
building, 115
chair, 107
cheap, 108
closet, 107
coffee table, 115
dark, 108
dining room, 107

downstairs, 111
dresser, 107
east, 120
expensive, 108
fire, 112
floor lamp, 115
furnished, 114
furniture, 114
garage, 109
goes off, 112
included, 119
kitchen, 107
lamp, 107
large, 108
laundry room, 109
living room, 107
microwave, 107

neighbor, 112
new, 108
north, 120
old, 108
one-bedroom
    apartment, 110
parking, 119
refrigerator, 107
rent, 108
road, 118
shower, 107
sink, 107
small, 108
sofa, 107
smoke, 112
smoke alarm, 112
south, 120

stove, 107
street, 118
studio, 115
sunny, 108
table, 107
table lamp, 115
two-bedroom apartment, 115
unfurnished, 114
upstairs, 111
utilities, 119
toilet, 107
wake up, 112
west, 120
yard, 109

UNIT 7

A.M., 126
always, 136
baby-sit, 129
bored, 141
busy, 128
check e-mail, 127
cook dinner, 127
clean, 134
do my homework, 135
do puzzles, 140
do the laundry, 135
eat breakfast, 127
eat dinner, 127
eat lunch, 127
employee, 133
excited, 141

exercise, 127
free, 134
free time, 138
go dancing, 135
go food shopping, 134
go running, 140
go swimming, 135
go to the beach, 135
go to the mall, 128
go to the park, 128
get dressed, 127
get home, 127
get up, 127
go to sleep, 127
go to work, 127
happy, 141

knit, 140
never, 136
P.M., 126
play basketball, 135
play cards, 135
play soccer, 128
play video games, 135
read the mail, 127
read the newspaper, 127
read the paper, 135
relax, 141
relaxed, 141
ride my bike, 135
sad, 141
see a movie, 128
sometimes, 136

spend time with someone, 134
stressed, 141
take a (computer) class, 129
take a hot bath, 140
take a long walk, 140
take a shower, 127
time in, 133
time out, 133
time sheet, 133
usually, 136
visit someone, 129
wash the dishes, 127
watch TV, 127
weekend, 134
work on my car, 135

UNIT 8

apple pie, 154
apples, 147
baked potato, 154
bananas, 147
beans, 147
beef, 147
bottle of water, 154
bread, 147
butter, 147
cabbage, 147
cabinets, 152
cake, 149
calories, 159
cereal, 147
cheese, 147
chef's salad, 154
chicken, 147
coffee, 154

cookies, 149
counter, 152
cucumbers, 161
cup, 154
dairy, 147
dessert, 155
eggs, 147
expiration date, 153
fat, 158
fish, 147
freezer, 152
fried, 160
fries, 154
fruit, 146
fruit cup, 154
grains, 147
grams (g), 159

green beans, 158
green salad, 154
grilled, 160
hamburger, 148
hungry, 148
ice cream, 154
iced tea, 154
keep (food), 152
lettuce, 147
meat, 146
menu, 155
milk, 147
milligrams (mg), 159
net weight, 159
oils, 147
olives, 161
onions, 147

oranges, 147
ounce (oz.), 157
pancakes, 149
pasta, 149
pepperoni pizza, 154
pizza, 148
pound (lb.), 157
red peppers, 161
rice, 147
roast beef, 161
salmon, 161
sandwich, 154
scrambled eggs, 149
sell by, 152
serving size, 159
shrimp, 161

soda, 154
sodium, 159
steak, 149
steamed, 160
sugar, 158
taco, 148
tomatoes, 161
tomato soup, 154
turkey, 161
use by, 152
vegetable oil, 147
vegetables, 146
yogurt, 147

UNIT 9

batteries, 173
boots, 180
candles, 173
cloudy, 167
cold, 167
cool, 167
drugstore, 175
ear muffs, 180
earthquake, 172
emergency, 172

fall, 167
first aid kit, 173
flashlight, 173
flood, 172
foggy, 169
gas station, 175
gloves, 180
grocery store, 175
hat, 180
heat wave, 172

hot, 167
humid, 169
hurricane, 172
light clothes, 180
matches, 173
medicine, 173
radio, 173
raincoat, 180
rainy, 167
scarf, 180

shorts, 180
small talk, 178
snowstorm, 172
snowy, 167
spring, 167
summer, 167
sun block, 180
sunglasses, 180
sunny, 167
thunderstorm, 172

tornado, 172
turn on, 175
umbrella, 180
warm, 167
weather report, 181
wild fire, 172
windy, 169
winter, 167

UNIT 10

around the corner from, 190
ATM, 187
bank, 187
baseball game, 200
bike, 191
bus, 191
bus stop, 187
car, 191
chocolate, 197

coffee shop, 187
concert, 200
courthouse, 189
DMV, 189
down the block from, 190
department store, 187
drugstore, 187
due date, 198
exact change, 194

fare, 194
fire station, 187
gas station, 187
get off/on, 194
grand opening, 200
hair salon, 187
laundromat, 187
library card, 198
near, 190
park, 187

parking lot, 187
police station, 187
post office, 187
public library, 198
subway, 191
supermarket, 187
taxi, 191
tissues, 197
train, 191
yard sale, 200

UNIT 11

alcoholic beverage, 213
ankle, 207
antibiotics, 220
arm, 207
back, 207
backache, 220
bones, 218
chest, 207
clap, 207
cold, 209
cough, 209
day before yesterday, 215
ear, 207
earache, 209
elbow, 207
eye, 207
face, 207
feel sick, 208

feel well, 208
feet, 207
fever, 209
flu, 209
foot, 207
get sick, 218
get strong, 218
hand, 207
have energy, 218
head, 207
headache, 208
heart, 218
heating pad, 220
hurts, 208
ice pack, 220
knee, 207
last night, 214

leg, 207
lie down, 212
look straight ahead, 212
lose weight, 218
make a fist, 212
mouth, 207
neck, 207
nod, 207
nose, 207
Open your mouth and say *Ahh*, 212
orally, 213
out of reach, 213
prevent health problems, 218
roll up your sleeve, 212
shake, 207

shoulder, 207
sit on the table, 212
sore throat, 208
step, 212
step on the scale, 212
stomach, 207
stomachache, 208
stuffy nose, 209
tablet, 213
take a deep breath, 212
teeth, 207
throat, 208
tooth, 207
toothache, 208
touch, 207
wrist, 207
yesterday, 215

UNIT 12

afternoon shift, 233
answer the phone, 227
body language, 238
clean floors, 227
day shift, 233
deliver packages, 227
drive a truck, 227
experience, 232
firmly, 238

first impression, 238
fix furniture, 229
fix things, 227
full-time, 232
hair stylist, 241
help people, 227
lap, 238
lean forward, 238
lift heavy boxes, 227

make cabinets, 229
make copies, 227
make eye contact, 238
night shift, 233
part-time, 232
smile, 238
stand three feet away, 238
supervise workers, 227
take care of grounds, 227

take inventory, 229
take messages, 227
take returns, 229
use a cash register, 227
use a computer, 227
want ad, 232

Audio Script

PRE-UNIT

Page 2, Use the Alphabet, Exercise C

1. A   2. F   3. y   4. B   5. Q   6. Z   7. H   8. J

Page 2, Use the Alphabet, Exercise D

1. A   2. E   3. I   4. O   5. U

Page 2, Use Numbers, Exercise C

1. 5   2. 70   3. 9   4. 50   5. 2
6. 8   7. 10   8. 90   9. 40   10. 6

UNIT 1

Page 8, Listen, Exercise B

Luisa: Hi, I'm Luisa Flores.
Ilya: Hi, I'm Ilya Petrov.
Luisa: Nice to meet you.
Ilya: Nice to meet you, too.

Page 8, Listen, Exercise C

Luisa: Hi, I'm Luisa Flores.
Ilya : Hi, I'm Ilya Petrov.
Luisa: Nice to meet you.
Ilya : Nice to meet you, too.
Luisa: Where are you from, Ilya?
Ilya: I'm from Russia. What about you?
Luisa: I'm from Peru.

Page 11, Practice, Exercise B

1.
A: Your name, please?
B: Michael Chen.
A: Can you spell your first name, please?
B: Sure. M-I-C-H-A-E-L.
A: M-I-C-H-A-E-L. OK, Mr. Chen. You want to take English classes, right?

2.
A: Your name, please?
B: Darya Kotova.
A: Can you spell your last name, please?
B: Sure. K-O-T-O-V-A.
A: K-O-T-O-V-A. OK, Miss Kotova. You want to take English classes, right?

3.
A: Your name, please?
B: Ana Lopez.
A: Can you spell your last name, please?
B: Sure. L-O-P-E-Z.
A: L-O-P-E-Z. OK, Ms. Lopez. You want to take computer classes, right?

Page 12, Listen, Exercise B

Luisa: Who's that?
Sen: That's Ilya.
Luisa: No, that's not Ilya.
Sen: Oh, you're right. That's Nikolai.
Luisa: Nikolai? Where's he from?
Sen: He's from Russia.

Page 12, Listen, Exercise C

Luisa: Who's that?
Sen: That's Ilya.
Luisa: No, that's not Ilya.
Sen: Oh, you're right. That's Nikolai.
Luisa: Nikolai? Where's he from?
Sen: He's from Russia.
Luisa: So, where's Ilya?
Sen: I don't know. I guess he's absent.
Ilya: I'm not absent. I'm here! Sorry I'm late.

Page 13, Conversation, Exercise B

1. She's a student.
2. He's in level 1.
3. He's late.

Page 18, Listen, Exercise B

Min Jung: Hi! So, what class are you in?
Ilya: We're in level 1.
Min Jung: Oh. How is it?
Kamaria: It's good. The teacher is great.
Min Jung: What about the students?
Ilya: They're great, too.

Page 18, Listen, Exercise C

Min Jung: Hi! So, what class are you in?
Ilya: We're in level 1.
Min Jung: Oh. How is it?
Kamaria: It's good. The teacher is great.
Min Jung: What about the students?
Ilya: They're great, too. There's just one problem.
Min Jung: Oh? What's the problem?
Ilya: English is *hard*.

UNIT 2

Page 28, Listen, Exercise B

Gabriela: So, what do you do?
Pierre: I'm a gardener. And I'm a student at Greenville Adult School.
Gabriela: Really? I'm a student there, too. And I'm an artist.
Pierre: Oh, that's interesting.

Page 28, Listen, Exercise C

Gabriela: So, what do you do?
Pierre: I'm a gardener. And I'm a student at Greenville Adult School.
Gabriela: Really? I'm a student there, too. And I'm an artist.
Pierre: Oh, that's interesting. I think Emilio is an artist, too.
Gabriela: No, he's not.
Pierre: Yes, he is. He's a painter.
Gabriela: Right, but he's a *house* painter, not an artist!

Page 31, Practice, Exercise B

nurses
gardeners
cashiers
waitresses
drivers

Page 32, Practice, Exercise A

1. five, one, two
2. seven, one, four
3. three, oh, five
4. seven, oh, eight
5. nine, one, nine
6. seven, eight, six

Page 33, Give Phone Numbers

1.
Hi, Than. This is Mr. Fernandez at Center Hospital. I'm calling about the gardener job. Please call me back at 562-555-1349. That's 562-555-1349.

2.
Hi, Maya. This is Grace Simms at Grace's Office Supplies. I'm calling about the cashier job. Please call me back. My number is 408-555-7821. That's 408-555-7821.

3.
Hi, Nara. This is Jin Heng Wu at Riverside Child Care. I'm calling about the child-care worker job. Please call me back at 773-555-9602. That's 773-555-9602.

4.
Hi, Juan. This is Ms. Rodriguez at Carla's Restaurant. I'm calling about the waiter job. Please call me back at 339-555-8851. That's 339-555-8851.

Page 34, Listen, Exercise B

Claudia: Who's that? Is she a teacher?
Ilya: No, she's not. She's a student. And she's a cashier at Al's Restaurant.
Claudia: Oh, that's interesting. And what do you do?
Ilya: I'm a cook.

Page 34, Listen, Exercise C

Claudia: Who's that? Is she a teacher?
Ilya: No, she's not. She's a student. And she's a cashier at Al's Restaurant.
Claudia: Oh, that's interesting. And what do you do?
Ilya: I'm a cook.
Claudia: A cook! I'm a cook, too.
Ilya: Really?
Claudia: Yes. I'm a cook, a waitress, a child-care worker, and a doctor.
Ilya: *Four* jobs?!
Claudia: Yes! I'm a homemaker!

Page 35, Conversation, Exercise B

1. Is she a teacher?
2. She's a student.
3. What do you do?
4. Are you a doctor?

Page 40, Listen, Exercises B and C

Dora: What do you do?
Miriam: I'm a nurse.
Dora: Really? Where do you work?
Miriam: I work at a school on Main Street. I'm a school nurse.
Dora: Oh. That's interesting.

Page 40, Listen, Exercise D

Dora: What do you do?
Miriam: I'm a nurse.
Dora: Really? Where do you work?
Miriam: I work at a school on Main Street. I'm a school nurse.
Dora: Oh. That's interesting. What about you, Pierre?
Pierre: I work at a school, too.
Dora: Oh. Are you a teacher?
Pierre: No. I'm a student.
Miriam: That's not a job, Pierre!
Pierre: Oh, yes it is. It's a *hard* job!

Page 44, Act It Out, Step 1

Paula: Minh, this is Sahra. Sahra, this is Minh.
Minh: Nice to meet you, Sahra.
Sahra: Nice to meet you, too, Minh. What do you do?
Minh: I'm a stock clerk. What about you?
Sahra: I'm a driver.
Minh: Oh. That's interesting. Where do you work?
Sahra: I work at Holiday Hotel. And you? Where do you work?
Minh: I work at a store—Gil's Supermarket.

UNIT 3

Page 48, Listen, Exercises A and B

Ms. Reed: OK, everyone. Are you ready for the test? Put away your books. Take out a piece of paper.
Aram: Chan, can I borrow a pencil?
Chan: Sure, Aram.

Page 48, Listen, Exercise C

Ms. Reed: OK, everyone. Get ready for the test. Don't look at your books. Take out your notebooks.
Aram: Chan, can I borrow a pencil?
Chan: Sure, Aram.
Ms. Reed: Uh-oh. Please turn off your cell phones, everyone.
Aram: Uhmm, Ms. Reed?
Ms. Reed: Yes?
Aram: I think that's *your* cell phone.
Ms. Reed: Oh!

Page 54, Listen, Exercise B

Carlos: What's this called in English?
Mei-Yu: It's a mouse.
Carlos: And these? What are these called?
Mei-Yu: They're CDs.

Page 54, Listen, Exercise C

Carlos: What's this called in English?
Mei-Yu: It's a mouse.
Carlos: And these? What are these called?
Mei-Yu: They're CDs.
Carlos: Nope. You're wrong.
Mei-Yu: What? I'm not wrong. That's a mouse and those are CDs.
Carlos: No, they're not. This is a *picture* of a mouse and that's a *picture* of CDs.
Mei-Yu: Very funny.

Page 58, Practice, Exercise B

1.
A: What page are we on?
B: Nineteen.

2.
A: How many of your classmates work?
B: Twelve.

3.
A: How many students are here today?
B: Thirty-five.

4.
A: Which room is the office?
B: Room fifty-nine.

5.
A: How many desks are in the classroom?
B: Forty.

6.
A: How many dictionaries are in the classroom?
B: Thirty.

7.
A: How many students in our class are from China?
B: Seventeen.

8.
A: How many students are in level 1?
B: Eighty-two.

Page 60, Listen, Exercise B

Ken: Excuse me. Is the computer lab open?
Berta: Sorry. I don't know. Ask him.
Ken: Oh, OK. But . . . Who is he?
Berta: He's the computer lab assistant!

Page 60, Listen, Exercise C

Ken: Excuse me. Is the computer lab open?
Berta: Sorry. I don't know. Ask him.
Ken: Oh, OK. But . . . Who is he?
Berta: He's the computer lab assistant!

UNIT 4

Page 68, Listen, Exercise B

Sen: That's a great photo. Who's that?
Dora: My father.
Sen: Oh, he looks nice.
Dora: Thanks.

Page 68, Listen, Exercise C

Sen: That's a great photo. Who's that?
Dora: My father.
Sen: Oh, he looks nice.
Dora: Thanks.
Sen: And is that your sister? She looks like you.
Dora: Thanks, but that's not my sister. That's my daughter!

Page 74, Listen, Exercises A and B

Zofia: Is your family here in this country?
Ernesto: My brother is here. He's a carpenter.
Zofia: Oh. What's he like?
Ernesto: He's great. He's a lot of fun.
Zofia: Does he look like you?
Ernesto: No. He's tall and thin and he has long hair.

Page 74, Listen, Exercise C

Zofia: Is your family here in this country?
Ernesto: My brother is here. He's a carpenter.
Zofia: Oh. What's he like?
Ernesto: He's great. He's a lot of fun.
Zofia: Does he look like you?
Ernesto: No. He's tall and thin and he has long hair. Here's a picture of him.
Zofia: Oh. He has a beard and a mustache, too.
Ernesto: He has one more thing, too.
Zofia: Oh, yeah? What's that?
Ernesto: He has a wife.
Zofia: Oh.

Page 78, Practice, Exercise C

1. January twenty-first
2. January fifth
3. January seventeenth
4. January eighth
5. January twenty-fourth
6. January eleventh
7. January thirtieth
8. January ninth

Page 79, Practice, Exercise F

1.
A: What's your date of birth?
B: It's March fourteenth, nineteen seventy-seven.

2.
A: When was your son born?
B: October second, two thousand and one.

3.
A: What's your sister's date of birth?
B: It's May twenty-eighth, nineteen eighty-eight.

4.
A: When was your daughter born?
B: August thirty-first, nineteen ninety-five.

5.
A: When was your father born?
B: December seventeenth, nineteen fifty-nine.

6.
A: What's your brother's date of birth?
B: It's September second, nineteen sixty-two.

Page 80, Listen, Exercise B

Assefa: Hi, Zofia. Where are you?
Zofia: I'm at my friend's house. I'm babysitting for her kids.
Assefa: Oh. How old are they?
Zofia: Well, her son is eleven. He's in the fifth grade. And her daughter is six. She's in the first grade.

Page 80, Listen, Exercise C

Assefa: Hi, Zofia. Where are you?
Zofia: I'm at my friend's house. I'm babysitting for her kids.
Assefa: Oh. How old are they?
Zofia: Well, her son is eleven. He's in the fifth grade. And her daughter is six. She's in the first grade.
Assefa: What are they like?
Zofia: Well, Kevin's great.
Assefa: Oh. And what about her daughter?
Zofia: Terry? She's really friendly, but my friend calls her "Terry the terrible."
Assefa: Why?
Zofia: I really don't know.

UNIT 5

Page 88, Listen, Exercises A and B

Zofia: I need a gift for my brother Robert. It's his birthday next week.
Carlos: How about clothes?
Zofia: Well, he *needs* clothes, but he *wants* a backpack!

Page 88, Listen, Exercise C

Zofia: I need a gift for my brother Robert. It's his birthday next week.
Carlos: How about clothes?
Zofia: Well, he *needs* clothes, but he *wants* a backpack!
Carlos: Then get two backpacks!
Zofia: Two?
Carlos: Yes. My birthday is next month and I want a backpack, too!

Page 93, Practice, Exercise A

1. **Customer:** Excuse me. How much is this blouse?
   Assistant: It's $11.95.

2. **Customer:** Excuse me. How much are these shoes?
   Assistant: They're $34.99.

3. **Customer:** Excuse me. How much is this watch?
   Assistant: It's $23.50.

4. **Customer:** Excuse me. How much are these pants?
   Assistant: They're $13.49.

Page 94, Listen, Exercise B

Assefa: Do you have this sweater in a large?
Assistant: No, I'm sorry. We don't.
Assefa: Too bad. It's for my sister and she needs a large.

Page 94, Listen, Exercise C

Assefa: Do you have this sweater in a large?
Assistant: No, I'm sorry. We don't.
Assefa: Too bad. It's for my sister and she needs a large.
Assistant: What about this sweater? Does she like blue?
Assefa: Yes, she does.
Assistant: Well, here you go.
Assefa: Great. Thanks.

Page 100, Listen, Exercises B and C

Matt: Good morning! This is Matt Spencer, and you're listening to *Shopping Time* on Greenville News Radio. Today's question is: Why do people return clothes? Right now, I'm in the popular clothing store Imagine. Many people are in line here at the customer service desk. Let's find out why they're here . . . Hello, Ma'am.
Woman 1: Hi.
Matt: Ma'am, can you tell us why you're here today?
Woman 1: Well, I need to return this shirt.
Matt: And why do you need to return it?
Woman 1: My husband doesn't like it. I need to get him a different gift!
Matt: Oh, too bad. It looks like a nice shirt to me! But I guess I'm not your husband. OK, how about over here—sir? What are you returning, and what's the problem?
Man 1: I'm returning these pants. They don't match my shirt.
Matt: Oh, no? So, you need a different color.
Man 1: Right. I want beige pants instead.
Matt: All right. Now, the next person in line is a young woman . . . Miss?
Woman 2: Uh, yeah?
Matt: What are *you* here for today?
Woman 2: I'm returning these pants. They don't fit. They're too big!
Matt: Ahh. Well, that's a good reason. OK, let's ask one more person . . . Sir? I see you're returning a jacket. What's the problem with it?
Man 2: The zipper doesn't work.
Matt: It doesn't work? You mean, it's broken?
Man 2: Yeah. I need a new one.
Matt: OK, well, good luck with that. . . . And that's all we have time for today! Join me tomorrow, for a discussion of the question: What's the best toy? We'll talk to Susan Ianello, the president of Good for You Toys . . .

UNIT 6

Page 108, Listen, Exercise B

Dan: Oh, wow! This house looks great!
Emily: Really?
Dan: Yes. There are two bedrooms and a large kitchen.
Emily: What about a dining room?
Dan: Well, no. There's no dining room.

Page 108, Listen, Exercise C

Dan: Oh, wow! This house looks great!
Emily: Really?
Dan: Yes. There are two bedrooms and a large kitchen.
Emily: What about a dining room?
Dan: Well, no. There's no dining room.
Emily: That's OK. The kitchen's large. How's the rent?
Dan: Not bad. It's pretty cheap. There *is* one problem, though.
Emily: Oh? What's that?
Dan: It's not in the United States. It's in Canada!

Page 114, Listen, Exercise B

Amy: Excuse me. Is there an apartment for rent in this building?
Manager: Yes, there is. There's a one-bedroom apartment on the second floor.
Amy: Oh, great. Is it furnished?
Manager: Well, yes and no. There's a dresser, but no beds.
Lei: Oh. Well, are there appliances?
Manager: Uh, yes and no. There's a stove, but no refrigerator.

Page 114, Listen, Exercise C

Amy: Excuse me. Is there an apartment for rent in this building?
Manager: Yes, there is. There's a one-bedroom apartment on the second floor.
Amy: Oh, great. Is it furnished?
Manager: Well, yes and no. There's a dresser, but no beds.
Lei: Oh. Well, are there appliances?
Manager: Uh, yes and no. There's a stove, but no refrigerator. So? Are you interested?
Amy: Well, yes.
Lei: And no!

Page 120, Listen, Exercise B

Thank you for calling Joe's Furniture Store. We're located at 231 Fifth Avenue in Riverside.

For store hours, please press 1. For directions, press 2.

For directions from the north, press 1.
For directions from the south, press 2.

Page 120, Listen, Exercise C

Thank you for calling Joe's Furniture Store. We're located at 231 Fifth Avenue in Riverside.

For store hours, please press 1. For directions, press 2.

For directions from the north, press 1.
For directions from the south, press 2.

You're coming from the south. Go north on 12th Street. Turn left on Fifth Avenue. Continue on Fifth Avenue for one block. Joe's is on the left, across from the hospital. Once again, go north on 12th street. Turn left on Fifth Avenue. Go one block. You can't miss it. So, hurry into Joe's and save!

UNIT 7

Page 128, Listen, Exercise B

Gloria: Are you free tomorrow? How about a movie?
Sen: Sorry, I'm busy. I work on Saturdays.
Gloria: Oh. Well, when do you get home?
Sen: At 8:00.

Page 128, Listen, Exercise C

Gloria: Are you free tomorrow? How about a movie?
Sen: Sorry, I'm busy. I work on Saturdays.
Gloria: Oh. Well, when do you get home?
Sen: At 8:00.
Gloria: That's not a problem.
Sen: No? What time is the movie?
Gloria: What do you mean?
Sen: What time does the movie start?
Gloria: It starts when we want. It's a DVD!

Page 134, Listen, Exercise B

Mei-Yu: Gee, I'm so glad it's Friday!
Ernesto: Me, too. What do you usually do on the weekend?
Mei-Yu: Well, I always clean the house on Saturdays, and I always spend time with my family on Sundays. What about you?
Ernesto: I usually shop for food on Saturdays, and I sometimes go to the park on Sundays.

Page 134, Listen, Exercise C

Mei-Yu: Gee, I'm so glad it's Friday!
Ernesto: Me, too. What do you usually do on the weekend?
Mei-Yu: Well, I always clean the house on Saturdays, and I always spend time with my family on Sundays. What about you?
Ernesto: I usually shop for food on Saturdays, and I sometimes go to the park on Sundays.
Mei-Yu: I love the weekend.
Ernesto: Yeah, especially Sunday.
Mei-Yu: Right. Saturday is for cleaning and shopping, and Sunday is for fun.
Ernesto: Exactly. In our house, we call Sunday "fun day."

Page 140, Listen, Exercises B and C

Hello. This is Sue Miller with *Life Styles*. Our program today is about relaxing. So, how often do *you* relax? Many people say: "Relax? I never relax." What about *you*?

How often do you take a long hot bath?

How often do you go running?

How often do you listen to music?

How often do you take a long walk?

Sometimes? Never? That's not good.

We're all busy, but we need to relax—and not just sometimes. You need to relax every day. It helps you study better, it helps you work better, and it helps you be a better parent.

Well, that's all for today. . . .

Thank you for listening to *Life Styles*. This is Sue Miller saying *relax* and good-bye from Greenville News Radio.

UNIT 8

Page 148, Listen, Exercise B

Marius: Wow, I'm hungry!
Gabriela: Yeah, me, too. What do you want for lunch?
Marius: Pizza! I love pizza! What about you?
Gabriela: I don't really like pizza, but I *love* tacos!

Page 148, Listen, Exercise C

Marius: Wow, I'm hungry!
Gabriela: Yeah, me, too. What do you want for lunch?
Marius: Pizza! I love pizza! What about you?
Gabriela: I don't really like pizza, but I *love* tacos! And look! There's a taco place over there!
Marius: Sounds good! But wait a minute. It's not time for lunch!
Gabriela: No?
Marius: No. It's only 10:30!
Gabriela: So, forget about lunch. Let's have pizza and tacos for breakfast!

Page 154, Listen, Exercise B

Waiter: Can I help you?
Greg: Yes, I'd like a hamburger and a soda.
Waiter: Is that a large soda or a small soda?
Greg: Large, please.
Waiter: OK, a large soda . . . Anything else?
Greg: Yes. A small order of fries.

Page 154, Listen, Exercise C

Waiter: Can I help you?
Greg: Yes, I'd like a hamburger and a soda.
Waiter: Is that a large soda or a small soda?
Greg: Large, please.
Waiter: OK, a large soda . . . Anything else?
Greg: Yes. A small order of fries.
Liz: A hamburger, fries, and a soda? You know, that's not very healthy! What about vegetables?
Greg: Well, there's lettuce on the hamburger.
Liz: OK . . . And what about fruit?
Greg: You're right! I need fruit. I know . . . I'll have a piece of apple pie, too.

Page 157, Compare Food Prices, Exercise B

1.
A: How much is the chicken?
B: It's three twenty-nine a pound.

2.
A: How much are the bananas?
B: They're ninety-nine cents a pound.

3.
A: How much is the yogurt?
B: It's three eighty-five.

4.
A: How much are the apples?
B: They're one ninety-nine a pound.

5.
A: How much are the onions?
B: They're eighty-nine cents a pound.

6.
A: How much is the bread?
B: It's two fifty-nine.

Page 160, Listen Exercises A and B

Hannah: Good morning. This is Hannah Charles with Greenville News Radio. You're listening to *The Food Show*. Do you have questions about food? Well, call and ask. Now here's our first caller . . .
Greg: Hi Hannah. I'm Greg Johnson. My wife says that I don't eat healthy food. She says, "Eat more fruit and vegetables." But I'm a meat and potatoes man.
Hannah: OK, Mr. Meat and Potatoes. Tell me, do you like chicken?
Greg: Sure. I eat a lot of chicken.
Hannah: And do you like grilled chicken or fried chicken?
Greg: I like grilled chicken *and* fried chicken.

Hannah: OK. Now, let me ask you a question. How many calories are there in a piece of fried chicken?

Greg: Hmm. I don't know.

Hannah: 250 calories.

Greg: 250 calories!

Hannah: That's right, but in a piece of grilled chicken there are only about 100 calories. So, the choice is easy. The next time you have chicken, eat grilled chicken, not fried.

Greg: OK. That's not so hard.

Hannah: Now another question. This is about potatoes. How much fat is there in an order of fries? Do you know?

Greg: A lot?

Hannah: You're right. There are 15 grams of fat in a small order of fries. But there's no fat in a plain baked potato. That's 15 grams in the fries and no grams in the baked! But remember, no butter! So, the next time you have potatoes, think baked, not fried.

Greg: Wow. I don't believe it!

Hannah: Yes. And one more thing, listen to your wife! . . . She's right. Those vegetables and fruit *are* good for you. Thanks a lot for calling *The Food Show*. We have time for one more call.

Page 163, Grammar

A: This omelet is really good. What's in it?

B: Eggs and cheese. Oh, and there's salt, but not much.

A: Eggs? How many eggs?

B: Three.

A: And how much cheese?

B: Just one slice.

A: What do you cook it in? Do you use butter or oil?

B: I use oil, but it's good with butter, too.

UNIT 9

Page 168, Listen, Exercises B and C

David: Hello?

Laura: Hi! It's me. How are you?

David: Fine, thanks. Where are you?

Laura: I'm in Tampa. I'm visiting family, but they're at work now.

David: Tampa! That's great! How's the weather there?

Laura: Well, it's cold and rainy.

Page 168, Listen, Exercise D

David: Hello?

Laura: Hi! It's me. How are you?

David: Fine, thanks. Where are you?

Laura: I'm in Tampa. I'm visiting family, but they're at work now.

David: Tampa! That's great! How's the weather there?

Laura: Well, it's cold and rainy.

David: Oh, that's too bad. It's beautiful here in Green Bay. It's not warm, but it's sunny.

Laura: Don't tell me that! Here I am in Tampa, and I'm just sitting in the living room and watching the rain!

Page 174, Listen, Exercise B

Dan: Are you watching the news?

Emily: No, I'm not. I'm reading a magazine.

Dan: Well, turn on the TV. A big storm is coming.

Emily: Really?

Dan: Yes. In fact, I'm coming home early. I'm at the supermarket now.

Page 174, Listen, Exercise C

Dan: Are you watching the news?

Emily: No, I'm not. I'm reading a magazine.

Dan: Well, turn on the TV. A big storm is coming.

Emily: Really?

Dan: Yes. In fact, I'm coming home early. I'm at the supermarket now.

Emily: Oh, good. Are you getting water?

Dan: Yes. I'm getting water, food, and a lot of batteries.

Emily: Great. Get matches, too.

Dan: OK. Do we need anything else?

Emily: Yes. We need good weather!

Page 181, Listen, Exercises A and B

Good morning. This is *Weather Watch* on Greenville News Radio. Here's the weather report for cities across the country.

It's cloudy and very hot in Los Angeles. The temperature is already 90 degrees. Wear light clothes and drink lots of water if you go outside.

It's a beautiful day in Atlanta! It's warm and very sunny now with a temperature of 75 degrees. So, go outside, take your sunglasses, and enjoy the nice weather!

It's raining in New York City, and the temperature is 62 degrees. Take your umbrella if you go out.

It's very windy in Chicago. The temperature is only 38 degrees. So, don't forget your scarf and gloves. It's pretty cold out there!

UNIT 10

Page 188, Listen, Exercise B

Berta: Excuse me. Can you help me? I'm looking for Foodsmart.
Mail Carrier: Sure. It's on Seventh between Hill and Oak.
Berta: Sorry?
Mail Carrier: It's on Seventh Avenue between Hill Street and Oak Street.
Berta: Thanks.

Page 188, Listen, Exercise C

Berta: Excuse me. Can you help me? I'm looking for Foodsmart.
Mail Carrier: Sure. It's on Seventh between Hill and Oak.
Berta: Sorry?
Mail Carrier: It's on Seventh Avenue between Hill Street and Oak Street.
Berta: Thanks. Uh… is that near here?
Mail Carrier: Yes. It's just around the corner.
Berta: They're having a grand opening. I guess there are a lot of people there.
Mail Carrier: No, not really. Only one or two workers.
Berta: Really? I don't understand.
Mail Carrier: Today is October 7. The grand opening is *tomorrow*, October 8!

Page 192, Practice

Conversation 1
A: Don't turn left here.
B: Oh, thanks. I'll turn at the next street.

Conversation 2
A: Be careful. There's a school near here.
B: You're right. I'll drive slowly. A lot of kids cross here.

Conversation 3
A: Be careful. There's a railroad crossing.
B: I know. Do you see a train?
A: Not right now, but be careful anyway.

Page 194, Listen, Exercise B

Tina: Excuse me. How do you get to Adams College?
Officer: Take the Number 4 bus, and get off at Second Street. It's not far from there.
Tina: Thanks. Oh, and how much does the bus cost?
Officer: Two dollars, but you need exact change.

Page 194, Listen, Exercise C

Driver: Second Street.
Matt: OK. Here we are at Second Street. Now what?
Tina: There's a woman. Let's ask her.
Matt: Excuse me. We want to go to Adams College. How do we get there?
Woman: It's easy! Study, study, study!

Pages 200–201, Listen, Exercises A and B

Welcome back to Greenville News Radio. It's time for our *Weekend Watch*.

What are your plans for this weekend? Are you looking for something to do? Well, here's what's happening in our community.

Foodsmart is having its grand opening on Saturday, October 8. They're giving away samples at 3:00. There'll be lots of food and drinks at this free event.

Saturday night, Greenville's very own Zeebees are singing at the community college. The concert begins at 8:00. Tickets are on sale now for five dollars.

There's a baseball game Sunday afternoon at one o' clock. Greenville High is playing Lincoln High in Greenville Park. Free with a student ID.

And also on Sunday there's a community yard sale at the Community Center across from the fire station. People are selling old toys, furniture, and clothes. The sale is from 10 A.M. to 4 P.M. Get there early. It doesn't cost just to look!

This is Simon Chan. Have a great weekend!

UNIT 11

Page 207, Show What You Know, Step 1

1. Touch your nose.
2. Clap your hands.
3. Close your eyes.
4. Shake your head.
5. Touch your arm.
6. Point to your chest.
7. Nod your head.
8. Point to your knee.

Page 208, Listen, Exercise B

Assistant: Good morning. Greenville Elementary.
Mrs. Lee: Hello. This is Terry Lee. I'm calling about my son Alex.
Assistant: Is that Alex Lee?
Mrs. Lee: Yes. He's sick today. He has a sore throat and a headache.
Assistant: I'm sorry to hear that. What class is he in?
Mrs. Lee: He's in Ms. Wong's class.

Page 208, Listen, Exercise C

Assistant: Good morning. Greenville Elementary.
Mrs. Lee: Hello. This is Terry Lee. I'm calling about my son Alex.
Assistant: Is that Alex Lee?
Mrs. Lee: Yes. He's sick today. He has a sore throat and a headache.
Assistant: I'm sorry to hear that. What class is he in?
Mrs. Lee: He's in Ms. Wong's class.

Assistant: OK. Thank you for calling. I'll tell Ms. Wong. I hope he feels better soon.

Daughter 1: Mom, my throat hurts!

Son: Mom, my head hurts!

Daughter 2: Mommy, my stomach hurts!

Mrs. Lee: Uh-oh. Can I call you back?

Page 213, Practice, Exercise A

Pain Away!

Pain Reliever. Fever reducer.

Directions: Take 2 tablets orally every 6 hours.

Warnings:
• Do not take more than 8 tablets per day.
• Take with food or milk.
• Do not drink alcoholic beverages.
• Do not give to children under twelve.
• Keep out of reach of children.

Page 214, Listen, Exercise B

Tuan: You weren't here yesterday.

Luisa: I know. My daughter was home sick. She had a bad cold.

Tuan: Oh, too bad. How is she now?

Luisa: A lot better, thanks. She's back at school.

Page 214, Listen, Exercise C

Tuan: You weren't here yesterday.

Luisa: I know. My daughter was home sick. She had a bad cold.

Tuan: Oh, too bad. How is she now?

Luisa: A lot better, thanks. She's back in school.

Tuan: Great. And what about your other kids?

Luisa: Well, they were sick *last* week, but they're OK now.

Tuan: That's good. Well, take care, Luisa, and have a good day.

Luisa: Oh, thanks, Tuan. I'll try.

Page 215, Conversation, Exercise B

1. Marie wasn't here yesterday morning.
2. The students were in class.
3. The teacher was absent.
4. We weren't at work.

Page 221, Listen, Exercises B and C

Dr. Garcia: Good evening. This is Dr. Elias Garcia with Greenville News Radio. You're listening to *Ask the Doctor*. I'm here to answer your health questions. . . . Our first call today is from Carl Gold. Carl?

Carl: Yes. Hello, Dr. Garcia. Here's my problem. I exercise. I know it's good to exercise but I get these terrible backaches. what should I do?

Should I use an ice pack?

Dr. Garcia: Yes, ice is good if your backache is from exercising. But only when you first feel the pain. Later, heat is better. You should take a long hot shower.

Carl: A hot shower?

Dr. Garcia: Yes. And you should use a heating pad, too.

Carl: OK, great. Thank you, Dr. Garcia.

Dr. Garcia: You're welcome. Hello, this is *Ask the Doctor*. Who's speaking?

Jon: Hello, Dr. Garacia. My name is Jon Kerins. I have a terrible toothache. What should I do? Should I put heat on it?

Dr. Garcia: Oh, no. You shouldn't put heat on a toothache. Heat might feel good, but it isn't good for you. Here's what you should do: You should eat a small piece of onion.

Jon: Onion?

Dr. Garcia: Yes! Believe it or not, onion helps the pain. Also, you should drink lime juice regularly —it helps prevent toothaches.

Jon: Wow. Lime juice. OK, thank you, Dr. Garcia.

Dr. Garcia: Thanks for calling. And now we have time for one more call. . . . Hello?

Dana: Hi, I'm Dana Jones. My husband, my son, and I all have the flu. What should we do?

Dr. Garcia: Gee, I'm really sorry to hear that. There's not much you can do. You should stay in bed and drink a lot of fluids.

Dana: You mean, like water?

Dr. Garcia: Yes, water, or tea, or even juice. You should drink as much as you can.

Dana: What about antibiotics?

Dr. Garcia: Unfortunately, antibiotics don't help the flu. You shouldn't take them.

Dana: OK. Well, thanks.

Dr. Garcia: I hope you all feel better soon. And that's all the time we have for today. . . .

UNIT 12

Page 228, Listen, Exercise B

Assefa: I noticed the "Help Wanted" sign. I'd like to apply for a job.

Dino: OK. Which job?

Assefa: Well, I'm a cook. I can make great hamburgers.

Dino: Can you make pizza?

Assefa: No, I can't make pizza, but I can learn.

Page 228, Listen, Exercise C

Assefa: I noticed the "Help Wanted" sign. I'd like to apply for a job.

Dino: OK. Which job?

Assefa: Well, I'm a cook. I can make great hamburgers.

Dino: Can you make pizza?

Assefa: No, I can't make pizza, but I can learn.

Dino: Good. As you can see, this place is really busy. The phone never stops.

Assefa: Well, I can answer the phone, too.

Dino: Great. Can you start now? Can you answer the phone?

Assefa: Sure. Dino's Diner. Can I help you?

Page 233, Practice, Exercise E

A: Hey, you're looking for a job, right?

B: That's right. Why?

A: Well, here's one in the paper. It says "no experience necessary."

B: Really? What's the schedule like?

A: Well, it's only part-time, but you can work any shift.

B: Oh, that's great. And how much do they pay?

A: Seven dollars an hour.

B: Hmmm. I guess that's not bad. How can I apply?

Page 234, Listen, Exercise B

Dana: Hi, I'm Dana.

Sam: Hi. I'm Sam. Wow. This store is really busy.

Dana: I know! Listen, I need a favor. Can you work this Saturday?

Sam: Uh, well, yes, I can.

Dana: Oh, great, thanks, because I can't. Can you work from 2:00 to 7:00?

Sam: Un, yes. I guess so.

Page 234, Listen, Exercise C

Dana: Hi, I'm Dana.

Sam: Hi. I'm Sam. Wow. This store is really busy.

Dana: I know! Listen, I need a favor. Can you work this Saturday?

Sam: Uh, well, yes, I can.

Dana: Oh, great, thanks, because I can't. Can you work from 2:00 to 7:00?

Sam: Um, yes. I guess so. . . . but, I don't understand. Why are you asking me all these questions?

Dana: Well, you're the new sales assistant, right?

Sam: No . . . I'm the elevator repair guy. I'm here to fix the elevator.

Page 240, Listen, Exercises B and C

Tina: Good afternoon. This is Tina Martins. You're listening to *Meet Your Neighbors*. Today I'm in Saigon, Greenville's first Vietnamese restaurant, and I'm talking with Bao Tran and Hanh Le. Hello. And congratulations! Your restaurant looks great.

Hanh: Thank you.

Bao: Thanks, Tina.

Tina: So, Bao, is this your first restaurant?

Bao: Yes, it is. But I worked in a restaurant before.

Tina: Oh. Was that here in Greenville?

Bao: Yes. The Greenville Café.

Tina: How long were you there?

Bao: Eight years.

Tina: And what did you do? Were you a cook?

Bao: Oh, I did a lot of things. I was a cashier, a waiter, *and* a cook.

Tina: Wow. So you really know the restaurant business.

Bao: Yes, I think so.

Tina: Hanh, were you in the restaurant business, too?

Hanh: No. I worked in people's homes. I took care of children and I cooked for the families.

Tina: That's interesting. When did you two come to this country?

Hanh: Twelve years ago.

Tina: Well, your English is great.

Hanh: Thanks. We were students at the Greenville Adult School. We also cooked at the school!

Tina: Really!?

Bao: Yes, we cooked for class parties.

Hahn: Right. We were good students, but we were *great* cooks! Just ask our teacher, Ms. Reed!

Hahn: Actually, Bao and I always loved to cook. And now we can cook for everyone here in Greenville. We want everyone here to visit us.

Bao: Yes. We're right across the street from the new Foodsmart. And we're open every day from noon to 11 P.M.

Tina: Well, it's almost noon now, and there are people waiting to get in. So business looks good, and the food smells delicious. For those of you listening today, make a reservation for Saigon at 555-8776. And thank you for listening to *Meet Your Neighbors*.

Page 244, Act It Out, Step 1

Angela: Hi, Miguel. I'm Angela Miller. Thanks for coming in today.

Miguel: Thank *you*. It's nice to meet you.

Angela: You can have a seat here. Now, as you know, we're looking for office assistants. I see you have some experience with that?

Miguel: Yes, I do. I worked for Newtown Auto Supplies.

Angela: How long were you there?

Miguel: Three years. And then my family moved here, to Greenville.

Angela: I see. And what are your skills? Can you use a computer?

Miguel: Yes, I can. I can also answer phones, make copies . . . And I can take inventory, too.

Index

Map of the United States and Canada

U. S. Postal Abbreviations

Alabama	AL		Montana	MT
Alaska	AK		Nebraska	NE
Arizona	AZ		Nevada	NV
Arkansas	AR		New Hampshire	NH
California	CA		New Jersey	NJ
Colorado	CO		New Mexico	NM
Connecticut	CT		New York	NY
Delaware	DE		North Carolina	NC
District of Columbia	DC		North Dakota	ND
Florida	FL		Ohio	OH
Georgia	GA		Oklahoma	OK
Hawaii	HI		Oregon	OR
Idaho	ID		Pennsylvania	PA
Illinois	IL		Rhode Island	RI
Indiana	IN		South Carolina	SC
Iowa	IA		South Dakota	SD
Kansas	KS		Tennessee	TN
Kentucky	KY		Texas	TX
Louisiana	LA		Utah	UT
Maine	ME		Vermont	VT
Maryland	MD		Virginia	VA
Massachusetts	MA		Washington	WA
Michigan	MI		West Virginia	WV
Minnesota	MN		Wisconsin	WI
Mississippi	MS		Wyoming	WY
Missouri	MO			

Canadian Postal Abbreviations

Alberta	AB		Nova Scotia	NS
British Columbia	BC		Nunavut	NU
Manitoba	MB		Prince Edward Island	PE
New Brunswick	NB		Quebec	QC
Newfoundland and Labrador	NL		Saskatchewan	SK
Northwest Territories	NT		Yukon	YT

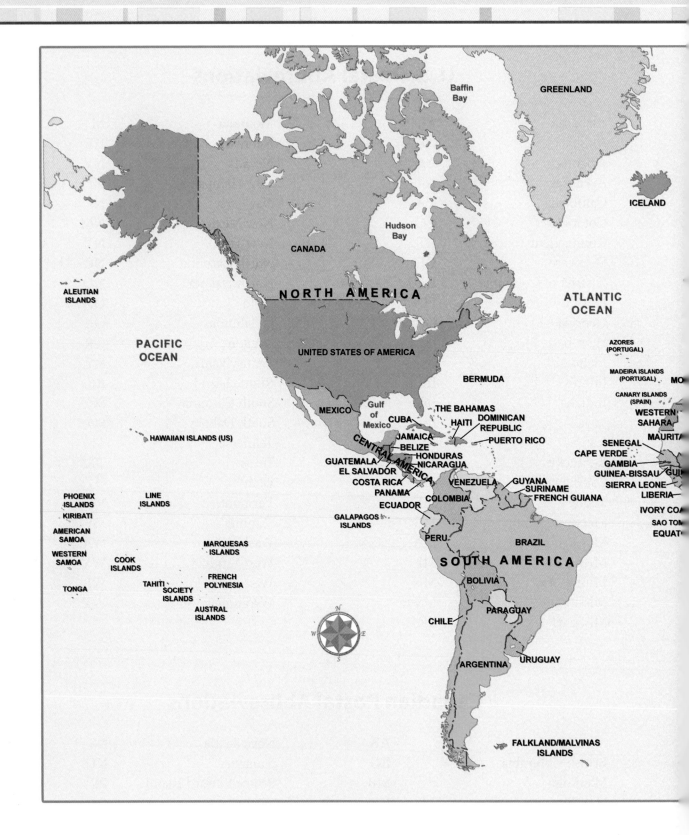

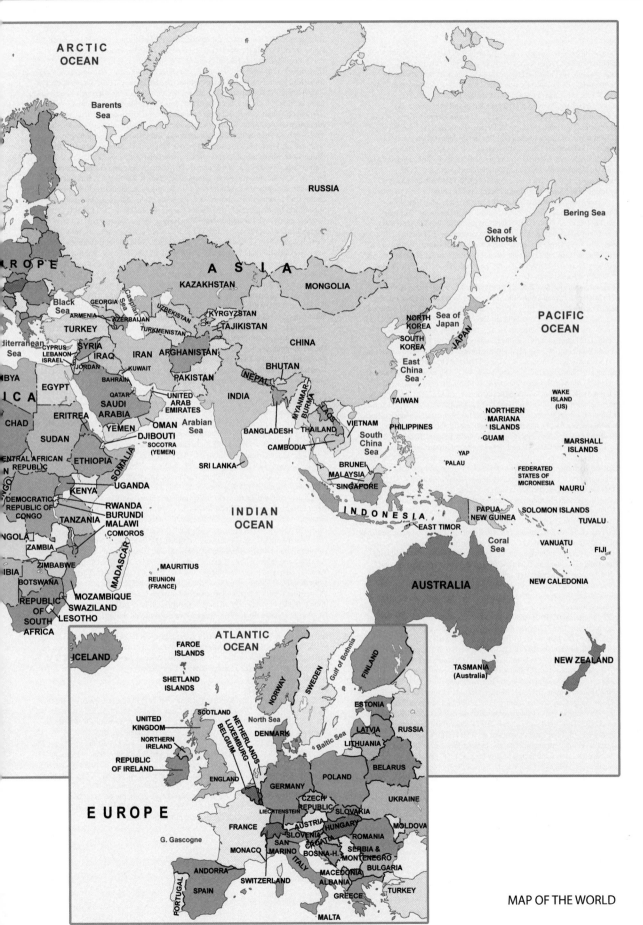

ARCTIC OCEAN

Barents Sea

RUSSIA

Bering Sea

Sea of Okhotsk

ASIA

KAZAKHSTAN

MONGOLIA

PACIFIC OCEAN

Black Sea
GEORGIA
Caspian Sea
ARMENIA
AZERBAIJAN
TURKMENISTAN
UZBEKISTAN
KYRGYZSTAN
TAJIKISTAN

NORTH KOREA
Sea of Japan
JAPAN

TURKEY

SOUTH KOREA

Mediterranean Sea
CYPRUS
LEBANON
ISRAEL
SYRIA
IRAQ
JORDAN
KUWAIT
BAHRAIN

IRAN
AFGHANISTAN
CHINA
BHUTAN
NEPAL

East China Sea

LBYA

EGYPT

QATAR
SAUDI ARABIA
UNITED ARAB EMIRATES

PAKISTAN

INDIA

MYANMAR BURMA
LAOS

TAIWAN

WAKE ISLAND (US)

ICA

ERITREA
YEMEN
OMAN
DJIBOUTI
SOCOTRA (YEMEN)

Arabian Sea

BANGLADESH
THAILAND
VIETNAM

PHILIPPINES

NORTHERN MARIANA ISLANDS
GUAM

CHAD
SUDAN

CAMBODIA

South China Sea

MARSHALL ISLANDS

CENTRAL AFRICAN REPUBLIC
N
ETHIOPIA
SOMALIA
UGANDA

SRI LANKA

BRUNEI
MALAYSIA
SINGAPORE

YAP
PALAU

FEDERATED STATES OF MICRONESIA

NAURU

KENYA

INDIAN OCEAN

INDONESIA

PAPUA NEW GUINEA

SOLOMON ISLANDS
TUVALU

DEMOCRATIC REPUBLIC OF CONGO
RWANDA
BURUNDI
TANZANIA
MALAWI
COMOROS

EAST TIMOR

Coral Sea

VANUATU
FIJI

NGOLA
ZAMBIA
ZIMBABWE
MADAGASCAR

MAURITIUS
REUNION (FRANCE)

AUSTRALIA

NEW CALEDONIA

IBIA
BOTSWANA
REPUBLIC OF SOUTH AFRICA
MOZAMBIQUE
SWAZILAND
LESOTHO

TASMANIA (Australia)

NEW ZEALAND

EUROPE

ATLANTIC OCEAN

FAROE ISLANDS

Gulf of Bothnia

FINLAND

ICELAND

SHETLAND ISLANDS

NORWAY
SWEDEN

ESTONIA
RUSSIA

SCOTLAND
North Sea

LATVIA
LITHUANIA

UNITED KINGDOM
NORTHERN IRELAND
NETHERLANDS
LUXEMBURG
BELGIUM
DENMARK

Baltic Sea

REPUBLIC OF IRELAND

ENGLAND

GERMANY
POLAND

BELARUS

EUROPE

LIECHTENSTEIN
CZECH REPUBLIC
SLOVAKIA

UKRAINE

G. Gascogne

FRANCE
AUSTRIA
SLOVENIA
HUNGARY

MOLDOVA

MONACO
SAN MARINO
CROATIA
BOSNIA-H.
ROMANIA
SERBIA & MONTENEGRO

ITALY
MACEDONIA
BULGARIA

ANDORRA
PORTUGAL
SPAIN
SWITZERLAND
ALBANIA
GREECE
TURKEY

MALTA

Credits

Photo credits

All original photography by David Mager. Page 4(R) David Ball/Alamy; 8(T) Shutterstock; 10(R) BigStockPhoto.com; 11(L) Ryan McVay/Getty Images, (M) Shutterstock, (R) Justin Horrocks/iStockphoto.com; 13(T) Michael Newman/PhotoEdit, (M) Don Mason/age fotostock, (B) Shutterstock; 16(T) Tanya Constantine/Getty Images, (M) Andersen Ross/Brand X/Corbis, (B) Pedro Coll/age fotostock; 25 Corbis/age fotostock; 26-27(1) Shutterstock, (2) Jeff Greenberg/PhotoEdit, (3) Stephe Simpson/Getty Images, (4) Photoshow/Dreamstime.com, (5) Gary Crabbe/Alamy, (6) Frank Herholdt/Getty Images, (7) Royalty-Free Division/Masterfile, (8) Kayte M. Deioma/PhotoEdit, (9) John Foxx/age fotostock, (10) David Lewis/iStockphoto.com, (11) Jim DeLillo/iStockphoto.com, (12) Index Stock Imagery, (13) David De Lossy/Getty Images, (14) Royalty-Free Division/Masterfile, (15) Medioimages/Photodisc/Getty Images, (16) Andersen Ross/age fotostock; 28(a) Shutterstock, (b) Shutterstock; 29(TL) Jim DeLillo/iStockphoto.com, (TR) Photoshow/Dreamstime.com, (ML) Jeff Greenberg/PhotoEdit, (MR) Medioimages/Photodisc/Getty Images, (BL) Kayte M. Deioma/PhotoEdit, (BR) Royalty-Free Division/Masterfile; 30(T) Redchopsticks.com LLC/Alamy, (B) Shutterstock; 32(1) Roy Ooms/Masterfile, (2) Picture Partners/age fotostock, (3) Stuart Cohen/The Image Works, (4) Michael Newman/PhotoEdit; 33 Photos.com/Jupiterimages; 34(L) Blend Images/Alamy, (ML) Royalty Free Division/Masterfile, (MR) Corbis/Jupiterimages, (R) Dennis MacDonald/PhotoEdit; 37(L) Sergio Barrenechea/epa/Corbis, (M) George Tiedemann/GT Images/Corbis, (R) Shutterstock; 38(TL) Shutterstock, (TR) Rob Van Petten/Getty Images, (ML) Dex Image/Getty Images, (MR) David Bacon/The Image Works, (BL) Eric Fowke/PhotoEdit, (BR) Royalty-Free Division/Masterfile; 39 Bob Daemmrich/PhotoEdit; 40(T) Dynamic Graphics/Jupiterimages, (a) Michael Newman/PhotoEdit, (b) David R. Frazier/PhotoEdit; 41(TL) Michael Newman/PhotoEdit, (TR) Jupiter Images/Comstock Images/Alamy, (BL) Spencer Grant/PhotoEdit, (BR) Jeff Greenberg/PhotoEdit; 42(T) John Birdsall/The Image Works, (M) David Urbina/PhotoEdit, (B) David Young-Wolff/PhotoEdit; 43(T) Corbis/Jupiterimages, (B) Amy Etra/PhotoEdit; 46-47(1) Brian Klutch/Getty Images, (2) Bill Aron/PhotoEdit, (3) Shutterstock, (4) Cre8tive Studios/Alamy, (6) Mark Lund/Getty Images, (7) BigStockPhoto.com, (8) Ryan McVay/Getty Images, (9) iStockphoto.com, (10) Shutterstock, (11) Stockbyte/Getty Images, (12) Michael Newman/PhotoEdit, (14) Felicia Martinez/PhotoEdit, (15) Shutterstock, (16) Shutterstock, 49(TL) Stockbyte/Getty Images, (TM) Shutterstock, (TR) Michael Newman/PhotoEdit, (BM) Shutterstock, (BR) Ryan McVay/Getty Images; 53 Sion Touhig/Corbis; 54(inset) Shutterstock, 55(TL) Shutterstock, (ML) Brian Klutch/Getty Images, (MR) Shutterstock, (BL) iStockphoto.com; 60(L) Michael Newman/PhotoEdit, (ML) Bob Daemmrich/PhotoEdit, (MR) Andersen Ross/age fotostock, (R) Radius Images/Masterfile; 61(L) ColorBlind Images/Blend/IPNStock, (R) Michael Newman/PhotoEdit; 65 Ryan McVay/Getty Images; 68(L) Getty Images, (R) Shutterstock; 71 Shutterstock, Shutterstock, Shutterstock, Shutterstock, Sharon Meredith/iStockphoto.com, Shutterstock, Shutterstock, Shutterstock, Shutterstock, (B) Ronnie Kaufman/Corbis; 76(1) Shutterstock, (2) Bartomeu Amengual/age fotostock, (3) Digital Vision Ltd./SuperStock, (4) Shutterstock, (5) Ariel Skelley/Getty Images, (6) Shutterstock, 81(T) Sean Justice/Corbis, (M) Jose Luis Pelaez, Inc./Blend Images/Corbis, (B) Shutterstock; 82(1) RPM Pictures/Getty Images, (2) Photononstop/SuperStock, (3) Mary Kate Denny/PhotoEdit, (4) Bill Bachmann/Photo Researchers, Inc., (5) Beathan/Corbis, (B) AP Images, AP Images, AP Images, AP Images; 86-87(2) Photos.com/Jupiterimages, (4) Index Stock Imagery, (7) Shutterstock, (8) Canstockphoto.com, (9) Robert Lerich/iStockphoto.com, (10) Shutterstock, (12) Shutterstock; 88(a) C Squared Studios/Getty Images, (b) Shutterstock, (c) Photos.com/Jupiterimages; 89(TL) Comstock/SuperStock, (TM) David Young-Wolff/PhotoEdit, (TR) Jose Luis Pelzez Inc./Blend/IPNStock, (BL) Photos.com/Jupiterimages, (BR) Photos.com/Jupiterimages; 90(T) Kevin Cooley/Getty Images, (inset) Photos.com/Jupiterimages, (B) Shutterstock, (inset) Shutterstock; 91 Shutterstock, Shutterstock, Shutterstock; 92(1) Bill Aron/PhotoEdit, (2) Lushpix/age fotostock, (3) M Stock/Alamy, (4) David Young-Wolff/PhotoEdit; 94(B) Thomas Northcut/Getty Images; 95(L) Shutterstock, (R) Shutterstock; 96 Jack Hollingsworth/age fotostock; 98(T) Lushpix/age fotostock; 100(T) Royalty-Free/Corbis, (MTL) Imagesource.com, (MTR) Big Cheese Photo LLC/Alamy, (MBL) Thomas Northcut/Getty Images, Dorling Kindersley; 101(L) Corsicarobase/Fotolia.com; 103 Digital Vision/Getty Images; 105 GOGO Images/SuperStock; 106-107 (A) Look Photography/Beateworks/Corbis, (C) Shutterstock, (D) BigStockPhoto.com, (E) Shutterstock, PNC/Getty Images, Dorling Kindersley, Rob Melnychuk/Getty Images, Shutterstock, Scott Van Dyke/Beateworks/Corbis, (B inset) Shutterstock; 115 Shutterstock; 121 Dennis MacDonald/PhotoEdit; 125 GoGo Image Corporation/Alamy; 126-127 Michael Newman/PhotoEdit; 128(T) John Eder/Getty Images, Jeff Greenberg/PhotoEdit, Mark Gamba/Corbis, Rob Van Petten/age fotostock, (BL) Directphoto.org/Alamy; 129(L) Nick White/Getty Images, (M) Tony Freeman/Getty Images, (B) Elyse Lewin/Getty Images; 134(T) BE&W agencja fotograficzna Sp. z o.o./Alamy, Tom Stewart/Corbis, Shutterstock, (L inset) Renault Philippe/age fotostock, (R inset) Kane Skennar/Getty Images; 135(T) Photofusion Picture Library/Alamy, Jupiter Images/BananaStock/Alamy, Ingram Publishing/Getty Images, Blend Images/Alamy, Mira/Alamy, Purestock/Getty Images, (B) Adam Crowley/Getty Images, Robert Warren/Getty Images, LWA-Dann Tardif/Corbis, Blend Images/Alamy, Phillip Jarrell/Getty Images, Tony Freeman/PhotoEdit; 140(T) Photos.com/Jupiterimages, (M) Royalty-Free Division/Masterfile, Asia Images Group/Alamy, Index Stock Imagery, (B) Mel Yates/Getty Images, Jack Hollingsworth/Getty Images, Shutterstock; 141(T) Creative Eye/MIRA.com, RubberBall/Alamy, Shutterstock, Stockbyte/Getty Images, Adamsmith/Getty Images, Bettmann/Corbis, (B) Shutterstock; 145 Digital Vision/Getty Images; 146-147(1) Shutterstock, (2) Shutterstock, (3) Shutterstock, (4) Shutterstock, (5) Shutterstock, (6) Shutterstock, (7) Shutterstock, (8) Shutterstock, (9) Shutterstock, (10) Shutterstock, (11) Shutterstock, (12) Shutterstock, (13) Shutterstock, (14) Shutterstock, (15) Ingram Publishing/SuperStock, (16) Shutterstock, (17) Shutterstock, (18) Shutterstock, (19) Shutterstock, (20) Shutterstock; 149(TL) Devilpup/Fotolia.com, (TR) Uyen Le/iStockphoto.com, (ML) Shutterstock, (MR) Shutterstock, (BL) Shutterstock, (BR) Shutterstock; 151 Shutterstock; 152 Shutterstock; 153 Image100/Corbis; 154(T) Shutterstock, Shutterstock, Uyen Le/iStockphoto.com, FoodCollection/SuperStock, Shutterstock, Shutterstock, Shutterstock, Shutterstock, Bobelias/Dreamstime.com, Kiransaleem/Dreamstime. com, Barry Gregg/Corbis, Rachel Weill/Jupiterimages; (B) Dennis MacDonald/Alamy; 156 Jeff Greenberg/PhotoEdit; 158(T) Shutterstock, Shutterstock, Pearson Education, Shutterstock, Westend61/Alamy, Shutterstock, Shutterstock, Shutterstock, (B) Shutterstock, Shutterstock, Shutterstock, Ingram Publishing/SuperStock, Shutterstock, Shutterstock, Shutterstock, Shutterstock; 160 Shutterstock, Bobelias/Dreamstime.com, Shutterstock, Shutterstock, Shutterstock, FoodCollection/SuperStock, Shutterstock, Shutterstock, Shutterstock, Shutterstock, Shutterstock; 161 Shutterstock, Shutterstock, Shutterstock, Shutterstock, Shutterstock, Shutterstock, Pg_cata/Dreamstime.com, Shutterstock; 163 SuperStock, Inc./SuperStock; 165 Radius Images (Photolibrary; 166(T) Keith Clarke/Fotolia.com, (B) Sylvain Grandadam/Getty Images; 167(L) Shutterstock, (R) Steve Dunwell/Index Stock Imagery; 168(T) Fabio Cardoso/age fotostock, (B) Andy Whale/Getty Images; 169(T) David Young-Wolff/PhotoEdit, (M) Don Johnston/age fotostock, (B) Jim Reed/Corbis; 172(1) David R. Frazier/PhotoEdit, (2) AP Images, (3) Jim Zuckerman/Corbis, (4) David Robert Austen/Getty Images, (5) Kent Wood/Photo Researchers, Inc., (6) Najlah Feanny/Corbis, (7) Shutterstock, (8) AP Images; 175(L) Robin Sachs/PhotoEdit, (M) Rob Casey/Jupiterimages, (R) Bill Aron/PhotoEdit; 177(L) AllOver Photography/Alamy, (M) ImageState/Alamy, (R) Jupiter Images/Creatas/ Alamy; 179 Tony Freeman/PhotoEdit; 180(1) Michael Newman/PhotoEdit, (3) Shutterstock, (4) Shutterstock, (5) Shutterstock, (6) Shutterstock, (7) Michael Newman/PhotoEdit, (8) Shutterstock, (9) Shutterstock, (10) Shutterstock, (11) Shutterstock, (12) Siede Preis/Getty Images; 181 Jacom Stephens/iStockphoto; 185 Roy McMahon/Corbis; 186-187(1) Swerve/Alamy, (2) David R. Frazier Photolibrary, Inc./Alamy, (3) Colin Young-Wolff/PhotoEdit, (4) Phil McCarten/PhotoEdit, (5) Will & Deni McIntyre/Corbis, (6) JG Photography/Alamy, (7) Jeffwqc/Dreamstime.com, (8) Index Stock Imagery, (9) Bob Daemmrich/The Image Works, (10) Shutterstock, (11) Jeff Greenberg/The Image Works, (12) M Stock/Alamy, (13) Geri Engberg/The Image Works, (14) Blend Images/Jupiterimages, (15) Royalty-Free Division/Masterfile; 189(T) Tom Carter/PhotoEdit, (BL) Javier Larrea/SuperStock, (BR) Ron Chapple/Getty Images; 190(TL) Shutterstock, (TM) Art Stein/ZUMA/Corbis, (TR) Shutterstock, (BL) Shutterstock, (BM) Shutterstock, (BR) Shutterstock; 192(1) Shutterstock, (2) Image Farm Inc./Alamy, (3) Shutterstock, (4) Shutterstock, (5) Shutterstock, (6) Shutterstock, (7) Shutterstock, (8) Shutterstock, (9) Shutterstock; 195(TL) Jon Hicks/Corbis, (ML) Jeff Greenberg/PhotoEdit, (BL) Lon C. Diehl/PhotoEdit, (M) Peter Bennett/Ambient Images; 197(T) Spencer Grant/PhotoEdit, (B) Shutterstock, Shutterstock, Shutterstock, Shutterstock; 199 Digital Vision/age fotostock; 205 Thinkstock/Jupiterimages; 206 Shutterstock; 208(TL) Phototake NYC, (TR) Ken Cavanagh/Photo Researchers, Inc., (ML) Lucidio Studio, Inc./Corbis, (MR) Guillermo Hung/Getty Images; 219 Jim Cummins/Getty Images; 221 Anthony Redpath/Corbis, Corbis/age fotostock, Florea Marius Catalin/iStockphoto.com, Shutterstock; 224 Image100/Corbis, MIXA/Getty Images, MedioImages/Corbis, Giantstep Inc/Getty Images; 225 Keith Brofsky/Getty Images; 226-227 (1) Lon C. Diehl/PhotoEdit, (2) John Birdsall/age fotostock, (3) Corbis/age fotostock, (4) Michael Newman/PhotoEdit, (5) Thinkstock/Corbis, (6) Tim Matsui/Alamy, (7) Blend Images/Jupiterimages, (8) Ann Marie Kurtz/iStockphoto.com, (9) Pfutze/zefa/Corbis, (10) Andrew Woodley/Alamy, (11) Jeff Greenberg/The Image Works, (12) Barros & Barros/Getty Images; 228(M) Shutterstock, Ron Fehling/Masterfile, Jeff Greenberg/PhotoEdit, (B) Shutterstock, FoodCollection/SuperStock, Shutterstock; 232 Getty Images; 237(L) David Young-Wolff/PhotoEdit; 239 Michael Newman/PhotoEdit; 241(T) MM Productions/Corbis, (TL) Shutterstock, (TR) Myrleen Ferguson Cate/PhotoEdit, (ML) Rob Casey/Jupiterimages, (MR) David Young-Wolff/PhotoEdit, (BL) David Young-Wolff/PhotoEdit, (BR) Jeff Greenberg/PhotoEdit; 244(L) TongRo Image Stock/Alamy, (M) David Young-Wolff/PhotoEdit, (R) Michael Newman/PhotoEdit; 246(TL) Andersen Ross/Brand X/Corbis, (TR) Marc Romanelli/Getty Images, (BL) Michael Newman/PhotoEdit, (BM) Jeff Greenberg/PhotoEdit, (BR) Stephe Simpson/Getty Images.

Illustration Credits

Steve Attoe, pp. 88, 97, 101; Kenneth Batelman, pp. 111, 123; Luis Briseno, pp. 18, 40, 52, 93, 109, 114, 150, 160-161, 173, 193; Laurie Conley, pp. 12, 31, 48, 51, 52, 55, 74, 83, 176, 194, 196, 121-213, 218; Deborah Crowle, pp. 6-7, 168,181; A Corazon Abierto/Marce Gomez & David Silva, pp. 18-19, 148, 209, 229; Brian Hughes, pp. 32, 50-51, 78, 94, 112-113, 117, 120, 122, 129, 152, 157, 162, 188-189, 190, 228, 244, 273; André Labrie, pp. 178, 182, 210, 214, 217, 231, 236, 238; Paul McCusker, pp.79, 120; Steve Mac eachern, pp. 15, 17, 33, 108, 119, 122-123; Luis Montiel, pp. 24, 44, 54, 64, 66-67, 70, 72-73, 75, 84, 144; Allan Moon, pp. 69, 71, 72, 214, 258, 261, 268; Roberto Sadi, pp. 59, 77, 184, 204; Michel Rabagliati, pp. 9, 36, 56, 62, 138, 207, 216 ,231; Steve Schulman, pp. 37,76,137,174; John Schreiner/Wolfe LTD, p159; Neil Stewart/NSV Productions, pp. 42, 124, 128, 155, 164, 173, 211, 213; Anna Veltfort, pp. 3, 20-21, 22,42,56-57,80,102,106,112,170-171,183,198,200-201,206,220,245,249,252; Rose Zgodzinski, pp139,166-167,222